COPYRIGHT LAW IN AN AGE OF
LIMITATIONS AND EXCEPTIONS

Copyright Law in an Age of Limitations and Exceptions brings together leading copyright scholars and the field's foremost authorities to consider the role of copyright law in shaping the complex social, economic, and political interactions that are crucial for cultural productivity and human flourishing. The book addresses defining issues facing copyright law today, including justifications for copyright law's limitations and exceptions (L&Es), the role of authors in copyright, users' rights, fair use politics and reform, the three-step test in European copyright law, the idea/expression principle with respect to functional works, limits on the use of L&Es in scientific innovation, and L&Es as a tool for economic development in international copyright law. The book also presents case studies on the historical development of the concept of "neighboring rights" and on Harvard Law School's pioneering model of global copyright education, made possible by the exercise of L&Es across national borders.

Ruth L. Okediji is the William L. Prosser Professor of Law and McKnight Presidential Professor at the University of Minnesota Law School. A leading scholar in international intellectual property law, she has authored several books, United Nations studies, and numerous articles. She serves as a policy advisor to many governments and intergovernmental organizations on issues relating to intellectual property, innovation, and economic development. She was a member of the U.S. National Academies Board on Science, Technology and Economic Policy Committee on the Impact of Copyright Policy on Innovation in the Digital Era.

Copyright Law in an Age of Limitations and Exceptions

Edited by

RUTH L. OKEDIJI

University of Minnesota Law School

CAMBRIDGE UNIVERSITY PRESS

CAMBRIDGE
UNIVERSITY PRESS

University Printing House, Cambridge CB2 8BS, United Kingdom

One Liberty Plaza, 20th Floor, New York, NY 10006, USA

477 Williamstown Road, Port Melbourne, VIC 3207, Australia

314-321, 3rd Floor, Plot 3, Splendor Forum, Jasola District Centre, New Delhi - 110025, India

79 Anson Road, #06-04/06, Singapore 079906

Cambridge University Press is part of the University of Cambridge.

It furthers the University's mission by disseminating knowledge in the pursuit of education, learning and research at the highest international levels of excellence.

www.cambridge.org
Information on this title: www.cambridge.org/9781107584846

© Cambridge University Press 2017

First published 2017
First paperback edition 2018

A catalogue record for this publication is available from the British Library

ISBN 978-1-107-13237-5 Hardback
ISBN 978-1-107-58484-6 Paperback

Dedication

To each of the authors in this volume—
your work continues to teach, challenge, provoke, and
inspire generations;
and to אֵל עֶלְיוֹן *(El Elyon), God Almighty,*
Who has blessed me with these.

Contents

Author Biographies

James Boyle is the William Neal Reynolds Professor of Law, School of Law, Duke University, Durham, North Carolina, USA.

Niva Elkin-Koren is Professor of Law and Director of the Haifa Center for Law and Technology, Faculty of Law, University of Haifa, Israel.

William W. Fisher III is the WilmerHale Professor of Intellectual Property Law, Harvard Law School, Harvard University, Cambridge, Massachusetts, USA.

Michael Geist is the Canada Research Chair in Internet and E-commerce Law, Faculty of Law, University of Ottawa, Canada.

Jane C. Ginsburg is the Morton L. Janklow Professor of Literary and Artistic Property Law, Columbia Law School, Columbia University, New York, USA.

Wendy J. Gordon is the William Fairfield Warren Distinguished Professor at the School of Law, Boston University, Boston, Massachusetts, USA.

P. Bernt Hugenholtz is Professor of Intellectual Property Law, Institute for Information Law at the University of Amsterdam, Amsterdam, Netherlands.

Justin Hughes is the William H. Hannon Distinguished Professor of Law, Loyola Law School, Loyola Marymount University, California, USA.

Jessica Litman is the John F. Nickoll Professor of Law and Professor of Information, University of Michigan Law School, Michigan, USA.

Ruth L. Okediji is the William L. Prosser Professor of Law and McKnight Presidential Professor, Law School, University of Minnesota, Minneapolis, Minnesota, USA.

William F. Patry is Senior Copyright Counsel, Google, USA.

Jerome H. Reichman is the Bunyan S. Womble Professor of Law, School of Law, Duke University, Durham, North Carolina, USA.

Sam Ricketson is Professor of Law, Melbourne Law School, University of Melbourne, Victoria, Australia.

Pamela Samuelson is the Richard M. Sherman Distinguished Professor of Law; Co-Director, Berkeley Center for Law & Technology, School of Law, University of California, Berkeley, California, USA.

Preface

This book did not begin as a volume about copyright limitations and exceptions. Having spent countless hours in research, writing, and policy work, and especially having served as one of the lead technical experts for the Africa Group during the long, winding road to the World Intellectual Property Organization's Marrakesh Treaty,[1] I most definitely did *not* want to contribute additional hours of my life to the study of copyright limitations and exceptions. My experience during the Marrakesh Treaty negotiations did, however, heighten my sensitivity to the trenchant tone of the global debate over the role of copyright law in promoting the public interest, more so in a pervasively digital world. The differences between those who believe that copyright law has run its course (or lost its way) and those who expect that copyright can live up to its goals (if we could only agree on what those are and how to achieve them) are most striking in the debate over copyright limitations and exceptions.

From the start, my principal interest was to consider whether copyright law could emerge intact given these intractable debates about what constitutes social welfare in our hyper-digital networked world. Do we need to strike a fundamentally different kind of social bargain? If so, what kind of values should undergird a well-informed copyright system — one that reflects how copyright can work more effectively for creators, users, and innovation? Importantly, my international policy work with developing and least-developed countries had left me dissatisfied with the conventional theories that have long nourished copyright's role in the production of cultural goods.

In a number of jurisdictions, copyright reform efforts had been stymied by competing claims, usually with little or inconclusive empirical support, about the appropriate design of copyright for the digital, globally networked economy. At the same

---

[1] The treaty is formally titled "Marrakesh Treaty to Facilitate Access to Published Works by Visually Impaired Persons and Persons with Print Disabilities." It was signed in Marrakesh, Morocco, on June 28, 2013.

time, widespread skepticism about copyright's relevance seemed at an all-time high; and this in an era characterized by an abundance of creativity and new business models for the distribution and consumption of content. Copyright's international public disfavor reinforced a prevalent view of copyright law as the last guard of an old, if glorious, age in which traditional content industries bartered with legislatures for new rules designed primarily to advance their own narrow interests. But, no matter the challenge or issue regarding copyright in the digital age, the policy discussions seemed frustratingly to devolve into justifications for more rights or battles over appropriate limitations and exceptions.

I chose not to embark on the traditional private intellectual journey of a scholar, but to bring together those who have spent most of their academic lives pondering copyright's past, present, and future. This book thus reflects the collective and distinctive wisdom of some of copyright law's greatest intellectual leaders. Their life's work and chief passion have been the development of a copyright law that delivers on its explicit social covenant to facilitate the production of, and access to, knowledge, and in so doing to improve the odds for sustainable social, economic, cultural, and political progress. I asked each author to write about what is important to him or her. I said "write from your heart," believing that whatever topic each author chose would speak to the conditions needed for copyright law to flourish, help us understand aspects of copyright's history better, and demonstrate new ideas for how copyright law could be improved. I believed that each author's topic choice would serve as a "GPS" of sorts for her or his strongly felt instincts, ideas, and arguments about what is important to copyright law today, and how to prepare for the future of copyright in a difficult and continuously evolving technological landscape.

In November 2014, many of the contributing authors convened in St. Helena, California, for a two-day workshop to discuss the first drafts of the chapters. This peer review process fostered debate, helped refine key arguments, encouraged reflection, and enhanced the level of engagement between authors and across topics. The book strongly reflects the benefits of those two days in St. Helena; the chapters collectively bring fresh perspective, new insight, and greater clarity to the unnecessary complexity of copyright law. Copyright law is fraught with tension, bloated in many respects and under great political pressure. Yet, as each author's contribution illustrates, it remains a subject important enough to demand fidelity to what makes copyright law important – the stewardship of human ingenuity for reward and progress.

I owe a large debt of gratitude to Bria Goldman who was my assistant at the University of Minnesota Law School until close to the finish of the book. Bria stewarded the manuscript through several versions, and oversaw all the logistics for the workshop with great skill and remarkable efficiency; that she did so in Minnesota's subzero temperatures while we enjoyed the sunny Napa countryside truly reflects her remarkable grace. Special thanks also are due to Professor Pam Samuelson who graciously offered her home to host several workshop participants and the workshop itself. Those who have experienced Professor Samuelson's generosity as a mentor, teacher, or friend, will not be surprised to learn that her hospitality extends well beyond reading and offering honest criticism of draft articles. She is famous for keeping conference "trains" on time (and on track!). I could not have asked for a more ideal venue to gather for serious conversation, rigorous feedback, delightful commentary throughout the day, and easy banter at night – all enhanced by a constant supply of good food.

Every successful book project requires a small army, and this one was no different. A number of anonymous academic reviewers started the process by giving Cambridge University Press (CUP) very positive reviews of my book proposal – you know who you are and I send you each my thanks. My discussions with Professor Peter Jaszi, Professor David Lange, and David Nimmer helped to clarify important aspects regarding the scope and content of the book; to each of them I owe thanks for their participation at different stages along the way. My editor, Matt Galloway, is without question one of the very best there is. Together with the team at CUP, he provided steady leadership, candid advice, and truly exceptional support throughout the process. Abundant thanks go to Ariane Moss, my research assistant at Harvard Law School. Ariane's meticulous proofreading, cite checking, and editing, were done with great enthusiasm and excellence. She supplied exactly what I needed to cross the finish line, earning her a place in the RA Hall of Fame. Finally, Tucker Chambers, a graduate of the University of Minnesota Law School, on the heels of completing a judicial clerkship, proofread the entire manuscript and added his usual touch of excellence.

There are no words to adequately thank my husband and best friend, Tade O. Okediji. He offered consistent encouragement and prayed for me through this project; he is my good and perfect gift from God (James 1:17).

Above all, my praise and thanksgiving go to the God of my Lord and Savior Jesus Christ; it is He who arms me with strength and makes my way perfect (Psalms 18:32).

Ruth L. Okediji
Minneapolis, Minnesota
December 2016

Introduction

Copyright law, particularly its Anglo-American variety, has never been about authors or users as ends in themselves. A law that encourages creativity by giving rights to creators is good for society if it is effectively reconciled with the public interest. Like all created objects, this law can fall short of its goals, and so it requires constant attention; yet, attention that produces no meaningful change is vain. Many of the efforts to improve copyright law certainly feel fruitless in retrospect. Discerning where along the spectrum from effective to irrelevant our present copyright system falls is no easy task, and the task grows harder when the criteria for judgment and the end goals have themselves become increasingly contentious. What seems clear to many observers is the level of worldwide dissatisfaction with the present state of copyright law.[1] Much of that dissatisfaction focuses on the role of limitations and exceptions (L&Es) in the perpetual search for balance among the goals of copyright law's various stakeholders, including the public. Some economic and business interests find themselves aligned with the public's desire for liberty of access, thus elevating the intensity of the debate about whether copyright works and, more importantly, about *how* copyright works as a driver of innovation.

This collection of chapters by leading copyright scholars reflects on various aspects of copyright law at a time when the subject of L&Es is arguably the most controversial in the field and is the focus of reform efforts nationally and internationally. Across jurisdictions, many of the economic, social, and cultural engagements characteristic of the digital era take place in the uncertain light of copyright L&Es. This reality has made it difficult to embrace the historically dominant narrative that holds out copyright's set of exclusive rights as the primary motivator of creative expression.

---

[1] *See e.g.*, Peter S. Menell, *This American Copyright Life: Reflections on Re-Equilibrating Copyright for the Internet Age*, 61 J. Copyright Soc'y U.S.A. 235 (2014) (addressing the "dismal state of copyright's public approval rating").

1

Instead, L&Es have assumed a prominent role in copyright law as tools for defining zones in which use, experimentation, and innovation can occur.

In Chapter 1, Professor Samuelson sets the stage for a systematic approach to understanding the nature and purpose of copyright L&Es. In *Justifications for Copyright Limitations and Exceptions*, she identifies a set of policy justifications that underpin different kinds of L&Es in U.S. law and in other jurisdictions. Her chapter establishes a framework for rationalizing the vast realm of copyright L&Es in a global context. Professor Samuelson's approach offers important levers for adjusting copyright law's required balance of interests in a more disciplined fashion, and it provides a pathway toward reducing the extensive work that the fair use doctrine currently is forced to do in the United States. Importantly, her analysis suggests that the distinction between countries with designated L&Es and those with more flexible L&Es is less marked than traditionally understood,[2] a point that Professor Hugenholtz's chapter later confirms. Bridging the gap between differing national approaches to L&Es is thus not only feasible but, in my view, also desirable.

In Chapter 2, *The Role of the Author in Copyright*, Professor Jane Ginsburg challenges the notion that copyright law's conventional author, who needs and responds to incentives to create, has grown less distinctive and significant to the creative enterprise in today's digital environment. She argues that, even in an age in which a combination of pervasive interaction over digital networks and minimalist criteria for copyright protection has given everyone a claim to authorship, the traditional author is still alive and deserving of copyright's solicitude, perhaps more so than ever before. Instead of making this traditional author irrelevant, Professor Ginsburg suggests that copyright in an era of digital technologies serves precisely to direct forms of creativity into more stable enterprise models, while taking advantage of new remuneration criteria that could ensure that the author's full range of interests – economic and moral – remain viable in the digital era. She then outlines ways in which new business models and digital network platforms afford opportunities to remain true to the authorial role that is essential to copyright's future.

William (Bill) Patry, drawing from his impressive career as a copyright lawyer, policymaker, scholar, and now Senior Copyright Counsel at Google, has written an unapologetically personal assessment of the professional and legal environment in which copyright law operates. In Chapter 3, *A Few Observations about the State of*

---

[2] *See, e.g.,* Jerome H. Reichman & Ruth L. Okediji, *When Science and Copyright Collide: Empowering Digitally Integrated Research Methods on a Global Scale,* 96 Minn. L. Rev 1362, 1375–89 (2012) (analyzing the closed list model of the European approach to L&Es and the U.S. hybrid approach that combines specific L&Es with a flexible approach, such as the fair use doctrine).

Copyright Law, Bill offers a piercing set of observations that challenge the utility of modern copyright law to accomplish any of its stated goals, be it the advancement of culture, the encouragement of creativity, or the safeguarding of the public interest. In reflecting on some of the major ailments of U.S. copyright law – its excessive breadth, long duration, statutory damages, and a complicated text that most citizens (including lawyers) strain to understand – today's copyright law, Bill argues, has inflicted damage on what should matter most, namely, creativity and learning. In his reflective and blunt critique, L&Es are not spared. He argues that they are no antidote to the challenge of a failed copyright law that is shaped increasingly by ideology and not facts. Bill's chapter emphasizes the need for a copyright law that actually advances the public good. Furthering the enterprise of learning should be the chief aim of copyright law, one that requires simplicity and flexibility for authors, users, and the public. He insists that the only legitimate question to which use of a copyrighted work should be subjected is "does th[at] use further learning?"

In Chapter 4, *Fetishizing Copies*, Professor Jessica Litman takes on one of copyright law's most sacred cows – the copy. Copy-fetish is "the idea that every appearance of any part of a work anywhere should be deemed a 'copy' of it, and that every single copy needs a license or excuse, whether or not anyone will ever see the copy, whether or not the copy has any independent economic significance, whether or not the so-called copy is incidental to some other use that is completely lawful." Professor Litman is unequivocal in her brilliant critique of the courts of appeals decisions that she identifies as giving rise to copy-fetish. She argues that any future copyright reform will require an explicit carve-out of readers', listeners', and viewers' rights because that is the only way to secure these liberties a place in today's political economy of copyright law.

In recent years, the concept of "users' rights" has become an important part of efforts to infuse normative content in various efforts to delineate the public's stake in the copyright system. The phrase encompasses the idea that freedom to engage in creative and learning practices, enabled by new technological platforms and fueled by the massive amount of online content, is central to the effective functioning of copyright law. Recognizing and identifying users' rights explicitly extends the boundaries of contemporary copyright policy by situating potential defendants as fundamentally important to the core purposes of copyright law.

In Chapter 5, *Copyright in a Digital Ecosystem: A User Rights Approach*, Professor Niva Elkin-Koren provides a formidable defense of users' rights. She argues that recognition of the role of users in promoting the purposes of copyright law could change our perspective about both the scope of copyright protection and what should be considered permissible uses. Professor Elkin-Koren argues for a users' rights approach that goes beyond a defense of users' right of access to cultural goods; her analysis forcefully reframes the object of copyright policy from authors' rights to the creative process itself, emphasizing the role of users as partners in promoting the objectives of copyright law.

Next, in Chapter 6, *The Canadian Copyright Story: How Canada Improbably Became the World Leader on Users' Rights in Copyright Law*, Professor Michael Geist gives an absorbing account of Canada's embrace of users' rights. Canada's experience reflects important aspects of the framework proposed by Professor Elkin-Koren. Canada is not the only country where copyright reform efforts have been intensely focused on users' rights and access to cultural goods, but it is one of the few to succeed in such an effort. Professor Geist attributes this success at least in part to the fact that copyright law is intertwined with the daily lives of most citizens. A growing awareness of how the exercise of exclusive rights could impact what had become routine activities for most citizens galvanized a movement that helped shift Canada's internal copyright calculus in recognition of the role of users in the digital economy.

In Chapter 7, *(When) Is Copyright Reform Possible?*, Professor James Boyle explores the distinctive reform effort that emerged in the United Kingdom via the Hargreaves Review of Intellectual Property. L&Es have formed an essential part of recent copyright reform efforts across the globe. Many of these reform efforts are sidelined, at impasse, or still embroiled in intense political debates, suggesting skewed outcomes consistent with the endemic dysfunction of copyright law-making with which scholars are all too familiar. Professor Boyles's chapter is an uncommon account of a successful reform effort explicitly driven by utilitarian considerations. It offers readers a compelling insider's view, demonstrating that there can be public-minded solutions that remain consistent with the economic considerations policy-makers often feel compelled to underscore. Professor Boyle identifies five factors he believes together account for the success of the United Kingdom. I will not spell out what those are here, but his analysis provides insight into the kind of copyright reform that works – both as a process that garners public trust and as a means for policy redirection embraced by people with widely diverging views. There is no suggestion in his chapter that this success story can happen for all countries or that it will ever happen again, even in the United Kingdom, in quite this way. But *something* made it attainable, and that something is an important aspect of how countries might imagine future reform processes and, in particular, the institutions and personalities that drive them.

The fair use doctrine, one can safely say, is a leading concern of copyright holders in the United States. Not only are its outer limits uncertain, but the discretion afforded courts has sometimes resulted in unjustified largesse to users at the expense of owners. This "most troublesome doctrine"[3] has long distinguished U.S. law in

---

[3]   Dellar v. Samuel Goldwyn, Inc., 104 F.2d 661, 662 (2d Cir. 1939)

international copyright relations, even slowing down U.S. ratification of the Berne Convention. But despite its constitutional status, and the United States' aggressive stance on copyright harmonization, no administration has sought to promote fair use as an international copyright norm. Nonetheless, the fair use doctrine has become the centerpiece of copyright's ideological wars on a world stage.

In Chapter 8, *Fair Use and Its Politics – at Home and Abroad*, Professor Justin Hughes takes on the controversial question of whether the fair use doctrine is consistent with the three-step test that has become the "gold standard" for L&Es in international copyright law. I have previously argued that the two approaches are incompatible; his chapter has made me think differently. Professor Hughes proposes a new analytical prism: he argues that the fair use doctrine is best understood as a mechanism for establishing specific copyright exceptions. Once fair use has been properly applied, it is *those* permitted uses that should be analyzed for consistency with the three-step test and not the fair use standard as such.

This is a compelling approach to a long-standing debate in international copyright relations, a debate that is most certainly grounded in the troubling politics of fair use in the United States. Professor Hughes identifies two challenges to his proposal: the inherent ambiguity of fair use and the question of whether judges should be the ones exercising such extensive law-making power. I would add the following related considerations: (1) fair use in the United States has become increasingly pressured both by technological changes and, at times, a far-reaching "transformative use" jurisprudence that has produced some troubling outcomes, and (2) fair use is quintessentially tailored to local conditions, but we live in an increasingly culturally ambiguous world.

These elements can make fair use seem (or function) more like "guidance" and less like a "standard," something likely to trouble those who view harmonization as a key goal of the international copyright system. To be clear, the uses or cases that are "special" for three-step test purposes will (and should) vary across jurisdictions. As Professor Hughes notes, nothing in international copyright law forecloses such variation in outcomes. But to the extent debates about fair use mostly embody competing ideological views of what copyright law should accomplish in today's society, internationalizing fair use is a road that, as Professor Hughes cautions, should be tread cautiously. This is prudent counsel, not only because fair use mutations will inevitably emerge and produce incoherence at a time when clarity is much needed for cross-border economic activity, but also because uncritical exportation of the fair use doctrine can impose costly institutional design problems for countries not yet equipped to manage the open-ended nature of the fair use inquiry.

Professor Bernt Hugenholtz addresses the opposite problem in Chapter 9: Can the continental authors' right system be made as flexible as its Anglo-American law counterpart? In *Flexible Copyright: Can the EU Author's Right Accommodate Fair*

Use?, Professor Hugenholtz describes an "unequivocal" recognition of the need for flexibility in the EU's copyright regulatory environment. One reason for flexibility is to equip courts for rapidly changing technological developments; another is to preserve the legitimacy and relevance of authors' right systems by aligning the law more realistically with new and growing societal expectations. In continental Europe and elsewhere, strict adherence to the exclusive rights that copyright law offers on paper is simply unworkable in today's networked environment where heavy reliance on copyrightable content is an essential part of daily life. Professor Hugenholtz's chapter, however, presents more than a pragmatic response to the technological pressures all jurisdictions face. He provides an astute assessment of the state of authors' right systems, describing a degree of flexibility inherent in these systems that was lost over time, in part due to the dictates of European harmonization. Professor Hugenholtz suggests that the political and cultural interests favoring greater flexibility in the EU authors' right system are reinforced by technological change, by proposals for revision of the 2001 Copyright Information Society Directive, and by the jurisprudence on fundamental freedoms emerging from the European Court of Justice, which gives EU states greater autonomy when copyright collides with these freedoms.

Professor Jerome Reichman questions the very effectiveness of L&Es to address new forms of creative collaboration and expression. He focuses on the scientific community where open-access movements and private, contractually designed semi-commons initiatives are proliferating in response to the needs of digital science. In Chapter 10, *The Limits of "Limitations and Exceptions" in Copyright Law*, Professor Reichman argues that both the "bean counter" methodology typically employed by countries adhering to the "designated exceptions" approach in the European Union and the more agile fair use exception rooted in U.S. law are equally overwhelmed by the needs of science. His chapter addresses three questions: (1) Can we really make a copyright law inherited from the Romantic view of authorship, and built around business models rooted in hardcopy print media, more friendly to the needs of both authors and users in the digital age? (2) If we managed to devise such a digitally friendly legal regime, is there even a remote chance of persuading legislatures to adopt it? and (3) If the answer to either of these questions is negative, what else can authors and users do to circumvent the existing legal barriers to construct regimes that foster innovation? Professor Reichman envisages only a limited role for copyright L&Es; he argues instead for open-access or semi-open access options, devised by scientists themselves and utilizing legal tools, such as standardized licenses or default liability rules, that facilitate access to knowledge goods. These default options also reduce transaction costs that currently stifle effective operation of even the most well-intentioned set of L&Es.

In Chapter 11, Professor William Fisher describes a unique model of online education that harnesses the power of new technologies to a deep conviction that persons all over the world should have access to high-quality knowledge about copyright law and policy. It is called CopyrightX. Now in its fourth year, CopyrightX is a distinctive community of "learners" – teachers and students – engaged in the study of copyright law. With roughly 500 students spread across 93 countries, the course safeguards classic pedagogic principles in the challenging context of immense online participation. As *Lessons from CopyrightX* makes clear, the course is exacting. It infuses the traditional U.S.-focused copyright syllabus with a rigorous comparative dimension, case studies to provide practical applications of doctrines learned, and live lectures from authors and other actors (including policymakers) in the copyright system. Additional important dimensions of this incomparable model of online education are highlighted by Professor Fisher in *Lessons from CopyrightX*, including key insights about financial and organizational dimensions.

Professor Reichman's concerns about the limits of L&Es are well illustrated by CopyrightX. Consider the permissions thicket that might have crippled this effort if every recorded lecture, case study, or audio-visual teaching aid used in the course required permission from the copyright owner. Even partially digital knowledge communities, such as CopyrightX, require more than L&Es to function effectively; achieving the high objectives of the course is possible only by reliance on a combination of licenses, well-defined L&Es equally applicable to real-time and online environments, and a fair use doctrine that accommodates flexibility and innovation in teaching. A clear takeaway of *Lessons from CopyrightX* is the importance of flexibility in the design of L&Es. This is especially true in a technologically vibrant environment with innumerable opportunities to construct communities of learning that can, more than any legislative outcome, fundamentally change the conditions in which copyright norms are implemented.

In *Lessons from CopyrightX*, one sees the potential for real copyright reform – reform that rises from the "bottom up" by *teaching* copyright law to as many as possible, thus developing a cadre of people equipped to think critically in their respective contexts about what sensible copyright laws should look like. This possibility of education-driven reform, pioneered by Professor Fisher, is without doubt, in my mind, one of the most important and valuable contributions to overcoming the recurring malaise characterstic of contemporary copyright relations, both national and global.

Professor Sam Ricketson, the world's leading authority on the Berne Convention, focuses on the challenge of obtaining protection for so-called neighboring rights, such as rights for producers of phonograms, performers, and broadcasters. In Chapter 12, *Rights on the Border: The Berne Convention and*

Neighbouring Rights, Professor Ricketson traces the evolution of the relationship between author's rights and neighboring rights, through the recommendations of the Samedan Committee. Both the Committee, convened by the Rome
International Institute for the Unification of Private Law (UNIDROIT), and its
work have remained largely ignored in the literature. As Professor Ricketson
painstakingly shows, this work was influential in the development of the Rome
Convention in 1961, and elements of that work continue to influence current
negotiations at the World Intellectual Property Organization (WIPO), such as
those for a Broadcasting Treaty.[4] A more critical observation is how copyright's
key requirements of authorship and intellectual creativity served to police the
scope of copyright protection in international copyright relations. Contrary to
popular wisdom that depicts an inexorable ratcheting up of exclusive rights in
the international system, the generous definition of "literary and artistic works"
in the 1886 Act of the Berne Convention gradually became narrowly tailored to
the list of works specified in the Convention. Limiting the scope of copyright to
works produced by "authors" thus once served as the most significant limit to
copyright protection.

Many important points emerge from Professor Ricketson's in-depth historical
analysis, but I wish to highlight one that bears upon dominant themes in this
volume: modern copyright law's broad definition of protected works facilitates
end runs around the prudent limits originally imposed by the Berne Convention.
Professor Ricketson notes, for example, that photographs did not make the cut for
protected works in the period 1884–1886, nor did works of architecture, choreographic works, cinematographic works, sound recordings, and others. Of these
early claimants for protection, some failed because the technologies that produced them had not yet come into existence (e.g., the phonograph), while others
failed as a result of serious concern about whether the work was the result of intellectual skill by an author (e.g., photographs). In both cases, however, protection
when it arrived did not apply unconditionally, given concerns about fidelity to
the qualifying criteria. The gradual but conditional acceptance of photographs as
copyrightable works in the Berne Convention, for example, reflects not only the
rigor with which the fundamental copyright standards were applied and upheld,
but also the importance of those standards in disciplining the scope of copyright
and the pace of its expansion. Return to a similar discipline in the application of
copyright standards would greatly help to curb the aggrandizement of contemporary copyright laws.

---

[4] *See Protection of Broadcasting Organizations – Background Brief*, WORLD INTELLECTUAL PROP.
     ORG., www.wipo.int/pressroom/en/briefs/broadcasting.html (last visited June 14, 2016).

Today, there exists an inexorable pull to overcome copyright's external limits by creating sui generis forms of protection, such as for databases, or enacting new forms of protection with similar (if unstated) rationales for industries that are part of the production chain for cultural goods. I agree strongly with Professor Ricketson that the wisdom and carefully thought-out approach to neighboring rights reflected in the recommendations of the Samedan Committee remain vitally important in the digital economy – both to inform how we might construe the fluid notions of "author" and corresponding concept of "works," and also more fundamentally in reconsidering how copyright's expansion unduly impacts the interests of those engaged in other creative industries.

In Chapter 13, *How* Oracle *Erred: The Use/Explanation Distinction and the Future of Computer Copyright*, Professor Wendy Gordon provides an important and new analysis of the copyright struggles between cyber-titans Oracle and Google. Drawing on statutory language, legislative history, caselaw, and policy, Professor Gordon expertly demonstrates that copyright gives no rights to control how others can use software (or other products) for purposes of interoperability. She shows that the primary assertions of control advanced by Oracle fall outside the "scope of right" that any copyright owner could properly hold. Her "scope of right" argument is a novel application of traditional copyright categories. It expands the ability of courts to terminate quickly cases where litigants attempt to employ copyright law to control behavior that belongs to the patent realm. Admittedly, as Professor Gordon notes, the judiciary already has one tool to resolve such cases quickly in the software arena, namely, to find a product "uncopyrightable." But denying copyrightability is a blunt instrument that some judges fear might endanger Congress's decision that at least some computer programs are copyrightable. By contrast, Professor Gordon argues, "scope of right" is a precise and surgical tool, limited in application to particular kinds of behavior, and one that does not eliminate all possibility of copyright protection for the plaintiff's product.

The Oracle case ended with a jury deciding that Google had engaged in "fair use" (a verdict that arrived months after Professor Gordon's article was completed). However, that belated victory for interoperability was highly fact- specific and might not be followed when interoperability questions arise in other circumstances. Therefore, the verdict neither eliminates nor undermines Professor Gordon's key points. "Scope of right" provides judges a valuable lens for evaluating the propriety of claims along the patent/copyright border. To allow copyright to impede interoperability distorts the overall scheme of federal intellectual property protections. Further, fairly clear rules and fairly swift dispositions could follow if, as Professor Gordon recommends, plaintiffs were explicitly required to prove, as part of their *prima facie* case, that a defendant's alleged behavior fell within the "scope" of behavior that copyright law governs.

Finally, in Chapter 14, *Reframing International Copyright Limitations and Exceptions as Development Policy*, I take on the longstanding but uncritical defense of copyright law as a sine qua non of economic development. In particular, I highlight the tension between the liberty-promoting goals of copyright law's well-established L&Es and the economic aspirations of developing and least-developed countries which, I argue, require different types of L&Es. Demands by these countries for new international instruments establishing mandatory L&Es for libraries, archives, and educational institutions at the World Intellectual Property Organization are examples of "development-facilitating" or "development-inducing" L&Es that have long been fiercely resisted in international copyright relations. Limitations and exceptions can promote the flourishing of creative individuals, facilitate cross-border access to diverse cultural goods, and advance the role of cultural institutions in ensuring access to knowledge. But this will not happen in the same way for all countries. Development-facilitating L&Es must be supported by institutional and cultural endowments that effectuate copyright's core commitment to human development. Drawing on insights from development and growth economics, I argue that all countries should have the policy space to enact L&Es in order to pursue a variety of both global and local goals. Developing countries may need even more space than others for this purpose because they lack the domestic institutions that can effectively maneuver within the ostensible rigidity of the international copyright system.

Technology has historically shaped the nature and scope of rights to which copyright holders feel entitled. As advancements in technologies that enable reproduction and distribution have become more pervasive and personal, copyright law as a regime directed at controlling creative content – how, when, and why it is used – is no longer unquestionably consistent with the public interest and is even less so with development. Technological change, while creating new opportunities to monetize content, also creates new conceptions of the social good and may require greater emphasis on copyright L&Es more than at any other time in modern history. New technologies have transformed how users and intermediaries imagine the future; these new user-creators intentionally rely on the opacity of L&Es to foster experimentation and creative processes. Rights granted by copyright law are necessary to consolidate some of the emerging business models; but creativity will not thrive without copyright L&Es. Neither will dynamic entrepreneurship or development policy.

The collective wisdom of the authors in this volume reveals at least three important themes. First, there is a call for copyright law to return to its foundations – promoting creativity and learning—and to do so with a statute that is practical, sensible, and accessible to the citizens whose interests it should represent. Second, there is an effort to identify workable ways to reconcile new forms of creativity, and new interests in how to market creativity, in the face of a technologically vibrant and culturally complex global society. Rewards for creativity, new business models, sustainable and flexible access to knowledge, and distributive justice are all part of copyright law's mosaic. Our rules, national and international, must meaningfully accommodate and equally advance these dimensions. Third, there is a compelling need to retreat from trenchant and increasingly ideological copyright debates. We must do so with a view to designing a new copyright framework in which the rules recognize the contributions and roles of workers, creators, users, and traditional authors.

Pragmatic, well-considered, and careful changes to the law and its enforcement are possible even as we work through the competing ethical, moral, and cultural values that might inform a larger policy transformation in copyright law. The chapters in this book reflect insightful ways to initiate the former, and how we might more constructively embark on the latter to ensure copyright law's continued and strengthened relevance for the future.

1

Justifications for Copyright Limitations and Exceptions

Pamela Samuelson[*]

ABSTRACT

Modern copyright laws grant authors a broad set of rights to control exploitations of their works. Typically tempering the reach of these broad rights are a series of limitations and exceptions (L&Es) adopted by legislatures or by courts through common law adjudication. L&E provisions in national copyright laws often seem like a hodge-podge of special purpose provisions whose policy justifications are sometimes difficult to discern.

This chapter discusses a set of policy justifications for L&Es and considers the relative utilities of specific and open-ended L&Es. Its principal focus will be on U.S. law, although it will feature examples of L&Es embodied in other national copyright laws and authorized by international treaties.

∾ ∾ ∾

1.1. INTRODUCTION

Modern copyright laws grant authors a broad set of rights to control exploitations of their works.[1] Typically tempering the reach of these broad rights is a set of limitations and exceptions (L&Es) adopted by legislatures or developed through common law

[*] Richard M. Sherman Distinguished Professor of Law, Berkeley Law School. I wish to thank Ashley Lin for excellent research support for this essay, Kathryn Hashimoto for research support, construction of the tables, and insightful editing, and Mike Carroll, Niva Elkin-Koren, Paul Geller, Mark Gergen, Daniel Gervais, Jane Ginsburg, Eric Goldman, Wendy Gordon, David Hansen, Bernt Hugenholtz, Justin Hughes, Jessica Litman, Mike Madison, Ruth L. Okediji, Jennifer Rothman, Matthew Sag, Josh Sarnoff, Martin Senftleben, Molly Van Houweling, Berkeley Law colleagues who commented on it during a faculty retreat, and students enrolled in the fall 2014 Berkeley Law Intellectual Property Scholarship seminar for their helpful comments on earlier drafts.
[1] *See, e.g.,* 17 U.S.C. § 106. An issue worth exploration in another essay is the extent to which the considerable breadth of the exclusive rights in modern copyright laws is justifiable.

adjudication.[2] L&Es generally enable free use of protected works under national copyright laws, although some L&Es are subject to equitable remuneration obligations.[3]

Copyright L&Es are, in general, quite specific as to the types of users, types of uses, and types of works that qualify for the safe harbors they provide.[4] These L&Es are largely the product of legislative deliberations about how far exclusive rights should extend and under what circumstances and to what extent those rights should be curtailed. Legislatures have recognized that authors need to be able to use some expression from existing works to create critical commentaries, parodies, biographies, and the like; news reporters need to quote from political speeches and public policy documents on issues of the day; teachers need to draw upon copyrighted materials to illustrate lessons for students; libraries and archives need to copy materials for preservation purposes; lawyers and judges need to make copies of documents as evidence; and ephemeral or incidental copies lacking in economic significance need to be exempted.[5]

It is eminently reasonable for legislatures to adopt specific L&Es to deal with these kinds of stable uses that legislatures can easily anticipate. The two main advantages of specific L&Es are, first, that they provide a reasonable measure of predictability,

---

[2] *See, e.g.*, 17 U.S.C. §§ 107–122. The distinction between "limitations" and "exceptions" is somewhat murky and the two terms are often used interchangeably in copyright discourse. "Exceptions" are probably best understood as outright exemptions from copyright liability. The term "limitations" includes provisions that create compulsory or statutory licenses; these permit certain acts, but subject them to an obligation to pay for the use. Whether L&Es should be understood as creating defenses to infringement claims or legal rights to engage in specified conduct is contested. *See, e.g.*, National Research Council, The Digital Dilemma: Intellectual Property in the Information Age 5 (2000). There are, of course, many other types of copyright limitations, including limits on copyright subject matter, originality and fixation requirements, the exclusion of ideas, and the duration of rights, among others.

[3] *See, e.g.*, Jane C. Ginsburg, *Fair Use for Free, or Permitted-But-Paid*, 29 Berkeley Tech. L.J. 1383, 1385–86 (2014) (recommending permitted-but-paid L&Es for many "redistributive" uses that American courts have ruled are fair, and pointing to foreign L&Es that permit uses subject to remuneration). Some European scholars have proposed a model copyright law for the EU under which some L&Es would be subject to remuneration. *See* The Wittem Project: European Copyright Code, art. 5 (April 2010) [hereinafter Wittem Project], *available at* www.copyrightcode.eu.

[4] Countries often have dozens of L&Es. Germany's copyright law, for instance, has thirty-seven L&E provisions. Act on Copyright and Related Rights, Sept. 9, 1965, § VI (Ger.), *available at* www .gesetze-im-internet.de/englisch_urhg/. Some common law countries (Canada, for example) have fairly long lists of specific L&Es as well. *See, e.g.*, Copyright Act of Canada (R.S.C., 1985, c. C-42), arts. 29–32.2. Even when European nations have adopted substantially the same exception, there may nonetheless be variations in scope. *See, e.g.*, P. Bernt Hugenholtz & Martin R.F. Senftleben, Fair Use in Europe: In Search of Flexibilities 6 (2011), *available at* www.ivir.nl/publications/ hugenholtz/Fair%20Use%20Report%20PUB.pdf (comparing European national implementations of quotation exceptions).

[5] *See, e.g.*, Directive 2001/29/EC of the European Parliament and of the Council of 22 May 2001 on the Harmonisation of Certain Aspects of Copyright and Related Rights in the Information Society, art. 5, 2001 O.J. (L 167) 10, 16–17 [hereinafter InfoSoc Directive] (setting forth permissible L&Es in the EU).

and second, that prospective users can make investments or engage in privileged activities in reliance on them. However, open-ended, flexible L&Es, such as the U.S. fair use doctrine, may also be useful because legislatures cannot foresee all circumstances in which L&Es may be needed.

Taken together, the L&E provisions of national copyright laws may, at first blush, seem a hodgepodge of special purpose provisions whose policy justifications are difficult to discern.[6] However, a closer examination suggests that the copyright L&Es are generally supported by a range of principled justifications.[7]

To lay a foundation for the discussion of these justifications, it is useful to understand how copyright L&Es have evolved over time.[8] Section 1.2 focuses on the history of L&Es in U.S. copyright law. During the first hundred years or so of this nation's existence, U.S. law had no L&Es mainly because the exclusive rights granted to authors were much narrower in scope than they became over time. In the late nineteenth and early twentieth centuries, U.S. courts invented the exhaustion of rights and fair use doctrines as the first common law limits on copyright's scope on the theory that Congress did not intend for exclusive rights to extend as far as some claimants asserted. The exhaustion doctrine was first codified in the Copyright Act of 1909. It was not until the Copyright Act of 1976 ("1976 Act") that the more open-ended fair use doctrine was codified. Both doctrines have continued to evolve in the decades since their enactments.[9] Less well-known, although quite important to those whom they affect, are dozens of other L&Es codified in the

---

6   *See, e.g.,* 17 U.S.C. §§ 107–122; InfoSoc Directive, *supra* note 5, art. 5. *See also* P. Bernt Hugenholtz, *Fierce Creatures: Copyright Exemptions: Towards Extinction?* Keynote Speech at IFLA/IMPRIMATUR Conference on Rights, Limitations and Exceptions: Striking a Proper Balance (Oct. 30, 1997), *in* 2 INTELLECTUAL PROPERTY RIGHTS: CRITICAL CONCEPTS IN LAW 232 (David Vaver ed., 2006) (noting the "bewildering variety" of L&Es in national copyright laws).

7   The Copyright Principles Project (CPP) (of which I was the convenor) made several recommendations about L&Es, including that they should be the product of principles, not just of lobbying. *See* Pamela Samuelson & Members of the CPP, *The Copyright Principles Project: Directions for Reform*, 25 BERKELEY TECH. L.J. 1175, 1228–34 (2010). The CPP started me on the quest for a principled approach to L&Es. In the winter of 2013–14, I gave talks about copyright L&Es at Waseda University, Osaka University, Tilburg University, and the European Parliament. The taxonomy of L&E justifications discussed in this chapter evolved as I studied the L&Es in the laws of Japan, the Netherlands, and the United States, as well as those authorized by the InfoSoc Directive, *supra* note 5. Subsequently, I discovered another scholar's effort to articulate principles for L&Es. *See* Daniel Gervais, *Making Copyright Whole: A Principled Approach to Copyright Exceptions and Limitations*, 5 U. OTTAWA L. TECH. J. 1 (2008). His article does not, however, map the proposed principles for L&Es with specific L&Es that are illustrative examples.

8   It is obviously not possible to discuss the evolution of L&Es in all national copyright laws. However, a crucial point of the U.S. story – that the need for numerous specific L&Es was recognized as legislatures expanded the exclusive rights granted to authors – is, I believe, generally true for other jurisdictions as well. Professor Gervais provides a table showing the evolution of exclusive rights and L&E provisions in the Berne Convention. *See* Gervais, *supra* note 7, at 8–9.

9   Sections 1.3 and 1.4 will discuss some of this evolution.

1976 Act, as well as L&Es that have been added to U.S. law since then, virtually all of which aim to mitigate the effects of an expansion of rights to authors. Most of the specific U.S. L&Es have counterparts in national copyright laws in other countries, although relatively few countries have an open-ended flexible L&E such as fair use.

Section 1.3 considers ten justifications for the existence of these L&Es, grouped into six larger clusters. One cluster focuses on protecting authorial interests and promoting ongoing authorship. A second acknowledges user interests, creating a buffer for personal autonomy and ownership interests of consumers. A third cluster aims to promote a broader set of public interests, including those that promote public access to information, activities of nonprofit institutions, and functions of public institutions. A fourth addresses economic issues, such as fostering competition and innovation, exempting incidental uses that lack economic significance, and addressing market failures. A fifth achieves politically expedient ends. A sixth type responds to the need for flexibility and adaptability over time. Although this section's principal focus is on U.S. law, it provides numerous examples of specific L&Es embodied in other national copyright laws that aim to achieve the same or similar objectives as U.S. L&Es.[10] Some L&Es are justified on more than one ground.

Section 1.4 considers in further detail the benefits of open-ended L&Es in national copyright laws and responds to critiques against them. It makes three main points. First, open-ended L&Es such as fair use have an advantage over specific L&Es in an era of rapid social, economic, and technological change by enabling copyright law to adapt to new circumstances and to evolve over time without the need for continual statutory amendments. Second, fair use is more predictable than some commentators believe, but fair use is not the only way to create flexibility in national copyright laws. Third, open-ended L&Es such as fair use are compatible with international treaty obligations.

This chapter concludes that the optimal policy for L&Es in national copyright laws may well be to have both specific exceptions and an open-ended exception such as fair use. Specific L&Es are useful for categories of justified uses that are relatively stable over time and for which predictability is more important than flexibility. Open-ended L&Es allow the law to adapt to new uses not contemplated by the legislature.

---

[10] For information about permitted and mandatory L&Es in international treaties, *see* P. Bernt Hugenholtz & Ruth L. Okediji, Conceiving an International Instrument on Limitations and Exceptions to Copyright: Final Report 51–55 (Mar. 6, 2008). Although some laws external to copyright – such as freedom of expression, competition, and consumer protection laws – may limit the reach of copyright, *id.* at 29–34, I concentrate in this chapter on L&Es internal to national copyright laws.

1.2. THE EVOLUTION OF COPYRIGHT L&ES IN U.S. LAW

Until the early twentieth century, copyright laws typically granted authors a fairly narrow set of exclusive rights and those rights were, in general, narrowly construed. When rights were narrow, it was unnecessary to create exceptions to limit those rights. As legislatures expanded authorial rights to cover a broader array of activities, they discovered the need to create limits on the exclusive rights. Table 1.1 illustrates the evolution of L&Es in U.S. copyright law.

1.2.1. *Copyright Law Had No Statutory Exceptions When Rights Were Narrow*

Shortly after the United States was founded, Congress passed the Copyright Act of 1790.[11] It granted to authors of books, maps, and charts a set of four exclusive rights that were conditioned on compliance with a set of formalities aimed at giving notice of copyright claims. The rights were to "print, reprint, publish or vend" those works.[12] Failure to comply with the required formalities caused the work to attain public domain status and be free for all manner of unlicensed uses.[13]

During the nineteenth century, the exclusive rights initially conferred in the 1790 Act continued to serve as the main legal protections for copyrighted works. Some new exclusive rights were, however, created. When Congress extended copyright protection to dramatic works in 1856, it granted their authors the right to control public performances.[14] When extending protection to works of art for the first time in 1870, Congress similarly granted artists new exclusive rights to control the "completing, copying, executing, [and] finishing" them.[15] Authors of books got two new rights in 1870, one to control translations of their works, and a second to dramatize nondramatic works.[16] Musical compositions became copyright subject matter in 1831,[17] but Congress did not grant composers a right to control public performances of them until 1897.[18]

---

[11] Act of May 31, 1790, ch. 15, 1 Stat. 124 (repealed 1831).

[12] *Id.* § 1 at 124.

[13] *Id.* § 3 at 125.

[14] Act of Aug. 18, 1856, ch. 169, 11 Stat. 138, 138–39 (repealed 1870).

[15] Act of July 8, 1870, ch. 230, § 86, 16 Stat. 198, 212 (repealed 1909).

[16] *Id.*

[17] Act of Feb. 3, 1831, ch. 16, § 1, 4 Stat. 436, 436 (repealed 1870). Musical compositions had sometimes been registered as "books." *See* R. Anthony Reese, *Innocent Infringement in U.S. Copyright Law: A History*, 30 COLUM. J.L. & ARTS 133, 136 (2007).

[18] Act of Jan. 6, 1897, ch. 4, 29 Stat. 481, 481–82. Under that act, only for-profit performances could infringe.

Through the mid-nineteenth century, copyright's exclusive rights were generally interpreted rather narrowly.[19] Fair abridgements,[20] dramatizations,[21] making improved versions of older works,[22] and translations[23] were generally regarded as noninfringing. For the most part, only exact or near-exact copying of protected works would infringe.[24]

The fair abridgement doctrine was curtailed significantly after 1841 under the influence of the *Folsom v. Marsh* decision.[25] In *Folsom*, Justice Story ruled that a biographer's unauthorized excerpting of 353 pages of George Washington's letters from a twelve-volume biography was an infringement because so much was taken that it would supplant demand for the original.[26] In *Folsom*, Justice Story articulated some factors to consider when undertaking an infringement analysis, which explains why *Folsom* is credited as the source of the four-factor fair use test.[27]

Even though a few late-nineteenth-century decisions mention fair use, those cases typically involved unconvincing infringement claims.[28] Fair use did not mature into a meaningful limitation on the scope of copyright until the early twentieth century. The 1903 case of *Bloom & Hamlin v. Nixon* invoked fair use in the modern sense of the term as a defense to infringement for the use of small parts of a song in a parody.[29]

---

[19] *See, e.g.,* Oren Bracha, *The Ideology of Authorship Revisited: Authors, Markets, and Liberal Values in Early American Copyright*, 118 YALE L.J. 186, 224–25 (2008); Matthew Sag, *The Prehistory of Fair Use*, 76 BROOK. L. REV. 1371, 1380–87 (2011) (tracing this view back to the Statute of Anne, 1710, 8 Ann. c. 19 (Eng.), and cases and treatises from the eighteenth century).

[20] *See, e.g.,* Gyles v. Wilcox (1740) 26 Eng. Rep. 489, 490 (Ch.) ("[A]bridgments may with great propriety be called a new book, because not only the paper and print, but the invention, learning, and judgment of the author is [shown] in them....").

[21] *See* Stewart v. Abend, 495 U.S. 207, 245–46 (1990) (Stevens, J., dissenting) (citing *Stowe v. Thomas*, 23 F. Cas. 201, 208 (C.C.E.D. Pa. 1853) (No. 13,514)). *See also* AUGUSTINE BIRRELL, SEVEN LECTURES ON THE LAW AND HISTORY OF COPYRIGHT IN BOOKS 155–56 (1899) (discussing the omission of unauthorized dramatizations of novels as infringements in English copyright law).

[22] *See, e.g.,* Matthewson v. Stockdale (1806) 33 Eng. Rep. 103 (Ch.) 105; 12 Ves. Jun. 270, 275 (noting that an improvement on an original is noninfringing); Sayre v. Moore (1785) (holding that the reuse of elements of a navigation map was noninfringing because of defendant's improvements), *cited in* Cary v. Longman (1801) 120 Eng. Rep. 138 (K.B.) 139 n.b; 1 East 358, 361 n.b.

[23] *See, e.g.,* Stowe v. Thomas, 23 F. Cas. 201 (C.C.E.D. Pa. 1853) (No. 13,514) (holding that an unauthorized German translation of *Uncle Tom's Cabin* did not infringe). This ruling was legislatively overturned in 1870. *See supra* note 16 and accompanying text.

[24] In addition to case law, *supra* notes 20–23, early copyright treatises endorsed this view. *See* ROBERT MAUGHAM, A TREATISE ON THE LAWS OF LITERARY PROPERTY 126 (1828); RICHARD GODSON, A PRACTICAL TREATISE ON THE LAW OF PATENTS FOR INVENTIONS AND OF COPYRIGHT 215 (1823).

[25] 9 F. Cas. 342 (C.C.D. Mass. 1841) (No. 4901).

[26] *Id.* at 349.

[27] *See, e.g.,* Bracha, *supra* note 19, at 229–30.

[28] *See, e.g.,* Simms v. Stanton, 75 F. 6, 10–11 (C.C.N.D. Cal. 1896) (mentioning fair use in considering infringement claim based on similarities in books on physiognomy).

[29] 125 F. 977 (C.C.E.D. Pa. 1903). For a history of fair use prior to its codification, see ALAN LATMAN, FAIR USE OF COPYRIGHTED WORKS, STUDY NO. 14, COPYRIGHT LAW REVISION, STUDIES PREPARED

The "first sale" or exhaustion of rights limit on copyright was, like fair use, the product of a common law process. In the 1908 Supreme Court decision in *Bobbs-Merrill Co. v. Straus*, the Supreme Court recognized this limit on the exclusive right to control the sale of copies of copyrighted works.[30] Bobbs-Merrill had sought to enforce a $1 per copy resale price through a notice printed in its books that "[n]o dealer is licensed to sell [the book] at a less price, and a sale at a less price will be treated as an infringement of the copyright."[31] The Court ruled that Straus's resales of the book at a lower price were not infringements because the first authorized sale of copies to Straus had exhausted Bobbs-Merrill's right to control sales of those copies.[32]

1.2.2. *The Copyright Act of 1909 Created the First Statutory Exceptions*

A year after the *Bobbs-Merrill* decision, Congress passed the Copyright Act of 1909.[33] That Act granted a more specific set of exclusive rights for each type of protected work. Authors of literary works were, for example, given a translation right, authors of nondramatic works a right to dramatize them, authors of dramatic works a right to convert them to novels, and authors of musical works the right to arrange or adapt their works.[34] Other exclusive rights were carefully cabined so that only certain types of works qualified for them and only for-profit performances could infringe rights in musical compositions.[35]

The 1909 Act had three L&E provisions. One was a codification of the exhaustion doctrine.[36] A second limited the newly created right of composers to control mechanical reproductions of their music in sound recordings by subjecting their works to a compulsory license.[37] Once a copyrighted song had been recorded once, anyone could re-record the song as long as they paid the license fee set forth in

---

FOR THE SUBCOMM. ON PATENTS, TRADEMARKS AND COPYRIGHTS, S. COMM. ON THE JUDICIARY, 86th Cong. 3, 8–14 (Comm. Print 1960) [hereinafter LATMAN STUDY].

[30] 210 U.S. 339 (1908).

[31] *Id.* at 341.

[32] *Id.* at 351. In *Bobbs-Merrill*, the Court expressed skepticism that Congress had intended the vending right to allow control of resales of copies of protected works. Some cases before *Bobbs-Merrill* had recognized limits on copyright owner rights to control repairs and renewals of copies of protected works. *See, e.g.,* Aaron Perzanowski & Jason Schultz, *Digital Exhaustion,* 58 UCLA L. REV. 889, 912–13 (2011).

[33] Act of Mar. 4, 1909, Pub. L. No. 60–349, 35 Stat. 1075 (repealed 1976).

[34] *Id.* § 1(b).

[35] *See id.* § 1(c) (lecture, sermon, address, or similar), § 1(e) (musical composition). Only dramatic works had a public performance right without regard to profit. *Id.* § 1(d).

[36] *Id.* § 41, 35 Stat. at 1091. In 1947, the provisions of the 1909 Act were renumbered, and the exhaustion doctrine became § 27. *See* Act of July 30, 1947, Pub. L. No. 80–281, 61 Stat. 652.

[37] Act of Mar. 4, 1909 § 1(e).

the statute.[38] A third exempted coin-operated music machines unless their owners charged for admission to the premises where the machines were located.[39]

~~As the twentieth century wore on, the uncodified fair use doctrine became the main common law limit~~ on copyright's exclusive rights. Cases typically involved parodies and burlesques, scholarly quotations, critical commentary, and news reporting, although not all of the defenses prevailed.[40] Some exhaustion cases were litigated as well.[41] Congress did not, however, create any new copyright exceptions during the first seventy years of the twentieth century.[42]

1.2.3. *Congress Created L&Es as It Expanded Rights in the 1976 Act*

By the mid-1950s, Congress initiated work toward a general revision of U.S. copyright law, authorizing the Copyright Office to commission a series of studies to inform the revision agenda.[43] In 1961, the Register issued a report to Congress with his analysis of the need for new legislation and some preliminary recommendations. One goal was to simplify and generalize the exclusive rights provisions to these four: to make and publish copies, to make new versions, to publicly perform, and to make recordings.[44]

The 1961 Report recommended adoption of only two exceptions to these exclusive rights: one to codify fair use and one to allow libraries to make single copies of journal articles for their patrons' research use.[45] The 1961 Report proposed to retain

---

[38] In adopting this license, Congress did not so much intend to allow "covers" of songs by unlicensed artists (although that has become its primary function). Its goal was to enable more than one sound recording company to record the music. *See infra* notes 168–73 and accompanying text for a discussion of this compulsory license.

[39] *Id.* § 1(e). This came to be known as the "jukebox" exception because of the industry that later grew up around it. The exception was originally intended to limit liability for coin-operated music machines perceived to have little economic significance. By 1961, however, the annual gross revenue of the jukebox industry was half a billion dollars, and the Register was determined to repeal the exemption. *See* H. COMM. ON THE JUDICIARY, 87TH CONG., COPYRIGHT LAW REVISION: REPORT OF THE REGISTER OF COPYRIGHTS ON THE GENERAL REVISION OF THE U.S. COPYRIGHT LAW 31–32 (Comm. Print 1961) [hereinafter REGISTER'S 1961 REPORT]. The "jukebox" exception is discussed further *infra* notes 178, 200 and accompanying text.

[40] *See, e.g.*, LATMAN STUDY, *supra* note 29, at 8–12 (discussing cases).

[41] *See, e.g.*, Fawcett Publ'ns v. Elliot Publ'g Co., 46 F. Supp. 717 (S.D.N.Y. 1942) (not infringement to combine and rebind sets of comic books); Bureau of Nat'l Literature v. Sells, 211 F. 379 (W.D. Wash. 1914) (not infringement to overhaul and reconstruct secondhand sets of copyrighted books).

[42] Bills were introduced to repeal the jukebox exception, but none passed. *See* REGISTER'S 1961 REPORT, *supra* note 39, at 31.

[43] *Id.* at ix. Five of the thirty-four studies concerned L&Es: one on fair use, one on photoduplication of copyrighted materials by libraries, one on limitations on performing rights, and two on compulsory license issues. These studies can be found at www.copyright.gov/history/studies.html.

[44] REGISTER'S 1961 REPORT, *supra* note 39, at 21–24.

[45] *Id.* at 24–26. This Report also proposed to repeal the two 1909 Act compulsory licenses. *Id.* at 31–36. It did not mention the exhaustion doctrine, which had been conceived as a limit on the vending right.

the "for profit" limit on the public performance right as to literary and musical works.[46]

By 1965, when the Register issued a supplementary report to accompany redrafted legislation,[47] many changes were evident. Under the 1965 draft legislation,[48] authors would have five exclusive rights, and each would be applicable to all types of works: a reproduction right, a derivative work right, a distribution to the public right, a public performance right, and a public exhibition right.[49] Although the proposed public exhibition right eventually became the public display right, these are exclusive rights in the 1976 Act.[50]

The new exclusive rights would, as before, be subject to fair use and exhaustion limitations.[51] In addition, because the 1965 Report proposed considerable expansions of authorial rights, the Register recommended two new kinds of exemptions, one set for certain nonprofit activities and the other to address certain industry-specific issues.

The need for the nonprofit exemptions arose because the 1965 exclusive rights provision would drop the for-profit limit on the public performance right, expand the public performance right to all types of works, and create a new public exhibition right. Four nonprofit exemptions from the public performance and exhibition rights were proposed in 1965: one for face-to-face classroom teaching; a second for closed circuit educational broadcasting; a third for reciting or singing literary and musical works during religious services; and a fourth for public performances and exhibitions of these works during nonprofit educational, religious, or charitable

---

[46] *Id.* at 28. However, the Register thought that motion pictures and choreographic works should have a public performance right without regard to the profit or nonprofit status of the use or user. *Id.*

[47] H. COMM. ON THE JUDICIARY, 89TH CONG., COPYRIGHT LAW REVISION PART 6: SUPPLEMENTARY REPORT OF THE REGISTER OF COPYRIGHTS ON THE GENERAL REVISION OF THE U.S. COPYRIGHT LAW: 1965 REVISION BILL (Comm. Print 1965) [hereinafter REGISTER'S SUPPLEMENTARY REPORT]. There was an intermediate draft between 1961 and 1965 that included a preliminary draft bill and commentary. *See* HOUSE COMM. ON THE JUDICIARY, 88TH CONG., COPYRIGHT LAW REVISION PART 3: PRELIMINARY DRAFT FOR REVISED U.S. COPYRIGHT LAW AND DISCUSSIONS AND COMMENTS ON THE DRAFT (Comm. Print 1964). In the interest of keeping a very long story shorter than it would otherwise be, this chapter focuses on the 1961 and 1965 reports as they set the parameters for the revision.

[48] H.R. 4347, 89th Cong., 2d Sess. (1965) and S. 1006, 89th Cong., 2d Sess. (1965).

[49] REGISTER'S SUPPLEMENTARY REPORT, *supra* note 47, at 15. The scope of the public exhibition right under the 1909 Act had been uncertain. *Id.* at 20. In 1965, the Register proposed to make the public exhibition right applicable to a broad set of works, but to treat exhibition of motion pictures under the public performance right. *Id.* at 20–21.

[50] 17 U.S.C. § 106(1)-(5). The public performance and public display rights, as enacted, did not apply to all types of works. Sound recordings, for instance, were omitted from the performance right for reasons discussed *infra* Section 1.3.5. The U.S. Copyright Office has called for extending the public performance right to sound recordings. *See* Maria A. Pallante, *The Next Great Copyright Act*, 36 COLUM. J.L. & ARTS 315, 324–25 (2013).

[51] REGISTER'S SUPPLEMENTARY REPORT, *supra* note 47, at 25–28 (fair use), 70–71 (first sale).

events under certain conditions.[52] With some modifications, these exemptions ended up in the 1976 Act.[53]

Among the 1965 Report's industry-specific exemptions was one to shield operators of broadcast signal "booster" technologies from copyright liability.[54] Another aimed to allow broadcasters to make ephemeral copies of programs in the course of their business operations.[55] The 1965 Report also proposed an L&E to ensure that the scope of copyright in pictorial, graphic, and sculptural (PGS) works would not extend to the design of any useful article depicted therein.[56] The 1976 Act adopted the ephemeral copy and PGS limits, and eventually adopted a complex new provision enabling cable systems to retransmit broadcast signals subject to a compulsory license.[57]

Five further exceptions proposed in the 1965 Report concerned the music industry. Although now endorsing the extension of copyright protection to sound recordings,[58] the Register perceived the need for limits on rights accorded to their owners.[59] One exception aimed to preclude a public performance right to sound recordings.[60] A second would restrict the scope of the reproduction right so that imitating another's recording would not infringe.[61] A third would retain, with some modifications, the

---

[52] *Id.* at 31–40. As the House Report later explained, "[t]he approach of the bill, as in many foreign laws, is first to state the public performance right in broad terms, and then to provide specific exceptions for educational and other nonprofit uses." H.R. REP. NO. 94–1476, at 62 (1976), *reprinted in* 1976 U.S.C.C.A.N. 5659, 5676.

[53] 17 U.S.C. § 110(1)-(4). By 1976, the closed circuit educational broadcasting exception was changed to a more technology-neutral and more general instructional use provision. *Id.* § 110(2). The charitable use exceptions is conditioned on a lack of payment to the performers, the event being held either without admission charges or with any surplus from the admission charge being used exclusively for educational, religious, or charitable uses. In addition, advance notice must be given to the copyright owner about the intended use. *Id.* § 110(4). This requirement was added so that copyright owners would not be forced to "donate" to charities they did not support. *See Bills for the General Revision of the Copyright Law, Title 17 of the United States Code, and for Other Purposes, Hearings on H.R. 4347, H.R. 5680, H.R.6831, H.R. 6835 Before Subcomm. No. 3 of the H. Comm. on the Judiciary*, 89th Cong., 1st Sess. (1966), Part 2 at 1130.

[54] However, the Register thought cable retransmissions of broadcast signals should fall within the new public performance right. REGISTER'S SUPPLEMENTARY REPORT, *supra* note 47, at 40–43. Eventually, the broadcast and cable industries negotiated a compromise provision, now embodied in 17 U.S.C. § 111, that provides a compulsory license for cable retransmission of copyrighted programs. This compromise is discussed *infra* notes 180–89 and accompanying text.

[55] REGISTER'S SUPPLEMENTARY REPORT, *supra* note 47, at 44–47. This exemption is now codified at 17 U.S.C. § 112.

[56] REGISTER'S SUPPLEMENTARY REPORT, *supra* note 47, at 47–49. Case law supported this limit on copyright scope. *See, e.g.*, Fulmer v. United States, 103 F. Supp. 1021 (Ct. Cl. 1952) (copyright in drawing did not extend to parachute design depicted therein).

[57] *See* 17 U.S.C. §§ 112 (ephemeral copies), 113(b) (useful articles in PGS works).

[58] REGISTER'S SUPPLEMENTARY REPORT, *supra* note 47, at 5.

[59] *Id.* at 49–52.

[60] *Id.* at 51.

[61] *Id.* at 51–53. Section 1.3.5 discusses the rationale for denying public performance rights to sound recordings.

compulsory license that had long allowed sound recordings to be made of music for a set fee.[62] A fourth would have granted jukebox operators a one year moratorium on copyright liability to give them time to negotiate license fees with music copyright owners.[63] A fifth would exempt from liability those who merely turned on radio or television sets with consumer-grade equipment.[64] With some refinements (and eventually a compulsory license for jukeboxes), these rules ended up in the 1976 Act.[65]

The 1965 Report backed away from the Register's earlier proposal to create an exemption so that libraries could make single copies of articles or excerpts from books for patrons engaged in research. This change was in response to strenuous opposition to the 1961 recommendation from all sides.[66] Authors and publishers thought it went too far, and librarians and educators thought it did not go far enough.[67] In the 1965 Report, the Register acknowledged that rights holders had some legitimate concerns about a library copying exception that might harm markets for their works.[68] The Register now proposed that library copying be dealt with under fair use.[69]

While the library copying issue was being debated in the halls of Congress, Williams & Wilkins, a publisher of medical research journals, decided to test library copying in court. It sued the U.S. government to challenge the policy of two federal research institutions whose staff regularly made photocopies of individual journal articles for researcher patrons of the library. In a split decision, the Court of Claims ruled that this practice was fair use, and an evenly divided Supreme Court affirmed that ruling.[70]

Notwithstanding the success in that litigation, library organizations wanted greater reassurances than the *Williams & Wilkins* decision provided. Ultimately, these organizations persuaded the Register and Congress to support a new exception that exempts many common library activities, including one for copying single articles for research patrons.[71]

---

[62] *Id.* at 53. The Register recommended some adjustments to the license. *Id.* at 53–59.

[63] *Id.* at 59–61.

[64] *Id.* at 44. This was meant to legislatively overturn *Buck v. Jewell LaSalle Realty Co.*, 283 U.S. 193 (1931), which had held a hotel proprietor liable for copyright infringement for having the radio playing in the hotel.

[65] *See* 17 U.S.C. §§ 114(a), 114(b), 115(a), 116, 110(5)(B).

[66] The 1961 proposal for a library copy exception may have initially seemed noncontroversial because it was consistent with the 1935 "gentlemen's agreement" under which publishers had accepted that libraries, archives, and museums could make single copies for researchers. *See* Peter B. Hirtle, *Research, Libraries, and Fair Use: The Gentlemen's Agreement of 1935*, 53 J. COPYRIGHT SOC'Y U.S.A. 545, 546 (2005).

[67] REGISTER'S SUPPLEMENTARY REPORT, *supra* note 47, at 26–27.

[68] *Id.* at xiv-xvi, 14–15.

[69] *Id.* at 27–28.

[70] Williams & Wilkins Co. v. United States, 487 F.2d 1345 (Ct. Cl. 1973), *aff'd by an equally divided court*, 420 U.S. 376 (1975).

[71] 17 U.S.C. § 108(d).

By 1965, educational use copying had become even more contentious than library copying.[72] Educators wanted a general exception for copying done for nonprofit educational purposes, but publisher and author groups strongly objected. The 1965 Report recommended that educational use copying be dealt with under the fair use doctrine,[73] and Congress concurred in this result.[74]

Educators were, however, able to influence the contours of the fair use provision in four ways: first, by successfully defending the inclusion of teaching, scholarship, and research as three of the six favored uses; second, by persuading Congress to insert "(including multiple copies for classroom use)" after "teaching" in the list of favored uses; third, by supporting language directing courts to consider "whether [the] use is of a commercial nature or is for nonprofit educational purposes" as part of the purpose-of-the-use factor; and fourth, by defeating some limiting language ("to the extent reasonably necessary or incidental to a legitimate purpose").[75]

Between 1965 and 1976, several new L&Es found their way into the copyright revision bills,[76] and those proposed in 1965 generally became wordier and more complicated. During the copyright revision process, debates over various L&Es were

---

[72] For a detailed discussion of the debate over educational uses, see, e.g., WILLIAM F. PATRY, THE FAIR USE PRIVILEGE IN COPYRIGHT LAW (1985).

[73] REGISTER'S SUPPLEMENTARY REPORT, *supra* note 47, at 27–28.

[74] *See* H.R. REP. NO. 94–1476, at 66–72 (1976). Some members of Congress urged educators and publishers to negotiate a set of fair use guidelines for educational use copying. *Id.* at 67. The result was two sets of negotiated guidelines which have had considerable influence on institutional practices. *See* Agreement on Guidelines for Classroom Copying in Not-for-profit Educational Institutions with Respect to Books and Periodicals (often referred to as the "Classroom Guidelines"), *id.* at 68–70; Guidelines for Educational Uses of Music, *id.* at 70–71. It remains controversial whether these guidelines are a "floor," with plenty of headroom for additional fair use copies for educational purposes, or a "ceiling," so that copying beyond the guidelines should be presumed unfair. *See* Kenneth D. Crews, *The Law of Fair Use and the Illusion of Fair Use Guidelines*, 62 OHIO ST. L.J. 601 (2001). Educational use copying and the negotiated guidelines remain controversial. *See* Cambridge Univ. Press v. Becker, 863 F. Supp. 2d 1190 (N.D. Ga. 2012), *rev'd sub nom.* Cambridge Univ. Press v. Patton, 769 F.3d 1232 (11th Cir. 2014). CUP charged that Georgia State University's electronic course reserve policy was unfair because it exceeded what was permissible under the Classroom Guidelines. *See* Brief of Appellants at 63, Cambridge Univ. Press v. Becker, Nos. 12-14676-FF, 12-15147-FF (11th Cir. Jan. 28, 2013). The legislative history viewed the guidelines as "a reasonable interpretation of the minimum standards of fair use." H.R. REP. NO. 94–1476, at 72.

[75] *Compare* 17 U.S.C. § 107 *with* REGISTER'S SUPPLEMENTARY REPORT, *supra* note 47, at 27 (draft language for the fair use provision).

[76] Between 1965 and 1976, three new compulsory licenses emerged: one for cable retransmissions of broadcast programming, one for jukebox performances of music, and one for certain uses of works in public broadcasts. These were codified in 17 U.S.C. §§ 111, 116, and 118. *See infra* notes 178–89, 201 and accompanying text for a discussion of the origins of these licenses. The nonprofit performance exceptions became more numerous in § 110. *See infra* notes 198–203 and accompanying text. The oddest exception in the 1976 Act was 17 U.S.C. § 117. It preserved the status quo (whatever that was) as to computer uses of copyrighted works while a National Commission on New Technological Uses of Copyrighted Works deliberated on these issues. *See* H.R. REP. NO. 94–1476, at 116.

among the most controversial issues with which the Register and Congress had to contend, especially those affecting the cable and jukebox industries, public broadcasters, and libraries and educational institutions.

Although several of the 1976 Act L&Es were highly controversial prior to enactment,[77] these controversies generally ceased after adoption. Only fair use and the small business public performance exception have attracted much litigation.[78] Since 1976, Congress has amended some of the 1976 Act L&Es as well as added new L&E provisions to the law, most of which have subsections setting forth more than one L&E.[79] These amendments have significantly contributed to the bulk of the U.S. copyright statute since its L&E provisions now constitute almost half of its considerable heft. The L&E provisions are, moreover, a motley crew. The next section will explain just how varied they are in substance and in policy justifications.

1.3. JUSTIFICATIONS FOR COPYRIGHT L&ES

Countries vary substantially in the number and types of L&Es in their laws.[80] Underlying the L&Es in national copyright laws, though, are discernible justifications.[81]

---

[77] *See supra* notes 66–74 and accompanying text for a discussion of the library and educational use controversies; other controversies are discussed *infra* notes 180–89, 196–201 and accompanying text.

[78] *See, e.g.,* Sailor Music v. Gap Stores, Inc., 516 F. Supp. 923 (S.D.N.Y 1981), *aff'd*, 668 F.2d 84 (2d Cir. 1981) (interpreting 17 U.S.C. § 110(5)). Fair use decisions are discussed at length in Section 1.4.

[79] Among the post-1976 new exceptions are 17 U.S.C. §§ 119 and 122 to deal with secondary transmissions of broadcast programming via satellite, both of which have compulsory license provisions, § 120 to limit the scope of copyrights in architectural works, and § 121 to facilitate greater access to nondramatic literary works for print-disabled persons. Some exceptions adopted in 1976 have been amended, most notably an L&E that allows certain copying and adaptations of computer programs in § 117 and provisions to address digital audio performance of musical works and sound recordings in §§ 114 and 115.

[80] Japan, for instance, has a large number of L&Es; France has very few. *See* Copyright Act, Law No. 43 of June 27, 2012, arts. 30–50 (Japan); Intellectual Property Code art. L122-5(1)-(5) (France). Professor Gervais points out how unharmonized L&Es are on the international level. Gervais, *supra* note 7, at 11–12.

[81] Professor Hugenholtz has identified three types of justifications for copyright L&Es: some to protect fundamental freedoms (such as free expression and privacy interests), some to fulfill public interests (such as library and disabled person exceptions), and others to address market failures (such as compulsory licenses). Hugenholtz, *supra* note 6, at 237–38. The Wittem European Copyright Code grouped L&Es into four categories: incidental uses, uses for purposes of freedom of expression and information, uses for social, political and cultural purposes, and uses that enhance competition. WITTEM PROJECT, *supra* note 3, art. 5. *See also* Daniel Gervais, *Fair Use, Fair Dealing, Fair Principles: Efforts to Conceptualize Exceptions and Limitations to Copyright*, 57 J. COPYRIGHT SOC'Y 499, 504–09 (2010) (discussing the Wittem Project's clustering of L&Es). The justifications set forth in this section overlap to some degree with the categorizations of L&Es proffered by other scholars. One reason for the differences is because my taxonomy is the product of a bottom-up process. That is, I examined the L&Es in various laws to cluster them, much as I did for my study of fair uses. *See* Pamela Samuelson, *Unbundling Fair Uses*, 77 FORDHAM L. REV. 2537 (2009).

Like the L&Es themselves, justifications can vary in type and range. Some rationales are grounded in normative values and perspectives on copyright, while others are more pragmatic responses to the complex difficulties inherent in the lawmaking process and the need to balance competing interests. Some L&Es may be justified in national laws based not only on the purpose of the use, but also on remuneration that goes to rights holders.[82] In some instances, more than one justification may apply.[83]

Many of the justifications for L&Es can be grouped in general categories, such as concerns about authorship, user interests, the public interest, economic rationales, political expediency, and the need for flexibility. Table 1.2 shows the categories of justifications, offering illustrative examples of L&Es from U.S. law as well as some representative L&Es drawn from other countries' laws and treaties.

Although this section concentrates mainly on justifications for L&Es found in U.S. law, this taxonomy should be useful in assessing justifications for L&Es in national laws more generally. By understanding, from a policy perspective, the justifications for existing L&Es, it may be possible to develop a more principled framework for assessing needs for L&Es going forward and work toward a more harmonized approach internationally.

1.3.1. *Some L&Es Promote Ongoing Authorship*

Authorship is an ongoing process of communicating knowledge and cultural expression among authors and their readers, viewers, and listeners. Authors routinely draw upon preexisting works in the process of creating new ones. As Justice Story famously noted in 1845, "in literature, in science and in art, there are, and can be, few, if any, things, which, in an abstract sense, are strictly new and original throughout. Every book in literature, science and art, borrows, and must necessarily borrow, and use much which was well known and used before."[84]

The premier international copyright treaty, the Berne Convention for the Protection of Literary and Artistic Works, recognizes the importance of promoting ongoing authorship by mandating that member states must adopt a right of fair quotation in their national copyright laws.[85] In keeping with this norm, most jurisdictions have specific L&Es allowing authors to quote from other authors' works,

---

[82] Ginsburg, *supra* note 3. Educational use and private copying L&Es are examples of permitted-but-paid uses in some national laws. *Id.*

[83] For example, L&Es allowing print-disabled access to works fulfill important social policy goals as well as responding to market failure problems. *See infra* notes 135, 189 and accompanying text.

[84] Emerson v. Davies, 8 F. Cas. 615, 619 (C.C.D. Mass. 1845) (No. 4,436).

[85] Berne Convention for the Protection of Literary and Artistic Works art. 10(1), *adopted* Sept. 9, 1886, S. TREATY DOC. NO. 99-27, 1161 U.N.T.S. 3 (amended Sept. 28, 1979) [hereinafter Berne Convention]. These quotations must, however, be compatible with fair practice and no more extensive than is justified by the purpose. *Id.*

and many have specific L&Es to allow parodies, satires, and other types of critical commentary.[86] Fair dealing provisions in the UK and Commonwealth countries allow researchers to make copies of protected works for purposes of study, a common practice among authors in preparing to create new works.[87]

Most of the breathing room for ongoing authorship in U.S. copyright law comes from the fair use doctrine.[88] Indeed, one of the most important functions of fair use in U.S. law is to promote ongoing authorship.[89] In its landmark decision *Campbell v. Acuff-Rose Music, Inc.*, the Supreme Court spoke of fair use as "permit[ting] ... courts to avoid rigid application of the copyright statute when, on occasion, it would stifle the very creativity which that law is designed to foster."[90] The facts of *Campbell* illustrate this point.

Acuff-Rose owns a copyright in the well-known Roy Orbison song, "Pretty Woman." Luther Campbell and his rap group 2 Live Crew recorded an identically named song that drew upon some of the lyrics, melody, and guitar riffs of the Orbison song in a parodic manner. The group went ahead with its rap parody after Acuff-Rose refused its request for permission.

In assessing Campbell's fair use defense, the Supreme Court observed that "[p]arody needs to mimic an original to make its point."[91] The Court noted that the 2 Live Crew song conveyed a very different message than the Orbison song: "2 Live Crew juxtaposes the romantic musings of a man whose fantasy comes true, with degrading taunts, a bawdy demand for sex, and a sigh of relief from paternal responsibility."[92] Although the group copied the first line of the Orbison song, it "thereafter departed markedly from the Orbison lyrics for its own ends."[93] The Court

---

[86] *See, e.g.,* InfoSoc Directive, *supra* note 5, art. 5(3)(d), (i), (k).

[87] *See, e.g.,* Copyright, Designs and Patents Act 1988, c. 48, §§ 29–30 (UK). As noted *supra* note 71 and accompanying text, U.S. law has a specific exception allowing libraries to make copies of articles or small parts of works for patron researchers. *See* 17 U.S.C. § 108(d).

[88] 17 U.S.C. § 107. An example of a specific L&E in U.S. law that promotes ongoing authorship is that which allows people to make photographs, paintings, and other representations of publicly visible buildings embodying architectural works. 17 U.S.C. § 120(a). Other reasons for this exception are the low likelihood of harm to the architects' market from these depictions and the difficulty, as a practical matter, of enforcing a rule that would make tourists into prima facie infringers. *See Architectural Design Protection: Hearings on H.R. 3990 and 3991 Before the Subcomm. on Courts, Intellectual Prop. and the Admin. of Justice of the H. Comm. on the Judiciary,* 101st Cong., 2d Sess. 15–18 (1990).

[89] *See, e.g.,* Ginsburg, *supra* note 3 (suggesting that the only legitimate function of fair use without compensation is to promote authorship).

[90] 510 U.S. 569, 577 (1994) (quoting *Stewart v. Abend,* 495 U.S. 207, 236 (1990)). The Supreme Court cited approvingly, *id.* at 576–9, to a classic law review article on fair use, namely, Pierre L. Leval, *Toward a Fair Use Standard,* 103 HARV. L. REV. 1105 (1990).

[91] Campbell, 510 U.S. at 580–81.

[92] *Id.* at 583.

[93] *Id.* at 589.

concluded that 2 Live Crew had taken no more than was necessary for its parodic purpose.

Many productive uses of an earlier author's work have been deemed fair by the courts. An example is *New Era Publications Int'l v. Carol Publishing Group*.[94] New Era owns copyrights in works authored by L. Ron Hubbard, the founder of the Church of Scientology. Carol published an unauthorized biography that contained 121 passages from 48 of Hubbard's writings. In an affidavit, the biographer explained that each quotation was necessary to support the book's thesis that "Hubbard was a charlatan and the Church [was] a dangerous cult."[95] The court agreed with the biographer that potential customers for an authorized biography of Hubbard would not be deterred from buying that book because of the disparaging biography Carol was publishing, so it upheld Carol's fair use defense.[96]

Productive uses may also be fair when they are neutral or positive about the works on which they draw. In *Bill Graham Archives v. Dorling Kindersley Ltd.*,[97] for example, Dorling Kindersley (DK), who published a cultural history of the Grateful Dead, included seven small-size images of Grateful Dead concert posters as part of its chronological timeline of the band's history. DK initially sought permission to reproduce the images in the book from copyright owner Bill Graham Archives (BGA), but ultimately used the images without permission after concluding that the price BGA offered was unreasonable. The Court of Appeals concluded that DK's use was fair because the images were very small and had been put in the book to illustrate cultural context and not to take advantage of the artistic merit of the posters.[98]

1.3.2. *Some L&Es Create a Buffer for User Autonomy and Personal Property Interests*

As important as it is for copyright to promote the interests of authors, this law also plays an important role in promoting the interests of users. As the U.S. Supreme Court has repeatedly recognized, "[t]he sole interest of the United States and the primary object in conferring the [copyright] monopoly lie in the general benefits derived by the public from the labors of authors."[99] To achieve those general

---

[94] 904 F.2d 152 (2d. Cir. 1990).

[95] *Id.* at 156.

[96] *Id.* at 161.

[97] 448 F.3d 605 (2d Cir. 2006).

[98] *Id.* at 611. Documentary filmmakers and appropriation artists also benefit from the breathing room that fair use provides. *See, e.g.*, Hofheinz v. A & E Television Networks, 146 F. Supp. 2d 442 (S.D.N.Y. 2001); Cariou v. Prince, 714 F.3d 694 (2d Cir. 2013).

[99] Fox Film Corp. v. Doyal, 286 U.S. 123, 127 (1932), *cited approvingly in* Sony Corp. of Am. v. Universal City Studios, Inc., 464 U.S. 417, 429 (1984). Professor Gervais asserts that balancing the interests of the public with those of authors is a goal of the international copyright system. Gervais, *supra* note 7, at 4.

benefits, there needs to be a buffer zone within which readers, viewers, and listeners can make unregulated uses of protected works. There are several ways copyright law builds this kind of buffer.

One significant way in which national copyright laws respect the autonomy and privacy interests of users of copyrighted works is through legislation that regulates only public – and not private – performances, displays, communications, and distributions of protected works.[100] Some nations have adopted similar buffers through special L&E provisions authorizing private or personal use copying.[101] Fair dealing and fair use provisions typically shield personal use copying for purposes of research, study, criticism, and review.[102]

The main U.S. fair use ruling to have addressed whether personal use copying could be fair use is *Sony Corp. of America v. Universal City Studios, Inc.*[103] Fair use was critical to the Supreme Court's decision that Sony was not liable for contributory infringement, even though it knew or had reason to know that many consumers were using their Betamax tape recorders to make infringing copies of copyrighted programs broadcast over public airwaves. The Court noted that the most common use of Betamax machines was to make time-shift copies of television programs to watch the programs at a later time. Because it regarded time-shifting as a fair use, the Court concluded that consumers had a legitimate interest in being able to buy Betamax machines for this and other noninfringing uses.[104]

Although time-shifting was the only personal use issue before it, the Court made general statements in *Sony* that private noncommercial copying should be presumed fair and that this presumption should be overcome only if there was evidence of a meaningful likelihood of harm to the market for the copyrighted works at issue.[105] *Sony* has provided support for personal uses being fair in subsequent appellate court decisions.[106]

---

[100] *See, e.g.,* 17 U.S.C. § 106(3)-(5). This and other lacunae in U.S. copyright law affecting personal uses are explored in Jessica Litman, *Lawful Personal Use*, 85 TEX. L. REV. 1871 (2007).

[101] *See, e.g.,* Copyright Act, Law No. 43 of June 27, 2012, arts. 30 (personal use), 31 (private study) (Japan).

[102] *See, e.g.,* Copyright, Designs and Patents Act 1988, c. 48 § 29 (UK); *Copyright Act 1968* (Cth) ss 43C, 47J, 109A, 110AA, 111 (Austl.).

[103] 464 U.S. 417 (1984). Although the Supreme Court split 5-4 on this issue in *Sony*, it was unanimous in its support of *Sony* on this issue in a later decision. *See* Metro-Goldwyn-Mayer Studios, Inc. v. Grokster, Ltd., 545 U.S. 913, 931 (2005).

[104] Sony, 464 U.S. at 442. The *Sony* case is discussed further *infra* notes 225–7 and accompanying text.

[105] *Id.* at 451.

[106] *See, e.g.,* Recording Indus. Ass'n of Am. v. Diamond Multimedia, Inc., 180 F.3d 1072, 1079 (9th Cir. 1999) (consumer space-shifting of music held to be fair use). There are very few private or personal fair use decisions in the United States, owing in part to difficulties in detecting such uses and the expense of litigation compared with likely recovery if the lawsuit succeeds. In peer-to-peer file-sharing cases that went to trial, fair use defenses have been unavailing. *See, e.g.,* Capitol Records v. Thomas-Rasset, 692 F.3d 899 (8th Cir. 2012).

Fair use, fair dealing, and specific personal use L&Es are far from the only mechanisms copyright laws contain to provide users with breathing room to exercise their autonomy interests as to copyrighted works. Users who own copies of protected works have personal property rights in those copies that confer freedom to make a range of uses of the copies, including sharing them with others, under the exhaustion of rights rules that are common in national copyright laws.[107] An owner can generally lend his copy to others, rent or lease it, use it as collateral for a loan, resell it, give it away, bequeath it to heirs, and/or destroy it if he so chooses.[108] Exhaustion also entitles the owner of a copy of a work to display his copy to the public.[109]

Some national copyright laws include L&Es that give consumers latitude to make specified uses of certain types of works. Many countries, for example, have special provisions that confer on owners of copies of computer programs the right to make copies necessary to use the programs, to make backup copies, and to adapt the programs as necessary to enable its use.[110] Another example is the special U.S. exception that allows owners of buildings embodying architectural works to renovate the buildings, which in the absence of this exception might arguably infringe the architects' derivative work rights.[111]

1.3.3. *Some L&Es Aim to Provide Public Benefits*

Consumers of copies of copyrighted works are not the only members of the public whose interests are respected in national copyright laws. Both authorial and broader public interests can justify L&Es that promote access to works and information. The public's interest in access to information is often implicated when unauthorized persons use copyrighted works without a license. The public interest may also be served by L&Es that promote education and other nonprofit activities and by those that enable uses of works in investigations, litigation, and the like.

Some L&Es Foster the Public Interest in Access to Information

The public has a keen interest in access to information, freedom of speech and expression, and cultural enrichment, all of which are part of copyright's mission.

---

[107] *See, e.g.*, 17 U.S.C. § 109(a); Copyright, Designs and Patents Act 1988, c. 48 § 18(3)(a) (UK); InfoSoc Directive, *supra* note 5, art. 4. *See also* Aaron Perzanowski & Jason Schultz, *Copyright Exhaustion and the Personal Use Dilemma*, 96 MINN. L. REV. 2067 (2012) (discussing consumer uses that may fall within the exhaustion right).

[108] Under U.S. law, exhaustion does not, however, apply to copies obtained by rental, lease, or lending. 17 U.S.C. § 109(d). The lending of computer programs and sound recordings is restricted under § 109(b).

[109] 17 U.S.C. § 109(c).

[110] *See, e.g.*, Copyright Act, Law No. 43 of June 27, 2012, art. 47*ter*, 47*quater* (Japan).

[111] 17 U.S.C. § 120(b).

Whenever an author forgoes the opportunity to reuse portions of another author's work out of fear that the use might be challenged as infringing, there is a loss not only to that author, but also to the public. The public cannot benefit from the insights that the second author's reuse of a first author's work would have enabled. There is, moreover, some loss to freedom of expression and to access to information when lawful reuses are forgone. Losses to the public may be more substantial when news is not reported or publications on matters of public concern are suppressed because of copyright concerns.

Many national copyright laws have specific L&E provisions to permit reuses of in-copyright materials to promote public access to information. Some L&Es allow copyrighted materials to be reproduced and disseminated in the course of news reporting on current political or economic events.[112] Other L&Es permit dissemination of political speeches.[113] The Berne Convention recognizes that member states may decide "to permit the reproduction by the press, the broadcasting or communication to the public by wire of articles published in newspapers or periodicals on current economic, political or religious topics, and of broadcast works of the same character."[114] These provisions grant latitude to those who disseminate information in copyrighted works on matters of public concern.

In the United States, the fair use doctrine is the principal way U.S. law fulfills this function.[115] For example, the public interest in "having the fullest information available on the murder of President Kennedy" played an important role in *Time, Inc. v. Bernard Geis Associates*.[116] Time owned the copyright in Abraham Zapruder's film of the presidential cavalcade in Dallas during which the President was shot. Because this film was the only documentation of the assassination, it was a significant piece of evidence for the Warren Commission's investigation of the President's death. Its report was important in the wider public debate over whether Lee Harvey Oswald was the sole assassin. Geis sought to publish a book aimed at proving that Oswald was not the only gunman. Its author relied heavily on several frames from the Zapruder film as evidence in support of his claim. After Time refused to license the use of these frames in the book, Geis prepared sketches of the frames for the book anyway. Time sued for infringement. The court ruled that

---

[112] *See, e.g.,* InfoSoc Directive, *supra* note 5, art. 5(3)(c).

[113] *See, e.g., id.,* art. 5(3)(f).

[114] Berne Convention, *supra* note 85, art. 10*bis.*

[115] Some specific L&Es in U.S. law promote public access to information. *See, e.g.,* 17 U.S.C. §§ 113(c) (exempting photographs or pictures of protected works for purposes of comment or news reporting), 108(f) (allowing libraries and archives to make and lend copies of broadcast news programs). The exclusion of U.S. government works from copyright protections also promotes public access to information. 17 U.S.C. § 105.

[116] 293 F. Supp. 130, 146 (S.D.N.Y. 1968).

Geis's inclusion of the sketches in the book was a fair use in part because of public interest in getting information about the assassination.[117]

Fair use also protected the Council on American-Islamic Relations against infringement claims based on its posting of four minutes of audio from a conservative radio talk show to prove that its host had made anti-Muslim statements.[118] The court observed that "it was not unreasonable for defendants to provide the actual audio excerpts, since they reaffirmed the authenticity of the criticized statements and provided the audience with the tone and manner in which plaintiff made the statements."[119] The court's opinion vindicated not only the Council's free speech interests in making the statements known, but also the public interest in getting accurate information about a radio personality's prejudicial remarks.[120]

More mundane, but nonetheless newsworthy, was the challenged use in *Nunez v. Caribbean Int'l News Corp.*[121] Caribbean News defended its publication of nude photos of a woman who became Miss Puerto Rico because its purpose was to inform public debate about whether she deserved to retain her title. The court noted that "the pictures were the story" and "[i]t would have been much more difficult to explain the controversy without reproducing the photographs."[122] Also significant was the fact that the newspaper used the photos for a very different purpose than the original (i.e., for a modeling portfolio). Under *Campbell*, uses for different purposes may be transformative, which generally tips in favor of fair use.[123]

Newsworthiness is, of course, no guarantee that a use will be fair, as witnessed by the Supreme Court's decision in *Harper & Row, Publishers, Inc. v. Nation Enterprises*.[124] The left-leaning news magazine published a 2,250 word story about the upcoming publication of Gerald Ford's memoirs. The story quoted verbatim 300 words from the book and paraphrased other passages. Ford's publisher sued The Nation for infringement. The Nation argued its use had been fair.

Several factors contributed to the Court's decision that the use was unfair. The most important was that the book was unpublished when The Nation's story appeared. The Nation, in the Court's view, intended to "scoop" the right of first publication that copyright provides to authors.[125] The Court also criticized The Nation for having "purloined" a copy of the book and for having extracted a qualitatively

[117] *Id.*
[118] Savage v. Council on American-Islamic Relations, Inc., No. C 07-6076 SI, 2008 WL 2951281 (N.D. Cal. July 25, 2008).
[119] *Id.* at *6.
[120] *Id.* at *8.
[121] 235 F.3d 18 (1st Cir. 2000).
[122] *Id.* at 22 (internal quotation marks omitted).
[123] Campbell v. Acuff-Rose Music, Inc., 510 U.S. 569, 579 (1994).
[124] 471 U.S. 539 (1985).
[125] *Id.* at 562.

substantial portion, namely, the part in which Ford discussed his decision as President to pardon Richard Nixon.[126] This was the very part of the book that Harper & Row had contracted with Time magazine to publish. That contract was canceled after The Nation's publication of the Nixon pardon material.

Although the public interest in access to information did not favor fair use in the *Harper & Row* decision,[127] it has reemerged as worthy of consideration since *Campbell*.[128] Indeed, the Court there observed that the public's interest in access to a subsequent work, even if its author took too much from the plaintiff's work to qualify as a fair use, might justify withholding injunctive relief and awarding damages instead.[129]

The public interest in access to information has also been a significant factor weighing in favor of fair use in a series of cases in which search engines have raised fair use defenses for making copies of texts and images to index their contents and make small portions available in response to user search queries.[130] Courts have also been sympathetic to fair use defenses for data-mining, which involves digitizing works and indexing their contents so that the texts can be analyzed by specialized software programs.[131] In *Authors Guild, Inc. v. HathiTrust*,[132] for example, the Second Circuit ruled that a nonprofit digital library made fair use of books from research library collections in developing a full-text searchable database that enabled researchers to run search queries for books on specific topics of interest.[133]

Some L&Es Serve Social Policy Goals

National copyright laws typically have sets of L&Es aimed at fulfilling social and cultural policy goals. Especially common are rules that enable the use of in-copyright materials in the course of face-to-face teaching in nonprofit educational institutions,[134] enable libraries and archives to reproduce works to preserve them,[135] and

---

[126] *Id.* at 562, 565.

[127] *Id.* at 557–58.

[128] Campbell, 510 U.S. at 578 n.10.

[129] *Id.*

[130] *See, e.g.,* Kelly v. Arriba Soft Corp., 336 F.3d 811 (9th Cir. 2003). Two legal databases won fair use defenses for digitizing briefs filed in litigated cases, which increased public access to legal information without harming the market for the briefs. *See* White v. West Pub. Corp., 29 F. Supp. 3d 396 (S.D.N.Y. 2014).

[131] For an in-depth discussion of copyright implications of data-mining issues, see, e.g., *Matthew Sag, Copyright and Copy Reliant Technology,* 103 Nw. L. Rev. 1607 (2009).

[132] 755 F.3d 87 (2d Cir. 2014). *See also* A.V. v. iParadigms, LLC., 562 F.3d 630 (4th Cir. 2009) (fair use to make copies of student papers so that a computer program could detect plagiarism).

[133] Japan has a special L&E for data-mining. *See* Copyright Act, Law No. 43 of June 27, 2012, art. 47*septies* (Japan).

[134] *See, e.g.,* InfoSoc Directive, *supra* note 5, art. 5(3)(a).

[135] *See, e.g., id.,* art. 5(2)(c).

enable the creation of special format works so print-disabled persons can have greater access to literary works.[136]

L&Es that allow teachers and students to make instructional uses of copyrighted works obviously promote societal objectives to educate students to expose them to their cultural heritage and to prepare them for their future roles as members of society. Preservation of cultural heritage ensures that future generations will have access to the cultural and intellectual artifacts of the past. Increased access for print-disabled persons allows them to participate more fully in the cultural life of their society and become more productive citizens.[137]

U.S. copyright law grants an outright exemption for classroom performances and displays of in-copyright works,[138] as well as a privilege allowing libraries and archives to make copies to preserve some in-copyright works,[139] to replace lost or damaged copies if other copies are unavailable at a reasonable price,[140] and to give to patrons for research purposes.[141] A special U.S. L&E facilitates making books and journals more accessible to print-disabled persons.[142] Fair use sometimes complements these specific exceptions. For example, in the *HathiTrust* case, the court upheld creation of a full-text searchable database containing millions of copyrighted books for purposes of preserving the books and of making them more accessible to print-disabled persons, both of which went beyond the contours of the statutory exceptions.[143]

Among the other exemptions in U.S. law that aim to foster social policy goals are those that exempt public performances of music and nondramatic literary works in the course of religious services[144] and other nonprofit educational, religious, or charitable events.[145] Public broadcasting also benefits from L&Es for certain uses of copyrighted works.[146] Veterans groups, fraternal organizations, and horticultural and agricultural fairs have also persuaded Congress that some of their activities should be exempt from copyright liability.[147]

---

[136] *See, e.g., id.*, art. 5(3)(b).

[137] The importance of enhancing access to works by disabled persons has recently been recognized in an international treaty. *See* Marrakesh Treaty to Facilitate Access to Published Works for Persons Who Are Blind, Visually Impaired, or Otherwise Print Disabled, WIPO Doc. VIP/DC/8 Rev (June 27, 2013), *available at* www.wipo.int/edocs/mdocs/copyright/en/vip_dc/vip_dc_8_rev.pdf.

[138] 17 U.S.C. § 110(1).

[139] *Id.* § 108(b).

[140] *Id.* § 108(c).

[141] *Id.* § 108(d).

[142] *Id.* § 121.

[143] Authors Guild, Inc. v. HathiTrust, 755 F.3d 87 (2d Cir. 2014).

[144] 17 U.S.C. § 110(3).

[145] *Id.* § 110(4). There are several conditions that must be satisfied for these events to qualify.

[146] *Id.* §§ 114(b), 118.

[147] *Id.* § 110(6), (10).

During the revision process, some Washington-savvy representatives of these groups must have realized that these institutions would soon face liability for activities in which they had long engaged without obtaining copyright licenses. They seem to have found a sympathetic ear in the Register and members of Congress by emphasizing the social benefits they provided to the public.[48]

Some L&Es Enable Public Institutions to Function

Many social policy exemptions allow beneficiaries to consume copyrighted works in ways that other actors (e.g., for-profit entities, individuals, and nonprofits that don't qualify for the exemption) have to pay for. In this respect, L&Es are like congressional subsidies for the activities of the exempt beneficiaries.

Very different are exemptions that permit government agencies, courts, and legislatures to make and distribute copies of, and possibly even to perform, copyrighted works for nonconsumptive governmental purposes (e.g., as evidence relevant to court proceedings). Many nations have special exemptions from liability for uses of in-copyright materials in investigations, adjudications, administrative proceedings, and the like.[149]

These exemptions are necessary because copyright is so ubiquitous in the modern era since rights attach automatically by operation of law to all original works of authorship.[150] The consequence is that works of all kinds, including memoranda, reports, letters, outlines, and photographs, just to name a few, are protected by copyright laws, even if their creation was not induced by copyright incentives. Reproducing and distributing copies of these documents may be necessary for discovery proceedings in civil cases, investigations of crimes, exhibits for trials or administrative proceedings, and legislative deliberations, and relevant to various other public institutional functions.

There is no specific L&E for governmental uses in U.S. copyright law, but fair use fills this gap. One case, for example, held that police had made fair use when copying and publicly displaying photographs of a crime victim in connection with the investigation of his murder for which the photographer was a suspect.[151] Fair use also shielded an investigator who recorded scenes from a sexually explicit film in a movie theatre to provide the district attorney with evidence that these depictions constituted a nuisance under local laws.[152] Patent lawyers have also been successful with fair use

---

[48] Yet one might question whether exemptions for religious and charitable events are justifiable subsidies. After all, churches and charities have to pay for many other products and services they consume. Singing music is such a regular part of religious services that it might have seemed logical to require churches to license the performance of copyrighted music.

[149] *See, e.g.*, Copyright Act, Law No. 43 of June 27, 2012, art. 42 (Japan).

[150] *See, e.g.*, 17 U.S.C. § 102(a). Under U.S. law, works must be fixed in a tangible medium to be protectable. *Id.*

[151] Shell v. City of Radford, 351 F. Supp. 510 (W.D. Va. 2005).

[152] Jartech, Inc. v. Clancy, 666 F.2d 403 (9th Cir. 1982).

defenses for copying and distributing copies of scientific and technical articles to fulfill their disclosure of prior art obligations to the U.S. Patent and Trademark Office in connection with patent applications.[153]

1.3.4. *Some L&Es Accomplish Economic Goals*

Some copyright L&Es accomplish classic economic goals, such as fostering commerce, competition, and ongoing innovation. Others exempt incidental uses lacking economic significance. Still others aim to cure or mitigate market failure problems, sometimes through compulsory or statutory licenses and sometimes through outright exemptions.

Some L&Es Foster Commerce, Competition, and Ongoing Innovation

One commerce-promoting L&E in U.S. law allows stores that sell sound recordings and equipment to play music to help customers decide whether to buy them.[154] Another exempts the public performance and display of coin-operated videogames so that customers can play them in public places.[155] Yet another limits copyrights in pictorial or sculptural works to clarify that the scope of protection does not extend to designs of useful articles depicted in them.[156] These designs are free for competitive copying and ongoing innovation unless patented.[157]

One type of L&E that promotes competition and ongoing innovation is that which permits software developers to make copies of another firm's computer program in the course of reverse engineering it. This is often done for the purpose of extracting information necessary to develop a program that can interoperate with the existing program. Reverse engineering is sometimes the only way to get that information without a license. But for a reverse engineering privilege, the developer of a first program would have complete control over who could make a computer program that could interoperate with its program. Some nations authorize reverse-engineering copies through a specific L&E.[158]

---

[153] *See, e.g.*, American Institute of Physics v. Schwegman Lundberg & Woessner, P.A., No. 12–528 (RHK/JJK), 2013 WL 4666330 (D. Minn. Aug. 30, 2013), *appeal dismissed*, No. 13–3351 (8th Cir. Feb. 19, 2014).

[154] 17 U.S.C. § 110(7).

[155] *Id.* § 109(e).

[156] *Id.* § 113(b).

[157] *See, e.g.*, Ralph S. Brown, *Eligibility for Copyright Protection: A Search for Principled Standards*, 70 Minn. L. Rev. 579 (1985).

[158] *See, e.g.*, Directive 2009/24/EC of the European Parliament and of the Council on the Legal Protection of Computer Programs, art. 6, 2009 O.J. (L 111) 19.

Fair use has allowed software reverse engineering in the United States. The principal case is *Sega Enterprises Ltd. v. Accolade, Inc.*[159] Accolade initially produced videogames for PCs, but wanted to adapt the games so they could be played on the popular Sega platform. So it bought copies of Sega games, reverse engineered them to discern the interface information, and then made a version of its games that could interoperate with the Sega system.

A U.S. appellate court ruled that Accolade's purpose favored fair use because the firm's goal was to extract information from the Sega programs to enable it to make a noninfringing interoperable program. The nature of the works favored fair use because programs are functional works and reverse engineering was sometimes the only way to get interface information. Although Accolade's copying was substantial, it was also intermediate (that is, part of the development process, not in the final product). Accolade games did not supplant market demand for Sega games, but merely competed on the merits with the Sega games.[160] Hence, Accolade's reverse engineering was fair use.

Another competition- and innovation-promoting fair use case is *Lewis Galoob Toys v. Nintendo of America.*[161] Galoob sold an add-on program called the Game Genie that allowed owners of videogames for the Nintendo platform to change temporarily the play of those games (e.g., increasing the number of lives of certain characters). Galoob asked a court to declare that its sale of Game Genies was noninfringing. The appellate court thought this was fair use because it enabled consumers to enjoy the games in the privacy of their homes, and the Game Genie did not supplant demand for Nintendo games.[162] This ruling freed others to develop add-on programs.[163]

Galoob was the principal precedent on which another software developer relied to justify its development of a program that enabled owners of DVD movies to block violent, sexually explicit, or otherwise offensive parts of movies to make them "family friendly."[164] Before a court could rule on the claim that this software infringed the

---

[159] 977 F.2d 1510 (9th Cir. 1992).

[160] *Id.* at 1527. One specific U.S. computer-related L&E that fosters competition is that which allows firms to copy computer programs in the process of repairing computers. *See* 17 U.S.C. § 117(c). The latter provision legislatively overturned the ruling in *MAI Systems Corp. v. Peak Computer, Inc.*, 991 F.2d 511 (9th Cir. 1993), which held that making RAM copies in the course of repairing a computer infringed copyrights in the programs.

[161] 964 F.2d 965 (9th Cir. 1992).

[162] *Id.* at 971–72.

[163] Another competition-fostering fair use involved the use of copyrighted images in advertising. Sony sued the developer of a program that emulated the functions of Sony's PlayStation platform, claiming it infringed copyright by publishing ads featuring screen shots of Sony games being played on Bleem's platform. The court found the advertising use to be fair. *Sony Computer Entm't Am., Inc. v. Bleem, LLC*, 214 F.3d 1022 (9th Cir. 2002).

[164] *Huntsman v. Soderbergh*, No. 02-M-1662 (D. Colo. Filed Aug. 19, 2002).

derivative work right, Congress enacted an L&E to enable the development of this type of software.[165]

Some L&Es Exempt Economically Insignificant Incidental Uses

It is sometimes necessary to make copies of copyrighted works in order to carry out legitimate economic functions. National copyright laws often recognize this through specific exceptions. One example in the 1976 Act is the ephemeral recording L&E adopted at the behest of broadcast television operators.[166] Broadcasters often make ephemeral copies of programming in anticipation of broadcasting them at a later time. As long as these copies are retained only for archival purposes and used solely by the transmitting broadcaster, they lack a separate economic significance that would warrant imposition of copyright liability.

Another example is a common exception permitting owners of computer programs to make copies essential to the utilization of the programs.[167] It is impossible to use a software program without the computer itself making numerous copies in the course of use. These copies are incidental to the normal operation of the program. It would make no sense to say that individuals or firms must pay once to obtain a copy of the program and then pay again to make copies necessary to use it.[168]

The European InfoSoc Directive recognizes that incidental copies made of digital works lack independent economic significance; it mandates that these incidental copies be exempted from copyright liability.[169] There is, interestingly enough, no equivalent provision in U.S. law. As a result, making incidental copies of music, photos, and texts when playing or viewing them on one's computer might seem to implicate the reproduction right because there is no statutory safe harbor for this activity akin to that created for computer programs. Fair use (or implied license) would almost certainly fill the gap for the missing equivalent to the software utilization exception. The Copyright Office has recently suggested that a more general incidental copying privilege should be given serious consideration.[170]

---

[165] 17 U.S.C. § 110(11). This exception concomitantly serves the autonomy interests of owners of DVDs to watch movies in a manner that suits their tastes and preferences. It does not, however, extend to editing offensive materials out of the DVD movies. *See* Clean Flicks of Colo. v. Soderbergh, 433 F. Supp. 2d 1236 (D. Colo. 2006).

[166] 17 U.S.C. § 112(a). The Berne Convention recognizes ephemeral broadcast copying as legitimate conduct to exempt from copyright liability. Berne Convention, *supra* note 85, art. 11*bis*.

[167] 117 U.S.C. § 117(a). Fair use also sometimes privileges incidental uses of copyrighted works. *See, e.g.,* Italian Book Corp. v. Am. Broad. Co., 458 F. Supp. 65 (S.D.N.Y. 1978) (incidental capture of music in news coverage of parade was fair use).

[168] 117 U.S.C. § 117(a) also permits owners of copies of computer programs to make backup copies.

[169] InfoSoc Directive, *supra* note 5, art. 5(1).

[170] Pallante, *supra* note 50, at 325–26.

Some L&Es Aim to Cure or Mitigate Market Failures

Some L&Es have been adopted in national copyright laws as a way to cure or mitigate perceived market failures. Copyright markets can fail to form or be dysfunctional for a number of reasons.[171] The transaction costs of negotiating licenses on a
work-by-work and rightsholder-by-rightsholder basis may, for instance, be prohibitive. The market power of some players in certain industry sectors can make it difficult or impossible to achieve or approximate competitive market pricing. Regulatory
interventions aimed at achieving noncopyright goals can, as a byproduct, thwart
efforts to reach competitive market results in particular industry sectors. Holdup
problems are among the factors that may make certain industry players unwilling to
license uses on terms that other players deem reasonable.

Compulsory licensing has been a frequent tool to resolve market failures in copyright industry sectors. The first compulsory license adopted in the United States
was that which allowed mechanical reproductions of musical compositions after
the first authorized sound recording of that music, subject to payment of a statutory
license fee.[172] This license was created out of fear of monopoly control of the sound
recording market.[173] While courts in the early 1900s were struggling over whether the
unauthorized manufacture and sale of piano rolls infringed music copyrights,[174] the
Aeolian Co. was quietly buying up exclusive licenses to make sound recordings of
popular music. Aeolian wanted to be the only firm that could make sound recordings of that music.

After the Supreme Court ruled that piano rolls were not copies of musical compositions under then-existing law, it was almost inevitable that Congress would be
asked to expand the exclusive rights of composers to control mechanical reproductions of their works. As this proposal was under consideration, great concern arose
about the competitive impact of Aeolian's exclusive licensing project. Adoption of
a compulsory license made it possible for firms other than Aeolian to participate in
the piano roll market as long as they provided statutorily prescribed compensation to
rights holders for the music they recorded. Piano rolls were the first of many sound
recordings that have been subject to this compulsory license.

By 1961, monopoly concerns no longer justified the existence of this compulsory
license, which is why the Register of Copyrights called for its abolition in the first
stage of the copyright revision process.[175] However, stable industry practices had

---

[171] *See, e.g.,* Wendy J. Gordon, *Excuse and Justification in the Law of Fair Use: Transaction Costs Have
Always Been Only Part of the Story,* 50 J. COPYRIGHT SOC'Y U.S.A. 149 (2003) (discussing the variety
of reasons why copyright markets may fail).

[172] *See supra* note 38 and accompanying text.

[173] REGISTER'S 1961 REPORT, *supra* note 39, at 32–36.

[174] *See, e.g.,* White-Smith Music Publ'g Co. v. Apollo Co., 209 U.S. 1 (1908).

[175] REGISTER'S 1961 REPORT, *supra* note 39, at 32–36.

grown up around the license. In 1965, the Register changed his mind about the desirability of this repeal.[176] However, he recommended adjustments to the compulsory license provision to make it fairer and less cumbersome.[177]

In keeping with the Register's recommendation, Congress retained the compulsory license for sound recordings of music. But it also created some new ones in the 1976 Act. One required jukebox operators to pay an annual, relatively small flat fee for public performances of musical works for each such machine on their premises.[178] A second benefited public broadcasters. Proponents used market failure arguments in support of this license, saying it was necessary to overcome a multitude of administratively cumbersome and very costly rights clearance problems that, left unchecked, would impair the vitality of public broadcasting.[179] A third resolved a longstanding bitter dispute between broadcasters and cable television systems.

During the copyright revision process, broadcasters brought two lawsuits challenging cable television retransmissions of television programs. They complained that cable systems were making significant amounts of money for retransmitting broadcast programs and paying nothing for that privilege.[180] To the keen disappointment of these broadcasters, the Supreme Court ruled in both cases that the 1909 Act's public performance right did not extend to passive retransmission of broadcast programs by cable systems.[181]

The highest priority for broadcasters in the copyright revision process was to ensure that cable retransmissions of broadcast programs would be covered by the public performance right under the new act. The Register supported this proposal in 1965.[182] However, "full scale verbal warfare" broke out in response to bills to codify

[176] REGISTER'S SUPPLEMENTARY REPORT, *supra* note 47, at 53–54.

[177] *Id.* at 53–59. The 1976 Act reduced some administrative burdens the 1909 Act license had imposed and increased the fixed rate for the license. H.R. REP. NO. 94–1476, at 107–11 (1976).

[178] 17 U.S.C. § 116 (as adopted in 1976). The House Report did not directly invoke market failure as a rationale for this license, although it noted that "the whole structure of the jukebox industry has been based on the existence of the copyright exemption" the industry enjoyed under the 1909 Act. H.R. REP. NO. 94–1476, at 113. That license is no longer in effect, however, because after the United States joined the Berne Convention in 1989, Congress amended the 1976 Act to encourage voluntary negotiations for jukebox licenses with a proviso that Copyright Royalty judges could step in as needed if voluntary negotiations failed. *See* 17 U.S.C. § 116 (as amended).

[179] H.R. REP. NO. 94–1476, at 116–17.

[180] By 1976, there were approximately 3,500 cable operators in 7,700 communities, reaching 10.8 million homes, and earning revenues of almost $770 million. H.R. REP. NO. 94–1476, at 88.

[181] Teleprompter Corp. v. Columbia Broad. Sys., Inc., 415 U.S. 394 (1974); Fortnightly Corp. v. United Artists Television, Inc., 392 U.S. 390 (1968).

[182] REGISTER'S SUPPLEMENTARY REPORT, *supra* note 47, at 40–42.

this position in 1967.[183] The failure of the copyright revision legislation that year was largely owing to this unresolved controversy.[184]

Further complicating resolution of the broadcaster-cable system copyright dispute was the important role that the Federal Communications Commission (FCC) played in regulating the broadcast industry. The FCC had initially declined to regulate cable television systems because it did not perceive them to threaten the viability of the broadcast industry.[185] By the mid-1960s, however, as cable systems grew larger and more robust, the FCC changed its mind and issued a rule forbidding cable systems operating in the 100 largest television markets from importing distant signals unless they satisfied stiff evidentiary requirements (which almost none undertook).[186] By the early 1970s, the FCC went further and required cable systems to transmit broadcast signals from local stations to cable customers; it also set limits on the number of distant signals cable systems could import, as well as specifying conditions under which cable systems could import these signals.[187]

The FCC's regulation of cable retransmissions of broadcast signals greatly complicated the task of figuring out what royalties and other terms would be "reasonable" because arms-length voluntary deals between broadcasters and cable systems on terms was implausible given the "must carry" rules. Requiring each of the nearly then-existing 3,500 cable systems to negotiate licenses with every rights holder of every protected work broadcast on television would be prohibitively expensive. A compulsory license thus seemed to be necessary to facilitate authorized uses.[188] Ultimately, an extremely complex interindustry negotiation resulted in the nearly incomprehensible compulsory license provision embedded in the 1976 Act establishing the compensation framework that is still in effect today.[189]

Other compulsory licenses have been created in the years following the 1976 Act: two affecting satellite transmission of broadcast signals and one affecting

---

[183] U.S. Copyright Office, Draft Second Supplementary Report of the Register of Copyrights on the General Revision of the U.S. Copyright Law: 1975 Revision Bill 122 (1975) [hereinafter Register's Second Supplementary Report].

[184] H.R. Rep. No. 94–1476, at 89.

[185] CATV and TV Repeater Services, 26 F.C.C. 403, 431 (1959).

[186] *See* Register's Second Supplementary Report, *supra* note 183, at 132–33. The cable industry had earlier challenged FCC's jurisdiction to regulate the cable industry. *See* United States v. Southwestern Cable Co., 392 U.S. 157 (1968) (upholding the FCC's jurisdiction over cable television insofar as it was "reasonably ancillary" to its jurisdiction over broadcast television).

[187] In the early 1990s, the "must carry" rules were codified at 47 U.S.C. §§ 534–35. Cable industry firms unsuccessfully challenged the "must carry" rules as a violation of their First Amendment-protected editorial judgments. *See* Turner Broad. Sys., Inc. v. FCC, 520 U.S. 180 (1997).

[188] Elements of the consensus finally achieved to resolve the cable-broadcast television controversy, including the compulsory license, are set forth in Register's Second Supplementary Report, *supra* note 183, at 134–37.

[189] 17 U.S.C. § 111.

satellite radio and webcasting. The satellite transmission compulsory licenses are very similar to the cable compulsory license adopted in 1976.[190] The prohibitively high transaction cost of negotiating with all possible rights holders was the principle rationale for the creation of a compulsory license for certain online public performances of sound recordings.[191]

Compulsory licenses are, of course, not the only way to address copyright market failures. Several of the outright exemptions from liability in U.S. law may partially be explained by market failure considerations. One U.S. example is the specific exception that allows authorized entities to make and distribute copies of literary works in special formats for blind persons. This L&E is justifiable not just because of a social policy to aid print-disabled persons, but also because markets for special format works are typically so small that publishers rarely serve them.[192]

Some U.S. exemptions may also be attributable to market failures that arise because the U.S. lacks comparable institutional infrastructures such as the collecting societies in Europe and elsewhere that license a wide range of nonprofit as well as commercial uses of literary and other works.[193] Without a one-stop-shop, low-cost licensing entity able to grant permission to copy and distribute large numbers of works owned by large numbers of rights holders, markets may fail to form. Outright exceptions may thus be justifiable to enable some socially desirable uses for which markets cannot effectively and efficiently operate.

Market failure may also have played a role in the fair use ruling in the *HathiTrust* case, as it would have been cost-prohibitive to clear rights for the seven-plus million in-copyright books to digitize them to allow preservation, full-text indexing for search, and access for print-disabled persons.[194]

[190] *See, e.g.*, Rob Frieden, *Analog and Digital Must-Carry Obligations of Cable and Satellite Television Operators in the United States*, 15 MEDIA L. POL'Y 230 (2006).

[191] *See, e.g.*, Amy Duvall, Note, *Royalty Rate-Setting for Webcasters: A Royal(ty) Mess*, 15 MICH. TELECOMM. TECH. L. REV. 267 (2008).

[192] 17 U.S.C. § 121. Senator Chafee noted the reluctance of publishers to produce special format works in his remarks in support of this legislation. *See* 142 Cong. Rec. 19674 (1996) (statement of Senator John Chafee).

[193] *See generally* COLLECTIVE MANAGEMENT OF COPYRIGHTS AND RELATED RIGHTS (Daniel Gervais ed., 2d ed. 2010).

[194] The district court cited to the declaration of expert witness Professor Joel Waldfogel, who calculated a total cost estimate of $569 million just to secure permissions, not including licensing fees. Authors Guild, Inc. v. HathiTrust, 902 F. Supp. 2d 445, 463 (2012), *aff'd in part, vacated and remanded in part*, 755 F.3d 87 (2d Cir. 2014). The Second Circuit remanded to the lower court to consider one small issue about possible uses of preservation copies. HathiTrust, 755 F.3d at 104. On Jan. 6, 2015, the parties settled upon stipulation by HathiTrust that it has complied with the Copyright Act's § 108(c) provision on replacement copies, thus apparently bringing the lawsuit to a close. *See* Krista Cox, *Authors Guild v. HathiTrust Litigation Ends in Victory for Fair Use*, ASS'N OF RESEARCH LIBRARIES NEWS (Jan. 8, 2015), www.arl.org/news/community-updates/3501-authors-guild-v-hathitrust-litigation-ends-in-victory-for-fair-use#.VMvTl2Pq-ZQ.

1.3.5. *Some L&Es Are Adopted for Politically Expedient Reasons*

Legislatures sometimes enact L&Es based less on principle than on political expediency.[195] During the revision process leading up to the 1976 Act, for example, the Register offered political expediency as an explanation for why sound recordings would not get public performance rights. This issue was, he said, so "explosively controversial" that "the chances of [the] passage [of the general revision bill] would be seriously impaired" if it included a proposal for a public performance right for sound recordings.[196] Broadcasters and owners of music copyrights strongly opposed the grant of this right.[197]

Radio and television stations had, of course, played recorded music for decades without paying royalties to recording companies because prior to 1972, sound recordings did not enjoy copyright or any other federal intellectual property protection in the United States.[198] On purely utilitarian grounds, nonpayment of royalties to sound recording companies was seemingly justified on the ground that broadcasts of music were like free advertising for the recordings. People who heard songs from the latest Beatles album on the radio were, for example, likely to go out to buy the album. (Indeed, sound recording companies sometimes paid broadcasters to play recordings to boost their popularity, a practice that was only legal if the radio station announced that it had taken money to play the music, which DJs did not always do.) Sound recordings that became "hits" on the radio were also in demand for jukeboxes.

Broadcasters were understandably not keen to support legislation that would cut into their revenue streams. After all, they were already paying hefty sums to the American Society of Composers, Authors and Publishers (ASCAP) and Broadcast Music, Inc. (BMI) collecting societies for licenses to broadcast music.

Composers, music publishers, and other owners of music copyrights were even stronger objectors to public performance rights for sound recordings.[199] They were miffed because sound recording companies had long benefited at their expense from

---

[195] Political expediency has a long pedigree in U.S. copyright lawmaking processes. *See, e.g.,* JESSICA LITMAN, DIGITAL COPYRIGHT 22–63 (2001).

[196] REGISTER'S SUPPLEMENTARY REPORT, *supra* note 47, at 51–52. S. 543, 91st Cong., 1st Sess. (1969) would have granted a public performance right to sound recordings; however, this provision was omitted in S. 22, 94th Cong., 1st Sess. (1975).

[197] REGISTER'S SUPPLEMENTARY REPORT, *supra* note 47, at 50–51.

[198] Some state laws and judicial decisions had provided legal protection against counterfeit recordings, but these laws and decisions have generally been thought not to confer public performance rights. *See, e.g.,* U.S. COPYRIGHT OFFICE, FEDERAL COPYRIGHT PROTECTION FOR PRE-1972 SOUND RECORDINGS 20–49 (2011). However, a recent decision has interpreted New York legal protections as extending to public performance rights. *See* Flo & Eddie, Inc. v. Sirius XM Radio, Inc., No. 13 Civ. 5784 (CM), 2014 WL 6670201 (S.D.N.Y. 2014).

[199] REGISTER'S SUPPLEMENTARY REPORT, *supra* note 47, at 51.

the low fixed rate (two cents per record) for the compulsory license fee to record music. Music copyright owners feared that broadcasters would demand lower payments for licensing music rights if broadcasters now had to pay royalties for public performances of sound recordings. Broadcasters could not easily pass on higher costs of licensing both music and sound recording copyrights to their consumers. Broadcasters were, after all, transmitting music over the public airwaves for free, and advertisers were likely to balk at higher rates.

The politically expedient compromise reached in the 1976 Act gave makers of sound recordings rights to control reproductions and distributions of their recordings, but not over public performances.[200]

Similarly politically expedient was the compulsory license adopted to benefit jukebox operators who threatened to stymie the copyright revision process unless they either retained their exemption or got a compulsory license.[201] This threat was real because there were jukebox operators in virtually every Congressional district and their owners were hopping mad about the proposed repeal of their exemption.

It is a fair question whether political expediency or principle explains some of the outright exemptions in the 1976 Act. Consider the L&E that permits governments and nonprofit agricultural and horticultural fairs to perform copyrighted music without a license.[202] A proponent of the agricultural/horticultural fair exemption emphasized the nonprofit educational purposes of these fairs, noting that they provided training programs for young people and for farmers so that they could, for instance, learn how to raise better livestock. Forcing fairs to pay copyright fees would, proponents said, threaten their existence because they are thinly funded.[203] This L&E may seem justified on principle if one analogizes these fairs to the exemption for classroom teaching. Yet, many other nonprofit groups, such as the Girl Scouts and Campfire Girls, engage in similar activities to these fairs without a similar exception.[204]

---

[200] The recording industry has continued to lobby for full public performance rights, but has yet to attain them. The U.S. Copyright Office has endorsed a general grant of public performance rights in sound recordings. *See* Pallante, *supra* note 50, at 324. However, sound recording copyright owners now enjoy only an exclusive right to control digital audio transmissions of their works. 17 U.S.C. § 106(6).

[201] The Register thought it would be "tragic" if their opposition would "cause the complete failure of a general revision bill that is urgently needed in the public and national interest." Yet, it would also be "deplorable" not to require jukebox operators to pay performance royalties. REGISTER'S SUPPLEMENTARY REPORT, *supra* note 47, at 60. A compulsory license at a low fixed rate per machine was the politically expedient way to resolve this controversy.

[202] 17 U.S.C. § 110(6). Professor Hugenholtz once identified this exception as the product of lobbying. *See* Hugenholtz, *supra* note 6, at 231.

[203] *Hearings Pursuant to S. Res. 37 on S. 597 Before the Subcomm. on Patents, Trademarks, and Copyrights of the Senate Comm. on the Judiciary Part 3*, 90th Cong., 1st Sess. 779–81 (1967).

[204] ASCAP has sometimes challenged Girl Scouts for unlicensed public performances of music. *See, e.g.,* Julien H. Collins III, *When In Doubt, Do Without: Licensing Public Performances by Nonprofit*

Consider also the exemption that nonprofit veterans' and fraternal organizations enjoy that allows them to perform nondramatic literary works and music without a license at their social functions.[205] In lobbying for this L&E, representatives of the American Legion, the Veterans of Foreign Wars, and the Shriners argued that they were as deserving of an exemption as agricultural fairs because they supported youth programs, scholarships, mental health programs, the Red Cross, and cancer research. Any funds that went to pay copyright royalties would reduce the amounts these organizations could use to support these worthy causes.[206] The American Legion reported that it was at the "top of the collection list" for music licensing and had been unable to reach an acceptable agreement with ASCAP.[207]

A lingering question is whether this or similar exemptions can be justified on principle as reasonable subsidies to worthy nonprofit organizations or whether they are simply the products of successful lobbying efforts. If such specific L&Es are justified, then a second inquiry asks whether there are other equally deserving nonprofit groups who should but do not have a similar subsidy. And if there are, how just is it that some deserving entities are exempt and others are not?

1.3.6. *Some L&Es Provide Flexibility in Copyright Laws*

Fair use, as we have seen, plays a considerable role in balancing the interests of rights holders and of users and the public in relation to many activities that the U.S. Congress has not created specific L&Es to address.[208] Indeed, in at least seven categories of L&E justifications proffered thus far, fair use does most of the work in regulating activities that do not fall within a specific statutory L&E. It even does some nontrivial work in addressing market failures. In *Campbell*, for instance, the Supreme Court noted the unlikelihood that copyright owners would voluntarily license parodies of their works because they may be unwilling to subject their works to the kind of critical commentary or ridicule that parodies are likely to bring about.[209] The only category in which fair use does not seem to play a role is the political expediency category.

Camping or Volunteer Service Organizations Under Federal Copyright Law, 75 Wash. U. L.Q. 1277 (1997) (proposing a new exemption for this kind of activity).

[205] 17 U.S.C. § 110(10).

[206] *Hearings on S. 2082 Before the Subcomm. on Improvements in Judicial Machinery of the S. Comm. on the Judiciary*, 96th Cong. 23–27 (1980).

[207] *Id.* at 27.

[208] *See, e.g.,* Lloyd L. Weinreb, *Fair's Fair: A Comment on the Fair Use Doctrine*, 103 Harv. L. Rev. 1137 (1990).

[209] Campbell v. Acuff-Rose Music, Inc., 510 U.S. 569, 592 (1994). Although the Supreme Court did not directly invoke market failure as a rationale for its fair use ruling in the *Sony Betamax* case, one influential article has interpreted the decision as mainly justified on that ground. *See* Wendy J.

Notwithstanding the chameleon-like character of fair use, the U.S. Congress has been remarkably comfortable with it as a flexible, open-ended limit on copyright. This doctrine gives courts discretion to develop the law in keeping with the long-standing American common law tradition. The legislative history of the 1976 Act characterized this doctrine as "one of the most important and well-established limits" on copyright with an "ample caselaw" applying it.[210] The bounds of fair use are not, of course, limited by the case law, for the legislative history gave numerous other examples of uses that should be fair.[211]

1.4. WHY OTHER COUNTRIES SHOULD ADOPT FLEXIBLE,
OPEN-ENDED L&ES

Civil law countries have generally been reluctant to adopt a flexible and open-ended L&E, such as fair use, for three principal reasons: first, legislatures in those countries are expected to define the balance of rights between copyright owners and the public; second, open-ended L&Es, such as fair use, are often thought to be unpredictable; and third, some think open-ended L&Es are incompatible with international treaty obligations.

This section will make three main points. First, open-ended, flexible L&Es such as fair use are important because legislatures cannot predict which L&Es may be needed. A key advantage of a flexible L&E in an era of rapid social, economic, and technological change is that it enables the law to adapt to new circumstances and evolve over time without the need for continual statutory amendments. Second, fair use is more predictable than some commentators have asserted and, in any event, it is not the only way to build flexibility in national copyright laws. Third, open-ended L&Es, such as fair use, are consistent with international treaty obligations.

1.4.1. *Open-ended L&Es Enable the Law to Adapt to New Circumstances*

The impossibility of foreseeing and accounting for all possible uses of in-copyright works in an era of considerable technological change was recognized by the U.S. Congress as a reason to codify fair use in U.S. copyright law.[212] Some other national legislatures have recently come to agree with this proposition; fair use is now part of the national copyright laws of several other countries, including Israel, Taiwan, and

---

Gordon, *Fair Use as Market Failure: A Structural and Economic Analysis of the* Betamax *Case and its Predecessors*, 82 COLUM. L. REV. 1600 (1982).
[210] H.R. REP. NO. 94–1476, at 65 (1976).
[211] *Id.* at 65–66.
[212] *Id.* at 66.

Korea.[213] Canada's fair dealing provision has been amended so that it now resembles the U.S. fair use doctrine.[214] Australian policymakers have proposed adoption of a U.S.-style fair use provision.[215]

There is, moreover, growing recognition in Europe of the need for flexible L&Es. Leading European scholars have observed that "[t]he need for more openness in copyright law is almost self-evident in this information society of highly dynamic and unpredictable change."[216] The European Commission's recent consultation paper posed the question whether Europe needs a U.S.-style fair use provision or other mechanism to provide greater flexibility in member state copyright laws.[217] Neelie Kroes, the Vice President of the European Commission, has urged that copyright laws in Europe be reformed to enable more flexibility in their application.[218] The Dutch Parliament has even expressed interest in fair use.[219]

In the last forty years, fair use has taken on an increasingly important role in enabling copyright law to adapt to new technological challenges not contemplated by the legislature.[220] *Williams & Wilkins v. U.S.* was arguably the first such case.[221] At issue was the photocopying policy of the National Institutes of Health (NIH) under which librarians made single copies of scientific research articles at the request of patrons. Congress did not anticipate in 1909 the development of photocopying or

[213] JONATHAN BAND & JONATHAN GERAFI, THE FAIR USE/FAIR DEALING HANDBOOK (2013).

[214] *See, e.g.,* Michael Geist, *Fairness Found: How Canada Quietly Shifted From Fair Dealing to Fair Use,* in THE COPYRIGHT PENTALOGY: HOW THE SUPREME COURT OF CANADA SHOOK THE FOUNDATIONS OF CANADIAN COPYRIGHT LAW (Michael Geist ed. 2013), *available at* www.michaelgeist.ca/2012/07/canada-now-fair-use/.

[215] AUSTRALIAN LAW REFORM COMMISSION, COPYRIGHT AND THE DIGITAL ECONOMY: FINAL REPORT 13 (2013) [hereinafter ALRC Report], *available at* www.alrc.gov.au/sites/default/files/pdfs/publications/final_report_alrc_122_2nd_december_2013_.pdf. The Australian government has, however, rejected this proposed reform. *See* Jeremy Malcolm, *International Copyright Law: 2014 in Review,* ELECTRONIC FRONTIER FOUNDATION (2014), www.eff.org/deeplinks/2014/12/2014-review-international-copyright-law.

[216] HUGENHOLTZ & SENFTLEBEN, *supra* note 4, at 2.

[217] PUBLIC CONSULTATION ON THE REVIEW OF THE EU COPYRIGHT RULES (EC), *available at* http://ec.europa.eu/internal_market/consultations/2013/copyright-rules/index_en.htm.

[218] Neelie Kroes, *Reform of EU Copyright Rules: Your Chance to Give Your Views!* EUROPEAN COMMISSION (2014), http://ec.europa.eu/commission_2010-2014/kroes/en/content/reform-eu-copyright-rules-your-chance-give-your-views.

[219] HUGENHOLTZ & SENFTLEBEN, *supra* note 4, at 8 n.19.

[220] It is important to note that fair use initially evolved as a limit on the scope of U.S. copyright law principally to balance competing interests in cases in which second comers made productive uses of a first author's work in creating a new one, not to balance interests in new technology cases. *See supra* Section 1.3.1.

[221] Williams & Wilkins Co. v. United States, 487 F.2d 1345 (Ct. Cl. 1973), *aff'd by an equally divided court,* 420 U.S. 376 (1975). *Williams & Wilkins* is discussed *supra* note 70 and accompanying text. Although the *Fortnightly* case, which predates *Williams & Wilkins,* involved a new technological use of copyrighted works, it concerned whether the retransmission of broadcast signals fell within the public performance right, not fair use. *See* Fortnightly Corp. v. United Artists Television, Inc., 392 U.S. 390 (1968).

how to respond to it. Once photocopy machines came into widespread use, the question arose whether using them to make copies of in-copyright materials for research purposes was infringement. The NIH and many researchers likened this to the hand-copying of passages from books and articles that had long been thought fair. Williams and Wilkins insisted that the copies were not fair use because they were excessive and thwarted the emergence of a licensing market for such uses. Because research is a favored use and the copying policy was limited in key respects, NIH prevailed in its fair use defense.[222]

Twenty years later, however, publishers successfully defeated a photocopying fair use defense raised by Texaco, whom the publishers sued because its staff routinely photocopied articles for the firm's research scientists. In *American Geophysical Union v. Texaco, Inc.*,[223] this practice was held unfair partly because, unlike NIH, Texaco was a commercial entity and the copies furthered its commercial interests. More importantly, though, American Geophysical Union (AGU) persuaded the court that this use caused market harm because a new collecting society had established a licensing regime for photocopying of copyrighted articles.[224] The existence of this licensing regime arguably cured the market failure that had cut in NIH's favor in the *Williams & Wilkins* case.

Perhaps the most significant of the new technology cases, however, has been *Sony v. Universal*, which was the first case in which copyright owners tried to stop the distribution of a technology because consumers could use it to make infringing copies of in-copyright works.[225] Universal claimed that Sony was a contributory infringer because it sold Betamax machines knowing or having reason to know that consumers would use them to make infringing copies of television programs. But the Court decided otherwise:

> One may search the Copyright Act in vain for any sign that the elected representatives of the millions of people who watch television every day have made it unlawful to copy a program for later viewing at home, or have enacted a flat prohibition against the sale of machines that make such copying possible.[226]

[222] Williams & Wilkins, 487 F.2d at 1362–63. Photocopying within the Classroom Guidelines, discussed *supra* note 74, is unquestionably fair. Library photocopying of single articles for patrons is privileged by 17 U.S.C. § 108(d).

[223] 60 F.3d 913 (2d Cir. 1994). *See also* Princeton Univ. Press v. Mich. Document Servs. Inc., 99 F.3d 1381 (6th Cir. 1996) (photocopying of in-copyright materials for educational coursepacks held unfair because licenses available from Copyright Clearance Center).

[224] Texaco, 60 F.3d at 929–30.

[225] Sony Corp. of Am. v. Universal City Studios, Inc., 464 U.S. 417 (1984). *See also* discussion *supra* notes 103–04 and accompanying text.

[226] *Id.* at 456.

The Court noted that most owners of Betamax machines used them for time-shifting purposes; that is, to make private noncommercial copies of television programs shown on public airwaves for free. Because Universal offered only speculative theories about harm to its markets, the Court ruled that this time-shifting was fair use, saying:

> [A] use that has no demonstrable effect upon the potential market for, or the value of, the copyrighted work need not be prohibited in order to protect the author's incentive to create. The prohibition of such noncommercial uses would merely inhibit access to ideas without any countervailing benefit.[227]

The Court ruled that consumers had legitimate interests in getting access to Betamax machines for their noninfringing uses, such as making time-shift copies of broadcast TV programs.

The *Sony* decision is widely understood as having established a safe harbor for technologies with substantial noninfringing uses, insulating their makers from infringement lawsuits (in the absence of evidence that the makers were inducing users to infringe).[228] This safe harbor has been an important shield against liability for the makers of many innovative information technologies, including iPods, MP3 players, scanners, and digital video recorders.

The *Sony* decision can also be credited with laying the conceptual groundwork for numerous other judicial decisions in new technology cases.[229] It was, for instance, an important precedent to the resolution of several other controversies involving reverse engineering of computer programs to extract interface information necessary for compatibility,[230] search engine copying of images on the Internet,[231] and mass digitization of books from research library collections to make a full-text searchable database.[232] It is no wonder, then, that some commentators consider fair use to be an important part of copyright's innovation policy,[233] and

---

[227] *Id.* at 450–51.

[228] *See* Metro-Goldwyn-Mayer Studios, Inc. v. Grokster, Ltd., 545 U.S. 913 (2005) (reaffirming the safe harbor but holding that it does not shield those who induce infringement).

[229] *See, e.g.*, Pamela Samuelson, *The Generativity of Sony v. Universal: The Intellectual Property Legacy of Justice Stevens*, 74 FORDHAM L. REV. 1831, 1850 (2006). Especially important has been *Sony's* recognition that copying the whole work does not preclude a finding of fair use and that when the statute is ambiguous, courts should be guided by the constitutional purposes of copyright. *Id.* at 1866.

[230] Sega Enters. Ltd. v. Accolade, Inc., 977 F.2d 1510 (9th Cir. 1992).

[231] Perfect 10, Inc. v. Amazon.com, 508 F.3d 1146 (9th Cir. 2007).

[232] Authors Guild, Inc. v. HathiTrust, 755 F.3d 87 (2d Cir. 2014).

[233] *See, e.g.*, Fred von Lohmann, *Fair Use as Innovation Policy*, 23 BERKELEY TECH. L.J. 829 (2008). *See also* THOMAS ROGERS & ANDREW SZAMOSSZEGI, FAIR USE IN THE U.S. ECONOMY: ECONOMIC CONTRIBUTIONS OF INDUSTRIES RELYING ON FAIR USE (CCIA, 2011).

why fair use is being adopted or considered by other nations who want to attract high technology investments.[234]

1.4.2. *Open-ended L&Es Can Produce Reasonably Predictable Outcomes*

One frequent complaint about fair use is its unpredictability.[235] That criticism has, however, been overstated. Fair use is not a completely open-ended doctrine, for the statute directs courts to consider various factors that bear on the fairness (or not) of any particular use. When codifying the fair use doctrine, the U.S. Congress identified a set of favored purposes – criticism, comment, news reporting, research, teaching, and scholarship – and set forth four factors that courts should weigh together in making determinations about whether a challenged use was fair or foul: the purpose of the challenged use, the nature of the copyrighted work, the amount and substantiality of the taking, and the harm likely to be caused to the market for the work.[236]

Because the fair use provision articulates these purposes and factors, the statute provides a framework within which courts can balance interests of copyright owners, of prospective users, of developers of new technologies or services, and of the public to decide whether a challenged use is or is not, on balance, harmful in ways that copyright laws are intended to address. Over time, reasonably predictable patterns of fair use decisions have emerged, as recent scholarship has shown.[237] In short, uses tend to be fair if the amount taken was reasonable in light of the challenged user's

---

[234] Fair use has other advantages that may help to explain why the concept is spreading to other nations. For one thing, it is a concept that ordinary people can understand. By learning about fair and unfair uses, people can adapt their behavior to conform to the fair ones. For another, fair use can avert a proliferation of specific exemptions that can make copyright laws read like the tax code. Most non-professional users of copyrighted works do not have the diligence or patience to wade through a long motley list of exceptions to find one that arguably applies to the specific activity in which they are engaged. Most users can, however, ask themselves a set of questions that will help them make fair use judgment (such as "is what I took from an author's work reasonable in light of my purpose for doing so, and how much (if any) harm might this cause to the copyright owner?"). Finally, fair use engenders respect for copyright law, for it avoids the rigidity that grants of exceptionally broad rights, tempered only by a few narrow exceptions, can cause. Codes of fair use best practices allow user communities to come to consensus about practices that enable reasonable uses that do not cause appreciable harm to authorial markets. *See, e.g.,* Patricia Aufderheide & Peter Jaszi, Reclaiming Fair Use (2011) (discussing the value of best practices).

[235] *See, e.g.,* David Nimmer, *"Fairest of Them All" and Other Fairy Tales of Fair Use,* 66 Law & Contemp. Probs. 263 (2003); Lawrence Lessig, Free Culture 187 (2004) (characterizing fair use as the "right to hire a lawyer").

[236] 17 U.S.C. § 107.

[237] *See, e.g.,* Barton Beebe, *An Empirical Study of U.S. Copyright Fair Use Opinions, 1978–2005,* 156 U. Penn. L. Rev. 549 (2008); Neil Weinstock Netanel, *Making Sense of Fair Use,* 15 Lewis Clark L. Rev. 715 (2011); Matthew Sag, *Predicting Fair Use,* 73 Ohio St. L.J. 47 (2012); Samuelson, *supra* note 81.

purpose and the use did not cause measurable harm to the market.[238] In addition, best practices guidelines can contribute to greater predictability about the scope of fair use as a flexible limit.[239]

Fair use is, of course, not the only way that copyright laws can be made more flexible. European scholars have proposed several ways to achieve this goal. For civil law jurisdictions, these alternatives may be preferable to a U.S.-style fair use doctrine. The Wittem Project's model European Copyright Code, for instance, identifies twenty or so specific exceptions that such a code should embody, but it also proposes an open-ended exception to allow other analogous uses to be deemed noninfringing.[240] In his influential report prepared for the UK Intellectual Property Office, Professor Hargreaves recommended that the UK adopt a flexible copyright limitation designed "to accommodate future technological change where it does not threaten copyright owners."[241]

Professors Hugenholtz and Senftleben report on other flexibilities in existing European copyright rules.[242] EU member states have, they assert, considerable freedom to craft flexible L&Es in keeping with the InfoSoc Directive's list of permissible exceptions.[243] Some European courts have reached flexible results in Internet search engine cases, either by applying the fair quotation exception in a creative way or by relying upon a doctrine of implied consent.[244] Flexibility can also be achieved if courts rule against digital infringement claims when defendants are engaged in acts that would be lawful if done with analog products.[245] External doctrines such as freedom of expression may provide further flexibility in copyright cases in Europe.[246]

1.4.3. *Flexible L&Es Can Be Compatible With International Treaty Obligations*

A lively scholarly debate exists about whether open-ended L&Es such as fair use are compatible with international treaty obligations.[247] To set the stage for this

---

[238] *See, e.g.,* Bill Graham Archives v. Dorling Kindersley Ltd., 448 F.3d 605 (2d Cir. 2006).

[239] *See, e.g.,* Niva Elkin-Koren & Orit Fischman-Afori, *Taking Users' Rights to the Next Level: A Pragmatist Approach to Fair Uses,* 33 CARDOZO ARTS & ENT. L.J. 1 (2015).

[240] WITTEM PROJECT, *supra* note 3, art. 5.

[241] IAN HARGREAVES, DIGITAL OPPORTUNITY: A REVIEW OF INTELLECTUAL PROPERTY AND GROWTH 5 (2011).

[242] HUGENHOLTZ & SENFTLEBEN, *supra* note 4, at 13–26.

[243] *Id.* at 14–16. Sweden, for instance, has a relatively open-ended fair quotation rule.

[244] *Id.* at 15–16.

[245] *Id.* at 23–24.

[246] *Id.* at 25–26.

[247] Some scholars have questioned whether open-ended, flexible L&Es are compliant with international treaty obligations. *See, e.g.,* Ruth L. Okediji, *Toward an International Fair Use Doctrine,* 39 COLUM. J.

discussion, it is necessary to understand the origins and evolution of the three-step test that lies at the heart of this debate.

The Berne Convention was revised in 1967 to harmonize national copyright rules on a broader authorial right to control reproductions of protected works than existed under previous versions of that treaty.[248] Because member states were not in complete agreement about just how broad that right should be, the treaty established a three-step test for nations to use when deciding whether to adopt an L&E to the reproduction right.[249]

The first step of this test calls for identifying the particular purpose the L&E would serve (i.e., it should be focused on "certain special cases"). The second step inquires whether the L&E would conflict with a normal exploitation of the work. The third step considers whether the L&E would otherwise unreasonably prejudice legitimate interests of the rights holder.[250] Berne Union members' copyright laws have adopted many L&Es to the reproduction right which they consider to be compliant with the three-step test.[251]

The three-step test was incorporated into the Agreement on Trade-Related Aspects of Intellectual Property Rights (TRIPS) in 1994 with three significant changes.[252] TRIPS extended the test so that it applies to all L&Es, not just to L&Es affecting the reproduction right.[253] It also recast the test so that it seems more of a constraint on national adoptions of L&Es than under Berne.[254] And TRIPS has provided a process by which member states can challenge another member state with violating a TRIPS norm, such as adopting an L&E that did not satisfy the three-step test.[255]

Several factors suggest that the U.S. fair use doctrine is consistent with the three-step test. For one thing, the United States, when it joined the Berne Convention in

TRANSNAT'L L. 75, 87 (2000). However, most scholars think that they are. *See, e.g.,* Christophe Geiger, Daniel Gervais, & Martin Senftleben, *The Three-Step Test Revisited: How to Use the Test's Flexibility in National Copyright Law,* 29 AM. U. INT'L L. REV. 581, 612–16 (2014). *See also* ALRC REPORT, *supra* note 215, at 116–22 (citing several academic experts in concluding that fair use complies with the three-step test).

[248] *See* MARTIN SENFTLEBEN, COPYRIGHT, LIMITATIONS AND THE THREE-STEP TEST: AN ANALYSIS OF THE THREE-STEP TEST IN INTERNATIONAL AND EC COPYRIGHT LAW 47 (2004).

[249] *Id.* at 48–51.

[250] Berne Convention, *supra* note 85, art. 9(2).

[251] The United States had adopted almost all of its L&Es before it joined the Berne Convention in 1989.

[252] Agreement on Trade-Related Aspects of Intellectual Property Rights, art. 13, Apr. 15, 1994, 1869 U.N.T.S. 299 (1994) [hereinafter TRIPS Agreement].

[253] *Id.* The TRIPS three-step test also applies to other intellectual property rights. *See id.* art. 26(2) (industrial designs), art. 30 (patents).

[254] Article 13 states that member states "shall confine" L&Es to those that satisfy the three-step test. *Id.* art. 13. The Berne provision is phrased more permissively, for it says that "[i]t shall be a matter for legislation" for nations "to permit the reproduction" of works in accordance with the three-step test. Berne Convention, *supra* note 85, art. 9(2).

[255] TRIPS Agreement, *supra* note 252, art. 64.

1989, asserted that its copyright law, including the fair use doctrine, was compatible with Berne norms, including the three-step test.[256] The United States must also have believed its fair use doctrine was compatible with its obligations under the TRIPS Agreement, of which it was a principal instigator.[257] Because fair use cases generally fall within quite predictable patterns,[258] the "certain special cases" requirement would seem to be satisfied. A use is unlikely to be fair under U.S. law if it would conflict with a normal exploitation of the work or otherwise unreasonably interfere with legitimate interests of rights holders. Hence, the argument that the U.S. fair use doctrine is compatible with the three-step test is convincing.

Several scholars have pointed to the drafting history of the three-step test, which "demonstrate[s] that [the test] was intended to serve as a flexible balancing tool offering national policy makers sufficient breathing space to satisfy economic, social and cultural needs."[259] They argue that the three-step test parallels the U.S. fair use doctrine because it considers the purpose of a challenged use, the risk of interference with normal exploitations (which inevitably must be assessed in light of the nature of the work and how much was taken), as well as other legitimate interests of rights holders (and the public) in assessing whether the three-step test is satisfied.[260] Indeed, the three-step test itself can be conceived as a treaty-compliant way to achieve flexibility in European copyright laws.[261]

1.5. CONCLUSION

Scholars have paid surprisingly little attention to the specific policy justifications for the wide range of L&Es set forth in national copyright laws.[262] This chapter has sought to fill this gap in the literature. It has explained how U.S. copyright law came

---

[256] *See, e.g.,* Geiger et al., *supra* note 247, at 615–16; PATRY ON FAIR USE § 8:2 (2014) (noting that in congressional activity leading to the Berne Convention Implementation Act of 1988, no changes to the U.S. fair use provision were recommended or made).

[257] ALRC REPORT, *supra* note 215, at 121 (citing submitted comments of Gwen Hinze, Peter Jaszi, & Matthew Sag, "The Fair Use Doctrine in the United States – A Response to the Kernochan Report," June 26, 2013, *available at* http://ssrn.com/abstract=2298833).

[258] *See, e.g.,* Samuelson, *supra* note 81, at 2541–42.

[259] Geiger et al., *supra* note 247, at 582. Thirty scholars, mostly from European universities, have endorsed a balanced interpretation of this test. *See* Christophe Geiger, Reto M. Hilty, Jonathan Griffiths & Uma Suthersanen, *Declaration: A Balanced Approach to the Interpretation of the "Three-Step Test" of Copyright Law,* 39 I.I.C. 707 (2008) *available at* www.ip.mpg.de/en/news/declaration_on_the_three_ step_test.html. *See also* Jerome H. Reichman & Ruth L. Okediji, *When Copyright Law and Science Collide: Empowering Digitally Integrated Research Methods on a Global Scale,* 96 MINN. L. REV. 1362, 1453–56 (2012) (analyzing the three-step test and endorsing the Geiger et al. Declaration).

[260] Geiger et al., *supra* note 247, at 612–13.

[261] *Id.* at 616–17.

[262] *But see* Gervais, *supra* note 7, at 21–22 (proposing several principles for copyright L&Es); RUTH L. OKEDIJI, THE INTERNATIONAL COPYRIGHT SYSTEM: LIMITATIONS, EXCEPTIONS,

to have a substantial number of very specific L&Es as well as the judicially developed fair use doctrine. It has identified numerous principled justifications for adoption of these L&Es, while recognizing that some L&Es have been adopted more out of political expediency than out of principle.[263]

Specific L&Es play an important role in copyright laws in identifying relatively stable sets of uses and users whose activities legislators have decided should be permitted notwithstanding the broad scope of exclusive rights granted to authors. But should all L&Es be specific? As a complement to specific L&Es, nations should consider adoption of some sort of flexible and open-ended L&E to enable courts to adapt copyright laws to respond to new circumstances.

Flexible L&Es are needed in an era of rapid technological change because legislators cannot possibly foresee the copyright implications of these developments or construct well-tailored specific provisions to deal with these developments. Nor can legislatures be expected to amend the law every time some new development raises questions not easily answerable under the existing statutory framework. The fair use doctrine has served the flexibility function well for U.S. copyright law, in part because fair use cases tend to fall into predictable patterns. Yet, some nations may prefer to achieve flexibilities in their national copyright laws in other ways.

Although some scholars have questioned whether open-ended L&Es, such as fair use, are consistent with international treaty obligations, many European as well as U.S. scholars make compelling arguments that fair use and other flexible L&Es are compatible with treaty obligations.

The optimal policy for copyright L&Es may well be for nations to have specific L&Es, for categories of justified uses that are relatively stable over time and for which predictability is more important than flexibility, and to have an open-ended exception, such as fair use, to allow the law to adapt to new uses not contemplated by legislatures.

AND PUBLIC INTEREST CONSIDERATIONS FOR DEVELOPING COUNTRIES, ICSTD ISSUE PAPER No. 15 (2006), *available at* www.ictsd.org/themes/innovation-and-ip/research/the-international-copyright-system-limitations-exceptions-and. *See also* SAM RICKETSON, WIPO STUDY ON LIMITATIONS AND EXCEPTIONS OF COPYRIGHT AND RELATED RIGHTS IN THE DIGITAL ENVIRONMENT (2003), *available at* www.wipo.int/meetings/en/doc_details.jsp?doc_id=16805 (assessing the compatibility of several types of L&Es with the three-step test).

[263] One important question not addressed in this chapter is whether or to what extent L&Es should be overridable by contracts, or in particular, mass-market license agreements.

TABLE 1.1. *Timetable for exceptions and limitations in U.S. copyright law*

	1790	1841	1880	1908	1909	1947	1973	1975	1976	1988	1990	1997	1998	1999	2005
Fair use									§ 107						
Useful articles depicted in drawings									§ 113(b)						
First sale					§ 41	§ 27			§ 109						
Compulsory license to make sound recordings of music					§ 1(e)				§ 115(a)						
Compulsory license for playing music via jukeboxes					§ 1(e)				§ 116						
Library copying									§ 108						
Small business reception of broadcasts									§ 110(5)(A)						
Face-to-face classroom teaching									§ 110(1)						
Distance education									§ 110(2)						
Performances in the course of religious services									§ 110(3)						
Nonprofit educational, religious, and charity performances									§ 110(4)						
Music performance at agricultural/ horticultural fairs									§ 110(6)						
Stores promoting sale of records/ audio equipment									§ 110(7)						
Nondramatic performances for the blind/handicapped									§ 110(8)						
Performance of dramatic works for the blind/handicapped									§ 110(9)						

Folsom v. Marsh — 1841

Baker v. Selden — 1880

Bobbs-Merrill v. Straus — 1908

Williams & Wilkins v. U.S. — 1973

20th Century Music v. Aiken — 1975

Williams & Wilkins v. U.S. (1978) — 1976

U.S. common law.

(continued)

TABLE 1.1 (continued)

	1790	1841	1880	1908	1909	1947	1973	1975	1976 (1978)	1988	1990	1997	1998	1999	2005
Cable retransmission of broadcast compulsory license									§ 111						
Ephemeral recordings of broadcast programs									§ 112						
No public performance right for sound recordings									§ 114(a)						
Exemption for public broadcasting of sound recordings									§ 114(b)						
Computer uses (1980 amendment for SW uses)									§ 117						
Public broadcaster compulsory license process									§ 118						
Nonprofit veterans/fraternal organizations										§ 110(10)					
Satellite local TV retransmission compulsory license										§ 119					
Limits on architectural works											§ 120				
Enhance print-disabled access to nondramatic literary works												§ 121			
Larger establishment broadcast performance													§ 110(5)(B)		
Satellite radio & webcasting compulsory license													§ 114(d)		
Satellite distant TV retransmission compulsory license														§ 122	
Blocking parts of motion pictures for home viewing															§ 110(11)
	1790	1841	1880	1908	1909	1947	1973	1975	1976 (1978)	1988	1990	1997	1998	1999	2005

Folsom v. Marsh (1841)
Baker v. Selden (1908), Bobbs-Merrill v. Straus (1909)
Williams & Wilkins v. U.S. (1973–1975)
20th Century Music v. Aiken (1975)

U.S. common law.

Table compiled by Kathryn Hashimoto.

TABLE 1.2 *Copyright L&E clusters*

	United States		Examples from other countries/international
	Examples of fair uses (case law)	Specific exceptions (statutory)	
AUTHORSHIP Promoting ongoing authorship	• song parody (*Campbell v. Acuff-Rose Music, Inc.*) • excerpts in unauthorized biography (*New Era Publ'ns Int'l v. Carol Publ'g Group*) • thumbnail images in historical account (*Bill Graham Archives v. Dorling Kindersley Ltd.*)	• architectural works: depictions of publicly visible works [§ 120(a)] • library copies for patron research [§ 108(d)]	• Berne: right of fair quotation [art. 10(1)] • InfoSoc Dir: quotation [art. 5(3)(d)]; caricature, parody, pastiche [art. 5(3)(k)] • UK: research, private study [§ 29]; criticism, review, news reporting [§ 30]; caricature, parody, pastiche [§ 30A]
USER INTERESTS Creating a buffer for user autonomy and personal property interests	• time-shift copying of television programs (*Sony Corp. of Am. v. Universal City Studios, Inc.*)	• first sale [§ 109] • motion pictures for home viewing [§ 110(11)] • architectural works: modification [§ 120(b)]	• Japan: personal use [art. 30]; private study [art. 31]; computer programs [art. 47*ter*, 47*quater*] • UK: research, private study [§ 29]; exhaustion [§ 18(3)(a)] • Australia: private-use time shifting [s 111], format shifting [ss 43C, 47J, 109A, 110AA] • InfoSoc Dir: exhaustion [art. 4(2)]

(continued)

TABLE 1.2 (continued)

	United States		Examples from other countries/international
	Examples of fair uses (case law)	Specific exceptions (statutory)	
PUBLIC BENEFITS			
Fostering the public interest in access to information	• film images in book (*Time, Inc. v. Bernard Geis Assocs.*) • radio segment posted on website (*Savage v. Council on American-Islamic Relations, Inc.*) • photos in news story (*Nunez v. Caribbean Int'l News*)	• photos for comment or reporting [§ 113(c)] • library uses: audiovisual news programs [§ 108(f)(3)]	• InfoSoc Dir: news reporting [art. 5(3)(c)]; use of political speeches [art. 5(3)(f)]
Serving social policy goals	• full-text searchable database (*Authors Guild, Inc. v. HathiTrust*)	• library uses: preservation [§ 108(b)]; lost/damaged copies [§ 108(c)]; research patrons [§ 108(d)] • classroom performances, displays [§ 110(1)] • performance in course of religious services [§ 110(3)] • nonprofit educational, religious, charity performances [§ 110(4)] • print-disabled access [§ 121]	• InfoSoc Dir: teaching/scientific research [art. 5(3)(a)]; benefiting people with a disability [art. 5(3)(b)]; library preservation [art. 5(3)(b)]

ECONOMIC GOALS			
Enabling public institutions to function	• law enforcement investigation (*Shell v. City of Radford; Jartech, Inc. v. Clancy*)		• Japan: investigations, adjudications, administrative proceedings [art. 42]
Fostering commerce, competition, and ongoing innovation	• reverse engineering (*Sega Enters. v. Accolade, Inc.*) • add-on programs (*Lewis Galoob Toys v. Nintendo of Am., Inc.*) • images used in advertising (*Sony Computer Entm't Am. v. Bleem, LLC*)	• phonorecord/audio equipment sales promotion [§ 110(7)] • motion pictures for home viewing [§ 110(11)] • useful articles depicted in PGS works [§ 113(b)] • computer repair [§ 117(c)]	• EU Dir 2009/24/EC: computer programs [art. 6]
Exempting economically insignificant incidental uses	fair use is likely but untested in the courts	• ephemeral recordings of broadcast program [§ 112(a)] • computer programs: essential copies [§ 117(a)]	• InfoSoc Dir: transient or incidental copies [art. 5(1)]
Aiming to cure or mitigate market failures		• compulsory license for cable TV retransmission [§ 111] • satellite radio & webcast compulsory license [§ 114(d)] • compulsory license to make sound recording [§ 115(a)] • compulsory license to play music via jukeboxes [§ 116] • satellite TV retransmit compulsory license [§§ 119, 122] • print-disabled access [§ 121]	

(continued)

TABLE 1.2 (continued)

	United States		Examples from other countries/international
	Examples of fair uses (case law)	Specific exceptions (statutory)	
EXPEDIENCY Enabling politically expedient outcomes		• performances at nonprofit agricultural/horticultural fair [§ 110(6)], veterans/ fraternal organization [§ 110(10)] • cable TV retransmissions [§ 111] • sound recordings: no public performance right [§ 114(a)]; public broadcasting exemption [§ 114(b)] • compulsory license to play music via jukeboxes [§ 116]	
FLEXIBILITY Enabling copyright laws to adapt to new circumstances	numerous	• § 107	

Table compiled by Kathryn Hashimoto

2

The Role of the Author in Copyright[*]

Jane C. Ginsburg[**]

ABSTRACT

Two encroachments, one long-standing, the other a product of the digital era, cramp the author's place in copyright today. First, most authors lack bargaining power; the real economic actors in the copyright system have long been the publishers and other exploiters to whom authors cede their rights. These actors may advance the figure of the author for the moral luster it lends their appeals to lawmakers, but then may promptly despoil the creators of whatever increased protections they may have garnered. Second, the advent of new technologies of creation and dissemination of works of authorship not only threatens traditional revenue models but also calls into question whatever artistic control the author may – or should – retain over her work. After reviewing these challenges, I will consider legal measures to protect authors from leonine contracts, as well as measures in the marketplace to obtain compensation for the exploitation of their rights, in order to assure authors better remuneration, and more power over the ways their works encounter the public.

The author's place in the future of copyright (assuming copyright has a future) will not be assured until the full range of her interests, monetary and moral, receives both recognition and enforcement. Online micropayment and other systems for remunerating individual authors (including by means of collective licensing), albeit often

[*] © Jane C. Ginsburg 2015.

[**] Morton L. Janklow Professor of Literary and Artistic Property Law, Columbia University School of Law. Thanks to Prof. Jessica Litman for trenchant criticisms, and to Jennifer Maul, Columbia Law School class of 2008, Emily Weiss, Columbia Law School class of 2009, and especially Allyson Mackavage, Columbia Law School class of 2015, for research assistance.

Parts of this chapter are based both on a lecture first given at the American Philosophical Society, Nov. 9, 2007 – later delivered at Willamette University College of Law, Sept. 10, 2008, and subsequently revised for publication in 153 PROC. AM. PHILOS. SOC. 147 (2009), also published at 45 WILLAMETTE L. REV. 381 (2009) – and on a lecture given in Nov. 2012 at Victoria University of Wellington (N.Z.) and subsequently published as *Exceptional Authorship: The Role of Copyright Exceptions in Promoting Creativity, in* EVOLUTION AND EQUILIBRIUM: COPYRIGHT THIS CENTURY 15 (Susy Frankel & Daniel Gervais eds., Cambridge University Press 2014).

embryonic, hold promise. But will these new means of remunerating authors (or for that matter older business models that, while often divesting authors of their rights, also often afforded them an income stream) remain viable in a digital environment in which paying for creativity increasingly seems an act of largesse? Most fundamentally, we need to appreciate authorship, and to recognize that a work in digital form is a thing of value, lest the old adage that "information" (meaning, works of authorship) "wants to be free" presage works of authorship that don't "want" to be created.

In the beginning was the Reader. And the Reader, in a Pirandello-esque flash of insight, went in search of an Author, for the Reader realized that without an Author, there could be no Readers. But when the Reader met an Author, the Author, anticipating Dr. Johnson, scowled, "No man but a blockhead ever wrote, except for money."

And the Reader calculated the worth of a free supply of blockhead-written works against the value of recognizing the Author's economic self-interest. She concluded that the author's interest is also her interest, that the "public interest" encompasses *both* that of authors and of readers. So she looked upon copyright, and saw that it was good.[1]

This, in essence, is the philosophy that informs the 1710 English Statute of Anne (the first copyright statute) and the 1787 U.S. Constitution's copyright clause. The latter states: "Congress shall have Power ... to promote the Progress of Science by securing for limited Times to Authors ... the exclusive Right to their Writings ...," U.S. CONST., art. I, § 8, cl. 8. In the Anglo-American system, copyright enabled the public to have what Thomas Babbington Macaulay heralded as "a supply of good books" and other works that promote the progress of learning.[2] Copyright did this by assuring authors "the exclusive Right to their ... Writings" – that is, a property right giving authors sufficient control over and compensation for their works to make it worth their while to be creative.[3]

Vesting copyright in authors – rather than exploiters – was an innovation in the eighteenth century.[4] It made authorship the functional and moral center of the

---

[1] Samuel Johnson, *in* BARTLETT'S FAMILIAR QUOTATIONS 328 (John Bartlett & Justin Kaplan eds., 17th ed. 2002) (quoting JAMES BOSWELL, LIFE OF JOHNSON (Apr. 5, 1776)).

[2] Thomas B. Macaulay, *Speech before the House of Commons* (Feb. 5, 1841), *in* MACAULAY: PROSE AND POETRY 733–4 (G. M. Young ed., 1970).

[3] U.S. CONST. art. I, § 8, cl. 8. Both the Statute of Anne (England 1710), and the U.S. Constitution's copyright clause highlight the role of exclusive rights in promoting the progress of learning.

[4] Before the Statute of Anne, the printing privilege system in force in many European states generally conferred the monopoly on printers, though authors too might receive privileges. Papal printing privileges appear to have been granted to authors at least as frequently as to printers or booksellers. *See* Jane C. Ginsburg, *Proto-property in Literary and Artistic Works: Sixteenth-Century Papal Printing Privileges*, 36 COLUM. J.L. & ARTS 345 (2013). Nonetheless, the Statute of Anne was the first legislation systematically to vest authors with exclusive rights.

system. But all too often in fact, authors neither control nor derive substantial benefits from their work. In the copyright polemics of today, moreover, authors are curiously absent; the overheated rhetoric that currently characterizes much of the academic and popular press tends to portray copyright as a battleground between evil industry exploiters and free-speaking users.[5] If authors have any role in this scenario, it is at most a walk-on, a cameo appearance as victims of monopolist "content owners."[6] The disappearance of the author moreover justifies disrespect for copyright – after all, those downloading teenagers aren't ripping off the authors and performers; the major record companies have already done that.[7]

Two encroachments, one long-standing, the other a product of the digital era, cramp the author's place in copyright today. First, most authors lack bargaining power; the real economic actors in the copyright system have long been the publishers and other exploiters to whom authors cede their rights. These actors may advance the figure of the author for the moral luster it lends their appeals to lawmakers, but then may promptly despoil the creators of whatever increased protections they may have garnered. Second, the advent of new technologies of creation and dissemination of works of authorship not only threatens traditional revenue models but also calls into question whatever artistic control the author may – or should – retain over her work. After reviewing these challenges, I will consider legal measures

---

[5] *See, e.g.,* JOHN TEHRANIAN, INFRINGEMENT NATION: COPYRIGHT 2.0 AND YOU 14 (2011) (describing today's copyright laws as "a legal regime that threatens to make criminal infringers of us all"); *id.* at 129 ("[T]he widening ambit of copyright protection has increasingly encroached upon critical First Amendment values, suppressing transformative uses of copyrighted works that advance creativity and free speech rights"); LAWRENCE LESSIG, FREE CULTURE: HOW BIG MEDIA USES TECHNOLOGY AND THE LAW TO LOCK DOWN CULTURE AND CONTROL CREATIVITY (2004); Electronic Frontier Foundation, *Intellectual Property, available at* www.eff.org/issues/intellectual-property (last visited Feb. 4, 2015) (noting that dysfunctional IP systems give "IP owners a veto on innovation and free speech"); Amanda Beshears Cook, *Copyright and Freedom of Expression: Saving Free Speech from Advancing Legislation,* 12 CHI.-KENT J. INTELL. PROP. 1, 20–21 (2013) (discussing the entertainment industry's efforts to push through legislation that would diminish First Amendment interests); Jenna Wortham, *With Twitter, Blackouts and Demonstrations, Web Flexes Its Muscle,* N.Y. TIMES, Jan. 18, 2012, *available at* www.nytimes.com/2012/01/19/technology/protests-of-antipiracy-bills-unite-web.html?pagewanted=all.

[6] *But see* PETER BALDWIN, THE COPYRIGHT WARS: THREE CENTURIES OF TRANS-ATLANTIC BATTLE (2014) (opposing the author-oriented continental copyright tradition against the public-minded Anglo-American copyright tradition and contending that undue attention to authors restricts access to culture and suppresses expression).

[7] David Cloyd, *Music Thievery Laid Bare: When Pirates Rip Off Working Class Artists,* THE TRICHORDIST, Feb. 8, 2014, *available at* http://thetrichordist.com/2014/02/08/music-thievery-laid-bare-when-pirates-rip-off-the-working-class-artist-guest-post-by-david-cloyd/ (noting that many pirates "see themselves as modern-day Robin Hoods, fighting against corporate greed and the tyranny of the big bad music industry"); Cord Jefferson, *The Music Industry's Funny Money,* THE ROOT, July 6, 2010, *available at* www.theroot.com/articles/culture/2010/07/the_root_investigates_who_really_gets_paid_in_the_music_industry.html?GT1=38002 (finding that the musicians receive about 13% of profits whereas the record label and distributors receive a combined 87%).

to protect authors from leonine contracts, as well as measures in the marketplace to obtain compensation for the exploitation of their rights.

2.1. AUTHORS AND COPYRIGHT OWNERSHIP

U.S. Copyright vests in a work's creator as soon as she "fixes" it in any tangible medium of expression.[8] But for many authors, ownership is quickly divested, and for some, it never attaches at all. The latter group of creators are "employees for hire," salaried authors who create works in pursuit of their employment, or freelancers who are commissioned to create certain kinds of works, and who sign a contract specifying that the work will be "for hire."[9] An author who is not an employee for hire starts out with rights that she may transfer by contract; unlike many continental European laws, the U.S. copyright law places few limitations on the scope of the rights she may transfer.[10] Moreover, unlike those foreign laws, the U.S. copyright law contains few mandatory remuneration provisions.[11] Thus it is possible for a U.S. author, "for good and valuable consideration" (which could be the mere fact of disseminating the work) to assign "all right, title and interest in and to the work, in all media, now known or later developed, for the full term of copyright, including any renewals and extensions thereof, for the full territory, which shall be the Universe."[12] I'm not making this up. The Roz Chast *New Yorker* "Ultimate Contract" cartoon was not so far off in further specifying: "and even if one day they find a door in the Universe that leads to a whole new non-Universe place, ... or everything falls into a black hole so nobody knows which end is up and we're all dead anyway so who cares, we'll STILL own all those rights...."[13] Worse, with one exception, this is a valid contract. The exception is not the extraterrestrial aspect; authors can, it seems, validly grant rights for Mars (at least if the grant is governed by U.S. law). It concerns the author's inalienable right to terminate grants of U.S. rights thirty-five years after the grant was executed. Thus, even if the contract purports to grant rights in perpetuity and for a lump sum, the author can nonetheless retrieve most of her U.S. rights thirty-five years after the

---

[8] *See* 17 U.S.C. § 102(a) (2006).

[9] *Id.* at §§ 101, 201(b).

[10] *Compare id.* § 204(a) (grant of exclusive rights must be in writing and signed by grantor) *with* France, Code of Intellectual Property, arts. L 131-1 – L 131-9, L 132-1 – L 132-34, *available at* www .wipo.int/wipolex/en/text.jsp?file_id=179120 (detailed provisions concerning contracts, including rules protecting authors against overreaching transfers).

[11] Certain compulsory licenses include mandatory set-asides or percentages for certain classes of creators. *See, e.g.,* 17 U.S.C. § 114(g)(2) ("Proceeds from Licensing of Transmissions").

[12] For examples of these kinds of contracts, see *Keep Your Copyrights, Clauses about General Assignment of Copyright, available at* http://web.law.columbia.edu/keep-your-copyrights/contracts/clauses/by-type/10/overreaching (last visited Feb. 4, 2015).

[13] Roz Chast, *The Ultimate Contract,* THE NEW YORKER, Aug. 11, 2003, *available at* www.condenaststore .com/-sp/The-Ultimate-Contract-New-Yorker-Cartoon-Prints_i8534476_.htm

conclusion of the contract.[14] This is a very important, but otherwise isolated, U.S. legislative nod to authors' weak bargaining position.[15] Unfortunately, authors or their heirs have not always fared well in court when they seek to enforce their termination rights. For example, courts have upheld grantees' assertions that the work was "for hire" and therefore not subject to termination,[16] and they have invalidated termination attempts for failure to comply with the statute's many prerequisites to effective exercise of the right.[17]

It is no accident that the copyright law of the United States and other common law countries favors easy alienability of authors' rights. Our legal system frowns on "restraints on alienation."[18] Perhaps ironically, the ability to freely part with property

---

[14] *See* 17 U.S.C. § 203. For extensive historical and doctrinal analysis of authors' reversion rights, see, e.g., Lionel Bently & Jane C. Ginsburg, *"The Sole Right Shall Return to the Author": Anglo-American Authors' Reversion Rights from the Statute of Anne to Contemporary U.S. Copyright*, 25 BERKELEY TECH. L.J. 1475 (2011).

[15] Thus, the U.S. copyright law lacks the kind of author-protective provisions now found in German and French law, which guarantee proportional or fair remuneration as well as some control over new modes of exploitation. See Copyright Act, Sept. 9, 1965, Federal Law Gazette Part I, at 1273 (Ger.), as last amended by Article 8 of the Act of Oct. 1, 2013 (Federal Law Gazette Part I, 3714), arts. 31–41; Code of Intellectual Property, arts. L. 131-1 – 131-6; L. 132-1 – 132-17 (Fr.), as modified by Ordonnance n° 2014-1348 of Nov. 12, 2014 modifying the provisions of the Code of Intellectual Property respecting publishing contracts, *Journal Officiel de la République Française* n°0262, Nov. 13, 2014, page 19101, *available at* www.legifrance.gouv.fr/affichTexte.do;jsessionid=3784253FD9F4E 4382CC4719AC49F50A3.tpdjo11v_1?cidTexte=JORFTEXT000029750455&dateTexte=20141114, discussed *infra*. For a review of EU legal restrictions on the scope of authors contracts and obligations to remunerate authors, see generally SÉVERINE DUSOLLIER ET AL., CONTRACTUAL ARRANGEMENTS APPLICABLE TO CREATORS: LAW AND PRACTICE OF SELECTED MEMBER STATES (Citizens' Rights and Constitutional Affairs, Policy Department ed., 2014), *available at* www.europarl.europa.eu/ RegData/etudes/etudes/join/2014/493041/IPOL-JURI_ET%282014%29493041_EN.pdf

[16] *See, e.g.*, Marvel Characters, Inc. v. Kirby, 726 F.3d 119, 143 (2d Cir. 2013) (concluding that Kirby's comic book characters were works made for hire, and therefore Kirby had no right to terminate transfer of copyright to Marvel); Siegel v. Warner Bros. Entm't, 542 F. Supp. 2d 1098, 1064–79 (C.D. Cal. 2008) (finding that certain "Superman" works were works made for hire, and therefore not within scope of termination right); Fifty-Six Hope Road Music Ltd. v. UMG Recordings, Inc., 99 U.S.P.Q. 1735, 2010 WL 3564258, at *9 (S.D.N.Y. 2010) (finding that certain works by Bob Marley were works made for hire, and therefore heirs were not entitled to renewal term).

[17] *See, e.g.*, DC Comics v. Pacific Pictures Corp., 545 Fed. App'x 678, 680 (9th Cir. 2013), *cert. denied*, 135 S. Ct. 144 (2014) (holding that agreement between copyright transferee and beneficiary of life pension granted to "Superman" co-creator Joseph Shuster waived right to termination by statutory heirs of termination right); Siegel, 542 F. Supp. 2d at 1118, 1126 (holding that elements of "Superman" comic books fell outside of the scope of termination based on the date of the notices; Statutory heirs of co-creator Jerry Siegel therefore failed to terminate copyright grants as to those elements); Burroughs v. Metro-Goldwyn-Mayer, Inc., 683 F.2d 610, 622 (2d Cir. 1982) (holding that termination notice's failure to list five *Tarzan* titles failed to terminate the copyright interest in those titles). *See generally* Bently & Ginsburg, *supra* note 14 at 1572–86 (discussing caselaw construing termination rights); *id.* at 1586–87 (concluding that legal limits on scope of transfers might serve authors better than termination rights).

[18] *See generally* 61 AM. JUR. 2D *Perpetuities* § 90 (2002); Bd. of County Supervisors of Prince William County, Va. v. United States, 48 F.3d 520 (Fed. Cir. 1995); Metro. Life Ins. Co. v. Strnad, 876 P.2d 1362 (Kan. 1994); Cole v. Peters, 3 S.W.3d 846 (Mo. Ct. App. W.D. 1999).

is a hallmark of its ownership. That this works to the benefit of the so-called content industries could traditionally be justified as consistent with the overall goals of the copyright scheme. These are not only to promote the care and feeding of authors but also – some would contend, primarily – to ensure the dissemination of works of authorship.[19] After all, the constitutional goal "to promote the progress of science" is not met merely by creating works; someone has to get them from the author's pen (or laptop) into the public's hands. To the extent that authors retard that process by endeavoring to withhold some rights, or make it more expensive by demanding more pay for rights granted, they can seem like pesky interlopers. Australian writer Miles Franklin (best known for her novel *My Brilliant Career*) captured this annoyance in *Bring the Monkey*, her 1933 parody of the English country house murder mystery. The conversation she imagined among members of Britain's budding motion picture industry anticipates what today's motion picture and television producers may have been fantasizing when the members of the Writers Guild went on strike a few years ago for a decent share of the income from new media "platforms" such as the Internet. Miles Franklin wrote:

> [T]hey [the "film magnates"] were generally agreed that the total elimination of the author would be a tremendous advance....

> "Authors," said this gentleman, "are the bummest lot of cranks I have ever been up against. Why the heck they aren't content to beat it once they get a price for their stuff, gets my goat." ...

> There was ready agreement that authors were a wanton tax on any industry, whether publishing, drama or pictures .....

> "I understand your point of view," [the film producer] said suavely. "That is why I want you to see my film – one reason." "It has been assembled by experts in the industry, not written by some wayward outsider." ...

> [And, indeed, in the film] [t]here was no suggestion of an author. [Instead, the suave producer] was listed twice, as continuity expert and producer.[20]

---

[19] *See, e.g.*, R. Anthony Reese, *A Map of the Frontiers of Copyright*, 85 TEX. L. REV. 1979, 1982–84 (2007); Jessica Litman, *Readers' Copyright*, 58 J. COPYRIGHT SOC'Y 325, 339 (2011); Julie E. Cohen, *Copyright as Property in the Post-Industrial Economy: A Research Agenda*, 2011 WIS. L. REV. 141, 143 ("[T]he purpose of copyright is to enable the provision of capital and organization so that creative work may be exploited."); Malla Pollack, *What Is Congress Supposed to Promote? Defining "Progress" in Article I, Section 8, Clause 8 of the United States Constitution, or Introducing the Progress Clause*, 80 NEB. L. REV. 754, 773, 809 (2001) (equating "progress" in the constitutional sense with the dissemination of ideas). *But see* Wendy J. Gordon, *The Core of Copyright: Authors, Not Publishers*, 52 HOUSTON L. REV. 613 (2014) (Congress does not have power to enact copyright laws for the benefit of disseminators if they do not also benefit authors).

[20] MILES FRANKLIN, BRING THE MONKEY 38–40, 74 (1933).

A copyright law for "continuity experts and producers" (also known as reality television coordinators) or, as the French might more pithily put it, *"le droit d'auteur
sans auteur"* – now *there* is a vision to spur illegal downloading and streaming as
civil disobedience: let's strike a blow for authors by stealing from the corporations
that fleece them.

2.2. WHAT IF AUTHORS RETAINED THEIR COPYRIGHTS?

What difference would it make were authors to retain their copyrights? If it is easy
to discredit copyright on the ground that authors have always served as a shill for
large, unlovable corporations,[21] would copyright's detractors rally to the cause of
exclusive rights to control the exploitation of works of authorship were authors the
true beneficiaries?[22] While authors' divestiture may enable copyright antagonists to
unmask the corporate wolves who strut the moral high ground in the sheep's clothing of romantic authorship,[23] I doubt that restoring romantic authors to their estates
will in fact enhance the popularity of their property rights. After all, proprietary
authorship implies not only economic power, but also control over the work's artistic
expression. That, in turn, may rankle not only the apostles of remix, but also those
who contest the concept of individual creativity in an environment that, as Peter
Jaszi predicted in the Paleolithic early 1990s, is making authorship an enterprise that
is "polyvocal … increasingly collective … and collaborative."[24] With the increasing
Wikipediafication of content, the "wisdom of crowds"[25] overtakes individual expertise in the production of works that everyone can pitch in to create, add to, or modify.

The advent of what I will call the "techno postmodernist participant," challenges
proprietary authorship in two ways. First, if creativity now is so dispersed, then no
one can claim to have originated a work of authorship, so perhaps no one can fairly
own a copyright, either. Second, the communal culture undermines the incentive
rationale for copyright. The Internet may have topped up our supply of Johnsonian
"blockheads."[26] In addition to the poets who burn with inner fire, for whom creation
is allegedly its own reward, and others (such as law professors) for whom other gain-
ful employment permits authorial altruism, we now have Internet exhibitionists (call

---

[21] *See, e.g.*, W. PATRY, MORAL PANICS AND THE COPYRIGHT WARS 76 (2009).

[22] *See, e.g.*, Jessica Litman, *War and Peace*, 53 J. COPYRIGHT SOC'Y 1, 19–20 (2006) (suggesting copyright
would win more hearts and minds were authors truly its beneficiaries).

[23] For exculpation of the "romantic author," see Lionel Bently, *R. v. The Author: From Death Penalty to
Community Service*, 32 COLUM. J.L. & ARTS 1 (2008).

[24] Peter Jaszi, *On the Author Effect: Contemporary Copyright and Collective Creativity*, 10 CARDOZO
ARTS & ENT. L.J. 293, 302 (1992).

[25] JAMES SUROWEICKI, THE WISDOM OF CROWDS (2004).

[26] *See* Tom W. Bell, *The Specter of Copyism v. Blockheaded Authors: How User-Generated Content
Affects Copyright Policy*, 10 VAND. J. ENT. TECH. L. 841, 852–54 (2008) (explaining that technological

them bloggers) and "crowdsources," masses of incremental contributors whose participation, whether occasional or obsessive, belies the Johnsonian calculus. These creators supposedly do not need the carrot of exclusive rights in order to produce works of authorship.

This is, of course, a very short-sighted view, for it describes motivations at a particular point in time. Filthy lucre may not have spurred the first endeavor; many new creators hunger for exposure over income. But to *remain* a creator requires material, as well as moral, sustenance. We may cheer those who generously give their works to the public; we may pause, however when they seek to impose that generosity on other authors' works.

Moreover, just as "copyright industries" may cynically have appropriated the rhetoric of romantic authorship, so may technology interests convert calls for communitarianism to their own benefit. A pre-Internet copyright-exploiting technology furnishes an example: as French legal historian Laurent Pfister has demonstrated, the rhetoric accompanying the rise of the radio in the 1920s and 1930s seems freshly ripped from a current blog. "The moral claims of the community trump the selfish interests of authors who should be obliged to abandon their works so that they may be distributed to the collectivity," urged a representative of the French broadcasting industry.[27] Authors' property rights reflect a spirit of individualism out of step with the times, he declared: "the author has moral obligations to the society which forms the cultural basis for his work. Society has the right to demand that he contribute his works to the cultural capital of the nation."[28] Even then, however, a jaundiced commentator observed "it is pure Pharisee-ism to claim that [the challenges to exclusive rights] had the goal of spreading knowledge of works of authorship; they never had any goal or result other than to allow industry to profit from the labors of authors."[29]

I would like to suggest that today's counterpart – or antidote? – to the romantic author, the techno postmodernist participant, is also a shill for big industry. The

---

advances have decreased the cost of producing and distributing expressive works, resulting in more blockhead authors). *But see* Graeme Austin, *Property on the Line: Life on the Frontier Between Copyright and the Public Domain*, 44 VICTORIA UNIV. WELLINGTON L. REV. 1, 12 (2013) (contrasting the "kid in the United States college dorm room, with ready access to bandwidth, hardware and software" with resource-strapped working adults, and pointing out that not all would-be creators can afford to be "blockheads": "Surplus time and money for amateur creativity probably sit somewhere near the top of the Maslovian hierarchy. Not all of us ever reach those toney heights. To champion amateur user-generated content uncritically, without interrogating these class implications, seems like an irresponsible basis for the formulation of social policy.").

27 Laurent Pfister, *La 'Révolution' de la communication radiophonique, une onde de choc sur le droit d'auteur?, in* LA COMMUNICATION NUMÉRIQUE. UN DROIT, DES DROITS, 183, 195 (B. Teyssié ed. 2012), *citing* F. Lubinski, *Droit d'auteur et radiodiffusion. Proposition de modification de l'article 11 bis de la Convention de Berne*, REV. JUR. INT. RADIODIF. 41 (1934, translation mine).

28 *Id.*

29 *Id., citing* PAUL OLAGNIER, LE DROIT D'AUTEUR, VOL. 1 (Paris: LGDJ), 73 (1934, translation mine).

instrumentalization of the author, or of the anti-author, still serves big business,[30] it is just that the business consumes copyrighted works, rather than producing them.

In the welter of interested challenges to authors' property rights in their creations, we should not forget that copyright advances the concerns of the collectivity: it promotes artistic freedom and free speech by enabling authors to earn (or perhaps more often, eke out) a living from their creativity.[31] As Victor Hugo proclaimed at the International Literary Congress convened in 1878 to urge international protection for authors:

> Literary property is in the public interest. All the old monarchic laws have rejected, and continue to reject literary property. To what end? In order to enslave. The writer who is an owner [of his literary property] is a writer who is free. To take his property away is to deprive him of his independence.[32]

So let us take seriously the proposition that proprietary authorship furthers the commonweal. That rather than suppressing speech, it advances it; by providing professional creators with the prospect of earning a living, it promotes a diversity of expressions that might otherwise remain unvoiced. Poverty is a kind of censorship, too.[33]

Regarding authorship in the digital era, I doubt neither that the web vastly enlarges the numbers of people who commit acts of authorship, nor that digital media promote new kinds of authorship, from wikis to mashups to fanzines to

---

[30] *Cf.* Anupam Chander & Madhavi Sunder, *The Romance of the Public Domain*, 92 CAL. L. REV. 1331, 1335–56 (2004) ("Just as the trope of the romantic author has served to bolster the property rights claims of the powerful, so too does the romance of the public domain. Resourcefully, the romantic public domain trope steps in exactly where the romantic author trope falters. Where genius cannot justify the property claims of corporations because the knowledge pre-exists any ownership claims, the public domain can.").

[31] Tj Stiles, *Among the Digital Luddites*, 38 COLUM. J.L. & ARTS 293 (2015).

[32] Société des Gens de Lettres de France, CONGRÈS LITTÉRAIRE INTERNATIONAL DE PARIS 1878 (Paris, 1879), 106 (translation mine).

[33] *See The impact of intellectual property regimes on the enjoyment of right to science and culture*, submission by the Kernochan Center for Law, Media and the Arts at Columbia University School of Law to the UN Special Rapporteur on the International Covenant on Economic, Social and Cultural Rights on the Impact of Intellectual Property Regimes on the Enjoyment of Rights to Science and Culture at 4 (Sept. 2014): "Censorship can be achieved by outright bans of authorial work. It can also be achieved by denying authors the ability to reach a market for their works through techniques such as putting authors on 'gray lists' that prevent them from finding publishers for their works. An especially effective way to censor creative authorship is to eliminate material rewards, so that few people, other than the economically elite, can undertake to be an author."

See also, Austin, *Property on the Line, supra* note 26, at 15 (citations omitted): The International Covenant on Economic, Social and Cultural Rights

> invites us to take seriously the idea that liberty interests can be furthered by participation in functional markets for creative work.... [T]he right to participate in private markets for creative work helps to carve out for authors "a zone of personal autonomy in which authors ... control their productive output, and lead independent, intellectual lives." These are things any free society needs, and they are nurtured by a system that enables authors to derive at least some of their income from a paying public (assuming they can find one) rather than

kinetic graphics to blogs and beyond. Professional authorship will nonetheless persist, I believe, whether because we still value individual genius (or at least expertise), and/or because not all readers/viewers/listeners will want to be participatory all the time. Recombinant and instant authorship may or may not be passing fancies; professional authors will still be with us. Moreover, they will be joined by a host of newcomers, for example, as bloggers become novelists or write book-length nonfiction, or simply persist in their online endeavors that they succeed in monetizing. At least, professional authors will remain as long as the writing and other creative trades furnish adequate remuneration.[34] As my former colleague, legal philosopher Jeremy Waldron, put it, the author may be dead, but she still responds to economic incentives. The question for the future of copyright, and for the author's place in it, is how to make those incentives meaningful for creators.

2.3. MAKING COPYRIGHT WORK FOR AUTHORS

That question entails two others. First, will authors retain their copyrights in the digital environment? Second, even if authors are copyright owners, will they be able to avail themselves of business models that succeed in reaping meaningful remuneration despite widescale unauthorized and unpaid use of their works?

2.3.1. *Authors and Publishers*

Some of the same factors that today cause copyright to be derided may also come to the aid of individual authors. The technology that brings works directly to users'

depending entirely on political or other forms of patronage. In other words, if the public domain were *all* we had, if property in creative outputs were dispatched over the line, we risk creating a new kind of thralldom.

[34] Writers themselves query whether professional authors will survive if, notwithstanding viral readerships, no one pays them for their work. *See, e.g.,* ROB LEVINE, FREE RIDE: HOW DIGITAL PARASITES ARE DESTROYING THE CULTURE BUSINESS, AND HOW THE CULTURE BUSINESS CAN FIGHT BACK 252–53 (2011) (arguing that the internet diminishes creators' potential to profit from their work because illegal activities and free content undermine the legitimate market); Barbara Garson, *If Only Pageviews Were Dollars,* PUBLISHERS WEEKLY, Sept. 12, 2014, *available at* http://publishersweekly .com/pw/by-topic/columns-and-blogs/soapbox/article/63987-content-provider-goes-bacterial-but-who-will-pay-her.html ("In the online era, who will send first-time authors those small checks that prove to their parents (and themselves) that they're professionals? . . . [H]ow will we pay writers in a world awash in free words?"); Authors' Licensing and Collecting Society, WHAT ARE WORDS WORTH?: COUNTING THE COST OF A WRITING CAREER IN THE 21ST CENTURY: A SURVEY OF 25,000 WRITERS 9 (2007), *available at* www.alcs.co.uk/Documents/Downloads/whatarewordsworth.aspx (surveying authors in Europe and finding that less than 15% of authors have received compensation for online uses of their work); ROBERT McCRUM, FROM BESTSELLER TO BUST: IS THIS THE END OF AN AUTHOR'S LIFE?, Mar. 2, 2014, *available at* www.theguardian.com/books/2014/mar/02/bestseller-novel-to-bust-author-life (citing the rise of free content on the Internet as a challenge for authors today and finding that writing is increasingly unprofitable for unknown authors).

computers and personal portable devices no longer requires traditional publishing's infrastructure of intermediaries. Techno postmodernism notwithstanding, maybe every reader is not truly an author, but every author can be a publisher. At least, every computer-equipped author can make her work directly available to her audience via the Internet. Availing oneself of the means of distribution is one thing, but making a *living* from the works one distributes is another,[35] particularly when the media that empower authors also empower users to acquire and disseminate works for free. Moreover, not every author or performer will want to self-publish. Many will prefer the assistance of distribution intermediaries (e.g., book publishers and record producers) to attend not only to the production and distribution, which authors and performers might now do themselves, but also to provide the credibility, publicity, and most importantly, the advances, that come from signing a publishing contract.

But must that signing also condemn the author to the Roz Chast-ian bargain evoked earlier? While, with the exception of the termination right, Congress has not sought to redress the imbalance of power between publishers and most authors, other countries' legislatures, particularly in the EU, have.[36] The French law on authors' contracts, including recent amendments to the regime of publishing contracts, warrants wistful contemplation as an example of how a copyright law might endeavor to ensure that authors either retain their copyrights or receive fair compensation for their alienation.

The French Code of Intellectual Property safeguards authors against leonine transfers in a variety of ways. In addition to mandating that publishing contracts, performance rights contracts, and audiovisual production contracts be in writing,[37] the law further requires that each right granted be distinctly specified in the contract, and that the scope of the grant be defined with respect to its purpose, its geographic

---

[35] *See, e.g.*, Brian Stelter, *For Web TV, a Handful of Hits but No Formula for Success*, N.Y. Times, Aug. 31, 2008, *available at* www.nytimes.com/2008/09/01/business/media/01webisodes.html?pagewanted=all (Striking Hollywood writers created independent "webisodes." "The strategy seemed simple: make money by going straight to the Internet. Months later, they are realizing that producing Web content may be easy but profiting from it is hard."); Trent Hamm, *The Truth About Making Money Online*, The Christian Science Monitor, Oct. 29, 2013, *available at* www.csmonitor.com/Business/The-Simple-Dollar/2013/1029/The-truth-about-making-money-online (describing how "the only way to make money consistently online is to produce a lot of content on a very consistent basis" and that proceeds are often realized in the long-term, not immediately after publication); Jim Edwards, *Yes, You Can Make Six Figures as a YouTube Star … And Still End Up Poor*, Business Insider, Feb. 10, 2014, *available at* www.businessinsider.com/how-much-money-youtube-stars-actually-make-2014-2 (finding that even YouTube content providers that generate high gross revenue see less than 50% of that revenue, resulting in unsustainable costs for building a business).

[36] *See supra* note 15. In addition, collective management associations representing authors and collectively licensing their rights are far more prevalent outside the U.S.

[37] France, Code of Intellectual Property, art. L131-2. U.S. Copyright law requires that the grant of any exclusive right must be in writing and signed by the grantor, 17 U.S.C. § 204(a).

extent, and its duration.[38] As a general rule, authors are to receive royalties, rather than a lump sum payment.[39] Amendments to the statutory provisions on publishing contracts, introduced at the end of 2014, further detail authors' rights in print and digital editions of literary works. These modifications seek to ensure that publishers will in fact exercise the rights that authors grant them, and will fairly account to authors for the fruits of those exploitations. Failure to publish the work within a certain time, or to pursue the exploitation of the rights in a consistent manner (exploitation permanente et suivie), or to reissue a book that has gone out of print, will result in reversion of print or electronic rights to the author.[40] The new provisions require the grant to distinguish print from digital editions, and impose additional author protections with respect to the latter. Notably, the contract must guarantee authors just and fair remuneration for all the revenues deriving from the commercialization and dissemination of digital editions.[41] In addition, contracts granting electronic rights must include a clause providing for periodic review of the economic conditions of the grant;[42] an accord between associations of authors and of publishers will determine the frequency of the reviews and will provide guidelines for dispute resolution.[43] The law also promotes the development of digital editions because a grantee who fails to disseminate a digital edition within the time set out in an accord between associations of authors and of publishers will lose those rights back to the author.[44] Moreover, as to contracts concluded before the law's effective date, the

---

[38] *Id.* art. L131-3 ("La transmission des droits de l'auteur est subordonnée à la condition que chacun des droits cédés fasse l'objet d'une mention distincte dans l'acte de cession et que le domaine d'exploitation des droits cédés soit délimité quant à son étendue et à sa destination, quant au lieu et quant à la durée"). The author may grant rights for future modes of exploitation unknown at the time of the contract, but such a grant must be explicit, and must provide for a share in the profits of the new form of exploitation. *Id.* art. L131-6 ("La clause d'une cession qui tend à conférer le droit d'exploiter l'œuvre sous une forme non prévisible ou non prévue à la date du contrat doit être expresse et stipuler une participation corrélative aux profits d'exploitation.").

[39] *Id.* art. L131-4 ("La cession par l'auteur de ses droits sur son œuvre peut être totale ou partielle. Elle doit comporter au profit de l'auteur la participation proportionnelle aux recettes provenant de la vente ou de l'exploitation.").

[40] *Id.* art. 132-17-1 – 5 (see www.legifrance.gouv.fr/affichCode.do;jsessionid=2D013356C523C269C9691 2FA8B0AE456.tpdjoo4v_3?idSectionTA=LEGISCTA000029759371&cidTexte=LEGITEXT000000060 69414&dateTexte=20150208).

[41] *Id.* art. 132-17-6 ("Le contrat d'édition garantit à l'auteur une rémunération juste et équitable sur l'ensemble des recettes provenant de la commercialisation et de la diffusion d'un livre édité sous une forme numérique.").

[42] *Id.* art. L.132-17-7 ("Le contrat d'édition comporte une clause de réexamen des conditions économiques de la cession des droits d'exploitation du livre sous une forme numérique.").

[43] *Id.* art. 132-17-8(8) ("L'accord mentionné au I fixe les modalités d'application des dispositions: 8° De l'article L. 132-17-7 relatives au réexamen des conditions économiques de la cession des droits d'exploitation d'un livre sous forme numérique, notamment la périodicité de ce réexamen, son objet et son régime ainsi que les modalités de règlement des différends.").

[44] *Id.* art. L. 132-17-5 ("Lorsque l'éditeur n'a pas procédé à cette réalisation [du livre sous une forme numérique], la cession des droits d'exploitation sous une forme numérique est résiliée de plein droit.").

law empowers authors two years thereafter to demand that the publisher produce a digital edition; the publisher's failure to do so within three months following proper notification results in reversion of the digital rights to the author.[45]

2.3.2. *Authors as Publishers*

Whether or not measures like France's will inspire the U.S. Congress, were it to embark on "the next great copyright act,"[46] to add author-protections to the rules on transfers of copyright, some authors will in any event choose to forego intermediary publishers (and others will fail to attract them). Having kept their copyrights, what are their prospects for exploiting them? To an increasing extent, every author can employ electronic copyright management, and/or copyright management collectives to set the financial and other terms and conditions for access to and copying of her work. Or, more rudimentarily, she can make the work available without technological restraints, and appeal to user generosity,[47] though, as Radiohead and Stephen King discovered, passing the hat may prove a precarious strategy.[48]

---

[45] Ordonnance n° 2014-1348 of Nov. 2, 2014, transitional provisions, art. 9. Arts. 11 and 12 provide for application of other author protections to contracts concluded before the law's effective date.

[46] *See* Maria A. Pallante, *The Next Great Copyright Act (26th Horace S. Manges Lecture)*, 36 COLUM. J.L. & ARTS 315 (2013).

[47] Crowdfunding sites, such as Kickstarter and similar websites (Go Fund Me, Indiegogo) can assist authors to generate the funding necessary to create their works in the first place, but are not a useful source of remuneration. On crowdfunding sites, creators are expected to estimate the amount they need to complete a specific project, and induce people to pledge to that project in exchange for rewards (e.g., prints of an art project or free downloads of a song). *See, e.g.,* Kickstarter, *Creator Questions, available at* www.kickstarter.com/help/faq/creator%2oquestions (last visited Feb. 4, 2015). On Kickstarter at least, the creator receives money only if the full amount asked for is funded. If pledges fall short, no money changes hands. For success rates, see Kickstarter, Stats, *available at* www .kickstarter.com/help/stats (last visited Feb. 4, 2015). If pledges exceed the cost of creation, then the creator may keep the difference. However, there are many costs additional to the cost of creation, for example fees to the hosting website or rewards to backers. Amanda Palmer made more than ten times what she needed during a Kickstarter campaign, but once all costs of the project, hosting, and rewards were paid, she cleared only about $100,000 (an 8% profit). Salvador Briggman, *How to Make Money on Kickstarter*, CROWDCRUX, *available at* www.crowdcrux.com/make-money-kickstarter/ (last visited Oct. 30, 2014). *Cf.* Cord Jefferson, *Amanda Palmer's Million-Dollar Music Project and Kickstarter's Accountability Problem*, GAWKER, Sept. 19, 2012, *available at* http://gawker.com/5944050/amanda-palmers-million-dollar-music-project-and-kickstarters-accountability-problem (questioning whether Amanda Palmer's reporting of an 8% profit was honest and pointing out that Kickstarter does not guarantee that the project actually gets completed or that the money is used to fund it).

[48] *See, e.g.,* Joshua Gans, *Pay-What-You-Want Experiments, From Stephen King to Kickstarter*, HARVARD BUSINESS REVIEW, May 3, 2011, *available at* https://hbr.org/2011/05/pay-what-you-want-experiments (describing Stephen King's abandoned experiment with pay-what-you-want); Eric Garland, *The "In Rainbows" Experiment: Did It Work?*, NPR, Nov. 16, 2009, *available at* www.npr.org/blogs/monitor mix/2009/11/the_in_rainbows_experiment_did.html (finding that although Radiohead, as a part of its pay-what-you-want scheme, "offered a legal free and low-cost option to obtain the album from its Web

Nonetheless, some variations on pass-the-hat may succeed. For example, The Humble Bundle service offers bundles of digital content, primarily video games and comic books. It makes each bundle available online for a limited amount of time. The user selects the price he is willing to pay (there is no suggested price, but the minimum is $1) and the division of his payment among the content creators, and website-designated charities. The pricing scheme has generated some revenue,[49] but many users continue to pirate works.[50]

Pay-what-you-want, moreover, may disadvantage lesser-known creators, since the desire to pay may decrease with the celebrity of the beneficiary.[51] As one commentator put it, pay-what-you-want can work where there is "a fair minded customer, strong relationship with customer, a product that can be sold credibly at a wide

site, piracy was up … at 10 times the rate of new releases from other top artists"). However some commentators believe Radiohead's experiment was in fact a success, in part because of the interest generated by the novel payment option. *See* Daniel Kreps, *Radiohead Publishers Reveal "In Rainbows" Numbers*, ROLLING STONE, Oct. 15, 2008, *available at* www.rollingstone.com/music/news/radiohead-publishers-reveal-in-rainbows-numbers-20081015 (reporting that although "more people downloaded the album for free than paid for it … [$3 million in sales] is a hugely-successful number considering the album was both given away for free and that it was actually downloaded more times via Bit Torrent than free and legally through Radiohead's own site.").

[49] In 2013, a Humble Bundle co-founder stated that the service had grossed over $50 Million. Interview by John Walker with John Graham, Co-Founder, Humble Bundle, Aug. 23, 2013, *available at* www.rock papershotgun.com/2013/08/23/interview-humble-bundle-on-humble-bundles/. A currently-available bundle on Humble Bundle has received an average of over $6 per download. *Statistics*, HUMBLE BUNDLE, *available at* www.humblebundle.com/ (last visited Feb. 4, 2015).

[50] The first bundle available online had a 75% sales rate, but nonetheless grossed $1.3 Million in revenue. Sam Machkovech, *Beyond Radiohead: Video Games One-Up the Pay-What-You-Want Model*, THE ATLANTIC, Dec. 14, 2010, *available at* www.theatlantic.com/entertainment/archive/2010/12/beyond-radiohead-video-games-one-up-the-pay-what-you-want-model/67921/.
Comedians have experimented with pay-what-you-want as well. In 2011, Louis C.K. offered videos of a live performance online and grossed over $1 million in the first two weeks. Press Release, A Statement from Louis C.K., Dec. 13, 2011, *available at* https://buy.louisck.net/news/a-statement-from-louis-c-k. He stated online that, "If anybody stole it, it wasn't many of you. Pretty much everybody bought it." He also stated that his profits (taking into account only short-term profits) were less than he would have made by allowing a large company to film and distribute the performance, but that they would have charged the consumer about $20 for an encrypted and restricted-use copy. Press Release, Another Statement from Louis C.K., Dec. 21, 2011, *available at* https://buy.louisck.net/news/another-statement-from-louis-c-k.

[51] For comedians specifically, it seems that less high-profile performers than Louis C.K. are using pay-what-you-want with mixed success. Comedian Steve Hofstetter released an album under a pay-what-you-want model (with a minimum of 1 cent) even earlier than Louis C.K. Although at the time, he was relatively unknown, he was coming off a successful first album. In the early stages of the offering, he averaged $6 per album, which is more than triple the royalty he would receive if it were distributed by a label. Daniel Langendorf, *Comedian Hofstetter Experiments with Pay-What-You-Want–And Provides Numbers*, LAST100, Dec. 14, 2007, *available at* www.last100.com/2007/12/14/comedian-hofstetter-experiments-with-pay-what-you-want-and-provides-numbers/.

range of prices, or a product with low marginal cost."[52] Even then, generosity does not always abound, neither in the proportion of users who pay, nor in the amount expended by those who do pay. For example, the website Tech Dirt, a blog and news source on technology news, provided a pay-what-you-scheme in its "Insider Shop." Customers could choose several options ($0, $5, $10, $20, or $50), although the $5 default payment somewhat masked the zero option. The site optimistically advertised the experiment as a success, although 51% of downloaders paid nothing and the average price paid was $2.41.[53]

Another variation on pay-what-you-want is Flattr, an online service to which internet consumers pay a fixed monthly fee. As Flattr's users peruse websites and see creations they like, they click the "Flattr" button (like the Facebook "like" button). Flattr tallies up all of the users' clicks in a month and divides their monthly subscription fees among the owners of the creations they clicked.[54] The service is a far cry from systematic remuneration for authors; indeed Flattr seems to characterize the payments more as donations than as license fees.[55]

"Freemium," a hybrid free-access/paid-access model, which allows access to the bottom tier of content for free, but charges per unit or by subscription for more or better content, or for content without advertising, offers another approach for authors' self-financing on the Internet.[56] The model has perhaps encountered its greatest

---

[52] Isamer Bilog, *Are "Pay What You Want" Models the Road to Success?*, SPINNAKR BLOG, May 2013, *available at* http://spinnakr.com/blog/ideas/2013/05/pay-what-you-want-pricing-model/ (describing various examples of successful pay-what-you-want models).

[53] By contrast, Cards against Humanity (an adult card game similar to Apples to Apples) offered an expansion pack under a pay-what-you-want model. It used social pressure to discourage people from the zero price, by shaming customers who attempted to pay nothing at all. Although almost 20% of customers still paid nothing, the average price paid was $3.89 (greater than the $3 per unit cost of manufacturing and shipping). *Holiday Stats*, CARDS AGAINST HUMANITY, *available at* http://cardsagainsthumanity.com/holidaystats (last visited Jan. 30, 2015).

[54] *How Flattr Works*, FLATTR, *available at* https://flattr.com/howflattrworks (last visited Nov. 2, 2014).

[55] *See, e.g.*, Mike Butcher, *Flattr Now Monetizes the Like Economy by Connecting Social Accounts With Payments*, TECH CRUNCH, Mar. 18, 2013, *available at* http://techcrunch.com/2013/03/18/flattr-now-monetizes-the-like-economy-by-connecting-social-accounts-with-payments/ (noting that "Flattr users can now give and receive micro-donations directly on other web services they already use … [including] Twitter, Instagram, Soundcloud, Github, Flickr, Vimeo, 500px and App.net" but "it's unlikely to make anyone rich just yet because it will require many more people to open Flattr accounts"); L.M., *Go on, Flattr Yourself*, THE ECONOMIST, Jan. 21, 2011, *available at* www.economist.com/blogs/babbage/2011/01/another_approach_micropayments (noting that "[f]or Flattr to have an impact on the way online content is consumed and produced, however, it would need to become massive").

[56] Currently, the principal successful exploiters of "freemium" models appear to be web services, rather than individual creators. Jason Cohen, *Reframing the Problems With "Freemium" By Charging the Marketing Department*, VENTUREBEAT, Apr. 19, 2013, *available at* http://venturebeat.com/2013/04/19/reframing-the-problems-with-freemium-by-charging-the-marketing-department/ (arguing that freemium is essentially a marketing strategy, and, given its expense, a difficult one to surmount without substantial resources and know-how); Sarah E. Needleman & Angus Loten, *Why*

success with digital phone applications.[57] The content provider hopes to attract a large number of free users and convert a percentage of them to premium users.[58] The freemium model typically begins as a loss-leader, until enough users become premium users to turn a profit.[59] Its success thus depends on attracting and retaining customers and efficiently developing and marketing the premium content.

Following its unhappy essay with pass-the-hat, Nine Inch Nails experimented with the freemium model for its album release of Ghosts I-IV. In conjunction with the release, the band proposed a number of different packages to consumers, including offering the first nine tracks of the album for free on their website and through BitTorrent. Premium packages ranged from $5 for a full album download to a $300 "ultra deluxe" package including CDs, vinyl LPs, and signed prints.[60] Within the first week, lead singer Trent Reznor made over $1.6 million on the release.[61]

Freemium Fails, WALL ST. J., Aug. 22, 2013, *available at* http://online.wsj.com/news/articles/SB10000872 396390443713704577603782317318996?mg=ren064-wsj&url=http%3A%2F%2Fonline.wsj.com%2Farticle %2FSB10000872396390443713704577603782317318996.html (concluding that freemium is a "costly trap" which can destroy businesses that lack the sophistication to implement it properly and that it is rarely executed well by start-ups in part because "[t]he freemium approach doesn't make sense for any business that can't eventually reach millions of users"). One example is Spotify Premium. With a free Spotify account, a user can stream unlimited music. However, every 10 minutes or so, there is a minute of advertising. A subscription to Spotify Premium for $9.99 per month removes advertising interruptions. It also allows users to download songs to listen to offline on their computers or phones. *See Premium*, SPOTIFY, *available at* www.spotify.com/us/?_ga=1.146397108.1257926096.1414689432#premium (last visited Oct. 30, 2014). Additional examples are Pandora, Angry Birds, and Xobni (a smart address-book service that compiles contact and social information from LinkedIn, Facebook, and Twitter), which remove advertising from the interface once the user pays for a premium account. *See* Michael Learmonth, *Why the "Freemium" Model is Bad for Advertisers*, ADVERTISINGAGE, Apr. 23, 2013, *available at* http://adage .com/article/digital/freemium-model-bad-advertisers/241042/.

[57] For recent statistics on how the monetization of mobile apps through the freemium model is working, see John Koetsier, *Mobile App Monetization: Freemium is King, But In-App Ads Are Growing Fast*, VENTURE BEAT, Mar. 27, 2014, *available at* http://venturebeat.com/2014/03/27/ mobile-app-monetization-freemium-is-king-but-in-app-ads-are-growing-fast/.

[58] It has been suggested that the most profitable model is continually to attract a large number of users, and focus on converting a modest percentage (research suggests successful companies range from 2% to 5%); indeed, even free users are valuable if they refer new users to the content. Vineet Kumar, *Making "Freemium" Work*, HARVARD BUSINESS REVIEW, May 2014, at 27.

[59] Glenn Peoples, *Business Matters: Spotify UK Shows that the Freemium Model is Not "Unsustainable*," BILLBOARD BIZ, Oct. 9, 2012, *available at* www.billboard.com/biz/articles/news/1083467/ business-matters-spotify-uk-shows-that-the-freemium-model-is-not (analyzing Spotify UK's profits over multi-year period and finding loss in early years does not indicate overall unprofitability of the freemium business model).

[60] Daniel Kreps, *Nine Inch Nails Surprise Fans by Web-Releasing New "Ghosts" Album*, ROLLING STONE, Mar. 3, 2008, *available at* www.rollingstone.com/music/news/nine-inch-nails-surprise-fans-by-web-releasing-new-ghosts-album-20080303.

[61] *See* Daniel Kreps, *Nine Inch Nails' "Ghosts I-IV" Makes Trent Reznor a Millionaire*, ROLLING STONE, Mar. 13, 2008, *available at* www.rollingstone.com/music/news/nine-inch-nails-ghosts-i-iv-makes-trent-reznor-an-instant-millionaire-20080313. The 2500 "ultra deluxe" packages available sold out within 30 hours of the release. *Id.*

Like pay-what-you-want, however, this approach may primarily benefit creators, and especially performers, who already enjoy a substantial fan base. But the scheme can apply more broadly, at least to recording artists. For example, Bandcamp, a music streaming and download website, allows artists to develop their own freemium pricing schemes. Artists upload their music and choose whether to price it free, pay-what-you-want, or for a fixed price.[62]

Freemium models, by placing some content behind paywalls, rely to a greater or lesser extent on technological protection measures to secure the paywall.[63] There has been much debate over whether technological protection measures (also referred to as DRM – digital rights management) are worth the candle, given their unpopularity and the relative ease with which consumers can elude them.[64] Some have contended that DRM decreases music sales, especially for less popular albums because it prevents sharing of the album when uninhibited redistribution would provide more exposure (and, supposedly, in the long run, sales) for the performing artists.[65] In fact, some technological measures are more obnoxious than others. Many people

---

[62] Bandcamp claims to have made $82 Million for musicians so far. *Artists*, BANDCAMP, *available at* http://bandcamp.com/artists (last visited Sept. 30, 2014).

[63] *See generally* Ashkan Soltani, *Protecting Your Privacy Could Make You the Bad Guy*, WIRED, July 23, 2013, *available at* www.wired.com/2013/07/the-catch-22-of-internet-commerce-and-privacy-could-mean-youre-the-bad-guy/ (describing various technological measures used to enforce paywalls including tracking cookies and browser fingerprinting). Some companies offer software to website and app developers that allows content providers to protect and monetize freemium content. *See, e.g., INSIDE Secure Protects Premium Content for Snap, Sky Deutschland's Online Media Application*, MARKETWATCH, June 4, 2014, *available at* www.marketwatch.com/story/inside-secure-protects-premium-content-for-snap-sky-deutschlands-online-media-application-2014-06-04 (reporting on software used to protect online and mobile premium video content); *Solutions*, OOYALA, *available at* www.ooyala.com/solutions (last visited Nov. 2, 2014) (offering software "protect premium content from unauthorized access").

[64] Even though the eluding, or aiding the eluding by distributing descramblers, is illegal, see 17 U.S.C. § 1201(a)(b). For recent entrants in the ongoing debate over the desirability and effectiveness of DRM, see, e.g., Andrew V. Moshirnia, *Giant Pink Scorpions: Fighting Piracy with Novel Digital Rights Management Technology*, 23 DEPAUL J. ART TECH. & INTELL. PROP. L. 1, 6–7 (2012) (describing various methods of DRM and noting that it has been largely ineffectual and that "[a] technologically-impervious DRM is unlikely to emerge"); (Jerry) Jie Hua, *Toward A More Balanced Model: The Revision of Anti-Circumvention Rules*, 60 J. COPYRIGHT SOC'Y U.S.A., 327, 328–30 (2013) (describing DRM as a preventative measure against piracy and noting criticism of the DMCA's overprotection of DRM technologies).

[65] Andrew Flanagan, *DRM Was a Bad Move: Sales Found to Increase 10% After Dropping the Chains (Study)*, BILLBOARD, Dec. 2, 2013, *available at* www.billboard.com/biz/articles/news/digital-and-mobile/5812288/drm-was-a-bad-move-sales-found-to-increase-10-after (reporting study finding that absence of DRM increased sales by 30% for albums that sold less than 25,000 copies and by 24% for albums that sold less than 100,000 copies; the study found no discernable increase in sales for the most successful albums, reasoning that those albums are already known and do not need sharing to increase awareness).

deplore copy controls on downloads.[66] For example, in 2009, Apple and Steve Jobs, whose iPod had been the most noteworthy and successful utilizer of download control technology, began offering DRM-free music in the iTunes Store.[67] DRM in the e-books market has also provoked opposition on the grounds that the protection measures prevent sharing and resale of e-books and reduce compatibility between devices.[68] By contrast, most people seem not to notice, much less denounce, the technology that controls streaming media[69] for example, the Netflix subscription that lets you watch unlimited quantities of movies but does not let you create retention copies[70] or the YouTube video clips that you can watch in more or less real time, but not download to keep.[71] And, to return to freemium, restricting access to the upper tier of content, or requiring payment after a certain number of free views or downloads (an increasing practice in the beleaguered journalism business[72]) seems to be gaining

---

[66] There is even a "Day Against DRM." *See* Katherine Noyes, *Four Ways to Celebrate "Day Against DRM" Today*, PC WORLD, May 4, 2012, *available at* www.pcworld.com/article/255066/four_ways_to_ celebrate_day_against_drm_today.html.

[67] Press Release, Apple, Changes Coming to the iTunes Store, Jan. 6, 2009, *available at* www.apple .com/pr/library/2009/01/06Changes-Coming-to-the-iTunes-Store.html. Other content, including e-Books, movies, and apps remain protected by DRM. Concerning Apple's motivations for abandoning DRM, see Jessica Litman, *Antibiotic Resistance*, *available at* www.umich.edu/~jdlitman/papers/ AntibioticResistance.pdf (discussing the initial role of DRM in contributing to Apple's dominance of market for MP3 players and the disadvantages of DRM once Apple had eclipsed its rivals).

[68] At least one e-book publisher has gone DRM-free, but the major publishers retain DRM protection. *See* Suw Charman-Anderson, *Macmillan's Tor Abandons DRM, Other Publishers Must Follow*, FORBES MAGAZINE, Apr. 25, 2012, *available at* www.forbes.com/sites/suwcharmananderson/2012/04/25/ macmillans-tor-abandons-drm-other-publishers-must-follow/.

[69] Note that while end users remain largely ambivalent, some internet entities are opposed to DRM in the streaming context. *See* Jeremy Kirk, *Mozilla Hates It, But Streaming Video DRM is Coming to Firefox*, PC WORLD, May 15, 2014, *available at* www.pcworld.com/article/2155440/firefox-will-get-drm-copy-protection-despite-mozillas-concerns.html (noting that Mozilla opposes DRM technologies and quoting CTO saying, "we would much prefer a world and a Web without DRM").

[70] *See* Anthony Park & Mark Watson, *HTML5 Video at Netflix*, NETFLIX TECHBLOG, Apr. 15, 2013, *available at* http://techblog.netflix.com/2013/04/html5-video-at-netflix.html (noting that DRM is a requirement for any premium subscription video service).

[71] While YouTube does not allow downloading, *see Download YouTube Videos*, GOOGLE SUPPORT, *available at* https://support.google.com/youtube/answer/56100?hl=en (last visited Nov. 1, 2014), it is possible to download free software that (illegally) circumvents copy controls and lets users to convert YouTube videos into mp4 files. *See, e.g.*, Jim Martin, *How to Download YouTube Videos – Save to Your PC, Laptop, iPhone, iPad or Android Device*, PC ADVISOR, Mar. 17, 2014, *available at* www .pcadvisor.co.uk/how-to/photo-video/3492830/how-download-youtube-videos/.

[72] *See* Rachel Bartlett, *News Corp Outlines "Freemium" Subscription Model for Australian*, JOURNALISM, June 7, 2011, *available at* www.journalism.co.uk/news/news-corp-outlines-freemium-subscription-model-for-australian/s2/a544630/ (reporting that News Corp was so "encouraged by the 'success' of paywalls at fellow News Corp titles the Times and Sunday Times" that on a third paper, it "will offer access to some content free … while others will require payment to view"); *New York Times*, FREEMIUM.ORG, *available at* www.freemium.org/new-york-times/ (last visited Nov. 2, 2014) (reporting statistics on implementation of the *New York Times*'s freemium model and

general public acceptance, despite its reliance on technological protection measures to separate the free and premium tiers.[73]

As a practical matter, the future of copyright for professional authors is likely to depend on the development of consumer-friendly payment and protection mechanisms. Free distribution can, of course, enhance the author's fame, but if the author cannot capitalize on her fame by exploiting her copyrights, then she will not have made much progress. (A starving artist's garret is still a garret, even if the address is well-known.) I am not sanguine about the non-copyright alternatives, most of which involve giving the copyrighted work away as a loss leader to get consumers to spend money on something else whose supply the author can control. This is sometimes called the "Grateful Dead model": I sell my song for a song, but make you pay real money for the t-shirts that allow you to express your affection for my band.[74] Some performing artists today may make money on everything from clothing lines and perfume to licensing their songs to TV shows and movies to uploading content to YouTube.[75] But that kind of licensing operation probably requires a distribution intermediary, and the increasingly popular "360 deal" in contemporary recording contracts, granting to the label the rights including merchandizing, film, and TV or guaranteeing the label a cut of profits from those activities,[76] significantly limits performers' revenues on rights peripheral to the recorded performance.

Furthermore, the success of these models assumes, counterfactually, that the demand for bundled goods or services is infinitely expandable, and even more counterfactually, that it is applicable to all kinds of works of authorship. For example, the public may be willing to purchase some successful performers' "allegiance

concluding that it "proved that freemium model can work in news industry"); Jasper Jackson, *BILD CEO on Freemium Paywalls, Protecting Ads and Being the Burger*, THE MEDIA BRIEFING, Mar. 24, 2014, *available at* www.themediabriefing.com/article/donata-hopfen-bild-axel-springer-paywalls-charging (describing Germany's highest circulation newspaper's new freemium model "which leaves some content outside the paywall on its mobile sites, but charges for content with more 'added value' and for access via apps").

73 *See* Vineet Kumar, *Making "Freemium" Work*, HARVARD BUSINESS REVIEW, May 2014, at 27 ("Over the past decade 'freemium' – a combination of 'free' and 'premium' – has become the dominant business model among internet start-ups and smartphone app developers").

74 For speculation about how to make money notwithstanding widespread unpaid digital uses, see, e.g., CORY DOCTOROW, INFORMATION DOESN'T WANT TO BE FREE: LAWS FOR THE DIGITAL AGE 53–63 ("How Do I Get People to Pay Me?") (2014).

75 Steve Knopper, *Nine Ways Musicians Actually Make Money Today*, ROLLING STONE, Aug. 28, 2012, *available at* www.rollingstone.com/music/lists/9-ways-musicians-actually-make-money-today-20120828. *See also* Peter Dicola, *Money from Music: Survey Evidence on Musicians' Revenue and Lessons about Copyright Incentives*, 55 ARIZ. L. REV. 301 (2013) (reporting results of survey regarding sources of revenue streams across 5,000 musicians).

76 Daniel J. Gervais, Kent M. Marcus, & Lauren E. Kilgore, *The Rise of 360 Deals in the Music Industry*, 3 LANDSLIDE 40, 41 (2011). An additional problem is that even though the labels hold these rights, they have "little legal obligation to help the artists develop those revenue streams." *Id.* at 43.

goods," but who ever heard of the non-performing artist *songwriter* whose works the singer performs, much less would be interested in paying to blazon her name across his chest? Or "bundling" *services* with intellectual content may work well for software, for which "helplines" can be an essential adjunct, but I see fewer prospects for a *service après vente* for a photograph.

More fundamentally, copyright is not just about money; it is also about artistic integrity. As Pulitzer Prize-winning playwright Doug Wright recently put it:

> [C]opyright guarantees us only one thing, one ephemeral, fleeting, but indispensable thing: our singularity as artists.

> Copyright acknowledges the innate worth of an individual author's voice; that a well-turned phrase by Philip Roth or an acerbic line of dialogue by Edward Albee, or the haunting melody of 'Sunrise, Sunset' by Jerry Bock is as special, as distinctive, as a thumb print or a strand of DNA.

> … Because of copyright, I get to be the CEO of my own imagination. When I create a work, copyright acknowledges that it belongs to me as fully as a newborn belongs to its mother. And just like a parent, I am granted responsibility for its future.[77]

Thus, copyright is also about maintaining control – both economic and artistic – over the fate of the work. Artistic control concerns authors' interests in receiving authorship credit and in maintaining the integrity of their works ("moral rights"), as well as their determination of when and how to release their works to the public. Artists who self-distribute on the Internet may exercise the latter form of control, for example, by first making their works available to a dedicated fan base on a site such as Bandcamp, before authorizing its broader dissemination via streaming platforms such as YouTube. Whether or not such strategies yield creators more money, the power to decide whether, when, and how to bring one's work to the public is both one that copyright law has long secured[78] and one of considerable importance to creators, including in the online environment.[79]

As for "moral rights," some developments suggest that the Web may not create an ineluctably hostile environment for these interests. For example, attribution and integrity clauses have long characterized licenses in the open source software

---

[77] Doug Wright, *Playwrights and Copyright*, 38 COLUM. J.L. & ARTS 301, 304 (2015).

[78] *See, e.g.*, Harper & Row v. Nation Enters., 471 U.S. 539, 554–55 (1985).

[79] *See, e.g.*, Interview with composer-cellist Zoë Keating, "Google Plays Hardball with Indie Musicians," *available at* www.studio360.org/story/google-plays-hardball-with-indie-musicians-zoe-keating/ (Feb. 5, 2015) ("I'm not going to [agree to YouTube's new contract for streaming music] at the expense of that control over releasing my music."); Holly Robinson, *Should You Self Publish? From Traditional to Indie and Back Again: One Hybrid Author Tells All*, HUFFINGTON POST, Aug. 7, 2013, *available at* www .huffingtonpost.com/holly-robinson/should-you-self-publish-f_b_3721206.html ("As an indie author, you have complete control. You decide when your book is ready for public consumption, and you decide what sort of indie publisher to take on as your partner.")

community.[80] Creative Commons (CC) offers a means to self-distribute over the Internet and preserve authors' moral rights of attribution and integrity. The default CC license requires attribution of authorship, and the author may also choose to include an "ND" (no derivatives) icon,[81] which might serve to instruct users not to alter or modify the work.[82] These licenses may even be enforceable.[83]

But CC licenses accompany works distributed online for free. For authors who seek to earn a living from their work online, the absence of a CC payment mechanism may pose an insuperable shortcoming. A CC-licensed work may help introduce an author to an audience, but at some point a professional author needs to be paid. Authors who self-distribute on the Web thus may face the prospect of respect for their names and their works, but without remuneration.[84] In effect if not

---

[80] *See, e.g.,* Nicolas Suzor, *Access, Progress, and Fairness: Rethinking Exclusivity in Copyright,* 15 VAND. J. ENT. TECH. L. 297, 339–40 (2013) (describing common license terms in free software license agreements); Rebecca Schoff Curtin, *Hackers and Humanists: Transactions and the Evolution of Copyright,* 54 IDEA 103, 115–16 (2014) (noting that free software "values a software author's moral rights over the kinds of exclusive rights conveyed by U.S. copyright law" and describing incorporation of rights of integrity and attribution into free software licenses); Greg R. Vetter, *The Collaborative Integrity of Open-Source Software,* 2004 UTAH L. REV. 563, 685 tbl. 2 (comparing the inclusion of rights of integrity and attribution in a few open source licenses and discussing the enforcement of the right of integrity under an open source license); *Various Licenses and Comments About Them,* GNU OPERATING SYSTEM, *available at* www.gnu.org/philosophy/license-list.html (last visited Feb. 9, 2015) (listing and assessing common licenses for open source software).

[81] *About the Licenses,* CREATIVE COMMONS, *available at* http://creativecommons.org/licenses/ (last visited Sept. 30, 2014); *Metrics/License Statistics,* CREATIVE COMMONS WIKI, *available at* https://wiki .creativecommons.org/Metrics/License_statistics#License_property_charts (last visited Feb. 9, 2015) (showing that more than 96% of creative commons licenses contain attribution provision and nearly 25% retain the integrity right).

[82] It is not clear whether the excluded "derivatives" are "derivative works" in the copyright sense, in which case the instruction might not bar all modifications or alterations, but only those which sufficiently transform the work to constitute new works of authorship. To the extent that modifications may compromise a work's integrity without necessarily yielding a new work, the ND icon would not fully correspond to the moral right of integrity. *See* Mira T. Sundara Rajan, *Creative Commons: America's Moral Rights?,* 21 FORDHAM INTELL. PROP. MEDIA ENT. L.J. 905, 928 (2011). On the other hand, CC's plain-English explanation of what ND means – "[t]his license allows for redistribution, commercial and non-commercial, as long as it is passed along *unchanged and in whole,* with credit to you," *id.* at 927 (emphasis added)– suggests a non-technical understanding of the term. *See also* Suzor, *supra* note 80, at 340 ("Each of these different licenses reflects a particular conception of harm, and it is only by building on copyright's exclusive rights that the licenses are able to strike a balance between access and integrity with which the author is comfortable.").

[83] Jacobsen v. Katzer, 535 F.3d 1373, 1380, 1383 (Fed. Cir. 2008) (finding that because "the terms of the Artistic License [requiring attribution of incremental software authorship] allegedly violated are both covenants and conditions, they may serve to limit the scope of the license and are governed by copyright law."). *See also* Victoria Nemiah, *License and Registration, Please: Using Copyright "Conditions" to Protect Free/open Source Software,* 3 NYU J. INTELL. PROP. ENT. L. 358, 387 (2014) (describing best practices for open source licensing enforcement).

[84] Professional publishing contracts, by contrast, in addition to providing for remuneration, may include clauses providing for authorship credit, *see, e.g.,* clause 1 of sample magazine publishing contract at

intention, Creative Commons proclaims that "money is nothing" and "[r]eputation is everything;"[85] if CC-implemented moral rights come at the price to authors of unpaid distribution of their works, then, the overall endeavor of authorship becomes devalued.[86] Authors' moral rights claims underscore their dignitary interests but, particularly in our society, money and dignity are closely intertwined.

In any event, for many authors, whether on principled objection to obligatory gratuity or out of necessity, the trade-off between money and artistic integrity often will favor the former.[87] It may be cynical to suggest that one can bear having one's artistic vision mangled, so long as the mangling occurs all the way to the bank. To the extent the observation is true, it brings us back to payment. Easing[88] or diversifying[89] legal means of accessing work may increase payments to authors and artists. Another way is advertising, and many big copyright battles, notably Viacom's suit against Google-YouTube,[90] have really been about who gets what cut of the

---

http://web.law.columbia.edu/keep-your-copyrights/contracts/samples/17, and occasionally, for author control over the work's integrity, *see e.g.*, clause 4 of sample book publishing contract at http://web.law.columbia.edu/keep-your-copyrights/contracts/samples/11. *See also* Professional Artists Client Toolkit, *Contracts*, ARTPACT.COM, *available at* www.artpact.com/Contracts (last visited Feb. 9, 2015) (website for illustrators offers model contracts, all of which contain an attribution clause in conjunction with the copyright notice). Many contracts, however, protect neither attribution nor integrity rights. *See e.g.*, "creator unfriendly" and "incredibly overreaching" contracts on the keepyourcopyrights.org website. Self-publishing through platforms like Amazon's Kindle Direct Publishing (KDR) may provide remuneration, but the KDR license contains neither explicit attribution nor integrity clauses. In fact, it allows Amazon to change the scope of rights at any time in its sole discretion. *See Kindle Direct Publishing Terms of Service*, KINDLE DIRECT PUBLISHING, *available at* https://kdp.amazon.com/help?topicId=APILE934L348N (last visited Feb. 9, 2015). As for whether self-publication in fact pays, *compare* Alison Flood, *Stop the Press: Half of Self-Published Authors Earn Less Than $500*, THE GUARDIAN, May 24, 2012, *available at* www.theguardian.com/books/2012/may/24/self-published-author-earnings, *with* Steve Henn, *Self-Published Authors Make A Living–And Sometimes A Fortune*, NPR, July 25, 2014, *available at* www.npr.org/blogs/money/2014/07/25/334484331/unknown-authors-make-a-living-self-publishing (reporting anecdotal evidence through Amazon e-books, "many relatively unknown authors are making a decent living self-publishing their work.").

[85] *See* Sundara Rajan, *supra* note 82, at 931.

[86] *Id.*

[87] *See, e.g.*, Wright, *supra* note 77 (maintaining copyright ownership over his plays allows him to control the integrity of his work, but not to earn a living from it; for the latter he writes screenplays, which pay well, but require him to give up any copyright interest).

[88] It has long been suggested that a way to compete with free music is in combination to lower the cost to consumers or decrease the effort required to download legal music. *See, e.g.*, Henry H. Perritt, Jr., *New Business Models for Music*, 18 VILL. SPORTS ENT. L.J. 63, 208 (2011).

[89] For example, Spotify, which provides unlimited on-demand music streaming services, reported that its availability reduced piracy in Australia by 20%. Max Mason & Paul Smith, *Artists Suffer as Online Piracy Worsens*, FINANCIAL REVIEW, Sept. 16, 2014, *available at* www.afr.com/p/technology/artists_suffer_as_online_piracy_5qsfQmSay6z8rbi5utnLvI.

[90] *See, e.g.*, Viacom Intern., Inc. v. YouTube, Inc., 676 F.3d 19 (2d Cir. 2012).

advertising revenue. But the advertising revenue can also go to authors, assuming that they retain the relevant copyright interests.[91]

Some major streaming services share ad revenue with creators. For example, YouTube pays record producers and songwriters a percentage of the revenue received from advertising accompanying videos.[92] But YouTube's policies in connection with its new Music Key streaming service appear to require artists and composers to sacrifice control over which platforms they post to first in exchange for receiving a share of advertising revenue through YouTube's Content ID service. In effect, YouTube will continue to add to its repertory not only content the creator had licensed to YouTube, but also works or performances that third parties have posted, and unless the creator agrees to the new terms instituted with the Music Key service, she will not be paid for any of the content.[93]

Spotify includes ad revenue in calculating the total amount of royalties it will pay out.[94] Blip, a free online distributer of web series, pays content providers 50% of the advertising revenue they generate.[95] It is not clear, however, that these services in fact generate meaningful income streams for authors,[96] or, for that matter that copyright

---

[91]   This approach has been suggested for blogs posting content by unpaid providers, which in theory could either pay a flat fee per article or create an ad-revenue sharing scheme. Nate Silver, *The Economics of Blogging and The Huffington Post*, N.Y. TIMES, Feb. 12, 2011, 12:28 P.M., *available at* http://fivethir tyeight.blogs.nytimes.com/2011/02/12/the-economics-of-blogging-and-the-huffington-post/ (also noting that the complications of a revenue-sharing model would outweigh the benefit of compensating unpaid contributors on the Huffington Post because 96% of traffic is directed to content by paid contributors).

[92]   Laura Sydell, *YouTube Shares Ad Revenue With Musicians, But Does It Add Up?*, NPR MUSIC (Sept. 27, 2012 12:01 A.M.), *available at* www.npr.org/blogs/therecord/2012/09/27/161837316/youtube-shares-ad-revenue-with-musicians-but-does-it-add-up.

[93]   *See Google Plays Hardball with Indie Musicians*, STUDIO 360, Feb. 5, 2015, *available at* www .studio360.org/story/google-plays-hardball-with-indie-musicians-zoe-keating/.

[94]   *Spotify Explained*, SPOTIFY, *available at* www.spotifyartists.com/spotify-explained/ (last visited Sept. 30, 2014).

[95]   *User Terms of Use*, BLIP, *available at* http://blip.tv/terms (last visited Sept. 30, 2014).
       BLIP (also known as Blip.tv), is a website that helps up-and-coming television and webisode producers develop and distribute work. Blip editors select web series to include on the site, and viewing content is free. Blip and its content providers are paid for by ad revenue. *See About*, BLIP, http://blip .tv/about (last visited Oct. 30, 2014). For a discussion of how the advertising works, see Janko Roettgers, *Blip to Publishers: We're Going to Monetize Your Videos, Whether You Like It or Not*, GIGAOM, Mar. 25, 2013, *available at* https://gigaom.com/2013/03/25/blip-preroll-ads/.

[96]   Spotify pays royalties ranging from $0.006 to $0.0084 to artists based on percentage of streams the artist receives of all users' plays. Victor Luckerson, *Here's How Much Money Top Musicians Are Making on Spotify*, TIME, Dec. 3, 2013, *available at* http://business.time.com/2013/12/03/heres-how-much-money-top-musicians-are-making-on-spotify/; *see also Spotify Explained*, SPOTIFY, *available at* www.spotifyartists.com/spotify-explained/ (last visited Sept. 30, 2014). Even with millions of streams, however, the sums add up to very little, *see* Phillip Pantuso, *The Best Way to Make Money on Spotify*, BROOKLYN MAGAZINE, Mar. 21, 2014, *available at* www.bkmag.com/2014/03/21/the-best-way-to-make-money-on-spotify/ ("Despite the growing user base, a microscopic proportion of bands with songs on Spotify (or Pandora and Rdio, for that matter) see any financial benefits whatsoever.") *See also*

owners, who may be receiving income from advertisements on online platforms, are in fact sharing it with authors.[97]

By contrast, author-oriented business models for aggregating sales of content, or that undertake micro-licensing of content for incorporation in other works, are beginning to emerge. Two examples, both from the independent music business, may point the way. CD Baby is an artist-run hub for sales of CDs and downloads by independent recording artists. The artists set the prices; CD Baby promotes and sells the recordings both direct to consumers and to online music retailers, returning most of the revenue to the artists.[98] CD Baby has also partnered with Rumblefish, a micro-licensing service for recording artists. Musicians place their music in the Rumblefish catalog and video-editors and app developers can license the recorded songs for incorporation in audiovisual works. Rumblefish then distributes license fees to the copyright owners.[99] YouTube and other social video sites link directly to Rumblefish so that uploaders can license their soundtracks as they upload video. So far, the Rumblefish catalog contains more than five million tracks, which have been licensed for more than 65 million videos' soundtracks, resulting, according to Rumblefish, in millions of dollars in royalties for its artists.[100]

U.S. COPYRIGHT OFFICE, COPYRIGHT AND THE MUSIC MARKETPLACE 73–80 ("Impact of Music Streaming Models") (Feb. 2015) (detailing diminution in songwriter and performer revenues as consumption shifts from purchases of copies to accessing streams of recorded musical compositions).

[97] *See, e.g.*, U.S. COPYRIGHT OFFICE, COPYRIGHT AND THE MUSIC MARKETPLACE, *supra* note 96, at 77 (lack of transparency about how – or whether – rights owner intermediaries distribute streaming revenues to creators "can create uncertainty regarding which benefits of the deal are subject to being shared with Artists at all," *quoting* submission of SAG-AFTRA and AFM). Jessica Litman has suggested that pro-author transparency could prove an attractive business strategy: online services which disclosed how much of the price of a stream or download will in fact be paid to creators of a work might garner more users than less transparent services, *see* Jessica Litman, *Fetishizing Copies*, in COPYRIGHT LAW IN AN AGE OF LIMITATIONS AND EXCEPTIONS 130 (Ruth L. Okediji ed., 2017).

[98] *Available at* www.cdbaby.com/about

[99] *Micro-Licensing*, RUMBLEFISH, *available at* http://rumblefish.com/micro-licensing/ (last visited Nov. 2, 2014).

[100] Press Release, Top YouTube Music Partner Rumblefish Breaks 1 Billion Monthly Views, Boasts 5 Million Copyrights under Management, Apr. 2, 2014, *available at* www.marketwired.com/press-release/top-youtube-music-partner-rumblefish-breaks-1-billion-monthly-views-boasts-5-million-1895259.htm.

For further discussion of evolving author-oriented micro-licensing business models, see, e.g., Peter Munters, *Digital Pioneers Explore the Social Economy of Music*, Apr. 26, 2014, *available at* www.ascap.com/eventsawards/events/expo/news/2014/04/digital-pioneers-explore-the-social-economy-of-music.aspx.

The "copyright industries" also are seeking to exploit the micro-licensing market. About a year ago, RIAA and NMPA announced they were creating a micro-licensing system, not to be "aimed at music-centric businesses but rather parties outside of the industry." Tom Pakinkis, *RIAA and NMPA Working on Micro-Licensing Platform That 'Could Unlock Millions,'* MUSICWEEK, June 13, 2013, *available at* www.musicweek.com/news/read/riaa-and-nmpa-working-on-micro-licensing-platform-that-could-unlock-millions/055036; *see also* Ed Christman, *RIAA & NMPA Eyeing Simplified Music Licensing System, Could Unlock 'Millions' in New Revenue*, BILLBOARDBIZ, June 13, 2013, *available at* www.billboard.com/biz/articles/news/record-labels/1566550/riaa-nmpa-eyeing-simplified-music-licensing-system-could (quoting RIAA officials discussing the untapped market of

2.4. CONCLUSION

The author's place in the future of copyright (assuming copyright has a future) will not be assured until the full range of her interests, monetary and moral, receives both recognition and enforcement. Online micropayment and other systems for remunerating individual authors (including by means of collective licensing), albeit often embryonic, hold promise. But will these new means of remunerating authors (or for that matter older business models, which, while often divesting authors of their rights, also often afforded them an income stream) remain viable in a digital environment in which paying for creativity increasingly seems an act of largesse? Most fundamentally, we need to appreciate authorship, and to recognize that a work in digital form is a thing of value,[101] lest the old adage that "information" (meaning, works of authorship) "wants to be free" presage works of authorship that do not "want" to be created.

"businesses[that] want licenses, but haven't a clue how to get them"). It is not clear whether the effort has gone further, although RIAA did respond to a Notice and Request for Public Comment urging the government to take action to promote and facilitate micro-licensing. Comments of the Recording Industry Association of America, Inc. to the U.S. Copyright Office, Docket No. 2014-03, *available at* http://copyright.gov/docs/musiclicensingstudy/comments/Docket2014_3/Recording_Industry_Association_of_America_MLS_2014.pdf (responding to Music Licensing Study: Notice and Request for Public Comment, 79 Fed. Reg. 14,739 (Mar. 17, 2014)).

[101] *See* T.J. Stiles, *Among the Digital Luddites*, 38 Colum. J.L. & Arts 293, 297 (2015) (deploring those who perceive value only in physical copies – and therefore unrestrainedly pirate digital instantiations – as "Digital Luddites").

3

A Few Observations about the State of Copyright Law

*William F. Patry**

ABSTRACT

Reflecting on my over thirty years in the copyright field, this chapter highlights why so many copyright laws are failing. They are failing due to blind adherence to an ideology that insists that unauthorized copying should by default be infringing, and that limitations and exceptions must be narrowly construed. These views – often put forth by those who profess their love for authors – are both ahistorical and inhibit creativity. My principal suggestion is that copyright law must be empirically fitted to the way that people actually create, and not according to the false belief that strong laws are necessary to encourage creativity. If the law is developed in this way, we will see that copyright laws must be flexible because creativity is inherently flexible. There should be one, and only one, inquiry, free of biases: does the work, or an unauthorized use of the work, further creativity and learning? The rest is a distraction.

3.1. MY PURPOSE

In 2004, before its IPO, Google filed an S-1 registration statement. The founders, Sergey Brin and Larry Page, styled this "An Owner's Manual for Google's Shareholders."[1] The first sentence was: "Google is not a conventional company. We do not intend to become one." Similarly, this is not a piece of conventional academic writing, and should not be judged as one. Conventionally, articles have a tripartite structure: the author sets out what the problem is, offers beliefs about how the problem arose, and then offers solutions. This structure is believed to be

---

* Senior Copyright Counsel, Google Inc. The views expressed here are mine alone. In a few places, I have included revised portions from my "How to Fix Copyright" (Oxford University Press, 2011).
[1] Available at: https://investor.google.com/corporate/2004/ipo-founders-letter.html

a requirement for having both direction and purpose; articles that depart from this structure are considered to be confusing.

I have no particular objection to this conventional "Elements of Style" approach to academic writing. Readers are able to quickly see if they are interested in the topic, and upon finishing the article, they can act like test proctors grading whether the author has fulfilled the defined purpose of the article. I have no interest in writing that way. I have, in fact, stopped all new academic writing[2] and decline all public speaking engagements. It's not that I have become a hermit. Rather, I have become convinced that what are sometimes called The Copyright Wars[3] have reached the point where sensible dialogue among people who have differing views is impossible. What we are left with is like-minded people talking only to like-minded people.

This is hardly unique to copyright. Public discourse about politics, climate control, alleged links between vaccines and autism, virtually all topics where strong opinions are held are rife with polarized shouting past each other. There is no reason debates about copyright should be any more illuminating than whether the U.S. government is planning to invade Texas by pretending to stage military preparedness exercises, and in my experience, the debates around copyright law are not more illuminating.

There is still very good academic work being done, as this book demonstrates, but my own interests lie elsewhere, in figuring out why we think what we do, why we believe what we do. Humans have an amazing ability to ignore facts and data. My mother once told me when I was on the verge of winning an argument with her, "Don't confuse me with the facts." A conventional article laying out facts and data, while calling for empirical decision-making, is a helpful resource but only for those with an open mind: such an article assumes that readers who have a different perspective will change those views once presented with evidence of how things really are. My mother, an otherwise sober Irishwoman, was not so easily moved when it came to a view she dearly held.

Perhaps it is genetics, but I too suffer from an inability to realize that what I take for facts are sometimes merely beliefs, and beliefs that are quite wrong. I am my own worst enemy, not those who hold diametrically opposed views. The purpose of this piece is to show some of the processes I have gone through in my personal efforts to separate the fact-sheep from the belief-goats. I will focus on two topics: (1) the belief that we need strong copyright laws, and, (2) the woefully wrong label of "limitations and exceptions." These topics stem from a single point: as a purpose-driven tool, copyright laws, including infringement analysis in courts, should be concerned with a single question: does the work in question, or an unauthorized use of that

---

[2]   I continue to update my treatises.
[3]   *See, e.g.*, WILLIAM PATRY, MORAL PANICS AND THE COPYRIGHT WARS (Oxford University Press, 2009).

work, encourage learning? Everything else, as the ancient rabbinic sage Hillel said, is commentary.[4]

3.2. WHY WE DON'T INHERENTLY WANT STRONG OR WEAK COPYRIGHT LAWS

I have been a full-time copyright lawyer for thirty-two years. I feel blessed to have known giants in the field, such as Alan Latman, Barbara Ringer, and Mel Nimmer. Unfortunately all three have died, but I keep their lessons alive in my memories. I feel fortunate to have started out in the pre-digital era. The training I received in the 1909 Copyright Act and the 1976 Act (as passed) gave me a strong grounding in copyright's traditional values of encouraging creativity and learning. The traditional copyright lawyers who taught me had a strong appreciation for the contributions that art, music, literature, and other forms of expression bring to our daily lives. Copyright law was their calling because culture was their love. As a life-long musician and music composition major in college, I took to copyright law like a fish to water.

The traditional copyright lawyers who were my mentors were extremely generous in taking me under their wing. In those days, law firms developed promising associates, giving them the time and resources to become specialists. The larger copyright bar, especially in New York City, was welcoming, inclusive, and academically inclined. It was, for me, a golden opportunity to learn from people I admired. I had a first-rate education from people who loved their field. My career would have been impossible without their generosity.

Those days are gone forever. The pressure to generate profits, as well as other changes in the profession, have led to few if any opportunities for young lawyers to have the time to develop expertise, nor to learn from patient and generous mentors. This in turn has severed what was for me a given: that copyright law and culture are twined – copyright law, like all the practice of all law, is now just a business. It isn't a profession or, more deeply, a calling. I don't for a minute suggest that those who became copyright lawyers in the digital era lack the same appreciation for culture that my mentors had. My point is that changes in the legal field, coupled with the persistent, difficult issues over digital creation and uses of copyrighted works have called into question the utility of copyright law in ways that didn't exist in the formative years of my career.

There are good reasons for digital-era copyright lawyers' skepticism: copyright law has bulked out to steroid-level strength bearing little resemblance to the law

---

[4] Hillel was referring to learning the Torah. See http://forward.com/culture/14250/the-rest-of-the-rest-is-commentary-02564/

I was trained in. This has led me, sadly and reluctantly, to abandon my decades-old inculcated belief that our copyright laws are inherently essential to culture and for the creation of cultural works. Once true, due to the present constitution of those laws, it is now false. Incredibly, copyright law has become a serious threat to culture and the production of new works. Common sense and empiricism have been shunted aside by the groundless belief (created by large corporate media companies' lobbying) that we allegedly need strong copyright laws, because only strong laws can encourage authors to create and further culture.

This is absurd. When we go to the doctor we don't automatically receive strong medicine, but rather the medicine that is the most effective for the illness at hand. Overdosing can lead to death or long-term side effects. Doctors are, of course, quite familiar with patients who insist they have illnesses they don't have and which the patient believes can only be cured by a favorite drug, as well as with patients who become addicted to drugs that are necessary but only for the short-term. Addiction is easy when drugs are easily available and when you believe they are the answer to your problems. Amending our copyright laws by making them stronger and stronger has become precisely such an addiction; one that we seem incapable or unwilling to either admit to or stop.

3.3. THE DAMAGE DONE BY OUR CURRENT COPYRIGHT LAWS

In my opinion, copyright law has become unmoored from its original purpose of providing a practical, effective way for authors to ensure that they will be able to control and profit from uses that are economically damaging. To be clear: I fully believe they should have that control. But the level of law required to do so is quite minimal. Based on the relatively short commercial life of the vast majority of works, the term of copyright rarely needs to last beyond a few decades, and certainly not life of the author plus seventy years.

Copyright law is also far too broad in the types of works it covers: protection is now granted to virtually everything we do that involves fixing thoughts into a tangible form, even though we had no thought of, or need for, having a copyright for such material. This has resulted in misuse of copyright for anti-competitive purposes and censorship. Potential statutory damages are so high that they have killed many innovative companies.

Things used to be different. In the United States, formalities such as mandatory notice and registration, coupled with a shorter term (but with a renewal period if applied for) provided a possibility of fifty-six years of protection, which was more than enough for almost all works, while eliminating from protection those works that no one had a continued interest in. No one complained that the 1909 Act was anti-author or that there was a lack of great works created between 1909 and 1978.

Aside from the advantages provided by this reasonable statute, in the formative years of Anglo-American copyright, courts were exquisitely sensitive to assuring that the fundamental purpose of copyright – encouraging learning – was the *only* lodestar. We would not be in the sorry state we are in if this were still the case. My fundamental point in this piece is that we need to return to this approach. We need to abandon our misplaced obsession with strong laws – a synonym for rights practically without boundaries – and the idea that boundaries represent an undesirable departure from an idealized natural state of grace in which all uses must either be compensated for or licensed. The Coase Theorem[5] and other right-wing economic excuses for the rich exercising absolute dominion to the great detriment of everyone else should be relegated to the dustbins of history, along with communism and other political failures.

Those who created the essentials of copyright law – the English common law judges – knew that creativity requires copying, often generously, and often without permission or payment.

3.4. WHAT THE OLD ENGLISH COMMON LAW JUDGES TAUGHT ME

In addition to the traditional copyright lawyers who taught me, I learned a great deal from reading the opinions of the early English common law judges who grappled with the bare bones 1710 Statute of Anne, the first general copyright law. That legislation said little more than that there is an exclusive right to publish your book. It had a legislative purpose of encouraging learning by encouraging the publication of books that otherwise wouldn't have been written. That was a simple and functional goal. The Statute of Anne was the tool to accomplish that purpose.[6] Late eighteenth century and early nineteenth century English common law judges, faced with only the Parliamentary purpose of encouraging learning, created all of the foundational elements of copyright: who is an author, what is an original work of authorship, the idea-expression dichotomy, when copying is de minimis, when copying is more than substantial but still not in violation of the statute. U.S. courts adopted these foundational elements lock, stock and barrel, as have most other courts around the world. Copyright, as we know it, was forged by these early judges.

Importantly, there were no separate "limitations and exceptions," no affirmative defenses to a prima facie case satisfied today by merely invoking a statutory right. Plaintiffs and defendants were on equal footing, unlike today where a copyright holder

---

5   *See, e.g.,* https://en.wikipedia.org/wiki/Coase_theorem
6   One could argue that breaking the Stationers' Guild previous monopoly over the book trade was another purpose, but the goal of all monopolies is to reduce choice and availability, and thus opening up choice would increase availability. In any event, there is no reason not to take at face value Parliament's own explanation of the law's purpose.

plaintiff is regarded as being in a protected class formerly reserved for children at risk. In copyright's formative period, there was a single judicial inquiry under a single legislative purpose of encouraging learning. Put simply by Lord Chancellor Eldon in the 1810 case of *Wilkins v. Aiken*: "The question upon the whole is, whether this is a legitimate use of the plaintiff's publication, in the fair exercise of a mental operation, deserving the character of an original work."[7] The original work referred to here is not plaintiff's, but defendant's. The early judges saw copyright law as a way to mediate between conflicting claims to creativity.[8] Where an unauthorized use was itself creative in its employment of a previous book, it was regarded as a "new book," and encouraged under the statute. This is clearly seen in unauthorized abridgments. In 1740, Lord Chancellor Hardwicke wrote that unauthorized "abridgments may with great propriety be called a new book, because not only the paper and print, but the invention, learning, and judgment of the author is shewn in them...."[9]

Unauthorized copying was thus not regarded as a social ill. Seven years before *Wilkins v. Aiken*, in 1803, Lord Ellenborough, in *Cary v. Kearsley*, had held:

> That part of the work of one author is found in another, is not of itself piracy, or sufficient to support an action; a man may fairly adopt the work of another: he may so make use of another's labours for the promotion of science, and the benefit of the public; but having done so, the question will be, Was the matter used fairly with that view[?][10]

Sometimes the answer was no, the work hadn't been used fairly, as in the 1752 case of *Tonson v. Walker*,[11] where Lord Chancellor Hardwicke condemned defendant's unauthorized copying of an edition of Milton's (public domain) poetry along with plaintiff's protected editorial notes but adding a few of defendant's own notes. The court rightly dismissed defendant's work as a "mere evasion" of plaintiff's copyright, and not as a bona fide abridgment.

The English courts' unified approach to furthering learning by a unified judicial inquiry arose from their understanding of the creative process. That understanding prevented them from falling prey to the accusation that copying is piracy, laziness, and free-riding, to be stamped out at every opportunity possible, and condemned as a moral and social shortcoming.

---

[7]   17 Ves. (Chancery) 422, 426 (1810).

[8]   Or other social benefits such as reviews and scientific discussions which used portions of the copyrighted work. From copyright's inception in Anglo-American law, sanctioned unauthorized uses extended beyond creating a second work.

[9]   Gyles v. Wilcox, 2 Atk. 141, 143 (1740). Later, in both the United Kingdom and the United States such fair abridgments would be considered as infringing derivative works by virtue of statutory changes, reflecting different market conditions.

[10]   4 Esp. 168, 170 (1803).

[11]   3 Swans. (App.) 672, 680 (1752).

Once a pragmatic tool for creativity, copyright law has been infested with a permission mentality in which all uses, no matter how trivial or remote from impacting authors' wallets, are declared licensable and therefore must be licensed. Unlicensed uses are to be avoided at all costs, and tolerated, if at all, only when there is "market failure," an abstract economic concept antithetical to the motivations for why people create and the ways in which they create. Culture is not based on hypothetical markets or fictional rational market "actors" but instead on real flesh and blood people expressing their emotions, their fears, and their hopes. They can only do so by copying from others who have similar emotions, fears, and hopes. Here's why.

3.5. WHAT BEING A MUSICIAN HAS TAUGHT ME

Culture can be built only out of a shared approach to knowledge. After all, you can't communicate with others unless you speak the same expressive language; even jokes depend on a high level of shared awareness and behavior. Authors and other creators depend on a mix of expectations and deviations from those expectations. The expectations come from a shared history of how things have been done in previous works. We see this in what the French call *scènes à faire*. The term was developed in the theatre with the classic dramatic setup: A scene occurs; a problem is presented; from that scene the audience knows that, inevitably, another scene will occur in which the problem created in the first scene will be confronted. Inevitability occurs only from shared cultural views about dramatic narrative; for example, that the "problem" really is a problem. How the inevitable problem is confronted is a question of art, of expression. This is also true in music, where we expect certain melodies or chords to be resolved in certain ways, or we expect rhythmic patterns to repeat. Our expectations are formed by prior works. Our expectations are met (or not) in subsequent works that copy from the earlier works that created the expectations in the first place.

Back in the days when copyright laws meshed with cultural creation, courts in the United States approached the issue of shared expressive language in a nuanced way, taking account of the intertwining of inevitability (not protectable) with deviations from our expectations (protectable).[12] The inevitable dramatic confrontation might, in a particular case, include material that inheres in any action or depiction of the *scènes à faire* – that is, stock or commonplace resolutions of the problem confronted (e.g., traditional happy Hollywood endings, as where a driven, hardworking man, through a crisis comes to realize the primacy of love and family over work). But the confrontation would also likely include the filmmaker's own expression too; it is the

---

[12]   *See generally* 1 PATRY ON COPYRIGHT §§ 4:24–4:25.

rare work that consists entirely of *scènes à faire*. We appreciate both the shared values and the new insights.

Culture is shared behavior, creatively duplicated and transformed. While some traditional copyright lawyers ignore the essential role of copying in creating culture, everyone has experienced it in their personal lives. I certainly have as a clarinet player, and in my college days as a music composition major. Children and adults who wish to learn how to play a musical instrument must do so by listening to the sounds their teachers make and then trying to replicate those sounds as closely as possible. Many times you play the same passage in unison so that your teacher's sound is imprinted in your brain. Tricky rhythms can only be learned by listening to others and by copying their playing over and over until you get it right. For most musicians, this process of copying continues throughout your life, as you seek out new sounds you want to copy and then incorporate them as *your* sound.

Professional musicians often have a particular performer they idolize and try to copy. The late Robert Marcellus was the principal clarinetist with the Cleveland Orchestra during its golden years with George Szell (roughly 1956–70). The 1961 recording of the Mozart Clarinet Concerto with Marcellus and Szell has long been an icon for classical clarinetists, who seek to replicate Marcellus's expressiveness. Here is a comment by one person about how important it was for him to copy Marcellus's sound:

> I was 12 years old. I hadn't formed any opinion of Mozart, and had never heard of Robert Marcellus. But when I heard that recording for the first time, I knew I wanted to be the one playing that piece someday. His tone was what hooked me. Marcellus had a haunting clarity, a round, dark ring to every note. I couldn't get that sound out of my ear, and I still strive for it.[13]

To deny people the ability to copy – whether from a book, a recorded performance (as in the Marcellus example), or from any other source – is to deny them their dream of becoming who they want to be. This also applies to groups of people, not just to individuals. European jazz exists only because European musicians were able to relentlessly copy American jazz musicians without permission or payment. The current rhetoric in Europe on copyright is wholly at odds with how post-World War II culture in Europe was created.

American performers religiously copied from their peers. Ray Charles described how he set out deliberately to copy Nat King Cole:

> I knew ... that Nat King Cole was bigger than ever.... Funny thing, but during all those years I was imitating Nat Cole, I never thought about it, never felt bad about

---

[13]   Remarks of David Thomas, quoted in: http://en.wikipedia.org/wiki/Robert_Marcellus.

copying the cat's licks. To me it was practically a science. I worked at it. I enjoyed it. I was proud of it, and I loved doing it.[14]

It has been a tradition for hundreds of years for aspiring painters to go to museums and faithfully copy works hanging there. Henri Rousseau (1844–1910), who painted magical works such as "The Hungry Lion Throws Itself on the Antelope," "The Dream," and "The Sleeping Gypsy," was self-trained and learned much of his technique from camping out at the Louvre and copying from the works on exhibit. Poets, choreographers, and novelists find their voice only after a long period of imitation. This is why Northrop Frey wrote: "Poetry can only be made out of other poems; novels out of other novels."[15] George Orwell confirmed this in "Why I Write," by stating that his first poem was, as he put it, a plagiarism of Blake's "Tiger, Tiger," and that he then moved on to imitating Aristophanes.[16] Creating your own poems and novels only occurs after you have thoroughly assimilated others and have created your voice out of theirs. James Joyce's Ulysses is closely patterned after Homer's The Odyssey, yet at the same time it was so closely of its own time that it has been said to be a "demonstration and summation of the entire [Modernist Literature] movement."[17]

Our greatest works of culture have been the result of creative copying, although one would not know this from the current discussions about copyright, discussions that too often are little more than sloganeering.

3.6. SOME EXAMPLES OF COPYRIGHT SLOGANEERING

Instead of a common sense, calm approach to solving problems, today we have been reduced to mere ideological and political sloganeering, across copyright's political spectrum. Here are a few examples:

"I stand with authors."

"I have to start with enforcement."

"You look at this and you say this is insane. It's insane. And if it is only Hollywood that has to deal with this, OK, that's fine. Let them be insane. The problem is their insane rules are now being applied to the whole world. This insanity of control is expanding as everything you do touches copyrights."

---

14 *See* Jonathan Lethem, *The Ecstasy of Influence: A Plagiarism*, HARPER'S MAGAZINE, Feb. 2007, *available at*: http://harpers.org/archive/2007/02/0081387.

15 Quoted in James Boyle, *Sold Out*, N.Y. TIMES, Mar. 31, 1996, *available at*: www.law.duke.edu/boylesite/Sold_out.htm.

16 GEORGE ORWELL, WHY I WRITE 2 (Penguin Books 2004) (1946).

17 Maurice Beebe, *Ulysses and the Age of Modernism*, 10 JAMES JOYCE QUARTERLY 172, 176 (Fall 1972).

None of these statements advance anything. The first statement sanctimoniously ignores that many copyright disputes are between two authors, and assumes falsely that authors create without copying from their predecessors. Given a dispute between two authors, what does it mean to stand up for authors? It is extremely rare for politicians to stand up for authors when that means standing up to a powerful corporation or trade association. Anyone who doubts this need only look at the reversionary rights provisions in U.S. law, or U.S. term extensions that were carefully crafted to ensure that those extensions go directly to corporations that had long ago bought the copyright from the author with no expectation of a longer term of copyright.

Nor is this a U.S.-only phenomenon. The World Intellectual Property Organization (WIPO) also says it likes to stand up for authors, even appropriating the title of Bob Marley's 1973 song "Get Up, Stand Up" for World Intellectual Property Day 2015. WIPO declared: "Today is a day to 'get up, stand up, for music' – to ensure that our musicians get a fair deal, and that we value their creativity and their unique contribution to our lives." Other politicians around the world used the same message.

Alas, standing up for author's rights doesn't include Marley himself or his heirs, given that in a 2010 litigation, Marley's record label, Island Records (part of Universal Music Group, the world's largest record label), successfully argued that all five of Marley's first, classic albums, including "Burnin," on which "Get Up, Stand Up" appears, are works for hire.[18] This means that Marley was stripped of his status as an author and is considered an employee, just like the janitor who mopped up at the recording studio. It also means that Marley's estate was stripped of its valuable reversionary rights. Since Marley is not an author, he was also stripped of any moral rights. The recordings were, the judge held, citing standard, non-negotiable recording industry contractual language, "the absolute property" of the record label. Standing up for author's rights doesn't seem to extend to the actual authors, but instead is limited to those who hire them. Talk is so very cheap.

The second example of political sloganeering ("I have to start with enforcement") evidences the delusion that inequitable and unpopular laws can be shoved down people's throats by making them even more inequitable and unpopular.

The final statement ("copyright law is insane") is simply a demagogic rant, but one that was quite popular in its speaker's day.

I have my own criticisms of the current state of copyright law, but my dissatisfaction is one "within the family," not outside of it. I am proud to be a traditional copyright lawyer. I do feel, though, as if I have a favorite relative who went off the edge and is doing destructive things. I want the relative back, to be his or her old fun self

---

[18] Fifty-Six Hope Road Music Ltd. v. UMG Recordings, Inc., No. 08 Civ. 6143 (DLC) (S.D.N.Y. Sept. 10, 2010).

again. My positioning of myself as a within-the-family critic is attributable to when I grew up professionally, whom I worked with and for, and where I practiced. In the interest of disclosure, here is my background.

3.7. MY EXPERIENCE WITH COPYRIGHT LAW

My thirty-two years in the field can be broken down as follows: eleven years in private practice, seven years on Capitol Hill (divided between the Copyright Office and the House of Representatives Judiciary Committee), five years as a full-time law professor, and the last nine years as in-house counsel at Google Inc. In my years in private practice, I represented many rights holder groups, such as the Association of American Publishers, the Motion Picture Association of America, and the National Music Publishers Association. I also represented individual rights holders, some of whom were plaintiffs and some of whom were defendants. I argued in court for the application of fair use[19] and against its application.[20]

During my years on Capitol Hill, I drafted many laws and committee reports, went on U.S. government delegations overseas seeking to improve U.S. rights holders' protections, worked on U.S. adherence to the Berne Convention, the Architectural Works Protection Act and Visual Artists Rights Act of 1990, repeal of the renewal requirement, revision of copyright criminal laws, abolition of the Copyright Royalty Tribunal, the 1992 amendment to fair use, the Audio Home Recording Act of 1992 (which had the first anti-circumvention provision), renewal of the Satellite Home Viewer Act, and the GATT implementing legislation. I also worked on versions of what became the Digital Performance Rights in Sound Recording Act of 1995. After leaving Congress, I testified before the House on term extension, and before the Senate on a proposal to move the Copyright Office to the Commerce Department.

My last nine years at Google have presented me with incredible experiences at a cutting edge technology company that faces the toughest copyright issues of the day, both under U.S. law and the laws of many other countries.

I detail my background simply to explain that my experience with copyright law is long, rich, varied, and hardly that of someone who is "anti-copyright." Not surprisingly, given thirty-two years in the field and many different experiences within it, some of my views have evolved. This is a good thing: our appreciation of past events deepens as we gain new knowledge and new perspectives. Such evolution is a sign of personal growth and is quite different from complete shifts in sides like Saul's conversion on the road to Damascus. Indeed, to my distress, many of the battles

---

[19] *See, e.g.*, Ty, Inc. v. Publications Int'l Ltd., 292 F.3d 512 (7th Cir. 2002).
[20] *See, e.g.*, Bill Graham Archives v. Dorling Kindersley, Ltd., 448 F.3d 605 (2d Cir. 2009).

over copyright law resemble the disputes among the first century CE Judean sects of Saul's time: the Pharisees, the Sadducees, the Essenes, and the ζηλωτής (transliterated Greek, zēlōtḗs), which may have been the sect Saul was a member of before he became Paul.

I have never felt the desire for zealotry, perhaps because I grew up in Marin County, Northern California, in the 1960s; indeed, being around so many false messiahs made me extremely wary of ideology, but not impervious to it. The mistakes I have made as a copyright lawyer – and there are a number – have been the result of a failure to think empirically and pragmatically and to instead act out of ideological beliefs I held at the time. Adherence to ideology is not the same as passion. One can be passionate about things without being a zealot. Paraphrasing A. J. P. Taylor, one may have "strong views, lightly held." Strong views strongly held is an inhibition to seeing things as they are or are likely to be, an obstacle to being able to change your views when you are wrong. Judge Pierre Leval once quipped to me, "The best way to know you have a mind is to change it." You can't change your mind if, blinded by ideology, you think you are always right. My friend German writer and publisher Rafael Seligmann told me during a visit to Berlin last year, "Neugierde ist die Triebfeder der menschlichen Entwicklung, und Angst ihr Hemmschuh": "Curiosity is the driving force of human development, and fear is her stumbling block." One of our biggest fears is being wrong, a fear I don't share. To the contrary, I am happy when someone points out I was wrong about something because I have then both learned something new, and unlearned something I thought true but wasn't.

3.8. WHAT BIKE RIDING HAS TAUGHT ME

It is much easier to admit mistakes when ideology and lobbying are not involved. If I make a wrong turn while driving, I don't regard it as a personal failing. I simply turn around and go the right direction. Correcting mistakes in law is much harder. First, there are vested interests in the status quo that will fight tooth-and-nail against any change. There is also a tendency to think laws have some sort of political and social imprimatur of validity, that they represent a considered, collective societal judgment. This is baloney. In my seven years on Capitol Hill, most copyright bills were brought up on the House floor and voted on by only two people: the chairman of the subcommittee and his Republican counterpart. In the Senate, bills were brought up *en masse* and voted on by only one person, the floor manager of that evening's proceedings, who likely knew nothing about any of the bills. Legislation represents only what was politically possible at the time, not necessarily what is the best (most effective) policy.

Law is simply a tool, a functional way of solving a problem. In our daily lives we have no problem testing tools to see if they work, and discarding them for other tools if they don't, or changing them so they work better. There is no ideology in this: you wouldn't keep using a hammer because you love hammers when the task at hand is tightening a screw. You wouldn't keep using the same paint if it didn't give you the result you wanted. You wouldn't use the same recipe over and over if the cake didn't come out the way you wanted; you would experiment by changing the ingredients until you get the desired end result. In short, we approach our daily lives empirically.

I am an avid road bicyclist. I live in a hilly area, which is good because I like climbing. I have a number of bikes from different eras, different weights, different gearing. This allows lots of performance comparisons, aided by the incredible amount of data available now through portable computing devices that you can attach to your handlebars, and which you can synch up with sensors and computerized power meters placed on your bike.

After a ride, you upload the data to a website, and, *voilà*, you have more data than you can imagine, along with graphs. The data includes not just how far you went and at what average speed, but also cadence (how fast you turn the pedals); power (measured in watts); heart beat; calories expended; elevation gained or lost; average temperature; minimums and maximums of speed; how you distributed the power between your left and right pedals; pedal smoothness; and how much time you spent riding in the saddle or pedaling while standing, to name the most common data points. As you are riding, many of these data points are available to you in real time, so that you can adjust your performance by changing a host of variables. You can even share your ride in real time with others via smartphones or social websites.

The performance I was interested in was finding the best way to climb hills with "best" meaning the fastest way that doesn't leave you so tired you have to stop and rest at the top, so you can continue on for a long ride.

There are two basic theories about how to climb "hills" (a term that includes mountains). The first, the "high cadence theory," is to ride using the smaller of the two front gears. The smaller front gear is called the "small chain ring." The larger front gear is called the "big chain ring." In order to move the bike forward, the front chain ring has to be paired with a rear gear sprocket via the pedals and a chain, thereby driving the power to the rear wheel.

After doing a lot of reading and watching video of some of the world's best past and present climbers. I concluded that the high cadence theory was the one for me. It was, after all, the style the best climbers used. The high cadence theory also, I confess, appealed to me on aesthetic, almost romantic grounds: the image of a lone cyclist pedaling his or her way gracefully up a high mountain in the Alps or Pyrenees is the stuff of legend, captured in numerous iconic photographs of the Tour de France or the Giro d'Italia.[21] Such elegant riding can also result in those rare mystical moments when you feel at one with the bike and your surroundings, when you feel the pedals are effortlessly moving through the air. Having the correct technique doesn't mean you will have this feeling, but without the correct technique you will never have it.

After investing in the proper equipment, and using the high cadence approach, I happily rode my way up the hardest hills I could find in our area. I wasn't tired at the top and followed the techniques that the best climbers used, although my speed was only average. Eventually, I decided to see how quickly I could go up a particularly short but tough hill. It is only half a mile long, but it has an average gradient of 10 percent with switchbacks, and at the end a gradient of 16 percent. Over the course of a few weeks on three different bikes, I conducted experiments. One bike weighs 13.5 pounds and has as its largest rear sprocket a huge 40 tooth sprocket; a second bike weighs 15.5 pounds and has as its largest rear sprocket 28 teeth; a third (an older Italian steel bike) weighing 18.5 pounds has the largest back sprocket of 25 teeth. All three had at the time the same size chain rings in the front: 50 teeth/34 teeth.

After many experiments, it turned out that my best time going up the target hill was on the heaviest bike with the hardest gears, 4 minutes and 1 second. That baffled me. My best time should have been, I thought, on my lightest bike with the easiest gears. Having no explanation, I ended the experiment until one day a few months later I was on a ride with a friend who is a much stronger rider. He is also over four decades younger, but we are about the same weight. We went on a 40-mile ride that included the target hill. My friend went up all the hills in his big front chain ring. I went up in my small front chain ring. He went faster up the hills than I did. At first, I attributed his quicker pace to his youth. But then I got back to wondering why I had done my own best time up the target hill with the hardest gear in the back. I wondered what would happen if I experimented with the second approach to climbing, the "big chain ring theory."

With this approach you use the larger gear in the front with as small a gear as you can turn in the back, frequently while standing out of the saddle while you pedal.[22]

---

[21] This is not so different from the copyright romantic vision of the lone, starving artist in his or her garret.

[22] Chain rings come in different sizes, the two most common are the "standard": 53 teeth as the largest, and 39 teeth as the smallest, and, the "compact": 50 teeth as the largest, and 34 teeth as the smallest. Compact chain rings are rarely used by professionals and are a compromise for amateurs, enabling them to use a lower gear (that is, a rear sprocket with more teeth) in order to make it easier to climb hills without changing speed. As a result of my experiment, I now have 53 x 39 chainrings.

This gives you more power, as you are able to use your whole body.[23] The principal advantage of the big chain ring is speed: if two riders are using the same sprocket in the back, and both are pedaling at the same cadence, the one using a larger sprocket in front will go faster. For example, a rider with a chain ring with 34 teeth in the front, paired with a 12 teeth sprocket in the back, pedaling at 100 rpm, will go at a speed of 17.3 kilometers per hour, while one with 39 teeth in the front paired with a 12 teeth sprocket in the back will go at a speed of 19.8 kilometers per hour.[24]

I began a series of experiments, on all kinds of rides, on all my bikes, using just the big front chain ring. The end result was a dramatic improvement in my speed on all rides, and a new fastest time going up the target hill of 2 minutes and 47 seconds. That is over a 30 percent improvement: from 241 seconds down to 167 seconds. The big improvement in performance caused me to reassess the way I had been riding. It required me to abandon beliefs I had developed after a fair amount of research – and investment in bikes and parts too. But the data was clear and I have followed it.

3.9. WHY CAN'T COPYRIGHT LAWS BE LIKE RIDING A BIKE?

I went through this description of bike riding because it demonstrates how we can experiment with problems in our daily lives and develop and refine our solutions based on what the evidence shows, even though we may have begun with a different belief about the best solution.

Why is abandoning beliefs easier with bike riding or any daily chore, than in drafting laws? After all, both a bike and laws are tools. It's not that bike riding is free of ideology: as I found out, once one technique works well in some experiments, it is very tempting to apply it to everything, to become a "believer." But ultimately in sports, at least at the professional level, you are judged by your performance results. If riding in the big chain ring all the time means others beat you, you will have to drop your ideology or drop out of the sport and find another way to make a living.

Our copyright laws are not performance based. They are not based on data or on experiments to see if they can accomplish what they set out to do. Despite changes in the length of copyright around the world from life of the author and fifty years post-mortem to life of the author plus seventy years post-mortem, based on the assertion that doing so would result in more works being created, no legislature ever undertook to examine whether there was an empirical basis for the assertion, and no legislature has ever undertaken a study to see, post-enactment, whether the assertion has proven true. And probably for good reason. The assertion is facially false – any

---

[23] *See, e.g.,* http://roadcyclinguk.com/how-to/technique/technique-from-bronze-to-gold-in-2013-part-six .html#oYiTmXROvoDwWDtF.97

[24] Thirty-four is in fact the small chain ring in the front on a compact crankset, while thirty-nine is the small chain ring on a standard crankset, but the math is the same for the big chain ring.

lengthening of the term of protection post-mortem cannot, by definition, lead the dead author to create more works. Nor has there been a single author anywhere in the world who could truthfully claim: "A term of copyright that only lasts for 50 years after I die is too short; I will not create a single new work unless copyright lasts 70 years after I die." Most works have a commercial life of only a few years, if any at all. No publisher or other distributor is going to give an author a single penny more based on a term of seventy years post-mortem rather than fifty years post-mortem. The only effect of term extension has been to reduce the number of new works created by those who wish to build on the works of their predecessors, and to restrict access to cultural works by the public.

Our unwillingness to test claims of copyright by the same approach we take to riding a bike, baking a cake, or diagnosing an illness is even worse than this: in those rare cases where a law *is* tested against its claims and comes up short, the law is nevertheless continued based on "perceptions" that it does something the evidence has proven false.

On March 11, 1996, the European Union adopted a directive covering databases. The directive had two goals, the first laudable, the second not. The first goal was to harmonize the level of originality required for a database to be protected under copyright laws. As a single market, the rules in that market should be consistent. Databases covered under this part of the directive include compilations of literary material, musical compositions, and audiovisual material.

The second goal was to create new, sui generis (non-copyright) rights over unoriginal databases: databases of facts, numbers, and other material that require investment to produce but which are not the result of creative activity of the sort recognized by copyright laws. This new right was made available to database compilers outside the European Union, but only on a reciprocal basis; that is, only if the non-EU country of origin extended the same rights to EU database compilers.[25] Like much of EU intellectual property law, this provision was directed solely at the United States, which, as a result of the 1991 Supreme Court opinion in *Feist Publications, Inc. v. Rural Telephone Services Co.*,[26] cannot, as a constitutional matter, extend copyright to non-original databases.

The *Feist* Court held that there was no author of facts and that arranging facts in alphabetical or similar lock-step ways did not meet the constitutional requirement of originality. (*Feist* involved a copyright claim in the white page listings of a telephone book.) In an attempt to get around the *Feist* opinion, database compilers in the United States attempted for many years to convince Congress to grant sui generis

---

[25] *See generally* INTELLECTUAL PROPERTY PROTECTION OF FACT-BASED WORKS: COPYRIGHT AND ITS ALTERNATIVES (Robert F. Brauneis ed., Edward Elgar 2009).

[26] 499 U.S. 340 (1991).

rights, but eventually gave up. Even if they had succeeded, it is likely the Supreme Court would have struck the law down. The database industry in the United States has nevertheless continued to thrive without any new rights.

The EU directive required a post-enactment impact statement in which the Commission would evaluate whether the goal of increasing the production of databases had been met. The first evaluative report was to have been submitted no later than January 1, 2001. It was not submitted until December 12, 2005.[27] There has been no second report. The report is remarkable in its candor, declaring that although "[i]ntroduced to stimulate the production of databases in Europe, the 'sui generis' protection has had no proven impact on the production of databases."[28] The evidence pointed in the opposite direction, to a reduction in the number of databases produced within the European Union. The report noted that the number of EU-based database entries in the Gale Directory of Databases dropped from 4,085 in 2001, to 3,095 in 2004, the year before the evaluation report was issued.

Recall that the sui generis right was conditioned on the United States granting reciprocal rights to EU databases. The United States did not, however, grant sui generis rights. Not only did the number of EU databases decline in absolute numbers, but so too did the relative global market share of EU databases to U.S. databases. Notwithstanding the evidence, the report recites how EU database producers continue to believe, completely falsely, that the sui generis right "has helped Europe catch up with the US in terms of investment."[29] The report disagreed, noting "there has been a considerable growth in database production in the US," whereas, in the EU, "the introduction of 'sui generis' protection appears to have had the opposite effect. With respect to 'non-original' databases, the assumption that more and more layers of IP protection means more innovation and growth appears not to hold up."[30]

Based on the failure of the directive to achieve its purpose, the only logical approach would have been to repeal it. This was the first option discussed in the report, but it was quickly dismissed – not on empirical grounds, since the evidence supported repeal – but instead based on the false insistence of EU database producers that the right was necessary. As the report noted: "While [EU database producers'] endorsement of the 'sui generis' rights is somewhat at odds with the continued success of US publishing and database production that thrives without the 'sui generis' type protection, the attachment to the new right is a political reality that seems very true for Europe."[31]

---

[27] DG Internal Market and Services Working Paper, First evaluation of Directive 96/9/EC on the legal protection of databases, Commission of the European Communities, Brussels, December 12, 2005
[28] Report at 20.
[29] Report at 23
[30] Report at 5.
[31] Report at 25.

The database directive shows the danger of enacting legislation that departs from economic reality: once enacted, even failures are left intact due to political pressure.

3.10. THE ATTACK ON SAFE HARBORS AND FAIR USE

In addition to having ineffective laws, we also face the reverse problem of attacks on laws that *do* work. One example is found in the Section 512(c) hosting safe harbors, enacted as part of the 1998 U.S. Digital Millennium Copyright Act. It is this provision that enables authors, artists, performers, and other creators, no matter where they live or how much money they have, to share their works directly with the whole world through YouTube, blogs, Twitter, Facebook, and thousands of other popular platforms. We are living in the most creative time in history as a result of Section 512. Yet, Section 512 and similar provisions in EU and other laws are under attack from gatekeeper groups as an unwise "limitation" on rights. The only limitation is on gatekeeper's ability to control what we can create, and what we, as a public, can have access to. The democratization of creativity made possible by safe harbors is a direct threat to the winner-take-all system facilitated by traditional copyright law.

Another provision that actually encourages the creation of new works in the United States is the fair use doctrine. Fair use is a part of traditional copyright law, hearkening back to the old English cases reviewed above. Judge Pierre Leval has written: "Fair use should not be considered a bizarre, occasionally tolerated departure from the grand conception of the copyright monopoly. To the contrary, it is a necessary part of the overall design."[32] Throughout his thirty-eight years as a member of the federal judiciary – sixteen years as a trial judge in the Southern District of New York, and twenty-two years as an appellate judge on the U.S. Court of Appeals for the Second Circuit in Manhattan – Judge Leval has gained a great deal of practical experience in deciding fair use cases. His more than three decades of experience in applying fair use has led him to a greater, not a lesser appreciation of the doctrine's importance in furthering creativity. He is not alone in this view: The Supreme Court has twice held that fair use is an essential "built-in accommodation of First Amendment interests."[33]

One would not recognize the critical role that fair use plays in the attacks on it by private interests. As revealed in the leaked Sony documents, Chris Dodd, head of the Motion Picture Association of America, described fair use as "extremely controversial and divisive" in an email to the United States Trade Representative Michael Froman.[34] This contradicts public statements by the MPAA, including a thoughtful

---

[32] Pierre Leval, *Toward a Fair Use Standard*, 103 HARV. L. REV. 1105, 1110 (1990)

[33] Golan v. Holder, 132 S.Ct. 873, 890 (2012); Eldred v. Ashcroft, 537 U.S. 186, 219 (2003).

[34] *See* www.techdirt.com/articles/20150416/17252230680/chris-dodds-email-reveals-what-mpaa-really-thinks-fair-use-extremely-controversial.shtml.

October 2013 MPAA blog post by its very experienced counsel Ben Sheffner. Mr. Sheffner was responding to comments about an MPAA brief submitted in litigation supporting fair use:

> [W]e do want to push back a bit on the suggestion in some of the commentary about our brief that the MPAA and its members somehow "oppose" fair use, or that our embrace of it in the Baltimore Ravens brief represents a shift in our position. That's simply false, a notion that doesn't survive even a casual encounter with the facts. Our members rely on the fair use doctrine every day when producing their movies and television shows – especially those that involve parody and news and documentary programs. And it's routine for our members to raise fair use – successfully – in court.
>
> ....
>
> No thinking person is "for" or "against" fair use in all circumstances. As the Supreme Court and countless others have said, fair use is a flexible doctrine, one that requires a case-by-case examination of the facts, and a careful weighing of all of the statutory factors. Some uses are fair; some aren't.[35]

I agree with these remarks completely. Yet, it has become common for those who know better to attack fair use for being fact-specific and therefore unpredictable, as being merely the right to hire a lawyer. The right-to-hire-a-lawyer argument applies equally to all litigation, and not just for the poor, but for the middle class too.[36] This is particularly a problem in criminal cases where the personal stakes are much, much higher. Some studies have indicated that the average hourly income of a person needing legal services (of any type) is $25, while the average hourly rate for a new lawyer is about $350. Thus, for every hour of a lawyer's time, the person hiring the lawyer would have to work an extra 12 hours just to break even, or almost an extra week for three hours of a lawyer's time.[37] That doesn't happen, and therefore many middle-class people (in addition to the poor) cannot access the courts. This is a national problem, not one of copyright law in general, much less fair use.

The argument that fair use is so fact-specific that it is unpredictable fails for the same reason: it is equally true of many concepts in law – the "reasonable person" in tort and negligence law, the "rule of reason" in antitrust law. These standards do not exist independently of the facts of the particular case.

---

[35] www.mpaa.org/mpaa-and-fair-use-a-quick-history/.

[36] *See Middle-Class Dilemma: Can't Afford Lawyers, Can't Qualify for Legal Aid*, July 22, 2010, *available at* www.abajournal.com/news/article/middle-class_dilemma_cant_afford_lawyers_cant_qualify_for_legal_aid.

[37] *See Is There Such a Thing as an Affordable Lawyer?*, May 30, 2014, www.theatlantic.com/business/archive/2014/05/is-there-such-a-thing-as-an-affordable-lawyer/371746/.

All of the foundational issues in copyright are equally fact-specific: did you contribute enough to be considered an author, did you imbue the work with enough originality for the work to be protected, is the material in question an idea or the expression of an idea. One of our greatest judges ever, Learned Hand, made this point in *Peter Pan Fabrics, Inc. v. Martin Weiner Corp.*: "Obviously, no principle can be stated as to when an imitator has gone beyond copying the 'idea,' and has borrowed its 'expression.' Decisions must therefore inevitably be ad hoc."[38] Yet, the idea-expression dichotomy is a bedrock of copyright laws around the world, and is not subject to criticism even though like fair use it is totally fact specific and therefore "unpredictable."

All of the other elements of copyright infringement litigation are similarly situated: Was the copying de minimis? If not, was the copying material enough for the two works to be substantially similar? As early as 1836, English courts held this inquiry involved multiple factors that could not form the basis for precedent, seen in this opinion by Lord Chancellor Cottenham:

> When it comes to a question of quantity [of copying], it must be very vague. One writer might take all the vital part of another's book, though it might be but a small proportion of the book in quantity. It is not only quantity but value that is always looked to. It is useless to refer to any particular cases as to quantity.[39]

This too is a bedrock of modern copyright law, never challenged or criticized as making copyright protection merely the right to hire a lawyer. The inquiry into whether one is a joint author is the same:

> [A] determination as to whether a work was created jointly involves an examination of both the quantity and quality of the parties' contributions as factors bearing on the ultimate question, intent. While a co-author's contribution need not equal the other author's, at least when the authors are not immediately and obviously collaborating, the co-authors contribution must be "significant" both in quality and quantity in order to permit an inference that the parties intended a joint work.[40]

---

[38] 274 F.2d 487 (2d Cir. 1960).

[39] 3 My. & Cr. (Ch.) 737, 738 (1836).

[40] Eckert v. Hurley Chicago Co., 638 F. Supp. 699, 704 (N.D. Ill. 1986). See also the very comprehensive opinions in *Marshall v. Marshall*, 2012 WL 1079550 (E.D.N.Y. March 30, 2012), *aff'd*, 2012 WL 6013418 (2d Cir. Dec. 4, 2012), and *Corwin v. Quinone*, 2012 WL 832600 (N.D. Ohio Mar. 12, 2012). A number of other courts have rejected claims of joint authorship on the ground that one party's contribution was too minimal. *See* Forward v. Thorogood, 985 F.2d 604, 607 (1st Cir. 1993) (in a common-law case involving pre-1976 Act sound recording, court held that individual who merely arranged and paid for musical group to create a demo tape and requested that certain songs be played was not a joint author; the court noted that "the band played th[e] songs in precisely the same manner it always played them"); M.G.B. Homes, Inc. v. Ameron Homes, Inc., 903 F.2d 1486, 1493 (11th Cir. 1990) (providing sketches and ideas for homes insufficient); BancTraining Video Sys. v. First Am. Corp., 956 F.2d 268

All of these foundational elements of copyright law involve exactly the same type of analysis as fair use determinations do. The criticism of fair use as unpredictable or unstable is hogwash. It is important to point out that those who make such criticisms or who regard fair use as inappropriate for other countries' copyright laws lack any practical experience in applying the doctrine. In the United States, everyday corporate lawyers make fair use determinations with substantial consequences. Many companies are both copyright owners and users. Viacom, Inc., a very large, litigious media company that has regularly spoken in favor of strong copyright rights, relied heavily on fair use for its popular "Daily Show with Jon Stewart" and "The Colbert Report." The idea that fair use reduces copyright owners' rights is belied by the regular practice of large U.S. media companies applying fair use in their everyday commercial decisions. The existence of a fair use defense does not mean any particular claim of fair use will succeed. I have argued cases in court in favor of fair use applying. I have argued cases in court against fair use applying. In all cases, the assessment is driven by whether the claimed fair use furthers the goals of copyright.

3.11. WHY WE NEED FLEXIBLE COPYRIGHT LAWS

I began this piece by stating a dual purpose of discussing why we don't inherently need strong (or weak) copyright laws, and, why the label "limitations and exceptions" is inapt and disguises the unitary nature of creativity. In addition to calls for strong copyright law, one also hears calls for flexible copyright laws. Laws have no animate nature: they do not need or aspire to be anything, neither strong nor flexible. They are simply tools for a purpose. Unlike the bare-bones Statute of Anne, copyright laws today cover a great range of activity, some of it highly regulatory in nature and impacting on other areas of law, as with broadcasting which works in tandem with communications law and policy.

Certainty in law is generally a very good thing. It is a global belief that people should not be held to have violated a vague law. When we pay our taxes, we want to know exactly how much we pay. When we drive, we want to know the exact speed limit. There are areas of copyright law where we want, and should have, precise provisions, as with compulsory licensing. This has nothing to do, though, with a law being strong, but rather with it being precise. There are elements in copyright law, like all laws, that cannot be precise because of the nature of the activity in question. These turn out to be the heart of traditional copyright law: who is an author, what is

(6th Cir. 1992) (supervision of production of a videotape and supplying ideas insufficient); Johannsen v. Brown, 797 F. Supp. 835, 841–42 (D. Or. 1992) (providing idea for Grateful Dead-style takeoff on Grant Wood's American Gothic insufficient to establish joint authorship); Kenbrooke Fabrics, Inc. v. Material Things, 1984 WL 532 (S.D.N.Y. 1984).

an original work of authorship, the idea-expression dichotomy, when copying is de minimis, when copying is more than substantial but still not in violation of the statute. The analyses of these questions have always been judge-made and fact-specific, for the simple reason that creativity is dynamic. For our copyright laws to be effective they too must be dynamic, a synonym of which is flexible. And they are: in the 1976 Act, Congress deliberately created a definition of copy, and a list of exclusive rights that are flexible. By continuing the common law fair use doctrine, it also continued that flexibility. As Judge Leval noted in the above quote, "Fair use should not be considered a bizarre, occasionally tolerated departure from the grand conception of the copyright monopoly. To the contrary, it is a necessary part of the overall design."[41] There is an overall design, and it is one design. The old English judges got it right. There should be one inquiry: does the use further learning? It is time to return that sensible approach.

---

[41] Leval, *supra* note 32.

4

Fetishizing Copies

*Jessica Litman** *

ABSTRACT

Our copyright laws encourage authors to create new works and communicate them to the public, because we hope that people will read the books, listen to the music, see the art, watch the films, run the software, and build and inhabit the buildings. That is the way that copyright promotes the Progress of Science. Recently, that not-very-controversial principle has collided with copyright owners' conviction that they should be able to control, or at least collect royalties from, all uses of their works. A particularly ill-considered manifestation of this conviction is what I have decided to call copy-fetish. This is the idea that every appearance of any part of a work anywhere should be deemed a "copy" of it, and that every single copy needs a license or excuse. In this chapter, I focus on two well-known instances of copy-fetish: the contention that any appearance of a work or part of a work in the random access memory of a computer or other digital device is an actionable copy, and the assertion that the mere posses-sion of a publicly accessible copy infringes the exclusive right to distribute copies to the public. Both arguments have their inception in difficult-to-justify court of appeals decisions, which were then embraced by copyright owners as tools to expand second-ary liability. Neither one makes much sense on its own terms. The political economy of copyright, however, makes it overwhelmingly likely that any comprehensive copyright revision bill will incorporate both of them. That makes it imperative that we recognize readers', listeners', and viewers' copyright liberties expressly, and protect them with explicit statutory provisions.

* John F. Nickoll Professor of Law and Professor of Information, University of Michigan. I'm grateful to Jon Weinberg, Pam Samuelson, Terry Fisher, Niva Elkin-Koren, Peter Jaszi, Justin Hughes, Ruth L. Okediji, and Jane Ginsburg, who read drafts of this chapter and made extremely useful suggestions for improving it.

The most important reason that we have copyright laws is to encourage authors to create books, music, art, theatre, films, computer software, and building designs, and to communicate those works to the public.[1] The most important reason we want authors to create and communicate new works is that we hope people will read the books, listen to the music, see the art, watch the films, run the software, and build and inhabit the buildings. That is the way that copyright promotes the Progress of Science.[2]

This assertion has become more contentious than it used to be. If the most important reason for copyright is to encourage readers, listeners, and viewers to experience works of authorship, that suggests that readers, listeners, and viewers have significant interests that the copyright laws should pay attention to. And that's controversial, even though it shouldn't be, because too many advocates for copyright owners have concluded that any explicit attention to the copyright interests of readers, listeners, and viewers might undermine the interests of owners.[3] Thus, over the past decade, we've seen ill-considered overstatements in copyright speeches and essays to the effect that there are no readers' rights under copyright law.[4]

The notion of readers' interests in copyright law wasn't invented by some 21st century cyber-radicals. The concept that the public (which is to say, readers, listeners, and viewers) have copyright interests that are as important and sometimes more important than the interests of authors and owners has a long scholarly pedigree;[5]

---

[1] Copyright laws may also accomplish other goals. Over the past few years, I have heard people mention such purposes as securing a favorable balance of trade, providing jobs, and exporting American values. *See* U.S. Department of Commerce Internet Policy Task Force, Copyright Policy, Creativity, and Innovation in the Internet Economy, www.uspto.gov/news/publications/copyrightgreenpaper.pdf (2013); Stewart Siwerk, Copyright Industries in the U.S. Economy: The 2013 Report (2013), www.iipa.com/pdf/2013_Copyright_Industries_Full_Report.PDF (prepared for the International Intellectual Property Alliance); Chris Dodd, *Copyright: A Leading Force for Jobs, Innovation and Growth,* Huffington Post (Nov. 19, 2013) www.huffingtonpost.com/chris-dodd/copyright-a-leading-forc_b_4302882.html. Those subsidiary purposes, though, are common to many different businesses, and are by-products of a functioning copyright system, rather than its core goals.

[2] *Accord* Jane C. Ginsburg, *Authors and Users in Copyright,* 45 J. Copyright Soc'y 1, 4–5 (1997) ("authors … enrich society by creating works which promote learning").

[3] *See* Henry Horbaczewski, *Copyright Under Siege: Reflection of an In-House Counsel, The Sixth Annual Christopher A Meyer Memorial Lecture,* 53 J. Copright Soc'y 387, 393–94 (2006); I. Fred Koenigsberg, *The Fifth Annual Christopher A. Meyer Memorial Lecture: Humpty-Dumpty in Copyrightland,* 51 J. Copyright Soc'y 677, 679 (2004). *See also* Ginsburg, *supra* note 2, at 20 ("Copyright is a law about creativity; it is not, and should not become, merely a law for the facilitation of consumption.").

[4] *See, e.g.,* David Johnstone, *Debunking Fair Use Rights and Copyduty Under U.S. Copyright Law,* 52 J. Copyright Soc'y 345 (2005); Koenigsberg, *supra* note 3, at 679.

[5] *See, e.g.,* Robert Gorman, Copyright Law 1 (1991); Benjamin Kaplan, An Unhurried View of Copyright (1967); L. Ray Patterson, Copyright in Historical Perspective (1968);

it appears in many of the Supreme Court copyright decisions handed down in the 20th Century,[6] and is expressed in the legislative history of every major copyright statute.[7] So why has it suddenly morphed into a dangerous idea?

Some of it, I think, is real fear caused by the rapid development of networked digital technology. The markets for works of authorship have evolved more swiftly than our 40-year-old statute can adjust to. A reader, viewer, or listener equipped with networked digital technology can look like a scary machine for disseminating millions of copies.[8] Another reason may be the sense that compensation for creators is already shockingly inadequate. Any suggestion that readers might be entitled to rights seems to threaten to shave off another portion of what has turned out to be a tiny share of the sloshing piles of money that inhabit the copyright system. Some of it is surely conviction, not grounded in either law or history, that copyright owners should be able to control, or at least collect royalties from, *all uses* of their works. That's never been true, either in fact or law, but representatives of copyright owners have gotten used to arguing that it should be true.[9]

A particularly ill-considered manifestation of this conviction is what I have decided to call copy-fetish. This is the idea that every appearance of any part of a work anywhere should be deemed a "copy" of it, and that every single copy needs a license or excuse, whether or not anyone will ever see the copy, whether or not the copy has any independent economic significance, whether or not the so-called copy is incidental to some other use that is completely lawful.

Copy-fetish inspired the Authors Guild to sue the HathiTrust for copyright infringement over copies that HathiTrust archived and indexed but didn't allow

THOMAS EDWARD SCRUTTON, THE LAWS OF COPYRIGHT (1883); Zechariah Chafee, *Reflections on the Law of Copyright*, 45 COLUM. L. REV. 503 (1945).

6   *See* Quality King v. L'Anza, 523 U.S. 135, 150 (1998); Fogerty v. Fantasy, 510 U.S. 517, 526–27 (1994); Feist v. Rural, 499 U.S. 340, 349–50 (1991); Sony v. Universal, 464 U.S. 417, 429 (1984); Twentieth Century Music v. Aiken, 422 U.S. 151, 156 (1975); Mazer v. Stein, 347 U.S. 201, 219 (1954); *see also* U.S. v. Loew's, 371 U.S. 38, 46 (1962); U.S. v. Paramount, 334 U.S. 131, 148 (1948); Fox Film v. Doyal, 286 U.S. 123, 127 (1932).

7   *See, e.g.,* S. Rep. No. 190, 105th Cong. 9 (1998); H.R. Rep. 2222, 60th Cong. 7 (1909).

8   *See, e.g.,* Departments of Commerce, Justice, State, the Judiciary and Related Agencies Appropriations for 2003: Hearings before a Subcomm. of the House Comm. on Appropriations, 107th Cong. 455–63 (2002) (testimony of Jack Valenti, Motion Picture Assn of Am); DAVID PRICE, SIZING THE PIRACY UNIVERSE (2013), at www.netnames.com//sites/default/files/netnames-sizing_piracy_universe- FULL report-sept2013.pdf (NetNames report commissioned by NBC Universal).

9   *See, e.g.,* Fair Copyright in Research Works Act: Hearing on HR 6845 Before the Subcomm. on Courts, the Internet, and Intellectual Property of the House Comm. On the Judiciary, 110th Cong., 50–51 (2009) (Serial # 110-204) (testimony of Ralph Oman, former Register of Copyrights); Performance Rights Act: Hearing on HR 848 Before the House Judiciary Comm., 111th Cong. 29 (2009) (testimony of Billy Corgan, MusicFIRST) (Serial # 111-8); Mark Helprin, *A Great Idea Lives Forever. Shouldn't Its Copyright?*, N.Y. TIMES, May 20, 2007, at www.nytimes.com/2007/05/20/opinion/20helprin.html.

anyone to see.[10] Copy-fetish has persuaded others that fair use has somehow run amok because copyright owners are losing lawsuits that they would probably never have brought if they didn't feel obliged to protect themselves from all unlicensed copies.[11] Copy-fetish is encouraging lobbyists to push the United States Trade Representative to negotiate bilateral free trade agreements that incorporate copyright provisions far more generous to copyright owners (and stingier to copy users) than anything in U.S. law.[12] Copy-fetish is impelling copyright's defenders to insist that readers, listeners, and viewers have and should have no rights under the copyright law, at least if attention to user rights might breed tolerance for unlicensed copies.[13] As a rhetorical strategy, that tack seems short-sighted. Without a wide swath of freedom for readers, listeners, and viewers to encounter and enjoy works of authorship, the copyright law accomplishes little and is hard to defend.

Every single one of us who writes books, or articles, or stories, or music, or makes art, or photographs, or major motion pictures does so, at least in part, as an act of communication. We want to convey our ideas, words, sounds, and images to audiences, so that they can enjoy them, appreciate them, interact with them, and learn from them. The copyright system works because, in addition to encouraging authors to create works and communicate them to the public, it encourages audiences to read, listen, look at, learn from, and interact with those works.

[10] *See* Authors Guild, Inc. v. HathiTrust, 755 F.3d 87 (2d Cir. 2014), *aff'g* 954 F. Supp. 2d 282 (S.D.N.Y. 2013). When the district court upheld HathiTrust's fair use defense, one rightsholder representative reportedly described the decision as the 21st century's *Plessy v. Ferguson. See* http://policynotes.arl .org/post/79876737815/recap-of-the-copyright-offices-roundtables-on-orphan; Preservation and Reuse of Copyrighted Works: Hearing Before the Subcomm. On Courts, Intellectual Property, and the Internet of the House Judiciary Comm., 113th Cong. (2014) (Serial # 113-88) (testimony of James Neal, Columbia University). That's silly. There are lots of copies in the HathiTrust archive, but nobody actually sees them; nobody can read them. The copies make it possible to index, to perform sophisticated digital analysis of the text, and to attach metadata that tells us who owns the copyright and when the work will enter the public domain. None of that has ever been an infringement of copyright. *See, e.g.,* New York Times v. Roxbury Data Interface, 434 F. Supp. 217 (S.D.N.Y. 1977). The digital copies allow remote readers to search the text and discover that a particular word is in the book, but not to see so much as a snippet of the text itself. They make it possible to generate readable copies for print-disabled readers, which is explicitly permitted under 17 U.S.C. § 121. No licensing market has arisen for these uses and it is difficult to imagine how such a market could be designed. For most of the works in the HathiTrust collection, there is no easy way to ascertain the identity of the people or businesses that would be entitled to give permission for these uses if permission were required. The primary objection to what HathiTrust is doing is the largely noneconomic objection that the archive has a bunch of digital copies that nobody sees or reads, and that it didn't get licenses for those copies.

[11] *See, e.g.,* White v. West Publishing, 12-CV-01340 (SDNY Feb. 11, 2013); Am. Inst. of Physics v. Winstead, 109 USPQ 2d 1661 (N.D. Tex. 2013); Shell v. City of Radford, Virginia, 351 F. Supp. 2d 510 (W.D. Va. 2005).

[12] *See, e.g.,* Margot Kaminski, *The Capture of International Intellectual Property Law Through the U.S. Trade Regime,* 87 S. CAL. L. REV. 977 (2014).

[13] *See, e.g.,* Darren Hudson Hick, *Mystery and Misdirection: Some Problems of Fair Use and Users' Rights,* 56 J. COPYRIGHT SOC'Y U.S.A. 485 (2008).

The opportunities for readers, listeners, and viewers to read, hear, see, learn from, enjoy, and use works of authorship have always been among copyright law's most crucial features. For U.S. copyright law's first two centuries, it was rarely important to worry explicitly about the copyright rights of readers, listeners, and viewers, because the law left reading, listening, and viewing alone. Copyright law might have burdened the enjoyment of copyrighted works by supporting a system in which copies were scarce, overpriced, or both, but it didn't impinge directly on reading, seeing, or hearing those works. Publishers or bookstores that distributed books that were plagiarized from other works might have faced liability under the copyright law,[14] but it was never unlawful to read the books. George Harrison's *My Sweet Lord* might have infringed Ronald Mack's *He's So Fine*,[15] but Harrison fans who heard the song over the radio or played it on their phonographs were not themselves doing anything illegal.[16] Indeed, if, upon learning that Harrison had lost a copyright infringement suit, fans had run out and bought recordings of *My Sweet Lord* on CDs, they would not have had to worry about copyright liability for their purchases. The owners of the Skyline Supperclub may have been willful infringers when the club's band played *Proud Mary* and *I Heard it Through the Grapevine* without a performance license,[17] but the customers who danced to the music were not. Museum patrons who saw an infringing photograph hanging on the wall of the museum and bought postcards of it in the museum shop did not face even theoretical liability for copyright infringement unless and until they chose to send the postcard through the mail. Even though McDonald's McDonaldland commercials infringed Sid and Mary Krofft's *H.R. PuffNStuff* programs,[18] children who watched the McDonaldland commercials on television were not liable for seeing them, nor for begging their parents to dine at McDonald's because they were fans of Mayor McCheese.

Copyright law has traditionally sheltered readers, listeners, and viewers from liability for enjoying infringing works. That shelter is not an inadvertent failure to extend the law's reach to its logical targets, but a crucial mechanism for encouraging the use and enjoyment of works of authorship, and thereby promoting the progress of science. Rather than giving owners a broad general right to control all uses of their works, the copyright law has always conferred bounded exclusive rights that

---

[14] *See, e.g.,* Salinger v. Colting, 607 F.3d 68 (2d Cir. 2010); Horgan v. Macmillan, 789 F.2d 157 (2d Cir. 1986).

[15] *See* Bright Tunes Music v. Harrisongs Music Ltd., 420 F. Supp. 177 (SDNY 1976), *aff'd in part, rev'd in part sub. nom.* ABKCO Music v. Harrisongs Music, 722 F.2d 988 (2d Cir. 1983).

[16] *But see* Worlds of Wonder Inc. v. Vector Intercontinental, 1 U.S.P.Q. 2d 1982 (N.D. Ohio 1986) (children who played unlicensed tapes in their Teddy Ruxpin toys created unauthorized derivative works; therefore the makers of the tapes were willful contributory infringers).

[17] *See* Broad. Music v. Davis, 1986 U.S. Dist Lexis 27005 (D.S.C. 1986).

[18] *See* Sid & Marty Krofft Television Prods. v. McDonalds Corp., 562 F.2d 1157 (9th Cir. 1977).

preserve sizeable zones of liberty for members of the public.[19] Copyright owners are not entitled to control many valuable uses of their works, including private distributions, performances, or displays. The challenges of adapting copyright law to the networked digital environment and copyright owners' effort to extend their exclusive rights to encompass control of any and all copies of their works are putting those zones of liberty at risk.

In the 21st century, we've seen significant erosion in reader liberties. Some of the erosion has been technological. Networked digital technology gives copyright owners and their agents abilities to monitor and meter what we read, hear, and see. This turns out to be useful if one seeks to sell our eyes and ears to advertisers.[20] Vendors of books, music, and movies use this information to recommend other items we might want to buy.[21] Publishers of digital textbooks convey detailed information about students' reading of assigned texts to their instructors to enable them to "assess student engagement" and intervene with individual students who may not have read the assignment with sufficient attention.[22] Because it can be both handy and profitable, businesses have equipped digital platforms for enjoying copyrighted works with technology that can identify, report, and disable users and their uses.[23]

Some of the erosion, though, has been legal. Vendors of works of authorship have moved from selling copies of works to a licensing model in which they detail which uses are permitted and which are prohibited.[24] They have yielded to the temptation to load the purported licenses up with multiple niggling conditions, exclusions, and bans.[25]

---

[19] *See generally* Jessica Litman, *Lawful Personal Use*, 85 Tex. L. Rev. 1871 (2007).

[20] *See, e.g.*, J. Howard Beales & Jeffrey A. Eisenach, An Empirical Analysis of the Value of Information Sharing in the Market for Online Content, Study conducted by Navigant Economics on behalf of the Digital Advertising Alliance, Jan. 2014, at www.aboutads.info/resource/fullvalueinfostudy.pdf; *Deliver One-To-One Personalization with Quantifiable Results*, Maxymiser, www.maxymiser.com/products/online-personalization (visited Aug. 4, 2014).

[21] *See, e.g.*, *About Recommendations*, Amazon.com, www.amazon.com/gp/help/customer/display.html/ref=hp_left_sib?ie=UTF8&nodeId=16465251 (visited Aug. 4, 2014); *iTunes: Genius*, Apple, www.apple.com/itunes/features/ (visited Aug. 4, 2014); Netflix, Netflix Taste Preferences and Recommendations, https://help.netflix.com/en/node/9898?catId=en%2F131 (visited Aug. 4, 2014).

[22] *See* www.coursesmart.com/.

[23] *See, e.g.*, Electronic Frontier Foundation, *Who's Tracking Your Reading Habits? An e_Book Buyer's Guide to Privacy*, Nov. 29, 2012, at www.eff.org/deeplinks/2012/11/e-reader-privacy-chart-2012-update; *About Canoe Ventures*, Canoe, www.canoe-ventures.com/about.html (visited Aug. 6, 2014); Chris Kanaracus, *Oracle Builds on Blue Kai Acquisition with Data Cloud*, PC World (July 22, 2014), at www.pcworld.com/article/2457000/oracle-builds-on-bluekai-acquisition-with-data-cloud.html; *About Leap Media Investments*, Leap Media, www.leapmediainvestments.com/about.php (visited Aug. 6, 2014).

[24] *See generally* Margaret Jane Radin, Boilerplate (2012); Aaron Perzanowski & Jason Schultz, *Reconciling Intellectual and Personal Property*, 90 Notre Dame L. Rev. 1211 (2015).

[25] *See, e.g.*, Cory Doctorow, *Even Amazon Can't Keep Its EULA Story Straight*, BoingBoing, Jan. 12, 2010, at http://boingboing.net/2010/01/12/even-amazon-cant-kee.html.

Publishers of some works of authorship have combined their copyright rights, license terms, and legal prohibitions on circumvention of technological protections into florid schemes of user control that interfere with reader, listener, and viewer enjoyment of the works they purchase.[26]

When the legal erosion in reader, listener, and viewer copyright liberties meets up with copyright owners' appetite for enhanced control over all uses of their works, the combination creates a genuine danger that our copyright system will discourage rather than encourage reading, listening, and viewing. Indeed, the notion that readers, listeners, viewers, and other members of the public have cognizable interests in the copyright system strikes many copyright lawyers as both radical and unreasonable. The public's interest, they insist, is entirely congruent with the interests of copyright owners in a strong copyright system with powerful enforcement mechanisms.[27] Their insistence is accompanied by bitter complaints painting members of the public as hordes of ravening freewatchers,[28] but they don't appear to notice the irony.

The archetypal copy-fetish, familiar to all copyright scholars, is copyright owners' inconstant devotion to the infringing Random Access Memory copy.[29] (I call the devotion inconstant because even the most enthusiastic backers of the notion that unlicensed RAM copies infringe copyrights ignore the possibility of RAM fixation when it suits them.[30]) It's difficult to argue with a straight face that Congress

---

[26] *See, e.g.*, Perzanowski & Schultz, *supra* note 24, at 1235-38; Nick Valery, *Difference Engine, Wanted: A Tinkerer's Charter, Babbage Science and Technology*, THE ECONOMIST, Aug. 4, 2014, at www .economist.com/blogs/babbage/2014/08/difference-engine.

[27] *See, e.g.*, MARK HELPRIN, DIGITAL BARBARISM: A WRITER'S MANIFESTO 131–35 (2009); Terry Hart, Copyright Is for the Author First and the Nation Second, COPYHYPE, Oct. 23, 2012, at www.copyhype .com/2012/10/copyright-is-for-the-author-first-and-the-nation-second/; Terry Hart, *Copyright, the Public Interest, and Free Trade*, COPYRIGHT ALLIANCE BLOG, Mar. 25, 2014, at https://copyrightalliance .org/2014/03/copyright_public_interest_and_free_trade; Koenigsberg, *supra* note 3, at 681–89.

[28] *See, e.g.*, Helprin, *supra* note 27, at 37–39; Terry Hart, *Expendables 3 and the Negative Effects of Piracy*, COPYHYPE, July 30, 2014, at www.copyhype.com/2014/07/expendables-3-and-the-negative-effects-of-piracy/; Koenigsberg, *supra* note 3, at 680; Tim League & Ruth Vitale, *Guest Post: Here's How Piracy Hurts Indie Film*, INDIEWIRE, July 11, 2014, at www.indiewire.com/article/guest-post-heres-how-piracy-hurts-indie-film-20140711; Ruth Vitale, *We're All Waiting Bittorrent*, CREATIVE FUTURE BLOG, July 31, 2014, at http://creativefuture.org/were-waiting-bittorrent/. *See also* Chris Ruen, *Fifteen Years of Utter Bollocks: How a Generation's Freeloading Has Starved Creativity*, NEW STATESMAN, July 16, 2014, at www.newstatesman.com/culture/2014/07/fifteen-years-utter-bollocks-how-generation-s-freeloading-has-starved-creativity

[29] *See* Jane C. Ginsburg, *Copyright 1992–2012: The Most Significant Development?*, 23 FORDHAM INTELL. PROP. MEDIA & ENT. L.J. 465, 467–71 (2013); Jane C. Ginsburg, *From Having Copies to Experiencing Works*, 50 J. COPYRIGHT SOC'Y 113, 121–22 & n.21 (2002); Aaron Perzanowski, *Fixing RAM Copies*, 104 NORTHWESTERN L. REV. 1067 (2010).

[30] *See, e.g.*, Digital Millennium Copyright Act Section 104 Report: Hearing Before the Subcomm. on Courts, Intellectual Property, and the Internet of the House Judiciary Comm., 107th Cong. 24 (2001) (Serial # 107-52) (testimony of Cary Sherman, Recording Industry Ass'n of Am.); Reply Memorandum

intended in 1976 to make RAM copies actionable; all the available evidence supports the contrary view. The doctrine that the reproduction right encompassed RAM copies, rather, resulted from a combination of ambitious lawyering, clueless judging, and dumb luck.

When Congress enacted the 1976 Act, it limited eligibility for copyright protection and the scope of the reproduction right to tangible embodiments of works. The statute's definitions of copies and fixation, Congress wrote, "would exclude from the concept purely evanescent or transient reproductions such as those projected briefly on a screen, shown electronically on a television or other cathode ray tube, or captured momentarily in the 'memory' of a computer."[31] In 1991, though, customer service manager Eric Francis and three of his coworkers left their jobs at MAI Computing to work for a competitor. In his new job, Francis serviced and maintained computers leased to customers by his former employer. MAI filed suit against Francis and his new employer on a variety of grounds, including copyright infringement, misappropriation of trade secrets, trademark infringement, false advertising, and unfair competition. Francis had signed non-disclosure and non-compete agreements with MAI. The district court judge was apparently convinced that he had grievously injured his former employer, because Judge Real granted MAI's motion for a summary judgment on the trade secrecy claim, and, for good measure, also granted MAI's summary judgment on the copyright, trademark, false advertising, and unfair competition claims.[32] The court based its copyright infringement determination on two uses: first, Peak had computers on its premises that ran MAI software for which it had not secured licenses, and second, Peak's employees ran MAI software on customers' MAI computers when they serviced them. The court reasoned that

> the loading of copyrighted computer software from a storage medium (hard disk, floppy disk, or read only memory) into the memory of a central processing unit ("CPU") causes a copy to be made. In the absence of ownership of the copyright or express permission by license, such acts constitute copyright infringement.[33]

Peak appealed to the 9th Circuit, which affirmed. The court of appeals agreed with MAI that when Peak employees turned on computers leased from MAI on its customers' premises, an infringing copy resulted.

> Peak concedes that in maintaining its customer's computers, it uses MAI operating software "to the extent that the repair and maintenance process necessarily involves

of Law in Further Support of Plaintiff's motion for Partial Summary Judgment at 5 n.1, Capitol Records v. Redigi, 934 F. Supp. 2d 640 (S.D.N.Y. 2013) (No. 12-Civ-0095); *infra* note 44 and accompanying text.
[31] H.R. Rep. 1476, 94th Cong. 53 (1976).
[32] MAI Systems v. Peak Computer, 991 F.2d 511 (9th Cir 1993), *aff'g* 1992 U.S. Dist. LEXIS 21829 (C.D. Cal. 1992).
[33] 1992 U.S. Dist LEXIS at *36-37.

turning on the computer to make sure it is functional and thereby running the operating system." It is also uncontroverted that when the computer is turned on the operating system is loaded into the computer's RAM. As part of diagnosing a computer problem at the customer site, the Peak technician runs the computer's operating system software, allowing the technician to view the systems error log, which is part of the operating system, thereby enabling the technician to diagnose the problem.

Peak argues that this loading of copyrighted software does not constitute a copyright violation because the "copy" created in RAM is not "fixed." However, by showing that Peak loads the software into the RAM and is then able to view the system error log and diagnose the problem with the computer, MAI has adequately shown that the representation created in the RAM is "sufficiently permanent or stable to permit it to be perceived, reproduced, or otherwise communicated for a period of more than transitory duration."[34]

This reasoning was unexpected.[35] Representative Joe Knollenberg introduced a bill to reverse the result.[36] Copyright owners, though, having been handed a shiny new tool, were loath to give it up. Colleagues persuaded Representative Knollenberg to narrow his legislation so that it permitted computer maintenance and repair firms, but not others, to turn on computers without incurring liability for copyright infringement.[37] Meanwhile, the Clinton Administration Task Force on the National Information Infrastructure seized on the RAM copy notion to support a vision of the Internet for which every individual would need copyright permission to look at or listen to anything posted online.[38] Congress enacted Knollenberg's narrowed

---

[34] 991 F.2d at 519.

[35] *See, e.g.,* Michael E. Johnson, *Note: The Uncertain Future of Computer Software Users' Rights in the Aftermath of MAI Systems,* 44 DUKE L.J. 327 (1994); Jule L. Sigall, *Comment: Copyright Infringement Was Never this Easy: RAM Copies and Their Impact on the Scope of Copyright Protection in Computer Programs,* 45 CATHOLIC U. L. REV. 181 (1995); Pamela Samuelson, *Legally Speaking: The NII Intellectual Property Report,* Communications of the ACM, at 21 (Dec. 1994).

[36] H.R. 533, 104th Cong. (1995).

[37] *See* H.R. 72, 105th Cong. (1997); 143 Cong. Rec. E21 (Jan. 1, 1997) (remarks of Rep. Knollenberg); 143 Cong. Rec. H7102 (remarks of Rep. Knollenberg). Congress enacted the narrowed legislation as Title III of the Digital Millennium Copyright Act.

[38] *See* INFORMATION INFRASTRUCTURE TASK FORCE, INTELLECTUAL PROPERTY AND THE NATIONAL INFORMATION INFRASTRUCTURE 64–66 (1995), at www.uspto.gov/web/offices/com/doc/ipnii/ipnii .pdf. The White House's Information Infrastructure Task Force authored a White Paper Report that became the basis for the 1998 Digital Millennium Copyright Act, Pub. L. 105–304, 112 Stat. 2860, and for the U.S. negotiating position in connection with some of the provisions of the World Intellectual Property Organization (WIPO) Treaties discussed *infra* notes 59–61 and accompanying text. The White Paper asserted that whenever a computer user viewed a file that resided on a remote computer, the image on the user's screen and the copies of the file made by every computer that helped to transfer the file would be potentially infringing copies. INFORMATION INFRASTRUCTURE TASK FORCE, *supra,* at 65–66.

legislation and asked the Copyright Office to study the issue.[39] The Copyright Office reported that RAM copies should be deemed within the scope of the copyright owner's reproduction right. "In establishing the dividing line between those reproductions that are subject to the reproduction right and those that are not, we believe that Congress intended the copyright owner's exclusive right to extend to all reproductions from which economic value can be derived."[40] A statutory exemption for temporary copies incidental to lawful uses was not warranted, the Copyright Office concluded, because advocates for users had failed to make a compelling case that such an exemption was necessary.[41] Meanwhile, the Office characterized the risks of adding a new privilege to the statute as "significant:"

> Copyright owners have pointed out with justification that the reproduction right is the "cornerstone of the edifice of copyright protection" and that exceptions from that right should not be made lightly. In the absence of specific, identifiable harm, the risk of foreclosing legitimate business opportunities based on copyright owners' exploitation of their exclusive reproduction right counsels against creating a broad exception to that right.[42]

Even though the Register of Copyrights explained to Congress that RAM copies should be deemed to be actionable reproductions,[43] she appears not to have fully believed it. When the introduction of software that allowed individual viewers to skip sexually explicit or violent scenes in DVDs they watched inspired a copyright infringement suit, the Register testified to Congress that there was no need to amend the copyright law because using the software did not infringe any copyrights. That was so, she insisted, because the censored versions of the film created by the software were never fixed.[44] But, of course, if RAM copies are copies, the censored versions of the film were

---

[39] Digital Millennium Copyright Act, Pub. L. 105–304 §§ 104, 301, 302, 112 Stat. 2860, 2876, 2886, 2887 (Oct. 28, 1998).

[40] U.S. COPYRIGHT OFFICE, DMCA SECTION 104 REPORT (2001), www.copyright.gov/reports/studies/dmca/sec-104-report-vol-1.pdf.

[41] *Id.* at 130.

[42] *Id.* at 142. The Copyright Office did support a narrow amendment to relieve licensed digital transmitters of sound recordings from liability for buffer copies that were incidental to the licensed transmissions. The Office thought that such buffer copies should be sheltered by the fair use privilege, but expressed sympathy for webcasters who faced copyright owners' demand for double compensation. *See id.* at 142–46.

[43] *See* The Digital Millennium Copyright Act (DMCA) Section 104 Report: Hearing Before the Subcomm. of Courts, Intellectual Property, and the Internet of the House Judiciary Comm., 107th Cong. 15 (2001) (Serial # 107-52) (Statement of MaryBeth Peters, Register of Copyrights) ("[W]e recommend against the adoption of a general exemption from the reproduction right to render non-infringing all temporary copies that are incidental to lawful uses. . . ."), also at www.copyright.gov/docs/regstat121201.html.

[44] *See* the Family Movie Act: Hearing on H.R. 4077 Before the Subcomm. of Courts, Intellectual Property, and the Internet of the House Judiciary Comm., 108th Cong. 28 (2004) (Serial # 108-94)

fixed in the DVD players' RAM. That is, after all, how the software enabled viewers to skip scenes.

Some courts adopted the 9th Circuit's reasoning,[45] although many decisions purporting to follow the decision applied it to indisputably fixed copies of software installed on computers and saved in durable computer storage.[46] Other courts reasoned around it.[47] In many other cases in which it might have had determinative effect, neither party raised it.[48]

Twenty years after the MAI opinion, a Commerce Department task force report characterized the RAM copy doctrine as well-settled:

> The right to reproduce a work in copies is the first and most fundamental of the bundle of rights that make up a copyright. In the online environment, this right is even more central, as copies are made in the course of virtually every network transmission of a digital copy. Temporary copies may be a key aspect of the value of the use in some circumstances, but merely incidental in others.

> The ability to control temporary copying in digital devices has long been important to rights owners. For software in particular, consumers increasingly engage in the exploitation of software they receive over a network without ever knowingly storing a permanent copy on their hard drive. Temporary copies are also prevalent in the context of streaming sound recordings and video, where "buffer copies" are a technologically necessary step in the delivery of content to the consumer.

> It has long been clear in U.S. law that the reproduction right is not limited solely to the making of "permanent" physical copies. The statutory definitions cover any fixation "sufficiently permanent or stable to permit it to be perceived, reproduced, or otherwise communicated for a period of more than transitory duration." In the seminal 1993 case *MAI Systems Corp. v. Peak Computer, Inc.*, the Ninth Circuit

(Statement of MaryBeth Peters, Register of Copyrights) ("There is no infringement of the reproduction right because no unauthorized copies of the motion pictures are made"). While agreeing with the Register that the censored versions of the films created by this technology were not fixed, the Motion Picture Association of America's Jack Valenti nonetheless opposed the bill because it threatened to undermine the right to make derivative works: "The law tells us, with great clarity, that the owner of a copyrighted work – and only that owner – has the authority to decide if someone else may produce a product derived from that copyrighted work ... The movie filtering bill would seriously erode that core right by legalizing businesses that sell technology, for a profit, which can 'skip and mute' scenes or dialogue to create an abridged version of a movie, as long as no 'fixed copy' of the altered version is created." *Id.* at 38.

[45] *See, e.g.*, Quantum Sys. Integrators, Inc. v. Sprint Nextel Corp., 338 Fed. App'x 329, 336–37 (4th Cir. 2009); Intellectual Reserve, Inc. v. Utah Lighthouse Ministry, Inc., 75 F. Supp. 2d 1290, 1294 (D. Utah 1999); Religious Tech. Ctr. v. Netcom, 907 F. Supp. 1361, 1368–73 (N.D. Cal. 1995).

[46] *See, e.g.*, Stenograph LLC v. Bossard Assocs., 144 F.3d 90 (D.C. Cir. 1998).

[47] See, e.g., Cartoon Network v. CSC Holdings, 536 F3d 121 (2d Cir 2008); DSC Commc'ns Corp. v. DGI Techs. Inc., 81 F.3d 597 (5th Cir. 1996); NLFC, Inc. v. Devcom Mid-America, Inc., 45 F.3d 231, 235–36 (7th Cir. 1995).

[48] *See, e.g.*, Flava Works v. Gunter, 689 F.3d 754 (7th Cir. 2013).

applied these definitions to hold that when a program is loaded into RAM, a copy is created. In a 2001 Report, the Copyright Office confirmed its agreement, noting that "[a]lthough it is theoretically possible that information ... could be stored in RAM for such a short period of time that it could not be retrieved, displayed, copied or communicated, this is unlikely to happen in practice."[49]

My own story about the RAM copy and the *MAI* case is that the 9th Circuit Court of Appeals just made a mistake – courts do that all the time.[50] MAI's victory on its copyright infringement claim was improbable, but once it fell into copyright owners' laps, they became determined to retain it, even if they couldn't figure out exactly how to use it. If we cling to the determination that all RAM copies are actually actionable, though, and if we take it seriously, the reproduction right morphs into an all-purpose use right, covering, e.g., playing DVDs on a DVD player, watching TV on a digital TV; reading any ebook; or listening to music on a smartphone or MP3 player. That's not sustainable. All private performances on digital devices turn into actionable reproductions. This would be a major incursion on the interests of readers, listeners, and viewers, who have until now been able to count on a significant zone of freedom within which they can enjoy works of authorship that they have purchased or licensed.

The problem with the RAM copy is that making a RAM copy is just another name for private performance or display, which is to say, reading, listening, and viewing.[51] Private performance and display are not actionable. The copyright act has historically divided reproduction and distribution, and later, public performance, from reading, listening, and watching. The copyright owner has (some) control over the former activities but not the latter, because unfettered reading, listening, and viewing are as crucial to the promotion of the progress of science as encouraging the creation of new works. One half of the equation is meaningless without the other.

It has never before been copyright infringement to read a book, even if it turns out that the book is plagiarized from an earlier book. I can listen to an infringing recording or look at an infringing photograph without fear of liability. The RAM copy notion suddenly imposes liability for seeing, hearing, or enjoying any work using digital technology. There's no policy justification for that expansion in copyright scope: yes, if my reading the wrong ebook makes me an infringer, one can sue the ebook publisher as a contributory infringer, but one can sue the ebook publisher as a direct infringer anyway, so the only real effect is to burden and deter reading.

[49] Department of Commerce Internet Policy Task Force Report, *supra* note 1, at 12–13 (footnotes omitted).
[50] *See, e.g.,* Bridgeport Music v. Dimension Films, 410 F.3d 792 (6th Cir. 2005).
[51] *See, e.g.,* Jessica Litman, *The Exclusive Right to Read,* 13 Cardozo Arts & Ent. L.J. 29, 31–32 (1994). Contrast the approach taken by the European Union. *See, e.g.,* Public Relations Consultants Ass'n v. Newspaper Licensing Agency Ltd. & Ors (Judgment of the Court) [2014] EUECJ C-360/13 (5 June 2014) (holding RAM copies non-infringing under EU Directive).

A copyright system designed to deter reading has completely lost its moorings and forgotten its purpose.

As we move to increasing reliance on cloud computing, the problem becomes more acute. Every time an individual views, hears, reads, or edits her files in the cloud, she creates potentially actionable RAM copies. If she commits prima facie infringement against the owners of rights in the songs, stories, software, movies, and other expression in those files whenever she consults them, then centuries of key reader liberties will have vaporized.

A more recent outbreak of copy-fetish has inspired the quest for an expansive "making available" right. The essence of infringement of the making available right is the possession of a copy (legitimate or not) that is accessible to other people. Again, the story begins with a difficult-to-justify opinion from a Court of Appeals. In *Hotaling v. Church of Jesus Christ of Latter Day Saints*, the Court of Appeals for the Fourth Circuit held that "a library distributes a published work, within the meaning of the Copyright Act … when it places an unauthorized copy of the work in its collection, includes the copy in its catalog or index system, and makes the copy available to the public."[52] Donna and William Hotaling sued the Mormon Church because Donna had discovered an unauthorized microfiche copy of her genealogical research in the Church library. The Church had purchased an authorized copy in 1985, and had made unlicensed microfiche copies for its branch libraries. In 1991, when the Hotalings discovered the unlicensed copies and complained, the church recalled and destroyed them, but retained a single microfiche copy as a replacement for its original purchased copy, which had been inadvertently destroyed.[53] In 1995, Donna visited the church's main library, discovered the microfiche copy, and filed suit. The church acknowledged having made the microfiche copy years earlier, but insisted that it had engaged in no reproduction or distribution within the 3-year limitations period. The library allowed patrons to consult materials on the premises, but did not permit them to check those materials out of the library.[54] Thus, the church insisted, it had not distributed any copies of the copyrighted work to the public.[55]

A divided Fourth Circuit concluded that the combination of possessing an unauthorized copy, listing the work in its card catalogue, and enabling members of the public to view the copy on its premises, should be deemed to be distribution, even though the copy didn't leave the library.[56] As an interpretation of statutory language

---

[52] Hotaling v. Church of Jesus Christ of Latter Day Saints, 118 F.3d 199, 201 (4th Cir. 1997).

[53] The church argued that its retention of this copy was authorized by 17 U.S.C. § 108(c). The 4th Circuit declined to reach that question. Hotaling, 118 F.3d at 204.

[54] *Id.* at 205 (Hall, J., dissenting).

[55] *Id.* at 203 (majority opinion).

[56] *Id.*

that restricts distribution to the conveyance of copies to the public "by sale or other transfer of ownership or by rental, lease, or lending," the decision seems indefensible.[57] Some observers theorized that the Fourth Circuit had been influenced by evidence that the library had engaged in unauthorized reproductions and distributions outside of the limitations period.[58]

Coincidentally, the phrase "making available" also appeared in a pair of copyright treaties negotiated in 1996 (a year before the *Hotaling* decision) and ratified by the United States in 1998 (a year after *Hotaling*). The WIPO Copyright Treaty and the WIPO Performances and Phonograms Treaty obliged signatory nations to protect authors' "exclusive right of authorizing the making available to the public of the original and copies of their works through sale or other transfer of ownership"[59] and their "exclusive right of authorizing any communication to the public of their works by wired or wireless means, including the making available to the public of their works...."[60] The two "making available" provisions limited themselves, in terms, to making available by transferring copies to the public and making available by transmitting works to the public by wired or wireless means. At the time that Congress implemented the treaties, supporters assured Congress that extant U.S. law amply provided for the exclusive rights of communicating a work to the public. The making available provisions of the treaties were coextensive with the U.S. statute's rights, under section 106 to distribute copies ("by sale or other transfer of ownership or by rental, lease, or lending") and to perform or display a work publicly.[61]

---

[57] *See, e.g.,* WILLIAM F. PATRY, PATRY ON COPYRIGHT § 13.9 (2014). *But see* Joseph F. Key, *Recent Decisions: the U.S. Court of Appeals for the Fourth Circuit,* 57 MD. L. REV. 1157, 1174 (1998) (arguing that the decision was correct even though it was inconsistent with the statutory language because of the "unique nature of non-circulating research material in the library context").

[58] *See, e.g.,* Robert Kasunic, *Making Circumstantial Proof of Distribution Available,* 18 FORDHAM INTELL. PROP. MEDIA & ENT. L.J. 1145, 1149 n.14, 1153 n.28 (2008).

[59] WIPO Copyright Treaty art. 6. *See also* WIPO Performances and Phonograms Treaty art. 8 ("Performers shall enjoy the exclusive right of authorizing the making available to the public of the original and copies of their performances fixed in phonograms through sale or other transfer of ownership.").

[60] WIPO Copyright Treaty art. 8; *see also* WIPO Performances and Phonograms Treaty art. 10 ("Performers shall enjoy the exclusive right of authorizing the making available to the public of their performances fixed in phonograms, by wire or wireless means, in such a way that members of the public may access them from a place and at a time individually chosen by them.").

[61] *See, e.g.,* WIPO Copyright Treaties Implementation Act and Online Copyright Liability Limitation Act: Hearing on HR 2281 and HR 2280 Before the Subcomm. on Courts and Intellectual Property of the House Comm. On the Judiciary, 105th Cong. 43- 54 (1997) (Serial # 105-33) (testimony of MaryBeth Peters, Register of Copyrights); *id.* at 72–3 (statement of Robert Holleyman, President, Business Software Alliance). As should be evident, the conduct at issue in *Hotaling* neither involved "sale or other transfer of ownership" nor "communication to the public by wired or wireless means," so it would have fallen outside the making available rights secured by the language of the treaties.

The *Hotaling* opinion's expansion of the statutory distribution right to encompass something it called "making available" that did not involve the transfer or loan of copies might have been limited to that case's particular circumstances were it not for the fact that the Fourth Circuit's analysis scratched an itch that troubled the recording industry. After Napster appeared on the scene, record labels faced difficulty demonstrating that their sound recordings had been reproduced or distributed to the public by the users of peer-to-peer file sharing software. It was easy for their investigators to ascertain that individual users had copies of particular recordings in the "share" files associated with their peer-to-peer clients, but not to determine where those copies had come from, nor whether other members of the public had copied them.

The recording industry seized on the *Hotaling* decision as a solution to that problem. Citing *Hotaling*, the labels argued that they did not need to introduce evidence of actual copying of any recordings because the presence of a file in a share directory, without more, violated the public distribution right by making the file available for copying.[62] Other copyright owners followed. Motion picture studios insisted that the making available right included in the treaties entitled copyright owners to control any offering of copyrighted works to the public, without regard to the actual distribution of copies.[63] The *Perfect 10* magazine and website argued that, under *Hotaling*, search engines violated its distribution right when they returned search results that included links to infringing copies of its erotic photographs.[64] Some courts were persuaded.[65] Other courts found the argument that "making available" should be deemed distribution of a copy to the public "by sale or other transfer of ownership or by rental lease or lending" inconsistent with the text of section 106(3).[66] Copyright scholar Peter Menell, in a highly selective exploration of the statute's legislative history, claimed to have discovered evidence that Congress had intended courts to find a violation of the distribution right whenever unlicensed copies were

---

[62] *See, e.g.*, Atl. Recording v. Howell, 554 F. Supp. 2d 976, 981–84 (D. Ariz. 2008); In re Napster, Inc. Copyright Litig., 377 F. Supp. 2d 796, 802–05 (N.D. Cal. 2005).

[63] *See* Brief of MPAA as Amicus Curiae, Capitol Records v. Thomas, 579 F. Supp. 2d 1210 (D. Minn. 2008) (No. 06-1497), at www.eff.org/node/55647.

[64] *See* Brief of Appellant Perfect 10, Perfect 10 v. Amazon.com, 508 F.3d 1146 (9th Cir. 2007) (No. 06-55405), 2006 US 9th Cir. Briefs 55406, at 41–42.

[65] *See, e.g.*, UMG Recordings v. Green, 2009 US Dist LEXIS 39305 (N.D.N.Y. 2009); Sony BMG Music v. Doe, 2008 US Dist LEXIS 106088 (E.D.N.C. 2008); Universal City Studios v. Bigwood, 441 F. Supp. 2d 185 (D. Me. 2006).

[66] *See, e.g.*, Atl. Recording v. Howell, 554 F. Supp. 2d 976 (D. Ariz. 2008); Capitol Records v. Thomas, 579 F. Supp. 2d 1210, 1216–26 (D. Minn. 2008); London-Sire Records v. Doe, 542 F. Supp. 2d 153 (D. Mass. 2008); Elektra Entm't v. Barker, 551 F. Supp. 2d 234 (S.D.N.Y. 2008). *See also* Capitol Records v. Thomas-Rasset, 692 F.3d 899 (8th Cir. 2012) (declining to reach issue); Arista Record v. Doe, 604 F.3d 110 (2010) (same); Maverick Recording v. Harper, 598 F.3d 193 (5th Cir. 2010) (same); Warner Bros. Records v. Walker, 704 F. Supp. 460 (W.D. Pa. 2010) (same).

made available to the public.[67] For the majority of courts, though, the difficulty of squaring that interpretation with the statutory language dissuaded them from interpreting the distribution right to encompass making available without the transfer of tangible copies.[68]

Advocates for copyright owners have continued to argue that *Hotaling* was correctly decided, that the *Hotaling* construction represented the true meaning of the "making available" language in the WIPO treaties, and that the U.S. adherence to the WIPO Treaties therefore requires U.S. copyright law to give owners a robust right to recover for the existence of unlicensed, publicly accessible copies, whether or not any transfer of copies or public transmission has occurred.[69] A broad making available right, untethered to actual distributions or public performances, would give copyright owners a formidable weapon to deploy against Internet-enabled digital video recorders, cyberlockers, search engines, and cloud storage. Having glimpsed a law that would empower them to lay claim to control all publicly accessible copies, copyright owners are disinclined to give it up.

The Copyright Office is currently conducting a study on the making available right.[70] The premise of the study appears to be that if the U.S. law's protection of a making available right falls short of the right as defined by *Hotaling*, Congress should intervene to correct the problem. At a hearing in May 2014, the office expressed its position that U.S. copyright law *should* include a broad making available right and indicated that it would focus its study on whether it was necessary

---

[67] Peter S. Menell, *In Search of Copyright's Lost Ark: Interpreting the Right to Distribute in the Internet Age*, 59 J. COPYRIGHT SOC'Y 201, 233–66 (2012).

[68] *See, e.g.,* Fox Broad. v. Dish Network, 905 F. Supp. 2d 1088 (C.D. Cal. 2012), *aff'd* 723 F.3d 1067 (9th Cir. 2013); Shannon's Rainbow LLV v. Supernova Media, 2011 US Dist LEXIS 9275 (D. Utah 2011). See generally Patry, *supra* note 57, § 13.9.

[69] *See, e.g.,* Capitol Records v. Thomas, 579 F. Supp. 2d 1210, 1226 (D. Minn. 2008); U.S. Copyright Office, Public Roundtable on the Right of Making Available 329–32 (May 5, 2014), at www.copyright .gov/docs/making_available/public-roundtable/transcript.pdf (remarks of Steve Tep, U.S. Chamber of Commerce); Comments of the MPAA and the RIAA Before the Copyright Office In the Matter of Study of the Right of Making Available 3 (April 4, 2014), www.copyright .gov/docs/making_available/comments/docket2014_2/MPAA.pdf ("Where a party provides the public access to copyrighted works via the Internet without authorization – as a download, a stream, a link or otherwise – that party infringes one or more of the affected copyright owner's exclusive rights under Section 106 of the Act. It is not necessary to prove that any user actually availed herself of such access."); Brief Amici Curiae of International Federation of the Phonographic Industry et al. at 13–15, ABC v. Aereo, 134 S. Ct. 2498 (2014) (No 13–461), at http:// sblog.s3.amazonaws.com/wp-content/uploads/2014/04/13-461_pet_amcu_ifpi-etal.authcheckdam .pdf; Thomas Syndor, *The Making Available Right Under U.S. Law*, 16 PROGRESS ON POINT 7, Progress & Freedom Foundation (Mar. 2009). *See* William F. Patry, *MPAA's Brief and Charming Betsy*, PATRY COPYRIGHT BLOG, June 24, 2008, at http://williampatry.blogspot.com/2008/06/mpaas-brief-and-charming-betsy.html.

[70] *See* http://copyright.gov/docs/making_available/.

to amend the law to make such a right robust, and, if so, how such an amendment should be cast.[71]

As the notion of actionable RAM copies transforms ordinary acts of reading, listening, and using into copyright infringement, a making available right potentially imposes liability for having copies, without more, as well as for posting hyperlinks or citations to copies one doesn't have. The combination of these two instances of copy-fetish jeopardizes copyright law's longstanding protection of the interests of readers, listeners, and viewers.

Copy-fetishists have demonstrated that they view the mere existence of any unlicensed copy as an invasion of their prerogatives. In the *HathiTrust* case, the Authors Guild was willing to spend millions of dollars in an effort to ensure that even invisible unlicensed copies were eradicated. The bare possibility that an unlicensed copy might somehow escape into the wild was, the Authors Guild argued, itself irreparable harm.[72] In *Capitol Records v. Thomas-Rasset*, the recording industry was willing to shell out for three jury trials and an appeal to the 8th Circuit against a judgment-proof defendant in the hope of establishing the illegality of having a file in the share directory of a peer-to-peer file sharing client. Neither lawsuit accomplished its larger doctrinal objective, but failing to persuade the courts appears to have galvanized copyright owners' determination to procure legislation that repudiates those losses.

As the U.S. Congress takes its first serious look in many years at a comprehensive revision of the copyright law, the possibility that readers' copyright interests will be swallowed up by a series of new copyright owner rights and remedies seems significant. Most people are aware that copyright statutes are made when lawyers for copyright owners and commercial and institutional copyright users get together and figure out a compromise that most of them can live with. It's not news that copyright-affected industries have thoroughly captured the Copyright Office, the White House, the Commerce Department, and Congress.[73] At least up until now, readers and listeners and viewers have never gotten an official seat at the negotiating table. Indeed, institutions, businesses, and NGOs who have claimed to be advancing the interests of users have found themselves demoted, and banished to the children's table. (That's the best description I can come up with for CONFU, the mid-1990s Conference on Fair Use that was devised to ensure that contentious

---

[71] U.S. Copyright Office, Public Roundtable on the Right of Making Available, May 5, 2014, at www .copyright.gov/docs/making_available/public-roundtable/transcript.pdf.

[72] Memorandum of Law in Support of Plaintiff's Motion for Summary Judgment at 23, Authors Guild v. Hathitrust, 902 F. Supp. 2d 445 (S.D.N.Y. 2012) (No. 11-Civ-6351), at www.thepublicindex.org/wp-content/uploads/sites/19/docs/cases/hathitrust/115-ag-sj-brief.pdf.

[73] *See, e.g.*, Kaminski, *supra* note 12, at 988-1005; Deborah Tussey, *UCITA, Copyright and Capture*, 21 CARDOZO ARTS & ENT. L.J. 319, 321–22 (2003).

disputes about the scope of fair use in the digital realm did not delay enactment of
the Digital Millennium Copyright Act.[74] It bears some explanatory power, as well,
for the Section 108 Study Group convened in 2005 to define the scope of new library
privileges.[75])

The Register of Copyrights has now called on Congress to enact the "next great
copyright act."[76] The House Judiciary Committee held 19 hearings on copyright
issues during the 113th Congress in what was billed as a comprehensive reexami-
nation of the copyright system.[77] The committee heard from scores of witnesses

[74]   *See* www.uspto.gov/web/offices/dcom/olia/confu/confurep.pdf. In connection with the enactment of
       the Digital Millennium Copyright Act, discussions on the appropriate scope of fair use in the digital
       environment were diverted to a conference of fair use, in which many stakeholders met, argued,
       and failed to reach consensus. Meanwhile, supporters of the new legislation shepherded it through
       Congress without allocating Congressional attention to fair use questions. When fair use nonetheless
       appeared late in the game in connection with the bill's anticircumvention provisions, those questions
       were themselves diverted to a triennial copyright office rulemaking. *See* JESSICA LITMAN, DIGITAL
       COPYRIGHT 122–45 (2006).

[75]   *See* www.section108.gov/docs/Sec108StudyGroupReport.pdf. The Section 108 Study Group was a
       group assembled by the Copyright Office and charged with recommending revision to the hope-
       less outdated library reproduction privileges in section 108 of the Copyright Act. The group was co-
       chaired by a librarian and a publisher; it included members from libraries, museums, archives, book
       publishers, journal publishers, film studios, and software publishers. Like CONFU, it failed to reach
       consensus on proposals to amend the law.

[76]   *See* http://copyright.gov/regstat/2013/regstat03202013.html; www.copyright.gov/docs/next_great_
       copyright_act.pdf.

[77]   *See* Copyright Issues in Education and For the Visually Impaired: Hearing Before the Subcomm.
       on Courts, Intellectual Property, and the Internet of the House Judiciary Comm., 113th Cong. (2014)
       (Serial # 113-119); Oversight of the U.S. Copyright Office: Hearing Before the Subcomm. on Courts,
       Intellectual Property, and the Internet of the House Judiciary Comm., 113th Cong. (2014) (Serial #
       113-116); Chapter 12 of Title 17: Hearing Before the Subcomm. on Courts, Intellectual Property, and
       the Internet of the House Judiciary Comm., 113th Cong. (2014) (Serial # 113-115); Copyright Remedies:
       Hearing Before the Subcomm. on Courts, Intellectual Property, and the Internet of the House
       Judiciary Comm., 113th Cong. (2014) (Serial # 113-107); Moral Rights, Termination Rights, Resale
       Royalty, And Copyright Term: Hearing Before the Subcomm. on Courts, Intellectual Property, and
       the Internet of the House Judiciary Comm.,113th Cong. (2014) (Serial # 113-103); Music Licensing
       Under Title 17 Parts One And Two: Hearing Before the Subcomm. on Courts, Intellectual Property,
       and the Internet of the House Judiciary Comm.,113 the Cong. (2014) (Serial # 113-105); Hearing: First
       Sale Under Title 17: Hearing Before the Subcomm. on Courts, Intellectual Property, and the Internet
       of the House Judiciary Comm., 113th Cong. (2014) (Serial # 113-98); Compulsory Video Licenses of
       Title 17: Hearing Before the Subcomm. on Courts, Intellectual Property, and the Internet of the
       House Judiciary Comm., 113th Cong. (2014) (Serial # 113-89); Hearing: Preservation And Reuse of
       Copyrighted Works: Hearing Before the Subcomm. on Courts, Intellectual Property, and the Internet
       of the House Judiciary Comm., 113th Cong. (2014) (Serial # 113-88); Section 512 of Title 17: Hearing
       Before the Subcomm. on Courts, Intellectual Property, and Internet of the House Judiciary Comm.,
       113th Cong. (2014) (Serial # 113-86); The Scope of Fair Use: Hearing Before the Subcomm. on Courts,
       Intellectual Property, and the Internet of the House Judiciary Comm., 113th Cong. (2014) (Serial #
       113-82); The Scope of Copyright Protection: Hearing Before the Subcomm. on Courts, Intellectual
       Property, and the Internet of the House Judiciary Comm., 113th Cong. (2014) (Serial # 113-81); Satellite
       Television Laws in Title 17: Hearing Before the Subcomm. on Courts, Intellectual Property, and the

testifying about what they thought was right and wrong with current copyright law. Witnesses speaking on behalf of readers, listeners, and viewers were in short supply.[78] As copyright owners have pressed Congress to recognize or clarify a more expansive scope for reproduction and distribution rights, supporters of enhanced copyright protection have deflected calls for recognition or clarification of readers' and listeners' liberties. They insist that readers have failed to make a compelling showing that current legal ambiguities cause them meaningful harm.[79] Any new or expanded privileges or exceptions, they argue, would pose a grave danger of injuring the creators and owners of copyrighted works.[80]

Internet of the House Judiciary Comm., 113th Cong. (2013) (Serial # 113-48); Innovation In America (Part I And II): Hearing Before the Subcomm. on Courts, Intellectual Property, and the Internet of the House Judiciary Comm., 113th Cong. (2013) (Serial # 113-47); A Case Study for Consensus Building: The Copyright Principles Project: Hearing Before the House Judiciary Comm., 113th Cong. (2013); The Register's Call for Updates to U.S. Copyright Law: Hearing Before the House Judiciary Comm., 113th Cong. (2013) (Serial # 113-20). See also The Role of Voluntary Agreements in the U.S. Copyright System: Hearing Before the Subcomm. on Courts, Intellectual Property, and the Internet of the House Judiciary Comm., 113th Cong. (2013) (Serial # 113-49) (subcommittee hearing on voluntary agreements to address piracy of copyrighted works); Unlocking Consumer Choice and Wireless Competition Act, Hearing on H.R. 1123 Before the Subcomm. on Courts, Intellectual Property, and the Internet of the House Judiciary Comm., 113th Cong. (2013) (Serial # 113-27) (subcommittee hearing on restoring the telephone unlocking exception to § 1201).

[78] Five of the hearings included witnesses from nonprofit organizations that represent some aspect of the public's interest in copyright. The Hearing on Copyright First Sale included witnesses Jonathan Band on behalf of an organization named the Owners Rights Initiative, which advances the rights of copy buyers, and Sherwin Sy for Public Knowledge. Sy testified again at a later hearing on copyright remedies. The Hearing on the Scope of Fair Use included novelist Naomi Novik testifying for the Organization for Transformative Works. The Hearing on the Scope of Copyright included Jamie Love for Public Knowledge International. The Hearing on Issues in Education and for the Visually Impaired included witness Scott LeBarre for the National Federation for the Blind and Jack Bernard for the Association of American Universities. In addition, several hearings included law professor witnesses, and some of the law professors testified that a wise copyright law would take the interests of members of the public seriously.

[79] *See, e.g.*, The Scope of Fair Use Hearing, *supra* note 77, at 104–11 (statement submitted by the Association of American Publishers); Copyright Office Section 104 Report, *supra* note 40, at 73–77, 96–101, 130; Department of Commerce Internet Policy Task Force Report, *supra* note 1, at 35–38.

[80] *See, e.g.*, Copyright Office, DMCA Section 104 Report, *supra* note 40, at 99; The DMCA Section 104 Report Hearing, *supra* note 43, at 18 (testimony of Carey Ramos on behalf of the National Music Publishers Ass'n); *id.* at 46 (testimony of Emery Simon, Business Software Alliance); Unlocking Consumer Choice and Wireless Competition Act: Hearing on H.R. 1123, *supra* note 77, at 54–58 (colloquy); First Sale Under Title 17, *supra* note 77, at 108–09 (testimony of Emery Simon, BSA|The Software Alliance); id. at 95–96 (testimony of John Villasenor, Brookings Institution fellow); Digital Media Consumers Rights: Hearing on HR 107 Before the Commerce Subcomm. of the House Energy & Commerce Com., 108th Cong. (2004) (Serial # 108-109) (testimony Of Cary A Sherman, Recording Industry As'sn of Am.); Recording Industry Association of America, Comments Concerning Promotion of Distance Education Through Digital Technologies, Docket No. 98-12A (Feb. 5, 1999), at http://copyright.gov/disted/comments/init023.pdf.

I've focused on two manifestations of copy-fetish that originated, I contend, in doctrinal mistakes by courts of appeals. Copyright owners' advocates are clinging to both of them, and have enlisted the support of the Copyright Office, the Patent Office, the Department of Commerce, the U.S. Trade Representative, and the White House in their efforts to incorporate them into the law. That doesn't make these expansions of copyright a done deal – the support of all of these actors for drastic "rogue websites" legislation didn't stop the defeat of the Stop Online Piracy Act (SOPA).[81] It makes it unlikely, though, that any significant copyright revision bill will fail to incorporate them. The extent to which both expansions of owner rights pose significant threats to readers' interests simply is not salient to most of the policy makers involved in the debate. If copyright owners insist that it isn't appropriate to consider the interests of readers when crafting the next great copyright act, we can predict with some confidence that readers' rights will get short shrift. And that should worry all of us.

If copyright owners' control of the copyright legislative process all but guarantees that copyright's exclusive rights will expand further to encroach on reader, listener, and viewer liberties, then it becomes important to make those liberties explicit in the statute, and to define them with sufficient generosity and flexibility that they will survive technological innovation. Just as we want to promote creative authorship, we should also seek to encourage creative readership. Imaginative readers are valuable for many of the same reasons we prize imaginative authors.[82] It may be that we could rely on fair use and implicit reader privileges to continue to shelter creative reading rather than making readers' copyright liberties explicit. It's even possible that fair use and implicit reader privileges would give creative reading a broader shelter than any express exception or limitation that copyright owners will permit Congress to enact. But, when we fail to include express protections for the interests of readers, listeners, and viewers in the law, we lose an opportunity to express the importance of readers' interests in the copyright system. Affirming the core importance of readers, listeners, and viewers in the copyright ecosystem is an essential step toward restoring the public's respect for the copyright law. Giving explicit voice to the importance of readers' interests, meanwhile, may remind copyright owners that Congress has given them exclusive rights at least in part in the service of larger goals.

---

[81]   *See, e.g.,* Jonathan Weisman, *In Fight Over Piracy Bills, New Economy Rises Against Old,* N.Y. TIMES, Jan. 18, 2012, at www.nytimes.com/2012/01/19/technology/web-protests-piracy-bill-and-2-key-senators-change-course.html.

[82]   Consider the problems and opportunities posed by fan works. In theory, the most challenging uses to authors' rights would be the creation and widespread dissemination of fan fiction, fan video, and fan art. Yet, as many copyright owners have discovered, noncommercial fan works redound to the benefit of the copyright owners' bottom line. This shouldn't be surprising: the author/reader relationship is interactive rather than static, and the most devoted readers are the ones who feel invited to participate in the experience that the author communicates to them.

So, when I speak of explicit statutory readers' rights, what am I imagining?

The copyright rights that readers, listeners, and viewers need are modest unless one is a copy-fetishist: Individuals who make lawful use of works should be entitled to take a variety of actions that may enhance those uses.[83] Such an individual should have the right to make copies incidental to the lawful use, and to adapt the work to suit her needs. She should be able to store those copies where and as she wants to. She should be entitled to extract and use any material that is not protected by copyright – facts, ideas, processes, or expression that is in the public domain – even if doing so requires making another copy or defeating technological protections. She should not face liability for using citations, hyperlinks, or other information location tools to refer other readers to the work. She should be able to time-shift or format-shift her copy of the work; she should be entitled to loan, sell, or give her copies away to someone else, whether those copies are analog or digital.[84] She should be encouraged to enjoy the work, interact with it, revise it, describe it, respond to it, and share her responses with others, privately or publicly.[85] She should be able to do all of this with a reasonable expectation that her intellectual privacy will be respected.[86]

Those are very modest rights. If my list sounds ridiculously radical to you, recall that all of these uses represent behavior that readers, listeners, and viewers engaged in, completely lawfully, every day, before the wide deployment of networked digital technology.[87] The fact that the whole world has been linked up over digital networks hasn't changed the essence of reading, and interactive engagement with works of authorship is as crucial an aspect of reading (and listening and viewing) today as it was 40 years ago. None of the freedoms I enumerated need morph into a privilege to commercialize a work. All of the user rights I mentioned will, I believe, encourage respect for the copyright system and the process of authorship, and promote reader engagement in copyright norms.

---

[83] *See, e.g.,* Ginsburg, *supra* note 2, at 12 ("Where one has a lawful access to the work, there may be an implied right to enjoy the work in a manner convenient to the consumer.").

[84] *See* Aaron Perzanowski & Jason Schultz, *Legislating Digital Exhaustion*, 29 BERKELEY TECH. L.J. 1535 (2014). The current section 117 of the Copyright Act limits the right to transfer consumers' copies of computer programs by requiring that any transfer include both the original copy and all copies made by the consumer. The same general principle could be extended to copies of other classes of works. *See id.* at 1546–57.

[85] *See* Rebecca Tushnet, *Scary Monsters, Hybrid Mashups, and Other Illegitimate Children*, 86 NOTRE DAME L. REV. 2133 (2011); Rebecca Tusnet, *I Put You There: User Generated Content and Anticircumvention*, 12 VAND. J. ART TECH. 889 (2010).

[86] *See* Julie E. Cohen, *What Privacy Is For*, 126 HARVARD L. REV. (2013); Julie E. Cohen, *Intellectual Privacy and Censorship of the Internet*, 8 SETON HALL CONST. L.J. 693 (1998); Neil M. Richards, *Intellectual Privacy*, 87 TEX. L. REV. 387 (2008).

[87] Those are the same core reader freedoms that copyright law has always given readers, until recently, by cabining the scope of copyright rights so that copyright impinges only minimally on reader liberties.

I imagine that some readers are thinking: "Why can't we rely on licensing to permit uses like this? If an author thinks that it's important to permit readers to make this use or that use, then surely the author will license those uses."[88]

We've learned that doesn't work. First, and most obviously, the author is often not the licensing agent. Most academic authors are delighted when scholars and teachers want to make use of their work in any way at all, but if the authors have assigned their copyrights to publishers, their enthusiasm for the use is worse than irrelevant.[89] The popular press is full of articles about performers whose record companies decline to release their recordings, but refuse to return them to the artists.[90] Recording artists who welcomed peer-to-peer file sharing had no grounds on which to overrule their labels.[91] While individual creators may prefer that their works be read, seen, heard, and used as widely as possible, owners of the copyrights in multiple works may have other interests: they may, for example, want to protect their more profitable works from the competition that might arise if their less profitable works were readily available. They may have business plans that do not rely on widespread licensing. Consider the sad story of George Clinton, who has said that he would happily offer inexpensive sample licenses for Funkadelic recordings.[92] That doesn't matter, because the Funkadelic sound recording copyrights were purchased by Bridgeport music, which is pursuing a different business model.[93]

In the 1990s, copyright lawyers were briefly seduced by the notion of subjecting all consumer uses to individually negotiated licenses managed by intelligent

---

[88] *See, e.g.*, Tom Sydnor, *A "Digital-first-sale" Doctrine – Do We Really Need (Another) One – or Two?*, TECHPOLICYDAILY.COM, Sept. 11, 2004, at www.techpolicydaily.com/technology/digital-first-sale-doctrine-really-need-another-one-two/. *See also* Jane C. Ginsburg, *Fair Use for Free or Permitted-but-Paid*, 29 BERKELEY TECH. L.J. 1383 (2014) (suggesting that many of the current non-creative fair uses should be subject to a new licensing regime). Ginsburg acknowledges that the difficulty of setting terms and royalties for consumer licenses would be formidable.

[89] *See* Am. Geophysical Union v. Texaco, 802 F. Supp. 1 (1992), *aff'd* 37 F.3d 881 (1994).

[90] *See, e.g.*, Aylin Zafar, *What It's Like When a Label Won't Release Your Album*, BUZZFEED, May 12, 2013, at www.buzzfeed.com/azafar/what-happens-when-your-favorite-artist-is-legally-unable-to.

[91] *See, e.g.*, Janis Ian, *The Internet Debacle*, *Performing Songwriter Magazine*, May 2002, www.janisian.com/reading/internet.php.

[92] *See, e.g.*, www.hiphopdx.com/index/news/id.18253/title.george-clinton-explains-saving-hip-hop-artists-on-samples-recalls-early-days-of-dr-dre-afrika-bambaataa-eminem.

[93] *See* Bridgeport Music v. UMG Recordings (6th Cir. 2009); *Tim Wu, Jay Z v. The Sample Troll*, SLATE, Nov. 16, 2006, at www.slate.com/articles/arts/culturebox/2006/11/jayz_versus_the_sample_troll.html. Since Bridgeport demonstrated the economic advantages of operating as a copyright troll, a number of other businesses have followed its example of buying up copyrights in order to bring multiple lawsuits against alleged infringers. Some of these businesses have sued thousands of individuals who are alleged to have unauthorized copies of works. *See, e.g.*, Righthaven v. Democratic Underground, 791 F. Supp.2d 968 (D. Nev. 2011); AF Holdings, LLC, v. Olivas, 108 U.S.P.Q. 2d 1151 (D. Conn. 2013).

software agents.[94] You remember: "okay, so I can download this track if I pay you 99 cents. I also want to convert the file format to something my hardware can read, include the recording in a compilation I want to put together for my girlfriend, and edit the recording so that I can use it as the soundtrack for my figure skating routine. May I do that for, say, $1.49?"

The vision of consumer licenses negotiated by intelligent software agents turned out to be a pipe dream. It isn't that we don't have the technology to do this. We do. Rather, it's that it makes no economic sense for owners to keep track of a multiplicity of individually tailored licenses when they can instead offer only one or two. If we say we're going to rely on voluntary licensing to take care of this sort of use, then, we've learned that means that it isn't going to happen. And while that might suit some copyright owners just fine, it would be bad for the copyright ecosystem, which is and should be designed to encourage creative reading as well as creative writing.

I said earlier that every author creates works, at least in part, as an act of communication. For some authors, that goal of communicating is the only important goal.[95] For others, an often more imperative goal is to earn money. Our copyright law is not yet well-designed to ensure that creators of works get paid. Indeed, we need to face the fact that our copyright system does an embarrassingly lousy job of funneling money to creators. That isn't the readers' fault; rather the blame belongs with the architecture of the system. The United States copyright law has never done an admirable job of helping creators to get paid.[96] The law encourages creators to convey their copyright interests to publishers, aggregators, and other intermediaries, and it does not pay much attention to whether they can take advantage of copyright's benefits once they have done so. I've written about this elsewhere.[97] But hamstringing readers is unlikely to help creators earn more money; it's merely going to prevent the copyright system from doing its job.

---

[94] *See generally* Julie E. Cohen, *Some Reflections on Copyright Management Systems and Laws Designed to Protect Them*, 12 BERKELEY TECH. L.J. 161 (1997).

[95] *See, e.g., About Us*, AUTHORS' ALLIANCE, www.authorsalliance.org/about/ (visited Aug. 22, 2014).

[96] *See, e.g.,* Peter DiCola, *Money from Music: Survey Evidence on Musicians' Revenues and Lessons About Copyright's Incentives*, 55 ARIZ. L. REV. (2013); Jane C. Ginsburg, *The Author's Place in the Future of Copyright*, 153 PROCEEDINGS OF THE AM. PHIL. SOC'Y 147, 148–51 (2009), at www.amphilsoc .org/sites/default/files/proceedings/1530204.pdf; Maureen O'Rourke, *A Brief History of Author-Publisher Relations and the Outlook for the 21st Century*, 50 J. COPYRIGHT SOC'Y 425 (2002). Indeed the classes of creators with the strongest copyright control of the exploitation of their works are often the classes with the least likely prospect of earning a decent living from their creation of works of authorship. Playwrights, for example, have by custom retained almost European control over their scripts. Even very successful playwrights, though, earn very little money from licensing productions of their plays. TODD LONDON & BEN PESNER, OUTRAGEOUS FORTUNE: THE LIFE AND TIMES OF THE NEW AMERICAN PLAY 50–63 (2009).

[97] Jessica Litman, *Real Copyright Reform*, 96 IOWA L. REV. 1, 8–12 (2010).

In the past 25 years, Congress has tweaked the copyright law repeatedly to enhance copyright owners' control over their works. None of those tweaks put more money in creators' pockets. If one of our goals in revising the copyright law is to ensure that creators are able to earn more money from their works – and I personally think that it should be – then we need to recognize that ratcheting up owner control yet again is unlikely to achieve it. Even when copyright revision results in increased copyright revenues, copyright owners have displayed a persistent reluctance to share their augmented revenues with creators.[98] The lesson of past copyright revisions is that even massive enhancement of the scope of copyright owners' rights and the robustness of their remedies doesn't effect a noticeable increase in author compensation.[99] We need to think instead about restructuring the system in ways that make money for creators a higher priority than control of copies. When we do that, though, we need to make sure that we are also paying attention to the rights of readers, listeners, and viewers. Rather than narrowing reader liberties, we should be looking at elements of current and past copyright laws that have helped creators to collect a larger share of copyright receipts. Statutory and collective licenses that include direct payments to authors,[100] termination of transfer and other reversion provisions,[101] a narrowing of the work for hire doctrine,[102] and author-favoring construction rules[103] all show some promise. Something as simple as requiring the disclosure of accurate information about how much of the price of a copy or subscription is actually paid to creators may assist the development of norms that support author compensation.

The impulse to radically expand the scope of copyright rights and control or suppress reader creativity may be motivated by panic about online piracy, but the

---

[98] *See, e.g.,* U.S. Copyright Office, Copyright and the Music Marketplace 76–78, 128–30 (2015).

[99] *Accord* Dan Hunter & Nicholas Suzor, *Why Australians Should Back Turnbull in the Stoush over Copyright,* The Conversation, Aug. 8, 2014, at http://theconversation.com/why-australians-should-back-turnbull-in-the-stoush-over-copyright-30198.

[100] *See, e.g.,* Comments of SAG, AFTRA, & AFM, Copyright Licensing Study, Docket No. 2014–13, (May 23, 2014), at www.copyright.gov/docs/musiclicensingstudy/comments/Docket2014_3/SAG_AFTRA_AFM_MLS_2014.pdf.

[101] *See, e.g.,* Moral Rights, Termination Rights, Resale Royalty, And Copyright Term, *supra* note 77 (testimony of Casey Rae, Future of Music Coalition).

[102] *See, e.g.,* Jeffrey Trexler, *Taking Back the Kirby Case,* The Comics Journal (Aug. 20, 2013), at www.tcj.com/taking-back-the-kirby-case/.

[103] In *Cohen v. Paramount,* 845 F.2d 851 (9th Cir. 1988), for example, the Court of Appeals for the Ninth Circuit adopted a rule of construction limiting an author's grant to encompass uses contemplated by the parties and to reserve to the author all uses the parties did not anticipate. *See also* Random House v. Rosetta Books, 150 F. Supp. 2d 613 (S.D.N.Y. 2001), *aff'd* 283 F.3d 490 (2d Cir. 2002) (construing grant of right to publish work in book form to exclude ebook publication).

creative engagement of readers, listeners, and viewers isn't what causes piracy. (Indeed, it usually enhances the copyright owners' bottom line.) More important, though, is that audience members' engagement greatly enriches the reader's, listener's, and viewer's experience of copyrighted works, and is precisely the sort of behavior that a copyright system is designed, and should be designed, to promote.

What makes this an easy choice is that proposals to further extend copyright rights or to subject reading, listening, and viewing to tight control are unlikely to discourage people from stealing access to works that they aren't able to buy. Those proposals are much more likely to discourage people from buying access to works that they would otherwise be eager to read, hear, or see.

But even if the choice were harder – if copyright owners came up with a new formulation of their exclusive rights or a new sort of control over their readers that seemed certain to produce a measurable reduction in infringement – if the control also created a significant burden on reading, listening, and viewing, then adopting it would pose a risk of ignoring half of copyright's purpose: the half that seeks to promote reading. That half is, as I've argued, crucially important to the copyright system. When we ignore it, the system breaks down.

5

Copyright in a Digital Ecosystem

A *User Rights Approach*

*Niva Elkin-Koren**

ABSTRACT

The rights of users of copyrighted materials are growing in significance. This is the result of fundamental changes in the creative ecosystem that pull in opposite directions: on the one hand, the flourishing of user-generated content places individual users at the forefront of creative processes, strengthening the need to facilitate unlicensed use of creative materials. On the other hand, digital distribution, cloud computing, and mobile Internet strengthen restrictions on the freedom of users to access, experience, transform, and share creative materials.

These changes necessitate a user-rights approach to copyright law. Users' interests are often examined through the prism of Limitations and Exceptions (L&E) to copyright. However, this narrow view overlooks the users' critical role in serving the goals of copyright law and may therefore ultimately lead to inefficient outcomes.

A user-rights approach holds that permissible uses under copyright law should be articulated and treated as rights. It deviates from the L&E approach at the theoretical level, with some potential doctrinal implications. At the theoretical level, this approach shifts the locus of copyright analysis from author's rights to the creative process, emphasizing the role of users as partners in promoting copyright objectives. Rather than being "parasites" that benefit – unjustly – from limits on the just rewards of authors, users actively participate in promoting the creation, dissemination, and use of cultural works. A user-rights approach further suggests that to achieve its goals, copyright law should be drafted, interpreted, and applied in ways that consider the rights and duties of both users and authors. Permissible uses that serve the objectives of copyright law should therefore be defined as rights rather than as a legal defense.

* Professor of Law, Faculty of Law, University of Haifa, Israel. I thank William Fisher, Michael Geist, Wendy Gordon, Eldar Haber, Justin Hughes, Peter Jaszi, Jessica Litman, Neil Netanel, Ruth L. Okediji, Pamela Samuelson, and Jerry Reichman for invaluable discussions and helpful comments on earlier versions of this chapter.

The purpose of this chapter is to offer a theoretical framework for developing a jurisprudence of user rights. It demonstrates how the recognition of the role of users in promoting the purpose of copyright law could change our perspective on the scope of copyright protection and what should be considered permissible use. The user-rights approach does not purport to offer a detailed prescription on the desirable level of unlicensed use. It does offer, however, a theoretical framework for deciding what should be the scope of permissible use in each particular case.

5.1. INTRODUCTION

The rights of users of copyrighted materials are growing in significance. This is the result of fundamental changes in the creative ecosystem that pull in opposite directions: on the one hand, the rise of user-generated content places individual users at the forefront of creative processes, strengthening the need to facilitate unlicensed use of creative materials. On the other hand, digital distribution facilitates a continuing expansion of copyright and strengthens restrictions on the freedom of users to access, experience, transform, and share creative materials.

We are now a quarter-century into the digital era, and recent changes in the digital ecosystem are threatening access to knowledge and civil liberties. The rise of cloud computing and mobile Internet has transformed the delivery of content from the sale of copies to the provision of services. Streaming gives content owners ongoing control over the use and distribution of copyrighted materials. Moreover, copyright restrictions on the use of online materials are supplemented by contractual restrictions and restraints on use embedded in the design. Access to creative works is often made possible by online intermediaries, using algorithms to filter, block, and disable access to some materials. Access is often subject to monitoring and surveillance. The robustness of algorithmic filtering, removal, and blocking practices is effectively changing copyright default: copyrighted materials were once available unless proven infringing, while now materials detected by algorithms are unavailable unless explicitly authorized by the copyright owner.

These changes in the digital ecosystem are shaping the creative processes. While digital networks created new potential for user participation in creative processes, this environment is also putting the rights of online users under siege. The growing dependency on digital content, coupled with stronger copyright protection, has led overall to the narrowing of user liberties.

In this chapter, I argue that these changes necessitate a user-rights approach to copyright law. That is due to several reasons: First, as users assume an ever greater role in the creative environment, it becomes necessary to understand the part they play in promoting copyright goals. Second, deeper understanding of the users' role in advancing the goals of copyright and the conditions required for this may offer a theoretical framework for developing user rights. Recognition of the interdependency of authors and users, and their respective roles in the creative process, may entail a different scope of protection, corresponding duties, and possibly procedural implications. Third, a user-rights approach may help set the boundaries between copyright and private ordering, based on a more balanced perspective informed by copyright goals. It creates a legal framework for reviewing contractual terms and setting limits on private ordering, thereby offering more robust safeguards to users' liberties in the digital ecosystem. Finally, a user-rights approach could help develop a broader perspective on the rights and liberties necessary to sustain freedom in the digital era. This broader perspective could also be tied to other user liberties, such as free speech, freedom of information, privacy, consumer protection, and freedom of occupation.

Users' interests are often examined through the prism of Limitations and Exceptions (L&E) to copyright. This perspective seeks to identify the circumstances under which it is justified to set limits on the full scope of rights assigned to copyright owners. However, this narrow view overlooks the users' critical role in serving the goals of copyright law and may therefore ultimately lead to inefficient outcomes.

A user-rights approach holds that permissible uses under copyright law should be articulated and treated as rights. It deviates from the L&E approach at the theoretical level, with some potential doctrinal implications. On the normative level this approach shifts the locus of copyright analysis from author's rights to the creative process, emphasizing the role of users as partners in promoting copyright objectives. Copyright law seeks to promote the creation of new works for the benefit of the public, and consequently should focus on stimulating activity that fosters creation, learning, intellectual enrichment, and progress.[1] Designing incentives to create requires consideration of the full range of activities involved in the creative process, including generating new works, transforming existing materials, absorbing, learning, expressing, and disseminating new knowledge. Users take part in some of these processes. Thus, rather than being "parasites" that benefit – unjustly – from limits on the just rewards of authors, users actively participate in promoting the creation, dissemination, and use of cultural works.

On the doctrinal level a user-rights approach suggests that copyright law should be drafted, interpreted, and applied in ways that consider the rights and duties of both users and authors. To achieve copyright goals and promote creation, it is necessary

---

[1]   Pierre N. Leval, *Toward a Fair Use Standard*, 103 HARV. L. REV. 1105, 1107 (1990).

to design rights and duties for both authors and users of creative works and to define permissible uses that serve the objectives of copyright law as rights rather than as a legal defense. The framing of permissible uses as rights offers a legal framework for analyzing the potential threats to desirable uses which serve copyright purposes. This is particularly important given the emerging threats to the freedom of users and access to knowledge.

The purpose of this chapter is to offer a theoretical framework, for developing a jurisprudence of user rights. It demonstrates how the recognition of the role of users in promoting the purpose of copyright law could change our perspective on the scope of copyright protection and what should be considered permissible use. The user rights approach does not purport to offer a detailed prescription on the desirable level of unlicensed use. It does offer, however, a theoretical framework for deciding what should be the scope of permissible use in each particular case.

The chapter proceeds as follows: Section 5.2 explains the growing need to develop a user-rights approach in the digital ecosystem, describing the rise of user-generated content (UGC) and the growing threats to users' freedom. Section 5.3 offers a theoretical framework for justifying user rights. It analyzes the role of use and users in copyright law and argues that to promote creation, copyright law should focus on the rights of authors and of users alike. Section 5.4 considers how the law should promote desirable unlicensed use: Is it sufficient to afford users a legal defense in some circumstances, or is it necessary to recognize a right to make permissible use? Section 5.5 concludes by demonstrating some legal implications of a user-rights approach.

5.2. USERS IN THE DIGITAL ECOSYSTEM: OPPORTUNITIES AND THREATS

The rise of user rights is linked to fundamental changes in the creative ecosystem that pull in opposite directions: the flourishing of UGC on the one hand and the stronger restrictions on the freedom of users to access, experience, transform, and share creative materials, on the other hand.

Digital technology has changed the way we create, share, and experience cultural works, placing users at the forefront of creative processes. The term *user* may refer to different types of players engaging with cultural works in a variety of ways: readers of books, eBooks and online journals; users of embedded-software and Apps for smartphones; music fans who play songs on YouTube, subscribers to Spotify, or buyers on iTunes; viewers of live streams and renters or buyers of movies from platforms such as Amazon or Netflix.

Users play a greater role in generating culture, as a result of a sharp reduction in the cost of producing and mass distributing content, and the popular availability of tools which make this possible.[2] Users blog, tweet, edit, take pictures, shoot videos, write software, compose music, report the news, and share pictures, news, and videos on social networks.[3] The digital format enables easy mix and match, cut and paste, edit and remix. Music fans create new remixes, users compose memes from images, buyers appropriate cultural icons to express a new meaning, and communities of users collaborate in authoring software and news.

The rise of UGC as a significant cultural force in the twenty-first century necessitates adjustment of copyright law tailored to serve the needs of mass production of content that dominated the twentieth century.[4] Indeed, the digital ecosystem still consists of commercial producers of creative content, which relies on the incentives schemes set by the existing copyright regime. However, mass production of content is increasingly supplemented by robust creative activity of individual users, working alone or collaborating online.

This new fabric of the creative environment warrants adjustments in copyright law. UGC creates a greater need to secure sufficient access to preexisting materials. Users often lack the necessary legal knowledge and skills required to acquire a license to use copyrighted materials, and even more importantly they often lack a business model for funding a license fee. The uncertainty regarding permissible uses and the risk of liability dampen users' engagement in cultural works and impede participation in generating culture.

Moreover, access to knowledge has become fundamental in this environment. Digital content embraces a whole array of everyday practices, from transactional and professional services to education and social and political interactions. We have become dependent on digital content for almost every aspect of life: from reading the news and sharing pictures on social media to watching films, listening to music, and managing our financial affairs. Therefore, the rights and duties pertaining to the use of digital content might be essential not only for professional and business matters but also for our social life, personal growth, and self-expression.

On the other hand, over the past two decades users' freedom to access, experience, transform, and share creative materials has constantly declined. Constraints

---

[2] *See* YOCHAI BENKLER, THE WEALTH OF NETWORKS: HOW SOCIAL PRODUCTION TRANSFORMS MARKETS AND FREEDOM 213 (2006); LAWRENCE LESSIG, REMIX: MAKING ART AND COMMERCE THRIVE IN THE HYBRID ECONOMY (2008); Niva Elkin-Koren, *User-Generated Platforms, in* WORKING WITHIN THE BOUNDARIES OF INTELLECTUAL PROPERTY: INNOVATION POLICY FOR THE KNOWLEDGE SOCIETY 111, 116–17 (Rochelle C. Dreyfuss, Diane L. Zimmerman, & Harry First eds., 2010).

[3] *See, e.g.*, Florence Le Borgne-Bachschmidt, Sophie Girieud, Marc Leiba, Silvain de Munck, Sander Limonard, Martijn Poel, Linda Kool, Natali Helberger, Lucie Guibault, Esther Janssen, Nico van Eijk, Christina Angelopoulos, Joris van Hoboken & Ewout Swart, USER-CREATED-CONTENT: SUPPORTING A PARTICIPATIVE INFORMATION SOCIETY 50–53 (2008).

[4] Elkin-Koren, *User-Generated Platforms, supra* note 2, at 116–17; Steven Hetcher, *User-Generated Confusion: The Legal and Business Implications of Web 2.0*, 10 VAND. J. ENT. & TECH. L. 863, 871 (2008).

on the freedom of users of digital works are due to technological, business, and legal developments.

The distributed network architecture, open access, and total availability of content, which characterized the evolution of the Internet from the early 1990s,[5] are sidelined by more centralized and closely monitored environment. We are now a quarter of a century into the digital era, and the digital ecosystem has changed, restricting access to knowledge and threatening civil liberties. The rise of cloud computing and mobile Internet has transformed the delivery of content from the sale of copies to the provision of services, facilitating ongoing control over the use and distribution of copyrighted materials.

Copyright law plays a central role in shaping access to content and informational resources, affecting users' ability to read, use, and reuse works. In recent decades copyright protection has expanded, extending protection to new types of works for longer periods of time, and broadening the scope of rights and remedies offered to copyright owners, nationally and internationally. This steady expansion of copyright, named by Boyle "the second enclosure,"[6] has narrowed user liberties.

Take, for instance, reselling and lending copies. For decades, copyright law has distinguished ownership in the copyright from ownership in a copy. While ownership of copyright in a novel confers the right to make copies, ownership of a copy entitled libraries to lend the books in their collection and enabled book buyers to resell their used books. Resale of digital content, however, may involve the creation of temporary copies, and a broad interpretation of the reproduction rights under copyright may render such copying a copyright infringement.[7] In a recent lawsuit brought by Capitol Records against Redigi for copyright infringement, the court gave such a broad interpretation to the reproduction right, rendering any unauthorized transfer of a digital copy a copyright infringement.[8] This interpretation affords

---

[5] This environment of total availability is eloquently described by Litman. *See* Jessica Litman, *Sharing and Stealing*, 26 COMM. ENT. L.J. 1 (2004).

[6] JAMES BOYLE, THE PUBLIC DOMAIN: ENCLOSING THE COMMONS OF THE MIND (2008).

[7] Capitol Records, LLC v. ReDigi Inc., 934 F. Supp. 2d 640 (S.D.N.Y. 2013).

[8] Redigi has developed a secondary marketplace, where consumers of digital music can resell their legally purchased copies. Selling digital copies has always raised a concern that the delivery of copies from one person to another would in fact generate additional unauthorized copies: the original would remain with the seller and duplicates would be sent to the buyers. Redigi's design attempted to ensure that the transfer of a copy from one location to another would not create an additional copy. As each packet of the file is uploaded to the Cloud Locker, that packet is immediately deleted from the user's hard disk, ensuring that no two copies of the work exist at the same time. Nevertheless, the court held that any transfer of copies inevitably involves reproduction within the meaning of copyright law, even when no additional copies were involved. The court held that "Because the reproduction right is necessarily implicated when a copyrighted work is embodied in a new material object, and because digital music files must be embodied in a new material object following their transfer over the Internet, the Court determines that the embodiment of a digital music file on a new hard disk is a reproduction within the meaning of the Copyright Act." *Id.* at 649–50.

rightholders absolute control over any exchange of copies, even when no additional copies are made. In the emerging environment of cloud computing, where many of the software, data, and services are kept beyond users' control, this decision means a complete loss of control over creative content that users have purchased.

Still, copyright is no longer the sole form of constraint on access to knowledge and use of cultural works. The steady expansion of copyright has also been accompanied by further expansion of neighboring rights. Legal restrictions on use set by copyright law are supplemented by contractual restrictions and embedded in the design. For instance, the shift to cloud distribution and mobile Internet has transformed the delivery of content from the sale of copies to the provision of services. Users of creative works are increasingly offered mere access to eBooks, music files, or movies for a monthly fee. Consequently, users lack control over a physical copy and their access to the content may expire at any time.

Access to creative works is made possible by online intermediaries, using algorithms to filter, block, and disable access to copyrighted materials. Access is often subject to monitoring and surveillance. The robustness of algorithmic filtering, removal, and blocking practices is effectively changing the copyright default: Copyrighted materials were once available unless proven infringing, while now materials detected by algorithms are unavailable unless explicitly authorized by the copyright owner.

With the shift from commodity to service, the scope of user rights is defined, for the most part, by a license and the design, using Digital Rights Management (DRM) Systems or Technological Protection Measures (TPM). Consequently, users are subject to ongoing and intermittent changes in the terms of access to their purchased copies (e.g., Apple reducing the number of authorized copies of the playlist) or alternatively their access to purchased content may be terminated altogether. A striking example of the lack of consumer control over a purchased digital copy is the Orwellian 1984 saga, in which Amazon.com remotely removed from Kindle purchased copies of George Orwell's book 1984 due to some copyright concerns. Following a public outcry, Amazon.com apologized and later settled a class action brought against it for violating its terms of service by remotely deleting purchased copies of the book.

Copyright law is also often invoked to prevent compatibility between digital content and different playing devices, using the right of reproduction or anticircumvention legislation. Lack of interoperability may prevent users from using copyrighted materials on other devices, for example, iBooks of Apple on Kindle of Amazon, or from transferring content from one platform to another. Users may also be banned from interacting with information acquired on another platform or merging several types of content obtained from different sources.

The use of DRMs/TPMs enables postpurchase control of eBooks, software, movies, and music, while statutory bans on circumvention further weaken the rights of users of digital content.[9] Built-in surveillance is an example: Adobe Spyware, which allegedly tracks and reports the reading habits of users of Adobe's e-book software, "Digital Editions," illustrates growing concerns for readers' privacy and security.[10] Widespread monitoring and automated filtering by online platforms (e.g., YouTube Content ID) create further layers of protection which may threaten user rights to privacy and freedom of expression.[11]

Other constraints on users' freedom to access and use copyrighted materials are contractual. Restrictions on users' rights to use or resell digital copies are set by End User License Agreements (EULAs) or by Terms of Use (TOU) which are often drafted by online mega-platforms. Digital content is often subject to EULAs, which greatly limit what may be done with a digital work. A license may define an expiration date or limit the right of perpetual use. Some EULAs attempt to extend protection to aspects of the work not covered by copyright protection,[12] or to restrict fair use, such as the right of software users to engage in reverse engineering.[13] EULAs often provide nonownership by the licensee in the licensed copy, and to set limits on the right to resell the copy.[14] Some EULAs restrict permissible use to designated reading devices (e.g., iBooks for iPad), or permit the making of only a limited number of backup copies.[15] Some licenses set limits on public e-lending by libraries. For instance, HarperCollins, a major publishing company, offers e-lending licenses to libraries, using a metered access model so that libraries are authorized to circulate each eBook only twenty-six times before the license expires and a new digital copy must be repurchased. Restricting the public lending privileges of libraries may undermine their ability to serve their public function by ensuring free access to knowledge which is guided by a professional code of ethics. Such limitation clauses directed at libraries also affect the public at large, limiting opportunities for accessing knowledge in an environment that is committed to the ethical principles of public libraries: diversity, pluralism, and freedom of speech.[16]

---

[9] *See, e.g.*, the anticircumvention provisions of the DMCA.

[10] *See* Corynne Mcsherr, *Adobe Spyware Reveals (Again) the Price of DRM: Your Privacy and Security* (Oct. 7, 2014) *available at* www.eff.org/deeplinks/2014/10/adobe-spyware-reveals-again-price-drm-your-privacy-and-security.

[11] Michael S. Sawyer, *Note, Filters, Fair Use & Feedback: User-Generated Content Principles and the DMCA*, 24 BERKELEY TECH. L.J. 363, 388–90 (2009); Ira S. Nathenson, *Civil Procedures for a World of Shared and User-Generated Content*, 48 UNI. LOUISVILLE L. REV. 912, 938–44 (2010).

[12] ProCD, Inc v. Zeidenberg, 86 F.3d 1447 (7th Cir. 1996).

[13] Bowers v. Baystate Technologies, 320 F.3d 1317 (Fed. Cir. 2003).

[14] Vernor v. Autodesk, Inc., 621 F.3d 1102 (9th Cir. 2010).

[15] *See* David R. Hansen, *A State Law Approach to Preserving Fair Use in Academic Libraries*, 22 FORDHAM INTELL. PROP. MEDIA & ENT. L.J. 1 (2011).

[16] *See* CIVIC AGENDA, LIBRARIES, ELENDING, AND THE FUTURE OF PUBLIC ACCESS TO DIGITAL CONTENT (2012), *available at* www.ifla.org/node/7447.

Overall, these developments in law, design, and business models limit users' free-dom to access, experience, transform, and dispose of copyrighted materials. The legal framework of L&E is simply insufficient to counterbalance this rapid expan-sion of copyrights and safeguard user liberties in the digital environment, as it always lags behind the ever increasing rights. The L&E framework takes the form of a defensive strategy, one which assumes the current regime as its baseline. The scope of exclusive rights is accepted as a given, and in turn sets a high threshold for any new exception. The continuous expansion of copyright over recent decades and the fencing of content through licenses and technical means, including cases where L&E would normally apply, strengthen the need to develop a different approach to securing freedom of uses.

5.3. FORMULATING A THEORY OF USER RIGHTS

5.3.1. *Moving beyond Limitations and Exceptions*

In copyright law users are often perceived through the prism of L&E to copyright. L&Es define circumstances where some uses of protected works could be made without authorization. Copyright law may define such circumstances by rules which apply to strictly defined users (e.g., nonprofit educational institutions), particular uses (e.g., temporary copying), or certain types of works (e.g., computer programs). Alternatively, L&E could be defined by standards such as *fair use* or *fair dealing* that leave it to the court to decide whether an unauthorized use should be allowed.[17] Fair use, for instance, permits the unauthorized use of copyrighted works based on a four-factor analysis applied retroactively by the court. In determining whether a use is fair, courts would consider the purpose and character of use, the nature of the used work, the amount taken, and the potential market harm.[18]

The literature on L&E offers several theoretical grounds to justify the limits on copyright. Such theoretical frameworks may prove useful in assisting the courts to identify the appropriate scope of L&E, and are crucial for the legal analysis of stan-dards, such as fair use or fair dealing, where the courts are expected to exercise broad discretion.

[17] *Fair use* defines an open norm for deciding permissible uses of copyrighted material based on a fairly ambiguous set of standards. The fair use provisions in the U.S. 1976 Copyright Act codified judicial opinions which developed this open norm. *Fair dealing* is a relatively narrow standard, which is com-mon in many common law jurisdictions, including the United Kingdom, Canada, and Australia. To qualify for fair dealing a use must fall under one of the enumerated uses defined by law. *See* Sarah Sklar-Heyn, Note, *Battling Clearance Culture Shock: Comparing U.S. Fair Use and Canadian Fair Dealing in Advancing Freedom of Expression in Non-Fiction Film*, 20 CARDOZO J. INT'L COMP. L. 233, 236 (2011).

[18] 17 U.S.C. § 107.

One set of justifications for L&E focuses on the need to balance author rights against a public interest. From this perspective, it is sometimes necessary to limit the rights of authors in cases where a rigid application of their rights would prevent socially beneficial uses and possibly conflict with the public interest in freedom of expression, competition, consumer protection, or innovation.[19] L&E are meant to balance interest in securing just rewards for authors with the public interest. To achieve a proper balance, L&E may come into play whenever the broad proprietary right of the copyright owner might endanger socially beneficial values. One example is where copyright enforcement may conflict with free speech.[20] Copyright protects "expressions," therefore it might compromise the free speech of nonowners who wish to use such expressions to state an opinion or voice their criticism. Fair use may offer a built-in safeguard which allows the court to balance the rights of authors and free speech.[21]

By and large, other approaches to L&E are grounded in general theories of copyright law.[22] Judge Pierre Leval has eloquently argued:

> Fair use should be perceived not as a disorderly basket of exceptions to the rules of copyright, not as a departure from the principles governing that body of law, but rather as a rational, integral part of copyright, whose observance is necessary to achieve the objectives of that law.[23]

The economic approach to copyright law, for instance, explains L&E in terms of market failures. It assumes that in the absence of a market failure, markets could regulate the efficient level of investment in developing new works and secure their efficient use. Copyright law assigns ownership in creative works in order to address the market failure of public goods associated with informational resources.[24] In a seminal article Wendy Gordon argued that fair use could justify some socially beneficial uses that would fail to occur due to a market failure.[25] One example is high

---

[19] Rebecca Tushnet, *Copy This Essay: How Fair Use Doctrine Harms Free Speech and How Copying Serves It*, 114 YALE L.J. 535 (2004); Malla Pollack, *A Listener's Free Speech, A Reader's Copyright*, 36 HOFSTRA L. REV. 1457 (2007).

[20] *See* NEIL W. NETANEL, COPYRIGHT'S PARADOX (2008).

[21] Eldred v. Ashcroft, 537 U.S. 186, 221 (2003). *See also* Michael Birnhack, *Copyright Law and Free Speech after Eldred v. Ashcroft*, 76 S. CAL. L. REV. 1275 (2003).

[22] *See e.g.*, William W. Fisher III, *Reconstructing the Fair Use Doctrine*, 101 HARV. L. REV. 1659 (1988) (arguing that copyright law in general, and fair use doctrine in particular, should be applied to facilitate a utopian vision of the good life and human flourishing).

[23] *See* Leval, *supra* note 1, at 1107.

[24] WILLIAM LANDES & RICHARD POSNER, THE ECONOMIC STRUCTURE OF INTELLECTUAL PROPERTY LAW 116 (2003).

[25] *See* Wendy J. Gordon, *Fair Use as Market Failure: A Structural and Economic Analysis of the Betamax Case and Its Predecessors*, 82 COLUM. L. REV. 1600 (1982) (Gordon argued that fair use should be awarded to the defendant in a copyright infringement action when there is a market failure, the

transaction costs. When transaction costs are higher than the expected benefits to the parties, a license agreement might not take place, and the use will not materialize even when it is likely to increase overall welfare. For instance, a school teacher who seeks to show a few video clips in class for educational purposes may give up the use altogether if she is required to acquire a license for each and every use: identify multiple owners, negotiate a license, and pay the license fee. Similarly, a socially beneficial use may not occur due to another market failure: externalities.[26] For instance, even though the public could benefit from compatible computer programs, which are likely to facilitate competitive prices and facilitate further innovation, a license might not be available. Rightholders may refuse to license a compatible program, or may overcharge for it, in order to minimize competition. In such circumstances, the market will fail to reach an efficient outcome, and consequently it would be justified to limit the rights of copyright owners and allow unauthorized use.[27]

Another theoretical approach to copyright focuses on what is sometimes perceived as conflicting goals of copyright law: on the one hand seeking to secure incentives to authors and on the other hand seeking to promote wide dissemination of works for the benefit of the public. Permitting too much unauthorized use extinguishes the economic incentive to create, which copyright is intended to provide, while strict copyright enforcement may stifle the dissemination of works and limit access by the general public, which is the ultimate goal that copyright seeks to promote in the first place.[28]

Several scholars have questioned the attempt to identify a grand theory that would offer a comprehensive explanation for L&E.[29] Instead they take a bottom-up approach, which extracts a set of organizing principles from existing exceptions.

---

transfer of the use to defendant is socially desirable, and fair use would not cause substantial injury to the incentives of the copyright owner).

[26] Externalities occur when a particular use of copyrighted materials could benefit parties other than the licensor and licensee. In those circumstances, the cost benefit analysis of the parties in deciding whether to license the use might be incompatible with public welfare. Niva Elkin-Koren & Eli E. Salzberger, The Limits of Analysis: Law and Economics of Intellectual Property in the Digital Age (2012).

[27] Gordon, *supra* note 25, at 1614. Note, however, that according to Gordon fair use will apply in the case of a market failure only when "transfer of the use to defendant is socially desirable" and fair use "would not cause substantial injury to the incentives of the plaintiff copyright owner."

[28] *See, e.g.*, Cambridge Univ. Press v. Patton, 769 F.3d 1232 (11th Cir. 2014) ("If copyright's utilitarian goal is to be met, we must be careful not to place overbroad restrictions on the use of copyrighted works, because to do so would prevent would-be authors from effectively building on the ideas of others. Some unpaid use of copyrighted materials must be allowed in order to prevent copyright from functioning as a straitjacket that stifles the very creative activity it seeks to foster. If we allow too much unpaid copying, however, we risk extinguishing the economic incentive to create that copyright is intended to provide.")

[29] Michael J. Madison, A *Pattern-Oriented Approach to Fair Use*, 45 Wm. Mary L. Rev. 1525, 1564 (2004).

These principles may justify treating L&E as a coherent category and consequently inform their interpretation.[30]

Overall, the literature pertaining to L&E has focused primarily on circumstances where copyright must be limited or where extending the full scope of rights to copyright owners would be unjustifiable. A shortcoming of this approach is that it takes ownership of copyright as its baseline and treats the circumstances where limits are justifiable as exceptions. This view overlooks the critical role of users in serving the goals of copyright law and fulfilling its objectives.

Users have traditionally enjoyed relatively little attention in copyright scholarship and legal discourse. The focus is mostly the original author and authors' rights. The functions and needs of users of copyrighted materials are generally under-researched. Also, relatively little attention is paid to the legal definition of L&E and the legal consequences they carry. The absence of a systematic account of the users' role in the creative environment has limited the perspective of courts and policy makers in shaping copyright policy. Users have been mostly viewed as "parasites" who benefit, undeservedly, from limits on the just rewards of authors. Consequently, permissible uses have been perceived as exceptions, offered sparingly and interpreted narrowly.

Indeed, users of copyrighted materials are sometimes mentioned by scholars and courts as the ultimate beneficiaries of copyright schemes. That is, copyright is designed to serve the public interest by rewarding authors so that they will continue to create for the benefit of readers, viewers, and listeners.[31] The use of copyrighted materials is thus viewed as the outcome of copyright law, fulfilling one of the law's objectives.[32] Yet even this reading of copyright law still emphasizes the need to reward authors alone, and users, by this view, are always secondary.[33] This view rests on superficial assumptions about the creative ecosystem, and therefore it may ultimately lead to inefficient outcomes.

---

[30] Pamela Samuelson, *Justifications for Copyright Limitations & Exceptions, in* COPYRIGHT LAW IN AN AGE OF LIMITATIONS AND EXCEPTIONS (Ruth L. Okediji ed., 2017).

[31] *See,* Authors Guild, Inc. v. HathiTrust, 755 F.3d 87 (2d Cir. 2014) (citing Pierre N. Leval "In short, our law recognizes that copyright is not an inevitable, divine, or natural right that confers on authors the absolute ownership of their creations. It is designed rather to stimulate activity and progress in the arts for the intellectual enrichment of the public."). *See also* Jessica Litman, *Readers' Copyright,* 58 J. COPYRIGHT SOC'Y 325–53 (2011).

[32] This approach is also consistent with the U.S. Constitutional authority: "To promote the Progress of Science and useful Arts, by securing for limited Times to Authors and Inventors the exclusive Right to their respective Writings and Discoveries." To promote progress in science and useful arts may require setting limits on exclusive rights that do not promote progress, such as the right to prevent the use of creative works for learning. *See, e.g.,* L. RAY PATTERSON & STANLEY LINDBERG, THE NATURE OF COPYRIGHT: A LAW OF USER RIGHTS (1991).

[33] *See, e.g.,* Jane C. Ginsburg, *Putting Cars on the "Information Superhighway": Authors, Exploiters and Copyright in Cyberspace,* 95 COLUM. L. REV. 1466 (1995).

In recent years, interest in users of copyrighted materials has grown. The literature increasingly centers on the *recipients* of copyrighted works.[34] Scholars stress the
significance of use of copyrighted materials for protecting freedom of speech[35] or
securing consumer sovereignty.[36] Others attempt to articulate users' interests within
the framework of copyright law.[37]

This chapter seeks to add to this literature by offering a framework for understanding the role of users in promoting copyright goals, and demonstrating how this
analysis could inform the scope of fair use. I argue that *use* is a fundamental part
of any creative process and therefore it must be an integral part of any copyright
policy. Drawing on the role of *users* in achieving copyright goals, I seek to identify
the interests of users wherein protection under copyright law is deemed to achieve
its intended purposes.

A focus on the role of users in the creative ecosystem may help us better understand the necessary conditions under which various players, including users, may
advance or impede copyright goals. These conditions could be manifested in part
as exceptions and limitations of copyright, and they may also have implications for
other copyright doctrines. For instance, an understanding of a user's role in achieving copyright goals could shape the definition of copyright subject matter (e.g., the
idea/expression dichotomy), or the scope of copyright exclusive rights.

5.3.2. *The Virtues of Using Creative Works*

The view of copyright as a legal regime seeking to stimulate creativity for the benefit
of the public entails a balance between two public interests: encouraging creativity and encouraging wide dissemination of copyrighted materials as the ultimate
goal of copyright law.[38] The focus on user rights brings these two interests together:
encouraging creativity by, *inter alia*, encouraging the use of creative works.

---

[34] *See, e.g.*, David Vaver, *Nimmer on Copyright Commemorative Essay: Copyright Defenses as User Rights*, J. COPYRIGHT SOC'Y (2013); Litman, *Readers' Copyright*, *supra* note 31; LESSIG, *supra* note 2; Pamela Samuelson, *Challenges in Mapping the Public Domain*, in THE FUTURE OF THE PUBLIC DOMAIN: IDENTIFYING THE COMMONS IN INFORMATION LAW (L. Guibault and P. Hugenholtz eds., 2006); Julie E. Cohen, *The Place of the User in Copyright Law*, 74 FORDHAM L. REV. 347, 370 (2005).

[35] *See, e.g.*, Tushnet, *Copy This Essay*, *supra* note 19; Malla Pollack, *A Listener's Free Speech, A Reader's Copyright*, 36 HOFSTRA L. REV. 1457 (2007).

[36] *See, e.g.*, Jessica Litman, *Lawful Personal Use*, 85 TEX. L. REV. 1871 (2007); Alan L. Durham, *Consumer Modification of Copyrighted Works*, 81 IND. L.J. 851 (2006); Joseph P. Liu, *Copyright Law's Theory of the Consumer*, 44 B.C. L. REV. 397 (2003).

[37] *See, e.g.*, Litman, *Readers' Copyright*, *supra* note 31; Niva Elkin-Koren, *Making Room for Consumers Under the DMCA*, 22 BERKELEY TECH. L.J. 1119–55 (2007); Julie E. Cohen, *The Place of the User in Copyright Law*, 74 FORDHAM L. REV. 347 (2005).

[38] *See, e.g.*, Glynn S. Lunney, Jr., *Fair Use and Market Failure: Sony Revisited*, 82 B.U. L. REV. 975 (2002).

It considers users and usage as *inputs* into a creative process rather than recipients of outputs from creative processes. This broader understanding of the way cultural works are created and shared recognizes the dynamic, interactive, and diffused nature of creative processes. It shifts the locus of creative processes from a single act of authoring "from thin air" to an ongoing process with multiple participants.

Creating new knowledge involves human capital, engagement in preexisting materials, and sharing a cultural language. It is in all these aspects of the creative ecosystem that the *use* of creative works comes into play.

Enhancing Human Capital

One type of use of creative works which encourages creativity is use for the purpose of learning. Learning was explicitly included in the full title of the 1710 Statute of Anne: "An Act for the Encouragement of Learning, by vesting the Copies of printed Books in the Authors or Purchasers of such Copies, during the Times therein mentioned."[39] Cultivating cultural progress requires learning, training, and an opportunity to absorb informational goods and interact with creative works. Advancing learning is a cornerstone of copyright policy. Copyright law recognizes the significance of learning by limiting the scope of protection to cover expressions but not ideas and including explicit exceptions for learning and teaching (i.e., fair use).

The use of copyrighted materials is crucial especially for learning, training, and acquiring the skills necessary to become an author.[40] Authors' creative skills and their ability to generate new works depend, *inter alia*, on opportunities to access previous works. Exposure to the books of the past, to modern art, or to available computer programs may all become essential for writing a new novel or developing a new app. Readers of novels learn to detect and better understand other people's emotions, a vital skill for inventing literary characters; the users of software acquire some programming skills and a better understanding of the way computer programs work. The use of creative works in this sense nurtures the human capital that may subsequently contribute to the production of additional works.

Human capital requires high-level training, good techniques and skills, but also knowledge of the current state of the art. Generating new creative output involves linking different types of content and turning information into meaningful knowledge. Creative processes often draw on creative works and knowledge inputs incurred through previous experiences. To become new authors, or develop authorship skills, users must be aware of the cultural context in which they act, for instance: existing works, classic genres, current trends, and artistic language.

---

[39] Statute of Anne, 1710, 8 Ann., c. 19.
[40] PATTERSON & LINDBERG, *supra* note 32.

Consequently, unrestricted access to copyrighted materials for the purpose of learning and teaching serves copyright goals.

Productive and Transformative Use

Another type of use that promotes creativity is the transformative use of preexisting materials. Creation is presumed to be incremental – new works are built upon previous works
– and current authors' rights are balanced against those of future authors. Authors are
often users of preexisting materials. Creative processes involve an ongoing interaction
with the cultural tradition and its dynamic present. Creative works are often the primary
resource for further creation. Software developers build on existing programs and apps;
artists refer to other works, borrow symbols, metaphors, and characters, and often quote
other works. Productive users, who transform preexisting works by adding something
original to preexisting materials, often become authors of a new derivative work.

The incremental nature of the creative process has long been recognized by copyright law, and reflected in copyright doctrines such as the low threshold of originality or
the exemption of transformative use.[41] The law presumes that authors do not create "out
of thin air," but in fact all authors are users of preexisting materials.[42] Here too, the balance between different authors, during the lifetime and evolvement of a creative work,
is implemented by various doctrines, such as the idea/expression dichotomy or fair use.
With the rise of UGC, users' freedom to use copyrighted materials without seeking a
license has become even more crucial for achieving copyright goals.

Generating Meaning

The role of users in creative processes is not limited, however, to transformative use
of preexisting materials. The use of creative works also promotes creativity by generating a shared cultural language.[43] In fact, the bulk of users' contribution to advance
the goals of copyright law is made through nontransformative uses.[44]

A better metaphor for creative processes is *interactive flow*, which generates
meaning. The view of creative processes as flow depicts the dynamic nature of such

---

[41] *See* Leval, *supra* note 1. Abraham Drassinower suggested that the centrality of user rights derives
from the notion of authorship which is fundamental to copyright law. Drassinower perceives authors
as users: "authors are not only producers or creators but simultaneously users of other pre-existing
materials." Abraham Drassinower, *Taking User Rights Seriously, in* IN THE PUBLIC INTEREST: THE
FUTURE OF CANADIAN COPYRIGHT LAW 462–79 (Michael Geist ed., 2005).

[42] PATTERSON & LINDBERG, *supra* note 32; Drassinower, *supra* note 41.

[43] ROSEMARY J. COOMBE, THE CULTURAL LIFE OF INTELLECTUAL PROPERTY: AUTHORSHIP,
APPROPRIATION AND THE LAW (1998); Niva Elkin-Koren, *Cyberlaw and Social Change: A Democratic
Approach to Copyright Law in Cyberspace*, 14 CARDOZO ARTS & ENT. L.J. 215 (1996).

[44] Rebecca Tushnet, *Copy This Essay, supra* note 19, at 535, 556 ("nontransformative uses" could be a
form of self-expression, persuasion, participation and affirmation).

processes where meaning occurs through interaction among human beings, using and developing a shared cultural language. Culture is a language which enables interaction and engagement with other people, objects, and nature. We use words, as well as musical notation, poems, and symbolic artifacts to communicate a message, and to understand one another as well as ourselves and to comprehend the world.

Reading books and newspapers, listening to music, and watching films, are not simply consumptive behaviors.[45] They are all creative practices which involve an interactive exchange of meaning. As Julie Cohen suggests, creative practices are diffused, interactive, relational, and carried out by users *through the use* of artifacts.[46] In this model of creativity, everyone is a *"user first* and a creator second."[47] The act of reading a book (or watching a film for that matter) engages the reader in a conversation with the text: a mutual productive experience of generating new meaning. These processes of generating meaning are part of a continuum: They are carried out not only by authors, but also through the use of cultural works. Authors share a symbiotic purpose with users of their works who engage in listening to, reading, or performing their works. Cultural practices therefore do not simply diffuse or exploit cultural works; they occur through engagement with cultural artifacts, which shapes their meaning.[48]

5.3.3. *A Rationale for User Rights*

The inquiry into user function in creative processes reveals a whole range of activities, including generating new derivative works but also absorbing, learning, and disseminating new knowledge. This suggests that users are not simply passive recipients of creative works but constitute an input in the creative process. Copyright law, which seeks to promote creative process, should therefore address the rights of both authors and users.

A view of the creative ecosystem as an interactive cultural flow may carry some implications for copyright policy. To encourage creativity, copyright law must focus on the ability of authors to benefit *ex-post*, but also on their ability *ex-ante* to access

---

45 *But see* Jane C. Ginsburg, *Authors and Users in Copyright*, 45 J. COPYRIGHT SOC'Y 1 (1997).
46 Julie Cohen describes creative practices as situated in a particular cultural context and carried out by users *through the use* of artifacts. Culture, she argues, is a process of engagement by individuals with cultural artifacts, negotiation of cultural pathways and the shaping of culture "through interactions between situated users, taste-making institutions, and social groups." *See* JULIE E. COHEN, CONFIGURING THE NETWORKED SELF: LAW, CODE, AND THE PLAY OF EVERYDAY PRACTICE 69–70, 84–88 (2012).
47 *Id.* at 66. *See, e.g.,* Cohen, *supra* note 37. Cohen proposes the notion of a *situated user*, who "engages cultural goods and artifacts found within the context of her culture through a variety of activities ranging from consumption to creative play." The situated user, she argues, appropriates cultural goods for four primary purposes: *consumption, communication, self-development* and *creative play.*
48 Niva Elkin-Koren, *Making Room for Consumers under the DMCA*, 22 BERKELEY TECH. L.J. 1119 (2007).

and use preexisting materials, acquire new skills, learn new techniques, be exposed to the cultural flow, and be inspired by new ideas. All these are necessary to stimulate new creation no less than establishing exclusive rights.

Users' freedom to use creative works may affect their ability to participate in the creative process. As suggested by Pamela Samuelson, limitations on the rights of copyright owners are necessary "to aid education, cultural participation, the creation of new works and the development of new forms of creative output."[49] Therefore, permissible uses are not simply odd exceptions, describing peculiar circumstances where the governing rule fails to apply, but important mechanisms for achieving copyright goals.

Moreover, to promote creativity, copyright law should focus on authors and users alike, as both are actively engaged in generating culture. This view assumes that two strategies are equally important in order to promote the goals of copyright law and maintain a proper balance between authors and users: ownership by authors and sufficient access by users. From this perspective, incentives to authors provide only one means of promoting creativity, while other, equally important mechanisms focus on securing adequate rights for users. In other words, authors' rights in their creative works (for incentives or just reward) and users' rights to use them (e.g., read, learn, disseminate, reuse, and transform) are different mechanisms for promoting copyright goals. This analysis suggests that copyright law is not confined merely to designing a proprietary regime in informational works: it also designs a regime where some uses fall beyond the scope of ownership and could be used without a license. This is the rationale of user rights.

5.3.4. *What Rights Do Users Need?*

What rights are necessary to enable users to participate in generating culture? There is no exhaustive list of user rights that can serve for reference. As a start, user rights may include the current list of L&E, which in part reflects some essential interests of users.[50] However, considering the role of users in applying L&E may reverse the direction of the inquiry: Rather than seeking to extract the overarching principles informing existing L&E, we should explore which uses are desirable to promote copyright goals and which actions should be permitted without a license.

Permissible uses may cover a wide array of aspects related to their role in the creative ecosystem. These rights may typically involve freedom to use creative works and knowledge resources for learning and teaching, freedom to create and develop,

---

[49] *See* Pamela Samuelson and Members of the Copyright Principles Project, *The Copyright Principles Project: Directions for Reform*, 25 BERKELEY TECH. L.J. 1175, (2010).

[50] *Id.*

and freedom to access and use. User rights might also be linked to a wide array of rights and privileges, such as consumer sovereignty, freedom of information, and freedom of expression.[51]

Obviously, not every action which contributes to user participation in creative processes should automatically gain protection as a user right. Balancing the rights of different players in the creative process may involve additional consideration, such as whether it is personal or commercial, whether it communicative or competing. Yet, the interest in promoting some uses should be considered and balanced against those of rightholders when courts are called to draw the boundaries of copyright protection under flexible norms such as fair use, or when legislators are considering new rights and new exemptions under copyright law.

Further understanding of the users' role in advancing the objectives of copyright law could help identify the conditions necessary to enable them to promote copyright goals.

Authoring

Copyright policy has long emphasized the importance of creative (transformative) use of preexisting works to achieve copyright goals. If the intended purpose of copyright is to promote the creation of works, the use of preexisting materials to create a new expression should be encouraged.

Copyright law creates serious impediments to creative use by user-authors, especially for UGC which is often generated by amateurs, in the margins of the commercial model facilitated by copyright law.[52] The need to acquire a license prior to each and every use of copyrighted materials could make it prohibitively expensive for individual users to make use of preexisting works. As previously noted, users often lack the legal expertise and necessary funding to determine which license is necessary, identify the different copyright owners, negotiate a license to use the work, and pay the license fee. The high costs involved in licensing are often greater than the anticipated benefits from the work, especially where amateurs are concerned and no commercial exploitation is expected.

Simply avoiding copyright infringement becomes a major challenge for amateur creators. Indeed, fair use permits some unlicensed transformative uses.

---

[51] Scholars have listed several examples of such rights, such as personal use (Litman, *Lawful Personal Use*, *supra* note 36), learning and educational use (Elkin-Koren & Fishman-Afori, *infra* note 108), breathing space for creation by user-authors (COHEN, CONFIGURING THE NETWORKED SELF, *supra* note 46), rights necessary for free speech and a participatory citizenry (Tushnet, *Copy This Essay*, *supra* note 19; NETANEL, COPYRIGHT'S PARADOX, *supra* note 20).

[52] *See, e.g.*, LESSIG, *supra* note 2; Diane Leenheer Zimmerman, *Living Without Copyright in a Digital World*, 70 ALBANY L. REV. 1375, 1376–77 (2007).

Transformative use is considered a cornerstone of fair use, and was widely recognized by courts and legislators, in both artistic[53] and technological contexts.[54] Yet fair use provisions are rather vague and indeterminate, creating a high risk of liability. The uncertainty as to permissible uses and the risk of liability may impede some uses, which are otherwise legitimate.

To encourage users' authorship, user rights should enable *productive use* of copyrighted materials, building on existing works to create a new creative content, putting works to new use, or adapting content for ongoing needs.[55] Such rights may cover the adaptation of digital content for personal use and the remixing of digital content for self-expression and noncommercial purposes.

Users' rights should foster more certainty by adding specific rights apart from fair use. An example is the newly introduced *Non-commercial User-generated Content* exception to copyright infringement under Canadian copyright law.[56] This provision explicitly permits individual users to use copyrighted materials in the creation of a new work for noncommercial purposes without authorization of the copyright owner.[57]

---

[53] *See, e.g., Campbell v. Acuff-Rose Music, Inc.*, 510 U.S. 569 (1994).

[54] *See, e.g., Perfect 10, Inc. v. Amazon.com*, 508 F.3d 1146 (9th Cir. 2007); *Authors Guild, Inc. v. HathiTrust*, 755 F.3d 87 (2d Cir. 2014).

[55] A related issue is interoperability. Interoperability can directly affect creativity and innovation. It enables experimentation and the creation of new content by using different sources. Restrictions on interoperability, either by design or license, may compromise users' ability to put their content to its most efficient use or generate new content.

[56] Canada *Copyright Act*, R.S.C. 1985, c. C-42 CCA, s. 29.21. [(29.21 (1) It is not an infringement of copyright for an individual to use an existing work or other subject-matter or copy of one, which has been published or otherwise made available to the public, in the creation of a new work or other subject-matter in which copyright subsists and for the individual – or, with the individual's authorization, a member of their household – to use the new work or other subject-matter or to authorize an intermediary to disseminate it, if

  (*a*) the use of, or the authorization to disseminate, the new work or other subject-matter is done solely for noncommercial purposes;

  (*b*) the source – and, if given in the source, the name of the author, performer, maker or broadcaster – of the existing work or other subject-matter or copy of it are mentioned, if it is reasonable in the circumstances to do so;

  (*c*) the individual had reasonable grounds to believe that the existing work or other subject-matter or copy of it, as the case may be, was not infringing copyright; and

  (*d*) the use of, or the authorization to disseminate, the new work or other subject-matter does not have a substantial adverse effect, financial or otherwise, on the exploitation or potential exploitation of the existing work or other subject-matter – or copy of it – or on an existing or potential market for it, including that the new work or other subject-matter is not a substitute for the existing one.]

[57] Peter Yu, *Can the Canadian UGC Exception Be Transplanted Abroad?*, 26 INTELL. PROP. J. 177–205 (2014).

Learning

The role of learning in promoting copyright goals highlights the importance of *educational use*. This includes self-learning, exploring, absorbing, tinkering, and interacting with creative works. It also includes use for teaching and training.

Educational use requires that access to learning materials remains affordable and that licensing fees do not hinder learning. Copyright law places several impediments for educational use. The most obvious reason is that publishers are granted a monopoly power to determine the price. High fees, however, are not the only obstacle to the use of copyrighted materials for educational purposes. Difficulties in acquiring a license for each particular use often create serious barriers to efficient use, and in some cases may eradicate the use altogether. The effort involved in identifying the relevant rightholders and negotiating a license may be prohibitive. High transaction costs may cause teachers or educational institutions to refrain from making materials available to their students for the purpose of learning, even though such use may promote copyright goals.

Facilitating education use may require consideration of some distinctive characteristics of learning, which often involve players who are not motivated by profits. First, learning often requires the assistance of teachers, guides, and educators, to facilitate materials and offer input and guidance on selecting materials, navigating knowledge, explaining, and interpreting. Incentives for learning should therefore address not only the students or end-users but also their teachers.[58] Second, many learning activities proceed through educational and learning institutions, such as schools, colleges, universities, and libraries, which are often nonprofit. Consequently, user rights may extend to these cultural institutions that facilitate learning. Third, while public interest in promoting learning is strong, a gap often exists between the public welfare and the interest of the individual teachers and institutions that facilitate learning. While these facilitators will presumably strive to invest optimal resources to enable learning, the effect of resources on learning is often difficult to measure, and the incentives of teachers and schools to offer optimal access to educational resources might be suboptimal.

Another impediment to use might be the high level of unpredictability. For instance, the high level of uncertainty regarding the scope of permissible use for educational purposes under fair use might have a strong chilling effect on making materials available to students for the purpose of teaching and learning. Educational institutions, which are often risk-averse, might obtain a license even when such a license is unwarranted, and avoid any unlicensed use for fear that courts would not

---

[58] The Supreme Court of Canada explicitly recognized this distinct characteristic of education, holding in *Alberta (Education)* that teachers share a symbiotic purpose with students who engage in private study. *See* Alberta (Education) v. Canadian Copyright Licensing Agency, 2012 S.C.C. 37.

find it fair. University professors cannot be expected to undertake a sophisticated analysis of fair use for each particular item to be included in their reading materials. Librarians cannot apply the fair use provisions to the thousands of reading items they are required to handle every semester. The only choice left to a university is to acquire a license for uses that are actually fair (therefore free) or to compromise their educational mission by refraining from making any materials available to their students throughout the educational process.[59] A vicious cycle arises: The more users seek permission for what is presumably fair use, the more others perceive such uses as nonfair; consequently, more people seek permission where such permission is in fact unnecessary. This results in a Clearance Culture, where every use is assumed to require a license.[60]

Consequently, user rights should give priority to enhancing predictability and lowering the cost of accessing creative works that are necessary to enable learning. Special attention should be given to measures that could lower transaction costs of acquiring licenses and promote certainty in educational use, thereby encouraging teachers and schools to facilitate educational use.

Educational use may also require some room for spontaneous use of copyrighted materials for educational purposes, to enable teachers to respond to matters in good time, without having to clear the rights months prior to the beginning of classes. The significance of spontaneous use arises, as open textbooks create new opportunities for learning communities to engage in preparing educational materials on an enduring basis, and enable etextbook users to access, use, copy, remix, and further adapt the works to their dynamic needs.

---

[59] The recent decision in the case of *Cambridge University Press v. Becker* demonstrates this deadlock. Several major academic publishers filed a lawsuit against Georgia State University (GSU), claiming that the university was responsible for infringing their copyrighted books in its electronic course reserve (e-reserve) system. GSU relied on its 2009 Copyright Policy which required each law professor to complete a "fair use checklist," determining whether each item included in the reading list was fair use. The court examined whether this contributed to infringements by professors who had uploaded materials to the e-reserve system. In an opinion exceeding three hundred pages, the district court analyzed each of the sampled ninety-nine instances of infringement claimed by the plaintiffs and held that copied excerpts did not qualify as fair use in only five instances. Indeed, the court praised GSU for adopting a fair use policy, admitting that "fair use principles are notoriously difficult to apply." Nevertheless, the court held that fair use is facts-intensive and specific to each individual case, and consequently held GSU liable for copyright infringement. Cambridge Univ. Press v. Becker, 863 F. Supp. 2d 1190 (N.D. Ga. 2012). The Court of Appeals for the Eleventh Circuit went even further in fostering the "case-by-case" approach, thus leaving university professors, librarians, and staff with very little guidance on what amounts to fair use for educational purposes. Cambridge Univ. Press v. Patton, 769 F.3d 1232 (11th Cir. 2014).

[60] PATRICIA AUFDERHEIDE & PETER JASZI, UNTOLD STORIES: CREATIVE CONSEQUENCES OF THE RIGHTS CLEARANCE CULTURE FOR DOCUMENTARY FILMMAKERS 17–19 (2004); James Gibson, *Risk Aversion and Rights Accretion in Intellectual Property Law*, 116 YALE L.J. 882, 895–98 (2007).

Learning often involves more than simple access to copyrighted materials. It may also entail interaction with copyrighted works, which involves some changes and modifications. Therefore, educational use should also include freedom to explore, tinker with, transform, and edit materials before making them available to students.

Finally, learning and teaching may also require some assurances of intellectual privacy. Freedom from ongoing monitoring is necessary to protect the intimacy and private nature of the educational experience that is essential for meaningful learning. Intellectual privacy is also important for maintaining academic freedom. Thus, monitoring the use of copyrighted materials for the purpose of collecting royalties may compromise this freedom.[61]

Participating

While the need to permit transformative use by potential authors is widely acknowledged in copyright doctrine, the nontransformative aspects of use have been less explored.

Non-commercial access and use of cultural works is essential for promoting the use of cultural works. Freedom to access books of diverse origin and perspective pertains to fundamental liberties such as freedom of expression, intellectual freedom, and privacy. Access to copyrighted materials is essential in order to exercise citizenship in the twenty-first century. As information becomes crucial to every aspect of everyday life, access to information may affect one's ability to participate in modern life as an independent, autonomous human being. For instance, some free access to academic publications is necessary in order to facilitate the monitoring and review of scientific research; however, it also enables people to read about potential treatments for their personal health problems, and civil society (NGOs, bloggers) to engage in public debate regarding health policy. Free – as in open – access to books, newspapers, and journals on a nondiscriminatory basis was once offered by libraries, but with the shift to cloud services public libraries may no longer guarantee sufficient public access.

Intellectual privacy also arises from the role of users as active participants in creating culture.[62] Digital distribution often involves built-in surveillance. When music or apps are downloaded to a smartphone, or an eBook is downloaded to an e-Reader such as Kindle, rightholders may collect and retain detailed information about users, their reading habits and intellectual preferences. This may turn the

---

[61] For instance, the plaintiff in the Georgia State University case asked to receive access to the e-Reserve system and to the original records on the use and during a period of three years in order to monitor use for the purpose of collecting royalties. *See* Cambridge Univ. Press v. Patton, 769 F.3d 1232 (11th Cir. 2014).

[62] Neil Richards, *Intellectual Privacy*, 87 TEXAS L. REV. 387 (2008).

reading experience, which used to be intimate and private, into public knowledge. Enabling users to freely participate in cultural discourse may require access without surveillance. This is not simply a matter of privacy but may also affect the ability of user-authors to participate actively in the creative process by generating and disseminating cultural works. Fear of monitoring may create a chilling effect, causing users to refrain from seeking specific knowledge resources or reading particular materials for fear of their interests being monitored and recorded. A recent survey among fiction and nonfiction writers in fifty countries found that writers were deeply concerned with surveillance, with a large percentage reporting self-censorship resulting in avoiding controversial topics in their work or in their personal communications.[63] Aside from the possible chilling effect of surveillance on reading and writing, it may also threaten independent thinking by penetrating the intimacy of reading. To promote creativity, copyright law should encourage freedom to explore any cultural, religious, professional, political, or other type of resource, without the knowledge of third parties.

Perpetual access to personal copies of creative works is another issue.[64] As consumers, users may be entitled to use a purchased copy on any of their devices and make copies for their own personal use.[65] However, copyrighted works are increasingly offered as a service (e.g., subscription, streaming). The courts' interpretation of exclusive rights (reproduction, distribution) tends to strengthen the view that digital copies are not owned by their users and cannot be sold without the permission of the copyright owner.[66] Moreover, even if users were considered owners of a particular copy, there is no guarantee that a right to perpetual use would be enforced. The consumer protection perspective is likely to be too narrow to secure a right of perpetual use in creative materials. The reason is that consumer protection laws generally focus on consumer expectations.[67] Consequently, if no warranties were made in the original license regarding a permanent right to access the materials, or alternatively an appropriate notice was given prior to the termination of access, consumer protection laws may not be an effective remedy.

From a user-rights perspective, a right to secure continued access to knowledge resources is essential for users' participation in cultural processes. The reason is that cultural works often incorporate users' identity and input. A right to access copies that one has read (news stories, books, films, music), might be necessary to protect one's autonomy. Such works often become part of one's identity and a point

---

[63] *See* Pen American Center, Global Chilling: The Impact of Mass Surveillance on International Writers (Jan. 5, 2015), *available at* http://pen.org/global-chill

[64] Litman, *Lawful Personal Use, supra* note 36, at 1878.

[65] *See* Cohen, *supra* note 37; Liu, *supra* note 36; Durham, *supra* note 36; Litman, *supra* note 36.

[66] *See supra* notes 5–8 and accompanying text.

[67] Elkin-Koren, *Making Room for Consumers, supra* note 37.

of reference for defining one's taste and preferences. Copies of works that have been read or watched by users are often used for manifesting an identity or expressing a political statement.

With the shift to cloud computing, users lose control over their data and applications as they are all stored in remote facilities and subject to the terms and condition of an online provider. The shift to cloud computing and streaming services puts users at a disadvantage. Users become completely dependent on access providers, and access to works could be terminated at any time.[68] In such circumstances, recognizing a right to perpetual use becomes ever more important. This does not necessarily mean that users should own copies of works. Yet, some minimal guarantees of perpetual access to the original work must be secured for users. Also, users may need to exercise some freedom in using creative works with additional works (their own or others), such as attaching pictures, linking to text or playing music for personal use.

5.4. USING RIGHTS TO PROMOTE DESIRABLE USES

The previous discussion suggested that to promote creation, copyright law should focus on authors and users alike as both are actively engaged in generating culture. This view assumes that two strategies are equally important in order to promote the goals of copyright law and maintain a proper balance between authors and users: ownership by authors and sufficient access by users. Assuming that some unlicensed uses should be promoted by law, what is the best way to achieve it? How should the law protect users' interests and secure a desirable level of unlicensed use? Is it sufficient to afford users a legal defense in some circumstances, or is it necessary to recognize a right to make permissible uses?

5.4.1. *The Rise of the Rights Discourse*

In recent years several commentators have suggested that permissible uses, such as fair dealing or fair use, should be treated as user rights.[69] About two decades ago, Ray Patterson and Stanley Lindberg coined the term "users' rights" in their seminal work *The Nature of Copyright: A Law of Users' Rights*. Patterson and Lindberg argued that the constitutional purpose of copyright law, to promote the progress of knowledge, mandates that copyright law should not simply focus on authors, but also on users

---

[68] *See supra* notes 5–16 and accompanying text.

[69] *See* Vaver, *supra* note 34. See also Hugh Breakey advocating the general applicability of rights language to describe user rights under copyright. Hugh Breakey, *User's Rights and the Public Domain*, 3 INTELL. PROP. Q. 312–23 (2010).

who are learning, absorbing, and disseminating knowledge.[70] More recently, Jessica Litman argued that copyright law secures readers' rights, or at the very least readers' liberties.[71]

In Canada, David Vaver has argued that the framing of permissible uses as rights is necessary in order to achieve a more balanced law, as no symmetry exists between authors' exclusive rights and users' narrow defenses. If copyright is to be understood as creating a reasonable balance between authors and users, it needs to be a balance between like and like, not between authors' *rights* and the public's *privileges*.[72] Taking an authorship-centered perspective Abraham Drassinower argues that copyright law should not be understood as a prohibition on copying, but instead as "an institutionalized distinction between permissible and impermissible copying."[73] Viewed from this perspective, copyright is a legal regime concerned with authorship, which applies both to authors and users.

Over the past decade courts have also addressed the legal status of L&Es. The Supreme Court of Canada was the first to explicitly address the issue in *CCH Canadian Ltd. v. Law Society of Upper Canada.* The Court held that the fair dealing exception, as well as the other exceptions in the Canadian Copyright Act, should be understood as "user rights."[74] Recently, in a series of precedential copyright decisions in 2012, the Canadian Court reaffirmed the user-rights approach to L&E.[75] Citing with approval Professor David Vaver, the Canadian Supreme Court explained: "*User rights are not just loopholes. Both owner rights and user rights should therefore be given the fair and balanced reading that befits remedial legislation.*"[76]

Those precedential decisions shift from a legal-defense approach to a user-rights approach to fair dealing. From this perspective, "user rights" are an integral concept in copyright law, and should be equally treated as the rights of authors. L&E do not simply represent a legal defense which only excuses a particular user from liability in certain circumstance, in what would otherwise constitute a copyright infringement. Instead, fair dealing, or fair use for that matter, should be interpreted as a right which is deemed necessary in order to achieve the goals that copyright law is designed to promote.

---

[70] PATTERSON & LINDBERG, *supra* note 32.

[71] Jessica Litman, Reader's Copyright, *supra* note 31 (2011).

[72] *See* Vaver, *supra* note 34; Drassinower, *supra* note 41, at 462–79.

[73] *See* Drassinower, *supra* note 41, at 462–79.

[74] CCH Canadian Ltd. v. Law Society of Upper Canada, 2004 S.C.C. 13 [2004] 1 S.C.R. 339 (Can.).

[75] Society of Composers, Authors and Music Publishers of Canada (SOCAN) v. Bell Canada, 2012 S.C.C. 36, [2012] 2 S.C.R. 326 (Can.); Alberta (Education) v. Canadian Copyright Licensing Agency, (Access Copyright), 2012 SCC 37, 2 S. C. R. 345 (Can.).

[76] *See* CCH v. Law Society, *supra* note 74, para. 48.

In Israel, which only recently introduced fair use into its new 2007 Copyright Act, the issue of user rights has already been tackled by the Israeli Supreme Court. Initially, in 2012 the Court explicitly rejected the position that fair use is a user right. The case, *Football Ass'n Premier League Ltd. v. Anonymous* (2012),[77] involved a petition to unmask the identity of an anonymous user who streamed unauthorized broadcasts of football matches owned by the English Premier League. Although the petition was dismissed on procedural grounds, the Court held that streaming constituted copyright infringement and fair use did not apply. Explicitly rejecting the user-rights approach, the Israeli Supreme Court explained that fair use should be understood as simply a legal defense.

Soon after, in *Telran Communications (1986) Ltd. v. Charlton Ltd.* (2013),[78] the Israeli Supreme Court questioned this approach. The case involved the legality of marketing decoding cards which enabled Israeli customers to decode the encoded broadcasts of the World Cup games, which were transmitted by foreign channels via satellite. The Court held that merely distributing the decoding cards did not amount to a copyright infringement, nor was it a contributory infringement, since simply watching copyrighted materials did not constitute a copyright infringement. The Court explicitly rejected the *defense* approach to fair use held by the Premier League Court, noting that fair use is not merely a technical defense for copyright infringement but a permissible use. Consequently, even if users of the decoding cards were making unauthorized copies, which were nevertheless considered fair use, there was no ground for holding the defendant liable for contributory infringement. According to Justice Zilbertal, users who exercise user rights do not commit an infringing act which is excused, but instead they act in a manner that is explicitly permissible by law, and therefore there is no infringement to begin with. Consequently, "when no infringement materializes, there is no infringement to 'contribute' to. Hence, since the end-users carried out a permissible act, the middleman 'contributed' to a permissible act – and in any event did not infringe any rights of the copyright owner, since these rights have not been violated in the first place."[79]

A few weeks later, in the case of *Safecom v. Raviv* (2013),[80] the Israeli Supreme Court reaffirmed this approach. The decision addressed the copying of drawings of a functional electric device in a patent application submitted to the USPTO. The Court cited with agreement the user-rights approach upheld in *Telran* and noted the judicial controversy on this issue, commenting that the time was ripe for an extended judicial panel consideration of this matter.

[77] CA 9183/09 Football Ass'n Premier League Ltd. v. Anonymous (2012) (Isr.).
[78] CA 5097/11 Telran Commc'ns (1986) Ltd. v. Charlton Ltd. (2013) (Isr.).
[79] *Id.*
[80] CA 7996/11 Safecom Ltd. v. Ofer Raviv (2013) (Isr.).

The rise of user-rights discourse in recent decisions in Canada and Israel suggests that the legal status of L&Es might may have far-reaching legal consequences. Such legal implications are further discussed in Section 5.5.

5.4.2. *The Formalistic Analysis of Rights*

Although L&E are frequently invoked in court, they only rarely trigger a serious analysis of their legal nature. Courts and commentators often refer to "user rights" as an all-encompassing category, loosely describing the public domain, exceptions and limitations and other permissible uses.[81] They have also used the term *user rights* without fully developing the legal implications of framing permissible uses as rights.[82]

One way to gain a better understanding of user rights is by mapping copyright entitlements and their corresponding duties. A classic view of copyright often describes the jural relations between owners and users within the matrix proposed by Wesley Hohfeld.[83] Copyright is generally understood as a bundle of *"rights-to-exclude"* enumerated uses. This approach entails the view that potential users are under a duty to refrain from any use which contradicts the exclusive rights and has not been authorized by the copyright owner. The view of copyright as a *"right to exclude"* assumes that the copyright owner is vested with a set of exclusive rights over the use of her copyrighted work. These rights impose correlative, *in rem*, duties on everyone else to refrain from any unauthorized use within the scope of the rights.[84] Put simply, a duty-holder must refrain from using the rights exclusively vested in the copyright owner, or else be subject to remedies.

This formalistic approach defines copyright in terms of rights accorded to right-holders and their correlative duties. Portraying the relationship between copyright owners and potential users of their copyrighted works in Hohfeldian terms demonstrates some of the conceptual difficulties arising from the view of "fair use" as

---

[81] For a critical review of these approaches, see Edward Samuels, *The Public Domain in Copyright Law*, 41 J. COPYRIGHT SOC'Y U.S.A. 137 (1993).

[82] There are a few exceptions, see Breakey, *supra* note 69; Vaver, *supra* note 34.

[83] In his seminal article Wesley Newcomb Hohfeld analyzes the various types of jural relations within a scheme of rights and correlative duties. *See* Wesley Newcomb Hohfeld, *Some Fundamental Legal Conceptions as Applied in Judicial Reasoning*, 23 YALE L.J. 16, 30–32 (1913).

[84] *See* Shyamkrishna Balganesh, *The Obligatory Structure of Copyright Law: Unbundling the Wrong of Copying*, 125 HARVARD L. REV. 1664, 1670 (2012) (arguing that copyright achieves exclusion by forbidding all others from copying the expression – creating a "duty not to copy."). Balganesh draws a distinction between the rights under property law, which "actively *enables* the exclusive use of the *res* and operates within the domain of positive liberty" and rights under copyright, which *disable* "others from copying the expression and operates as a form of negative liberty." This is based on a distinction between negative freedom, namely, *freedom from* interference, and positive freedom, *freedom to* "which involves the affirmative *conferral* of the ability to undertake an action."

a *limitation* and the advantages of articulating fair use as user rights. This point is further discussed in the next section.

5.4.3. *Is Fair Use an Affirmative Defense?*

In the few occasions where the legal status of fair use was mentioned by the U.S. Supreme Court, it was in the context of procedural burden, holding that since fair use is an affirmative defense the burden of proof in demonstrating that it applies lies with the defendant.[85]

The view of fair use as an affirmative defense assumes that copyright law grants authors absolute property rights within the scope of their exclusive rights, though in some circumstances it may excuse the behavior of a particular user and will not impose liability for what otherwise might still be an infringing behavior.[86]

The defense approach to fair use raises several difficulties. One issue is conceptual, in that the notion of a legal defense presupposes the existence of a legal duty. Fair use sets limits on the exclusive rights of rightholders, thereby creating a legal space where, at a minimum, nonowners are not subject to any duty. Thus in this context the copyright held by rightholders is limited by the circumstances that fall under fair use, and in such circumstances *no duty* befalls the user to avoid unauthorized use. This analysis suggests that fair use, closely examined, cannot be described as merely a *legal defense*.[87] One does not need to assert a legal defense if one is not under a duty to act in a particular way or avoid a particular action. Whether a nonowner is under a *duty* to refrain from making particular use of a copyrighted work depends on whether such use falls under *fair use* or any other permissible use defined by law. In fair use circumstances, a user is free to exercise fair use, and under no duty whatsoever to avoid such use. Obviously, a user is under no duty to make limited use of copyrighted materials for parody, nor is he under a duty to avoid making a parody that constitutes fair use. This analysis suggests that fair use is a legal regime where users of copyrighted materials are subject to no-duty, or in Hohfeldian terms, nonowners have a *privilege* or, as later described by several commentators, a *liberty*.[88]

Another reason to question the narrow view of fair use as a legal defense is normative. Conceiving of fair use as a legal defense neglects the central role of

---

[85] *See* Harper & Row, Publishers, Inc. v. Nation Enters., 471 US 539, 561 (1985); Campbell v. Acuff-Rose Music, Inc., 510 US 579, at 590 (1994); Cambridge Univ. Press v. Patton, 769 F.3d 1232 (11th Cir.2014).

[86] Balganesh, for instance, argues that fair use merely offers an excuse for circumstances in which an otherwise infringing act (copying) will not impose liability. *See* Balganesh, *supra* note 84, at 1684–85.

[87] Those who believe L&E should be viewed as a legal defense, find support for this view in the fact that the burden of proof in fair use rests on the user/defendant. Yet, there are other examples of rights where the burden of proof rests with the rightholder.

[88] It has been suggested that the term "liberty" should replace the term "privilege" to better reflect the essence of the legal relations. *See, e.g.*, Breakey, *supra* note 69.

permissible uses in promoting copyright goals. The view of user rights as a mechanism for promoting copyright goals, that is, enhancing creativity, mandates that not only authors' rights but also users' rights are protected by copyright law. Copyright law must therefore not only secure incentives to authors, it must also promote learning, absorption, transformation, and dissemination of knowledge. From this perspective, fair use is not wrongful, albeit excusable, copying in exceptional circumstances, but rather a central measure for achieving copyright goals.

Along the same line, a third reason why fair use should not be interpreted as merely a defense arises from copyright policy. Fair use, and other L&Es, must ensure that copyright law serves its intended purpose, therefore they should encourage uses, such as fair transformative use, that foster creative activity. A use that the law seeks to promote must be permitted *ex-ante*, as a permissible use, and not simply excused *ex-post*. Recognizing permissible uses as rights also communicates a strong normative message that such uses are legitimate and should be pursued. Such a clear message of permissible uses may offer legitimacy and guidance to the public on use without the copyright holders' permission when such use is necessary to promote the intended objectives of copyright law.

Finally, the narrow view of fair use, and other L&Es for that matter, as an affirmative defense could be easily overridden by a license. Indeed, some courts have interpreted fair use as an implied license. For instance, the Court of Appeals in the *Georgia State University* case explained:

> In a sense, the grant to an author of copyright in a work is predicated upon a reciprocal grant to the public by the work's author of an implied license for fair use of the work.[89]

This narrow view of fair use assumes that the author implicitly authorized such uses that fall within the boundaries of fair use. Yet some rightholders may seek to limit fair use by including in a contract or a license agreement explicit restrictions on activities that would otherwise be typically considered fair use under the law. The defense approach to fair use might be insufficient to counterbalance such practices.

5.4.4. *Objections to the User-Rights Approach*

The user-rights approach may raise several objections. Focusing on the correlativity of copyright law, several commentators rejected the view that fair use, and other L&E, should be understood as user rights.[90] Accordingly, fair use cannot be treated

---

[89] Cambridge Univ. Press v. Patton, 769 F.3d 1232 (11th Cir. 2014).

[90] *See* Samuels, *supra* note 81; John Cahir, *Right or Liberty?*, *in* INTELLECTUAL PROPERTY: THE MANY FACES OF THE PUBLIC DOMAIN 35, 38 (Charlotte Wealde & Hector L. MacQueen eds., 2007).

as a right as it does not create any correlative duties on copyright owners to enable such permissible uses. This view reflects however a narrow understanding of rights. Users' rights could be protected by a wide variety of legal measures.[91] At a minimum, they correlate with the duty not to interfere. In other instances, user rights may correlate with some strict duties – in which case they might be considered *rights* in the strong sense. So the issue is not whether user rights should be protected but how the law should protect these interests of users of copyrighted materials. The choice of whether to protect permissible uses as rights in the strong sense or as liberties may depend on policy, and is not necessarily driven by the intrinsic nature of the rights themselves.

Another objection to the user-rights approach is that fair use is an indeterminate standard. This legal standard is intended to enable the courts to accommodate the law to rapid social, economic, and technological developments. Since courts may exercise wide discretion in determining what is fair on a case-by-case basis, fair use cannot qualify as a right since its scope is unknown. Moreover, as a matter of policy, a user-rights approach cannot achieve its intended goals to encourage permissible uses by offering clear guidelines. Arguably, the purpose of the rights approach is to define permissible uses, *ex-ante*, as rights, thus increasing certainty and encouraging permissible use. But fair use lacks the necessary specificity to offer guidance on what might be considered permissible. It suffers from a high level of uncertainty and it is often unclear *ex-ante* whether a particular use would be considered fair. The rights discourse cannot eliminate this high level of uncertainty arising from fair use.

Certainly, fair use allows the courts a great degree of flexibility in applying the legal principles to particular circumstances. At the same time, however, fair use adjudication does generate substantive rules of conduct. Recent studies have identified some systematic patterns in courts' four-factor analysis,[92] so some rules of practice may be extracted from existing fair use jurisprudence and provide answers to real cases.

More fundamentally, the indeterminacy of fair use does not detract from its nature as a right.[93] Indeed, the scope of rights accorded by law to copyright owners is also defined by a set of legal standards, such as *originality* and the *idea/expression*

---

[91] Hohfeld describes "right" in the broad sense, to cover not only rights in the narrow sense (which correlates to a duty), but also privileges, powers, and immunities. *See also* David Vaver, *Copyright Defenses as User Rights*, 60 J. COPYRIGHT SOC'Y U.S.A. 661 (2013).

[92] *See, e.g.*, Barton Beebe, *An Empirical Study of U.S. Copyright Fair Use Opinions, 1978–2005*, 156 U. PA. L. REV. 549 (2008); Neil Netanel, *Making Sense of Fair Use*, 15 LEWIS CLARK L. REV. 715 (2011); Matthew Sag, *Predicting Fair Use*, 73 OHIO ST. L.J. 1 (2012); Pamela Samuelson, *Unbundling Fair Uses*, 77 FORDHAM L. REV. 2537, 2540 (2009).

[93] *See also* Pascale Chapdelaine, *The Ambiguous Nature of Copyright Users' Rights*, 26 INTELL. PROP. J. 1–45 (2013) (arguing that the "lack of certainty, i.e., whether certain acts fall within the scope of an exception to copyright infringement, should not be a bar per se to qualify exceptions as rights giving rise to claims").

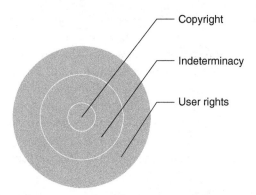

FIGURE 5.1. The scope of rights.

dichotomy. These legal standards are no less indeterminate than fair use and are also construed and applied by the courts without detracting from the characterization of copyrights as rights.

Moreover, the uncertainty associated with fair use may affect owners' and users' rights equally. Indeterminacy characterizes uses which have not been adjudicated by courts so far, and may fall inside or outside the copyright owner's sovereignty. But once a court decides that a particular use is fair, it falls within user rights and outside the boundaries of copyright (see Figure 5.1).

Finally, a plausible objection to the rights discourse may focus on power. This line of argument echoes the "critique of rights" developed by critical legal studies (CLS) theorists.[94] The critique of rights maintains that rights discourse might be less useful in promoting a progressive agenda, and may actually impede democracy and justice. CLS scholars have argued that negative liberties, which protect citizens from government interference, may offer powerful players protection from government intervention and in many cases simply release the government from any responsibility for ensuring that persons can exercise their liberties effectively (positive rights).[95]

The rights discourse in copyright reflects different challenges, however. While the CLS critique of the rights discourse focuses on constitutional rights, the user rights approach in copyright applies to private law. Indeed, it is arguable that user rights, like any legal rights, could benefit the more powerful players who may enjoy better information about their rights and significant advantages in access to justice. In fact, in recent years fair use has been claimed by powerful repeat players,

---

[94] *See generally* William W. Fisher, *The Development of Modern American Legal Theory and the Judicial Interpretation of the Bill of Rights, in* A CULTURE OF RIGHTS: THE BILL OF RIGHTS IN PHILOSOPHY, POLITICS, AND LAW-1791 and 1991 (Michael J. Lacey & Knud Haakonssen eds., 1991).

[95] *See* Mark Tushnet, *An Essay on Rights*, 62 TEX. L. REV. 1363, 1392 (1984).

for example, Google and Amazon.[96] The outcome of these cases, however, facilitated more access to end users and served to promote the rights of individual users. A rights discourse in copyright could equally apply to individual users, and rights could be invoked to restrain the power of facilitating intermediaries, as further demonstrated in the following discussion in the next section. True, a user-rights approach might be blind to consideration of power, but overall, the focus on permissible uses may empower individual users and strengthen their claim for permissible unlicensed access.

5.5. LEGAL IMPLICATIONS OF USER RIGHTS

The foregoing discussion pointed to a need to secure the rights of users of copyrighted materials. I argued that users in the digital era require more freedom in order to access knowledge and participate in cultural processes, but in fact their freedom is under siege. I also argued that given these threats to users' freedom, a narrow approach to L&E may defeat copyright's intended purpose, and a user-rights approach might be necessary to encourage permissible uses and serve copyright goals. What might the legal consequences of recognizing user rights be? How is the treatment of fair use as a right likely to shape the scope of copyright and the legal relationship between owners and nonowners vis-à-vis creative works? This section addresses these questions in greater detail.

Much attention has been focused on the procedural implications of protecting user interests as an affirmative defense, considering that the burden of proof in demonstrating fair use rests on the defendant. There might be good reasons to place the burden of proof on the defendant after the plaintiff has demonstrated that her exclusive rights in the copyrighted work has been used without authorization. Yet even so, fair use might still be considered a *right*. It is often the case that claimants exercising a right must still carry the burden of proving their rights.[97] The legal implications of the user-rights approach may extend far beyond procedural consequences, however. It may affect the legal interpretation of fair use and facilitate a legal oversight of private ordering.

5.5.1. *Legal Interpretation*

A narrow view of fair use as an affirmative defense takes the scope of copyright protection as a given, and treats fair use as the exception. It assumes that fair use could

---

[96] *See, e.g.,* Perfect 10, Inc. v. Amazon.com, 508 F.3d 1146 (9th Cir. 2007); Authors Guild, Inc. v. HathiTrust, 755 F.3d 87 (2d Cir. 2014).

[97] A classic example is the right of self-defense: A person who was attacked, is free to use sufficient force to repel the attack. Notwithstanding this privilege (right in the broad sense), the defended still carries the burden to prove his allegations that he was attacked.

only excuse some behaviors in particular circumstances that would otherwise be infringing. The dominant focus on authors may permit some level of unlicensed use, only to enable would-be authors to build on the works of others.[98] Accordingly, the affirmative defense approach would tend to limit fair use to circumstances where unpaid use could be tolerated and would not extinguish the economic incentives to create that copyright law aims to offer. Potentially, there is harm in each and every unauthorized use, as it detracts from the potential benefits which could be considered part of the legitimate expectations of the copyright owner.[99]

While an affirmative defense is likely to be given a strict interpretation, a legal interpretation inspired by user rights may give more prominence to the interests of users in applying copyright law in general, and fair use in particular.

A user-rights approach conveys a normative message that may shape legal interpretation. It expands the locus of copyright law from the confines of *author rights* to the broader sphere of creativity by addressing both authors and users.[100] For instance, considering the interests of users, the Supreme Court of Canada held that a library is not liable for copyright infringement for reproducing works for the purpose of research by practicing lawyers. The Court reasoned that that since fair dealing is not simply an exception but a user right, "it must not be interpreted restrictively."[101]

---

[98] *See, e.g.,* Cambridge Univ. Press v. Becker (11th Cir. Oct. 17, 2014) ("Some unpaid use of copyrighted materials must be allowed in order to prevent copyright from functioning as a straightjacket that stifles the very creative activity it seeks to foster.")

[99] Consider for instance the analysis of the Court of Appeals in *Cambridge University Press v. Becker* (11th Cir. Oct. 17, 2014). The court failed to seriously consider the merits of educational use in promoting copyright goals, thus assuming rather narrow rights of use to the university and students. The analysis of the partial dissent is particularly telling. Judge Vinson described the switch from paper to digital as an attempt of the university to avoid legitimate fees: "In short, GSU went from paper coursepacks (for which they had 'obtained the copyright permission and paid the royalties to the publishers') to digital coursepacks (for which they did not), and they did this not because there was any real difference in the actual use but, rather, in large part to save money." *Id.* This view fails, however, to acknowledge the transformative nature of every educational use, which adds "something new" to teaching materials, by offering intellectual guidance to students in their learning process. A digital format is not "merely another way of displaying the same paginated materials as in a paper format and for the same underlying use." The shift from paper to digital may reflect an entirely different pedagogy, a truly different approach to learning and knowledge in a completely different world. It replaces the fixed selection of copies with a dynamic selection of materials that could be hyperlinked and connected to other online materials. It enables interaction with the students, developing a learning community around content, where students and other participants are expected to contribute materials to the specific course. Finally, in a digital environment of wide availability the alternative to eReserve is often not, as assumed by the court, sending students to buy the books from which excerpts were copied. Instead, professors are likely to ask students to locate the materials all by themselves, thus depriving them of educational guidance in authenticating, locating, selecting, compiling, and engaging with a community of learners in building its own knowledgebase.

[100] A similar approach was reflected in the decision of the Courts of Appeals in *Authors Guild, Inc. v. HathiTrust*, 755 F.3d 87 (2d Cir. 2014).

[101] CCH Canadian Ltd. v. Law Society of Upper Canada, [2004] 1 S.C.R. 339, 2004 S.C.C. 13.

More recently the Canadian Supreme Court gave a liberal interpretation to fair dealing. Canadian copyright law permits fair dealing for particular purposes which are strictly enumerated by the law, including *research* and *private study*.[102] In *Alberta (Education)* the Court broadly interpreted *private study* under *fair dealing* to include also copying by teachers, explaining that teachers share a symbiotic purpose with the students who engage in private study.[103]

Similarly, in *SOCAN* the Canadian Supreme Court broadly interpreted *research* to include sampling during consumer research for online purchasing of music.[104] The Court explained:

> Limiting research to creative purposes would also run counter to the ordinary meaning of "research," which can include many activities that do not demand the establishment of new facts or conclusions. It can be piecemeal, informal, exploratory, or confirmatory. It can in fact be undertaken for no purpose except personal interest. It is true that research can be for the purpose of reaching new conclusions, but this should be seen as only one, not the primary component of the definitional framework.[105]

In all these cases the user-rights approach focused the legal analysis on the permissible uses that copyright law seeks to promote. The focus on users further led the Court to give priority to the purpose and needs of end-users served by the defendants, rather than focusing the legal analysis on the organizations which facilitate the use (sometimes for commercial purposes).[106]

Moving beyond an affirmative defense approach might be particularly important in the case of liability of facilitators. An affirmative defense would be determined on a case-by-case basis. Finding fair use in particular circumstances does not negate the infringing nature of the activity. Consequently, in some circumstances third parties that substantially contributed to such user activity may be held liable in contributing liability (provided there is knowledge). A user-rights approach would consider the use permissible (rather than excused), therefore no contributory liability would apply.[107]

---

[102] Following the Canadian Supreme Court decisions, the law was amended in 2012 to expand the categories of fair dealing. These categories before the amendment were: research, private study, criticism review, and news reporting. The amendment added parody, satire, and education see *Bill C-11, An Act to amend the Copyright Act*, First Session, Forty-first Parliament, 60 Elizabeth II, Sep. 29, 2011.

[103] Alberta (Education) v. Canadian Copyright Licensing Agency, 2012 S.C.C. 37.

[104] In *SOCAN* the Court denied the claims of the music licensing organizations, that the use of previews to facilitate sales of music via online distribution require a license.

[105] *See* Society of Composers, Authors and Music Publishers of Canada (SOCAN) v. Canadian Assn. of Internet Providers, [2004] 2 S.C.R. 427, 2004 S.C.C. 45, para. 22.

[106] *See Alberta*, 2012 S.C.C. 37, para. 23 (holding that the teacher/copiers share a symbiotic purpose with the student/user who is engaging in research or private study); SOCAN, 2004 S.C.C. 45, paras. 28–30. For a similar approach in the United States, see *Authors Guild, Inc. v. HathiTrust*, 755 F.3d 87 (2d Cir. 2014).

[107] This approach was reflected in the analysis of the Israeli Supreme Court, see *supra* notes 78–79.

Recognizing user rights may not only affect the interpretation of exceptions. It may also influence the scope of rights. The framework of user rights may enable adjustment of the principles to new types of uses which are made possible by technological developments and the changing legal regime. A robust notion of user rights may further facilitate new modes of analysis and tease out appropriate policies to maximize the preconditions for user liberties. Articulating user rights, rather than focusing on L&E or legal defenses, may also facilitate exploring other strategies beyond L&E. User rights could also be addressed, for instance, through a limitation on remedies for good faith assertions of fair use.[108]

5.5.2. *Legal Oversight of Private Ordering*

The user-rights approach may facilitate legal oversight of contractual restrictions on fair use applied by private ordering. It has become common practice to limit permissible uses by private ordering. Use restrictions may apply by End User License Agreements (EULA), which often include restrictions on fair use.[109] Online access to copyrighted works is often governed by a handful of online intermediaries. Economies of scale lead to the domination of online services by a small number of multinational mega platforms, such as Google, Amazon, Apple, and Facebook. Access is subject to Terms of Use (ToU) that often include restrictions on the use and reuse of copyrighted materials.

Can user rights be overridden by nonnegotiated standard contracts such as EULA and ToU? User rights could offer a framework for reviewing such restraints and identifying the way they might conflict with copyright goals.[110] It may also help distinguish between legitimate licensing practices and invalid restrictions on fundamental user freedoms. Restrictions in EULAs on the use of copyrighted materials are often beyond the reach of copyright L&E. A legal defense can only be invoked in a lawsuit for copyright infringement. The framework of user rights may help bridge such doctrinal gaps. Indeed, user rights might be alienable or at a minimum could be waived by users. But transfer or waiver would require a contract, and in some jurisdictions such contracts may require a higher standard of consent that is often absent in standard form contracts.

EULAs are often conceived of as a *property license*, which is not a contract[111] but a unilateral legal action whereby rightholders can exercise their rights and define the

---

[108] Niva Elkin-Koren & Orit Fischman-Afori, *Taking Users' Rights to the Next Level: A Pragmatist Approach to Fair Use*, 33 CARDOZO ARTS & ENT. L.J. 1 (2015).

[109] *See generally* MARGARET JANE RADIN, BOILERPLATE: THE FINE PRINT, VANISHING RIGHTS, AND THE RULE OF LAW 10–12 (2013).

[110] *See* Chapdelaine, *supra* note 93.

[111] *See, e.g.,* Jacobsen v. Katzer, 535 F.3d 1373 (Fed. Cir. 2008).

scope of the authorized use. The binding force of a property license does not derive from exercising autonomous will—it does not require any evidence of consent by the user. The binding force stems from the rightholder's property right: Copyright law empowers owners to exclude others from making certain use of the work, and a license is necessary to permit what the law otherwise prohibits. Under this view of EULAs as property licenses the burden of proof rests on the user, who must show that the use was properly authorized by the rightholder. Yet provisions that pertain to user rights (e.g., limits on fair use) fall beyond the bundle of rights defined by the property rule. Consequently, a property license cannot unilaterally restrict user rights, and stronger evidence of voluntary consent may be required to make such provisions enforceable.

Similarly, restrictions on user rights could also be invoked to claim "copyright misuse"[112] or under the U.S. doctrine of preemption, arguing that a contract purports to supersede rights entitled by law.[113] If user rights are secured by copyright, a contract that conflicts with them may be deemed unenforceable, particularly in the case of nonnegotiated contracts. These EULA are unilaterally drafted by copyright owners, and due to systematic public failure the provisions of such licenses will not be balanced by market pressure or public review. The robustness of these licenses raises the risk of practically deviating from copyright's delicate balances and distorting its intended policy.

User rights should not be confined merely to creating an exemption from liability. Rights discourse may also facilitate the imposition of duties on suppliers of digital content or on platforms implementing copyright enforcement procedures, so as to avoid any violation of users' rights. A proper articulation of rights may offer a framework for developing a set of corresponding duties on the part of suppliers.

The user-rights approach thus offers more robust safeguards for users' liberties in the digital ecosystem.

5.6. CONCLUSION

The growing significance of users in the creative ecosystem and blurring distinction between authors and users raise the need to develop a user-rights approach to copyright law. The new threats to users' freedom and to access to knowledge make such rights essential. A user-rights approach would acknowledge the role of users

---

[112] Mark A. Lemley, *Beyond Preemption: The Law and Policy of Intellectual Property Licensing*, 87 CAL. L. REV. 111 (1999).

[113] 17 USC § 301 (2012). Niva Elkin-Koren, *A Public-Regarding Approach to Contracting over Copyrights, in* EXPANDING THE BOUNDARIES OF INTELLECTUAL PROPERTY: INNOVATION POLICY FOR THE KNOWLEDGE SOCIETY 191 (Rochelle Cooper Dreyfuss, Diane Leenheer Zimmerman & Harry First eds., 2001).

in advancing the goals of copyright and may offer a framework for analyzing limits on permissible uses set by private ordering. Even though a user-rights approach is grounded in copyright law, it should also be understood in the context of civil liberties. Our ability to access, process, and share information with others is key to our freedom in the information ecosystem. Hence, limits on access to copyrighted materials may not only restrict users' ability to engage in generating culture, innovate, and compete as producers of new content; they may also affect users' ability to actively participate as citizens in political discourse and shape culture. Expansive copyrights and licenses may threaten free speech, consumer protection, privacy, and access to knowledge. This risk is growing in significance as we move to an environment of more robust algorithmic copyright enforcement by online intermediaries.[114]

Consequently, developing a user-rights approach in copyright may only be a first step. Understanding user rights as a matter of freedom, within the context of online liberties such as freedom of speech, freedom of information, the right to privacy, and consumer rights may strengthen the theoretical basis for user rights. Articulating user rights as civil liberties may also facilitate the guarantee of these rights by pursuit of different doctrinal schemes.

---

[114] *See* Maayan Perel & Niva Elkin-Koren, *Accountability in Algorithmic Enforcement: Lessons from Copyright Enforcement by Online Intermediaries* (Working Paper 2015).

6

The Canadian Copyright Story

How Canada Improbably Became the World Leader on Users' Rights in Copyright Law

*Michael Geist**

ABSTRACT

Given the long history of copyright reform battles in Canada that date back to the 1880s, there was little reason to think that when the Canadian government launched a public consultation on digital copyright issues in the spring of 2001 that the effort would mark the beginning of a dramatic shift in approach in which thousands of people would become politically engaged in copyright policy and pressure the government to rethink how it struck the copyright balance. Yet a decade of public debate culminated in copyright reforms that were among the most user-friendly in the world, emphasizing user rights and featuring an expansion of fair dealing, a host of new consumer exceptions, innovative new technology focused exceptions, limitations on liability for noncommercial infringement, and notable safeguards for user privacy in Internet service provider liability rules.

  This paper explores the stunning evolution of Canadian copyright law, highlighting how technology, the Internet, and a growing awareness of the wider implications of copyright policy for education, commerce, creativity, and everyday consumer uses sparked a users' rights movement that helped shape copyright policy long before the better-known digital rights successes involving SOPA/PIPA in the United States and the Anti-Counterfeiting Trade Agreement in Europe. The Canadian copyright story demonstrates how individuals were able to leverage social media and a strong scholarly foundation to not only stop legislative proposals, but

* Canada Research Chair in Internet and E-commerce Law, University of Ottawa, Faculty of Law. My thanks to Ruth L. Okediji for the invitation to participate in this project and her guidance on this piece, to the peer reviewers for their exceptionally helpful suggestions, Sarah Rooney for her terrific research assistance, and to the Social Sciences and Humanities Research Council of Canada and the Canada Research Chair Program for their financial assistance. Any errors or omissions are the sole responsibility of the author.

to proactively forge a positive copyright agenda that placed users at the center of policy development.

Copyright reform has seemingly always been a contentious policy issue. In the 1880s, publishers battled authors. In the early 1900s, piano roll manufacturers clashed with a nascent sound recording industry. In the late 1990s, rights holder groups, comprised primarily of the recording industry, Hollywood, and copyright collectives challenged librarians and the education community. Decade after decade, the battle for an appropriate copyright balance remains the same, though the players involved in the debate occasionally change.[1]

The same has been true in Canada, where disputes over Canadian copyright date back to the 1880s, when the country found itself sandwiched between the United States and Great Britain over copyright and was unable to pass its own domestic legislation.[2] Given the long history of copyright reform battles, there was little reason to think that when the Canadian government launched a public consultation on digital copyright issues in the spring of 2001 that the effort would mark the beginning of a dramatic shift in approach in which thousands of Canadians would become politically engaged in copyright policy and pressure the government to rethink how it struck the copyright balance.[3]

In many respects, there was little to distinguish Canadian copyright law at the time. Previous attempts at reform were characterized primarily by the influence of the largest lobby groups, particularly the entertainment industry, which had successfully navigated the Canadian copyright policy framework to achieve successes that eluded the user community, represented for most of the 1980s and 1990s by education and library associations.

For example, the previous round of reforms, which concluded in 1996, featured a new private copying levy worth millions to the recording industry. The inclusion of a new levy was the culmination of years of lobbying efforts dating back almost fifteen years. It started with a 1982 government study that noted the emergence of home recording equipment and recording industry concerns that home taping would result in declining revenues for the industry and royalties for artists. A detailed economic analysis found that the impact on the industry was actually relatively small, however, leading to the conclusion that it was premature to introduce a home taping compensation levy.[4]

[1] *See, e.g.,* RONAN DEAZLEY, RETHINKING COPYRIGHT: HISTORY, THEORY, LANGUAGE (Cheltenham: Edward Elgar 2006); LIONEL BENTLY, GLOBAL COPYRIGHT: THREE HUNDRED YEARS SINCE THE STATUTE OF ANNE, FROM 1709 TO CYBERSPACE (Cheltenham: Edward Elgar 2010).

[2] *See, e.g.,* SARA BANNERMAN, THE STRUGGLE FOR CANADIAN COPYRIGHT: IMPERIALISM TO INTERNATIONALISM 1842–1971 (Vancouver: UBC Press 2013).

[3] INDUSTRY CANADA, CONSULTATION PAPER ON DIGITAL COPYRIGHT ISSUES (June 22, 2001), online: www.ic.gc.ca/eic/site/crp-prda.nsf/eng/h_rp01102.html.

[4] Michael Geist, *Groundhog Day* (June 13, 2005), online: www.michaelgeist.ca/2005/06/groundhog-day/.

The recording industry was undaunted, however, and increased the pressure for a levy system. A parliamentary committee signaled its agreement in 1985, finding that the proliferation of audio recording devices meant that home copying was a real threat to the traditional revenue streams of copyright owners.[5] The committee also made it clear that the levy system should be technology neutral. It presciently noted that "future recording devices might not use blank tape, thereby making a tape royalty obsolete. The work could be stored in a computer memory with no independent material support at all."[6] The committee therefore declined to limit the levy to any particular technology, instead proposing that the royalty "be based upon both the material support used to store the work and on the machine used to make the reproduction."[7] The Canadian Recording Industry Association (CRIA) applauded the decision with then President Brian Robertson claiming that home copying was costing the industry between $250 and $600 million per year. He stated that for every one purchased record, there was one record taped at home without compensation, leading to "no growth" in the industry between 1979 and 1986.[8]

In 1994, the Department of Canadian Heritage established the Task Force on the Future of the Canadian Music Industry, co-chaired by Robertson and the Canadian Independent Record Production Association President Brian Chater.[9] The Task Force concluded that delays in copyright reform threatened to "seriously penalize Canada's music industry, to deprive Canadian performers of the proceeds from their work, of their moral and financial rights, and to place Canada in the ranks of the under-developed countries in terms of protection of intellectual property." Based on claims that three private copies were being made for every retail sale, the Task Force recommended enacting private copying levies.

In 1996, the government introduced legislation to create a private copying system. CRIA responded by celebrating fifteen years of lobbying efforts. However, Robertson lamented that "I think the lack of it over the past ten years has literally killed dozens of (music) careers. I think this is going to make a huge difference for artists, in terms of letting them make one more album or do one more tour that will give them the ability to prolong and develop their careers."[10]

---

[5] House of Commons, Standing Committee on Communications and Culture, A Charter of Rights for Creators – Report of the Subcommittee on the Revision of Copyright (Ottawa: Supply and Services Canada 1985).
[6] *Id.* at 75.
[7] *Id.* at 76.
[8] Geist, *supra* note 4.
[9] Task Force on the Future of the Canadian Music Industry, A Time for Action (Ottawa: Department of Canadian Heritage 1996), online: http://epe.lac-bac.gc.ca/100/200/301/cdn_heritage/task_force_ music-e/final-e.pdf.
[10] Geist, *supra* note 4.

Having concluded two rounds of reforms in the late 1980s and 1990s that not only added private copying but also codified moral rights and statutory damages, copyright reform in Canada was typified by the limited consideration of user concerns leading to a law that featured few significant copyright limitations or exceptions.[11] Fair dealing was viewed as an exception that necessitated a narrow interpretation and most other exceptions were tailored to specific sectors or technologies with little room for expansion.

The reform process itself was confined primarily to a small group of stakeholders comprising the entertainment associations, broadcasters, publishers, copyright collectives, educational institutions, and libraries. Few individuals had participated in past consultations and copyright garnered little national media attention. Moreover, the major Canadian political parties were largely aligned on copyright with the Liberal government and the opposition parties jockeying for positions to demonstrate their support for artists by increasing copyright protections.

The relative lack of interest in copyright and users' rights was not limited to the political world. The Supreme Court of Canada evinced little interest in the issue, releasing an average of one major copyright case every ten years. At the time, the most recent significant copyright case was *Bishop v. Stevens*, a 1990 decision that involved the recording of a song without permission.[12] In that case, Justice McLachlin (as she then was) suggested that since the *Copyright Act* was based on UK law, it was adopted with a single object: "namely, the benefit of authors of all kinds, whether the works were literary, dramatic or musical."[13]

That singular focus was evident in *Michelin v. CAW Canada*, a 1997 Federal Court case involving a suit against a union's distribution of leaflets during a labor dispute that included the image of the Michelin man logo.[14] The union argued that the use of the logo was a parody and thus qualified as criticism under the fair dealing exception.[15] The court rejected that argument, emphasizing the need to strictly interpret the fair dealing provision, while maintaining that parody was not an enumerated exception within the *Copyright Act* and that further, it was not synonymous with criticism.

---

[11] *See* Bill C-60 passed in 1998 (Phase One of copyright reform process) and Bill C-32, passed in 1997 (Phase Two of copyright reform process).

[12] [1990] 2 SCR 467, online: http://canlii.ca/t/1fsv7, 72 DLR (4th) 97.

[13] *Id.* para. 58.

[14] [1997] 2 FC 306, online: www.canlii.org/en/ca/fct/doc/1996/1996canlii3920/1996canlii3920.html.

[15] *See* Jane Bailey, *Deflating the Michelin Man: Protecting Users' Rights in the Canadian Copyright Reform Process, in* IN THE PUBLIC INTEREST: THE FUTURE OF CANADIAN COPYRIGHT LAW 125 (Michael Geist ed., Toronto: Irwin Law 2005).

Eleven years later, Canadian copyright law and policy bore little resemblance to the situation in 2001. A decade of public debate culminated in copyright reforms that were among the most user-friendly in the world, featuring an expansion of fair dealing, a host of new consumer exceptions, innovative new technology focused exceptions, limitations on liability for noncommercial infringement, and notable safeguards for user privacy in Internet service provider liability rules. In just over a decade, copyright emerged as a major policy issue in Canada and the broader public became a vocal, active, and influential participant in the process.

The dramatic changes were not limited to the policy and legislative realms. The Supreme Court of Canada released nearly as many copyright decisions during that eleven-year period as it did in the prior 100 years. Its copyright decisions are unrecognizable when contrasted with the *Bishop* approach. Today, Canadian copyright law is best known for having affirmatively adopted the view that exceptions are more properly regarded users' rights, the incorporation of technological neutrality as a foundational principle of copyright law, and the affirmation of an expansive approach to fair dealing, which Canada's highest court views as the most important users' right. Indeed, while Niva Elkin-Koren's chapter highlights the emergence of a users' rights discourse in Israeli law,[16] Canada remains the only country in the world where the highest court has positively (and repeatedly) affirmed the principle of users' rights within copyright law.

This paper explores the stunning evolution of Canadian copyright law, highlighting how technology, the Internet, and a growing awareness of the wider implications of copyright policy for education, commerce, creativity, and everyday consumer uses sparked a users' rights movement that helped shape copyright policy long before the better-known digital rights successes involving SOPA/PIPA in the United States and the Anti-Counterfeiting Trade Agreement in Europe. Indeed, the Canadian copyright story demonstrates how individuals were able to leverage social media and a strong scholarly foundation to not only stop legislative proposals, but to proactively forge a positive copyright agenda that placed users at the center of policy development.

The paper is divided into two parts. The first part tracks Canada's unlikely path to users' rights in copyright. Starting in 2002, it chronicles many of the important political, policy, and caselaw developments that ultimately resulted in one of the world's most user-friendly copyright reform bills. Part two explores what the Canadian experience can teach others by identifying some of the key ingredients to the copyright policy success story.

---

[16] *See* Niva Elkin-Koren, *Copyright in a Digital Ecosystem: A User Rights Approach, in* COPYRIGHT LAW IN AN AGE OF LIMITATIONS AND EXCEPTIONS (Ruth L. Okediji ed., 2017).

6.1. CANADA'S UNLIKELY PATH TO USERS' RIGHTS IN COPYRIGHT

6.1.1. 2002 – *Signs of Change?*

With the passage of the World Intellectual Property Organization's (WIPO) Copyright Treaty and the WIPO Performances and Phonograms Treaty in 1996, copyright regimes worldwide underwent significant reform to comply with these new treaty requirements.[17] The United States took the lead in 1998, enacting the highly contentious Digital Millennium Copyright Act.[18] The European Union followed in 2001, passing a similarly controversial Copyright Directive that brought European copyright law into conformity with the WIPO treaty requirements.[19]

Canadian officials had long expressed some concerns with the treaty. According to internal government documents, during the last round of negotiations in 1996, officials acknowledged that "in certain areas, the proposed treaty language has not been the subject of adequate debate within Canada – or indeed internationally."[20] Perhaps arising from these concerns, the memo concluded by noting "the delegation will not have full powers to sign a treaty."[21]

Moreover, the position of the Canadian government at the WIPO Diplomatic Conference was to support provisions that would not result in major changes to domestic law or were sufficiently flexible in implementation. In particular, the memo states that "Canada will also support provisions that constitute minor changes to domestic policy, or which provide flexibility to adopt measures compatible with Canadian policy."[22]

In the aftermath of the WIPO Diplomatic Conference, Canadian authorities remained noncommittal about how (and for a period whether) Canada would implement the treaties. Although it was clear that some reforms were coming, observers were unsure about whether a Canadian version of the Digital Millennium Copyright Act (DMCA) was on the horizon. In 2001, the government released a series of proposals that suggested that though it was committed to establishing some new protections, it planned to tread cautiously while the full impact of the digital environment on copyright remained uncertain. The proposals covered four key

---

[17] WIPO Copyright Treaty, Dec. 20, 1996, I-38542, online: www.wipo.int/treaties/en/ip/wct/; WIPO Performances and Phonograms Treaty, Dec. 20, 1996, I-38543, online: www.wipo.int/treaties/en/ip/wppt/.

[18] *Digital Millennium Copyright Act*, Pub. L. No. 105–304, 112 Stat. 2860 (1998).

[19] *Directive on the Harmonisation of Certain Aspects of Copyright and Related Rights in the Information Society*, 2001/29/EC, L167, 2001-06-22, p 10, L6, 2002-01-10, p 70 (2001).

[20] Michael Geist, *Canada and the WIPO Internet Treaties: Flexibility Was Always Key* (Dec. 23, 2009), online: www.michaelgeist.ca/2009/12/canada-and-wipo-treaty/.

[21] *Id.*

[22] Geist, *supra* note 20.

issues – a new Internet "making available" right, the legal protection afforded to technical measures such as encryption to digitally "lock" content, rights management information, as well as the liability of Internet service providers for copyright infringement.[23]

To the surprise of many in the government, the consultation attracted more than 700 responses, the vast majority of which came from individuals and user-oriented groups.[24] Most respondents had not previously participated in copyright policy and provided an early sense of an emerging, ad-hoc coalition of user perspectives on copyright that would mushroom over the following decade.

For example, over one hundred computer scientists responded to the government's call for comments, expressing concern that following the U.S. lead on copyright could result in researchers refraining from public presentations of their research for fear of inviting industry-sponsored lawsuits or, worse, landing in jail as Russian computer programmer Dmitri Sklyarov did in the United States after he delivered a presentation in Las Vegas on his company's latest software program.[25]

The education community, including virtually every provincial minister of education, voiced concern that new technical measures provisions might result in diminished fair dealing rights for students and teachers. Moreover, they argued that the use of content on the Internet might need a specific educational use exemption to ensure that valuable materials may be used in schools.

Librarians also worried about the loss of balance in copyright law that technical measures protections might bring. For example, the Canadian Library Association argued that "the introduction to the Copyright Act of sanctions against the circumvention of technological measures used by copyright owners to protect their works has the potential of providing copyright owners an unchallenged means of overriding all limitations on their statutory rights and of denying users their legitimate rights of access to protected works."[26] Meanwhile, several archivist organizations pointed out the importance of historical materials and raised their concern that statutory changes could diminish the ability of Canadians to access their own history.

Yet despite the early emergence of a user voice on copyright, the government remained largely indifferent to those perspectives. In late 2002, it issued the Section

---

[23] Industry Canada, *supra* note 3.

[24] *Response from Canadians: Submissions Received Regarding the Consultation Papers* (Ottawa: Industry Canada and Department of Heritage 2001), online: www.ic.gc.ca/eic/site/crp-prda.nsf/eng/h_rp01105 .html.

[25] *US v. ElcomSoft Sklyarov*, Electronic Frontier Foundation, online: www.eff.org/cases/us-v-elcomsoft-sklyarov.

[26] *Canadian Library Association Response to the Consultation Paper on Digital Copyright Issues* (Sept. 14, 2001), online: www.ic.gc.ca/eic/site/crp-prda.nsf/eng/rp00347.html.

92 report, a statutorily mandated roadmap of short-, medium-, and long-term copy-right policy priorities. Many individuals argued that Canada did not need to reform its copyright legislation in order to ensure that it was compliant with the WIPO Internet treaties, but it became apparent that the government did not agree, as the report left no doubt that Canadian legislation would be amended in response to them.

While the government's perspective on copyright showed little sign of change, the Supreme Court of Canada began to shift its view on the issue in 2002. The perspective evident in *Bishop* and *Michelin* remained firm for ten years – including throughout the 1997 *Copyright Act* reform process – until *Théberge v. Galerie d'Art du Petit Champlain Inc.*, a decision that featured explicit support for a copyright balance and due consideration for copyright's effect on innovation.[27] In doing so, the case marked the beginning of the departure from the *Bishop's* perspective of a single purpose for copyright toward a dual purpose that incorporated the interests of both creators and users.

The case involved a challenge by Claude Théberge, a Quebec painter with an international reputation, against an art gallery that purchased posters of Théberge's work and proceeded to transfer the images from paper to canvas. The gallery's tech-nology was state of the art – it used a process that lifted the ink off the poster and transferred it to the canvas. The gallery did not actually create any new images or reproductions of the work, since the poster paper was left blank after the process was complete. Théberge was nevertheless outraged – he believed he had sold paper posters, not canvas-based reproductions – and he proceeded to sue in Quebec court, requesting an injunction to stop the transfers, as well as the seizure of the existing canvas-backed images.

Although the Quebec Court of Appeal ruled in favor of the seizure, the majority of the Supreme Court overturned that decision, finding that the images were merely transferred from one medium to another and were not reproduced contrary to the *Copyright Act*. Writing for the majority of the Court, Justice Ian Binnie stated:

> [T]he proper balance among these and other public policy objectives lies not only in recognizing the creator's rights but in giving due weight to their limited nature … Once an authorized copy of a work is sold to a member of the public, it is gener-ally for the purchaser, not the author, to determine what happens to it.[28]

Binnie also emphasized the dangers of copyright law that veers too far toward copy-right creators at the expense of both the public and the innovation process. He noted that "[e]xcessive control by holders of copyrights and other forms of intellectual

[27] [2002] 2 S.C.R. 336, 210 D.L.R. (4th) 385.
[28] *Id.* para. 31.

property may unduly limit the ability of the public domain to incorporate and embellish creative innovation in the long-term interests of society as a whole, or create practical obstacles to proper utilization."[29]

It is fair to say that many in the Canadian copyright bar may have initially underestimated the shift that was underway. For example, Roger Hughes, one of Canada's leading copyright experts (now a federal court judge) told one reporter that "Théberge really does not impact on digital copyright or digital situations that may arise, for instance, out of (the U.S. Digital Millennium Copyright Act)."[30] Jay Kerr-Wilson, then a counsel with the Canadian Cable Television Association, said "people will probably try to use this by analogy to argue digital stuff, but it's not a digital case. Canvas and paper isn't bits and bytes."[31]

6.1.2. 2003–2005 – *The Recognition of Users' Rights*

By late 2003, the entertainment industry was growing increasingly impatient with the lack of Canadian progress on copyright reform. In fact, earlier that year, historians, academics, and individuals banded together to defeat a small copyright provision that had been inserted into a bill dealing with the Library of Canada archives. The provision called for the extension of the term of copyright for unpublished works of deceased authors.

Dubbed the "Lucy Maud Montgomery Copyright Term Extension Act" – referring to a controversial copyright term extension bill in the United States that was passed with the active support of the Disney Corporation that sought to delay Mickey Mouse's entry into the public domain – the Canadian bill arose at the request of the heirs of author Lucy Maud Montgomery of Anne of Green Gables fame, who wrote ten volumes of diaries during her lifetime that were not published until after her death. When it became clear that those works would enter into the public domain in 2004, the heirs sought a copyright extension from the government to maintain exclusive control over her works until 2018.[32]

Opponents of the change noted that the proposed change did little more than transfer the value of the work from the general public to Ms. Montgomery's heirs, while failing to create any new work or providing society with any tangible benefit.

---

[29] *Id.* para. 32.
[30] *Théberge Supreme Court Case Divides Experts on Digital Copyright Applicability*, THE WIRE REPORT (May 1, 2002), online: www.thewirereport.ca/news/2002/05/01/th%C3%A9berge-supreme-court-case-divides-experts-on-digital-copyright-applicability/13513.
[31] *Id.*
[32] Bill C-8, *The Library and Archives of Canada Act*, 2nd Sess, 38th Parl 2004 (assented to Apr. 22, 2004), RSO 2004, c 11, online: www.parl.gc.ca/About/Parliament/LegislativeSummaries/bills_ls.asp?ls=C8&Parl=37&Ses=3.

Those concerns seemed to resonate with a parliamentary committee considering the bill since it agreed to drop the provisions just before the House of Commons recessed for the summer.

With copyright reform stalled in the House of Commons and even minor reforms facing a backlash, supporters of more immediate reform turned to the Standing Committee on Canadian Heritage and its chair Sarmite Bulte, a Liberal Member of Parliament whose support for the entertainment industry was well known. The committee conducted brief hearings on copyright in the fall of 2003, leading to a recommendation in the "strongest possible terms" to the responsible ministers that they instruct their officials to prepare draft legislation by February 10, 2004, in order that the government might ratify the WIPO Internet treaties.[33] In fact, Canadian Heritage Minister Sheila Copps remarkably urged the committee to look to CRIA for the necessary wording, noting "at this point I would suggest that the best course of action to achieve your objectives might be to hear from CRIA to see what would be an acceptable wording."[34]

When that failed to move the responsible ministers, the committee conducted more extensive hearings in the spring of 2004 and released a second set of recommendations that almost completely neglected user perspectives on copyright.[35] These included recommendations for the swift ratification of the WIPO Internet treaties and increased liability for Internet service providers. The hearings were widely viewed as one-sided, with few user groups or interests represented. In fact, on the day the committee examined education and copyright, only one representative from the education community was invited, prompting one Member of Parliament to note that the representative was "the odd man out."[36]

Not only did the committee reject fair dealing reform or new copyright exceptions, but it instead recommended creating a new licence to cover Internet-based works. This new licence would require schools to pay an additional fee for works found on the Internet. Although it acknowledged that some work on the Internet is intended to be freely available, the committee recommended the adoption of the narrowest possible definition of publicly available, covering only those works that

---

[33] House of Commons, Standing Committee on Canadian Heritage (Nov. 2003), online: www
.parl.gc.ca/HousePublications/Publication.aspx?DocId=1169804&Language=E&Mode=1&Parl=37&
Ses=2.

[34] Id.

[35] House of Commons, Standing Committee on Canadian Heritage, *Interim Report on Copyright
Reform* (May 2004), online: www.parl.gc.ca/HousePublications/Publication.aspx?DocId=1350628&L
anguage=E.

[36] House of Commons, Standing Committee on Canadian Heritage (Apr. 2004), online: www.parl
.gc.ca/HousePublications/Publication.aspx?DocId=1329168&Language=E&Mode=1&Parl=37&
Ses=3.

were not technologically or password protected and contained an explicit notice that the material could be used without prior payment or permission.

The committee report would prove to be the high water mark in Canada for a copyright approach without a user perspective. The education community, led by provincial ministers of education, loudly protested the recommendations, while Canada's information technology community issued a public letter warning of its danger to that economic sector. Months later, a national election also altered the long-term impact of the report. The committee lost many of its original members, with at least one, former MP Paul Bonwick, wasting little time in signing up as a paid lobbyist for Access Copyright, a leading copyright collective.[37]

After the election, a newly constituted committee adopted a decidedly different tone. Although it re-tabled the report, Liberal MP Marlene Catterall, the new committee chair, publicly expressed a desire to learn more from both sides about the issues. New Democratic Party (NDP) committee member Charlie Angus, who was elected for the first time in the 2004 election, was even more direct, warning that "the recommendations could herald the end of the Internet as a digital intellectual commons."[38] The Angus position was particularly notable since it marked the first time that there was clear division among political parties in Canada. Moreover, Angus brought enormous credibility to the issue as he was a working musician before entering politics and remained an active performer.

The policy reversal came full circle in March 2005 as the government released its official response to the committee report.[39] Setting out the immediate path for Canadian copyright reform, it rejected virtually every committee recommendation. In late June, Bill C-60, the first copyright bill, followed with flexible anti-circumvention rules and some user-focused provisions (notably a "notice-and-notice approach" for Internet Service Providers), but no expansion of fair dealing and no significant new user exceptions.[40]

Bill C-60 did feature new educational and library exceptions, but even those were saddled with onerous restrictions. For example, the bill purported to promote Internet-based learning by permitting schools to communicate lessons featuring copyrighted materials via telecommunication. The bill restricted that new right, however, by forcing schools to destroy the lesson within thirty days of the conclusion

---

[37] Michael Geist, *Time to Clean up Canadian Copyright* (Jan. 15, 2006), online: www.michaelgeist .ca/2006/01/time-to-clean-up-canadian-copyright/.

[38] Russell McOrmand, *Holly Heffernan (Calgary Southwest, NDP) Replies to Questions* (Jan. 11, 2006), online: www.digital-copyright.ca/node/1712.

[39] Michael Geist, *Canada Rejects One-Sided Approach to Copyright Reform*, Toronto Star (Mar. 28, 2005).

[40] Bill C-60, *An Act to Amend the Copyright Act*, 1st Sess, 38th Parl, 2005, online: www.parl.gc.ca/About/ Parliament/LegislativeSummaries/Bills_ls.asp?ls=C60&Parl=38&Ses=1.

of the course. Moreover, schools were required to retain, for three years, records that identified the lesson as well as the dates it was placed on a tangible medium and ultimately destroyed.

The library provisions were even more restrictive, compelling librarians to restrict access to knowledge in order to provide it. The bill allowed libraries and archives to provide digital copies of materials; however, in order to do so they were required to limit further communication or copying of the digital files and ensure that the files could not be used for more than seven days.

Users were not the only groups unhappy with the bill. The U.S. government voiced its concern with the legislation, using the Special 301 Report process weeks before its introduction to identify the key concerns: anti-circumvention rules and ISP liability standards:

> The U.S. copyright industry is concerned about proposed copyright legislation regarding technological protection measures and internet service provider (ISP) liability, which if passed, would appear to be a departure from the requirements of the WIPO Internet Treaties as well as the international standards adopted by most Organisation for Economic Co-operation and Development (OECD) countries in the world. The United States urges Canada to adopt legislation that is consistent with the WIPO Internet Treaties and is in line with the international standards of most developed countries. Specifically, we encourage Canada to join the strong international consensus by adopting copyright legislation that provides comprehensive protection to copyrighted works in the digital environment, by outlawing trafficking in devices to circumvent technological protection measures, and by establishing a "notice and takedown" system to encourage cooperation by ISPs in combating online infringements.[41]

Once introduced, a U.S. State Department cable noted that some stakeholders were so unhappy with the bill that "faced with such a flawed document, some industry representatives are stuck hoping that the legislation, for which they pushed so long and hard, will die in committee."[42] The U.S. influence would shape the Canadian legislation in the years to come as the requirements for WIPO Internet treaty ratification would emerge as one of the most contentious domestic copyright issues.

Bill C-60 also generated considerable academic commentary with the release of *In the Public Interest: The Future of Canadian Copyright Law*.[43] I served as editor for

---

[41] USTR, SPECIAL 301 REPORT (2005), online: www.ipophil.gov.ph/images/IPEnforcement/Special301 Review/2005USTRSpecial301Report.pdf.

[42] US DEPARTMENT OF STATE, EVOLUTION OF INDUSTRY RESPONSE TO CANADA'S DRAFT COPYRIGHT AMENDMENT LEGISLATION (Ottawa: Mission Ottawa, Oct. 31, 2005), Cable No 05OTTAWA3244 at para. 7, online: https://cablegatesearch.wikileaks.org/cable.php?id=05OTTAWA3244&q=kipr.

[43] IN THE PUBLIC INTEREST: THE FUTURE OF CANADIAN COPYRIGHT LAW (Michael Geist ed., Toronto: Irwin Law 2005).

the book, which brought together the majority of Canadian academics researching and writing about intellectual property. In all, there were nineteen peer-reviewed chapters, all of which were made available under a Creative Commons license. The book signaled a desire for a new generation of copyright academics to engage in Canadian policy and its contributions have since been cited numerous times by the Supreme Court of Canada.

It also marked the emergence of scholarship focused on users' rights within copyright. For example, Professor Abraham Drassinower wrote *Taking User Rights Seriously*, in which he argued that users' rights are an incidence of authorship and therefore cannot be mere exceptions.[44] Meanwhile, Professor Teresa Scassa picked up on the users' rights issue in *Interests in the Balance*, which emphasized the departure by the Supreme Court of Canada in its assessment of the copyright balance.[45]

While Bill C-60 later died with yet another election call, the leading Supreme Court of Canada copyright decision of the period had a far more lasting effect. The March 2004 release of *CCH Canadian v. Law Society of Upper Canada*, in which a unanimous Supreme Court strongly affirmed its support for a balanced approach to copyright law, breathed new life into fair dealing.[46]

The case involved a dispute between the Law Society of Upper Canada and several legal publishers. The Law Society, which maintains the Great Library, a leading law library in Toronto, provided the profession with two methods of copying cases and other legal materials. First, it ran a service whereby lawyers could request a copy of a particular case or article. Second, it maintained several stand-alone photocopiers that could be used by library patrons. The legal publishers objected to the Law Society's copying practices and sued for copyright infringement. They maintained that the materials being copied were entitled to copyright protection and that the Law Society was authorizing others to infringe on their copyright.

The Law Society emerged victorious on most counts in this regard, as the court ruled that it had neither infringed the publishers' copyright nor authorized others to do so. In its decision, the court provided a detailed discussion of the fair dealing exception, concluding that the exception should be granted a large and liberal interpretation.[47] In fact, the court remarkably fashioned exceptions to copyright

---

[44] Abraham Drassinower, *Taking User Rights Seriously, in* IN THE PUBLIC INTEREST: THE FUTURE OF CANADIAN COPYRIGHT LAW 462 (Michael Geist ed., Toronto: Irwin Law 2005).

[45] Teresa Scassa, *Interests in the Balance, in* IN THE PUBLIC INTEREST: THE FUTURE OF CANADIAN COPYRIGHT LAW 41 (Michael Geist ed., Toronto: Irwin Law 2005).

[46] [2004] 1 S.C.R. 339, 2004 S.C.C. 13, available on CanLII.

[47] *Id.* paras. 48–60.

infringement as users' rights that must be balanced against the rights of copyright owners and creators.[48]

> Before reviewing the scope of the fair dealing exception under the Copyright Act, it is important to clarify some general considerations about exceptions to copyright infringement. Procedurally, a defendant is required to prove that his or her dealing with a work has been fair; however, the fair dealing exception is perhaps more properly understood as an integral part of the Copyright Act than simply a defence. Any act falling within the fair dealing exception will not be an infringement of copyright. *The fair dealing exception, like other exceptions in the Copyright Act, is a user's right. In order to maintain the proper balance between the rights of a copyright owner and users' interests, it must not be interpreted restrictively.*[49]

Having characterized fair dealing as a users' right that must not be interpreted restrictively, the Court then illustrated the appropriate application of a fair dealing analysis:

> The fair dealing exception under s. 29 is open to those who can show that their dealings with a copyrighted work were for the purpose of research or private study. "Research" must be given a large and liberal interpretation in order to ensure that users' rights are not unduly constrained. I agree with the Court of Appeal that research is not limited to non-commercial or private contexts.[50]

The importance of the *CCH* decision to the application of the fair dealing provision cannot be overstated. In a single decision, the Supreme Court elevated fair dealing from a limited exception that was viewed as largely ineffectual to a users' right that must not be interpreted restrictively and cannot be unduly constrained. While the *Copyright Act* grants copyright holders with a large basket of rights, the *CCH* decision provided a powerful reminder that those rights are not absolute.

The *CCH* decision drew a mixed reaction. The academic community emphasized its importance with articles by the likes of Craig[51] and Drassinower[52] that focused on the important shift in copyright.[53] The Supreme Court later cited both articles in its 2012 copyright decisions.

---

[48] *Id.* para. 12.

[49] *Id.* para. 48 (emphasis added).

[50] *Id.* para. 51.

[51] Carys J. Craig, *The Changing Face of Fair Dealing in Canadian Copyright Law: A Proposal for Legislative Reform*, OSGOODE DIGITAL COMMONS, Paper 76 (2005), *online*: https://apps.osgoode .yorku.ca/osgmedia.nsf/0/9D7E0F2555DC3E1E852571CD0054E156/$FILE/The%20Changing%20 Face.pdf.

[52] Abraham Drassinower, *Taking User Rights Seriously* (2005), *online*: www.irwinlaw.com/sites/default/ files/attached/Three_02_Drassinower.pdf.

[53] *See also* Daniel Gervais, *Canadian Copyright Law Post-CCH*, 18 I.P.J. 131 (2004); and Teresa Scassa, *Recalibrating Copyright Law? A Comment on the Supreme Court of Canada's Decision in CCH Canadian Ltd. v. Law Society of Upper Canada*, 3 CJLT 89 (2004).

The rights holder community alternated between dire warnings and denial. On the dire warnings side, Roger Hughes told one reporter: "who would (now) do a mathematical text or an encyclopedia or something like that without thinking, my goodness, who's going to be handing out copies of this and why and under what circumstances?"[54] More common was the denial side, with arguments that users' rights was simply a metaphor and that little had changed. For example, Access Copyright's immediate reaction was "this ruling does not change the fact that most copying of copyright protected works does not fall under fair dealing. The Supreme Court stated definitively that copyright does exist in original works, and that is why organizations must sign an Access Copyright licence or risk breaking the law."[55]

6.1.3. 2006–2008 – *The Fair Copyright Fight*

An election call in late 2005 consigned Bill C-60 to the dustbin, but copyright played a surprisingly important role in the election campaign that straddled 2005 and 2006. Liberal MP Sarmite Bulte, the parliamentary secretary for Canadian Heritage and chair of the standing committee on Canadian Heritage, found herself embroiled in a controversy over a fundraiser for her benefit hosted by the leaders of the major entertainment lobby groups four days before voters were scheduled to go to the polls.[56]

The fundraiser attracted national media attention as it sparked debate about the influence of campaign financing within the Canadian policy framework. Moreover, the issue marked one of the first effective online campaigns to raise awareness about copyright, which led *Maclean's*, Canada's national newsweekly, to label the fight "Bulte vs. the Bloggers."[57]

While it is unlikely that a copyright fundraiser alone changed the course of voting in the riding, there is little doubt that the copyright questions had an impact on Bulte's effectiveness on the campaign trail. When she first faced the issue, she

---

54 *Supreme Court Finds Law Society's Fax Service Not In Breach of Copyright Laws*, THE WIRE REPORT (Mar. 17, 2004), online: www.thewirereport.ca/news/2004/03/17/supreme-court-finds-law-society%E2%80%99s-fax-service-not-in-breach-of-copyright-laws/11788.

55 *Supreme Court Rules Copyright Existed in Works Copied by Law Society of Upper Canada, But Copyright Was Not Violated*, ACCESS COPYRIGHT (Mar. 4, 2004), online: http://web.archive.org/web/20040407013109/http://accesscopyright.ca/resources.asp?a=145.

56 *Liberal MP Takes Flak for Lobbyists' Fundraiser*, CBC NEWS (Jan. 6, 2006), online: www.cbc.ca/news/arts/liberal-mp-takes-flak-for-lobbyists-fundraiser-1.609390; *Bloggers Trample on MP's Hopes for Re-election*, CANADIAN PRESS (Jan. 26, 2006), online: www.canada.com/topics/technology/story.html?id=4bd9d3d7-5397-4ae5-91ea-0648a608feb9&k=24795.

57 Colin Campbell, *Wrath of the Bloggers*, MACLEAN'S MAGAZINE (Jan. 18, 2006), online: https://web.archive.org/web/20060220062959/http://www.macleans.ca/topstories/politics/article.jsp?content=20060123_120006_120006.

focused on transparency and characterized criticisms as "egregious."[58] She later told an all-candidates meeting that she would not let Michael Geist, the Electronic Frontier Foundation (EFF), and "pro-user zealots" intimidate and silence her.[59] Moreover, she alternately claimed that it wasn't a fundraiser[60] and threatened to sue me for posting on the issue. On election day, Bulte lost by thousands of votes, one of only two ridings in the Greater Toronto Area to change hands from the prior election held eighteen months earlier.

Bulte was not the only one to lose during that election. More than ten years of Liberal rule came to an end with the election of the Conservatives and their leader, Stephen Harper. The change in government provided an opportunity for a pause in the increasing tensions over copyright policy in Canada. The new Conservative government promised swift action, but it was not until late 2007, nearly two years after being elected, that a comprehensive bill finally appeared on the House of Commons order paper.

During the intervening two years, new groups focused on users' rights and copyright emerged as an increasingly prominent issue on the Canadian scene.

The most influential new group was the Canadian Music Creators Coalition, which included well known Canadian musicians such as Steven Page, Andrew Cash, and Brendan Canning.[61] The musicians argued that the recording industry did not represent their interests and they disavowed legal strategies that involved suing individual file sharers. The group garnered significant media attention and obtained meetings with Industry Minister Maxime Bernier and Canadian Heritage Minister Bev Oda. Soon after, more than 500 Canadian art professionals formed another coalition to call on the government to adopt a balanced approach to copyright reform. Appropriation Art: A Coalition of Arts Professionals included arts organizations from Alberta, BC, Quebec, Ontario, and Saskatchewan along with hundreds of artists from across Canada.[62]

The copyright issue spilled over to other areas as well. For example, then-Privacy Commissioner of Canada Jennifer Stoddart issued a public letter to the ministers in which she expressed "concerns about the pervasive threat of surveillance that these new technologies represent [referring to technological protection measures]" and

[58] Steve Janke, *Sarmite Bulte, Copyright Laws, and Her Staged Debate*, THE RECLUSIVE ANTIQUARIAN (Jan. 1, 2006), online: http://minx.cc:1080/?post=149779.

[59] Ian Irving, *Election Night in Canada: Parkdale/High Park All Candidates Debate*, FALSE POSITIVES (Jan. 11, 2006), online: www.falsepositives.com/index.php/2006/01/11/election-night-in-canada-parkdale-high-park-all-candidates-debate/.

[60] Michael Geist, *It's a Celebration* (Jan. 17, 2006), online: www.michaelgeist.ca/2006/01/its-a-celebration/.

[61] Steven Page, *A Barenaked Guide to Music Copyright Reform*, NATIONAL POST (May 1, 2006), online: www.canada.com/nationalpost/news/issuesideas/story.html?id=3367a219-f395-4161-a9b9-95256 c613824.

[62] *Appropriation Art Coalition*, online: http://appropriationart.ca/portfolio/the-coalition/.

welcomed the opportunity to meet with the government before a copyright bill is introduced and to appear before the relevant parliamentary committee during hearings on a bill.[63]

The corporate sector also became increasingly engaged on the issue. The Digital Security Coalition, composed primarily of new technology companies, issued a public letter calling for the adoption of a fair use approach in Canada, arguing that Canada's more restrictive copyright approach placed them at a competitive disadvantage:

> In our view, debates over copyright policy have focused myopically on the demands of the multinational content industry, and not enough on Canada's needs for laws that foster innovation and security in a digital environment. Canadian innovators rely on the unacceptably narrow defence of fair dealing for the legality of reverse engineering and security research. Our American competitors face no such uncertainty with respect to the broader US defence of fair use, which clearly captures reverse engineering. It is time to address this competitive disadvantage by harmonizing fair dealing with fair use.[64]

Telus, Canada's second largest telecommunications company, also jumped into the political fray with an open letter that recommended a "living fair use" model:

> the Government should ensure Canadians are able to use new technologies to fully enjoy copyrighted materials they have legally obtained or accessed in a manner that does no real measurable harm to copyright owners' legitimate interests. For example, customers of TELUS and other Canadian broadcasting distribution undertakings (BDUs) should be able to use new technologies to record, store and access television programming, for their own private enjoyment, at a time of their choosing ("time-shifting"). Similarly, Canadians should be able to transfer content they own from one device to another for ease and flexibility of access for their private use ("space-shifting").[65]

The delay was aided by the government's decision to introduce anti-camcording legislation in May 2007, following extensive pressure from the movie industry. In fact, Bev Oda, the Minister of Canadian Heritage, held a private meeting in Ottawa with Canadian Motion Pictures Distributors Association President Douglas Frith one year earlier, at which Frith provided the government with draft

---

[63] Letter from Jennifer Stoddart, Federal Privacy Commissioner, to Beverley J. Oda, Minister of Canadian Heritage and Maxime Bernier, Minister of Industry (May 17, 2006), online: www.privcom .gc.ca/media/let/let_ca_060517_e.asp.

[64] Michael Geist, *Canadian Digital Security Companies Warn Against Anti-Circumvention Laws* (June 22, 2006), online: www.michaelgeist.ca/2006/06/canadian-digital-security-companies-warn-against-anti-circumvention-laws/.

[65] Michael Geist, *Telus Joins Call for Fair Use* (Aug. 15, 2006), online: www.michaelgeist.ca/2006/08/telus-letter/.

legislation – legislation that the association itself had crafted – that likely served as the basis for the anti-camcording bill.[66]

The Canadian Motion Picture Distributors Association (CMPDA) meeting focused on several issues, including counterfeiting and signal theft, yet it was a movie piracy amendment to the Criminal Code that was clearly top of mind. An advance CMPDA briefing document claimed that legislative reform was needed to address the growth of unauthorized camcording in Canadian movie theatres. Much like the bill that ultimately passed, which contained a maximum jail term of five years for the recording of a movie in a theatre for the purposes of commercial distribution without the consent of the theatre owner, the CMPDA draft bill similarly envisioned a maximum of five years imprisonment for "any person who knowingly operates the audiovisual recording function of any device in a public place while a cinematographic work is being exhibited."[67]

Department officials were not persuaded by the proposal, however, warning in the Ministerial briefing note that the penalty provisions in the Copyright Act already constituted criminal offences and that "it is unclear how these measures would prove more efficient." That conclusion was consistent with comments from Justice Minister Rob Nicholson, who initially rejected the calls for movie piracy legislation by noting that "the country is not completely bereft of laws in this area."[68]

In light of the tepid governmental response, the industry went on the offensive, threatening to delay the release of movies in the Canadian theatres, cancelling Canadian pre-screenings, enlisting the support of the U.S. officials, and floating inconsistent claims of Canadian responsibility for global camcording that ranged from 20 to 70 percent (the Oda briefing note stated that Montreal alone was responsible for 40 percent of unauthorized film reproductions in the world market, twice what CMPDA later claimed for all of Canada).[69]

The industry's lobby efforts were clearly successful. Ignoring the inconsistent claims, the absence of evidence that Canadian films were being affected, and the contrary internal advice, a bill was quickly drafted and introduced during a visit from then-California Governor Arnold Schwarzenegger.[70] The bill sailed quickly through Parliament in just three weeks with little study and no desire among opposition parties or other stakeholders to actively oppose it.[71]

---

[66] Michael Geist, *Behind-scenes Action led to Camcording Bill*, TORONTO STAR (June 11, 2007), online: www.thestar.com/business/2007/06/11/behindscenes_action_led_to_camcording_bill.html.

[67] *Id.*

[68] *Id.*

[69] *Id.*

[70] *Harper Pledges Law to Combat Camcording in Cinemas*, CBC NEWS (May 31, 2007), online: www .cbc.ca/news/arts/harper-pledges-law-to-combat-camcording-in-cinemas-1.654149.

[71] Bill C-59, *An Act to Amend the Criminal Code* (unauthorized recording of a movie), 1st Sess, 39th Parl, 2007, online: www.parl.gc.ca/HousePublications/Publication.aspx?DocId=2993072&Language =e&Mode=1.

The anti-camcording bill relieved some of the lobbying pressure on copyright reform, but a meeting in August 2007 in Montebello, Quebec between Canadian Prime Minister Stephen Harper and then-U.S. President George W. Bush put the copyright issue back on the legislative agenda. According to a U.S. State Department cable:

> senior GOC officials, especially Industry Minister Prentice, repeatedly assured the Ambassador and senior Mission Canada officers that the copyright bill would be introduced "soon." Specifically, assurances were given that the legislation had been finalized and would be introduced prior to the Christmas recess, and then again immediately upon Parliament's return in January.[72]

Three months after the meeting between the two leaders, the copyright bill appeared on the House of Commons notice paper with a plan to table it in early December 2007.[73]

However, just days before, I had started a Facebook group called Fair Copyright for Canada that ultimately galvanized opposition to the forthcoming bill.[74] Within a week, 10,000 members joined the group, within two weeks there were 25,000 members, and within months more than 90,000 Canadians had joined the Facebook group.[75] Moreover, local Facebook chapters sprung up in communities across the country as the public sought out ways to influence government policy.

While Facebook was not the only source of activity – there was mounting coverage from the mainstream media along with hundreds of blog postings – the momentum was unquestionably built on thousands of Canadians who were determined to have their voices heard in light of plans to introduce a bill with no advance public consultation.

Much to the surprise of skeptics who painted government as unable or unwilling to listen to public concerns, those voices had an immediate impact. Ten days after the Facebook group's launch, then-Industry Minister Jim Prentice delayed introducing the new copyright reforms, seemingly struck by the rapid formation of concerned citizens who were writing letters and raising awareness.[76] The move shocked traditional stakeholders. ACTRA, the leading actors' union, urged Prentice

---

[72] Michael Geist, *Wikileaks Cables Show Massive U.S. Effort to Establish Canadian DMCA* (Apr. 29, 2011), *online*: www.michaelgeist.ca/2011/04/wikileaks-cables-on-us-copyright-lobby/.

[73] *Notice Paper* (Dec. 10, 2007), *online*: www.parl.gc.ca/HousePublications/Publication.aspx?DocId=318 7201&File=11&Language=E&Mode=1&Parl=39&Ses=2.

[74] *Online*: www.facebook.com/FairCopyrightCanada.

[75] Blayne Haggart, *Fair Copyright for Canada: Lessons from the First Facebook Uprising*, ORANGESPACE (June 7, 2013), *online*: http://blaynehaggart.wordpress.com/2013/06/07/fair-copyright-for-canada-lessons-from-the-first-facebook-uprising/.

[76] *Government Retreats on Copyright Reform*, CBC NEWS (Dec. 13, 2007), *online*: www.cbc.ca/news/technology/government-retreats-on-copyright-reform-1.657296.

"to do the right thing" by ignoring the protests of a "vocal minority."[77] Several music associations also issued a press release expressing their "growing concern" with the legislative delays.[78]

A U.S. State Department cable confirmed the role that users played in delaying the introduction of the bill:

> From December 2007 to mid-February, senior GOC officials and well-informed private sector contacts assured the Embassy that legislative calendar concerns were delaying the copyright bill's introduction into Parliament. Our contacts downplayed the small – but increasingly vocal – public opposition to copyright reform led by University of Ottawa law professor Dr. Michael Geist. On February 25, however, Industry Minister Prentice (please protect) admitted to the Ambassador that some Cabinet members and Conservative Members of Parliament – including MPs who won their ridings by slim margins – opposed tabling the copyright bill now because it might be used against them in the next federal election. Prentice said the copyright bill had become a "political" issue. He also indicated that elevating Canada to the Special 301 Priority Watch List would make the issue more difficult and would not be received well.[79]

Not only had tools like Facebook had an immediate effect on the government's legislative agenda, but the community that developed around the group also led to a "crowdsourcing" of knowledge. Canadians shared information, posed questions, posted letters to politicians, and started a national conversation on copyright law in Canada. The initiative was not without its detractors, however. For example, Barry Sookman took the Fair Copyright for Canada Facebook group to task for "the unbalanced manner in which information and arguments about the Government's proposed copyright bill and its likely effects have been presented at the site."[80]

The Fair Copyright for Canada backlash succeeded in delaying the bill, but it did not kill it. Bill C-61 was later introduced in June 2008, six months after first appearing on the notice paper.[81] Despite the growing interest of users in copyright reform and the emergence of tools to make their voices heard, the bill sought to tilt Canadian law toward greater enforcement and restrictions on the use of digital

---

[77] *Id.*

[78] *Government's Delay in Introducing Copyright Reforms Concerns Canadian Music Industry*, CNW Group (Dec. 14, 2007), online: www.newswire.ca/en/story/132273/government-s-delay-in-introducing-copyright-reforms-concerns-canadian-music-industry.

[79] US Department of State, Canada: Special 301 (Ottawa: Mission Ottawa, Oct. 31, 2005), Cable No 08OTTAWA311, online: https://wikileaks.org/cable/2008/02/08OTTAWA311.html.

[80] Barry Sookman, *Facebook Fair for Copyright of Canada: Replies to Professor Geist*, Osgoode Digital Commons (2008), online: http://digitalcommons.osgoode.yorku.ca/cgi/viewcontent.cgi?article=1014&context=ohrlp.

[81] Bill C-61, *An Act to Amend the Copyright Act*, 2nd Sess, 39th Parl (2008), online: https://openparliament.ca/bills/39-2/C-61/.

content, leading Liberal Industry critic MP Scott Brison to warn that it could result in a "police state."[82] With the opposition Liberal party now also criticizing the government's approach, copyright emerged as a divisive political issue in Canada.

Like its predecessor, Bill C-61 ignored fair dealing with no expansion to the exception. In fact, the decision to avoid reforms to fair dealing came despite internal departmental analysis that even with the broader interpretation to fair dealing arising from the *CCH* decision, it was still far from certain that uses such as parody and satire were adequately protected by Canadian copyright law.[83] The bill did include a series of new consumer-focused exceptions, including a time shifting provision that legalized recording of television programs, a private copying of music provision that allowed consumers to copy music onto their iPods, and a format shifting provision that permitted transferring content from analog to digital formats. The new rules were subject to a host of limitations, however, since users could not retain recorded programs or create backups of popular consumer products such as DVDs.

Most controversial were the anticircumvention rules, which were far more restrictive than those found in the previous Bill C-60. The law created a blanket prohibition on circumventing the digital locks that frequently accompanied consumer products such as CDs, DVDs, and electronic books.

The public and political reaction to Bill C-61 was decidedly negative. For example, polling firm Angus Reid released the results of a poll two weeks after the bill was introduced, which found 39 percent of the public wanted their Member of Parliament to vote against it as compared with 32 percent who supported the bill.[84] More tellingly, 76 percent agreed with the statement that the proposed amendments "are being introduced as a result of lobbying by the North American music market."[85]

The opposition parties also voiced their concern with the bill. The NDP, which had long been associated with artists and creative communities, focused on both the need for compensation for creators and improved rights of access for consumers:

> The NDP is strongly opposed to this bill and we are calling on MPs from other parties to listen to their constituents and join us in the growing chorus against it. Rather, we are pushing for legislation that will ensure that artists and creators are

---

[82] Peter Nowak, *Copyright Could Result in Police State: Critics*, CBC NEWS (June 12, 2008), online: www.cbc.ca/news/technology/copyright-law-could-result-in-police-state-critics-1.707544.

[83] Industry Canada, Advice Paper, Treatment of Parody and Satire under the Current Copyright Exceptions Framework (May 21, 2008), online: http://storage.blogues.canoe.ca/davidakin/pdf/0805 copyright.pdf.

[84] Michael Geist, *Angus Reid Poll on Copyright Reveals Strong Opposition to C-61* (June 19, 2008), online: www.michaelgeist.ca/2008/06/angus-reid-on-copyright-2/.

[85] *Id.*

compensated for their work but that also ensures consumers are able to enjoy reasonable rights of access.[86]

Once again, the public led the way with a sustained, grassroots campaign against the bill throughout the summer. Industry Canada received more than 30,000 physical letters opposing the bill within weeks of introduction, while the local Fair Copyright for Canada chapters began meeting in community venues to strategize on how they could effectively oppose the bill.[87] Critics leveraged the Internet to raise awareness, conducting a YouTube contest,[88] tracking media coverage, and posting thousands of comments about the implications of the bill. Indeed, the effort was so effective that several Members of Parliament held town hall meetings in their constituencies to discuss the copyright bill.[89]

Yet just like Bill C-60, Bill C-61 also died soon after it was introduced as there was an election call in September 2008, meaning that the bill was never debated in the House of Commons. After a summer of public discussion and negative media coverage, however, the government was prepared to consider a new approach.

6.1.4. 2009 – Hitting the Reset Button

Following two failed bills and mounting political opposition over copyright reform, the government responded in 2009 with some significant changes. Tony Clement became the Minister of Industry, providing a fresh copyright perspective that was more receptive to users' rights and demonstrating an obvious enthusiasm for new technologies. His counterpart at Canadian Heritage, James Moore, was similarly supportive of social media and new technologies and the two ministers seemed to signal a willingness to re-examine previous legislative choices.

The first major step was a national copyright consultation in the summer of 2009 that actively engaged government ministers and thousands of Canadians.[90] It included a website that offered Canadians several ways to ensure that their voices were heard. There was a direct submission process, an online discussion forum, and a calendar that included information on roundtables (which were by invitation

---

[86] Michael Geist, *NDP Response to the Prentice DMCA* (June 18, 2008), online: www.michaelgeist .ca/2008/06/ndp-on-c-61-2/.

[87] Michael Geist, *CRIA Launching Grassroots Campaign for Canadian DMCA* (Apr. 9, 2009), online: www.michaelgeist.ca/2009/04/cria-grassroots-for-dmca/.

[88] *C-61 in 61 Seconds*, YOUTUBE (July 16, 2008), online: www.youtube.com/watch?v=igu-7jDIjSU.

[89] *See, e.g.*, www.facebook.com/events/19588553894/.

[90] INDUSTRY CANADA, GOVERNMENT OF CANADA LAUNCHES NATIONAL CONSULTATIONS ON COPYRIGHT MODERNIZATION (July 20, 2009) online: www.ic.gc.ca/eic/site/008.nsf/eng/04020.html.

only) and town hall meetings that were open to the public and streamed online. The site also features an RSS feed, audio and video transcripts of the roundtables, and an official Twitter feed.

Clement used the consultation to identify a new concern: in an era of rapidly changing technology, Clement wondered aloud how the government could ensure that a new copyright bill was built to last.[91] Clement's focus on longevity appeared to be a tacit acknowledgement that Bill C-61 had not been sufficiently forward looking. Indeed, with specific references to VHS tapes, emphasis on digital rights management, and blocks on the use of network-based personal video recorders, critics argued that the bill was past its best-before date the moment it was introduced.

According to a U.S. State Department cable, the consultation concerned both the established stakeholders and the U.S. government. The cable noted:

> The large scale of these consultations concerns some stakeholders. Some have told the Embassy that at best, the consultations look like a stall tactic to delay the introduction of a copyright reform bill, and at worst, cover for the Government to walk back from support for strong, WIPO-compliant copyright reform ... . Most interested parties agree that the howls of protest from grassroots consumer groups virtually guarantee that the copyright bill will be more 'consumer friendly' than the last iteration.[92]

The consultation ultimately generated more than 8,300 responses, an unprecedented number for a government consultation of this nature.[93] The success led some to criticize the use of form letters in the public participation in the 2009 copyright consultation.[94] It is certainly true that some of the largest public participation initiatives on digital policies have leveraged social media to encourage the public to register its support through online petitions, form letters, and social media support. Yet the practices were not dissimilar to those employed by the incumbent stakeholders. In the 2009 copyright consultation, form letters were so widely used that Industry Canada segregated the submissions. The form letters included submissions from

---

[91] Industry Canada, Roundtable on Public Hearings on Copyright (July 29, 2009), online: www.ic.gc.ca/eic/site/008.nsf/eng/h_04028.html.

[92] US Department of State, Copyright Reform in Canada: Day 4,235 (Oct. 31, 2005), Cable No. 09OTTAWA583, online: www.wikileaks.org/plusd/cables/09OTTAWA583_a.html.

[93] Simon Doyle, *Industry Canada Responds to Consultation Criticism, Says Process Was a 'Tremendous Success,'* THE WIRE REPORT (Apr. 23, 2010), online: www.thewirereport.ca/news/2010/04/23/industry-canada-responds-to-consultation-criticism-says-process-was-a-tremendous-success/20686.

[94] *Richard Owens, Noises Heard: Canada's Recent Online Copyright Consultation Process – Teachings and Cautions*, IP OSGOODE, online: www.iposgoode.ca/2010/04/noises-heard-canadas-recent-online-copyright-consultation-process/.

employees working in the music industry,[95] music rights holders,[96] and employees of a publishing company.[97]

In fact, traditional stakeholders used the emergence of significant individual participation to encourage their own members to more actively engage in the consultation. For example, Access Copyright, a leading copyright collective rights management organization, told members that "it is vital that you also get involved to ensure that your voice is heard," warning:

> It's a simple fact that users outnumber us. But Canadian users involved in the online debate are so adept at leveraging the internet and social networks to their advantage, there's a danger that your voices as Canadian creators and publishers will be drowned out by the chatter. Your interests need to be expressed as forcefully as possible, and it's up to you to get involved to make that happen.[98]

Moreover, the traditional stakeholders were active participants in the consultation process and warned the government against expanding users' rights within copyright. Access Copyright argued that the Supreme Court of Canada's *CCH* decision pointed to the need to create new statutory restrictions on fair dealing:

> Rather than an expansion of fair dealing, Access Copyright believes that it may be necessary to qualify the fair dealing provision as set out by the Supreme Court of Canada in the CCH decision, in order to ensure that Canada is compliant with the three-step test. Access Copyright contends that the fair dealing provision as interpreted by the Supreme Court of Canada conflicts with the normal exploitation of a work and causes an unreasonable loss of income to creators and publishers.[99]

6.1.5. *2010–2012 – Copyright Closure: A Bill Passes and the Court Releases a Pentalogy of Cases*

Emboldened by the consultation's success and the evident interest in the issue, Clement and Moore promised new legislation by the summer of 2010 and lived up to this commitment with Bill C-32, tabled in the House of Commons in June

---

[95] Industry Canada, *I Work in Canada's Music Industry* (Mar. 1, 2010), online: www.ic.gc.ca/eic/site/008 .nsf/eng/01616.html.

[96] Industry Canada, *Letter Requesting Changes to the Copyright Act* (Mar. 1, 2010), online: www.ic.gc.ca/ eic/site/008.nsf/eng/01227.html.

[97] Industry Canada, *I am an Employee of a Publishing Company* (Mar. 1, 2010), online: www.ic.gc.ca/eic/ site/008.nsf/eng/01617.html.

[98] *Copyright Debate Takes Aim at Your Livelihood*, Magazines Canada (Nov. 16, 2009), online: www.magazinescanada.ca/search-news-results/pub:1852/Copyright-Debate-Takes-Aim-at-Your-Livelihood#.VUYkM2RDs0N.

[99] Michael Geist, *Access Copyright: Reduce Fair Dealing, No Taping TV Shows or Format Shifting* (Oct. 14, 2009), online: www.michaelgeist.ca/2009/10/access-copyright-copycon-submission/.

2010.[100] From the moment of its introduction, it was readily apparent that the bill would be the target of unprecedented scrutiny and public debate. Virtually every copyright stakeholder group wasted little time in posting their quick analysis, often welcoming the introduction of the bill, but reserving judgment on the fine print. Those groups were joined by the tens of thousands of Canadians who over the prior two years had joined Facebook groups, raised copyright concerns with their elected representatives, or participated in the copyright consultation.

The government also mobilized with a media campaign characterizing the bill as "balanced copyright." The campaign represented a re-framing of the government's prior positioning, which had emphasized a "made in Canada" approach. Clement and Moore actively engaged with the public, responding to dozens of comments posted on Twitter and assuring the public that they were open to potential amendments. "Balance" became the watchword of the legislation, as even CRIA adopted it by providing financial backing for a website called Balanced Copyright for Canada that urged users to tweet at parliamentarians, respond to opinion pieces in the media, and write directly to Members of Parliament.[101]

The claims of balance were based largely on efforts to find compromise positions on some of the most contentious copyright issues. Bill C-32 included sector-specific reforms with something for almost everyone: new rights for performers and photographers, a new exception for Canadian broadcasters, new liability for BitTorrent search services, as well as the legalization of common consumer activities such as recording television shows and transferring songs from a CD to an iPod. In fact, there was even a "YouTube" user-generated content remix exception that granted Canadians the right to create remixed work for noncommercial purposes under certain circumstances.[102]

There were a number of areas where the government worked toward a genuine compromise. These included reform to fair dealing. The government rejected both pleas for no changes as well as arguments for a flexible fair dealing that would have opened the door to courts adding their own purposes to the fair dealing categories of research, private study, news reporting, criticism, and review. Instead, it identified some specific new exceptions that assist creators (parody and satire), educators

---

[100] Bill C-32, *An Act to Amend the Copyright Act*, 3rd Sess, 40th Parl (2009), online: www.parl.gc.ca/About/Parliament/LegislativeSummaries/bills_ls.asp?Language=E&ls=C32&Mode=1&Parl=40&Ses=3&source=library_prb.

[101] Peter Nowak, *Consumer Groups Blast Moore over Copyright*, CBC News (June 16, 2010), online: www.cbc.ca/news/technology/consumer-groups-blast-moore-over-copyright-1.868095.

[102] Teresa Scassa, *Acknowledging Copyright's Illegitimate Offspring: User-Generated Content and Canadian Copyright Law*, in THE COPYRIGHT PENTALOGY: HOW THE SUPREME COURT OF CANADA SHOOK THE FOUNDATIONS OF CANADIAN COPYRIGHT LAW 431 (Michael Geist ed., University of Ottawa Press 2013).

(education exception, education Internet exception), and consumers (time shifting, format shifting, backup copies).[103]

The Internet provider liability similarly represented a compromise, as the government retained a "notice-and-notice" system that required providers to forward allegations of infringement to subscribers. The system was costly for the providers, but had proven successful in discouraging infringement.[104]

It also compromised on the statutory damages rules that create the risk of multimillion dollar liability for cases of noncommercial infringement. The new rules reduced noncommercial liability to a range of $100 to $5,000 for all infringements, well below the $20,000 per infringement maximum that applied to cases of commercial infringement.

Critics of the bill argued that these attempts at balance were ultimately undermined by the anticircumvention provisions found in Bill C-32.[105] Those provisions – widely referred to as digital lock rules – adopted a foundational principle that anytime a digital lock is used, it trumps virtually all other rights.[106] The digital lock rules quickly became the primary focus of public debate, with criticism from all opposition parties and dozens of public interest and education groups.

Having experienced the social media backlash against Bill C-61, traditional stakeholders and the government itself mimicked the approach in an effort to curry support for the new bill. Canadian Heritage Minister James Moore urged incumbent stakeholders to emulate the public participation approach. In a speech to the Canadian Intellectual Property Council weeks after the tabling of the bill, Moore stated:

> These voices that are out there, these people that are out there who pretend to be experts that the media cite all the time. They don't believe in any copyright reform whatsoever. They will find any excuse to oppose this bill, to drum up fear, to mislead, to misdirect, and to push people in the wrong direction and to undermine

---

[103] Graham Reynolds, *Towards a Right to Engage in the Fair Transformative Use of Copyright-Protected Expression, in* From Radical Extremism to Balanced Copyright: Canadian Copyright and the Digital Agenda 395 (Michael Geist ed., Toronto: Irwin Law 2010).

[104] Gregory R. Hagen, *'Modernizing' ISP Copyright Liability, in* From Radical Extremism to Balanced Copyright: Canadian Copyright and the Digital Agenda 361 (Michael Geist ed., Toronto: Irwin Law 2010).

[105] Carys Craig, *Locking out Lawful Users: Fair Dealing and Anti-Circumvention in Bill C-32* (Toronto: Irwin Law 2010), online: www.irwinlaw.com/sites/default/files/attached/CCDA%2007%20Craig.pdf.

[106] Ian Kerr, *Digital Locks and the Automation of Virtue, in* From Radical Extremism to Balanced Copyright: Canadian Copyright and the Digital Agenda 247 (Michael Geist ed., Toronto: Irwin Law 2010); and David Lametti, *How Virtue Ethics Might Help Erase C-32's Conceptual Incoherence, in* From Radical Extremism to Balanced Copyright: Canadian Copyright and the Digital Agenda 327 (Michael Geist ed., Toronto: Irwin Law 2010).

what has been a meaningful comprehensive year-long effort to get something right. When they speak, they need to be confronted. If it's on Facebook, if it's on Twitter, or if it's on a talk show or if it is a newspaper, confront them and tell them they are wrong.[107]

The bill also sparked another collaborative publishing effort from Canadian copyright academics. Borrowing from a Moore comment that only groups of radical extremists would oppose the bill, *From Radical Extremism to Balanced Copyright: Canadian Copyright and the Digital Agenda* featured nineteen contributions examining both the bill and copyright more generally.[108] I again served as editor of the volume, which tackled the history of Canadian copyright, technology issues, the link between copyright and creativity, as well as education and access issues. The book was invoked regularly during the legislative hearings, with some Members of Parliament citing from it during House of Commons debates.[109]

The bill took two years to work its way through the legislative process as a parliamentary prorogation forced the reintroduction of the bill after months of committee hearings. The hearings themselves were generally inclusive, with opportunities afforded to virtually all stakeholders from copyright collectives to consumer groups to voice their support or concerns.

As a compromise bill featuring numerous new exceptions, the bill gained support from the user community, though the U.S.-style implementation of the anticircumvention rules garnered widespread criticism. Many creator groups were particularly upset with the implementation of new users' rights within the bill. For example, Access Copyright stated:

> Copyright laws need to give creators and consumers the tools they need to engage with trust and confidence in the digital marketplace. A copyright framework that is principles based, flexible enough to deal with new technologies and that balances the interests of creators, innovators, consumers and intermediaries is the foundation of a digital economic strategy that promotes creativity and creation, innovation, economic growth, and competition. Bill C-32 does none of this.[110]

Several writers groups also focused on the expansion of fair dealing with the inclusion of education as a fair dealing purpose:

[107] Michael Geist, *James Moore's Attack on Fair Copyright* (June 23, 2010), online: www .michaelgeist.ca/content/view/5138/125.

[108] From Radical Extremism to Balanced Copyright: Canadian Copyright and the Digital Agenda (Mitchael Geist ed., Toronto: Irwin Law 2010).

[109] Open Parliament, *Debates of May 14th*, 2012, 1st Sess, 41st Parl, online: https://openparliament.ca/ debates/2012/5/14/scott-simms-8/?page=19.

[110] Michael Geist, *Access Copyright Slams C-32* (July 14, 2010), online: www.michaelgeist .ca/2010/07/ac-on-c-32/.

From our perspective the biggest weakness in the bill is the addition of the word 'education' to the purposes of fair dealing without clear legislative guidance on how this amended provision of the Copyright Act will work in conjunction with other, more specific exceptions for education. We think that this new fair dealing provision will result in serious damage to the cultural sector and to Canada's embryonic knowledge economy and, together with other new exceptions, negatively affect Canada's professional writers.[111]

Some of the bill's other exceptions drew the ire of the music industry. J. P. Ellson, the Chair of the Canadian Council of Music Industry Association, argued that:

Among Bill C-32's objectives is to put the pirate download and file-sharing sites out of business. But the provisions of the Bill that permit user-generated content and transferring digital files to other formats would in fact, keep the pirate flag flying and their sites in business.[112]

In an earlier era, these criticisms would have been sufficient to stop the user-oriented reforms. Yet after two years of review, the government ultimately left the bill largely unchanged, opting for a series of modest amendments and keeping the new copyright exceptions intact.

The Canadian government completed its legislative overhaul in late June 2012 as the bill received royal assent just hours before the summer break. Two weeks later, the Supreme Court of Canada waded in with its views in the "copyright pentalogy," releasing a remarkable five copyright decisions in a single July 2012 day. While the court had issued several notable decisions since the 2004 *CCH* decision, the fair dealing issue and users' rights had yet to again take center stage. For those opposed to the CCH users' rights model, these cases represented the best, possibly last, hope to reverse the trend.

Justice Binnie, who wrote the Theberge majority, had retired from the court and two new Harper appointees, Justices Michael Moldaver and Andromache Karakatsanis had just joined. With no prospect of significant legislative copyright reform for five to ten years and no real likelihood of the Supreme Court grappling with copyright to this degree for the foreseeable future, this was it.

The arguments against CCH and users' rights were unsurprisingly found throughout the briefs of numerous interveners. For example, in a case pitting Access Copyright against provincial ministers of education over classroom copying, the

---

[111] Letter from Joanne Elder et al. to Ministers Tony Clement and James Moore (Aug. 3, 2010), online: Literary Translators Association of Canada, www.attlc-ltac.org/node/518.

[112] Michael Geist, *Canadian Music Industry Association Chair: Format Shifting, User Generated Content Keep Piracy Sites Going* (Sept. 15, 2010), online: www.michaelgeist.ca/2010/09/ellson-comments/.

Canadian Publishers' Council intervention argued the meaning of "users' rights" was overstated:

> The Appellants and other Intervenors rely extensively on the concept of "users' rights" to promote a view of fair dealing that would substantially curtail copyright holders' rights and permit extensive copying on behalf of others. Their use of the term to justify this severe curtailment of exclusive rights illustrates the dangers of treating the word 'user rights' literally, rather than as a metaphor to express the importance of user interests.[113]

Access Copyright focused on the same concern:

> In CCH this Court raised expectations when it held that fair dealing is a "user's right". Those raised expectations have led users like the appellants to ask that the right be clarified and made more predictable. However, this should not come at the expense of upsetting the balance between users' and creators' rights under the Act.[114]

In *SOCAN v. Bell*, another fair dealing case involving questions of whether song previews on popular digital music services could be characterized as consumer research for the purposes of fair dealing, Canadian Musical Reproduction Rights Agency (CMRRA), a copyright collective, argued that users should be given "low weight in the balance intended to encourage the dissemination of artistic and intellectual works in the public interest."[115] SOCAN also focused on the dangers of users' rights in the song previews case:

> This Court has called fair dealing a 'users' right." But, as the text of the Act and this Court's jurisprudence reveal, this 'user's right' is not an unlimited right to use. The limited purposes for which the fair dealing defence is available and this Court's guidance on determining whether a particular dealing is fair circumscribe the defence of fair dealing and restrict its application to those circumstances where the user herself is participating in an activity that furthers the public interest purposes of the Act.[116]

---

[113] Memorandum from the Canadian Publishers' Council, the Association of Canadian Publishers, and the Canadian Educational Resources Council (2012), online: www.scribd.com/doc/73790862/CPC-SCC-Interveners-Memorandum.

[114] Factum from Access Copyright (2012), online: www.scc-csc.gc.ca/WebDocuments-DocumentsWeb/33888/FM020_Respondent_Canadian-Copyright-Licensing-Agency-Operating-as-Access-Copyright.pdf.

[115] Factum from CMRRA (2012), online: http://scc-csc.gc.ca/WebDocuments-DocumentsWeb/33800/FM040_Respondent_CMRRA-SODRAC-Inc.pdf.

[116] Factum from the Society of Composers Authors and Music Publishers of Canada (2012), online: http://scc-csc.gc.ca/WebDocuments-DocumentsWeb/33800/FM010_Appellant_Society-of-Composers-Authors-%20and-Music-Publishers-of-Canada_Redacted.pdf.

In seeking to establish these limits, SOCAN argued that research under fair dealing was limited to "the systematic investigation into and study of materials and sources in order to establish facts and reach new conclusions."[117]

CRIA intervened in the same case, attempting to rework CCH by focusing on balance not constraining rights owners and users:

> the proper approach to the construction of the Act is to focus upon a construc-
> tion that achieves the appropriate balance. A large and liberal construction of the
> Act that unduly constrains the rights owners or users should be avoided. In weigh-
> ing the balance a court must also give consideration to Canada's obligations under
> the TRIPS Agreement discussed below.[118]

Given these submissions, if the Supreme Court wanted to backtrack from CCH and users' rights, it certainly had ample opportunity to do so. Yet rather than back-track, it doubled down on users' rights and then added yet another foundational lens in technological neutrality to examine copyright that is likely to favor users.

The Court's copyright pentalogy addressed a range of copyright issues, but fair dealing assumed a central role in two cases. In *Alberta v. Access Copyright*, the court addressed the use of fair dealing within education, arriving at several conclusions that expanded both the breadth of education-related purposes and how such uses should be analyzed within the fair dealing six-factor test.

For example, the court assessed the scope of the "private study" purpose, arriv-ing at a broad definition that rejected both spatial limitations and the require-ment for isolation. Writing for the majority, Justice Rosalie Abella concluded that: "[T]he word 'private' in 'private study' should not be understood as requir-ing users to view copyrighted works in splendid isolation. Studying and learning are essentially personal endeavours, whether they are engaged in with others or in solitude."[119]

The scope of the research purpose was also given a large and liberal interpretation in *SOCAN v. Bell Canada*. Once again, Abella adopted a strong stand in favor of fair dealing. After reiterating that fair dealing is a user's right, Abella argued for a very broad approach to the fair dealing research category:

> Limiting research to creative purposes would also run counter to the ordinary
> meaning of "research", which can include many activities that do not demand
> the establishment of new facts or conclusions. It can be piecemeal, informal,

---

[117] *Id.*

[118] Factum from the Canadian Recording Industry Association (2012), online: http://scc-csc.gc.ca/ WebDocuments-DocumentsWeb/33800/FM050_Respondent_Canadian-Recording-Industry-Asso ciation.pdf.

[119] Alberta (Education) v. Canadian Copyright Licensing Agency, 2012 S.C.C. 37, para. 27, online: www .lexisnexis.ca/documents/2012scc37.pdf.

exploratory, or confirmatory. It can in fact be undertaken for no purpose except personal interest. It is true that research can be for the purpose of reaching new conclusions, but this should be seen as only one, not the primary component of the definitional framework.[120]

The *Access Copyright* and *SOCAN* decisions not only articulated an expansive approach to the enumerated purposes under fair dealing, but also provided guidance on the broad and liberal interpretation of the six-factor fair dealing test that is used to determine whether the dealing is fair.

These rulings added significant flexibility to fair dealing that extends far beyond the CCH case.[121] Had the court stopped there, they would have represented a major victory for users' rights. But the court went further, articulating a second principle with which to consider copyright claims: technological neutrality. The court identified technological neutrality as a matter of balance within the Copyright Act and as a means to avoid the "double dipping" that occurs when new fees or restrictions are layered onto new technologies.[122]

The net effect was to firmly reject claims that users' rights are merely a metaphor. In the eyes of the Supreme Court of Canada, it is an essential component of Canadian copyright law that is integral to achieving the purpose of copyright it identified in *Théberge* in 2002 – a balance that "lies not only in recognizing the creator's rights but in giving due weight to their limited nature."

The full impact of the copyright pentalogy has yet to be felt, but the decisions did give rise to a third collaborative book on copyright by Canada's copyright academics. *The Copyright Pentalogy: How the Supreme Court of Canada Shook the Foundations of Canadian Copyright Law*, featured fourteen articles on copyright written by independent scholars from coast to coast.[123] The diversity of contributors provides a rich view of the copyright pentalogy, with analysis of the standard of review of copyright

---

[120] SOCAN v. Bell, [2012] 2 S.C.R. 326, 2012 S.C.C. 36, para. 22 available on CanLII.

[121] For the view that Canada has always had such flexibility, see Ariel Katz, *Fair Use 2.0: The Rebirth of Fair Dealing in Canada*, in THE COPYRIGHT PENTALOGY: HOW THE SUPREME COURT OF CANADA SHOOK THE FOUNDATIONS OF CANADIAN COPYRIGHT LAW 93 (Michael Geist ed., University of Ottawa Press 2013).

[122] For a more detailed examination of the implications of technological neutrality, see *Carys Craig, Technological Neutrality: (Pre)Serving the Purposes of Copyright Law*, in THE COPYRIGHT PENTALOGY: HOW THE SUPREME COURT OF CANADA SHOOK THE FOUNDATIONS OF CANADIAN COPYRIGHT LAW 271 (Michael Geist ed., University of Ottawa Press 2013); and Gregory R. Hagen, *Technological Neutrality in Canadian Copyright Law*, in THE COPYRIGHT PENTALOGY: HOW THE SUPREME COURT OF CANADA SHOOK THE FOUNDATIONS OF CANADIAN COPYRIGHT LAW 307 (Michael Geist ed., University of Ottawa Press 2013).

[123] THE COPYRIGHT PENTALOGY: HOW THE SUPREME COURT OF CANADA SHOOK THE FOUNDATIONS OF CANADIAN COPYRIGHT LAW (Michael Geist ed., University of Ottawa Press 2013).

decisions, fair dealing, technological neutrality, the scope of copyright law, and the implications of the decisions for copyright collective management.

6.2. WHAT THE CANADIAN EXPERIENCE TEACHES

Canada is certainly not the only country in which public engagement on digital issues, particularly copyright, has taken policy makers and politicians by surprise. In 2009, thousands of people in New Zealand launched an Internet blackout campaign against proposed "three strikes and you're out" copyright legislation that would have led to Internet users losing access based on three allegations of infringement. Users blacked out websites and profiles on Facebook and Twitter and the New Zealand government responded by withdrawing the legislation.[124]

In January 2012, protests over the Stop Online Piracy Act (SOPA), hailed by some as the Internet Spring, saw millions speak out against restrictive legislative proposals that posed a serious threat to an open Internet. On a single day, Wikipedia reported that 162 million people viewed its blackout page during the 24-hour protest period.[125] The protest launched a political earthquake as previously supportive politicians raced for the exits, and the contentious bill was legislatively dead by the end of the week.[126]

Meanwhile, in Europe, thousands took to the streets throughout the spring of 2012 to protest against the Anti-Counterfeiting Trade Agreement, which featured Canada as a participant and initial signatory. The European Parliament ultimately voted overwhelmingly to reject the agreement, striking a major blow to the hopes of supporters who envisioned a landmark agreement that would set a new standard for intellectual property rights enforcement.

Yet the Canadian experience may be unique given the grassroots nature of the campaigns and the shift in approach within both the legislature and the courts. Moreover, unlike other protests that have focused on stopping legislation, the Canadian experience emphasized pro-user changes to the law. As a result, Canada is home to an expansive list of new copyright exceptions and the leading voice for treating limitations and exceptions within copyright as users' rights. What might the Canadian experience teach? While every circumstance is different, there are some lessons that may translate more readily to other countries.

---

[124] Cheryl Cheung, *New Zealand Withdraws Controversial Copyright Law*, DEETH WILLIAMS WALL (Apr. 8, 2009), online: www.dww.com/?p=1443.

[125] *Wikipedia Blackout Supports Free and Open Internet*, WIKIMEDIA FOUNDATION (Jan. 19, 2012), online: http://wikimediafoundation.org/wiki/Press_releases/Wikipedia_blackout_supports_free_and_open_internet.

[126] Dan Nguyen, *SOPA Opera Update: Opposition Surges*, PROPUBLICA NERD BLOG (Jan. 19, 2012), online: www.propublica.org/nerds/item/sopa-opera-update.

6.2.1. *Users as Copyright Stakeholders*

The biggest shift within the Canadian copyright reform framework was not a specific provision or law, but rather the emergence of the broader public as a recognized stakeholder within the policy process. While government officials would likely protest that the public has always been welcome within the policy-making process, the reality is that the system was largely stacked against individual participation. Copyright law can be highly technical, making it difficult for a nonexpert to assess the implications of legislative proposals. Moreover, policy officials often work with "stakeholder lists" that do not readily account for broader public participation.

The Canadian experience demonstrates that these barriers can be overcome. Once the public interest in copyright became evident, government officials conducted open consultations designed to maximize public participation. The use of social media, plain language explanations and backgrounders, town halls, online discussion fora, and other techniques were crucial in bringing users to the table and granting them a voice in the policy process. The openness to user perspectives continued during the hearings on Bill C-32, with several individuals invited to appear before the committee to provide their perspectives.

6.2.2. *The Internet as a Tool for Participation*

The ability for the public to become engaged in the copyright policy process was aided and facilitated by the Internet, which provided the mechanisms to ensure their voices were heard. Social media sites such as Facebook and Twitter, blogs, and online video provided an avenue for Canadians to become informed about copyright and the means to speak out.

The Canadian copyright story consistently demonstrates the potential of these tools to raise awareness and influence the policy process. For example, the 2007 copyright advocacy campaigns originated on Facebook at a time when government was still unsure about how to react to mass Internet-based advocacy.

While the effectiveness of online tools waxes and wanes over time – there is no simple recipe for success – there is no denying the importance of Internet-based advocacy in Canada with respect to copyright. Indeed, the significant shifts in copyright – and digital policies more broadly – in Canada over the past decade would likely not have occurred without the continuous feedback loop provided by Internet-based tools.

6.2.3. *The Role of Academics in the Policy Process*

Traditional copyright groups are often dismissive of academics, using "ivory tower" rhetoric to suggest that they do not understand the business implications of copyright policy, do not share the concerns of creators, or are "anti-copyright." Yet the Canadian experience demonstrates that academics can play an integral role in advancing the law within both the legislature and the courts. Indeed, the origin of "users' rights" in Canadian law lies in the work of Professor David Vaver, who was cited with approval by the Supreme Court of Canada in its adoption of the term.[127]

The copyright pentalogy cases feature many citations of academics from articles published in the books noted above. Professors Carys Craig,[128] Ariel Katz,[129] Margaret Ann Wilkinson,[130] and Abraham Drassinower[131] were all cited, pointing to the influence that academic scholarship can have on the court's deliberations. Academics such as Katz and Jeremy deBeer also intervened before the court in those cases.

Moreover, academics were also active participants during the policy process. Many appeared before legislative committees or submitted detailed briefs during the 2009 copyright consultation. The active participation in copyright policy suggests that Canadian copyright scholars increasingly view their role as doing more than just interpreting decisions and legislation, but rather also influencing the shape and scope of future reforms and caselaw.

6.2.4. *Users' Rights Have a Strong Policy Foundation*

Critics of recent Canadian policy developments sometimes suggest that the shift toward users' rights is a populist approach devoid of a solid policy foundation. Yet the reality is that both the Supreme Court's decisions on user rights and the government's legislative reforms have been premised on a clearly articulated policy approach. The Supreme Court's emphasis on users' rights draws a direct connection to the *Théberge* decision and Binnie's emphasis on the dangers inherent in both overprotecting work as well as under-protecting it. That perspective was the spark that soon after led to the emphasis on copyright balance and users' rights. Moreover, it continues to provide the policy foundation for assessing emerging copyright issues.

From a governmental perspective, the policy that underlies its copyright bill was support for the market (anticircumvention rules were viewed as facilitating market entry) and strong enforcement against commercial infringement (the government included an "enabler" provision to target websites that facilitate infringement and

---

[127] CCH Canadian v. Law Society of Upper Canada, [2004] 1 S.C.R. 339, 2004 S.C.C. 13, paras. 12–13, 51–54; SOCAN v. Bell, [2012] 2 S.C.R. 326, 2012 S.C.C. 36, para. 10; *ESA v. SOCAN*, 2012 S.C.C. 34, [2012] 2 S.C.R. 231, paras 6, 11, 96, 112, 127.

[128] See cases cited *supra* note 127.

[129] See cases cited *supra* note 127.

[130] Rogers Commc'ns Inc. v. SOCAN, 2012 S.C.C. 35, [2012] 2 S.C.R. 283, para. 65.

[131] SOCAN v. Bell, 2012 S.C.C. 36, para. 21.

maintained significant statutory damages for commercial infringement). However, the government was also supportive of removing personal, noncommercial activity from the scope of criminal and costly civil copyright enforcement. That view led to the inclusion of numerous new personal exceptions, the expansion of fair dealing, the introduction of the noncommercial user-generated content exception, as well as a cap on liability for noncommercial infringement.

6.2.5. *International Flexibility Allows for Users' Rights*

International copyright treaties are often used to convince policy makers that they face legal obligations that severely limit their ability to enact domestic reforms. The Canadian experience demonstrates that concern over international treaties is greatly overstated.[132] Early Canadian bills recognized the flexibility in the WIPO Internet treaties, adopting anticircumvention rules that remained subject to exceptions such as fair dealing.[133] While the final bill mirrored the U.S. DMCA approach, that was primarily a function of U.S. political pressure, not international treaty obligations.

Moreover, the introduction of new exceptions for noncommercial user-generated content, the expansion of fair dealing, and the inclusion of new personal exceptions for backup copies led critics to claim that Canada was offside its international copyright obligations. The government carefully studied the issue and concluded that international law offers sufficient flexibility to permit these reforms. The Canadian experience in this regard is clear: international law need not be viewed as a significant barrier to users' rights.

6.2.6. *Trade and Copyright*

The link between trade – particularly trade agreements – and intellectual property is well-known. The annual U.S. Trade Representative Special 301 list, Congressional watchlists, as well as trade negotiations such the Trans Pacific Partnership and

---

[132] *See, e.g.*, David Vaver, *Canada's Intellectual Property Framework: A Comparative Overview*, 17 I.P.J. 125 (2003); Blayne Haggart, *North American Digital Copyright, Regional Governance, and the Potential for Variation*, in FROM RADICAL EXTREMISM TO BALANCED COPYRIGHT: CANADIAN COPYRIGHT AND THE DIGITAL AGENDA 45 (Michael Geist ed., Toronto: Irwin Law 2010); Myra Tawfik, *History in the Balance: Copyright and Access to Knowledge*, in FROM RADICAL EXTREMISM TO BALANCED COPYRIGHT: CANADIAN COPYRIGHT AND THE DIGITAL AGENDA 69 (Michael Geist ed., Toronto: Irwin Law 2010); and Michael Geist, *The Case for Flexibility in Implementing the WIPO Internet Treaties: An Examination of the Anti-Circumvention Requirements*, in FROM RADICAL EXTREMISM TO BALANCED COPYRIGHT: CANADIAN COPYRIGHT AND THE DIGITAL AGENDA 185 (Michael Geist ed., Toronto: Irwin Law 2010).

[133] Michael Geist, *Fairness Found: How Canada Quietly Shifted from Fair Dealing to Fair Use*, in THE COPYRIGHT PENTALOGY: HOW THE SUPREME COURT OF CANADA SHOOK THE FOUNDATIONS OF CANADIAN COPYRIGHT LAW 157 (Michael Geist ed., University of Ottawa Press 2013).

the Canada – European Union Trade Agreement have the potential to influence domestic policy in a manner that leaves skeptics concerned that national laws are drafted in Washington or Brussels. It is certainly true that trade negotiations played a major role in the Canadian copyright process. In particular, the adoption of U.S. DMCA-style anticircumvention rules within the 2012 legislation was unquestionably a function of U.S. pressure and the recognition that a more flexible approach would face opposition in most other ongoing trade negotiations.

However, the impact of U.S. pressure and international trade negotiations can be overstated. Canadian officials have long dismissed the Special 301 process as a lobby document with little credibility.[134] Further, Canada has demonstrated a willingness to hold firm on key issues during trade negotiations. For example, the European Union sought a wide range of copyright reforms as part of the Canada and European Union (EU) Comprehensive Economic and Trade Agreement (CETA) negotiations, including copyright term extension, re-sale rights, and broadcaster rights.[135] None were included in the final document. Similarly, the United States voiced its objection to Canada's rules for Internet service providers, yet the government left them unchanged within the bill and seems likely to do so again within the Trans Pacific Partnership Agreement.

6.2.7. People Matter

While the public often views governments as a monolith, the Canadian experience demonstrates the profound impact that individuals can have on domestic copyright policy. For example, Charlie Angus, the NDP MP and musician, single-handedly altered the debate on copyright within the Standing Committee on Canadian Heritage by reversing longstanding party policies that ignored user concerns. Angus succeeded in both moving his party toward a user-oriented position and ensuring that committees moved beyond unanimous support for rights holder policies and perspectives.

The Canadian legislative journey involved numerous Industry Ministers, with the Conservatives alone having Maxime Bernier, Jim Prentice, Tony Clement, Christian Paradis, and James Moore occupying the post during the six-year period from 2006 to 2012. The public may not recognize the differences, but each had different perspectives on copyright. Indeed, it is unlikely that Bill C-32 would have included many of the exceptions if not for Clement's support at the time that the bill was being drafted.

---

[134] *House of Commons, Standing Committee on Public Safety and National Security*, 1st Sess, 39th Parl (Mar. 27, 2007), online: www.parl.gc.ca/HousePublications/Publication.aspx?DocId=2806944& Language=E&Mode=1&Parl=39&Ses=1.

[135] Michael Geist, *Billions at Stake if Canada Caves on Drug Patent Demands* (Aug. 14, 2012), online: www.michaelgeist.ca/2012/08/ceta-ip-demands-2/.

The role of individuals is also felt within the courts. For example, before the copyright pentalogy, Abella was rarely identified as a leader on copyright. Yet Abella has written reasons on virtually every copyright case before the court since her appointment to the bench in 2004.[136] As copyright evolved at the Supreme Court, her support for users' rights emerged as the majority view, providing further evidence of the crucial role that individuals can make on the state of the law.

Indeed, Canada's improbable journey from a country of relatively restrictive copyright rules to the world leader in users' rights over the span of a decade ultimately lies in the efforts of individuals. The Canadian copyright story is one of government ministers open to re-examining copyright policies, opposition MPs willing to break from longstanding party policy, judges committed to a balance in copyright law, scholars ensuring their research is factored into the policy process, and thousands of individuals – both expert and nonexpert – demanding that their voice be heard. The copyright story is still being written with new court cases and demands for reform, yet any changes must now be developed through a prism that prominently features user rights and an engaged public interest.

---

[136] Margaret Ann Wilkinson, *The Context of the Supreme Court's Copyright Cases, in* THE COPYRIGHT PENTALOGY: HOW THE SUPREME COURT OF CANADA SHOOK THE FOUNDATIONS OF CANADIAN COPYRIGHT LAW (Michael Geist ed., University of Ottawa Press 2013).

7

(When) Is Copyright Reform Possible?

*James Boyle**

ABSTRACT

Most discussions of the limitations on, and exceptions to, copyright start from an assumed set of malfunctions in the policy process. They include collective action problems, professional ideologies that are resistant to empirical evidence, "race to the top" effects in international political negotiations, the defensive reaction of incumbent industries to technological innovation, revolving doors and industry capture of the regulatory process, the unreflective imposition of ideas drawn from real property on the world of the intangible and many more. Those malfunctions have a disproportionate effect on attempts to set the boundaries of copyright more narrowly – whether in time, in scope, in the behavior that it regulates, or in the safe harbors that it protects.

This chapter explores a particular – albeit localized and partial – counterexample to the normal tale of the futility of reform; the Hargreaves Review of Intellectual Property, an independent review of the UK intellectual property system commissioned by the UK government in 2010. The Hargreaves Review was remarkable in that, in certain limited ways, it seemed to evade this tangle of regulatory malfunction in its assessments of the copyright system. More remarkable still, its policy proposals were – for the most part – concerned with limitations and exceptions to copyright, and most of them were actually enacted into law. In this chapter, I try to see if we can learn

* James Boyle is the William Neal Reynolds Professor of Law at Duke University. One of the founding board members of Creative Commons, he served as an external adviser to the Hargreaves Review.

James Boyle © 2015. Licensed under a CC BY:NC:SA license. This chapter would not have been possible without incredibly helpful comments about the UK process from Lionel Bently, Andres Guadamuz and Ian Hargreaves. In addition, the Intellectual Property Office (IPO) staff and my fellow "advisers" provided invaluable information. Jack Knight, John de Figueiredo, and Jennifer Jenkins gave very useful editorial feedback. The title of the chapter is a reference (and homage) to Pam Samuelson's extremely thought-provoking article, *Is Copyright Reform Possible*, 126 HARVARD L. REV. 740 (2013). Apart from Pam's work, Bernt Hugenholtz's œuvre was a continuing inspiration. Needless to say, none of those I thank are responsible for my conclusions or for the errors or omissions that remain.

anything about copyright's general state of regulatory *impasse* from this apparent partial counterexample.

In the five months we have had to compile the Review, we have sought never to lose sight of David Cameron's "exam question." Could it be true that laws designed more than three centuries ago with the express purpose of creating economic incentives for innovation by protecting creators' rights are today obstructing innovation and economic growth? The short answer is: yes. We have found that the UK's intellectual property framework, especially with regard to copyright, is falling behind what is needed. Copyright, once the exclusive concern of authors and their publishers, is today preventing medical researchers studying data and text in pursuit of new treatments. Copying has become basic to numerous industrial processes, as well as to a burgeoning service economy based upon the internet. The UK cannot afford to let a legal framework designed around artists impede vigorous participation in these emerging business sectors.

Ian Hargreaves, Foreword: Hargreaves Review (2011).[1]

7.1. THE STRUCTURE OF COPYRIGHT POLICY MAKING

Is copyright reform possible? Copyright scholars can give a litany of the features of the copyright system that seem deeply problematic.

- We have repeatedly extended copyright retrospectively. This clearly provides no new incentives to those who have already created – many of whom are dead. It benefits only a tiny number of authors, those whose creations are still economically viable after the end of the existing term, but locks up vast numbers of orphan works – still under copyright, but with unknown rightsholders – and makes the digitization of twentieth century culture all but impossible. This is social policy that imposes large social cost, with tiny private benefits, one that flies directly against copyright's central rationale of promoting *access* to works.[2]
- The copyright term is far too long – at least if copyright is judged by its effective incentives.[3] A copyright term that required renewal – which used to be the U.S. system – would provide almost all of the benefits to those copyright owners whose works remained valuable, while leaving the rest of society free of

---

[1] Ian Hargreaves, Digital Opportunity: A Review of Intellectual Property and Growth 1 (2011).

[2] *See, e.g.*, James Boyle, The Public Domain 222–29 (2008), and sources cited therein.

[3] *See, e.g.*, Raymond Shih Ray Ku, Jiayang Sun & Yiying Fan, *Does Copyright Law Promote Creativity? An Empirical Analysis of Copyright's Bounty*, 62 Vand. L. Rev. 1669 (2009); Paul J. Heald, *How Copyright Keeps Works Disappeared* (Ill. Public L. Research Paper No. 13–54, 2013); and Ivan Png & Qui-Hong Wang, *Copyright Law and the Supply of Creative Work: Evidence from the Movies* (2009).

the dead weight loss of the very long term for all other works. Far from adopting such a system, we have made it impossible by treaty.

- Copyright used to require formalities – which cut down on search costs (important in solving licensing problems or orphan works tangles) while requiring an affirmative act to enter the domain of copyright.[4] Again, we have abolished these requirements and made their reintroduction extremely difficult because of our treaty obligations. As an added "benefit," this sweeps all of informal culture into copyright. Every home movie, blog entry, diary, or snapshot is pulled into copyright's domain, irrespective of the wishes of the creator. This will create nightmarish orphan works problems for the documentarians, historians, and archivists of the future.

- We make copyright policy in an evidence-free environment;[5] depending on anecdote and, to quote the Hargreaves Review, "lobbynomics," and never revisiting our policies to see if they produced the benefits claimed for them. We have repeatedly extended rights and strengthened penalties without evidence that this is cost-justified or indeed that costs do not outweigh benefits.

- We say we harmonize copyright internationally but generally harmonize only the rights, which are mandatory, while making exceptions optional. This leaves a terrain that is in fact *not* harmonized. Think of a practice that depends on a limitation or exception – that decompilation of software is fair use, for example – present in one country but not another. More generally, the disparate treatment of rights and exceptions ignores the fact that the limitations on copyright are as central a feature of its operation as the rights themselves.

- We allow technological happenstance to sweep activities in and out of copyright's domain without considering whether it promotes copyright's goals to do so. To read a paper book or to turn a light on, I commit no "copyright significant act." But to read a *digital* text or turn on a *software* switch I must create a temporary and limited copy of the work involved. Should the copyright holder therefore be able to regulate my activity in a fine-tuned and granular way? For example, by conditioning my *license* to use the program or book on all kinds of conditions that copyright law itself does not impose?

- We now have the ability to do digital "text-mining" in a way that seems to have enormous scientific potential, cross referencing discoveries in unrelated fields that no human eye could discover. But that text-mining is hobbled by the licenses and digital fences that encumber scientific texts – frequently texts that lay out the results of publicly funded research. Those licenses and digital fences are backstopped, ultimately, by copyright.

---

[4] Jessica Litman, *Sharing and Stealing*, 27 HASTINGS COMM. ENT. L.J. 1, 14–18 (2004).
[5] BOYLE, *supra* note 2, at 208–29.

- We say we want to provide new, legal, ways of streaming and providing access to digital content internationally, but the businesses that try to do so find themselves in a Gordian knot of licenses and collecting societies, each country with its own particular set of rules. As technologies have developed, copyright has added right after right, intermediary after intermediary. If someone wants to play a song on the radio in France, the process is clear and the number of rights involved limited. But if someone wants to *stream* a song across all Europe? That is a nightmare. Consumers want cheap and legal access to content. Artists and distributors want to enable it. But the law (and the intermediaries built to collect the revenue streams which each right enables) have combined to produce a tangled anti-commons through which it is hard to make progress.

Each copyright scholar has their own list of the flaws in our copyright policy, though the ones above would probably be common to many of them. To be sure, not all of these are uncontroversial. Retrospective copyright term extension or the treatment of orphan works is one thing – that meets with almost universal disapproval from anyone whose scholarly focus is on copyright's instrumental effects. Even many rightsholders find the orphan works effects an embarrassment when they lobby for yet another increased copyright term. But text-mining, or licensing reform, are more complex. In those cases, rightsholders and intermediaries such as collecting societies may have strong reasons to prefer the status quo, even if it is socially wasteful. As for evidence-based policy making, that attracts little support from rightsholders – in part because they correctly perceive that in those areas where the data is clear, it is likely to provide no support for the rights they cherish. The empirical studies on the effects of copyright term extension, the availability of public domain works as opposed to those under copyright, and the EU's study on the effect of the Database Directive are all cases in point.[6]

To some, these problems are explained by a simple "public choice" theory of regulation. Mancur Olson's *The Logic of Collective Action*[7] provides an elegant, almost algebraic, account: repeat players with highly concentrated economic interests will lobby effectively for those interests, while an unorganized and under-informed public, whose interests are individually small but collectively larger than the repeat players, will thus be the victims of policies that are socially irrational yet which convey great benefits to the lobbyists. Copyright adds to this happy account of ubiquitous legislative malfunction the added attraction that its focus is partly on technological innovation. By definition, the industries of the future are not present at the

---

[6] *See, e.g.,* BOYLE, *supra* note 2, at 209–13, 217–20, 225–29; empirical studies *supra* note 3.
[7] MANCUR OLSON, JR., The Logic of Collective Action: Public Goods and the Theory of Groups (1965).

bargaining table and thus their technologies will be vulnerable to incumbents who may wish to legislatively hamper them in order to preserve a current business model.

One can add to these two factors the scholarship on regulatory capture[8]: Regulators grow comfortable with those whose industries they regulate. Increasingly, they will come to adopt their worldviews. Partly, this can be explained as a rational reaction to the future benefits to be gleaned when they leave public service and go to work for the companies they once regulated. (A recent article on the "revolving door" between the U.S. Trade Representatives Office and the content and pharmaceutical industries provides some eye-opening examples.[9]) A public servant who unceasingly promotes the interests of the rightsholders while in office will not want for lucrative employment after her departure. But it is also a form of "herd psychology." If one is surrounded, every day, by a group whose ideological tenets, economic baselines, and assumptions about the effects of regulation are homogeneous, it will produce cognitive dissonance to take a contrary position, even when the evidence clearly indicates that position has merit.

To be sure, not all lobbying is socially dysfunctional. Some is actively beneficial. Corporate lobbying brings important perspectives before regulators. It may help to solve coordination problems – effectively representing scattered creators, such as songwriters, whose interests might otherwise get lost in the process. Collective action problems can also work in reverse – when a diffuse population can cause *harm* rather than benefit to incumbents, harm that is individually small but collectively substantial. Technology can give private individuals around the world the power to cause economic harm – for example by illicit downloading – on a scale that was formerly the preserve of industrial enterprises. Rightsholders see themselves locked in combat to repair that damage – the extent of which is hotly debated, as the Hargreaves Review carefully notes. Given that framing, they may see their comparative over-representation in the policy-making process, and their hold on both the worldview and the future job prospects of policy makers, as a necessary balance to the massive, decentralized danger posed by the Internet. (This of course does not explain the policy making in the areas where such threats are absent.)

Of course there are some offsetting forces to the processes I am describing here, two of which demand particular attention. First, the consumer electronics industry and online intermediaries sometimes provide a counterweight in the policy-making process to some of the proposals put forward by copyright holders.[10] Google and

---

[8] For a nice review of the literature, see Ernesto Dal Bó, *Regulatory Capture: A Review*, 22 OXFORD REV. ECON. POLICY (Summer) 203–22 (2006).

[9] Timothy B. Lee, *Here's Why Obama Trade Negotiators Push the Interests of Hollywood and Drug Companies*, THE WASHINGTON POST, Nov. 26, 2013, *available at* www.washingtonpost .com/blogs/the-switch/wp/2013/11/26/heres-why-obama-trade-negotiators-push-the-interests-of-hollywood-and-drug-companies/ (last accessed Dec. 9, 2014).

[10] It is worth noting that this was very nearly not the case. The consumer electronics industry has flourished partly because of the protection of rules like that put forward in the *Sony* case – even if the

Apple now have a seat at the table and *their* interests include having the freedom to do things that copyright law might attempt to prohibit – the making of backup copies of your library of songs or copying the entire web every day in order to index it, for example. In fact, the Hargreaves Review was apparently begun because of conversations that David Cameron, the British Prime Minister, had with the founders of Google.[11] Second, copyright law has been transformed in the last forty years from an arcane form of inter-industry horizontal regulation into a body of laws that affects citizens on a daily basis in their technological and digital interactions. The result has been an increasing level of popular engagement with issues ranging from access to knowledge to Internet regulation.[12]

These two changes are important – clearly very important in the case of online intermediaries, and particularly so in the case of this Review. I will discuss that point further in my conclusion. Nevertheless, the changes have palpable limits. The process of democratic engagement is still in its infancy. The intermediaries and consumer electronics companies have a wide range of economic and policy interests, including as rightsholders themselves. Intellectual property issues do not have the primacy for them that they do with the content industries. More importantly, their agendas do not cover all of the policies involved, nor do they inevitably reflect the public interest, merely a different private interest than that presented by the content industry. At the moment, that often aligns with many of those seeking to defend an open Internet and a vibrant technological industry, but this is hardly something on which one can depend. Moreover, despite these important counterweights, the dominant voice in intellectual property policy making is still that of rightsholders. The dominant *philosophy* is that of maximalism – in which increases in rights are always presumed to produce increases in innovation, and where exceptions are viewed with a grudging hostility. To quote the Hargreaves Review:

> In the case of IP policy and specifically copyright policy, however, there is no doubt that the persuasive powers of celebrities and important UK creative companies have distorted policy outcomes. Further distortion arises from the fact (not unique to this sector) that there is a striking asymmetry of interest between rights holders,

---

predominant use of a product is to infringe copyright, the manufacturer is not liable if it has current or possible future substantial noninfringing uses. (Think of an iPod that can contain 10,000 songs – how much would that cost to fill *legally*?) In the online world, without the exceptions and limitations provided by the DMCA's 512 and the European E-Commerce Directive, Google, YouTube and Facebook would be impossible in their current form, as would most Internet Service Providers. Both of those safe harbors were very close battles. *Sony* was a 5–4 decision. The WIPO Copyright Treaties contain no requirement for safe harbors and the Clinton Administration's original plans for copyright online promoted the idea of strict liability for all intermediaries.

11 HARGREAVES, *supra* note 1, at 44.

12 *See, e.g.,* Amy Kapczynski, *The Access to Knowledge Mobilization and the New Politics of Intellectual Property*, 117 YALE L.J. 804 (2008).

for whom IP issues are of paramount importance, and consumers for whom they have been of passing interest only until the emergence of the Internet as a focus for competing technological, economic, business and cultural concerns.[13]

In my case, all of this sets the stage for a particular encounter with the policy-making process. I was one of five outside experts asked to advise the Hargreaves Review, a comprehensive review of intellectual property ordered by the British government in 2011. I wish to temper your expectations. The Hargreaves Review is very far indeed from being a solution to the problems I described earlier. But it did address some of them. In this chapter, I will lay out the main findings of the Review, which ranged from the structure of the copyright policy-making process, to orphan works reform, the legality of data mining, educational use, and copyright licensing. I hope these conclusions may be of interest for their own sake to copyright scholars around the world. After doing so, I will spend a little while discussing whether this personal experience caused any revision in or inflection of my scholarly assessment of the possibilities of copyright reform. The experience is merely an N of one, of course. No general conclusions can be deduced from it. On the other hand, it is an N of one and not zero.

7.2. THE REVIEW

It started with an email titled "Invitation from Baroness Wilcox." That went immediately into the spam folder that contains "invitations" from Saudi princes with investment schemes, the sons of Nigerian oil ministers with pressing needs for foreign bank accounts, and Ukrainian girls "who just need a friend." Then my subconscious tickled me – was Baroness Wilcox not the Undersecretary of State responsible for the Hargreaves Review of Intellectual Property – the comprehensive review of Britain's intellectual property regime recently announced by David Cameron? The email was a real one – an invitation to be one of the five expert advisors to that Review.[14] Though the invitation was obviously an honor, the decision whether to accept was more complex. Partly because of the dynamics of the policy-making process, participating in such projects is often deeply frustrating for academics. In 2006, the UK had conducted another review of intellectual property. Called the Gowers Review, it had conducted a thoroughgoing study of the field. The analysis was of an extremely high quality; the empirical analysis of the effects of copyright extension for sound recordings, for example, was state of the art. The Gowers Review called for fifty-four specific reforms of British law, and proposed that, in general, intellectual

---

[13] HARGREAVES, *supra* note 1, at 93.
[14] The other four experts – whose comments I found extremely useful – were Roger Burt, Mark Schankerman, David Gann, and Tom Loosemore.

property policy needed to become more data-driven. Academics loved it. Its suggestions were thoughtful, clearly laid out, and well-grounded in the data. The majority of them were also ignored.

This fate is by no means unusual. To participate in such efforts is normally to spend a great deal of time trying to make thoughtful arguments in the text of the report, most of which will be removed by the political compromises of the drafting process and then to see the few suggestions that do survive fail to become law. The Hargreaves Review turned out to be rather different.

7.2.1. *Evidence-Based Policy Making*

> Evidence. Government should ensure that development of the IP System is driven as far as possible by objective evidence. Policy should balance measurable economic objectives against social goals and potential benefits for rights holders against impacts on consumers and other interests. These concerns will be of particular importance in assessing future claims to extend rights or in determining desirable limits to rights.[15]

To those unfamiliar with intellectual property policy, these words seem like the merest *pablum*. Insiders know better. As I explained earlier, in the strange world of copyright policy it is controversial to suggest that the debate on extension or limitation of rights should be driven by evidence and by a utilitarian calculation of social and economic costs and benefits, or to suggest that extensions of rights can have negative impacts on consumers and other interests. The Hargreaves Review followed Gowers in embracing a largely utilitarian framework, rather than one based on moral rights, and an evidence-based framework which considers both incentive effects and negative externalities on consumers, competing business models, and other technologies.[16] For me, this was one of the most important aspects of the Review and one of the places in which my advice was most "forceful." (The experts offered advice to the Review team, but it was agreed that we would not be bound by its conclusions.)

I was impressed by the quality and professionalism of the staff at the Intellectual Property Office, the UK's equivalent of the Patent and Trademark Office (PTO), by their knowledge of the academic literature and the sophistication of their economic analysis of the problems we discussed. The IPO had already made a considerable effort to hire professional economists and to harness their insights. The staff had already reviewed and digested the empirical literature and the Review itself produced several studies. One of the other advisors, Professor Mark Schankerman of LSE, was himself an expert in the economic and empirical investigation of

---

[15] HARGREAVES, *supra* note 1, at 8.
[16] *Id.* at 6–7, 21–22.

intellectual property. Finally, the framework of the Review was built around the call for evidence from stakeholders – which put great stress on the importance of submitting *data* – the submissions by library bodies were particularly strong in this regard. But how far can an evidence-based approach go? The Review's conclusions here were thoughtful:

> There are three main practical obstacles to using evidence on the economic impacts of IP: [1] There are areas of IPRs on which data is simply difficult to assemble ... [2] The most controversial policy questions usually arise in areas (such as computer programs, digital communication and biosciences) which are new and inherently uncertain because they involve new technologies or new markets whose characteristics are not well understood or measured. [3] Much of the data needed to develop empirical evidence on copyright and designs is privately held. It enters the public domain chiefly in the form of "evidence" supporting the arguments of lobbyists ("lobbynomics") rather than as independently verified research conclusions. Dealing with these obstacles requires an approach to evidence which makes the most of the available research where data can be developed, applies the lessons learned in those areas where we do have data to areas where we don't, in ways which make credible use of economic theory, [and] demands standards of transparency and openness in both methodology and data. It also presupposes an institutional environment which encourages the relevant public authorities to build, present and act upon the evidence. This cannot be achieved if relevant institutions of Government lack access to the data upon which corporate lobbying and other positions are constructed.[17]

All of this is welcome – it was not long ago that both the World Intellectual Property Organization and the IPO themselves hired their first economists. But will it play out in reality? The Gowers Review was equally forceful in stressing the importance of data to policy. One of its most compelling examples was an exhaustive study – both economic modeling and empirical research – that came down firmly against retrospective extension of copyright terms. There was a proposal on the table to extend the term of copyrights over sound recordings. Gowers also pointed out the very limited benefits that any such extension would give to its supposed beneficiaries, the musicians themselves. Effectively ignoring this advice, the government then supported sound recording copyright term extension at the EU level. So, even if evidence of economic effects begins to trickle into the policy-making process, is anyone listening? I came to believe that this would depend in part on the culture among professional civil servants – in this case in the IPO. The pressures towards institutional capture will always be there, of course, but Hargreaves at least took a step towards stressing the need for an institution that did not think that its "clients"

---

[17] *Id.* at 18–19.

were only the rightsholders. To repeat, and expand upon, a quote from the Review that I used earlier:

> Lobbying is a feature of all political systems and as a way of informing and organising debate it brings many benefits. *In the case of IP policy and specifically copyright policy, however, there is no doubt that the persuasive powers of celebrities and important UK creative companies have distorted policy outcomes. Further distortion arises from the fact (not unique to this sector) that there is a striking asymmetry of interest between rights holders, for whom IP issues are of paramount importance, and consumers for whom they have been of passing interest only until the emergence of the internet as a focus for competing technological, economic, business and cultural concerns.*[18]

I was shocked by how harshly critical the Review was willing to be of the current policy-making process and, in particular, how frank it was about the distorting pressures I mentioned in my introduction. (Note the neat paraphrase of Olson's collective action theory which was discussed at the beginning of this article.) The Review closed by calling for the IPO to have a role in "future-proofing" the copyright system, providing advice and data on proposed reforms and offering advisory opinions on the interpretation of copyright law. It also proposed that the IPO have a role in assessing after the fact the impact of any policy changes made as a result of the Review. For many years I have been arguing that it should be a basic principle of copyright policy making that we undertake prospective weighing of costs and benefits and then a retrospective "environmental impact assessment" of actual effects. It is too soon to tell whether this version of that call will produce more real world results than other similar ones in the past.

7.2.2. *Limitations and Exceptions*

Government should firmly resist over-regulation of activities which do not prejudice the central objective of copyright, namely the provision of incentives to creators. Government should deliver copyright exceptions at national level to realize all the opportunities within the EU framework, including format shifting, parody, non-commercial research, and library archiving. The UK should also promote at EU level an exception to support text and data analytics. The UK should give a lead at EU level to develop a further copyright exception designed to build into the EU framework adaptability to new technologies. This would be designed to allow uses enabled by technology of works in ways which do not directly trade on the underlying creative and expressive purpose of the work. The Government should also legislate to ensure that these and other copyright exceptions are protected from override by contract.[19]

---

[18] *Id.* at 93 (emphasis added).
[19] *Id.* at 99.

The central focus of the Hargreaves Review was on exceptions and limitations to copyright. UK copyright law has a "closed-end" list of copyright limitations – the fair dealing provisions. Sections 28–31 of the Copyright, Designs and Patents Act of 1988[20] provide the basic structure, and are followed by a series of particular exemptions from copyright liability. To U.S. eyes two things are notable. First, the structure of the system; this is a closed list not, as in the United States, an open-ended provision with a series of factors that can be applied flexibly to new problems and new technologies. Second, the list is remarkably incomplete; for example, there was no exception for parody, for "format shifting," for "text-mining" for academic research, for library archiving, or for access to copyrighted works by those with disabilities.

It was the first point – the closed nature of copyright's exceptions – that was the main origin of the Hargreaves Review. In a speech quoted prominently in the Review itself, David Cameron, the British Prime Minister, provided the basic rationale.

> The founders of Google have said they could never have started their company in Britain. The service they provide depends on taking a snapshot of all the content on the internet at any one time and they feel our copyright system is not as friendly to this sort of innovation as it is in the United States. Over there, they have what are called "fair use" provisions, which some people believe gives companies more breathing space to create new products and services.[21]

Cameron's assessment was both right and wrong. Fair use *had* enabled U.S. copyright law to adapt to new technologies. In cases involving video recorders, decompilation of computer programs, search engine "spiders" and image thumbnails, and even the gargantuan Google Book search project, fair use's four factors and flexible, teleological structure had been used to carve out breathing space for new technologies without prejudicing the central incentives provided to copyright holders. For example, reverse engineering a physical product violates no intellectual property right and promotes competition. Reverse engineering a *software* product requires the creation of a copy during the process of decompilation. Is competition and

---

[20] Copyright, Designs and Patents Act, 1988, c. 48, *available at* www.legislation.gov.uk/ukpga/1988/48/ enacted (as enacted); Copyright, Designs and Patents Act, 1988, c. 48, *available at* www.legislation .gov.uk/ukpga/1988/48 (as amended) (last accessed Dec. 9, 2014). In addition, sections 32–76 provide an additional closed list of actions that do not infringe copyright.

[21] David Cameron, November 2010, announcing the Review of IP and Growth. Quoted in Hargreaves, *supra* note 1, at 44. The Review added an important caution, however. "Does this mean, as is sometimes implied, that if only the UK could adopt Fair Use, East London would quickly become a rival to Silicon Valley? The answer to this is: certainly not. We were told repeatedly in our American interviews, that the success of high technology companies in Silicon Valley owes more to attitudes to business risk and investor culture, not to mention other complex issues of economic geography, than it does to the shape of IP law. In practice, it is difficult to distinguish between the importance of different elements in successful industrial clusters of the Silicon Valley type. This does not mean that IP issues are unimportant for the success of innovative, high technology businesses." Hargreaves, *supra* note 1, at 45.

the promotion of interoperability therefore forbidden? Courts used fair use to say "no." As I have observed elsewhere,[22] fair use became the "duct tape" of copyright – used everywhere there was a problem of technologies being pulled into copyright's domain in ways that might actually retard rather than promote progress and no prospect of an immediate legislative fix. Fair use allowed U.S. law to, in the words of the Review, "resist over-regulation of activities which do not prejudice the central objective of copyright, namely the provision of incentives to creators." But Cameron's comments – and those of Google's founders if they were reported accurately – were also an oversimplification. Fair use was an important limitation, but others – particularly the "safe harbors" contained in Section 512 of the U.S. Copyright Act and in the E-commerce Directive in the EU – were also vital. The thrust of the question was correct, however: how to "future-proof" copyright?

Fair use attracted passionate, almost hysterical opposition "on the grounds that it would bring … massive legal uncertainty because of its roots in American case law; an American style proliferation of high cost litigation; and a further round of confusion for suppliers and purchasers of copyright goods." While conceding these were concerns, the Review noted sardonically,

> In response to the arguments against Fair Use, it is also worth noting that the creative industries continue to flourish in the US in the context of copyright law which includes Fair Use. It is likewise true that many large UK creative companies operate very successfully on both sides of the Atlantic in spite of these differences in law. This may indicate that the differences in the American and European legal approaches to copyright are less troublesome than polarised debate suggests. But this does not stop important American creative businesses, such as the film industry, arguing passionately that the UK and Europe should resist the adoption of the same U.S. style Fair Use approach with which these firms coexist in their home market.[23]

(For those who do not speak British as their first language, the last sentence can be fairly translated as "Cough. [*sotto voce*] '*Hypocrites!*' Cough." That is, however an unofficial translation, not sanctioned by the authors of the Review.) The legal staff of the IPO ultimately concluded that – whether or not it was a good *idea* – adopting a U.S. style, flexible fair use standard was incompatible with the general EU Copyright Directive.[24] That is not an unreasonable interpretation, although I disagree. First, the EU Copyright Directive is hardly a model of clarity. In the words of the inimitable Bernt Hugenholtz:

---

[22] BOYLE, *supra* note 2, at 120.
[23] HARGREAVES, *supra* note 1, at 45.
[24] 2001 O.J. (L 167/10) Directive 2001/29/EC of the European Parliament and of the Council of May 22, 2001 on the harmonization of certain aspects of copyright and related rights in the information society.

Surprisingly, the Directive does deal extensively with an issue mentioned only incidentally in the Green Paper: copyright exemptions, or "exceptions" as the Commission prefers to call them (*nomen est omen*). In view of the vast differences in purpose, wording and scope of limitations existing at the national level, many of which reflect local cultural traditions or business practices, one would have expected some more study and reflection before stirring up this hornet's nest.... As any less ambitious person could have foreseen, combining these various projects into a single legislative package has turned out be a disastrous mistake. The intense pressure from the copyright industries and, particularly, from the United States (where the main right holders of the world reside), to finish the job as quickly as possible, has not allowed the Member States and their parliaments, or even the European Parliament, to adequately reflect upon the many questions put before them. The result of this over-ambitious undertaking has been predictable. The Directive is a badly drafted, compromise-ridden, ambiguous piece of legislation. It does not increase "legal certainty," a goal repeatedly stated in the Directive's Recitals (Recitals 4, 6, 7 and 21), but instead creates new uncertainties by using vague and in places almost unintelligible language.[25]

Second, the Directive relies on the Berne "three-step test." "It shall be a matter for legislation in the countries of the Union to permit the reproduction of such works in certain special cases, provided that such reproduction does not conflict with a normal exploitation of the work and does not unreasonably prejudice the legitimate interests of the author." But the test contains a well-known circularity. The limitations on copyright will *define* the "normal exploitation of the work" and the "legitimate interests of the author." If I have a right to copy your work for educational use, then licensing educational copies will not be something within the "normal exploitation of the work" and the right to prevent that copying will not be an interference with "the legitimate interest of the copyright holder." There are lengthy debates on how to interpret these words so as to make them less circular – ovoid, perhaps – but I will not enter them here. Suffice it to say, that I believed that there were ways to implement a flexible fair use standard within the EU system.[26] The Review team took the opposite position.

Now we get to a point – and this is relevant for the discussion of the limits to copyright policy making – where, in my view, Ian Hargreaves exercised considerable political skill. (What follows is entirely my subjective interpretation of events and should be imputed neither to him nor the IPO team.) The opposition to fair use was intense. The Review team had concluded early on that a fully flexible U.S. style fair

---

[25] Bernt P. Hugenholtz, *Why the Copyright Directive is Unimportant, and Possibly Invalid,* 11 EUR. INTELL. PROP. R. 501 (2000), *available at* http://dare.uva.nl/document/2/9021 (last accessed Dec. 9, 2014).

[26] My own analysis was strongly influenced by an incisive discussion of the issue provided to the Review by Lionel Bently, the Herchel Smith Professor of Intellectual Property at Cambridge.

use provision was legally impossible under EU law. The Review process effectively made fair use the "punching bag," focusing all opposition upon it, while actually introducing support for a relatively substantial set of limitations and exceptions. "Legalized text-mining for research purposes, that can't be forbidden by contract?" "Sure, but no fair use." "Caricature, pastiche and parody?" "Sure, but no fair use." Private copying and format shifting? "Sure, but no fair use." Copying for private study? Educational exceptions? Library archiving? Exceptions for the visually impaired or disabled? "Sure, but no fair use." "Support for an EU-wide change to introduce more general technology sensitive flexibilities into a copyright?" "Perhaps, but no fair use." Hargreaves was able to use the fixation on the *label* "fair use" and the implication of the Prime Minister's strong support for reform to introduce more flexibilities. The Review proposed a "twin track approach."

> In order to make progress at the necessary rate, the UK needs to adopt a twin track approach: pursuing urgently specific exceptions where these are feasible within the current EU framework, and, at the same time, exploring with our EU partners a new mechanism in copyright law to create a built-in adaptability to future technologies which, by definition, cannot be foreseen in precise detail by today's policy-makers. This latter change will need to be made at EU level, as it does not fall within the current exceptions permitted under EU law. We strongly commend it to the Government: the alternative, a policy process whereby every beneficial new copying application of digital technology waits years for a bespoke exception, will be a poor second best.[27]

On the first point, the Review argued that we must decouple those occasions when a new technology enters copyright's world because it just so happens that the technology itself requires copying in order to function, from those occasions where the technology is actually infringing on the author's interests in the traditional exploitation or control of her work.

> We therefore recommend … that the Government should press at EU level for the introduction of an exception allowing uses of a work enabled by technology which do not directly trade on the underlying creative and expressive purpose of the work (this has been referred to as "nonconsumptive" use). The idea is to encompass the uses of copyright works where copying is really only carried out as part of the way the technology works. For instance, in data mining or search engine indexing, copies need to be created for the computer to be able to analyse; the technology provides a substitute for someone reading all the documents. This is not about overriding the aim of copyright – these uses do not compete with the normal exploitation of the work itself – indeed, they may facilitate it. Nor is copyright intended to

---

[27] Hargreaves, *supra* note 1, at 47.

restrict use of facts. That these new uses happen to fall within the scope of copyright regulation is essentially a side effect of how copyright has been defined, rather than being directly relevant to what copyright is supposed to protect.[28]

Thus, the Review does advocate a future-oriented, open-ended, non-technology-specific exception but concludes this must be done at the European level.

When it came to the specific exemptions for research, text-mining and so forth, the focus that the Review put on gathering evidence proved its worth. I will quote just one example, because I think it goes to the reasons that the Report was able to gain support for the exceptions and limitations it put forward. The evidentiary submissions gave a clear sense of both the arbitrariness and the human costs of the current formalistic system, and the Review was able to use those stories to make its point. Here is one example drawn from its pages.

> About five per cent of the world's population is infected with malaria, a parasitic infection which kills around 800,000 people annually (mainly children)…. During the first half of the twentieth century tens of thousands of patients with neurosyphilis were intentionally infected with malaria. This treatment, which cured a proportion of patients, is unique in the history of medicine, and the resulting literature contains a wealth of knowledge relating to the biology of the disease. The Mahidol-Oxford Tropical Medicine Research Unit, based in Thailand and supported by the Wellcome Trust, is interested in making generally available to researchers a set of some 1,000 journal papers from the first half of the twentieth century describing malaria in indigenous peoples, soldiers, and details of malaria therapy – a unique and unrepeatable experiment. This information offers potentially significant insights for the development of methods for preventing and treating malaria today. It is often impossible to establish who are the copyright holders in these articles, many of which appeared in long defunct journals – they are orphan works. Copying them to make them generally available in online form would break the law. Reproducing individual illustrations and diagrams in articles is not possible. If the orphan works problem could be overcome it would still not be possible to text mine them – copy the articles in order to run software seeking patterns and associations which would assist researchers – without permission from the copyright holders who can be found, since there is no exception covering text mining. Even overcoming those obstacles would not guarantee that text mining would be possible in future cases. For that any new text mining exception must also include provision to override any attempt to set it aside in the words of a contract.[29]

---

[28] *Id.*
[29] *Id.* at 46–47.

The Review proposed all of the specific limitations I have described – from private copying and private use for research, through format shifting, parody, pastiche, caricature, archival copying, educational use, use in public administration, text-mining, and limitations to enable the making of copies for the visually impaired. Even more strikingly, these proposals did not merely languish in a dusty report on a shelf. They were eventually enacted into law, through secondary legislation.[30] I was, to use the technical legal jargon, "gobsmacked." My hope – based on painful observation of prior "Reviews" – was to fight to get a few true sentences into a report that would then be ignored by the legislature and the civil service but *perhaps* make the next report or review a little easier. The implementation of the Hargreaves Review has huge limitations but it is perhaps sad to say, achieving any *actual* reform whatsoever was something I simply never envisaged.

Text-mining for academic, and particularly scientific, research was the exception that I focused on most intently during our discussion in the Review drafting process. (I will come to the treatment of orphan works, another central focus, in a moment.) Some years ago, John Wilbanks and I laid out the reasons why text-mining (among other techniques for increasing the power and speed of research) is *so* important, why it has such enormous promise to save lives.[31] The quotation earlier about malaria research gives some sense of this, yet the potential is even greater than that quotation indicates. But for text-mining to achieve its potential, it first has to be legal.

On the one hand, the text-mining provision has limitations. It only applies to non-commercial text-mining – for example, academic research. Thus, commercial entities such as Google cannot take advantage of it. And it only applies to text-mining on documents you already have in your possession. (No hacking through digital fences in order to text-mine.) On the other hand, the provision most important to me – that the exception could not be contractually waived – made it through the Review drafting process and into the implementing legislation. It is a beginning.

---

[30] *See, e.g.,* The Copyright and Rights in Performances (Personal Copies for Private Use) Regulations 2014, S.I. 2014/2361, *available at* www.legislation.gov.uk/uksi/2014/2361/contents/made; The Copyright and Rights in Performances (Quotation and Parody) Regulations 2014, S.I. 2014/2356, *available at* www.legislation.gov.uk/uksi/2014/2356/contents/made; The Copyright and Rights in Performances (Disability) Regulations 2014, S.I. 2014/1384, *available at* www.legislation.gov.uk/uksi/2014/1384/contents/made; The Copyright (Public Administration) Regulations 2014, S.I. 2014/1385, *available at* www.legislation.gov.uk/uksi/2014/1385/contents/made; The Copyright and Rights in Performances (Research, Education, Libraries and Archives) Regulations 2014, S.I. 2014/1372, *available at* www .legislation.gov.uk/uksi/2014/1372/contents/made (last accessed Dec. 9, 2014).

[31] JOHN WILBANKS & JAMES BOYLE, INTRODUCTION TO SCIENCE COMMONS (2006), *available at* http://sciencecommons.org/wp-content/uploads/ScienceCommons_Concept_Paper.pdf (last accessed Dec. 9, 2014). Science Commons – a part of Creative Commons – was founded to implement this vision and made some progress. Sadly, much of that work remains undone. The science efforts have been reintegrated within the larger organization.

7.2.3. *Orphan Works*

As the Hargreaves Review was being drafted, the EU was debating an Orphan Works Directive.[32] The best that can be said about it is that it is a start – which is more than the United States has managed. As we discussed the EU scheme during the Review process, it became clear that it was going to have some significant shortcomings. In brief, the scheme is heavily institutional, statist, and inflexible. Its provisions can really only be used by educational and cultural heritage institutions, only for nonprofit purposes, with lengthy and costly licensing provisions designed to protect the monetary interests of – almost certainly – nonexistent rightsholders. The EU seemed never to grasp the idea that *citizens* also need to have access to orphan works for uses that almost certainly present no threat to any living rightsholder.

Laws cannot choose to prevent error, but they can choose *where* errors occur. The presumption of innocence is a classic example. Orphan works reform can choose to focus on false positives or false negatives. Should a large-scale digitization be made almost impossibly costly because of the possibility that one rightsholder would turn up? Or is that result even more of a social cost than the *possibility* that the revenant rightsholder be undercompensated – something which itself could be solved by risk-spreading insurance? Unfortunately, the Directive's provisions effectively picked the former option. European libraries in particular have been extremely disappointed with its provisions.

> Orphan works pose significant challenges because they prevent libraries from making these works available to their users in digital formats. European library groups welcomed the desire to seek solutions to the orphan works problem, and put forward practical proposals that would enable the unlocking of culturally valuable collections for the benefit of all. The library community believes that the Directive will be useful only for small scale, niche projects, and regrets that the aim to facilitate large-scale digitization of Europe's cultural and educational heritage … has not been achieved. The main problem is the presumption that the re-use of orphan works is likely to be unfair to their untraceable rightholders, and should be restricted as far as possible.[33]

Among the many other problems listed are the onerous search and record keeping requirements, the need separately to clear "included works" (for example, drawings

---

[32] 2012 O.J. (L 299/5) Directive 2012/28/EU of the European Parliament and of the Council of 25 October 2012 on certain permitted uses of orphan works. *See also* European Commission, *The EU Single Market: Orphan Works, available at* http://ec.europa.eu/internal_market/copyright/orphan_works/index_en.htm (last accessed Dec. 9, 2014).

[33] Electronic Information for Libraries (EIFL), *The European Orphan Works Directive – an EIFL Guide, available at* www.eifl.net/european-orphan-works-directive-eifl-guide#directive_problems (last accessed Dec. 9, 2014).

or pictures in a book) the absence of sensitivity to the scale of a project and so on. To be fair, at least Europe has made a start on the problem of orphan works, which is something the United States has conspicuously failed to do.

The Review team realized early on that the EU approach was not going to be enough. We did not know exactly what the final Directive would look like, but it was clear that the focus would be on institutions (particularly state institutions) and on nonprofit uses. Consequently, the Hargreaves Review pushed for a complementary approach, one that would allow individual uses and for-profit uses. So far, so good. Unfortunately, though it is too soon to be certain, the implementation of that idea seems to have taken the same attitude towards risk that the EU Directive took.

My suggestions to the Review were based on the idea of a legal privilege. Entities that wanted to use an orphan work would have to go through the stages of a diligent search – though the search requirements would "scale" to the project involved. A mass nonprofit digitization for archival purposes would, of necessity, have fewer search requirements than the for-profit use of a single work; otherwise the digitization would be impossible. The privilege would allow *individuals* to exhume works from the cultural graveyard, so that the decentralized citizen archivists of the Net could add their enthusiasms to the efforts of the great state repositories. If a rightsholder did appear, despite the diligent search, liability would be "capped" at a statutory *post hoc* payment schedule. If there were a "license" to use the orphan work, that license should be viewed – in essence – as an insurance scheme that used the law of large numbers to spread the (small) risk over the entire risk pool, thus requiring minimal *premia* but guaranteeing adequate compensation. In other words, if I wish to license an orphan work, I do not pay the price of that work were it to be guarded by an assiduous rightsholder, but rather that price discounted by the considerable likelihood that there is no rightsholder at all. Finally, if the rightsholder insisted, there would be the alternative of a "takedown," except in cases where a derivative work had been created. In that case, a mutually agreeable "fair and reasonable royalty" would be negotiated, depending on the relative creative contributions of the parties involved.

The drafters of the Review chose to go with expanded collective licensing *ex ante*, rather than limited liability *post hoc*. The difference was acute. With collective licensing *ex ante*, I have to pay to use *even though it is most likely that no rightsholder exists!* European governments love requiring licenses to do things nearly as much as they like creating state bodies or collection societies to administer those licenses. (I say this as a European myself.) This was no exception.

To its credit, the UK government actually did implement the Review's proposals. They did allow individual use and for-profit use, complementing the EU Directive's proposals. With great fanfare ("UK Opens Access to 91 million Orphan Works," said the press release)[34] the licensing scheme was announced in October of 2014. But the details remain fuzzy. Licenses are to be provided at "market rates." What does that mean? In a rational licensing scheme, users would be charged a fee set at a level that would be adequate – on the level of the entire *scheme* – to compensate a revenant rightsholder should one appear. This would, of course, be discounted by the probability that a rightsholder would not in fact appear. Thus if there was a 1/1,000 chance a rightsholder would make a claim, and a market rate for such a (post hoc) license would be 10,000 pounds, I would be able to purchase the license for ten pounds. If the rightsholder did appear, she would be fully compensated by the licensing scheme. The 999 users who rescued a work from its orphan work purgatory would pay the fees that compensated the 1,000th rights owner who in fact did appear asking payment. Works would be used and not overpriced – thus satisfying the firm directive of (and to) the Review that we consider public benefit – the public availability of the works, which in all probability have no rightsholders, balanced against the payment of those rightsholders should they appear. Works would be available. Rightsholders would be fully compensated. Is that what market rate means here?

Sadly, it appears that the answer is "no." At least so far. One of my major criticisms of the implementation of the Review's ideas is its plan for pricing orphan works licenses. At present, (the licensing scheme is in beta test, so there is hope that this may change), the IPO seems to understand "market rate" to mean the full, undis-counted, cost of a license – even though the probability is that no one will appear to demand payment. But this is an obvious economic mistake. Imagine a world of uncertain property rights in *physical* land. Land records are in disarray. As a result, half of the land in the UK is being dramatically under-used. Fields lie fallow, for why till and plant if you are unsure whether your labor will result in a trespass suit? No one builds on open plots. The cost of usable land, food grown on that land, houses and other property-related goods is thus distorted, to the great benefit of those who do in fact hold clear title and the great cost of the public.

After many years of dithering, responding to this obvious social irrationality and economic dead weight loss, the government finally introduces an orphan fields scheme. People may apply to the Indeterminate Property Office for a "license" to use the land. Two proposals for pricing the licenses are put forward. One follows my suggestion – licenses are to be discounted by the risk that the land owner will appear. This can be estimated at first, but will become more and more certain as the scheme goes into effect and is publicized. The second, strongly supported by

---

[34] Department for Business, Innovation & Skills, Intellectual Property Office and Baroness Neville Rolfe, *UK Opens Access to 91 Million Orphan Works*, Oct. 29, 2014, *available at* www.gov.uk/government/news/uk-opens-access-to-91-million-orphan-works (last accessed Dec. 9, 2014).

those who have clear title to their lands, is very different. They *like* the distorted market that exists. Even though the legal system (by having irrational title rules) has created the distortion in the first place, and even though the legal system (through the Indeterminate Property Office) has been charged with *fixing* this problem, the incumbent land owners propose a different rule. They say that the license for the right to use these new "orphan plots" should be priced at current market rates for *known* plots, thus using as a baseline entitlement the very distortion that the scheme was set up to remedy. The result, as they well know, will be to chill the usage of these orphan plots – *indeed that is their goal*. They defend their proposal by saying no new scheme should negatively impact their current business model; that is, they assert a "right" to the profit margin they receive under the current-distorted-scheme, which the IPO has been told to remedy.

Unfortunately, after heavy lobbying by incumbent rightsholders, the actual IPO seems to have bought this line of reasoning – at least in its beta test. Its licenses will be at full market rates, lest the business models of current rightsholders be affected. This effectively assumes an "entitlement" to the profits available in a distorted market. My price for licensing my photo of the Eiffel Tower can be set high because copyright law says that all those ownerless snapshots from years past cannot be used. And I am entitled to have this irrationality continue! Indeed the government should step in and help me. Nice work if you can get it.

Just to be clear, the current pricing scheme is distorted in two ways. First, it assumes as a reference for the license cost the current prices of copyrighted works in an admittedly distorted market. Prices under conditions of unnecessary and irrational state-mandated "shortage" are obviously artificially inflated and thus are an inappropriate baseline. Second, it fails to discount for risk – that is, for the probability that there is no rightsholder out there. The market price for a license should not be the full cost of a currently available work anymore than the market price for home-owner's annual fire insurance *premia* should be the *full cost of the house*. If the government mandated that as a price for home-owner's insurance it would of course distort the market, guaranteeing that insurance was under-used, just as orphan works will be under this scheme. But this ignores the metric of public benefit. Rather than fix a market in which many valuable cultural items are unavailable, it prolongs it, market distortions and all. Many institutions proposing large-scale digitization of orphan works believe that – as a result – this orphan works reform will suffer from the same problems as the EU Directive or actually be less effective. As for the commercial use of orphan works, I would predict a resounding failure. The bold promise of "91 million orphan works" made available will not be realized. On this one, the IPO's implementation of the Hargreaves Review deserves – at best – a gentleman's "D" grade. We can only hope that better sense will prevail.

Perhaps the economists in the IPO can explain that one does not fix distorted markets by setting as a moral baseline an entitlement among incumbents to the distorted price. Nor does one fix them by ignoring in the pricing the very issue that made the orphan works problem so tragic in the first place; in all probability there is no rights owner to compensate and thus the works should be available at a price no higher than necessary, on the level of the entire licensing scheme, to compensate one, should she return. That price, needless to say, is not the *full* price.

7.2.4. *Patent Thickets*

Many scholars have pointed out the dysfunctions of our current patent system.[35] The Hargreaves Review was largely focused on copyright and so expectations should be adjusted appropriately. Nevertheless, some positive recommendations (from my point of view) emerged. The first was with a focus on "patent thickets," or the so-called anti-commons, in which a proliferation of rights actually blocks innovation. The second was a strong statement on the inadvisability of patents offered in areas in which scholars have generally found them to be of low utility, such as business methods and "nontechnical" computer software. The most objectionable members of the latter class of patents attempts to elude restrictions on patentable subject matter by adding to a simple algorithmic instruction the words "by means of a computer."

> **Patent thickets and other obstructions to innovation:** In order to limit the effects of these barriers to innovation, the Government should: take a leading role in promoting international efforts to cut backlogs and manage the boom in patent applications by further extending "work sharing" with patent offices in other countries; *work to ensure patents are not extended into sectors, such as non-technical computer programs and business methods, which they do not currently cover, without clear evidence of benefit;* investigate ways of limiting adverse consequences of patent thickets, including by working with international partners to establish a patent fee structure set by reference to innovation and growth goals rather than solely by reference to patent office running costs. *The structure of patent renewal fees might be adjusted to encourage patentees to assess more carefully the value of maintaining lower value patents, so reducing the density of patent thickets.*[36]

---

[35] *See, e.g.,* BOYLE, *supra* note 2, at 251–53; James Boyle, *Open Source Innovation, Patent Injunctions, and the Public Interest,* 11 DUKE L. TECH. R. 30 (2012); Arti K. Rai, *Who's Afraid of the Federal Circuit?,* 121 YALE L.J. 335 (2011); Robert P. Merges, *As Many as Six Impossible Patent before Breakfast: Property Rights for Business Concepts and Patent System Reform,* 14 BERKELEY TECH. L.J. 577 (1999); JAMES BESSEN & MICHAEL J. MEURER, PATENT FAILURE: HOW JUDGES, BUREAUCRATS, AND LAWYERS PUT INNOVATORS AT RISK (2009); ADAM B. JAFFE & JOSH LERNER, INNOVATION AND ITS DISCONTENTS: HOW OUR BROKEN PATENT SYSTEM IS ENDANGERING INNOVATION AND PROGRESS, AND WHAT TO DO ABOUT IT (2004).

[36] HARGREAVES, *supra* note 1, at 63 (emphasis added).

Since the IPO is the UK's equivalent of the PTO, one might hope that these recommendations will gain some real traction. The experimentation with patent renewal fees as a way of curtailing lower value seems very promising, but the resolution to avoid the "subject matter creep" that has so beset the U.S. system is of particular importance.[37]

7.2.5. *Miscellaneous Recommendations*

The Hargreaves Review process had limits. Until the penultimate draft, I had hopes that it would hold firm to the empirical evidence that increasing severity of penalties and upping enforcement was an ineffective method of ensuring compliance with copyright laws. These efforts largely fail to achieve their goals, though they do produce costs – both to privacy and to speech technologies. On balance, it is better to provide cheap, convenient and legal access to copyrighted works, something that has been shown to reduce illicit copying but something that copyright's spectacular tangle of rights makes particularly hard in areas such as music. The final draft of the Review was weaker on this point and while it did stress the importance of legal access it did not come out firmly against the belief that the cure for copyright's ills is ever more severe penalties.

A relatively visionary "pro-business" aspect of the Review, and one I supported, though with doubts about the practicality of its implementation, was the creation of a Digital Rights Exchange.

> Numerous responses to the Review's Call for Evidence drew attention to defects in licensing procedures, among them those of the CBI, News Corporation, Pearson, Reed Elsevier, an alliance of UK photographers and the European Publishers Council. Having studied these and several other proposals, including the Google Books Agreement recently struck down by the courts in the United States, the Review proposes that Government brings together rights holders and other business interests to create in the UK the world's first Digital Copyright Exchange. This will make it easier for rights owners, small and large, to sell licences in their work and for others to buy them. It will make market transactions faster, more automated and cheaper. The result will be a UK market in digital copyright which is better informed and more readily capable of resolving disputes without costly litigation.

The difficulty, of course, is that many of the obstacles to such an exchange are intermediaries who currently *profit* from the inefficiencies in the licensing system and would not necessarily be happy to be replaced by a "one stop shop" of easy and

---

[37] For some graphs giving sobering empirical evidence of the effects of those tendencies on the U.S. system see JAMES BOYLE & JENNIFER JENKINS, INTELLECTUAL PROPERTY: AN OPEN COURSEBOOK 635–37 (2014).

transparent digital licensing. The government followed up on this proposal with a feasibility study by Richard Hooper and Dr. Ros Lynch.[38] That report concluded that industry had already begun streamlining the licensing process since the Hargreaves Review and that a "nonprofit, industry led" Digital Hub should be created to continue the effort. The government has allocated 150,000 pounds to this effort,[39] which seems obviously insufficient. It is unclear whether, in the absence of strong pressure by government threatening legal reform and the simplification of licensing rights, an "industry led" process will ever overcome inertia long enough to transform the current system. That is particularly true of one whose members include those who are currently profiting from the friction in the current system, The Digital Rights Exchange remains, at the moment, an aspiration.

Finally, the Review team was the subject of heavy lobbying for increased design protection. Its actual recommendation was largely for further study, though with some suggestion that design rights be strengthened and harmonized.

> **Recommendation: The design industry.** The role of IP in supporting this important branch of the creative economy has been neglected. In the next 12 months, the IPO should conduct an evidence-based assessment of the relationship between design rights and innovation, with a view to establishing a firmer basis for evaluating policy at the UK and European level. The assessment should include exploration with design interests of whether access to the proposed Digital Copyright Exchange would help creators protect and market their designs and help users better achieve legally compliant access to designs.[40]

Unfortunately, despite interesting evidence that at least in some types of design, *weaker* protection has actually fuelled innovation,[41] the main upshot was that new liability for design infringements – including criminal liability – was introduced in the Intellectual Property Act of 2014.

7.3. LESSONS FOR REFORM?

Are there any lessons we can draw from the Hargreaves Review about intellectual property policy making and the possibilities for copyright reform more generally? In the strict sense, no. As I said before, the Review was an "N of one." On the other hand, it did some things that seemed very unlikely given the normal world

---

[38] Richard Hooper & Ros Lynch, *Copyright Works: Streamlining Copyright Licensing for the Digital Age*, *available at* www.copyrighthub.co.uk/Documents/dce-report-phase2.aspx.

[39] Helen Wilkins, *The UK's Copyright Hub and Digital Exchange*, *available at* www.own-it.org/news/the-uk-s-copyright-hub-and-digital-rights-exchange.

[40] HARGREAVES, *supra* note 1, at 66.

[41] *See* Kal Raustiala & Christopher Sprigman, *The Piracy Paradox*, 92 VIRGINIA L. REV. 1687 (2006).

of copyright policy making that I described in the first part of this chapter. It was strikingly straightforward about the "distortions" in our policy produced by the lobbying of the content industry. (Indeed, it placed more emphasis on the role of that lobbying than I would. I think the sincerely held ideology of intellectual property maximalism – "more rights equals more innovation" – is at least as much to blame.) It produced not just a robust defense of evidence-based policy making, but an institutional location for that evidence-based policy making. The jury is still out on whether the IPO will enthusiastically continue – or be *allowed* to continue – with this role, but it is a significant beginning. Most importantly, unlike other reviews of copyright policy, the Hargreaves Review got most of its central recommendations implemented into law in a relatively short period of time. Billed as the "fair use" review, it concluded that a general flexible fair use provision would be desirable, but had to be pursued at the EU level. Yet it not only put forward, but got implemented, fairly far reaching proposals on limitations and exceptions. These ranged from format shifting, private copying and academic text-mining to educational use and greater access to copyrighted works for those with disabilities. The text-mining limitation strikes me as particularly significant. The Hargreaves Review also proposed and got implemented significant orphan works reform. That scheme will not in fact produce the revolution in access that the IPO's press release suggested, but it is an important complement to the EU Orphan Works Directive and perhaps a building block for future further reforms. It is certainly a step ahead of anything the United States has been able to do.

Why did these things happen? Is this a "black swan" event – so unlikely that it tells us little about the normal functioning of the system? I think that five factors came together to make the Review's proposals (and their implementation) more likely.

1. **Counterbalancing Interests/Counterbalancing Worldviews:** For the first time in UK copyright policy making, policy makers were made *fully* aware that there was a powerful industry force, or set of industry forces, counterbalancing the lobbying but also the worldview, the *perspective*, of the content industry. This counterbalance was complicated. Take Google's role. The Hargreaves Review was billed by some as the "Google Review" – because of David Cameron's comments and the admiration held by some of his team for Google-style disruptive innovation. This appellation was given greater credibility by the fact that Google did push for similar Reviews in other countries, such as Ireland. I can say that, from the inside, the reality seemed much more complex.

In European politics to say "Google is behind this" is to produce kneejerk and sometimes frankly paranoid hostility. It evokes a cluster of fears: from perceived American industry dominance, to privacy concerns, to claims of monopoly. The EU has just finished imposing a well-intentioned but poorly thought out "right to be forgotten" that makes the job of both search engines and newspaper archives incredibly complex and is currently debating imposing far-reaching competition law limitations on Google. Thinking that having Google behind something was automatically a *plus* from a European perspective, is like thinking that "the Microsoft Review of Antitrust Law" or "the Exxon Review of Environmental Law" would be an unequivocal plus in U.S. politics.

From my own very limited point of view, while Google was extremely important starting the Review process, the actual recommendations succeeded in part despite, rather than because of, Google's specific lobbying. Instead, the effective argument was an existence proof posed by a whole *range* of industries. From search engines and social media sites, to user-generated content portals and consumer electronic industries there were a set of actually existing institutions worth billions of pounds that could say "without the limitations and exceptions in copyright our technologies and platforms for speech would have been stifled." The argument that won the day was that copyright would hold back technology and innovation in ways that would be against British national interests and would slow entrepreneurial experimentation in the high-tech industries. As well as "more rights equals more innovation" policy makers were also hearing "tangles of outmoded rights slow technological development against the public interest." And the sound bite – "a strict application of copyright law in the way favored by the content industry would have made the world wide web as we know it illegal" – was simple and fairly obviously true. Lobbying from well-known tech companies was clearly important, but contrary to the facile cynicism of political insiders (and some political scientists) ideas and worldviews also mattered a great deal.

2. A Perception of Political Support from the Top: The Review started with a clear display of support from the prime minister. The bureaucratic and legislative importance of this cannot be overstated. Whether that support was in fact maintained at the same level, or whether reform was a high priority, is a more complex question, but the very complexity of the question gave Ian Hargreaves and the IPO staff a great deal more leeway. One can contrast this with U.S. President Obama who sent a number of signals that he "understood the digital world." He appointed some excellent people. There was even some progress on patent reform. On copyright, however, the situation quickly returned to the *status quo ante*. From secret intellectual property treaties to "copyright czars" drawn exclusively from former (and subsequent) representatives of the content industries, the Administration's policies were far from balanced. In fact, despite claiming sympathy with the digital world, the Administration was apparently as shocked as the content industry by the massive wave of protest against SOPA (the Stop Online Piracy Act.) Colleagues who worked in government tell me that the Vice President's office was perceived to be a

robust friend of the content industry. Whatever the truth of that point, the perception proved powerful in squelching efforts towards reform, just as the perception of
Cameron's support proved vital in encouraging it.

3. A Skilled Professional Staff and a (Relatively) Apolitical Institutional Structure:
I cannot say enough about the sophistication, quality, and professionalism of the people I worked with at the IPO. They were extremely well-read in the relevant academic
disciplines. They had a wide range of backgrounds – from economics to literature.
They approached the task of the Review with what seemed to be a long-throttled frus-
tration with some of the manifest irrationalities of the current copyright system (such
as our treatment of orphan works). Above all, they wanted to get it right, to make the
system work for all of its stakeholders – including the public, which was refreshing. Let
me say quickly that I have long also been impressed by the quality of people working
for the U.S. government. The difference is a matter of how much those people could
achieve. Here the IPO had managed to defend a norm of independent professionalism that made it less likely a political appointee could merely order his staff to parrot
industry talking points, or that all proposals would be seen as mere rhetoric overlying
some industry agenda. They had just a little more working-room and that proved vital.

Fundamentally, and with some regret given where I currently live, I found that the
culture of British politics was less debased than that of the United States. Every staffer
was not assumed to be implicitly lobbying for an industry job on exit. Every academic
was not assumed to be a hired gun for some industry group. Expertise was given due
weight, but so was genuine (rather than astroturfed) popular support. Cynicism did
not strangle every reform effort. (Of course, if the IPO is *successful* in carving out
an important, independent, evidence-based role in intellectual property policy, the
pressures to co-opt it will increase.) We all know that there are both benefits and problems – ranging from insularity to the danger of professional blindness – in relying on
expertise-based administration. But politics is always a matter of "worse than what?"
Given the woeful state of our current copyright policy-making structure, encouraging
a more balanced, expertise-based, institutional structure would clearly be a plus.

4. Popular Engagement with Copyright: I once wrote that we needed the equivalent of an environmental movement for intellectual property, encompassing both
an intellectual movement (ecology, the economics of externalities) and a political
transformation through the creation of a conceptual linkage (connecting the perceived self-interest of hunters and birdwatchers, hikers and organic food lovers.)
The world of intellectual property has certainly not been transformed in that way
yet but it is very different from what it was twenty years ago. Citizens are forced –
willy nilly – into the world of copyright. They find that its rules are not what they
believed them to be. For example, the Review heard again and again the popular perception was that there already *was* a private copying and format shifting

privilege. Every copyright professor could make the same point about the reactions of lay people – and even law students and lawyers – to the actual rules of copyright. When given the historical nugget that, during the first attempts to adapt copyright law to the internet in the 1990s, the original proposal of the content industries was for strict liability for all online copies, my students respond derisively "that would make Google illegal! That would make the Internet illegal!" (Yes, that was the *idea*.)

The basic point is simple. Citizens' relationship to copyright law has changed. Now individual citizens can point to particular technologies, particular speech tools that they use every day that depend on copyright's limitations and exceptions. The Review was clearly affected, often in ways that were hard to quantify, by this change. It might be an MP learning that ripping his legally purchased CDs onto his iPhone was breaking the law, or a staffer hearing that there was no exception in UK copyright law for parody – even if it were on YouTube. It might be a journalist who had seen the role of social media – unfiltered social media – in the Arab Spring. It might be an historian who used Google Book Search or Ngrams or a scientist who wanted to text-mine his journal articles on malaria and was told that *copyright law* forbade it. For all of those people, the ideas that the rules and the technologies of the digital age should be defined solely around the interests of the content industry seemed ... well, silly. That had its effect. (It was also humbling. Learning from the IPO staff that an eight-year series of articles I wrote for the Financial Times were more influential than all the scholarship behind those articles was both the kind of smack to the ego that every academic needs periodically and a reminder of the need to *communicate* what we learn as scholars.)

5. Policy Entrepreneurship: The Right Person at the Right Time: Last, but not least, the Hargreaves Review convinced me that – sometimes – individuals matter, that acts of *policy* entrepreneurship as well as business entrepreneurship can be transformative. I did not know Ian Hargreaves before the Review and I have hardly seen him since. Nevertheless, his political skill in negotiating the process seemed clearly to make a difference. For those who imagine that politics is all the objective correlation of lobbying, money, and opinion polls, this point seems dubious. But at many stages of the process – when 10 Downing Street's attention was elsewhere, when there was a drumbeat of attacks on fair use, when the IPO staff could have bought into the process or could have doubted it – Hargreaves was consummately skillful. The human touch still matters. For me, this is reassuring.

7.4. CONCLUSION

I hope that both the specific reforms put forward by the Hargreaves Review and the thoughts I have offered here on the more general possibility of reform are of some interest. But on the latter point, even if my assessment is correct, how common are the factors I list here? Clearly, not very. Yet I think there are two mildly positive takeaways. First, it is *possible* to break the logjam apparently dictated by collective action problems, ideologies of maximalism, impenetrable subject matter, revolving doors and so on. The results may not be all we would wish: they certainly were not with the Hargreaves Review.[42] But it is not impossible for us to reform copyright law to make it a little more rational – just very, very hard. Second, in at least some of the factors I list here – particularly the rise of countervailing worldviews and increasing popular engagement – the process seems to be continuing and even accelerating. Neither of these points is cause for resounding optimism, but both of them are far more positive than the current consensus in the academic literature on the possibilities of reform.

---

[42] The patent reform process that resulted in the America Invents Act – which had many very real defects but still did some good, might be another example. That process also shared many of the five factors I mentioned here.

8

Fair Use and Its Politics – at Home and Abroad

*Justin Hughes**

ABSTRACT

The chapter "Fair Use and Its Politics – at Home and Abroad" explores how the United States' fair use doctrine – a "standard" in a world of statutory copyright rules – has become an arena of ideological struggle over intellectual property policy.

At the international level, this debate frequently plays out in terms of how 17 U.S.C. § 107 meets or fails the "three-step test" of Berne and TRIPS. The chapter reasons that asking whether section 107 complies with the three-step test is asking the wrong question: section 107 structure is not *an* exception – it is a *mechanism* to establish particular exceptions. When the fair use doctrine works properly, it produces discrete *de facto* exceptions, such as a parody exception following *Campbell* or intermediate copying exception for software following *Sega* and *Connectix*. Section 107 is almost certainly "compliant" with the three-step test; it is particular applications of the doctrine that might be attacked in the future as failing the three-step test. The chapter also describes how fair use has proliferated – in different permutations – to other jurisdictions as well as why the United States does not – and should not – strenuously lobby other countries on whether or not to adopt fair use-style mechanisms.

8.1. INTRODUCTION

If there were popularity contests in the United States for intellectual property (IP) doctrines, my guess is that fair use would win hands down. What makes the fair use doctrine so well known? Perhaps in a sociopolitical tradition imbued with the idea of "justice as fairness" a doctrine labeled "fair" *anything* gets an automatic groundswell

* Hon. William Byrne Professor of Law, Loyola Law School, Los Angeles. My thanks to Kyoung-Shin Park and all the other contributors to this volume for helpful suggestions and guidance. Thanks to Emile Nijmeh, Justin Paull, and Justin Thiele for research assistance. The remaining errors are the exclusive intellectual property of the author. Copyright © 2014 by the author.

of support. Perhaps in a world of complex laws – I mean tax regulations and street parking signs, not IP – everyone likes the idea of a rule that is both general and exculpatory. Perhaps fair use is both *fun* and *safe* for scholars, students, and bloggers because "when you're applying a multi-factor test … it's very difficult to be clearly wrong."[2]

But part of the notoriety of fair use is because the doctrine has become an important arena in the struggle between advocates and opponents of IP. This political fight centered on the doctrine is built around one unstated, perhaps unadmitted (perhaps even unconscious) conception of fair use: as the *open-ended possibility of the negation of copyright protection*. This implicit understanding of fair use undergirds its popularity among scholars and activists, both inside and outside the United States. It is also the source of the anathema copyright owners increasingly have toward fair use.

Fair use as a battleground for *the open-ended negation of copyright* leads naturally to the "three-step test" of the Berne Convention, a limitation on limitations which has now percolated throughout the international IP system. In a very real sense, the three-step test has become the "evil twin" of fair use. The three-step test has become the darling of copyright interests who see it as the principal bulwark against erosion of copyright protection through exceptions and limitations. And precisely because it is favored by copyright owners, the three-step test has become a subject of much scholarly and activist critique.

The two sides of this struggle tend to adopt different strategies in relation to their chosen doctrines. On the one side, low protectionists cheer when new jurisdictions adopt fair use and copyright holders tend to oppose any expansion of fair use to other countries, just as they are bound to oppose expansive interpretations of fair use when it is litigated in court.

On the other side, since the three-step test has already promulgated through the international IP regime, copyright holders defend the three-step test(s) already in situ and use it to oppose widening exceptions and limitations.[3] As a counter-measure, those concerned about copyright law's expansion promote their own reinterpretations of the three-step test. And that's a perfectly respectable effort in a legal tradition

[1] Steven Pinker, *The Moral Instinct*, N.Y. TIMES, Jan. 13, 2008 (describing research showing "fairness" as a universal moral concept), *available at* www.nytimes.com/2008/01/13/magazine/13Psychology-t.html?pagewanted=1&_r=0.

[2] Alex Kozinski & Christopher M. Newman, *What's So Fair About Fair Use?*, 46 J. COPYRIGHT SOC'Y U.S.A. 513, 514 (1999).

[3] *See, e.g.,* Andre Lucas, *For a Reasonable Interpretation of the Three-Step Test*, 32 EUR. INT. PROP. REV. 277 (2010) ("[R]ight owners already automatically make use of [the three step test] to oppose users.")

in which a photograph can be a "Writing,"[4] a piece of paper can be a "book,"[5] and a scent can be a "work."[6]

This chapter discusses the fair use doctrine in relation to the three-step test, proposing that fair use is better understood as a *mechanism* for establishing specific exceptions and limitations rather than as a specific copyright exception in its own right. This perspective – hinted at by a few commentators – makes it much easier to reconcile American fair use and the three-step test. From there, we will survey the spread of the fair use doctrine to other jurisdictions, the United States' own posture toward other countries' embrace of fair use, and what all this means for the politics of international copyright.

8.2. AMERICAN FAIR USE DOCTRINE AND THE THREE-STEP TEST

When the United States joined the Berne Convention in 1988, the number one topic was the elimination of formalities.[7] Other top topics were moral rights – whether the United States complied with the requirements of Berne Article 6bis[8] – and the protection of works that either had fallen into the public domain or never been protected at all.[9] Further down the list, one of the abiding questions was whether American fair use was compatible with the Berne Article 9(2) three-step test. This was a political question in the sense that (a) people knew that fair use was not something the United States would abandon for the sake of Berne and (b) once the United States was party to Berne – and there was a tacit acceptance of fair use as compatible with the Berne framework – the American doctrine *could* become influential with other jurisdictions.

In that context, let us consider the nature of 17 U.S.C. § 107 fair use and a better way to understand it in relation to the three-step test.

---

[4] Burrow-Giles Lithographic Co. v. Sarony, 111 U.S. 53 (1884).

[5] *Storace v. Longman*, 2 Camp. 27 (1788), following Lord Mansfield's decision in *Bach v. Longman*, 2 Cowp. 623 (1777).

[6] Kecofa B.V. v. Lancome Parfums et Beauté, Supreme Court of the Netherlands (First Chamber), No. C04/327HR (June 16, 2006).

[7] For example, a group of consultants assembled by WIPO in 1978 was of "the general view ... that the principle, if not the only, obstacle to the accession of the United States would seem to be certain provisions on formalities contained in the United States' law." WIPO, REPORT OF THE GROUP OF CONSULTANTS (June 14, 1978). A few years later, a State Department official called this group's report "the most serious consideration" that had been done of the problems of U.S. accession to Berne. *Out of UNESCO and Into Berne: Has United States Participation in the Berne Convention for International Copyright Protection Become Essential?*, 4 CARDOZO ARTS & ENT. L.J. 203, 213 (1985) (remarks of Harvey J. Winter).

[8] *See, e.g.*, Justin Hughes, *American Moral Rights and Fixing the Dastar Gap*, 2007 UTAH L. REV. 659 (Dec. 2007) (describing arguments surrounding U.S. compliance with Berne Article 6bis).

[9] *See, e.g.*, David Nimmer, *The Impact of Berne on United States Copyright Law*, 8 CARDOZO ARTS & ENT. L.J. 27 (1989).

8.2.1. *Rules, Standards, and Fair Use*

We are all familiar with the juridical distinction tracing back at least to Bentham[10] between "rules" and "standards." Over the years, a wide range of commentators have recognized that the fair use doctrine is a *standard* sitting in what is otherwise a body of rules setting out the metes and bounds of exceptions to copyright protection in the United States.[11] Not only is fair use obviously a standard (instead of a rule), but the realm of copyrighted works provides almost a perfect poster child environment for where the rational policy maker would want to deploy a standard.

Standards and rules can be imagined as the extremes on a spectrum of degrees of precision in law. "Rules" establish *ex ante* exactly what kinds of behavior are permitted versus what kinds of behavior attract liability.[12] But legal categories often do not map cleanly onto reality, producing situations where something like the rule should apply, but the rule as written clearly doesn't (underinclusiveness) and situations where the rule seems to apply, but we think it should not (overinclusiveness).[13] In contrast, "standards" give more vague direction to citizens; a standard is "fuzzy" because of the flexibility it gives to the decision maker to carry out the law's intent. As Vincy Fon and Francesco Parisi put it, "from an efficiency perspective, standards

---

[10] Bentham captured the idea in different ways, i.e., as the difference between "a more precise rule" and a "loose and general rule," Ch. I, ¶ 41, as well as between "particular injunctions" and "general rules." Ch. V, ¶ 10. Bentham reasoned, "since it is impossible, in so great a multitude, to give injunctions to every particular man, relative to each particular action, therefore the state establishes general rules for the perpetual information and direction of all persons, in all points, whether of positive or negative duty." Jeremy Bentham, A Fragment on Government (1774) Ch. V, ¶ 2, *available at* www.constitution .org/jb/frag_gov.htm.

[11] *See, e.g.,* Matthew Sag, *God in the Machine: A New Structural Analysis of Copyright's Fair Use Doctrine,* 11 Mich. Telecomm. Tech. L. Rev. 381, 401–02 (2005); Daniel Gervais, *Fair Use, Fair Dealing, Fair Principles: Efforts to Conceptualize Exceptions and Limitations to Copyright,* 57 J. Copyright Soc'y U.S.A. 499, 501–02 (2010) ("It may be that empiricism will teach us that formulating standards that leave courts broader discretion in determining appropriate E&Ls or limits on remedies– such as whether an injunction should necessarily be issued because a use is infringing or whether statutory damages are adequate for any infringement – is a better option than stricter rules when outcomes are evaluated critically to see if desired results were obtained.").

[12] *See, e.g.,* Hans-Bernd Schäfer, *Rules versus Standards in Rich and Poor Countries: Precise Legal Norms as Substitutes for Human Capital in Low-Income Countries,* 14 Sup. Ct. Econ. Rev. 113, 116 (2006) ("Rules are legal commands that differentiate legal from illegal behavior in a comprehensive and clear manner. Standards are general legal criteria that are unclear and fuzzy and require complicated judicial interpretation.")

[13] A classic example is *Pokora v. Wabash Railway Co.,* 292 U.S. 98 (1934) in which Justice Cardozo recommended "the need for caution in framing standards of behavior that amount to rules of law" reasoning that "[e]xtraordinary situations may not wisely or fairly be subjected to tests or regulations that are fitting for the common-place or normal." *Id.* at 105–6.

allow *ad hoc* custom-tailoring of the law to the circumstances of the case at bar, reducing problems of over-inclusion and under-inclusion."[14]

Commentators have noted a number of factors that should go into a rational choice between whether to regulate a particular activity with a rule or a standard. One factor is the frequency with which a fact pattern will come before judicial authorities: the more frequent the decision making, then *ceteris paribus* the better off we will be with a rule. If drivers accused of driving at excessive speeds are frequently brought before the justice system, better to have a fixed rule – 75 miles per hour – than a standard like "reasonable and proper" speed.[15]

Another factor in the choice between rules and standards is how quickly the nonlegal reality changes, that is "detailed rules are more sensitive to exogenous, unforeseen changes in the regulated environment and thus are more prone to obsolescence."[16] As Fon and Parisi have observed, "the fact that more specific rules become obsolete at a faster rate should imply that the optimal level of specificity of legal rules should depend on the expected rate of change of the external environment."[17] In that context, there is nothing new in observing that the increasing speed of technological change (in information technologies) and the concomitant need for "more responsive and flexible mechanisms" might tilt

---

[14] Vincy Fon & Francesco Parisi, *On the Optimal Specificity of Legal Rules*, 3 J. INSTITUTIONAL ECON. 147, 149 (2007). *See generally* VINCY FON & FRANCESCO PARISI, THE ECONOMICS OF LAWMAKING (2009).

[15] From 1995 to 1998, this was the standard for excessive driving speed in Montana. Section 61-8-303(1) of the Montana Code Annotated (MCA) provided the following:

> A person operating or driving a vehicle of any character on a public highway of this state shall drive the vehicle in a careful and prudent manner and at a rate of speed no greater than is reasonable and proper under the conditions existing at the point of operation, taking into account the amount and character of traffic, condition of brakes, weight of vehicle, grade and width of highway, condition of surface, and freedom of obstruction to the view ahead.

This multifactor test was ruled unconstitutionally vague, at least as to criminal prosecution, by the Montana Supreme Court in *State of Montana v. Stanko*, Dec. 23, 1998, para. 30 ("[W]e conclude that that part of § 61-8-303(1), MCA, which makes it a criminal offense to operate a motor vehicle "at a rate of speed no greater than is reasonable and proper under the conditions existing at the point of operation" is void for vagueness on its face and in violation of the Due Process Clause of Article II, Section 17, of the Montana Constitution.")

[16] Sag, *supra* note 11, at 400 ("[L]aws that are more specific have a lower cost of administration, but that same specificity makes them more likely to produce undesirable or paradoxical results in response to unforeseen situations. In other words, specific laws are prone to obsolescence."); Louis Kaplow, *Rules versus Standards: An Economic Analysis*, 42 DUKE L.J. 557, 615–17 (1992). See generally RICHARD POSNER, ECONOMIC ANALYSIS OF THE LAW (5th ed. 1998).

[17] Fon & Parisi, *supra* note 14, at 150; Schäfer, *supra* note 12, at 119–20 ("Rapid change makes precise rules obsolete after a short period of time, after only a small number of cases have been decided.").

norm-making away from legislative processes and toward administrative and judicial law making.[18]

At the same time, the choice between using a rule or a standard is not a one-time event: over time, precise rules can be generated off standards as fact patterns become standardized. Justice Holmes' approach in *Baltimore & Ohio Railroad v. Goodman Administratrix*[19] is largely understood this way: while recognizing that contributory negligence and "the question of due care very generally is left to the jury," Holmes reasoned that in the case of what a driver should do at a railway crossing, "the standard is clear [and] it should be laid down once for all by the Courts."[20] By the time of Holmes' decision, railway technology was old-hat, automobile technology had become commonplace,[21] and the expected rate of technological change in that environment (cars and trains) was low – but even then the rule later seemed to suffer from the problem of over/underinclusiveness.[22]

It is clear that the exceptions menu of U.S. copyright law uses both rules and standards – *or* many rules and *one* standard. Sections 120 (exception for architectural works) and 121 (exception for the blind) are precise rules with little gray zone for their application; this is even more true of the exceptions that resulted from complex and lengthy negotiations among affected parties, such as the section 119 exception regime for "[s]econdary transmissions of distant television programming by satellite." In the midst of these precise, often byzantine, rules there is one standard: fair use. The difference between the fair use doctrine in section 107 and the other statutory provisions for exceptions is partly evident even in their length[23]:

Section	Total words
§107	**175**
§108	1401
§109	962

---

[18] *See, e.g.*, Shira Perlmutter, *Convergence and the Future of Copyright*, 24 COLUM.-VLA J.L. & ARTS 163, 165 (2001) (observing that given the "speed of technological development ... [i]t seems plausible that the mix of legislative versus administrative and judicial law making, and the mix of government regulation versus private sector agreements and standards, will shift toward a greater preponderance of the latter.")

[19] 275 U.S. 66 (1927).

[20] *Id.* at 70.

[21] *See, e.g.*, *U.S. History – Pre-Columbian to the New Millennium, Chapter 46a: The Age of the Automobile, available at* www.ushistory.org/us/46a.asp ("By 1920, there were over 8 million registrations. The 1920s saw tremendous growth in automobile ownership, with the number of registered drivers almost tripling to 23 million by the end of the decade.").

[22] Perhaps exemplified by the back and forth between Justice Holmes' 1927 *Baltimore & Ohio Railway v. Goodman* decision and Justice Cardozo's 1934 *Pokora v. Wabash Railway Co.* analysis.

[23] These are approximate word counts, without titles.

Section	Total words
§110	2431
§111	5299
§112	2218
§113	621
§114	7380
§115	2724
§116	383
§117	402
§118	945
§119	9191
§120	112
§121	485
§122	3032

The length of these provisions demonstrates how rules tend to become *more* and *more* precise as rights and obligations are conditioned on increasingly detailed fact patterns. Of course, rules can be stated succinctly too. Section 120 is quite short and breaks into two distinct rules concerning architectural works. But each of the rules in sections 108 to 122 applies to specific situations – most deal with specific kinds of works (as defined in sections 101 and 102) and/or specific kinds of uses. The section 107 fair use standard applies *across the entirety of the copyright world*, meaning that in some conceptual ratio of words to coverage, the standard in section 107 has extreme succinctness compared to each of the rules in sections 108 to 122.

8.2.2. *The Three-Step Test and Its Angst*

When the 1967 Stockholm Revision Conference of the Berne Convention agreed to establish a general right of reproduction in the revised Convention, the immediate issue was how to legitimize the exceptions and limitations that then existed in various national copyright laws. The delegates settled on a general formulation of permissible exceptions and limitations to the right of reproduction.[24] Berne Article 9(2) provides the now familiar three-step test:

> It shall be a matter for legislation in the countries of the Union to permit the repro-
> duction of such works in certain special cases, provided that such reproduction

---

[24] For discussions of this history, see Gervais, *supra* note 11, at 510–12; MIHÁLY FICSOR, THE LAW OF COPYRIGHT AND THE INTERNET § 5.51 (2002).

does not conflict with a normal exploitation of the work and does not unreasonably prejudice the legitimate interests of the author.

In Berne, this "three-step test" applies only to the reproduction right (and arguably translations); to the degree Berne acknowledges exceptions and limitations to other rights those exceptions are found in a few specific provisions, such as Article 10(2) and the *aquis* to the Convention.

The three-step test might have remained an obscure component of Berne, but the drafters of the TRIPS Agreement saw it as a general template for how to handle exceptions and limitations. In the TRIPS Agreement and subsequent World Intellectual Property Organization (WIPO) treaties, the three-step test was expanded to apply to all copyright rights;[25] the test also became the foundation for slightly differing tests for permissible exceptions and limitations to patent, trademark, and industrial design protection in TRIPS.

As the moniker implies, the traditional interpretation of Berne Article 9(2) and its progeny is that each of the elements – [a] certain special cases, [b] no conflict with normal exploitation, and [c] no unreasonable prejudice of legitimate interests – is its own analytic "step." The records of the Stockholm Diplomatic Conference indicate that the elements were considered as distinct – or at least the second and third elements were considered as distinct from one another.[26] Treating each element as subject to its own analysis fits with standard principles of treaty interpretation and was the path taken by the two WTO dispute resolution panels that have reviewed three-step test provisions.[27]

Commentators concerned that this approach is too restrictive have proposed that instead of the test being three steps considered sequentially, the three-step test

---

[25] The Agreement on Trade-Related Aspects of Intellectual Property Rights, Apr. 15, 1994, Marrakesh Agreement Establishing the World Trade Organization, Annex 1C, 108 Stat. 4809, 1869 U.N.T.S. 299 [hereinafter TRIPS Agreement], Article 13; WIPO Copyright Treaty (WCT), article 10(1), Dec. 20, 1996, S. TREATY DOC. NO. 105–17 (1997), 36 I.L.M. 65, *available at* www.wipo.int/treaties/en/ip/wct/; WIPO Performances and Phonograms Treaty (WPPT) article 16(2), Dec. 20, 1996, S. TREATY DOC. NO. 105–17 (1997), 36 I.L.M. 76, *available at* www.wipo.int/treaties/en/ip/wppt/; Beijing Treaty on Audiovisual Performances, article 13(2), June 24, 2012, *available at* www.wipo.int/treaties/en/ip/beijing/; Marrakesh Treaty Facilitate Access to Published Works for Persons Who Are Blind, Visually Impaired, or Otherwise Print Disabled, article 11, June 27, 2013, *available at* www.wipo.int/treaties/en/ip/marrakesh/.

[26] WIPO, *Records of the Intellectual Property Conference of Stockholm June 11 to July 14, 1967*, Geneva: WIPO 1971, Report on the Work of Main Committee I, pp. 1145–46.

[27] *United States – Section 110(5) of the U.S. Copyright Act*, WT/DS 160/R (June 15, 2000) [hereinafter *United States – Section 110(5)* decision], *available at* www.wto.org/wto/ddf/ep/public.html. Both the United States and the European Union agreed that three conditions of three-step test apply cumulatively, *id.* at 27, para. 6.74. *Canada – Patent Protection of Pharmaceutical Products*, WTO doc. WT/DS114/R (Mar. 17, 2000) (holding that failure to meet the requirements of any one of the three steps results in a violation of Article 30 TRIPS).

should be interpreted "holistically,"[28] as "an indivisible entity,"[29] or, at a minimum, in a more "integrated approach … that does not disregard the connection between the three criteria."[30] A 2008 "Declaration" by a group of principally European academics states, "[w]hen correctly applied, the Three-Step Test requires a comprehensive overall assessment, rather than the step-by-step application that its usual, but misleading, description implies." Despite this statement, probably few of the academics who signed the declaration would disagree about the facts of the Berne negotiations or the WTO decisions. In this sense, "correct" and "misleading" are just in the ideological eyes of the beholder.

My own view is that people are unduly concerned about "sequential" analysis of the three-step test. The concern about sequential analysis is often expressed as a hypothetical of a national law exception somehow passing muster under two of the steps, yet failing against a third. But how likely are we to have exceptions in national laws that are judged compatible with "normal exploitation of the work" but also *unreasonably* prejudicing the "legitimate interests" of a copyright owner? Or vice versa? No matter how much prose a tribunal throws into keeping the second and third steps analytically distinct, for practical purposes the second and third steps will always (or almost always) overlap.

8.2.3. *Fair Use, Meet Three Step; Three Step, Meet Fair Use*

So does section 107 fair use violate the three-step test? I think most people agree that the second and third prongs of the three-step test are not *prima facie* problems for section 107; individually and in conjunction, factors one, three, and four of the fair use test should ensure that any recognized fair uses neither "conflict with a normal exploitation of the work" nor "unreasonably prejudice the legitimate interests of the author."[31] The real issue is the first step.

---

[28] Christopher Geiger, Daniel Gervais & Martin Senftleben, *The Three-step Test Revisited: How to Use the Test's Flexibility in National Copyright Law*, PIJIP Research Paper no. 2013-04 (2013) at 25, *available at* http://digitalcommons.wcl.american.edu/cgi/viewcontent.cgi?article=1041&context=research; P. Bernt Hugenholtz & Ruth L. Okediji, *Contours of an International Instrument on Limitations and Exceptions* 10 (recommending that "a 'holistic' approach would do more justice to the proportionality test that in essence underlies the three-step test").

[29] MAX PLANCK INSTITUTE FOR INTELLECTUAL PROPERTY AND THE SCHOOL OF LAW AT QUEEN MARY, UNIVERSITY OF LONDON, DECLARATION: A BALANCED INTERPRETATION OF THE 'THREE-STEP TEST' IN COPYRIGHT LAW (2008). Christopher Geiger, Reto M. Hilty, Jonathan Griffiths, and Uma Suthersanen were the principal drafters of the document [hereinafter 2008 MAX PLANCK QUEEN MARY DECLARATION].

[30] Geiger, Gervais & Senftleben, *supra* note 28, at 29 ("Regardless of the position taken on sequentiality or holism, sequentiality must not be applied too rigidly, … A more integrated approach should be followed that does not disregard the connection between the three criteria.")

[31] For other commentators sharing this view, see, e.g., Martin Senftleben, *The International Three-Step Test: A Model Provision for EC Fair Use Legislation*, 1 JIPITEC 67, 74, para. 44 (2010) ("The prohibition

As to "certain special cases," commentator Sam Ricketson believed that this meant an acceptable exception must be considered against two distinct aspects:

> First, the use in question must be for a quite distinct purpose: a broad kind of exemption would not be justified. Secondly, there must be something 'special' about this purpose, 'special' here meaning that it is justified by some clear reason of public policy or some other exceptional circumstance.[32]

If Ricketson's second, teleological aspect of "certain special cases" means there must be *some* public policy reason at the domestic level, this is surely a trivial requirement: a government that has established an exception or limitation presumably has its own public policy justification – in *that* polity. If Ricketson's proposed public policy requirement means that the domestic exception must have a public policy basis acceptable at the international level, this interpretation certainly *could* be rejected on grounds of the 1967 negotiating history.

In the negotiating history the first ancestor to the phrase "certain special cases" was arguably the phrase "for specified purposes" – this was the phrase used in a preparatory text recognizing exceptions that had been proposed by the Government of Sweden/BIRPI Study Group.[33] The Study Group pointed out that exceptions for "certain special purposes" in other Berne Articles could be carried through to the right of reproduction by the proposed phrase[34] (making "specified purposes" and "certain special purposes" arguably equivalent). In response to this proposal, a Working Group of the 1965 Committee of Governmental Experts offered the following alternative:

> "it shall be a matter for legislation in the countries of the Union to permit the reproduction of such works,
> (a) for private use;
> (b) for judicial or administrative purposes;

---

of a conflict with a normal exploitation, for instance, recalls the fourth factor of the U.S. fair use doctrine 'effect of the use upon the potential market for or value of the copyrighted work.'")

32 SAM RICKETSON, THE BERNE CONVENTION FOR THE PROTECTION OF LITERARY AND ARTISTIC WORKS 1886–1986, at 482 (1987); Mihály FICSOR, THE LAW OF COPYRIGHT AND THE INTERNET ¶ 5.55, at 284 and ¶ 10.03, at 516 (2002) (supporting same). But see 1 SAM RICKETSON & JANE C. GINSBURG, INTERNATIONAL COPYRIGHT AND NEIGHBOURING RIGHTS: THE BERNE CONVENTION AND BEYOND (2006), §§ 13.10–13.14, at 763–67 (adopting view that "certain special cases" should not have a "normative interpretation")

33 The entire proposal was the following: "However, it shall be a matter for legislation in the countries of the Union, having regard to the provisions of this Convention, to limit the recognition and the exercising of that right, for specified purposes and on the condition that these purposes should not enter into economic competition with these works." WIPO, *Records of the Intellectual Property Conference of Stockholm June 11 to July 14, 1967* (Geneva: WIPO 1971), at 112.

34 *Id.*

(c) in certain particular cases where the reproduction is not contrary to the legitimate interests of the author and does not conflict with the normal exploitation of the work."[35]

The British delegation suggested chopping off the first two parts of this proposal and it was this same British proposal that changed "certain particular cases" to "certain special cases."[36] The British proposal was, in turn, accepted by a "Working Group"[37] and the working group's proposal was adopted up by the Main Committee on June 26, 1967 in a vote of 21 to 4 (with eight abstentions).[38]

One could *arguably* find some support for Ricketson's early claim that "certain special cases" means "justified by some clear reason of public policy" in the French text, where the counterpart of the phrase "does not unreasonably prejudice" is "ne cause pas un préjudice injustifié" – *does not cause an unjustified prejudice*.[39] Technically, the French text of the Berne Convention is authoritative for interpretative ambiguities.[40] But there is no basis in the *travaux preparatoires* to give significance to the word choice in French – indeed, just the opposite. Much of the discussion in the Main Committee about what became Berne Article 9(2) was over the correct French word for "unreasonably." Delegates discussed "inéquitable," "appréciable," and "injustifié" as alternatives;[41] the chairman proposed the word "injustifié" to replace "inéquitable" in the original translation of the British proposal on the grounds that *injustifié* "had the advantage of being closer to the English text than the other words which had been proposed."[42] The chairman was German, so it is unclear where his French expertise came from.[43] But much more importantly, the 21 to 4 vote that accepted the three-step test language as Berne Article 9(2) was on the "understanding that the various questions of wording which had been raised in the discussion" – and these were principally about the word choice in French – "would

---

[35] *Id.* at 113.

[36] *Id.* at 687 (Document S/42 – proposal from the United Kingdom).

[37] *Id.* at 696 (Document S/109 – report from Working Group of Main Committee 1).

[38] *Id.* at 881, 883.

[39] As a group of scholars note, "[p]ut differently, the English (original) version imposes a test of reasonableness while the French (official) text … imposes a test of justification." Geiger, Gervais & Senftleben, *supra* note 28, at 5.

[40] Berne Article 37(1)(c).

[41] WIPO, *Records of the Intellectual Property Conference of Stockholm June 11 to July 14, 1967* (Geneva: WIPO 1971), at 883–5, paras. 1058.3, 1060.1, 1061, 1066.2.

[42] *Id.* at 885, para. 1072.2.

[43] Professor Eugene Ulmer (Federal Republic of Germany), *id.* at 837. According to colleagues who worked with him, Professor Ulmer was probably not fluent in French, but he had a long-standing Francophone assistant and at the Stockholm conference was undoubtedly working closely with WIPO's Patrick Masouyé, also a Francophone. So, we cannot really know what expertise was behind Ulmer's comment on the better French translation. My thanks to Professor Annette Kur for help on this point.

be referred to the Drafting Committee."[44] After that, there was no substantive debate in the Main Committee about Article 9(2).

In other words, the French text provides no real support for the idea that the three-step test requires "justif[ication] by some clear reason of public policy." That approach *was* more present in the proposal of the Government of Sweden/BIRPI Study Group that preceded the Stockholm diplomatic conference,[45] but the Study Group's language was pushed aside in favor of the formulations that eventually became the three-step test.[46]

Consistent with this history, a "public policy" interpretation of "certain special cases" *was rejected* by the only international tribunal to interpret the copyright three-step test language, the WTO panel decision in *United States – Section 110(5) of the U.S. Copyright Act*.[47] Since no one ever expects a case interpreting Berne Article 9(2) to go to the International Court of Justice, this WTO decision – and lack of reaction against it – serves as the pragmatic authoritative interpretation of the provision.[48]

Now shorn of any public policy dressings, "certain special cases" seems only to "requir[e] some clear definition of the contours of an exception."[49] In the words of the 2000 WTO panel, certain special cases mean that "an exception or limitation in national legislation must be clearly defined" such that "the scope of the exception is known and particularized."[50] No one questions that such exceptions would be statutory provisions that say there is no copyright infringement in, for example,

(a) "use of another person's published work for purposes of the user's own personal study, research or appreciation"
(b) "appropriate quotation from another person's published work in one's own work for the purpose of introducing or commenting a certain work, or explaining a certain point"

---

[44] *Id.* at 885, para. 1072.2.
[45] The prediplomatic conference Study Group had elaborated that "[e]xceptions should only be made for clearly specified purposes, e.g., private use, the composer's need for texts, the interests of the blind. Exceptions for no specified purpose, on the other hand, are not permitted." *Id.* at 112. See also FICSOR, *supra* note 32, ¶ 5.50, at 281.
[46] As Ficsor notes, the British formulation (which was the three-step test) was proposed "to cut the Gordian knot of conflicting amendments" that had been tabled in the actual diplomatic conference. *Id.* ¶ 5.53, at 283, suggesting no basis to believe that the Study Group's conclusion is embodied in the phrase "certain special cases."
[47] *United States – Section 110(5)* decision, *supra* note 27.
[48] Gervais, *supra* note 11, at 514 (recognizing that WTO panels are the "arbiter of international intellectual property disputes concerning both the TRIPS Agreement and the Berne Convention").
[49] *Id.* at 514.
[50] *United States – Section 110(5)* decision, *supra* note 27, para. 6.108.

(c) "uses, for the benefit of people with a disability, which are directly related to the disability and of a non-commercial nature, to the extent required by the specific disability"

(d) "use during religious celebrations or official celebrations organised by a public authority"

(e) "by making a temporary reproduction of the work or adaptation as part of the technical process of making or receiving a communication."[51]

Each of these is a "certain special case," in the form of *a type of activity, a type of user, a type of work,* or a combination thereof.

But unlike any of the domestic law exceptions above, section 107 can apply in *any* circumstance: it can apply to reverse engineering computer software, making special format copies of books for a disabled person's education, private copying for amusement, bots scraping online material for a search engine, parodists making fun of advertising jingles, and pop artists profitably lifting images from other artists. In that sense, it does *not* seem to be limited to "certain special cases" and some commentators have said as much.[52]

From 1988 until 1995, whether fair use met the three-step test was a parlor game for bored copyrati. When the TRIPS Agreement became effective, the question became a few degrees more practical – in the sense that any WTO Member dissatisfied with the breadth of section 107 could challenge it as inconsistent with the TRIPS three-step test. I say "a few degrees" more practical because anyone who understands the international IP system knows that a frontal challenge to the fair use doctrine would be *politically* disastrous.

In truth, there have only been the most modest of skirmishes about fair use. In the early years of the WTO, a few countries asked the United States to explain section 107's compatibility with TRIPS Article 13, but these may have only been political exercises both to placate domestic constituencies and to provide some give and take in the fledgling TRIPS Council. Nowadays, when doubts are raised about the fair use doctrine's compliance with the three-step test these doubts are usually couched in third person terms – "questions have been raised" "concerns have been

---

[51] As to these provisions, "a" and "b" come from China's copyright law. Copyright Law of the People's Republic of China, as last amended at the 13th Meeting of the Standing Committee of the Eleventh National People's Congress on Feb. 26, 2010, Article 22(a) and (b); "c" and "d" come from EU copyright law. See DIRECTIVE 2001/29/EC OF THE EUROPEAN PARLIAMENT AND OF THE COUNCIL OF 22 MAY 2001 ON THE HARMONISATION OF CERTAIN ASPECTS OF COPYRIGHT AND RELATED RIGHTS IN THE INFORMATION SOCIETY, Article 3(b) and 3(g), respectively, *available at* http://eur-lex.europa.eu/LexUriServ/LexUriServ.do?uri=CELEX:32001L0029:EN:HTML. Finally, "e" comes from the Australia Copyright Act 1968, as last amended Act No. 13, 2013. Article 43A(1).

[52] *See, e.g.,* Ruth L. Okediji, *Toward an International Fair Use Doctrine,* 39 COLUM. J. TRANSNAT'L L. 75, 127 (2000) ("[T]he fair use doctrine ... clearly is not limited to 'special' cases.").

expressed" – by commentators who themselves support fair use[53] and are perhaps using the shadow of the three-step test to critique the three-step test itself, not fair use. There is actually relatively little direct criticism of 17 U.S.C. § 107 as noncompliant with TRIPS Article 13.[54]

Still, the panel opinion in the *United States – Section 110(5)* dispute suggest that both the WTO panel and the parties were conscious that the question of fair use sits on the not too distant horizon. In giving their interpretation of "certain special cases," the panel prefaced their statement that such exceptions must be "particularized" by saying "[h]owever, there is no need to identify explicitly each and every possible situation to which the exception could apply"[55] – a clear attempt to give some breathing room to fair use and fair dealing doctrines. In response to the EU argument that the home-style amendment was "imprecise and a 'moving target' ... vague and open-ended,"[56] the United States raised the stakes by calling into question the EU's willingness to accept common law adjudication: "the fact that judges have weighed the various factors slightly differently in making their individual decisions is simply a typical feature of a common-law system."[57] That's a line of reasoning that would also apply to a gestalt defense of fair use – and the Panel certainly understood it as such, agreeing that an evolution of home-style standards would not prevent the exception from being a "certain special case."

So to my mind whether section 107 fair use in domestic American law passes the three-step test remains principally a theoretical question. But this is also where the ideological battle intensifies: low protection activists want to both promote fair use and to enshrine the most flexible interpretation of the three-step test possible.

---

[53] *See, e.g.,* Geiger, Gervais & Senftleben, *supra* note 28, at 31 ("Restrictive interpretations of the test, however, have cast doubt upon the compliance with the test of open-ended national doctrines such as U.S.-style fair use, as well as with more open and flexible versions of 'fair dealing' standards in place in a number of common law jurisdictions. It has been asserted, for instance, that fair use and fair dealing systems did not qualify as 'certain special cases.' "); Infojustice, *Public Statement on the U.S. Proposal for a Limitations and Exceptions Clause in the Trans-Pacific Partnership,* Aug. 2, 2012 ("[Q]uestions have been raised by some as to whether the first step of the test – requiring that limitations and exceptions be limited to 'certain special cases' – should prevent countries from adopting limitations and exceptions that, like U.S. fair use rights, turn on more abstract and flexible balancing criteria, applied on a case-by-case basis in a wide range of circumstances.") [hereinafter infojustice.org, August 2012 statement], *available at* http://infojustice.org/archives/26799.

[54] Exceptions might be Lucas, *supra* note 3, at 278 ("The matter before all concerns the American fair use; it is quite questionable whether in this regard, fair use complies with the test.") and Okediji, *supra* note 52, at 117 ("[T]he indeterminacy of the fair use doctrine violates the Berne Convention."); *id.* at 148 ("It would be disingenuous to assert without qualification that the fair use doctrine is consistent with Berne Article 9(2).").

[55] *United States – Section 110(5)* decision, *supra* note 27, para. 6108.

[56] *Id.* para. 6138.

[57] *Id.* para. 6137.

For them it is imperative to promote interpretations of the three-step test that allow fair use, that is, a three-step test that "does not prevent … legislatures from introducing open-ended limitations and exceptions."[58] Copyright owners, on the other hand, come to the fight with one hand tied behind their back: since they cannot directly attack fair use (a central pillar of U.S. copyright law), they must argue for as restrictive an interpretation of the three-step test as possible that still permits the fair use doctrine, or at least a fair use doctrine with a century of precedential guidance behind it.

A vivid example of this ideological rancor comes from a recent EU survey that asked "is there a need to provide for a greater degree of flexibility in the EU regulatory framework for limitations and exceptions?" and then asked, if the answer to the preceding question was yes, whether the right approach would be "built-in flexibility, e.g. in the form of a fair-use or fair dealing provision / open norm, etc.?" One of the most pointed responses came from the Hungarian Copyright Association that wrote:

> We strongly reject the idea of extending the US fair use system to Europe or even considering it as a possible option. It is well known that this idea is promoted by certain "copyright minimalist" ideologues and NGOs behind which it would be difficult not to see some big and prosperous online intermediaries who believe (wrongly even from the viewpoint of their own genuine long-term interests) that they benefit from an as low level of copyright protection as possible. In Europe, the introduction of a fair use system, in the absence of underlining traditions and of a rich case law, dangerous legal uncertainty would emerge. It would be detrimental to European cultural creativity and productivity in the current atmosphere when many politicians tend to give in to populists slogans and "mass movements" (among the generators, financers and aggressive promoters of which again we can see certain profit-hungry actors of the IT industries).[59]

This is a pretty good exemplar of the level of distrust and acrimony in the global discussion about fair use.

8.2.4. *A Thought Experiment on the Three-Step Test*

Recognizing that both fair use and the three-step test are standards, let's start with a thought experiment: *would the three-step test, if implemented in a national law, itself pass the three-step test?*

---

[58] 2008 MAX PLANCK QUEEN MARY DECLARATION, *supra* note 29, at 4.

[59] Responses by the Hungarian Copyright Association to the Public Consultation on the review of the EU copyright rules (Mar. 3, 2014), *available at* www.copyrightseesaw.net/archive/?sw_10_item=57.

Imagine two countries – say, Elbonia and Latveria[60] – each having a list of copyright exceptions as shown in section (C) above. The Latverian parliament decides to add the following to the list:

Article 1938

In addition to and in keeping with these limitations and exceptions, any court hearing a copyright dispute shall have the power to permit the unauthorized use of a copyrighted work in any certain special case, provided that such use does not conflict with a normal exploitation of the work and does not unreasonably prejudice the legitimate interests of the author.

Meanwhile, the Elbonian Congress decides to *abolish* the list of copyright exceptions and limitations in Elbonia's copyright act and replace it with the following:

Article 09-06

In order to ensure that copyright law maintains the appropriate balance between incentives for creativity, protection of author's interests, and public access to information, any court hearing a copyright dispute shall have the power to permit the unauthorized use of a copyrighted work in any certain special case, provided that such use does not conflict with a normal exploitation of the work and does not unreasonably prejudice the legitimate interests of the author.

Would either or both of these national law provisions pass the three-step test in international copyright law?

Let's start with the Elbonian law. The argument that this three-step test in national law could not pass the three-step test in international law would be that the court has absolutely no guidance and *anything* could be declared permissible by a court. The Latverian law might fare better because the retention of the specific exceptions and the requirement that any decision to excuse some prima facie infringement be "keeping with the spirit of these existing limitations and exceptions" provides considerably more context for what a court might do. At least one scholar, Martin Senftleben, has proposed just this sort of mechanism for the European Union.[61]

---

[60] Both apologies and homage to Scott Adams' "Dilbert" (in which projects are outsourced to the corrupt and mud-filled land of Elbonia) and Marvel Comics' "Fantastic Four" (in which Latveria is a central or eastern European kingdom controlled by Fantastic Four nemesis, Dr. Doom).

[61] After writing an initial draft of this section, I discovered Martin Senftleben's largely parallel thinking. Senftleben has proposed replacing the current Article 5(5) of the E.U. Information Society Directive with the following:

In certain special cases comparable to those reflected by the exceptions and limitations provided for in paragraphs 1, 2, 3 and 4, the use of works or other subject-matter may also be exempted from the reproduction right provided for in Article 2 and/or the right of communication and making available to the public provided for in Article 3, provided that such use

As we will discuss below, the Witten Group's scholarly proposal for a "European Copyright Code" does something similar.

Of course, American statutory fair use falls somewhere between the Elbonian and Latverian laws. Section 107 sits in a compendium of more specific exceptions and limitations, but does not explicitly refer to those other exceptions as providing a context for fair use decisions. Instead, section 107 includes a chapeau that recites specific contexts and circumstances that Congress believed would be especially prone to findings of fair use.

8.2.5. *Clustering Fair Use; Fair Use as a Mechanism for Establishing Exceptions*

One could argue that American fair use is more like the Latverian three-step test, that is, a discretionary tool for judges that is not directly moored to existing exceptions. But we all know a court does not make a section 107 decision equipped *only* with the statutory language and the facts of the case; there is a rich body of fair use case law, prior decisions that often include operative facts similar as the dispute before the court.

Over the years, a number of copyright commentators have gone further, recognizing that fair use decisions fit into groups or clusters[62] – an invitation to the taxonomist's spirit in each of us to categorize and classify the fair use decisions. In 1958, Alan Latman offered perhaps the first taxonomy of fair use decisions;[63] William Patry offered his own classification in the 1990s,[64] as did Michael Madison in 2004.[65] Pamela Samuelson has done the same in her 2009 review of fair use case law.

> does not conflict with a normal exploitation of the work or other subject-matter and does not unreasonably prejudice the legitimate interests of the rightholder.
>
> Senftleben, *supra* note 31, at 76, para. 54. In addition to wanting an open-ended exceptions mechanism, Senftleben opposes the "double" portal system of the Directive: first, the national law must fit the precise exception category and, second, the national law (as written or applied) must pass the three-step test. I am less critical of the directive's approach since it is reasonable to have *some* mechanism to guide the scope of national exceptions; simply saying a "private copying exception" is not enough without saying what the reasonable scope or outer bounds of such private copying might be.

[62] *See, e.g.*, Paul Goldstein, *Fair Use in Context*, 31 COLUM. J.L. & ARTS 433, 439–41 (2008) (suggesting that fair use cases tend to fall into distinct classes, but not attempting a systematic taxonomy).

[63] Alan Latman, Fair Use of Copyrighted Works, *Study No. 14, Copyright Law Revision, Studies Prepared for the Subcommittee on Patents, Trademarks and Copyrights, S. Comm. on the Judiciary*, 86th Cong. 3, 8–14 (Comm. Print 1960). Latman's 1958 study had eight categories of fair uses: of fair uses: (1) incidental uses; (2) review and criticism; (3) parody, satire, and burlesque; (4) scholarly uses; (5) personal and private uses; (6) news; (7) use in adjudicatory processes; and (8) use for nonprofit or government purposes.

[64] WILLIAM PATRY, THE FAIR USE PRIVILEGE IN COPYRIGHT LAW (2d ed. 1995). Patry describes seventeen (17) sorts of uses. But he also separates fair uses into five part types.

[65] Michael J. Madison, *A Pattern-Oriented Approach to Fair Use*, 45 WM. MARY L. REV. 1525, 1645–65 (2004). Madison's eight categories are (1) journalism and news reporting; (2) parody and satire;

When commentators develop taxonomies of fair use, it is usually for the purpose of claiming that some fair use cases are more predictable than others. In his empirical study of fair use case law, Barton Beebe observed that "critical uses" cases had a 62 percent fair use win rate, while news reporting cases had a 78 percent fair use win rate.[66] Pam Samuelson also believes that once the case law is properly classified into clusters, "[i]f one analyzes putative fair uses in light of cases previously decided in the same policy cluster, it is generally possible to predict whether a use is likely to be fair or not."[67]

Let us push this clustering analysis a little further: instead of viewing the fair use doctrine as a *single* exception to be measured against Berne Article 9(2) and TRIPS Article 13, let us imagine section 107 as a mechanism to establish discrete, particularized exceptions on issues and questions that never came before Congress – and could never have been expected to come before Congress.

Of course, this is not a completely new line of reasoning. The U.S. Government has long argued that American fair use meets the three-step test because the existing case law makes the "scope" of fair use adequately "known and particularized." A 2008 Declaration from a group of mainly European copyright academics argued that the three-step test "does not prevent . . . courts from . . . creating further limitations and exceptions."[68] Geiger, Gervais, and Senftleben have also reasoned that "[w]ith every court decision, a further 'special case' becomes known, particularized and thus 'certain' in the sense of the three-step test."[69] My goal here is to more fully develop this view.

The base assumption for the standard three-step test critique of American fair use is that the *national legislature* applies the first step. For example, we can see this assumption in the analysis of a distinguished continental copyright scholar, Andre Lucas:

---

(3) criticism and comment; (4) scholarship and research; (5) reverse engineering; (6) legal and political argument; (7) storytelling; and (8) comparative advertising, information merchants, and personal use.

[66] Barton Beebe, *An Empirical Study of U.S. Copyright Fair Use Opinions, 1978–2005*, 156 U. Pa. L. Rev. 549, 609–10 (2008).

[67] Pamela Samuelson, *Unbundling Fair Uses*, 77 Fordham L. Rev. 2537, 2540 (2009). *See also* Annette Kur, *Of Oceans, Islands, and Inland Waters – How Much Room for Exceptions and Limitations Under the Three-Step Test*, 8 Rich J. Global L. Bus. 287, 297 (2009) (noting that U.S. fair use case law "offer[s] a relatively stable basis for parties to plead their case and structure their arguments")

[68] 2008 Max Planck Queen Mary Declaration, *supra* note 29, at 4.

[69] Geiger, Gervais & Senftleben, *supra* note 28, at 33. They add "[a] sufficient degree of legal certainty thus may follow from established case law as well as in detailed legislation." *Id.* Senftleben makes a similar argument in his 2010 piece. Senftleben, *supra* note 31, at 76, para. 52 ("Legal certainty is not necessarily an exclusive task of the legislator. It may be divided between law makers and judges . . . With every court decision, a further 'special case' becomes known, particularized, and thus 'certain' in the sense of the three-step test.")

The fact that the first step leaves a wide discretion to the states or to the judges when applying the second and third steps does not at all allow anyone to disregard the wording of the text concerning the first step.[70]

This perspective impliedly assumes that the *national legislature* ("the states") apply the first step while national judges can apply the second and third steps in the dispatch of their duties.[71] But this is arguably a significant difference between the Berne Article 9(2) and its progeny – TRIPS Article 13, WCT Article 10, WPPT Article 16(2), and Beijing Article 13(2). Berne Article 9(2) says "[i]t shall be a matter for legislation in the countries of the Union to permit the reproduction of such works" according to the three-step test, but from TRIPS Article 13 forward the three-step test is that "[m]embers" or "Contracting Parties" "shall confine limitations or exceptions to exclusive rights" via the three-step test.[72] In TRIPS Article 13, the specification of the national legislature is removed, a point easily overlooked.[73]

There is nothing in the TRIPS Agreement that specifies how a country is to establish its copyright laws – or the exceptions therein. If Singapore chooses to empower a Minister to issue regulations with new copyright exceptions and China's Supreme People's Court issues "interpretations" on copyright law to guide the lower courts, those are just the workings of a domestic legal system and TRIPS guarantees that WTO Members are "free to determine the appropriate method of implementing the provisions of this Agreement within their own legal system and practice."[74] This means, in the words of one WTO panel, that Singapore, China, and the United States each has the "freedom to determine the appropriate method of implementation of the [TRIPS] provisions to which they are required to give effect"[75] and "that the TRIPS Agreement does not mandate specific forms of legislation."[76]

---

[70] Lucas, *supra* note 3, at 279.

[71] For example, in his discussion of Berne Article 9(2), Claude Masouye wrote "[t]he legislator's task is not an easy one. This paragraph with its two conditions, provides him with certain guidelines." CLAUDE MASOUYE [WIPO], GUIDE TO THE BERNE CONVENTION (1978), para. 9.13, at 57.

[72] To be completely accurate, this is most true of TRIPS, WPPT, and the Beijing Treaty. The WCT uses this more abstract formulation in relation to exceptions for Berne Convention rights, but as to exceptions to the rights granted by the WCT itself, WCT Article 10(1) says, "Contracting Parties may, in their national legislation, provide for limitations of or exceptions to the rights granted to authors of literary and artistic works under this Treaty in certain special cases..." That strikes this author as intermediary to the Berne and TRIPS formulations. The Agreed Statement to WCT Article 10 is, again, couched in terms of what the "Contracting Parties may" do, i.e., "devise new exceptions and limitations that are appropriate in the digital network environment." It does not say that the national legislature must device the new exceptions.

[73] For example, a scholar as careful as Annette Kur assumes that Article 13 speaks to legislatures. Kur, *supra* note 67, at 310 (describing TRIPS Article 13 as "emphasiz[ing] the constraints for Members' legislatures when permitting for exceptions or limitations ('Members shall confine...')").

[74] TRIPS Agreement, *supra* note 25, at Article 1(1).

[75] *China – Measures Affecting the Protection and Enforcement of Intellectual Property Rights*, WT/DS362/R, Jan. 26, 2009, at paragraph 7.513.

[76] After quoting the third sentence of TRIPS Article 1(1), the Panel noted "[t]his provision confirms that the TRIPS Agreement does not mandate specific forms of legislation." *Id.* para. 7.602.

If the 17 U.S.C. § 107 four-factor analysis were an administrative process to establish new exceptions before statutorily designated executive branch officers, I think that there would be no question that it was an acceptable process – in terms of WTO legal norms – for the creation of domestic law. Do we really experience anything so different when the Supreme Court makes a fair use ruling *or* when 2–3 influential Circuit Court opinions line up on roughly the same fair use issue? (I am speaking here of international IP norms, not constitutional issues.)

For example, the Supreme Court's determination in *Universal City Studios v. Sony* surely established a "rule" that there is no copyright liability for private copying for later consumption/enjoyment (when no copy is retained and the copyright owner made the work available). Some might reasonably believe that the Court established a broader rule, that is, that private copying *for any purposes* is exempt from copyright liability; viewed that way, subsequent courts have further refined the rule, that is, P2P litigations establishing that the rule does not extend to acts of *distribution* nor to copies made from unauthorized sources. Whatever the precise parameters, it would be quite difficult to argue that the zone of private copying permitted directly through the *Universal City Studios v. Sony* application of the fair use mechanism runs afoul of the three-step test.[77] The Supreme Court's decision in *Campbell v. Acuff-Rose*[78] also established an effective "rule" that parodies are exempt from copyright liability; this de facto rule established through the fair use mechanism in American jurisprudence does not seem operationally different from the precise statutory exemption for parody in the laws of Malaysia,[79] Nigeria,[80] or Senegal.[81]

In other words, if fair use were ever seriously questioned before an international body or tribunal, the United States could credibly claim that the fair use doctrine is a *mechanism* to allow *specific* judicially created exceptions to copyright liability

---

[77] Article 9(2) originated in a proposal to permit exceptions for private use, judicial and administrative use, and any other uses that meant the second and third steps of TST. As Ricketson writes of private use, "[t]his, again, was a special category which was included in the programme proposal, and it is similarly to be assumed that it continues to fall within the scope of article 9(2)." RICKETSON, *supra* note 32, at 483. Ricketson opines this private copying would not extend to all new technologies, but thinks that it would include when "video recordings of broadcast programmes are made purely on a 'time shift' basis so that the programme may be viewed at a more convenient time after which the copy is deleted." *Id.* at 486–87 (without citing *Universal City Studios v. Sony*).

[78] 510 U.S. 569 (1994).

[79] Article 13(2)(b) of the Malaysia Copyright Act 1987 [as amended up to Jan. 1, 2006] exempts from liability "the doing of any of the acts referred to in subsection (1) by way of parody, pastiche, or caricature."

[80] The Copyright Act of Nigeria, Second Schedule [Exceptions from Copyright Control] provides, "[t]he right conferred in respect of a work by section 5 of this Act does not include the right to control … *(b)* the doing of any of the aforesaid acts by way of parody, pastiche, or caricature."

[81] Article 43 of Law No. 2008–09 of Jan. 25, 2008 on Copyright and Neighboring rights in Senegal provides "[t]he author may not prohibit the reproduction or communication of the work in the form of a parody, where the rules of the genre are observed."

in situations in which "courts are faced with a use not contemplated by Congress"[82] and that this is the intentional design of the 1976 Act, by which "Congress transferred significant policy making responsibility to the courts by incorporating fair use as a flexible standard."[83] Beyond copyright law, scholars have noted that the U.S. Congress arguably adopts incomplete policies and relies on court-created legal norms more than comparable nations.[84] As Hans-Bernd Schäfer writes in describing the general interaction of rules and standards, "[g]radually, by way of many different court decisions, which become unified by Supreme Court rulings, the imprecise standard is gradually transformed into precise rules."[85]

So, before our imaginary WTO panel, the United States could plead that with a dynamic socioeconomic system and a gridlocked checks-and-balances political system, we have improvised a system to produce copyright exceptions as needed. We have done this because, as Matthew Sag puts it, "Congress is institutionally incapable of legislating on copyright with the frequency that would be demanded under a system with more specific rights and exemptions due to the daily changes in the environment in which those rights are exercised."[86]

Those who are convinced that fair use does not meet the three-step test have another, related problem that is generally unacknowledged: it is difficult to imagine a facial challenge to section 107 *en toto* – any challenge is usually premised on some *particular application(s)* of fair use. For example, when the European Union questioned section 107 in the TRIPS Council, the query was couched in terms of "how the fair use doctrine ... particularly in connection with a 'parody' that diminishes the value of a work, is consistent with TRIPS Article 13."[87] Australia's questioning of fair use in the TRIPS Council the same year focused on the results in *Sega Enterprises v. Accolade* and *Princeton University Press v. Michigan Document Services Inc.*[88]

If the fair use doctrine is actually working as a process *to establish de facto particularized copyright exceptions*, then we might expect to see a few things. First, it should not only be that case outcomes become reasonably predictable – as scholars

---

[82] Gervais, *supra* note 11, at 509.

[83] Sag, *supra* note 11, at 410.

[84] P. S. ATIYAH & ROBERT S. SUMMERS, FORM AND SUBSTANCE IN ANGLO-AMERICAN LAW 298 *et seq.* (1987).

[85] Schäfer, *supra* note 12, at 119–20.

[86] Sag, *supra* note 11, at 411–12.

[87] Review of Legislation on Copyright and Related Rights – Questions Posed by the European Communities and their Member States, WTO document IP/C/W/26 (June 18, 1996) at 5.

[88] Review of Legislation on Copyright and Related Rights – Questions Posed by Australia, WTO document IP/C/W/30 (June 18, 1996) at 1 ("Please explain, having regard to the decisions in *Sega Enterprises v. Accolade* and *Princeton University Press v. Michigan Document Services Inc.* and any similar cases whether and how the U.S. law of fair use complies with Article 9(2) of the Berne Convention and Article 13 of TRIPS.")

have discussed – *but that case law ends*, that is, no one goes to court on that issue anymore. In other words, if over time application of a standard makes it clear that X category of behavior *is* permitted and Y behavior *is* forbidden, we should see fewer and fewer court challenges concerning either X or Y category of behavior. Indeed, the disappearance of these particular disputes from the docket should be the indicia that the judge-created exception via section 107 has stabilized into a "rule." Pam Samuelson wrote that the initial reverse engineering fair use decision, the 1992 *Sega* case, was "followed in a steady stream of cases involving reverse engineering of computer software,"[89] but the stream was never more than a trickle and has now, for all intents and purposes, dried up.[90] This is *precisely what we would expect* if we have an adjudicatory process that is establishing de facto new rules.

Second, we might expect that the disputes that produce the new, particularized exceptions take a long time to resolve. Perhaps bearing on this, Chris Cotropia and Jim Gibson have found that as compared to both general civil litigation and patent/trademark suits, copyright litigations "end up in about the same place – a settlement or voluntary dismissal – but take longer to get there." Cotropia and Gibson note that this may be because of copyright's "complexity, uncertainty, and standard- and fact-driven doctrine."[91] Looking at their own data and the 2007 "Docketology" study of civil litigation generally, Cotropia and Gibson conclude that copyright law does not seem to generate *more* "difficult" cases, but when a case gets difficult, it gets *really* difficult, generating a higher average number of substantive decisions (2.28 versus 4.65).[92] It is interesting to think how this difficulty may relate to producing new rules from standards.

Finally, there also might be some categories of activity where, despite repeated tries, the fair use "mechanism" fails to produce enduring bright-line categories – for example, Beebe and Samuelson both conclude that fair use outcomes in educational and research use situations remain unpredictable.[93]

The discussion here would not be complete without considering some significant criticisms of this idea. First, judge-made rules developed from legal standards are usually second-best when it comes to transparency. As one critique of fair use

---

[89] Samuelson, *supra* note 67, at 2608.
[90] From 2005 to 2014, there were only six reported federal court decisions citing *Connectix* and/or *Sega Accolade*, two of those decisions involving the same high stakes litigation (*Oracle v. Google*). There were no reported decisions at all citing the two cases in 2005, 2008–11, and 2013. My thanks to Justin Thiele for the yeoman's work on this point.
[91] Christopher A. Cotropia & James Gibson, *Copyright's Topography: An Empirical Study of Copyright Litigation*, 92 Tex. L. Rev. 1981, 2006 (2014).
[92] *Id.* at 2010.
[93] Beebe, *supra* note 66, at 609–10; Samuelson, *supra* note 67, at 2545 ("Sharply divergent views on fair use exist in the educational and research use caselaw, and it is in this cluster that fair uses are least predictable.")

sensibly observed, "[c]ertainly, a law, even if badly drafted, is easier to decrypt for non-specialists than case law that is inevitably fluctuating."[94] When people criticize fair use as being opaque, it is not only a matter of hiring lawyers for the unsettled questions,[95] but getting lawyers or legal materials to explain even the settled fact patterns.

A second criticism is more important: that it is just *wrong*-headed to be willing to recognize judges as crafting new exceptions and limitations because this is an abandonment of democratic ideals. As even a proponent of fair use observed in 2004, "one may doubt whether it is suitable to delegate to the judge questions that are so delicate, and that imply principally political choices. Is it not in the first place the task of the legislature to provide for a foreseeable framework for the users …?"[96] One is reminded of *Chakrabarty v. Diamond*,[97] the 1982 dispute over the patenting of microorganisms. Against claims that patenting genetically modified organisms would produce a "parade of horribles" the U.S. Supreme Court said that they were "without competence to entertain these arguments" which really went to "a matter of high policy for resolution within the legislative process after the kind of investigation, examination, and study that legislative bodies can provide and courts cannot."[98] At least some of what happens under fair use arguably fits that description: for example, one could reasonably think that the Second Circuit's decision in *Google Books* was "a matter of high policy for resolution within the legislative process," not a decision for (randomly) assigned federal judges.

8.3. WHAT HAPPENS WHEN FAIR USE GOES ABROAD

In the years immediately before and following U.S. adherence to the Berne Convention, there were intermittent observations on the relationship between section 107 fair use and the three-step test beyond the simple does-107-violate-Berne debate. Some expressed the concern that the Berne three-step test would serve to constrain and possibly narrow the findings of section 107 fair use.[99] Others pointed

---

[94] Lucas, *supra* note 3, at 282.

[95] LAWRENCE LESSIG, FREE CULTURE: HOW BIG MEDIA USES TECHNOLOGY AND THE LAW TO LOCK DOWN CULTURE AND CONTROL CREATIVITY 187 (2004) (characterizing fair use as "the right to hire a lawyer").

[96] CHRISTOPHE GEIGER, DROIT D'AUTEUR ET DROIT DU PUBLIC À L'INFORMATION 420 (2004) (translated by the author of this chapter).

[97] 447 U.S. 303 (1980).

[98] *Id.* at 317.

[99] In 1985, Michael Keplinger of USPTO recognized that some people "could consider that the Berne Convention might exert some adverse influence on the development of the doctrine of fair use." *Out of UNESCO and Into Berne: Has United States Participation in the Berne Convention for International Copyright Protection Become Essential?*, 4 CARDOZO ARTS & ENT. L.J. 203, 229 (1985).

out – as we recognized above – that the three-step test and the fair use doctrine were similar, generalized tests for exceptions, such that American adherence to Berne might provide "impetus toward a generalized fair-use type approach" in national law exceptions.[100] That did not happen during the first decade of TRIPS, but things started to change in the second decade.

8.3.1. *The Spread of Fair Use to Other Jurisdictions*

It appears that Sri Lanka got things rolling in 2003 with a near verbatim reproduction of section 107 as Chapter 1, section 11 of their Intellectual Property Act, No. 36 of 2003. After section 9 sets out the copyright owner's exclusive rights, section 11 closely follows 17 U.S.C. § 107.[101] The Sri Lanka law does not replicate the post-*Harper & Row* addition to § 107 and is followed by a section 12 that separately addresses private copying, but otherwise the Sri Lanka law looks like a full attempt to transpose U.S.-style fair use into their national system.

Singapore's copyright law had long-standing provisions on "fair dealing," at least as to criticism, review, and reporting current events.[102] In 2004, Singapore expanded the range of its fair dealing exception(s), arguably giving their law the same breadth as 17 U.S.C. § 107 and expressly identifying "research and study" as suitable activities

---

Keplinger elaborated that "[s]ome concern has been expressed informally that the general tenor of the Berne Convention, particularly the moral rights provisions, might influence a court, when confronted with a particular fact situation, to interpret 'fair use' in a less expansive fashion than under the present United States jurisprudence." *Id.* at 229 n.50.

[100] Perlmutter, *supra* note 18, at 173.

[101] Section 11 provides as follows:

"(1) Notwithstanding the provisions of subsection (1) of section 9, the fair use of a work, including such use by reproduction in copies or by any other means specified by that section, for purposes such as criticism, comment, news reporting, teaching (including multiple copies for classroom use), scholarship or research, shall not be an infringement of copyright.

(2) The following factors shall be considered in determining whether the use made of a work in any particular fair use case is

(a) the purpose and character of the use, including whether such use is of a commercial nature or is for non-profit educational purposes;

(b) the nature of the copyrighted work;

(c) the amount and substantiality of the portion used in relation to the copyrighted work as a whole; and

(d) the effect of the use upon the potential market for, or value of, the copyrighted work."

Section 11, Sri Lanka Intellectual Property Act, No. 36 of 2003, *available at* www.wipo.int/wipolex/en/details.jsp?id=6705.

[102] Singaporean Copyright Act, § 36 (fair dealing for purpose of criticism or review) and § 36 (fair dealing for purpose of reporting current events).

for fair dealing in Singapore. In this new, general "fair dealing" provision the operative language is verbatim § 107, but adds a fifth factor:

> In determining whether a dealing with a literary, dramatic, musical or artistic work or with an adaptation of a literary, dramatic or musical work, being a dealing by way of copying the whole or a part of the work or adaptation, constitutes a fair dealing with the work or adaptation for any purpose other than a purpose referred to in section 36 or 37 shall include –
> (a) the purpose and character of the dealing, including whether such dealing is of a commercial nature or is for nonprofit educational purposes;
> (b) the nature of the work or adaptation;
> (c) the amount and substantiality of the part copied taken in relation to the whole work or adaptation;
> (d) the effect of the dealing upon the potential market for, or value of, the work or adaptation; and
> (e) the possibility of obtaining the work or adaptation within a reasonable time at an ordinary commercial price.[103]

Obviously, the addition of this fifth market failure condition could make Singaporean fair dealing more palatable to copyright owners. It is worth noting that the structure of the Singaporean law seems to now make fair dealing for research and study, for criticism and review, and for "reporting current events" *not* subject to this five factor test – suggesting that the five factor balancing test is intended for unforeseen categories of activity that might not traditionally have been considered "fair dealing" in Commonwealth jurisdictions.

In 2007, Israel adopted U.S.-style fair use even more expressly. Sections 19 through 32 of the new Israeli Copyright Act[104] provide a set of exceptions and limitations – called "permitted uses." As with the exceptions and limitations in U.S. law (sections 107 through 122), the first permitted use in the Israel statute is fair use:

> Section 19
> (a) Fair use of a work is permitted for purposes such as: private study, research, criticism, review, journalistic reporting, quotation, or instruction and examination by an educational institution.

---

[103] Singaporean Copyright Act, Chapter 63, § 35(2). Section 109 repeats this five factor test in relation to fair uses of audiovisual works where the use is not covered by two other sections, section 110 (for purpose of criticism or review) or section 111 (for purposes of news reporting). Those uses of audiovisual works are apparently not constrained by any balancing of factors.

[104] Israel's Copyright Act of 2007 passed the Israeli Parliament (the Knesset) on Nov. 19, 2007, and was published in "Reshumot" (official gazette), 2007 Law Statutes of Israel, Issue 2199, at 34 on Nov. 25, 2007. Pursuant to section 77 the Act came into force on May 25, 2008.

(b) In determining whether a use made of a work is fair within the meaning of this section the factors to be considered shall include, inter alia, all of the following:

    (1) The purpose and character of the use;

    (2) The character of the work used;

    (3) The scope of the use, quantitatively and qualitatively, in relation to the work as a whole;

    (4) The impact of the use on the value of the work and its potential market.

Compared to the Sri Lankan and Singaporean efforts, the language here is a slight simplification of § 107[105] but with no apparent differences in effect. Finally, the section provides that the Minister of Justice may make "regulations prescribing conditions under which a use shall be deemed a fair use."[106]

In 2011, Korea added a new twist to the fair use saga by enacting a fair use provision that also mixes in the second and third elements of the three-step test. Section 35–3 of the Korean Copyright Act adopted on December 2, 2011 provides as follows:

Section 35–3

(1) Other than the cases stipulated from Article 23 to Article 35–2, Article 101–3 to Article 101–5 it shall be permissible to use works for purposes such as news reporting, criticism, education, or research which do not conflict with a normal exploitation of the work and do not unreasonably prejudice the legitimate interests of the right holder.

(2) The following four factors must be considered in determining whether a particular use is fair:

    1. the purpose and character of the use, including whether such use is of commercial nature or is for nonprofit purposes;

    2. the nature of the copyrighted work;

    3. amount and substantiality of the portion used in relation to the copyrighted work as a whole; and

    4. the effect of the use upon the actual and potential market or value of the copyrighted work.

It is important to note that the Korean law followed on the heels of the 2007 United States-Korea Free Trade Agreement (KORUS FTA); the particular construction of the

---

[105] Whereas section 107 says "criticism, comment, news reporting, teaching (including multiple copies for classroom use), scholarship, or research," section 19 says "private study, research, criticism, review, journalistic reporting, quotation, or instruction and examination by an educational institution." Section 19 drops "including whether such use is of a commercial nature or is for nonprofit educational purposes" from the first factor, perhaps reflecting the drafters' awareness of transformative uses doctrine in the United States. Like the other laws discussed already, this does not include the post-*Harper & Row* addition to section 107, "The fact that a work is unpublished shall not itself bar a finding of fair use if such finding is made upon consideration of all the above factors."

[106] Section 19(c).

Korean fair use provision clearly reflects a footnote in the KORUS FTA text recognizing fair use.[107]

The Philippine Congress has also adopted a fair use provision using the four section 107 factors. The chapeau of the provision arguably makes Philippine fair use stricter than its U.S. counterpart. As amended in 2012, before reciting the four factors, section 185 of the Philippine Intellectual Property Code provides:

> The fair use of a copyrighted work for criticism, comment, news reporting, teaching including multiple limited number copies for classroom use, scholarship, research, and similar purposes is not an infringement of copyright. Decompilation, which is understood here to be the reproduction of the code and translation of the forms of the computer program to achieve the inter-operability of an independently created computer program with other programs may also constitute fair use, under the criteria established by this section, to the extent that such decompilation is done for the purpose of obtaining the information necessary to achieve such inter-operability. In determining whether the use made of a work in any particular case is fair use, the factors to be considered shall include … [*the remainder of the statute then goes on to spell out the classic four fair use factors*].

Where section 107 provides its list of activities as examples ("including … for purposes such as criticism, comment, news reporting, teaching (including multiple copies for classroom use), scholarship, or research") section 185 of the Philippine law arguably provides a closed list ("The fair use of a copyrighted work for") with the possibility of related expansion ("and similar purposes").[108]

This gives the reader a sense of the post-2000 expansion of fair use globally, but there are other jurisdictions one would add in any comprehensive account; these

---

[107] A footnote to the parties commitment to a right of reproduction, KORUS FTA provides as follows:

> Each Party shall confine limitations or exceptions to the rights described in paragraph 1 to certain special cases that do not conflict with a normal exploitation of the work, performance, or phonogram, and do not unreasonably prejudice the legitimate interests of the right holder. For greater certainty, each Party may adopt or maintain limitations or exceptions to the rights described in paragraph 1 for fair use, as long as any such limitation or exception is confined as stated in the previous sentence.

United States-Korea Free Trade Agreement (KORUS FTA), June 30, 2007, Chapter 18 (Intellectual Property Rights) Article 18.4(1), note 11, *available at* www.ustr.gov/sites/default/files/uploads/agreements/fta/korus/asset_upload_file273_12717.pdf.

[108] The 2012 amendment of this provision arguably tightened Philippine fair use further from what it had been. Prior to amendments passed by a bicameral (Senate-House) conference committee on Nov. 26, 2012, "limited number copies" had read "multiple copies" and the possibility of fair use decompilation was not conditioned on "to the extent that such decompilation is done for the purpose of obtaining the information necessary to achieve such inter-operability."

include jurisdictions that have added the four section 107 factors to their fair dealing provisions (for all or *some* activities) and national legislatures that have simply retitled their fair dealing provisions as "fair use." For readers who want such a comprehensive account, as of 2015, Jonathan Band and Jonathan Gerafi had produced the most or one of the most complete compendiums of fair use provisions in national laws.[109]

To echo a Singaporean jurist, now that section 107-inspired provisions have entered so many national copyright laws "of particular interest is how the courts will apply the new open-ended 'U.S.-style' fair dealing defense[s]."[110] It is time to start monitoring these jurisdictions to see how the new provisions are being applied by courts – not just as to results, but as to method.

What will courts use as points of reference for their analyses? Of course, courts can be expected to use their own case law as a starting point. For example, Singapore courts can be expected to use old fair dealing cases and their contexts;[111] Korean courts seem likely to rely on their precedent related to Article 28 of Korea's copyright law, an older section of the law, which provides that "it is permissible to quote a work already made public for news reporting, criticism, education, and research, etc., within a reasonable limit and in compliance with fair practices." That article was already functioning as a de facto fair use provision.[112] There is also the critical question of how much American fair use case law will be used by courts in other jurisdictions in the application of these fair use provisions – it seems reasonable to think there will be a substantial reliance on the American case law.[113]

---

[109] JONATHAN BAND AND JONATHAN GERAFI, THE FAIR USE/FAIR DEALING HANDBOOK (May 2013), *available at* http://infojustice.org/wp-content/uploads/2013/05/Fair-Use-Handbook-05072013.pdf

[110] George Wei, *A Look back at Public Policy, the Legislature, the Courts and the Development of Copyright Law in Singapore*, 24 SINGAPORE ACADEMY L.J. 867, 886 (2012). Of course, then-Professor, now Judge Wei was speaking in the singular about Singaporean law.

[111] See, e.g., Bee Cheng Hiang Hup Chong Foodstuff v. Fragrance Foodstuff, [2003] 1 S.L.R. 305 (interpreting prior Singaporean fair dealing provision liberally). See also Wei, *supra* note 110, at 890 (suggesting that in application of Singapore's new open-ended fair dealing provision "[p]urposes that fall within the shadow of established categories are likely to be more sympathetically treated than purposes that are far removed.")

[112] Korean courts had already been applying Article 28 to cover classic fair use fact patterns. In a case preceding the fair use provision by five years, the Korean Supreme Court concluded that a search engine providing thumbnail photographs was "fair practices" under Article 28; the court considered factors that parallel fair use: the purpose of the use, the type of copyrighted work, the content and amount of the portion used, and whether the new work could substitute for the original work in the marketplace. Decision 2005 Do 7793 (Korean Supreme Court, 2006). In a 2010 decision, the Seoul District Court concluded that 15 seconds of a sound recording being used in a UGC video of a child dancing would have no adverse market effect on the sound recording and was permissible. Decision 2009 GaHap 18800 (Seoul Southern District Court, 2010). My thanks to Kyoung-Shin Park for guiding me to these cases.

[113] David Tan, *The Transformative Doctrine and Fair Dealing in Singapore*, 24 SINGAPORE ACADEMY L.J. 832 (2012) (generally assuming American cases will substantially influence Singapore provision). *Id.* at 837–38 (citing situations in which Singapore courts refer to U.S. copyright law).

There remain reasonable concerns among copyright owners that newly minted fair use provisions may be misunderstood by courts and misused by plaintiffs. As Ruth L. Okediji observed in 2000, we need to be mindful of jurisdictions that might "cite the fair use doctrine as the justification for their own derogations" from copyright protection "notwithstanding that their local judicial institutions may not be developed enough to exercise a balanced application of the doctrine."[114] In a 2006 paper, Schäfer provided a more theoretical model for Okediji's observation, reasoning that "in low-income countries there are reasons for having a more rule-based system, which allows for relatively simple decisions by the judiciary and the civil service."[115] Discussing the on-the-ground capacity of judicial officials in developing countries is a delicate subject, but it is something that at least *national* legislators should do in relation to their own judiciary when contemplating adding standard-based mechanisms to their own laws.

8.3.2. *Fair Use and the Global Activist Community*

In international IP policy circles, NGO and academic advocates of "strengthening exceptions and limitations" in copyright seem to take different views of the importance of advancing fair use concepts; there is certainly no uniform advocacy for fair use. The 2011 *Washington Declaration on Intellectual Property and the Public Interest* says only that such "open-ended" exceptions should be discussed[116] while the *Max Planck Principles for Intellectual Property Provisions in Bilateral and Regional Agreements*[117] and the 2013 *Global Congress Declaration on Fundamental Public Interest Principles for International Intellectual Property Negotiations*[118] do not mention fair use (or fair dealing) at all. On the other hand, "fair use" and "fair

---

[114] Okediji, *supra* note 52, at 154.

[115] Schäfer, *supra* note 12, at 114.

[116] The document – the result of "over 180 experts from 32 countries and six continents to help re-articulate the public interest dimension in intellectual property law and policy" – included as one of its policy objectives "[p]romote discussion of employing 'open-ended' limitations in national copyright legislation, in addition to specific exceptions." Note that this objective only says "promote discussion" and not that such 'open-ended' exceptions be adopted. And "fair use" is not mentioned by name – that only occurs once in the document in a descriptive statement of the IP system ("Limitations and exceptions are woven into the fabric of intellectual property law not only as specific exceptional doctrines ('fair use' or 'fair dealing,' specific exemptions,' etc.), but also as structural restrictions on the scope of rights"). The Global Congress on Intellectual Property and the Public Interest, Washington Declaration on Intellectual Property and the Public Interest 3 (Aug. 27, 2011).

[117] Available at www.ip.mpg.de/files/pdf2/Principles_for_IP_provisions_in_Bilateral_and_Regional_Agreements_final1.pdf.

[118] This document was adopted at the Third Global Congress on Intellectual Property and the Public Interest, University of Cape Town, South Africa, Dec. 13, 2013, *available at* http://infojustice.org/draft-trade-agreement-principles.

dealing" figure prominently in the *Public Domain Manifesto*[119] – drafted by a group of European, American, and Brazilian NGOs and nonprofits.

The quandary over open-ended exceptions was clearly in the minds of the "Wittem Group" of European academics in their drafting of their streamlined 2010 "European Copyright Code."[120] The Code's chapter on exceptions and limitations "reflects a combination of a common law style open-ended system of limitations and a civil law style exhaustive enumeration."[121] After establishing a series of specific exceptions and limitations, the proposed Code provides a (somewhat) open-ended mechanism for "extension" of exceptions and limitations as follows:

Art. 5.5 – Further limitations

Any other use that is comparable to the uses enumerated in art. 5.1 to 5.4(1) is permitted provided that the corresponding requirements of the relevant limitation are met and the use does not conflict with the normal exploitation of the work and does not unreasonably prejudice the legitimate interests of the author or rightholder, taking account of the legitimate interests of third parties.[122]

This might be likened to the hypotheticals above except that the Wittem Project proposal is clearly intended to be more limited. The footnote to Article 5.5 provides "Note that art. 5.5 does not allow new limitations by blending the criteria of articles 5.1 to 5.3"[123] and a cross-reference further clarifies that "the possibility of flexibility is narrowed down in two ways." One of these ways is the direct reference to the second and third steps of the three-step test; the other way is that "the extension applies to uses 'similar' to the ones expressly enumerated. Thus, a certain normative effect is bestowed on these examples; the courts can only permit uses not expressly enumerated insofar as a certain analogy can be established with uses that are mentioned by the Code."[124] In short, whether as their own first choice or as acknowledgment of the political realities of European copyright, the Wittem Group participants chose a path *in the direction of* fair use, but without fair use as the announced destination.

8.3.3. *The Posture of the U.S. Government on the Fair Use Doctrine in International Negotiations*

One of the criticisms of the U.S. Government's position in trade and/or IP negotiations is that the United States seeks to export U.S. standards for IP protection, but does

---

[119] Available at www.publicdomainmanifesto.org/node/8.
[120] The Wittem Group, The Wittem Project: European Copyright Code (Apr. 2010), *available at* www.copyrightcode.eu.
[121] *Id.* at 19 n.48.
[122] *Id.* at 22.
[123] *Id.* at 22 n.55.
[124] *Id.* at 19 n.48.

nothing to export U.S. exceptions and limitations. This is largely true, but the reality is more complicated than the sound bite.

For example, at least one commentator[125] credits the rise of fair use provisions partly to U.S. negotiators recommending fair use to countries in lieu of the specific exceptions to protection in the European Union's Software Directive.[126] And American negotiators have not been intransigent on open-ended exceptions, as shown by the KORUS FTA and, more recently, the Trans-Pacific Partnership (TPP) negotiations.

When it comes to the TPP, U.S. negotiators under the guide of the Obama Administration should be given credit for adopting a more balanced view of exceptions and limitations. The IP chapter of the TPP includes a general provision on exceptions and limitations that heretofore had not been seen in free trade agreements negotiations:

Article 18.66

Each Party shall endeavor to achieve an appropriate balance in its copyright and related rights system, among other things by means of limitations or exceptions that are consistent with Article 18.65 (Limitations and Exceptions), including those for the digital environment, giving due consideration to legitimate purposes such as, but not limited to: criticism; comment; news reporting; teaching, scholarship, research and other similar purposes; and facilitating access to published works for persons who are blind, visually impaired, or otherwise print disabled.[127]

While this is not a multifactor balancing test as 17 U.S.C. § 107, the exemplary list comes direct from the chapeau of section 107: the order of the words – exactly the same as section 107 – is a telltale sign. The additional language at the end on exceptions for print disabilities (attributed to the United States and other delegations) comports with the United States role in the negotiations that produced the Marrakesh Treaty to Facilitate Access to Published Works for Persons Who Are Blind, Visually

---

[125] Jonathan Band & Masanobu Katoh, Interfaces on Trial 2.0, at 136 (MIT Press 2011) (claiming that "USTR and the U.S. software firms preferred the fair-use approach to the Software Directive approach" in negotiations with several Asian jurisdictions over software protection).

[126] Directive on the Legal Protection of Computer Programs, Council Directive 91/250/EEC of May 14, 1991, *available at* www.wipo.int/edocs/lexdocs/laws/en/eu/euo20en.pdf, replaced by Directive of the European Parliament and the Council on the Legal Protection of Computer Programs, 2009/24/EC, May 25, 2009, *available at* http://eur-lex.europa.eu/LexUriServ/LexUriServ.do?uri= OJ:L:2009:111:0016:0022:EN:PDF.

[127] Available at https://ustr.gov/sites/default/files/TPP-Final-Text-Intellectual-Property.pdf. Trans-Pacific Partnership Agreement, Nov. 12, 2015, Chapter 18 (Intellectual Property). The author participated in interagency discussions of the exceptions and limitations language that USTR negotiators introduced in TPP negotiations. Article 18.65, referenced above, is a restatement of the TPP Members' commitment to the three-step test.

Impaired, or Otherwise Print Disabled.[128] It is disappointing that some critics have failed to acknowledge this evolution in the United States negotiating posture.[129]

But this still does not address the question whether the United States should advocate section 107 fair use to other jurisdictions. Personally, I do not think that advocating our particular fair use doctrine to other countries is the best use of American diplomatic resources. My perspective comes, first, from a general view of the "granularity" of the concepts we should promote and, second, because the arguments for why we should lobby for section 107 fair use in the domestic laws of other countries are relatively weak.

Granularity

When the United States is helping other countries establish democratic governments, as a general rule we press them to adopt neither the Electoral College nor our campaign finance laws; when we are helping other countries establish corporate laws and banking systems, we don't insist that they adopt our so-called generally accepted accounting principles (GAAPs). Indeed, the International Financial Reporting Standards, as used by the EU, are arguably better. In all these cases and scores of others, we Americans have a particular system that serves us (one can debate how well) and we recognize that we got to that system through a highly contingent historical path.

In the context of IP law, the picture is admittedly mixed. The United States does not expressly demand that other countries adopt the details of our trademark dilution law, our elaborate compulsory licensing system for cable and satellite retransmissions, or our clunky library exceptions. It is true, as discussed above, that the United States *has convinced (and continues to try to convince)* free trade agreement partners to accept certain patent law and data exclusivity provisions drawn from U.S. law as well as highly detailed exceptions for Internet secondary liability and technological protection measures (modeled on the 1998 Digital Millennium Copyright Act). But in the case of these copyright provisions, that

---

[128] *Available at* www.wipo.int/treaties/en/ip/marrakesh/. The author was the U.S. chief negotiator for the 2013 Marrakesh Treaty to Facilitate Access to Printed Materials for the Visually-Impaired.

[129] An example is Krista Cox's statement in a law review article: "The United States' proposals have reflected aggressive provisions reflecting high standards of intellectual property protection that generally provide new rights to rightholders, without adequate balancing provisions for the public interest." Krista L. Cox, *The Intellectual Property Chapter of the Trans-Pacific Partnership Agreement and Investment in Developing Countries*, 35 U Pa. J. Int'l L. 1045, 1049 (2014). While Cox's piece focuses on patent law issues, it paints the copyright provisions with the same brush, even criticizing the "proposals on … Internet service provider (ISP) liability" without characterizing them for what they are: *limits* on copyright liability. *Id.* at 1056. Ms. Cox was a lobbyist for a Washington-based NGO at the time of her work on the quoted article. On the other hand, some NGOs have acknowledged the shift in U.S. position. *See, e.g.,* infojustice.org, August 2012 statement, *supra* note 53.

granularity has always struck me as a mistake; it is now a mistake that has come back to haunt us.[130]

Although the analogy is quite loose, the environmental protection jurisprudence of the World Trade Organization might merit some attention on this point. The United States has been the respondent in a set of GATT/WTO disputes in which the United States sought to export its own regimes for the protection of dolphins and sea turtles in fishing industry practices. In one of these disputes, the United States had required since 1973 that all American shrimp trawling vessels to use "Turtle Excluder Devices" (TEDs) to protect sea turtles, an endangered species.[131] In 1989, the United States imposed a ban on importation of shrimp caught without the use of TEDs, effectively extending its own endangered species protection law to any foreign fishing fleets supplying the U.S. market. India, Malaysia, and Thailand challenged the U.S. laws before a WTO panel in the 1998 *United States – Shrimp/Turtle* case.[132]

As a general matter, the WTO upheld the right of the United States to impose *some* harvesting requirements on imported shrimp in order to protect an endangered species – the panel did this under the GATT exception that permits free trade commitments to be curtailed by measures "relating to the conservation of natural resources." But the WTO Appellate Body found that the actual *implementation* of the U.S. laws ran afoul of WTO obligations because the United States *"require[d]* other WTO Members to adopt a regulatory program that is not merely *comparable,* but rather *essentially the same* as that applied to the United States trawl vessels."[133] The WTO Appellate panel was quite blunt: "[I]t is not acceptable, in international trade relations, for one WTO Member to use an economic embargo to require other Members to adopt essentially the same comprehensive regulatory program, to achieve a certain policy goal."[134]

Of course, the factual and juridical details of this WTO dispute were quite different, but the point is that even for an objective as important as safeguarding

---

[130] In the wake of a public outcry over "locked" smartphones, the Obama Administration supported the idea of "narrow legislative fixes in the telecommunications space" to make it clear that unlocking cellphones is legal. R. David Edelman, *It's Time to Legalize Cell Phone Unlocking* (Official White House Response to "We the People" petition), *available at* https://petitions.whitehouse.gov/response/its-time-legalize-cell-phone-unlocking. The choice of the words "in the telecommunications space" suggests the White House's awareness that in the "copyright space" the permissible exceptions to protection of technological measures have been baked into several free trade agreements.

[131] Then and now, www.nmfs.noaa.gov/pr/species/turtles/. And turtle deaths as a side effect of fishing remains the main cause. *See* www.nmfs.noaa.gov/pr/interactions/#turtle ("Incidental take in fishing operations, or bycatch, is one of the most serious threats to the recovery and conservation of marine turtle populations.") (last visited Nov. 14, 2014).

[132] The actual name of the dispute was *United States – Import Prohibition of Certain Shrimps and Shrimp Products,* WT/DS58/AB/R (Report of the Appellate Body, Nov. 6, 1998).

[133] WT/DS58/AB/R, ¶ 138.

[134] *Id.* ¶ 164.

biodiversity, it would be a principled position to say that a country should push other countries to improve their laws, it should not try to impose its *own particular regulatory regime* on other sovereign states. In other words, the goal should be to get negotiating countries to a common view of the desirable "eco-system" and one should accept efforts to establish and safeguard that eco-system that are *comparable* without being insistent that any particular way is the right way.[135]

The staunch fair use advocate may reply that fair use *is* a critical part of a good information eco-system; in my experience, there are two variants on this argument and neither is convincing.

Fair Use, Democracy, and Innovation

The first variant emphasizes that the American fair use doctrine is necessary for freedom of expression, civil liberties, and robust cultural development. Indeed, we all recognize that in our system the fair use doctrine is part of what allows the Copyright Clause and the First Amendment to cohabitate comfortably. But freedom of expression *as a global goal* is not the same thing as First Amendment jurisprudence. Again, this is a place where we should not export a particular recipe that works for us, but is a highly contingent result of history. For example, many of us do not want the United States exporting First Amendment jurisprudence that might throw into jeopardy hate speech laws in many western democracies.

More importantly, there is no indication that freedom of expression, representative democracy, or cultural progress have been systematically retarded anywhere for lack of a fair use doctrine. Does anyone really want to claim that cultural progress is *slower* in France or Brazil or India than in the United States, let alone that such a difference could be attributed to fair use? If, over time, one could prove that the fair use doctrine makes representative democracy more robust in South Korea than, say, in Japan – that would be the sort of evidence that might justify arguing strenuously for the fair use doctrine's embrace by other jurisdictions. No one expects that such empirical evidence can be found; the other, uncontrolled variables will always overwhelm.

Second, there is the argument that we should promote fair use because it is part and parcel of an optimal information economy. Google has made this argument

---

[135] Indeed, when Congress has charged the executive branch with trade promotion authority it has usually been understood that the goal is "similar" protection of intellectual property, not exactly the same. See, e.g., Bipartisan Congressional Trade Priorities Act of 2014, H.R. 3830, 113th Congress, introduced Jan. 9, 2014, Section 2(b)(5)(A)(i)(II) ("ensuring that the provisions of any trade agreement governing intellectual property rights that is entered into by the United States reflect a standard of protection similar to that found in United States law"), *available at* www.govtrack.us/congress/bills/113/hr3830/text. This is the same standard as existed in the trade promotion authority granted in the Trade Act of 2002, codified at 19 U.S. Code § 3802, (b)(4)(A)(i)(II), *available at* www.gpo.gov/fdsys/pkg/PLAW-107publ210/html/PLAW-107publ210.htm.

in the context of the TPP, lobbying U.S. Government officials that "no other TPP country has a copyright regime, such as the U.S. fair use doctrine codified at 17 U.S.C. § 107, with sufficient flexibility to keep up with fast-paced technological change and innovation."[136] At times, Google has proposed that the TPP have a specific, mandatory fair use provision[137] and at other times the company has backed away from American-style fair use but still told negotiators that it believed that "[m]andatory exceptions will ensure access to TPP markets that offer significant commercial opportunities for U.S. enterprises and individuals that rely on fair use, including global market-leading U.S. Internet companies."[138]

This entire argument that the United States should advocate "fair use" as *innovation policy* immediately turns on itself. As much as our political discourse is dominated by notions of "free trade," the truth is that our economic system – and that of *all* our trading partners – is a mix of interventionist policies and free markets. In that free market/interventionist mix, American companies continue to dominate the Internet globally.[139] If one believes that the fair use doctrine has been a central

---

[136] Google, *The United States Must Insist on Mandatory TPP IP Provisions that are Essential for U.S. Internet Companies to Succeed in the Asia-Pacific Region* 2 (Mar. 14, 2011) (on file with author) [hereinafter Google 2011 lobbying document].

[137] In 2010, Google lobbied for the inclusion of the following fair use provision in the TPP:

> Each party shall provide for limitations and exceptions that permit the unauthorized use of works of authorship as well as works covered by related rights in special cases where such use does not conflict with a normal exploitation of the work and does not unreasonably prejudice the legitimate interests of the author. Examples include, but are not limited to criticism, comment, parody, news reporting, teaching (including multiple copies for classroom use), scholarship, research, reverse engineering of software to enable interoperability, private copying, reproduction for the purpose of indexing, and activities that permit the ordinary operation of search engines and other online service providers. Consistent with the foregoing, each Party shall provide that its competent authorities have the authority to permit unauthorized uses upon due consideration of appropriate factors, including (1) the purpose and character of the use, including whether such use is of a commercial nature or is for private or nonprofit purposes; (2) the nature of the copyrighted work; (3) the amount and substantiality of the portion used in relation to the copyrighted work as a whole, and (4) the effect of the use upon the potential market for or value of the work.

> Google, *Alignment of Proposed TPP Text with the Limitations/Exceptions to Trademark and Copyright Under US Law* 1-2 (Dec. 21, 2010) (on file with author). It is also completely understandable that Google would propose a mandatory exceptions provision for *trademarks* to "avoid the creation of barriers to legitimate activity, including electronic commerce and innovation." *Id.* at 1.

[138] Google 2011 lobbying document, *supra* note 136, at 4.

[139] As former U.S. Ambassador to the OECD Karen Kornbluh noted in 2014, "Countries around the world are envious of U.S. companies' dominance of the Net. The United States is still the headquarters of the majority of the top Internet companies, and it dominates the app economy and LET, the next generation of high-speed wireless." Karen Kornbluh, *Beyond Borders: Fighting Data Protectionism*, 34 DEMOCRACY: A JOURNAL OF IDEAS (Fall 2014), *available at* www.democracyjournal .org/34/beyond-borders-fighting-data-protectionism.php?page=all.

element in the innovation environment that has made Silicon Valley wildly successful, *why would we want to promote other countries adopting a policy that, by
this account, is a competitive advantage?* If Google is right, people worried about
America's competitive edge would want to keep fair use to ourselves.

In other words, if all kinds of information processing tasks really depend on fair
use, one could reason that we would have a better chance of keeping those jobs
in the United States if our fair use doctrine is robust and well known while other
countries' counterpart doctrines are obscure and uncertain. We could speculate that
the South Koreans and Israelis have adopted fair use because they believe it might
help their information technology sectors – but if that were true, that doesn't give
a U.S. policy maker who is concerned about preserving American competitiveness
and American jobs a reason to promote fair use globally.

Beyond the strategic logic of the argument, U.S. government policy makers still
have little meaningful evidence of what impact, if any, the fair use doctrine has
on technological development. The argument rests on the largely unproven meme
that the fair use doctrine *"makes it possible* for large commercial entities to build
tools such as search engines that make the Internet work and to create platforms
such as YouTube and Facebook."[140] If "makes it possible" means a *necessary condition*, this is pretty much demonstrably false. Search engines developed, deployed,
and functioned quite well without any determination that fair use shielded their
activities; for those of us who worked on Internet law issues in the early days (late
1990s), we assumed that the copying that occurred with indexing activities would
be impliedly licensed by people who willingly put material on the Internet and do
not disallow crawling in the robots.txt file – a conclusion reached by at least one
American court and by the German Federal Court of Justice (as the basis for permitting Google's image search activities).[141] Truly user-generated content (UGC) on
YouTube is licensed for YouTube's public performance by the creators who post it;
more traditional copyright owners who find their works on YouTube but agree to
leave the material there for the monetization offered by "ContentID" are, again,
licensing the use. Almost all the personal material that is posted by Facebook users
is material of their own creation (text or photos) which is, again, licensed by them;
the many links people post on Facebook would be *prima facie* infringing only if
those links were acts of distribution. That issue is hotly debated in Europe, but not
so much in the United States.

In short, if the fair use doctrine was what "made it possible" for search engines,
YouTube, and Facebook to exist, then to use an overused rhetorical trope, the

---

[140] Matthew Sag, *Predicting Fair Use*, 73 OHIO ST. L.J. 47, 85 (2012).
[141] Bundesgerichtshof, Apr. 29, 2010, case 1 ZR 69/08, *available at* www.bundesgerichtshof.de.

Internet would be "broken" pretty much everywhere except the United States. All this leads me to conclude that when technology companies claim that they "need" fair use that need is akin to claims that they *need* minimalist laws on data privacy, something that many jurisdictions have thankfully rejected.[142]

Finally, if the "made it possible" analysis were correct, we would expect that companies like Dailymotion, Baidu, and SAP would be engaged in the same sort of "precision" or "targeted" lobbying with their own governments, urging those governments to adopt fair use. If anyone can find evidence of this [real lobbying, not blog posts by scholars and activists], it would be great to see.

In our own technological environment, there is actually little targeted lobbying in Washington for fair use. Combining Wikipedia's lists of the top software, top Internet, and top "information technology" companies, one gets the following list of (mostly) well-known players: Adobe, Amazon, Apple, CATechnologies, Dell, eBay, Facebook, Fiserv, Google, Hewlett-Packard, IBM, Intel, Intuit, Microsoft, Oracle, Priceline, Salesforce.com, Symantec, VMware, and Yahoo. Besides Google, to the best of my knowledge, all of these companies have been individually quiet about the fair use doctrine.

What Washington policy makers have gotten intermittently is a "Fair Use in the U.S. Economy" study, sponsored by the Computer and Communications Industry Association (CCIA).[143] These reports are intended to counteract the studies from copyright industries on how important they are to our economic vibrancy – in other words, they are part of the *atmospherics lobbying* that is continuous in Washington. The CCIA's 2007 announcement is characteristic of the tone of its effort: "[m]uch of the unprecedented economic growth of the past 10 years can actually be credited to the doctrine of fair use, as the Internet itself depends on the ability to use content in a limited and nonlicensed manner."[144]

The core idea of these annual reports is interesting and worthwhile, but the reports are not really about "fair use" itself in a way that would help policy making. The reports try to estimate all the information activity in the economy that "copyright leaves unregulated" – it is that activity that is being christened the "fair use economy." The report's

---

[142] Mark Scott, *Where Tech Giants Protect Privacy*, N.Y. Times, Dec. 14, 2014, at SR 5 (discussing privacy laws in the European Union, Brazil, India, South Africa, and Korea with which Facebook, Google, and Microsoft must comply).

[143] And, as befits the complexities of Washington, while Microsoft, Yahoo, and Google belong to this trade association, IBM, Oracle, Hewlett-Packard, Symantec, Apple, Adobe, Cisco, and Dell do not belong to the "Computer and Communications Industry Association." Some of these companies belong to the Business Software Alliance (SBA) or the Software and Information Industry Association (SIIA). Video game companies have their own trade group, the Entertainment Software Association (ESA).

[144] Thomas Claburn, *Fair Use Worth More to Economy Than Copyright, CCIA Says*, InformationWeek (Sept. 12, 2007), www.informationweek.com/fair-use-worth-more-to-economy-than-copyright-ccia-says/d/d-id/1059122 (quoting CCIA President Ed Black).

authors are upfront that their "fair use economy" includes everything from the idea/expression dichotomy to ISP safe harbors to the *public domain*, that is, all that is permitted by 17 U.S.C. §§ 102(a), 102(b), 105, 107, 108, 109, 112, 114(a), 117(a), 302–304, and 512.[145] Anyone who does something that would fall under one of these provisions is called a "beneficiary of fair use."[146]

So, these reports are really just about the *information economy unprotected/unregulated by copyright*. As I said, this is an interesting idea; many of us have written in defense of robust application of the different bells and whistles of the copyright machine that keep the system calibrated.[147] But a report that extolls the virtues of the whole structure of the copyright system – the idea/expression dichotomy, the fact/expression dichotomy, "limited times" protection, no copyright in government works, and so forth – is not very useful to policy makers in addressing any particular question, whether it is fair use or the protection of digital rights management information.

Preparing the Garden

While there is not yet a compelling case for American diplomatic resources to be used in strenuous advocacy of fair use, it should be recognized that significant American resources are used in activities that – in a principled world – should make it easier (and better) for other jurisdictions to adopt fair use-inspired provisions. Those resources are the time, money, and energy that the United States puts into training of IP judges from other countries. The U.S. Patent and Trademark Office itself "conducted 119 training programs for foreign government officials" in fiscal 2014[148] and in fiscal 2012 the USPTO "provided training to 9,217 foreign officials from 129 countries on a variety of intellectual property topics."[149] The U.S. Copyright Office has also conducted its own, small training programs for international officials

---

[145] Andrew Szamosszegi, "Fair Use in the US Economy," Powerpoint Presentation, July 11, 2011, slide 3 (on file with author).

[146] *Id.* slide 4.

[147] For myself, I have been particularly concerned about the "minimum size" principle in copyright law and nuanced application of the fact/expression distinction in situations where the putative © owner "created" the facts. For the former, see Justin Hughes, *Size Matters (or Should) in Copyright Law*, 75 FORDHAM L. REV. 575 (2005); *Banxcorp v. Costco*, Case No. 09-CV-1783 (KMK) (S.D.N.Y. Oct. 17, 2013) (holding short strings of numbers uncopyrightable). For the latter, see Justin Hughes, *Created Facts and the Flawed Ontology of Copyright*, 83 NOTRE DAME L. REV. 43 (2007).

[148] From the "data visualization dashboard" *available at* www.uspto.gov/dashboards/externalaffairs/main .dashxml#dlink_ZB_vxIT_2j4Y. The trainings were conducted by the USPTO's "Global Intellectual Property Academy" which reports that 93 percent+ of its program participants "respondents agree or strongly agree that they have a better appreciation for international intellectual property rights and enforcement policy strategies."

[149] USPTO Global Intellectual Property Academy, *available at* www.uspto.gov/ip/training/.

in recent years.[150] Assuming that a moderate fraction of the participants in all these efforts are judges, that is a substantial amount of judicial training in IP.

Increased training of judges should make them better at knowing when to find parties liable or not liable for IP infringements. More importantly, increased sophistication of judges should make them better able to handle "standards" handed down from their legislatures instead of precise rules; that is, if "in the course of economic development judges and civil servants receive better training combined with a general increase in the level of education, it becomes efficient to have less precise and more goal-oriented legal norms."[151] In that way, the substantial resources the United States invests in training judges from other jurisdictions in IP topics should rebound to the benefit of advocates of fair use.

8.4. CONCLUSION

Many people – particularly those who had dedicated English teachers in high school (as I did) – will remember this scene from Shakespeare's *Taming of the Shrew*:

PETRUCHIO

> I say it is the moon that shines so bright.

KATHARINA

> I know it is the sun that shines so bright.

* * *

PETRUCHIO

> I say it is the moon.

KATHARINA

> I know it is the moon.

PETRUCHIO

> Nay, then you lie: it is the blessed sun.[152]

Sometimes groups, like individuals, disagree because they are supposed to disagree – or because they have gotten into a deep pattern of disagreement.

There is no question that in the 1960s some copyright advocates opposed the codification of fair use in the 1976 Act and there is no denying their continuing angst

---

[150] U.S. Copyright Office 2012 International Training Program, *available at* www.copyright.gov/docs/ici/2012/; U.S. Copyright Office 2010 International Training Program, *available at* www.copyright.gov/docs/ici/.

[151] Schäfer, *supra* note 12, at 131.

[152] William Shakespeare, *Taming of the Shrew*, Act 4, Scene 5.

over the doctrine.[153] The question is whether that angst has been made worse as fair use has increasingly become the favored tool for those opposed to strong copyright protection, coupled with some American judges' strange, unpredictable application of the "transformativeness" test of the first fair use factor.[154]

Whatever the causes, these days fears of fair use among some copyright advocates appear as irrational and strident as low protectionists' advocacy for it – and there is no question in my mind that the two feed on each other. As I said at the beginning, this is a struggle in which fair use is implicitly perceived by both sides as the *open-ended possibility of the negation of copyright protection*. That formulation may take some people aback. In response to an earlier draft of this chapter, a colleague proposed to amend my characterization to "an open-ended regulator of copyright protection … a device to withdraw copyright protection in all circumstances in which such protection would fail to advance the underlying purposes of the copyright system." But that is really not what fair use does.

First, fair use is more aptly described as the "negation" of copyright because a successful use of the doctrine simply turns off the copyright: the doctrine is not an "open-ended regulator of copyright protection" as much as a kill-switch. It offers only a "blunt response" to situations in which full-blown copyright protection would not advance the purposes of the system.[155] Notice also that I said the *"open-ended possibility of the negation of copyright,"* not the "possibility of the *open-ended* negation of copyright." No single fair use decision – not even *Google Books* – will wipe out copyright. Fair use decisions are NOT about global policy determinations "to withdraw copyright protection in all circumstances in which such protection would

---

[153] *See, e.g.*, Kimberly Kindy, *Filmmakers' Group Tries to Reshape Treaty that Would Benefit the Blind*, WASHINGTON POST, June 22, 2013 (describing how, in the context of the Marrakesh Treaty negotiations, "Hollywood is strongly resisting language in the draft that mirrors the concept of 'fair use,' long embodied in U.S. copyright law"), *available at* www.washingtonpost.com/politics/filmmakers-group-tries-to-reshape-treaty-that-would-benefit-the-blind/2013/06/22/f98e6130-d761-11e2-9df4-895344c13c30_story.html. *See also IPA Criticizes Fair Use Proposal in Australia*, PUBLISHERS WEEKLY, Feb. 14, 2014, *available at* www.publishersweekly.com/pw/by-topic/industry-news/publisher-news/article/61069-ipa-criticizes-fair-use-proposal-in-australia.html.

[154] Not to say that the outcomes are wrong, but one can see an overreliance and sometimes wild-eyed application of the transformative analysis in some cases. I am thinking of *White v. West Publ'g*, 2014 WL 3057885 (S.D.N.Y. July 3, 2014); *SOFA Entm't Inc. v. Dodger Prods. Inc.*, 709 F.3d 1273 (9th Cir. 2013); *Monge v. Maya*, 96 USPQ2d 1678 (C.D. Cal. Sept. 30, 2010), *rev'd*, 688 F.3d 1164 (9th Cir. 2012); *Rightshaven, LLC v. Jarra*, 2011 U.S. Dist. LEXIS 43952 (D. Nev. Apr. 22, 2011). In all these cases, the courts could have reached the same result with a more balanced application of the four statutory factors and a less strained "transformative" analysis.

[155] The phrase comes from the article first cited in this chapter: Kozinski & Newman, *supra* note 2, at 525 (noting that all fair use can do "is choose between … two blunt responses.") Kozinski and Newman ask, "even if we decide that a use should be allowed why does it follow that no compensation is due to the owner of the infringed work?" *Id.* at 524.

fail to advance the underlying purposes of the copyright system." They are determinations made case-by-case whenever someone wants to do something and (reasonably or unreasonably) does not want copyright to get in their way. If the analysis of this chapter is correct, fair use is a *serial mechanism* for establishing new exceptions – and it is precisely that nature that alarms copyright owners.

If we are comfortable saying, as Gerald Dworkin has, that "[s]ome copyright laws are precise, allowing little discretion for judges to do more than apply them; other copyright legislation leaves some scope for judicial discretion ... to implement and develop the law in accordance with perceived policy considerations,"[156] it seems only a small step to say that in a system in which the legislature has mandated an open-ended copyright exception, the legislative act is really a *mechanism* for more precise *exceptions* to be established through judicial discretion. In short, 17 U.S.C. § 107, Section 185 of the Philippine IP Code, Section 35-3 of the Korean Copyright Act, and their ilk are not *exceptions per se*, but mechanisms for the establishment of exceptions.

Fair use is neither the #1 problem for copyright owners nor the #1 solution for users. For most copyright holders, the real issue is enforcement against commercial scale piracy, not *most* of the practice of statutory exceptions and exceptions created under fair use doctrines. (The increasingly acrimonious interaction of book publishers and libraries may be different.) For most users in most circumstances, well delineated statutory exceptions make for a more transparent world than judge-created doctrine. It is not just that the debate about fair use is acrimonious, but the fact that so much attention now focuses on fair use speaks to how acrimonious the broader copyright debate became. Until the dynamics between the two sides change, policy makers looking at reform of domestic copyright law or negotiators trying to improve international copyright incrementally would be well-advised to steer carefully when approaching the angry shoals of fair use.

---

[156] Gerald Dworkin, *Judicial Control of Copyright on Public Policy Grounds, in* INTELLECTUAL PROPERTY AND INFORMATION LAW: ESSAYS IN HONOUR OF HERMAN COHEN JEHORAM (Jan Kabel & Gerard Mom eds., Kluwer Law International 1998).

9

Flexible Copyright

Can the EU Author's Rights Accommodate Fair Use?

P. Bernt Hugenholtz[*]

ABSTRACT

Almost everyone agrees that modern copyright law needs to be flexible in order to accommodate rapid technological change and evolving media uses. In the United States, fair use is the flexible instrument of choice. Author's rights systems in Europe are generally deemed to be less flexible and less tolerant to open-ended limitations and exceptions. But are they really?

This chapter makes the case that (1) author's rights systems can be made as flexible as copyright systems, and (2) that the existing EU legal framework does not preclude the development of flexible norms at the national level.

9.1. INTRODUCTION

Like the European Union (EU) itself, the law of copyright in the EU seems to be in a state of perennial crisis. Surely, a major cause of this crisis is the increasing gap between the rules of copyright law in Europe and the social norms that are shaped by states of technology. Of course, technological development has *always* outpaced the process of lawmaking, but with the spectacular advances in information technology of recent years the law-norm gap in copyright has become so wide that the system is now almost at a breaking point. In the EU, this problem is exacerbated by two additional factors. One is the complexity of the EU lawmaking machinery, which may require many years for a harmonization directive to be adopted or revised, and thereafter implemented in national law. The other is the general lack of flexibility in the law of copyright in the EU and its Member States, which – unlike the United

---

[*] This chapter is partly based on a study by P. Bernt Hugenholtz & Martin R. F. Senftleben, *Fair Use in Europe: In Search of Flexibilities* (Nov. 2011), *available at* http://ssrn.com/abstract=1959554. The author wishes to thank James Boyle and Lisa Ramsey for comments on a previous version.

States – does not generally permit "fair use" and thus allows less leeway for new uses not foreseen by the legislature.

Consequently, there is an increasing mismatch between the law of copyright and emerging social norms in Europe. Examples abound. Whereas social media have become essential tools of social and cultural communication, current copyright law leaves little room for sharing user-generated content that builds upon pre-existing works. By the same token, the law in most Member States fails to take into account emerging educational and scholarly practices, such as the use of copyright protected content in PowerPoint presentations, in digital classrooms, on Blackboard sites, or in webinars. The law of copyright in the EU also finds it very hard to accommodate information location tools, such as search engines and aggregation sites. By hindering these and other uses that many believe should remain outside the reach of copyright protection (and would probably be qualified as "fair use" in the United States), the law impedes not only cultural, social, and economic progress, but also undermines the social legitimacy of copyright law.

Copyright laws in the Member States of the EU traditionally provide for closed lists of limitations and exceptions that enumerate uses of works that are permitted without the authorization of rightholders. Examples of such uses are: quotation, private copying, library archiving, and uses by the news media. These exceptions are sometimes very detailed and connected to specific states of technology, and therefore easily outdated. To complicate matters, the EU legal framework leaves Member States limited room to update or expand existing limitations and exceptions. The Copyright in the Information Society Directive of 2001 lists twenty-odd limitations and exceptions that Member States may provide for in their national laws, but generally does not allow exceptions beyond this "shopping list."

While *fair use* in Europe is often regarded as an oxymoron or even a taboo in classic author's rights doctrine, the idea of introducing a measure of flexibility in the European system of circumscribed limitations and exceptions is now gradually being received in European political discourse, both in common law and civil law states and at the EU policy level. Already in 2006, the Gowers Review in the United Kingdom recommended that an exception be created for "creative, transformative or derivative works," particularly in the context of user-generated content.[1] In 2008, the European Commission took this suggestion on board in its Green Paper on Copyright in the Knowledge Economy, which however did not lead to amendment of the EU legal framework.[2] The Dutch Government has repeatedly stated its commitment to initiate a discussion at the European political level on a European-style fair use rule.[3] In 2011, the

---

[1]   Gowers Review of Intellectual Property (December 2006), Recommendation 11.
[2]   EUROPEAN COMMISSION, GREEN PAPER ON COPYRIGHT IN THE KNOWLEDGE ECONOMY BRUSSELS, COM(2008) 466/3 (16.07.2008), at 19–20.
[3]   Kamerstuk (Parliamentary Record) 21501–34, no. 155.

Hargreaves Review in the United Kingdom recommended "that the UK could achieve many of its benefits by taking up copyright exceptions already permitted under EU law and arguing for an additional exception, designed to enable EU copyright law to accommodate future technological change where it does not threaten copyright owners."[4] While the UK Government's response to the Review[5] and recent amendments to UK copyright law[6] reflect many of the Hargreaves proposals for new exceptions to British copyright law, the Government shied away from promoting the introduction into EU law of a U.S. style fair use exemption. In 2013, the Irish Copyright Review Committee advised the Irish Government to consider the introduction of a general fair use rule to complement existing limitations and exceptions in the law.[7] The European Commission's consultation document accompanying its public consultation on the review of the EU copyright rules, which took place in 2014, specifically addressed the issue of (more) flexibility:

> Finally, the question of flexibility and adaptability is being raised: what is the best mechanism to ensure that the EU and Member States' regulatory frameworks adapt when necessary (either to clarify that certain uses are covered by an exception or to confirm that for certain uses the authorisation of rightholders is required)? The main question here is whether a greater degree of flexibility can be introduced in the EU and Member States regulatory framework while ensuring the required legal certainty, including for the functioning of the Single Market, and respecting the EU's international obligations.[8]

Most recently, the idea of introducing (more) flexibility in EU copyright law was unequivocally embraced by MEP Julia Reda in her draft report for the European Parliament's influential Legal Committee on the implementation of the Information Society Directive.[9]

---

[4] IAN HARGREAVES, DIGITAL OPPORTUNITY: A REVIEW OF INTELLECTUAL PROPERTY AND GROWTH 5 (May 2011).

[5] UK GOVERNMENT, MODERNISING COPYRIGHT: A MODERN, ROBUST AND FLEXIBLE FRAMEWORK, *available at* www.ipo.gov.uk/response-2011-copyright-final.pdf.

[6] *See* Copyright and Rights in Performances (Research, Education, Libraries and Archives) Regulations 2014, entered into force 1 June 2014; Copyright and Rights in Performances (Personal Copies for Private Use) Regulations 2014, entered into force 1 Oct. 2014; Copyright and Rights in Performances (Quotation and Parody) Regulations 2014, entered into force 1 Oct. 2014.

[7] COPYRIGHT REVIEW COMMITTEE, MODERNISING COPYRIGHT, Dublin, 2013, *available at* www .enterprise.gov.ie/en/Publications/CRC-Report.pdf.

[8] European Commission, Public Consultation on the Review of the EU Copyright Rules, Brussels, Dec. 2013, *available at* http://ec.europa.eu/internal_market/consultations/2013/copyright-rules/docs/ consultation-document_en.pdf, p. 16.

[9] Draft Report on the implementation of Directive 2001/29/EC of the European Parliament and of the Council of 22 May 2001 on the harmonization of certain aspects of copyright and related rights in the information society (2014/2256(INI)), Committee on Legal Affairs, Rapporteur Julia Reda, 14 Jan. 2015.

This chapter looks at copyright flexibilities in EU law from an author's rights perspective. Why is there a need for flexibilities today and to what extent are open norms compatible with the author's rights system that prevails in the EU? Does the EU legal framework leave Member States, in particular those states that subscribe to the tradition of *droit d'auteur*, discretion to adopt in their national laws open "fair use" style limitations and exceptions to copyright? Does the European Convention on Human Rights, in particular the European Court's recent case law on copyright v. freedom of expression, create (additional) flexibilities?

This chapter is structured as follows. Section 9.2 provides a general discussion of open norms in copyright regimes, and seeks to explain why author's rights regimes have lost much of their flexibility. Section 9.3 explores the policy space that the European legal framework, in particular the Information Society Directive, leaves to Member States aspiring to introduce flexible copyright exceptions. Section 9.4 analyses recent decisions of the European Court on Human Rights on the conflict between copyright and freedom of expression. Section 9.5 offers conclusions.

9.2. COPYRIGHT, *DROIT D'AUTEUR* AND OPEN NORMS

Copyright is confined by a subtle structure of limits and limitations. In the ideal copyright system these limits and limitations are essential balancing tools, calibrated to allow users of copyright works sufficient freedoms to interact with these works without unduly undermining copyright's multiple rationales. While the general limits of copyright define the subject matter, scope of protection, and duration of the exclusive rights, the statutory limitations (or "limitations and exceptions" as they are usually called today) accommodate more specifically a variety of cultural, social, informational, economic, and political needs and purposes. Flexibilities may be found in all elements of this structure. For example, the notion of "originality" and the idea/expression dichotomy allow courts certain ad hoc freedoms to decide what is and what is not copyright protected. By the same token, the rules on copyright infringement leave courts some discretion, particularly in jurisdictions where the scope of copyright protection is determined by the (level of) originality of the appropriated portion of the work.[10] Regardless of the relative fluidity of these and other core concepts of copyright law, limitations and exceptions are obviously the main instruments of flexibility.

Like any other structure of rulemaking, copyright law must mediate between the maxims of legal certainty, which favours precisely defined legal provisions that provide optimal predictability *ex post*, and of fairness, which favours open and flexible

---

[10] CJEU, 16 July 2009, case C-5/08, Infopaq International v. /Danske Dagblades Forening.

legal concepts that allow a wide margin of judicial appreciation *ad hoc*. In modern civil law, this compromise between certainty and fairness is usually achieved by codifying relatively abstract legal provisions that spell out the general rules without impeding civil courts to apply general normative principles, such as "reasonableness and fairness" (in Dutch: *redelijkheid en billijkheid*; in German: *Treu und Glauben*), to arrive at fair judgments. In the common law codified norms tend to be more precise and extensive, since they constrict rather than empower the court's mandate to apply the common law to distinct cases.[11] In copyright law, these conflicting traditions of codification are still visible today in the relatively concise, abstractly phrased codes of the *droit d'auteur* tradition, and the much more voluminous and detailed codifications of Anglo-American copyright law. Whereas, for example, the Dutch Copyright Act comprises some 75 provisions laid down in a mere 20 pages, the U.S. Copyright Act amounts to well over 200 pages.

These systemic differences to some extent explain why general rules of fairness are mostly absent from the codified laws of the *droit d'auteur* tradition. The relatively flexible norms that civil law jurisdictions traditionally provided never necessitated codifying a general rule of fairness. By contrast, such a rule – originally developed by the U.S. courts in the course of more than a century of case law – eventually did find its way into the U.S. Copyright Act.[12]

An example of a fairly open exception commonly found in laws of the author's rights tradition is the quotation right. Article 10(1) of the Berne Convention requires Contracting States to provide for copyright limitations that permit quotations subject to certain conditions "provided that their making is compatible with *fair practice*." The corresponding provision of Article 5(3)(d) of the Information Society Directive similarly refers to "fair practice," whereas its implementation into Dutch law (Article 15(a) of the Dutch Copyright Act) requires the quotation to be "commensurate with what might reasonably be accepted in accordance with social custom and the number and size of the quoted passages are justified by the purpose to be achieved." References to fair practice also appear in other limitations and exceptions in civil law jurisdictions. For example, the French parody exemption that inspired the inclusion of parody in the Information Society's list of permitted limitations and exceptions refers to "the rules of the genre."[13]

---

[11] A. STROWEL, DROIT D'AUTEUR ET COPYRIGHT 147 (1993).

[12] U.S. Copyright Act, Section 107, provides that uses for such purposes as criticism, comment, news reporting, teaching, scholarship and research are fair and non-infringing depending on four factors: the purpose and character of the use; the nature of the copyrighted work; the amount appropriated from the copyrighted work; and the effect of the use upon the potential market for or value of the copyrighted work.

[13] Intellectual Property Code (France), Article L122-5(4).

Unfortunately, as Prof. Strowel has explained,[14] *droit d'auteur* codifications have lost much of their original flexibility in the course of the twentieth century, as copyright laws were updated ever more frequently to accommodate the needs of a changing society, so as to respond to technological development and to implement the dictates of European harmonization. Thus, much of the original conciseness, elegance, and openness of the laws following the *droit d'auteur* tradition has been lost.

Another, more important reason why laws of the author's rights tradition have become less tolerant to unauthorized but "fair" uses, lies in the natural rights philosophy that in the course of the twentieth century increasingly came to dominate the discourse on copyright in continental Europe, and which eventually became the main underpinning of the author's rights paradigm. If protecting author's rights is, indeed, essentially a matter of natural law, limitations to this right must remain "exceptions."[15] Following this line of reasoning, courts in *droit d'auteur* jurisdictions such as France, have developed a rule of restrictive interpretation of copyright limitations.[16] By contrast, the U.S. copyright system that has its main justification in utilitarian considerations ("to promote the progress of science and useful arts"),[17] more easily absorbs "fair" uses that are in line with its main goal of optimizing the production and dissemination of creative works.

In parallel with this tendency towards closure of the author's rights system, and inspired by economic theories (and, of course, powerful lobbies) that posit copyright as "property," the economic rights that the law grants to copyright owners are increasingly perceived, by courts, politicians and some scholars alike, as absolute. According to these theories, just as property rights in tangible goods warrant complete and perpetual control, making unauthorized uses unlawful as a matter of principle, copyright should ideally become a perpetual and absolute right that tolerates few "free" uses.[18]

Paradoxically, as author's rights systems have gradually lost much of their openness, the need for flexibility in copyright law has greatly increased. Whereas, legislatures of the nineteenth and early twentieth century could still anticipate and adequately respond to the main technological changes that required modification of the law, the

---

[14]　STROWEL, *supra* note 11, at 149.

[15]　Martin Senftleben, *Bridging the Differences Between Copyright's Legal Traditions – The Emerging EC Fair Use Doctrine*, 57 J. COPYRIGHT SOC'Y U.S.A. 524–25 (2010).

[16]　*See, e.g.*, ANDRÉ LUCAS & HENRI-JACQUES LUCAS, TRAITÉ DE LA PROPRIÉTÉ LITTÉRAIRE ET ARTISTIQUE 259–60 (3d ed. 2006). A similar rule of narrow construction of exceptions, based however on principles of EU law, was articulated by the European Court of Justice in *Infopaq International v. Danske Dagblades Forening*, CJEU 16 July 2009, case C-5/08; see below text accompanying note 53.

[17]　Article I, Section 8 of the U.S. Constitution.

[18]　Christophe Geiger, *Flexibilising Copyright – Remedies to the Privatisation of Information by Copyright Law*, 39 INT'L REV. INTELL. PROP. & COMPETITION L. 178 (2008).

accelerating pace of technological change in the early twenty-first century no longer allows such legislative foresight. Conversely, the length of the legislative cycle in copyright has become ever longer, as copyright law is no longer perceived as a mostly "technical" legal matter but has become highly politicized. Aggravating matters, the European harmonization machinery has added an additional, complex and lengthy legislative cycle. As a result, in Europe the total legislative response time to a new technological development may easily exceed ten years.[19]

All in all, current calls for reinstating (or introducing) a measure of flexibility in the law on author's rights in the EU should come as no surprise. These appeals often go by the name of "fair use."[20] While fair use is indeed an appealing concept and its political potential undeniable – who would dare disagree with "fair"? – there are conceptual and systemic dangers here. The doctrine of fair use has its origin in the common law of the United States. Simply transplanting this doctrine into civil law-based *droit d'auteur* might lead to unintended consequences and ultimately systemic rejection.[21]

More generally, there are obvious risks and drawbacks to a legal structure of open norms, such as fair use. There is a vast scholarly literature that analyses the pros and cons of "vague norms" from various perspectives such as legal philosophy,[22] law and economics,[23] and legal practice,[24] which need not be rehearsed here. The main arguments against overly open or vague norms relate to the tradeoff between precise lawmaking by the legislature and ad hoc adjudication by the courts. While vague norms allow justice to be served more fairly in concrete cases – something that civil courts are generally well accustomed to – this enhanced fairness comes at the price of reduced legal certainty. Rules are generally more efficient than vague standards

---

[19] Mireille van Eechoud A.O., Harmonizing European Copyright Law. The Challenges of Better Lawmaking 298 (Kluwer Law International 2009).

[20] *See, e.g.*, the Dutch Government's letter to the Parliament confirming its commitment to initiate a discussion at the European political level on a European-style fair use rule; Kamerstuk (Parliamentary Record) 21501–34, no. 155; see www.boek9.nl/?//Kabinet%3A+discussie+starten+over+een+uitzonder ing+voor+fair+use///27678/.

[21] Nonetheless, this step has been proposed by J. Griffiths, *The 'Three-Step Test' in European Copyright Law – Problems and Solutions*, Intell. Prop. Q. 489 (2009), *available at* http://ssrn.com/abstract=1476968. With regard to the introduction of fair use in Israel, see O. Fischman Afori, *An Open Standard 'Fair Use' Doctrine: A Welcome Israeli Initiative*, Eur. Intell. Prop. Rev. 85 (2008); G. Pessach, *The New Israeli Copyright Act – A Case-Study in Reverse Comparative Law* 41 Int'l Rev. Intell. Prop. & Competition L. 187 (2010).

[22] Frederick Schauer, Playing by the Rules: A Philosophical Examination of Rule-based Decision-making in Law and in Life (Clarendon Press 1993).

[23] Louis Kaplow, *Rules versus Standards*, 42 Duke L.J. 557 (1992).

[24] *See, e.g.*, J. M. Barendrecht, Recht als model van rechtvaardigheid: Beschouwingen over vage en scherpe normen, over binding aan het recht en over rechtsvorming (Deventer: Kluwer 1992).

given that they better inform citizens of their rights and obligations upfront, and allow those seeking justice to assess their legal position without needing to resort to the courts. Moreover, an obvious constitutional objection against vague norms is that political decisions are effectively delegated from the legislator to the courts without the necessary democratic checks and balances. While open norms may thus be "easy" and relatively inexpensive for lawmakers to produce, the costs of the law-making process are effectively shifted to the judicial apparatus, and to those seeking justice at the courts. Conversely, vague standards are generally more efficient, and will lead to fairer outcomes, in hard (marginal) cases and in situations that lawmakers cannot predict.

Both in Europe and in the United States opponents of fair use often cite fair use's supposed lack of predictability, or even arbitrariness, as a reason not to (further) go down this road.[25] This criticism, however, seems to overlook the fact that vague norms may eventually become more predictable as sufficient jurisprudence is created by the courts. As recent studies by American scholars Barton Beebe, Pamela Samuelson, and Neil Netanel suggest, this now seems to be the case for fair use.[26] As analysed by Samuelson, fair use case law "tends to coalesce in consistent patterns."[27] Netanel concludes that this scholarly work "provides a convincing and salutary corrective to the widespread view that fair use is fundamentally arbitrary and ad hoc."[28]

Opponents of infusing author's rights systems with a measure of flexibility also tend to ignore that in civil law jurisdictions open and abstract norms are quite common, and civil courts are generally well versed in applying vague norms to hard cases. For example, in the Netherlands – a civil law jurisdiction – an entire body of unfair competition law was created by the courts based on a single, flexible provision in the Civil Code generally prohibiting "unlawful acts."[29]

Moreover, the advantage of legal certainty that is usually ascribed to the European system of precisely defined exceptions should not be overstated. In the first place, courts unhappy with the literal application of a precise norm in a given case will sometimes find solace in overriding (and usually vague) norms external to the law

---

[25] *See, e.g.*, David Nimmer, *"Fairest of Them All" and Other Fairy Tales of Fair Use*, 66 DUKE U. L.J. 263 (2003); Herman Cohen Jehoram, *Fair use – die ferne Geliebte'*, AMI/Tijdschrift voor auteurs-, media- en informatierecht 174 (1998); Herman Cohen Jehoram, *Restrictions to Copyright and their Abuse*, 27 E.I.P.R. 359 (2005).

[26] Barton Beebe, *An Empirical Study of U.S. Copyright Fair Use Opinions, 1978–2005*, 156 U. PA. L. REV. 549 (2008); Pamela Samuelson, *Unbundling Fair Uses*, 77 FORDHAM L. REV. 2537 (2009); Neil Weinstock Netanel, *Making Sense of Fair Use*, 15 LEWIS & CLARK L. REV. 715 (2011).

[27] Samuelson, *supra* note 26.

[28] Netanel, *supra* note 26, at 718.

[29] *See* R. W. de Vrey, *The Netherlands, in* INTERNATIONAL HANDBOOK ON UNFAIR COMPETITION (2013), Ch. 18, 399 ff.

of copyright, such as abuse of right,[30] implied consent,[31] or freedom of expression.[32] Secondly, the introduction into the fabric of EU law of the "three-step test,"[33] and its literal implementation in several laws of the Member States, has considerably reduced legal certainty, since courts are now invited to examine and (re)interpret statutory exceptions in the light of this entirely open-ended norm.[34]

In conclusion, what copyright laws in Europe ideally need today is a statutory system of limitations and exceptions that guarantees both a level of legal certainty and fairness, by combining relatively precise norms with sufficient flexibility to allow a fair outcome in hard or unpredictable cases. An example of such a semi-open structure of limitations and exceptions can be found in the *European Copyright Code* that was drafted as a model law by a group of European scholars.[35] Article 5.5 of the Code permits the application by analogy of all limitations and exceptions specifically enumerated in the Code – both compensated and uncompensated – subject to the application of the three-step test.

9.3. IN SEARCH OF FLEXIBILITIES INSIDE THE EU ACQUIS

In the EU, the uneven ground of limitations and exceptions has been partly harmonized by the Copyright in the Information Society Directive of 2001.[36] Article 5 of the Directive enumerates exhaustively the types of limitations that member states may implement in their national law.[37] The list includes a single mandatory limitation

---

[30] *See generally* for France: C. Caron, *Abuse of Rights and Author's Rights*, 176 R.I.D.A. 2, 4 (1998).

[31] *See, e.g., Google thumbnails*, Federal Constitutional Court (Germany), April 29, 2010, case I ZR 69/08

[32] *See, e.g., Germania 3 Gespenster am toten Mann*, Federal Constitutional Court (Germany), 29 June 2000, [2000] Zeitschrift für Urheber- und Medienrecht (ZUM) 867; *HFA v. FIFA*, Court of Cassation (France), Oct. 2, 2007, 214 R.I.D.A. 338 (2007).

[33] Information Society Directive, Article 5.5. See below, text accompanying note 48.

[34] For an overview of the application of the three-step test by national courts, see Jonathan Griffiths, *The 'Three-Step Test' in European Copyright Law – Problems and Solutions*, INTELL. PROP. Q. 489 (2009), *available at* http://ssrn.com/abstract=1476968; Martin Senftleben, *Bridging the Differences between Copyright's Legal Traditions – The Emerging EC Fair Use Doctrine*, 57 J. COPYRIGHT SOC'Y U.S.A. 521 (2010), *available at* http://ssrn.com/abstract=1723902; Martin Senftleben, *Fair Use in the Netherlands: A Renaissance?*, 33 Tijdschrift voor Auteurs, Media en Informatierecht (A.M.I.) 1 (2009), *available at* http://ssrn.com/abstract=1563986.

[35] Wittem Group, European Copyright Code, *available at* www.copyrightcode.eu.

[36] *See generally* L. GUIBAULT ET AL., STUDY ON THE IMPLEMENTATION AND EFFECT IN MEMBER STATES' LAWS OF DIRECTIVE 2001/29/EC ON THE HARMONISATION OF CERTAIN ASPECTS OF COPYRIGHT AND RELATED RIGHTS IN THE INFORMATION SOCIETY (2007) (Report to the European Commission). For national implementations see G. WESTKAMP, PART II: THE IMPLEMENTATION OF DIRECTIVE 2001/29/EC IN THE MEMBER STATES (2007).

[37] The exhaustive character of the Directive's list of permitted limitations has inspired interest among several Member States in more open, fair use-like exemptions; *see* P. Bernt Hugenholtz & Martin R. F. Senftleben, *Fair Use in Europe: In Search of Flexibilities* Nov. 2011, *available at* http://ssrn.com/abstract=1959554.

permitting transient copying incidental to digital communications,[38] and a menu of twenty optional limitations from which Member States may choose.[39] The limitations approved by the European legislature concern not only such generally accepted uses as photocopying, private copying, archival and ephemeral copying, educational uses, news reporting, quotation, and parody, but also more arcane uses, such as the use of works in religious celebrations, "use in connection with the demonstration or repair of equipment," etc. The Directive does allow some pre-existing minor "analogue" exemptions (i.e., those dating from pre-digital times) to survive in national law. However, it does not permit any limitations or exceptions beyond the list, and therefore most likely would not allow a Member State to provide for a generally worded American-style "fair use" provision.[40] Moreover, any limitation implemented at the national level must comply with the "three-step test."[41]

The Directive's complex structure of one mandatory and twenty optional exceptions subject to the overriding norm of the three-step test has attracted considerable criticism.[42] According to Martin Senftleben, "the current EC system provides neither sufficient flexibility for copyright limitations nor sufficient legal certainty for users of copyrighted material. It combines the two disadvantages of the Anglo-American and the continental-European approach."[43] Nevertheless, there does appear to be at least a measure of flexibility in the EU acquis due to the way many of the limitations in the Directive's smorgasbord are drafted.[44] While some provisions in Article 5 are formulated in rather precise language, requiring (near)literal implementation by national legislatures,[45] most others are framed in more general terms, loosely describing the type, function or purpose of the permitted exception. According to the European Court of Justice, such provisions leave the Member States "a broad

---

[38] E.C. Copyright in the Information Society Directive Art. 5(1). See § 11.3.2, below.

[39] E.C. Copyright in the Information Society Directive Art. 5(2), (3).

[40] A Member State desiring to take full advantage of all policy space available under the Information Society Directive, and thus maximize flexibilities available at the EU level, might achieve this literally transposing the Directive's entire catalogue of exceptions into national law. In combination with the three-step test, this could in theory lead to a semi-open norm almost as flexible as the fair use rule of the United States. *See* Hugenholtz & Senftleben, *supra* note 37, at 17–18.

[41] E.C. Copyright in the Information Society Directive Art. 5(5).

[42] *See, e.g.,* Bernt Hugenholtz, *Why the Copyright Directive is Unimportant, and Possibly Invalid,* 11 E.I.P.R. 501–2 (2000). Martin Senftleben, *Bridging the Differences between Copyright's Legal Traditions – The Emerging EC Fair Use Doctrine,* 57 J. COPYRIGHT SOC'Y U.S.A. 521–52 (2010).

[43] Senftleben, *supra* note 42, at 529.

[44] *See* L. Bently, *Exploring the Flexibilities Available to UK Law,* submission to the HARGREAVES REV., 3 Mar. 2011, *available at* http://webarchive.nationalarchives.gov.uk/20140603093549/http://www.ipo .gov.uk/ipreview-c4e-sub-bently.pdf.

[45] For example, Article 5(3)(n): "use by communication or making available, for the purpose of research or private study, to individual members of the public by dedicated terminals on the premises of establishments referred to in paragraph 2(c) of works and other subject-matter not subject to purchase or licensing terms which are contained in their collections."

discretion" to tailor national exceptions to their domestic needs.[46] As a consequence, the scope and breadth of national exceptions within the EU may differ markedly. For example, whereas the French copyright law notoriously allows quotation only under the strictest of conditions,[47] Nordic copyright law presents the quotation right as a relatively open rule of reason.[48]

While the broad wording of many of the Directive's permitted exceptions in principle leaves plenty of policy space to national legislatures, this space is reduced by various constricting factors. In the first place, Article 5(5) subordinates all national exceptions and limitations within the ambit of the Directive to the overriding norm of the "three-step test." Exceptions "shall only be applied in certain special cases which do not conflict with a normal exploitation of the work or other subject matter and do not unreasonably prejudice the legitimate interests of the rightholder." This provision, which obviously has its roots in international copyright law,[49] affects and constricts copyright exceptions at two levels. National legislatures are not allowed to provide for limitations that, although within the literal confines of the exceptions enumerated in Article 5(2) and (3), would not comply with the three-step test. For example, in the *ACI Adam* case the European Court of Justice held that a provision in Dutch copyright law exempting private copying without distinguishing between private copies made from legal or illegal sources, overstepped the test, in particular the second (no conflict with normal exploitation of works) and the third (no unreasonable prejudice to rightholders).[50] Moreover, several Member States, including France and Spain, have seen fit to transpose Article 5(5) into their national copyright law.[51] As a consequence, national courts are generally invited to interpret national exceptions in line with the three-step test. Remarkably, even in countries where the

---

[46] Eva-Maria Painer v. Standard VerlagsGmbH, Axel Springer AG, Süddeutsche Zeitung GmbH, Spiegel-Verlag Rudolf Augstein GmbH & Co KG, Verlag M. DuMont Schauberg Expedition der Kölnischen Zeitung GmbH & Co KG, ECJ 1 Dec. 2011, case C-145/10, ECR [2011] I-12533, para. 101.

[47] Intellectual Property Code (France), Article L122-5(3), provides: "Once a work has been disclosed, the author may not prohibit: [...] 3°. on condition that the name of the author and the source are clearly stated: a) analyses and short quotations justified by the critical, polemic, educational, scientific or informatory nature of the work in which they are incorporated [...]."

[48] Copyright Act of Sweden, Article 22 reads: "Anyone may, in accordance with proper usage and to the extent necessary for the purpose, quote from works which have been made available to the public." Translated text *available at* www.regeringen.se/content/1/c6/01/51/95/20edd6df.pdf. *See generally* Ole-Andreas Rognstad, *Opphavsrett*, Universitetsforlaget 2009, at 241–52.

[49] Notably Article 9(2) *Berne Convention*, Article 13 TRIPS and Article 10 WIPO Copyright Treaty.

[50] ACI Adam BV and Others v. Stichting de Thuiskopie and Stichting Onderhandelingen Thuiskopie vergoeding, CJEU 10 April 2014, case C-435/12, paras. 39–40.

[51] *See* Jonathan Griffiths, *The 'Three-Step Test' in European Copyright Law – Problems and Solutions*, INTELL. PROP. Q. 489, 495 (2009), *available at* http://ssrn.com/abstract=1476968.

three-step test has not been implemented, such as the Netherlands, courts have also applied the test to exceptions codified in national law.[52]

A second constricting factor is the "principle" announced in the CJEU's landmark *Infopaq* decision and regularly repeated afterwards that limitations and exceptions must be narrowly construed. This, according to the European Court, is not so much a matter of natural law, but rather an established maxim of EU law according to which exceptions to a rule in a directive are to be strictly interpreted.[53] According to the Court, "[t]his is all the more so given that the exemption must be interpreted in the light of Article 5(5) of Directive 2001/29, under which that exemption is to be applied only in certain special cases which do not conflict with a normal exploitation of the work or other subject-matter and do not unreasonably prejudice the legitimate interests of the rightholder."[54]

By contrast, recent decisions of the European Court reflect a more liberal manner of interpreting limitations and exceptions. While still providing lip service to the rule of narrow construction, these decisions emphasize the need to interpret the limitations in the EU acquis in line with their purpose or objective[55] and in light of the need for EU copyright law to achieve a *fair balance* of rights and interests between the rightholders and users involved. This balancing principle, which is expressly enshrined in the preamble of the Information Society Directive,[56] has increasingly become the cornerstone of the European Court's jurisprudence in the area of copyright and related rights.[57]

---

[52] Martin Senftleben, *Bridging the Differences Between Copyright's Legal Traditions – The Emerging EC Fair Use Doctrine*, 57 J. COPYRIGHT SOC'Y U.S.A. 530–532 (2010).

[53] CJEU, 16 July 2009, case C-5/08, Infopaq International/Danske Dagblades Forening, *available at* www.curia.eu, paras 56–57.

[54] CJEU, *supra* note 53, para. 58.

[55] *See, e.g.*, Football Association Premier League Ltd and Others v. QC Leisure and Others; and Karen Murphy v. Media Protection Services Ltd, ECJ 4 Oct. 2011, joined cases C-403/08 and C-429/08, para. 164; Johan Deckmyn and Vrijheidsfonds VZW v. Helena Vandersteen and Others, CJEU 3 September 2014, case C-201/13, paras 22–25. *See* European Copyright Society, Limitations and Exceptions as Key Elements of the Legal Framework for Copyright in the European Union – Opinion on the Judgment of the CJEU in Case C-201/13 Deckmyn, *available at* http://papers.ssrn.com/sol3/papers.cfm?abstract_id=2564772.

[56] Recital 31 of the Directive reads: "A fair balance of rights and interests between the different categories of rightholders, as well as between the different categories of rightholders and users of protected subject-matter must be safeguarded."

[57] *See, e.g.*, Johan Deckmyn and Vrijheidsfonds VZW v. Helena Vandersteen and Others, CJEU 3 Sept. 2014, case C-201/13, paras. 26–27; Technische Universität Darmstadt v. Eugen Ulmer KG, CJEU 11 Sept. 2014, case C-117/13, para. 31; Copydan Båndkopi v. Nokia Danmark A/S, CJEU 5 Mar. 2015, case C-463/12, para. 77. See also Jonathan Griffiths et al., *European Copyright Society, Limitations and Exceptions as Key Elements of the Legal Framework for Copyright in the European Union – Opinion on the Judgment of the CJEU in Case C-201/13 Deckmyn*, *available at* http://papers.ssrn.com/sol3/papers.cfm?abstract_id=2564772.

In sum, EU law's closed list of permitted limitations and exceptions does leave Member States considerably more room for flexibilities than its closed list of permitted limitations and exceptions, and than EU law's maxim of narrow interpretation of exceptions *prima facie* suggests. In the first place, the enumerated limitations are in many cases broadly worded prototypes rather than precisely circumscribed exceptions, thus leaving the Member States a broad margin of implementation, as is confirmed by actual legislative practice. In the second place, recent decisions of the European Court of Justice underscore the need to interpret EU copyright law's limitations in line with their objectives, and in light of the need to fairly balance the interests of rightholders and users.

While this policy space would probably not permit Member States to introduce a fair use rule as open and flexible as the American original, EU law does leave room for an array of semi-flexible norms at the national level. For example, the Dutch Copyright Committee that advises the Ministry of Justice on matters of copyright law and policy proposes to permit the use of user-generated content by way of amending the quotation right.[58] The proposed legislative solution would, according to the Committee, stay well within the discretion left by EU law to the national legislature.

9.4. FLEXIBILITIES IN FREEDOM OF EXPRESSION

Additional flexibilities may arise from the body of human rights law that guarantees, inter alia, freedom of expression. In Europe, freedom of expression is recognized as a fundamental right at three levels, that of national constitutions or "basic laws," that of the European Convention on Human Rights[59] and that of the much more recent Charter of Fundamental Rights of the European Union.[60] In civil law countries, where copyright limitations and exceptions are often narrowly circumscribed and exhaustively enumerated, free speech may offer a safety valve when application of the letter of the law would lead to unjust results. Freedom of expression defences

---

[58] Commissie Auteursrecht, Advies aan de Staatssecretaris van Veiligheid en Justitie over de mogelijkheden van het invoeren van een flexibel systeem van beperkingen op het auteursrecht. Deel 1: Een flexibele regeling voor user-generated content, Oct. 2012, *available at* www .rijksoverheid.nl/documenten-en-publicaties/rapporten/2012/10/30/advies-een-flexibele-regeling-voor-user-generated-content.html.

[59] European Convention on Human Rights (ECHR), signed in Rome on November 4, 1950. Article 10 (1) ECHR reads: "Everyone has the right to freedom of expression. This right shall include freedom to hold opinions and to receive and impart information and ideas without interference by public authority and regardless of frontiers." In many European states the norms of the Convention are deemed self-executing, i.e., may be invoked directly before the courts.

[60] Charter of Fundamental Rights of the European Union (2000/C 364/01).

have in the past been particularly successful before national courts in Europe in cases where literal copying was considered inevitable, for example, for purposes of literal quotation or in cases of "live" broadcasting of works of art.[61]

In early 2013, the European Court of Human Rights – the highest judicial authority in Europe on human rights – for the first time pronounced itself on the interface between author's rights and freedom of expression, in two different cases. In *Ashby and Others v. France*[62] the Court addressed a complaint by three fashion photographers who were convicted in France and faced considerable criminal penalties and damages for infringing the copyrights of French fashion houses by posting photos of fashion shows on their website. According to the Court, disseminating photographs over the Internet is an act protected by freedom of speech, and the plaintiffs' conviction under French law therefore constituted an interference to be assessed under the three-part test of Article 10(2) of the ECHR.[63] While the tests of legality ("prescribed by law") and legitimate aim ("protection of the … rights of others") were easily met, the Court's application of the proportionality requirement (was the interference "necessary in a democratic society"?) is less straightforward. In line with its established case law on Article 10, the Court posits, first, that states enjoy a "margin of appreciation" when applying this test. In cases involving commercial speech, such as the case at hand, this margin is "broad," and it is even broader in cases like where freedom of speech needs to be balanced against a right (i.e., copyright) that is in itself protected by the Convention, notably by Article 1 of the First Protocol.[64] In sum, France had enjoyed "a particularly wide margin of appreciation" in balancing

---

[61] See P. Bernt Hugenholtz, *Copyright and Freedom of Expression in Europe*, in EXPANDING THE BOUNDARIES OF INTELLECTUAL PROPERTY: INNOVATION POLICY FOR THE KNOWLEDGE SOCIETY 343–63 (Rochelle Cooper Dreyfuss, Diane L. Zimmerman & Harry First eds., 2001).

[62] Donald Ashby and Others v. France, European Court of Justice, 10 Jan. 2013, No. 36769/08, full text available in French only at http://hudoc.echr.coe.int/sites/eng/pages/search.aspx?i=001-115845, summary in English *available at* http://hudoc.echr.coe.int/sites/eng/pages/search.aspx?i=002-7393.

[63] Article 10(2) ECHR reads: "The exercise of these freedoms, since it carries with it duties and responsibilities, may be subject to such formalities, conditions, restrictions or penalties as are prescribed by law and are necessary in a democratic society, in the interests of national security, territorial integrity or public safety, for the prevention of disorder or crime, for the protection of health or morals, for the protection of the reputation or rights of others, for preventing the disclosure of information received in confidence, or for maintaining the authority and impartiality of the judiciary."

[64] ECHR, Paris, 2 March 1952, Article 1 reads: "Every natural or legal person is [ ]eful enjoyment of his possessions. No one shall be deprived of his possessions [ ] interest and subject to the conditions provided for by law and by the general [ ]tional law. The preceding provisions shall not, however, in any way impair the [ ]orce such laws as it deems necessary to control the use of property in accordance [ ]rest or to secure the payment of taxes or other contributions or penalties."

copyright against the complainants' speech. Consequently, the Court held that no violation of Article 10 had taken place.

In another case decided only a month later, the European Court reiterated that copyright interferes with freedom of expression, but that states enjoy a "particularly wide margin of appreciation" in mediating between copyright and free speech. In this case Fredrik Neij and Peter Sunde, founders of the *The Pirate Bay* file sharing platform, complained that their rights to freedom of expression had been infringed by their conviction by a Swedish criminal court to hefty prison terms.[65] According to the ECHR, these convictions stayed within Sweden's margin of appreciation; again, no violation of the Convention was found.

Whereas the apparent ease with which the European Court in both cases has let copyright trump freedom of expression raises eyebrows, and its holding that in such cases states enjoy "a particularly wide margin of appreciation" is questionable, the ECHR's decisions do send an important signal to national courts and legislatures across Europe. The Strasbourg Court's case law essentially requires legislatures and courts to perceive copyright protection as a limitation to freedom of expression, and to assess – both generally at the legislative level, and in individual cases before the courts – whether the positives of copyright protection outweigh the negatives of encroachment of free speech. Although the Court leaves national authorities broad discretion, the Court's subordination of copyright to freedom of expression is significant, not only in theory, but probably also in practice.[66] While in normal situations covered by the rights and limitations enshrined in copyright law it is unlikely a violation of Article 10 will be found, the Strasbourg case law might play a role whenever new technology creates uses unforeseen by the legislature.

Moreover, as recent case law of the European Court of Justice illustrates, other fundamental rights may come into play as well, such as the right to privacy[67] or the freedom to conduct a business,[68] a novel fundamental right enshrined in the EU Charter.[69] Why in such cases, where multiple fundamental rights collide, states would always enjoy "a particularly wide margin of appreciation," as the Strasbourg Court's case law seems to suggest, is difficult to comprehend. The Luxembourg

---

[65] Fredrik Neij and Peter Sunde Kolmisoppi v. Sweden, European Court of Human Rights, 19 Feb. 2013, No. 40397/12, *available at* http://hudoc.echr.coe.int/sites/fra/pages/search.aspx?i=001-117513.

[66] *See, e.g.,* GS Media v. Sanoma a.o., Supreme Court of the Netherlands (Hoge Raad), 3 Apr. 2015 [intellectual property and freedom of speech are equivalent fundamental rights; freedom of speech may override copyright not just in exceptional cases; which right takes precedence depends on facts of the case, including whether or not expression serves general public interest, or is merely commercial].

[67] Productores de Música de España (Promusicae) v. Telefónica de España SAU, ECJ 29 Jan. 2008, case C-275/06, ECR [2008] I-00271.

[68] Scarlet Extended SA v. Société belge des auteurs, compositeurs et éditeurs SCRL (SABAM). ECJ 24 Nov. 2011, case C-70/10, ECR [2011] I-11959.

[69] EU Charter, Article 16.

Court's approach makes much more sense: between copyright and conflicting fundamental freedoms a *fair balance* must be found.[70]

9.5. CONCLUSION

There are good reasons and ample opportunity to (re)introduce a measure of flexibility in the national copyright systems of Europe. The need for more openness in copyright law is almost self-evident in this "information society" of highly dynamic and unpredictable change. A historic perspective also suggests that, due to a variety of circumstances, copyright law in the civil law jurisdictions of Europe has lost much of its flexibility in the course of the past century. In other words, making author's rights regimes more flexible would not go against the tide of legal tradition.

Ironically, as copyright law has gradually lost its openness, with the accelerating pace of technological change in the twenty-first century the need for flexibility has greatly increased. Concomitantly, the process of revising copyright law has become much more complex and time-consuming as national lawmakers in the Member States of the EU are increasingly constricted by European harmonization, making the need for flexible copyright norms – both at the EU and the national levels – ever more urgent. As this chapter has demonstrated, EU law leaves considerably more room for flexibilities than its closed list of permitted limitations and exceptions initially suggests. Additional flexibilities may be inferred from recent European case law juxtaposing copyright and freedom of expression.

This need not necessarily imply the introduction into European copyright law of an American-style *fair use* provision. There are drawbacks and risks associated with instituting a completely open norm into copyright systems that, like those of the author's rights tradition in the EU, traditionally provide for circumscribed limitations and exceptions that offer a good deal of predictability and legal certainty. Instead, introducing a measure of flexibility *alongside* the existing structure of well-defined limitations and exceptions would better fit the European tradition of author's rights, combining the advantages of legal certainty and technological neutrality.

Will the EU legislature follow suit? The Copyright in the Information Society Directive of 2001 is currently under review, and the Commission's proposals for revision are expected in late 2015. With copyright reform in the EU a clear priority of the newly elected Commission,[71] adding flexibility to EU copyright law will, in all

---

[70] Johan Deckmyn and Vrijheidsfonds VZW v. Helena Vandersteen and Others. ECJ 3 Sept. 2014, case C-201/13.

[71] *See* Jean-Claude Juncker (President of the European Commission), Mission Letter to Günther Oettinger, Commissioner for Digital Economy and Society, Brussels, 1 Nov. 2014, *available at* http://ec.europa.eu/commission/sites/cwt/files/commissioner_mission_letters/oettinger_en.pdf.

likelihood, be on the table. In her draft report for the European Parliament's Legal Committee, MEP Julia Reda "[c]alls for the adoption of an open norm introducing flexibility in the interpretation of exceptions and limitations in certain special cases that do not conflict with the normal exploitation of the work and do not unreasonably prejudice the legitimate interests of the author or rightholder."[72] If the Reda Report is a sign of things to come, fair use European-style is already in the making.

---

[72] Draft Report on the implementation of Directive 2001/29/EC of the European Parliament and of the Council of 22 May 2001 on the harmonization of certain aspects of copyright and related rights in the information society (2014/2256(INI)), Committee on Legal Affairs, Rapporteur Julia Reda, 14 Jan. 2015.

10

The Limits of "Limitations and Exceptions" in Copyright Law

*Jerome H. Reichman**

ABSTRACT

The "designated exceptions" approach in the European Union and elsewhere becomes obsolete when faced with the needs of digital science to scrutinize and analyze all relevant research results pertinent to any scientific inquiry. Even the fair use exception rooted in U.S. law, while more agile on a case by case approach, is challenged by the scientific communities' need to reproduce and analyze all available material relevant to any given research project and by the ability of automated knowledge discovery tools to do just that. A more promising model for reform is the "some rights reserved" concept of private ordering that has recently afforded scholars and scientists alternative standard deals that better serve both their private interests and those of the public at large. This article explores the possibility of legislatively encouraging authors and artists in general to consider a more nuanced set of standard legal options than the one size fits all model inherited from the eighteenth century.

≈ ≈ ≈

10.1. SOME HISTORICAL MILESTONES

There is something quaint and vaguely antiquated about the nomenclature we are asked to evaluate in regard to the future of copyright law, namely, "Limitations and Exceptions to the Exclusive Rights of Authors." It evokes the world of the printing press and related technologies, in which publishers mapped out relatively stable profit-making strategies while legislatures weighed the space in which to preserve certain public-good uses of copyrighted works against the resulting sacrifices imposed on both authors and the intermediaries on whom they depended.[1]

---

* The author wishes to thank Peter Jaszi for insightful comments on an early version of this chapter.

[1] *See, e.g.,* 1 SAM RICKETSON & JANE C. GINSBERG, INTERNATIONAL COPYRIGHT AND NEIGHBORING RIGHTS: THE BERNE CONVENTION AND BEYOND 84–134 (2d ed. 2006).

Underlying an erratic regulatory process, in which the public-interest side usually lagged well behind the proprietary drivers of legislation, one nonetheless discerned a comforting vision of established business models that could reliably muddle on regardless of the gamesmanship at the margins.

In that not too distant past, limitations and exceptions sometimes played a major role in designing both domestic and international copyright laws, even if that role seldom delivered optimal results.[2] Since the very earliest period, for example, the private use exception recognized in most Continental copyright laws helped to free academic and scientific researchers from onerous legal constraints otherwise imposed by the authors' exclusive reproduction right, at least until the advent of photocopying machines.[3] The fair use standard, codified in United States copyright law since 1976,[4] widened the scope of this liberating tool and implemented it more effectively by allowing courts to provide case by case adjustments to all the exclusive rights of authors, especially for what later became known as "transformative uses."[5] A fair use exception thus lessened the need to draft and update designated exceptions in U.S. copyright law, as compared with European copyright laws,[6] although both approaches increasingly depended on the moral or express support that human rights, especially freedom of speech, has provided in recent years.[7]

Particularly dramatic examples of the potential impact of limitations and exceptions on the design of international copyright law occurred at the Stockholm Conference to revise the Berne Convention in 1967. Until then, it had not been possible to codify even the authors' exclusive reproduction right in the Berne Convention, because the Berne Union members had not agreed on limitations and

---

[2]   *See id.* §§ 13.01–13.93; Pamela Samuelson, *Justifications for Copyright Limitations and Exceptions, in* COPYRIGHT LAW IN AN AGE OF LIMITATIONS AND EXCEPTIONS (Ruth L. Okediji ed., 2017) [hereinafter Samuelson (2017)].

[3]   *See, e.g.,* J. A. L. STERLING, WORLD COPYRIGHT LAW 435, ¶ 10.03 (2d ed. 2003). For the continuing importance of a private use exception in the digital environment, see Jessica Litman, *Fetishizing Copies, in* COPYRIGHT LAW IN AN AGE OF LIMITATIONS AND EXCEPTIONS (Ruth L. Okediji ed., 2017).

[4]   17 U.S.C. § 107 (2012).

[5]   Campbell v. Acuff-Rose Music, 520 U.S. 569, 578–79 (1994); 2 PAUL GOLDSTEIN, GOLDSTEIN ON COPYRIGHT §§ 10.1.2–10.1.4 (3d ed. 2005). See most recently Justin Hughes, *Fair Use and Its Politics— at Home and Abroad, in* COPYRIGHT LAW IN AN AGE OF LIMITATIONS AND EXCEPTIONS (Ruth L. Okediji ed., 2017) [hereinafter Hughes (2017)].

[6]   *See, e.g.,* Jerome H. Reichman & Ruth L. Okediji, *When Copyright Law and Science Collide: Empowering Digitally Integrated Research Methods on a Global Scale*, 96 U. MINN. L. REV. 1362, 1376–78 (2012).

[7]   *See, e.g.,* Guido Westkamp, *The "Three-Step Test" and Copyright Limitations in Europe: European Copyright Law Between Approximation and National Decision Making*, 56 J. COPYRIGHT SOC'Y U.S.A. 1, 34–36 (2008); Paul Edward Gellar, *A German Approach to Fair Use: Test Cases for a TRIPS Criteria for Copyright Limitations*, 57 J. COPYRIGHT SOC'Y U.S.A. 553, 555–601 (2010). *See also* DAVID LANGE & JEFF POWELL, NO LAW: INTELLECTUAL PROPERTY IN THE IMAGE OF AN ABSOLUTE FIRST AMENDMENT 305–24 (2009); Lea Shaver, *The Right to Science and Culture*, 2010 WIS. L. REV. 121.

exceptions to the most basic of all the author's exclusive rights in the print media. That impasse was resolved in 1967, with the adoption of the three-step test in Article 9(2), as an outer limit to any codified exceptions in domestic laws to the reproduction right set out in Article 9(1) of the Berne Convention.[8] Few could then have predicted that this compromise solution in the name of expedience was destined to haunt the process of devising limitations and exceptions to all the exclusive rights of copyright law after the TRIPS Agreement of 1994,[9] or that it would seriously hinder access to and use of the global scientific and cultural heritage that digital networks later made readily available.[10]

The Stockholm Conference of 1967 also witnessed a major revolt by the developing country members of the Berne Union, who demanded new limitations and exceptions geared to their own cultural and economic development needs. This revolt produced a Protocol that temporarily responded to these needs, but was never ratified by the developed country members of the Berne Union.[11] That Protocol was ultimately abandoned and replaced by a set of so-called concessions to developing countries, codified in 1971,[12] that are so cumbersome and unworkable as to have almost never been implemented in practice.[13] The seeds of disaffection planted by this "triumph" of developed-country intransigence still undermine the prospects for copyright reform today, while motivating some leading developing countries to strike out on their own.

As late as the 1990s, efforts to adopt a multilateral regime to protect transmissions of copyrighted works over the Internet were stymied by the need to address the role of limitations and exceptions in a manner acceptable to all the relevant

---

[8] Berne Convention for the Protection of Literary and Artistic Works, arts. 9(1) and (2), Sept. 9, 1886, 828 U.N.T.S. 221 [hereinafter RBC 1967] (as revised at Stockholm on July 14, 1967) (not ratified); *see* Berne Convention for the Protection of Literary and Artistic Works, arts. 9(1) and (2), Sept. 9, 1886, 1161 U.N.T.S. 61 [hereinafter RBC 1971] (as last revised July 24, 1971); RICKETSON & GINSBURG, *supra* note 1, § 3.58.

[9] Agreement on Trade-Related Aspects of Intellectual Property Rights, arts. 13, 31, Apr. 15, 1994, 108 Stat. 4809, 1869 U.N.T.S. 299 [hereinafter TRIPS Agreement]. *See also* WIPO Copyright Treaty, art. 10, Dec. 20, 1996, 112 Stat. 2860, 2186 U.N.T.S. 152 [hereinafter WCT 1996] and Diplomatic Conference on Certain Copyright and Neighboring Rights Questions, Dec. 2–20, 1996, Agreed Statements Concerning the WIPO Copyright Treaty, WIPO Doc. CRNR/DC/96 (Dec. 20, 1996) [hereinafter WCT Agreed Statements], *available at* www.wipo.int/treaties/en/ip/wct/statements.html.

[10] *See, e.g.*, Reichman & Okediji, *supra* note 6, at 1475; Christophe Geiger, *Promoting Creativity through Copyright Limitations: Reflections on the Concept of Exclusivity in Copyright Law*, 12 VAND. J. ENT. TECH. L. 515, 518–24 (2010). *But see* Martin Senftleben, *Bridging the Differences Between Copyright's Legal Traditions – The Emerging EC Fair Use Doctrine*, 57 J. COPYRIGHT SOC'Y U.S.A. 521, 524–27 (2010).

[11] *See generally* RICKETSON & GINSBURG, *supra* note 1, §§ 3.64, 3.66.

[12] *See* RBC 1971, *supra* note 8, at Appendix, art. 1.

[13] Ruth L. Okediji, *Sustainable Access to Copyrighted Digital Information Works in Developing Countries*, *in* INTERNATIONAL PUBLIC GOODS AND TRANSFER OF TECHNOLOGY UNDER A GLOBALIZED INTELLECTUAL PROPERTY REGIME 142–87 (K. E. Maskus & J. H. Reichman eds., 2005).

stakeholders. Only when the full range of permitted uses under existing domestic and international copyright laws, including the fair use exception in United States law, was made formally available to all signatory countries[14] did it become possible to codify an agreement that obliged these same countries to respect the electronic fences destined to surround copyrighted works transmitted online under the WIPO Copyright Treaty (WCT) of 1996.[15] Given this historic compromise at the international level, however, few then predicted that both the governments of the United States and the European Union, while pretending to implement the WCT, would virtually obliterate all the preexisting limitations and exceptions in the online universe that the negotiators in Geneva had taken such pains to preserve.[16]

In retrospect, the Digital Millennium Copyright Act in the United States and the Directive on the Information Society in the European Union were collectively watershed events that downgraded the importance of limitations and exceptions in their respective copyright laws.[17] Technically, the dominant rule in Europe had become the three-step test, with its "exceptions should be narrowly construed" judicial mantra, and its built-in triple "yes" requirement that shrank the space in which positivist courts could apply any codified limitation or exception that might otherwise survive.[18]

The fair use standard in the United States did nonetheless continue to operate outside digital fences, and it was especially successful in preserving space for the use of search engines.[19] But these very successes obscured the extent to which

---

[14] WCT 1996, *supra* note 9, art. 10 and Agreed Statement.

[15] *Id.* arts. 11–12; *See, e.g.,* Reichman & Okediji, *supra* note 6, at 1369; Jerome H. Reichman, Graeme Dinwoodie & Pamela Samuelson, *A Reverse Notice and Takedown Regime to Enable Public Interest Uses of Technically Protected Copyrighted Works,* 22 BERKELEY TECH. L.J. 981, 983–85 (2007) [hereinafter Reichman et al. 2007].

[16] *See* Digital Millennium Copyright Act, 17 U.S.C. §§ 1201–1205 (2012); Council Directive 2001/29, 2001 O.J. (L 167) 10, 16 (EC) [hereinafter InfoSoc Directive]; Reichman & Okediji, *supra* note 6, at 1416–17. *See also* Niva Elkin-Koren, *Copyright in a Digital Ecosystem: A User Rights Approach, in* COPYRIGHT LAW IN AN AGE OF LIMITATIONS AND EXCEPTIONS (Ruth L. Okediji ed., 2017) [hereinafter Elkin-Koren 2017].

[17] *See supra* notes 14–16; P. BERNT HUGENHOLTZ & RUTH L. OKEDIJI, CONCEIVING AN INTERNATIONAL INSTRUMENT ON LIMITATIONS AND EXCEPTIONS TO COPYRIGHT 7 (2008), *available at* www.soros .org/sites/default/files/copyright_20080506.pdf.

[18] Infosoc Directive, *supra* note 16, art. 5; Christophe Geiger, Reto Hilty, Jonathan Griffiths & Uma Suthersanen, *Declaration: A Balanced Interpretation of the "Three-Step Test" in Copyright Law,* 39 INT'L REV. INTELL. PROP. & COMPETITION L. 707, 708 (2008) [hereinafter Max Planck Declaration on the Three-Step Test]. *But see* Senftleben, *supra* note 10.

[19] *See* Perfect 10, Inc. v. Amazon.com, Inc., 508 F.3d 1146, 1163–67 (9th Cir. 2007) (finding the use of thumbnail images to be a highly transformative); Kelly v. Arriba Soft Corp., 336 F.3d 811 (9th Cir. 2003) (holding the use of thumbnail images in search engines as fair use); *see also* A.V. v. IParadigms, L.L.C., 562 F.3d 630, 638–40 (4th Cir. 2009) (finding fair use for archival copies of student papers stored in digital form to help detect and prevent plagiarism); Field v. Google Inc., 412 F. Supp. 2d 1106, 1118 (D. Nev. 2006). More recent cases have preserved the idea of fair use and transformative use when searching through and providing "snippets" of digitized books. *See generally* Authors Guild,

the digital universe as a whole now responded to a different legal logic, rooted in a notice and takedown regime rather than codified limitations and exceptions in copyright law as such.[20] In this environment, it was the relatively stable set of business models and institutional practices still rooted in the print media and its technical limitations that conferred a patina of familiar continuity on the everyday economics of copyright law.

If we now fast forward to the twenty-first century, we see that the digital revolution has in fact upended both the business models and the institutional practices that copyright law had previously sustained.[21] As that old world recedes before our eyes under the onslaught of new technological platforms for creating and distributing cultural artifacts, publishing intermediaries push legislatures to defend their interests by ever more restrictive measures, now typically negotiated in secret.[22] In response, adversely affected user communities devise new ways to circumvent these same measures, or to defeat them by means of private ordering,[23] mass-digitization projects,[24] and increasingly, the distribution of artistic outputs directly from creators to users.[25]

In this new environment, the ever more restrictive copyright protection that literary and artistic works automatically attract in WTO member countries[26] often seems

---

Inc. v. Hathitrust, 755 F.3d 87 (2d Cir. 2014); Authors Guild, Inc. v. Google Inc., 954 F. Supp. 2d 282 (S.D.N.Y. 2013) [hereinafter Authors Guild Cases].

[20] 17 U.S.C. § 512 (2006); Reichman et al., *supra* note 15, at 986; Dan L. Burk, *Anticircumvention Misuse*, 50 U.C.L.A. L. REV. 1095, 1099–102 (2003).

[21] *See, e.g.*, Michael A. Carrier, *Copyright and Innovation: The Untold Story*, 2012 WIS. L. REV. 891, 894–97, *available at* http://ssrn.com/abstract=2099876. *See also* JAMES BOYLE, THE PUBLIC DOMAIN: ENCLOSING THE COMMONS OF THE MIND (2008).

[22] *See* Anti-Counterfeiting Trade Agreement, Dec. 3, 2010, *opened for signature* Mar. 1, 2011 [hereinafter ACTA], *available at* www.ustr.gov/webfm_send/2417 (last accessed Sept. 16, 2014); TRIPS Agreement, *supra* note 9; Patrick B. Fazzone, *The Trans-Pacific Partnership – Towards a Free Trade Agreement of Asia-Pacific?* 43 GEO. J. INT'L L. 695 (2012) (discussing the proposed Trans-Pacific Strategic Economic Partnership Agreement and predecessor agreements); Margot Kaminski, *The Capture of International Intellectual Property Law Through the U.S. Trade Regime*, 87 S. CAL. L. REV. 977, 985–90 (2014).

[23] *About the Licenses*, CREATIVE COMMONS, *available at* https://creativecommons.org/licenses/; *see also* Paul W. Jeffreys, *The Developing Concept of e-Research*, in WORLD WIDE RESEARCH: RESHAPING THE SCIENCES AND HUMANITIES 51, 51–2 (W. H. Dutton & P. W. Jeffreys eds., 2010) (noting that cooperation between research groups is necessary to perform complex research and analysis, and describing the pooling of "computational resources and research skills"); Jorge L. Contreras, *Data Sharing, Latency Variables, and Science Commons*, 25 BERKELEY TECH. L.J. 1601 (2011).

[24] *See* Authors Guild Cases, *supra* note 19.

[25] *See, e.g.*, Paul Thompson, *Radiohead's In Rainbows Successes Revealed*, PITCHFORK (Oct. 15, 2008, 12:30 PM EDT), *available at* http://pitchfork.com/news/33749-radioheads-in-rainbows-successes-revealed/ (discussing the success of the band's effort to license digital rights to its new album directly to consumers through the band's web store).

[26] TRIPS Agreement, *supra* note 9, art. 9.1.

more of a nuisance than a benefit even to many authors and artists for whom the system was originally devised. The limitations and exceptions of copyright law, largely excluded by domestic legislative fiat from the digital universe in developed countries,[27] become increasingly less relevant in practice, even if the fair use standard in the United States still retains a certain vitality worth emphasizing.[28] Meanwhile, the value, role, and tactics of the publishing intermediaries that continue to drive this regulatory frenzy are questioned as never before,[29] and direct engagement between creators and their audience, without the intervention of these same intermediaries, has begun to flourish.[30]

10.2. OBSOLESCENT OR MERELY INADEQUATE LEGAL TOOLS?

As the older, more established business models supported by copyright laws teeter, there is as yet no correspondingly clear or certain vision of the new business models that should emerge, either from a public-good perspective or even as the result of commercial trial and error. Consider, for example, Professor Carrier's revealing inquiry into the failure of the music industry to respond sensibly to the challenges of digital technology.[31] Again and again, farsighted tech-savvy experts proposed novel ways to exploit digital technologies for the creation and profitable diffusion of recorded musical works, only to be overruled by higher-level executives determined to bend the public appetite for facilitated access under a wider range of artistic options to their established business strategies. The sorry state of that industry today attests to the collective lack of business acumen and judgment thus displayed. Nevertheless, the novel forms of digital delivery that continue to emerge have so far not resulted in any detectable diminution in the supply of music available to the public.[32] Meanwhile, apart from the role of fair use in validating the operations of

[27] *See supra* notes 16–21 and accompanying text.
[28] *See* Cambridge Univ. Press v. Patton, 769 F.3d 1232, 1237–38 (11th Cir. 2014); *see also* Authors Guild cases, *supra* note 19.
[29] Contreras, *supra* note 23, at 1652–57; Robert Terry & Robert Kiley, *Open Access to the Research Literature: A Funder's Perspective, in* OPEN ACCESS: KEY STRATEGIC, TECHNICAL AND ECONOMIC ASPECTS 101, 101–03 (Neil Jacobs ed., Chandos Publishing 2006). *See generally* Reichman & Okediji, *supra* note 6; DANIEL J. GERVAIS, COLLECTIVE MANAGEMENT OF COPYRIGHT AND RELATED RIGHTS (2d ed., Kluwer Law International 2010).
[30] *See* Joel Waldfogel, Copyright Protection, Technological Change, and the Quality of New Products: Evidence from Recorded Music Since Napster (Working Paper 17503, National Bureau of Economic Research, 2011), *available at* http://nber.org/papers/w17503; *see also* Thompson, *supra* note 25.
[31] *See* Carrier, *supra* note 21, at 925–36 (discussing the various ways in which the record labels, when faced with the "innovators dilemma," failed to adapt to new technology or even heed the warnings of some of their own executives).
[32] *See, e.g.,* Waldfogel, *supra* note 30.

search engines generally,[33] it is hard to evaluate the role that limitations and exceptions to exclusive rights may yet have to play, if any, in enabling authors to connect directly with potential purchasers without the aid of traditional intermediaries.[34]

An intriguing new example is the casebook that Professors Boyle and Jenkins have prepared for the introductory course on "Intellectual Property Law," as taught at most law schools in the United States.[35] This fully digitized set of materials can be updated instantly, disaggregated, or recombined at will, and it is freely available online at barely more than the marginal cost of distribution. Alternatively, it can be acquired in book format from Amazon at a cost of $24, most of which is kept by the authors. Query what role limitations and exceptions to copyright law, geared to pre-existing business models, will continue to play if textbook publishing becomes the product of a direct discourse between authors, teachers, and governments without further dependence on either publishing intermediaries or the business models for which those legal measures were largely devised.

To see just how far this process of creative destruction can be carried, in relation to any meaningful discussion of limitations and exceptions in copyright law, one has only to look at how organized scientific research has responded to the challenges and opportunities of Big Data, and the extent to which that response has progressively liberated publicly funded researchers from some of the tentacles of copyright laws.[36] In a recent article, Ruth L. Okediji and I surveyed all the national, regional, and multilateral restrictions applicable to published scientific research results in the name of copyright law and related rights.[37] Among other things, this task required us to analyze database protection laws in addition to copyright laws, plus all the digital locks envisioned at the multilateral level, but diversely implemented in national and regional laws since the WCT of 1996.[38] To complete the picture, one should also consider claims that developing countries are asserting to own and control all data derived from uses and applications of genetic resources taken from their territories without Prior Informed Consent and Access and Benefit-Sharing Agreements under the Nagoya Protocol to the Convention on Biological Diversity.[39] Having compiled this massive array of

---

[33] See Authors Guild Cases, *supra* note 19. *But see* Cambridge v. Patton, 769 F.3d at 1237–38 (11th Cir. 2014) (focusing more on market harm where transformative use may not be present).

[34] *Cf.* Sony Corp. of Am. v. Universal City Studios, Inc., 464 U.S. 417, 454–56 (1984) (finding that Betamax producers did not infringe on the rights of television producers because some private recording for later viewing could fall into the fair use exemption).

[35] JAMES BOYLE & JENNIFER JENKINS, INTELLECTUAL PROPERTY: LAW & THE INFORMATION SOCIETY – CASES & MATERIALS (Center for the Study of the Public Domain 2014) [hereinafter BOYLE & JENKINS 2014].

[36] See *supra* note 29 and accompanying text.

[37] See generally Reichman & Okediji, *supra* note 6.

[38] See *id.* at 1372–425.

[39] Convention on Biological Diversity arts. 5–8, *opened for signature* June 5, 1992, 1760 U.N.T.S. 79 [hereinafter CBD]; and Tenth Meeting of the Conference of the Parties to the Convention

proprietary legislation, we found the task of articulating an effective set of limitations and exceptions to facilitate the use of digitally integrated knowledge discovery tools that might ever be enacted into law daunting, to put it mildly.

Simply stated, the narrow "bean counting" methodology typically employed by countries adhering to the "designated exceptions" approach in the European Union and elsewhere risks being overwhelmed and discredited when faced with the needs of digital science to scrutinize and analyze all published research results pertinent to any major scientific inquiry.[40] The fair use exception in the United States has so far proved itself better equipped to defend the intermediate copying needs of digitally integrated knowledge discovery tools, at least on a case-by-case approach.[41] Even the fair use doctrine, however, will be challenged by the scientific communities' need to reproduce and analyze all available material relevant to any given research project and by the ability of automated knowledge discovery tools to do just that. Moreover, apart from the difficulties of exporting it to other countries,[42] fair use becomes subject to the uncertain implications of the three-step test in international copyright law as an outer limit on domestic copyright legislation; to the digital locks that publishers may impose on scientific works transmitted online; and to their ability to contractually override any applicable limitations and exceptions that may still apply in that context.[43]

Formidable as these obstacles may be, one must concede that efforts to address them through pro-science reforms of copyright law scored one notable success in the United Kingdom's recent enactment of a data-mining exception

on Biological Diversity, Nagoya, Japan, Oct. 18–29, 2010, Nagoya Protocol on Access to Genetic Resources and the Fair and Equitable Sharing of Benefits Arising from their Utilization (ABS) to the Convention on Biological Diversity (entered into force Oct. 12, 2014) [hereinafter Nagoya Protocol], *available at* www.cbd.int/abs/doc/protocol/nagoya-protocol-en.pdf (last accessed Mar. 16, 2015). *See generally* Jerome H. Reichman, Paul F. Uhlir & Tom Dedeurwaerdere, Governing Digitally Integrated Genetic Resources, Data, and Literature: Global Intellectual Property Strategies for a Redesigned Microbial Research commons, Part One (Cambridge University Press 2016).

[40] *See, e.g.*, Reichman & Okediji, *supra* note 6, at 1399–405.

[41] *See* Matthew Sag, *Copyright and Copy-Reliant Technology*, 103 Nw. U. L. Rev. 1607, 1607–16 (2009) (finding the fair use doctrine to be an integral part of information dissemination); *also* Author's Guild Cases, *supra* note 19; Cambridge v. Patton, 769 F.3d at 1237–38.

[42] *See* Hughes (2017), *supra* note 5; Elkin-Koren (2017), *supra* note 16 (developments in Canadian case law); *see further* below nn. 55–58 (proposed Brazilian legislation). *But see* Paul Goldstein, The Americanization of Global Copyright Norms, Frey Lecture, Duke Law School, Sept. 16, 2015 (predicting expansion of fair use beyond the six countries that now recognize that doctrine).

[43] *See* Ruth L. Okediji, *Towards an International Fair Use Doctrine*, 39 Colum. J. Transnat'l L. 75 (2000); Jerome H. Reichman & Paul F. Uhlir, *A Contractually Reconstructed Research Commons for Scientific Data in a Highly Protectionist Intellectual Property Environment*, 66 Law & Contemp. Probs. 315, 319–22, 396–413 (2003). *See also* Reichman et al., *supra* note 15.

to the exclusive rights of copyright law.[44] The Hargreaves Review[45] – spawned
by the United Kingdom government – first produced a discerning critique of a
science-hostile legal environment, and then followed it up with an ambitious set of
proposals for reform legislation, some of which were actually adopted. As a result,
a legislated exception has been enacted that directly enables the use of automated
knowledge discovery tools, without recourse to the four-step evaluations of a U.S.-
style fair use exception. Still more remarkable, publishers cannot override this
text-mining exception by contract, a precedent one hopes to see repeated many
times over in the future.[46]

However, even this well-intentioned legislative endeavor ran up against the digital fences and digital locks, rooted in the WCT of 1996, which the U.K. authorities
declined to penetrate.[47] In this respect, the U.K. law still resembles its U.S. counterpart,
in the sense that a would-be user must gain lawful access to the electronically fenced
scientific publications before that user can invoke the data-mining exception to search
the contents of all the works stored behind the fence.[48] Under the U.K. law, however,
once a publisher allows a scientist through the digital locks, that publisher cannot arguably override by contract the scientist's right to text-mine the contents of the collection
to which he or she has gained lawful access.[49] One must still await possible scrutiny by
the European Court of Justice as to the ultimate legal viability of these reforms, which
to some extent deviate from the list of permissible reforms set out in the European
Commission's Infosoc Directive of 2001.[50]

On still another front, one may hope that some European Community courts might
be inclined to apply the three-step test more flexibly in given cases affecting scientific
research, either in response to the Max Planck Institute's Declaration on the Three-Step
Test of 2012, or in response to appeals sounding in fundamental human rights,[51] or

---

[44] *See* The Copyright and Rights in Performances (Research, Education, Libraries, and Archives)
Regulations 2014, S.I. 2014/1372, *available at* www.legislation.gov.uk/uksi/2014/1372/contents/made
(last accessed Feb. 21, 2014) (amending the Copyright, Designs, and Patent Act 1988, c. 48 (U.K)).

[45] IAN HARGREAVES, DIGITAL OPPORTUNITY: A REVIEW OF INTELLECTUAL PROPERTY AND GROWTH
46–47 (2011) [hereinafter HARGREAVES REVIEW].

[46] *See* Copyright (Research, Education, Libraries, and Archives) Regulations 2014, *supra* note 43, at 49A;
James Boyle, *(When) Is Copyright Reform Possible?*, *in* COPYRIGHT LAW IN AN AGE OF LIMITATIONS
AND EXCEPTIONS (Ruth L. Okediji ed., 2017), *available at* www.thepublicdomain.org/2015/01/14/
is-copyright-reform-possible.

[47] *See* Copyright (Research, Education, Libraries, and Archives) Regulations 2014, *supra* note 44,
at 49A.

[48] *Compare* Copyright (Research, Education, Libraries, and Archives) Regulations 2014, *supra* note 44,
with 17 U.S.C. § 1201 (2006), *supra* note 16. *See* Reichman et al., *supra* note 15.

[49] That, at least, seems to be the intention of the drafters; *see* Boyle, *supra* note 46.

[50] *See* Infosoc Directive, *supra* note 16, art. 5, which applies the three-step test to all limitations and
exceptions in the domestic copyright laws of the European Union.

[51] *See* Max Planck Declaration on the Three-Step Test, *supra* note 18; BGH, Mar. 11, 1993, 1994 GRUR
206 and 191, 1993 ZUM 534 and 537; OLG Munich, Mar. 26, 1998, 1998 ZUM 417. *See also* Laurence

to some combination of these same sources of law.[52] The Max Planck Institute's Declaration would, in particular, nudge the three-step test closer to a European version of fair use, in which each step would be examined and weighed separately, as part of an overall evaluation of the steps, and a "yes" answer to each prong of the test would no longer be required.[53] Whether the positivist leanings of civil law courts can accommodate these proposed flexibilities remains to be seen.[54]

Meanwhile, Brazil's long pending copyright reforms have aggressively tackled the challenge of reconciling U.S.-style fair use with the European Community's predilection for the three-step test.[55] In so doing, Brazil's proposed legislation, if enacted, could become the first copyright law to implement the more flexible approach to the three-step test proposed by the Max Planck Institute's Declaration of 2012. It would also provide a set of interpretative tools that could bridge the divide between the "fair use" and the "designated exception" approaches generally.[56] The proposed reforms of Brazilian copyright law could thus take a major step toward achieving at least an experimental synthesis of the different approaches that seems well worth testing in practice.

Moreover, the pending Brazilian reforms would go well beyond "fair use" in a concerted effort to exploit the opportunities for a digitally interconnected universe of creators and users.[57] Besides emphasizing the idea-expression dichotomy, along with the flexible fair-use regime described above, these proposals envision:

- An expanded private use exception;
- A regime supporting interoperability and portability;
- Broad exceptions for libraries, science, and education;
- Explicit measures to prohibit the privatization of public domain works;
- A liability rule for orphan works;
- A regime of international exhaustion;
- Express measures prohibiting Technical Protection Measures from overriding uses permitted by law;
- Regulatory measures enabling peer-to-peer file sharing in the public interest;
- And measures limiting the liability of internet service providers.[58]

Helfer, *The New Innovation Frontier? Intellectual Property and the European Court of Human Rights*, 49 HARV. INT'L. L.J. 1–52 (2008).

[52] *See* Max Planck Instit., Draft Declaration on the Principal Uses of Copyright (2015) (unpublished pending declaration on copyright law) (on file with the author).

[53] Max Planck Declaration on the Three-Step Test, *supra* note 18.

[54] *See* Reichman & Okediji, *supra* note 6, at 1409–11.

[55] Pedro Paranaguá, Brazil's Copyright Law Reform – Tropicalia 3.0? 19–20 (2014) (unpublished SJD thesis, Duke University School of Law) (on file with the Goodson Law Library, Duke Law School).

[56] *See* Reichman & Okediji, *supra* note 6, 1450–57.

[57] *See* Paranaguá, *supra* note 55.

[58] *See generally id.*

If these proposals – expressly designated as "users' rights"[59] – were eventually enacted into law, Brazil's reforms would provide an example of how to design a more digital-friendly copyright regime of interest to both developed and developing countries. At the moment, however, these proposals are still languishing after more than ten years of discussion, and the growing power of the publishers' lobby may ensure that the reform bill is never passed in the end. Whether this well-documented set of proposals could influence reforms elsewhere, even if never enacted into Brazilian law, remains to be seen and partly depends on the ability of law professors to spread the word.

That uncertainty raises a core question about the viability of limitations and exceptions in copyright law generally, assuming that one remains persuaded of their continued vitality.[60] Even in the best of times, designated exceptions tend to lag well behind the needs of users, in part because they take time to enact, and mainly because there is usually no powerful interest group with the political clout and financial resources to support their adoption. At present, big financial interests – which Professor Thomas Cottier has labeled a "global cartel"[61] – dictate the mindless expansion of further restrictions on access to and use of the copyrighted culture, backed up by ever more intrusive enforcement machinery and increasingly supplemented by criminal sanctions.[62] The capacity to mount effective legislative action favoring limitations and exceptions in this climate remains doubtful, notwithstanding the recent reforms enabled by enlightened government action in the United Kingdom. On the contrary, the multimillion-dollar circus needed to produce the recent treaty on exceptions in copyright laws for the visually impaired dramatically illustrates the obstacles that any more ambitious reform effort would have to overcome.[63]

---

[59] For an eloquent elaboration and defense of the "users' rights" rhetoric, *see* Elkin-Koren (2017), *supra* note 16.

[60] For a strong case in that regard, *see* Samuelson (2017), *supra* note 2. *See also* Goldstein, Frey Lecture (2015), *supra* note 42.

[61] Remarks of Prof. Thomas Cottier, World Trade Institute, University of Bern, at the International Center for Trade and Sustainable Development's (ICTSD) Conference on Trips at 20 and Beyond (Geneva, Switzerland, Oct. 30–31, 2014).

[62] *See, e.g.,* TRIPS Agreement, *supra* note 9, arts. 41–61; Fazzone, *supra* note 22; Kaminski, *An Overview and the Evolution of the Anti-Counterfeiting Trade Agreement* (PIJIP Research Paper no. 17. American University Washington College of Law, Washington, DC, 2011); Kaminski, *supra* note 22, at 985–90.

[63] *See* WIPO, *Marrakesh Treaty to Facilitate Access to Published Works for Persons Who Are Blind, Visually Impaired, or Otherwise Print Disabled,* art. 3, WIPO Doc. VIP/DC/8 Rev. (July 31, 2013) [hereinafter *Marrakesh Treaty*]; Press Release, WIPO, Historic Treaty Adopted, Boosts Access to Books for Visually Impaired Persons Worldwide, WIPO Doc. PR/2013/741 (June 27, 2013). *See also* Marketa Trimble, *The Marrakesh Puzzle,* 45 I.I.C. 768 (2014). However, some see the adoption of this treaty as a harbinger of more exceptions in the future. *See, e.g.,* Goldstein, Frey Lecture (2015), *supra* note 42.

Short of a wholesale revision "to link creators and users in a digital age" (in the manner of the Brazilian proposals),[64] any piecemeal reform undertaking could end in another set of narrow compromises that might actually make matters worse, especially if it reinforced obsolete business models. In my opinion, almost any set of designated limitations and exceptions that is not tied to a supplementary fair use regime remains intrinsically questionable, in part because a key function of that regime is to reveal and chart empirically relevant user needs over time.[65] Absent judicial or legislative acceptance of the Max Planck Institute's modified three-step test proposals,[66] one may doubt that fair use will become widely adopted in developed countries,[67] as witnessed by the inability of even the Hargreaves Review in the United Kingdom to overcome the resistance of STEM publishers to such a proposal.[68]

We should also recall that the U.S. National Academies recently sponsored a major study of this topic, with specific regard to limitations and exceptions, only to have reached a stalemate that left them with a set of issues in search of any authoritative solutions.[69] That stalemate resulted from the role of publishers on the Academies' Advisory Board, who rejected any serious reform proposals that might otherwise have emerged from a very expensive undertaking. Yet, without the *bene placito* of publishers, there is little hope of enacting any such reforms in the first place.[70]

One may nonetheless logically enquire about the future role that developing countries might play in rescuing limitations and exceptions from incipient obsolescence.[71] There is the Brazilian example on the table, as reviewed earlier,[72] and those proposals may already have influenced reforms underway in South Africa.[73] Moreover, the African delegations that were largely responsible for the successful

---

[64] *See* Paranaguá, *supra* note 55.

[65] *Accord* Hughes (2017), *supra* note 5.

[66] Max Planck Institute's Declaration on the Three-Step Test, *supra* note 18.

[67] For evidence of a more positive trend, see Elkin-Koren (2017), *supra* note 16; *see also* Hughes (2017), *supra* note 5.

[68] *See* HARGREAVES REVIEW, *supra* note 45.

[69] *See* NATIONAL ACADEMIES' BOARD ON SCIENCE, TECHNOLOGY, AND ECONOMIC POLICY, COPYRIGHT IN THE DIGITAL ERA: BUILDING EVIDENCE FOR POLICY 1–6 (Nat. Acad. Press 2014).

[70] For a more optimistic view, based on the National Academies' contribution to patent law reform, see BOYLE & JENKINS 2014, *supra* note 35.

[71] *See generally* Jerome H. Reichman, *Intellectual Property in the Twenty-First Century: Will the Developing Countries Lead or Follow?*, 46 HOUS. L. REV. 1115 (2009).

[72] *See supra* notes 55–57 and accompanying text.

[73] *See* Draft National Policy on Intellectual Property, 2013 (South Africa), Government Gazette 36816, Sept. 4, 2013, *available at* www.gov.za/documents/National-Policy-Intellectual-Property-draft; Tobias Schonwetter, Yousuf A. Vawda, Caroline Ncube, Andrew Rens, Brook K. Baker, Andre Louw, Bernard Maister & Bram de Jonge, Comments, Draft National Policy on Intellectual Property (IP) of South Africa, Oct. 17, 2013 (Joint Submission by Academics), at 13–16 (stressing need for more adequate exceptions for educational materials and a ban on contractual overrides). *See also* ACCESS TO KNOWLEDGE IN AFRICA: THE ROLE OF COPYRIGHT (C. Armstrong, J. de Beer, D. Kawooya, A. Prabhala & T. Schonwetter eds., 2010).

adoption of the Marrakesh Treaty on exceptions for the visually impaired also remain vigilant in pressing an agenda for limitations and exceptions at WIPO.[74] These positive developments, however, are offset by the fact that the proposed Brazilian reforms have languished on the table for ten years and may yet fail, while the African governments' legislative reform efforts in copyright law are often undermined by technical assistance emanating from the developed countries.[75] Overhanging all other initiatives are the ever-expanding national and regional Free Trade Agreements, in which Professor Cottier's alleged global cartel[76] attempts to circumscribe everyone else's access to the digitally available cultural heritage in secret negotiations, backed by massive campaign contributions to relevant legislators.[77]

10.3. HEADING FOR THE EXIT?

Meanwhile, the scientific community – faced with thickets of legal obstacles to reuse of published research results as well as to the use of automated knowledge discovery tools[78]– has been actively engaged in "contractually constructing [its own] research commons in a highly protectionist intellectual property environment," as Paul Uhlir and I advocated in 2003.[79] Besides a growing open-access movement that has enveloped published scientific research in the last decades,[80] there were groundbreaking decisions by certain federal agencies and private foundations, especially the National Institutes of Health in the United States and the Wellcome Trust in the United Kingdom, to mandate the pooling of government-funded research results in the human genome project and related endeavors.[81] Since then, the scientific

---

[74] *See, e.g., Marrakesh Treaty, supra* note 63.

[75] *See, e.g.,* Ana Santos, Music as an Instrument of Economic Development – Lessons from the African Experience (2015) (unpublished SJD thesis, Duke University School of Law) (on file with author).

[76] Cottier, Remarks, *supra* note 61.

[77] *Cf.* Kaminski, *The Capture of International Intellectual Property Law, supra* note 22, at 1036–37 (discussing the capture of the USTR in part due to Congress's inclusion of special interest groups as advisors and exclusion of the public).

[78] Reichman & Okediji, *supra* note 6, at 1368–70.

[79] Reichman & Uhlir, *supra* note 43.

[80] *See* REICHMAN ET AL., *supra* note 39, chapter 7 (citing authorities).

[81] *See, e.g.,* Summary of Principles Agreed at the First International Strategy Meeting on the Human Genome Sequencing, Bermuda, Feb. 25–28, 1996 [hereinafter Bermuda Principles (1996)], *available at* http://web.ornl.gov/sci/techresources/Human_Genome/research/bermuda.shtml#1 (as reported by HUGO); Summary of the Report of the Second International Strategy Meeting on Human Genome Sequencing, Bermuda, Feb. 27–Mar. 2, 1977 (as reported by HUGO) [hereinafter Bermuda Principles (1997)]; The Wellcome Trust, Sharing Data from Large-Scale Biological Research Projects: A System of Tripartite Responsibility, report of a meeting organized by the Wellcome Trust, Ft. Lauderdale. Florida, 14–15 Jan. 2003 [hereinafter Ft. Lauderdale Principles (2003)], *available at*

community has experimented with an ever growing number of both mandatory and voluntary data-pooling initiatives that result either in semicommons frameworks open to qualified participants working on related problems or in fully open-access research commons, in which data and information are made available to the world at large.[82]

Our forthcoming book on *Governing Digitally Integrated Genetic Resources, Data, and Literature*[83] tracks and examines some important exemplars of this trend. With specific regard to the voluntary formation of hypothesis-driven semicommons, we have identified one particular format, on the cutting edge of today's knowledge commons movement,[84] in which data repositories and custom-made software tools are merged together in a single knowledge hub subject to dynamic governance features, unlike anything we are accustomed to seeing in large-scale scientific endeavors. Paul Uhlir has called these novel sharing ventures "Open Knowledge Environments" (OKEs),[85] and we have described these novel and ambitious models of collaborative research in the following terms:

> Such initiatives would move beyond providing passive, research-supporting infrastructure to spawning dynamic research-generating platforms. This transformation occurs when a given thematic community or subcommunity organizes its upstream research assets, its technical and computational research tools, and its hypothesis-driven research goals in such a way that it successfully generates a set of self-sustaining activities, supported by a constantly evolving infrastructure that transcends the very notion of "repository" or "portal" to become an autonomous knowledge hub.

> The empirical evidence suggests that initiatives along these lines are already emerging in the life sciences, including microbiology. A small but growing number of sharing initiatives have moved beyond the familiar data-pooling arrangements. These undertakings combine reference data with hypothesis-driven data; they can also integrate both materials and even open literature – "gray" or peer reviewed – into their digitized infrastructure. Such resources, in turn, serve the entire thematic community or subcommunity as a whole, which necessitates a more formal governance structure to manage both the research assets that constitute its infrastructure and the research activities that the community supports and generates.[86]

---

www.genome.gov/pages/research/wellcomereporto303.pdf. *See most recently* Exec. Order No. 13,642, 2 C.F.R. 335 (2013) (increasing access to the results of federally funded scientific research).

[82] For empirical evidence, see also REICHMAN ET AL., *supra* note 39, chapter 8.

[83] REICHMAN ET AL., *supra* note 39.

[84] *See generally* BRETT M. FRISCHMANN, MICHAEL J. MADISON & KATHERINE J. STRANDBURG, GOVERNING THE KNOWLEDGE COMMONS (2014); *see also* REICHMAN ET AL., *supra* note 39, chapters 8–10.

[85] *See* REICHMAN ET AL., *supra* note 39, chapter 8, section III.

[86] *Id.*

We examine five different examples of incipient OKEs on the frontiers of microbiology: namely, the Genomic Standards Consortium; the Community Cyberinfrastructure for Advanced Marine Microbial Ecology Research and Analysis (CAMERA); the System Biology Knowledge Base at the U.S. Department of Energy; and the Sloan Foundation's Program on Microbiology of the Built Environment (MoBE).[87] Since then I have become an external adviser to another such initiative, the MICRO-B3 Project of the Max Planck Institute for Marine Biology at the University of Bremen, Germany, which exceeds, in both breadth and potential discoveries, any of the projects reviewed in our book.[88]

Meanwhile, ever more ambitious data-pooling initiatives are underway at the international level. For example, the Group on Earth Observations has taken steps to pool and coordinate the disparate national GPS systems into an integrated toolbox for addressing weather related disasters and other public-interest issues.[89] The National Science Foundation has sponsored the Belmont Forum Project, which is seeking to unite the science-funding agencies of some twenty-three countries in an effort to construct a Global E-Infrastructure for Climate Change Research Results.[90] Jorge Contreras and I, as members of the U.S. delegation working on this project, have written about the different models that research funders can adopt when they impose common default rules on grantees and common metadata parameters, in order to link an array of national research data repositories in one distributed knowledge hub.[91]

For present purposes, the point is that copyright and database protection laws pose such a threat to digitally integrated research methods that the scientific community's medium- and long-term collective responses necessarily dwarf the role of even the most enlightened set of limitations and exceptions likely to emerge from any foreseeable legislative initiatives, including those spawned by the Hargreaves Review.[92] Here, instead, the scientific community as a whole, as well as a growing number of research subcommunities, have begun to organize and implement their own open-access policies, along with the concerted efforts of funders to support and

---

[87] *Id.*, chapter 8, section III.A.

[88] *See, e.g., Homepage,* THE MICRO B3 PROJECT, *available at* www.microb3.eu/ (last accessed Mar. 18, 2015).

[89] REICHMAN ET AL., *supra* note 39, chapter 9, section II.B.3

[90] BELMONT FORUM: E-INFRASTRUCTURE AND DATA MANAGEMENT COLLABORATIVE RESEARCH ACTION–, STEERING COMMITTEE MEETING 5, FULL WORKSHOP REPORT (May 2015), *available at* www.bfe-inf .org/type-document/final-report. *See also* Belmont Forum Steering Committee, A Place to Stand: e-Infrastructures and Data Management for Global Change Research (June 2015).

[91] Jorge L. Contreras & Jerome H. Reichman, *Sharing by Design: Data and Decentralized Commons,* 350 SCIENCE 1312 (2015).

[92] *See supra* notes 45–46 and accompanying text.

eventually lead research and data-sharing initiatives well beyond the levels anyone could have imagined only a decade ago.[93]

One may ask whether this sort of broad-scale, collective response to legal barriers impeding digital integration of the copyrighted culture can be replicated or adapted outside the scientific community, where the sharing principle rests on a strong normative foundation. The evidence suggests an affirmative answer to that question. We see digital libraries exploding on both sides of the Atlantic;[94] we see major universities mandating open-access publishing for their faculties and leading university presses – now including Cambridge and Yale – institutionalizing the open access principle.[95] Moreover, there are growing possibilities for any author who wishes to communicate directly with his or her potential public, without the intervention of publishing intermediaries, to make their works freely available in one form or another.

10.4. SOME PREMISES FOR REFORM

My pessimism about the limits of limitations and exceptions under present-day political and institutional constraints does not obviate the need to consider proposals for legislative reform of existing copyright laws. Given the wealth of literature already emerging on this topic,[96] I will briefly summarize a few basic premises that follow from the preceding discussion.

First, we should not deny authors and artists the means to earn a livelihood from their works in our efforts to avoid the problems that thickets of rights increasingly pose for future creativity, research, and the public at large. In the digital age,

---

[93] For details and examples, see generally REICHMAN ET AL., *supra* note 39, chapter 8.

[94] *See generally* MAURIZIO BORGHI & STAVROULA KARAPAPA, COPYRIGHT AND MASS DIGITIZATION (2013); Avraham Osterman, Digital Libraries in the Age of Mass Digitization (2012) (unpublished SJD thesis, Duke University School of Law) (on file with the Goodson Library, Duke Law School).

[95] *See* Policy Recommendations for Open Access to Research Data in Europe (RECODE), Seventh Framework Programme for Science and Society, Feb. 1, 2013, *available at* www.recodeproject-eu. *See also* Eric Priest, *Copyright and the Harvard Open Access Mandate*, 10 Nw. J. TECH. INTELL. PROP. 377, 381–82 (2012); Alma Swan et al., Open Access Policy: Numbers, Analysis, Effectiveness (2015), Pasteur 40A Work Package 3, Report Open Access Policies, *available at* http://eprints.soton .ac.uk.3759854 (reporting a total of 663 institutional or funder open-access policies worldwide as of March 2015, over half of them mandatory).

[96] *See, e.g.,* Pamela Samuelson, *Is Copyright Reform Possible?: A Critical Evaluation of Two Major Contributions to the Copyright Reform Literature*, 126 HARV. L. REV. 740 (2013) (reviewing JASON MAZZONE, COPYFRAUD AND OTHER ABUSES OF INTELLECTUAL PROPERTY LAW (2013)); Jessica Litman, *Real Copyright Reform*, 96 IOWA L. REV. 1 (2010); Boyle, *supra* note 46; Marco Ricolfi, *The New Paradigm of Creativity and Innovation and Its Corollaries for the Law of Obligations*, *in* 1 KRITIKA: ESSAYS ON INTELLECTUAL PROPERTY 134 (2015).

nonetheless, everyone becomes potentially an author for certain purposes, and most of these unselfconscious authors lack any intent to profit from their own creations or otherwise to free-ride on those who do profit from such endeavors.[97] The default rules of a reformed copyright regime could, accordingly, be designed to accommodate the needs and interests of all authors as they evolve over time, and not just the interests of commercially motivated authors and their respective intermediaries.

By the same token, intermediaries should be paid for the value they add to the creative endeavors of authors, but copyright laws should not be designed to protect the "sacred rights" of intermediaries.[98] Sorely needed, instead, is some transnational antitrust authority to regulate concerted efforts on their behalf, which Professor Thomas Cottier has rightly deemed a global cartel.[99]

If disinterested legislators truly focused on the needs of authors in a digital age, they should be able to devise a menu of standard options from which artists and authors could choose, at different times, by entering a digital portal to be established for this purpose. Two objectives should be kept in mind. First, let us consider expanding the availability of – and knowledge about – the possibilities of standard, common-use licenses of copyrighted literary works for noncommercial purposes beyond the scientific and academic communities, where these options are already widely used. Second, let us consider developing a new range of standard, common-use licenses for copyrighted literary works expressly designed for commercial purposes that could attenuate search and transaction costs prevalent in the current system.

The first objective is hardly radical. Rather than needlessly obstructing all uses in the hope of controlling *ex ante* commercial benefits that may never materialize, a suitably framed standard deal could permit most noncommercial uses, in the manner of existing Creative Commons licenses and other private ordering initiatives.[100] In this case, however, the copyright authorities themselves would be encouraging artists and authors generally to follow the lead of academics and scientists who routinely adopt common use licenses for noncommercial uses of published research results.

The second, and more ambitious objective would deliberately establish a set of standardized, common-use licenses that could offer would-be users a menu of options to choose from when considering their commercial objectives. Such

---

[97] *Cf.* Jane C. Ginsburg, *The Role of the Author in Copyright, in* COPYRIGHT LAW IN AN AGE OF LIMITATIONS AND EXCEPTIONS (Ruth L. Okediji ed., 2017).

[98] The "most sacred form of property" goes back to the legislator who presented the first French copyright law to Parliament in 1793. Jane C. Ginsburg, *A Tale of Two Copyrights: Literary Property in Revolutionary France and America*, 64 TUL. L. REV. 991, 1007 (1990).

[99] Cottier, Remarks, *supra* note 61.

[100] *See, e.g.*, RECODE, *supra* note 95; REICHMAN ET AL., *supra* note 39, chapters 7–8.

licenses would implement a standardized liability rule, that is, a "take and pay" rule, that would require payment of the authors' predetermined, set royalties for specified uses to a collection society established for this purpose. Those standard deals offering built-in liability rules would thus avoid "free riding," as properly redefined, while still ensuring that authors obtained a fair share of any eventual commercial uses that actually occurred.[101] Other commercial uses not pre-authorized under the standard options would remain subject to case-by-case, bargained-for permissions.

In either cases of noncommercial or commercial uses, the proposed standard-form models could also require attribution while restricting the making of derivative works except on the conditions specified in the common use licenses.[102] Even a termination clause, with safeguards for reliance parties, could be built into these or other standard deals in order to enable authors to opt out of any selected, open-access platform if and when changing circumstances so required, with appropriate notice and protection for reliance parties. What the proposed standard deals would not do, unless expressly selected by any given author, is to needlessly restrict all uses without permission in a legal straightjacket that most of today's authors do not need or want.

If proposals to legislatively establish a standard set of copyright licenses that authors could opt into or out of from the outset sounds radical, at least from a domestic copyright law perspective, it has become a regular feature of at least two international treaties, not to mention the practices generated by private ordering. Consider in this light the Standard Material Transfer Agreements (SMTAs) that facilitate access to genetic resources for research and applications under the United Nations' Food and Agricultural Organization's (FAO) International Treaty on Plant Genetic Resources for Food and Agriculture of 2001[103] and the World Health Organization's (WHO) Pandemic Influenza Framework Agreement of 2014.[104] These SMTAs mediate tensions between private intellectual property rights rooted in the TRIPS Agreement of 1994 and sovereign territorial rights in plant, animal, and microbial genetic resources emanating from provider

---

[101] *Cf.* Jerome Reichman, *Of Green Tulips and Legal Kudzu: Repackaging Rights in Subpatentable Innovation*, 53 VAND. L. REV. 1743, 1776–86 (2000).

[102] *Cf.* Creative Commons License: CC BY-ND. *See About The Licenses*, www.creativecommons.org/licenses (last visited Aug. 6, 2016).

[103] International Treaty on Plant Genetic Resources for Food and Agriculture, *opened for signature* Nov. 3, 2001, 2400 U.N.T.S. 303 (entered into force June 29, 2004) [hereinafter ITPGRFA].

[104] World Health Organization (WHO), *Pandemic Influenza Preparedness Framework for the Sharing of the Influenza Viruses and Access to Vaccines and Other Benefits*, World Health Assembly Res. WHA645 (May 24, 2011); *see also* Marie Wilke, *The World Health Organization's Pandemic Influenza Preparedness Framework as a Public Health Resources Pool*, in COMMON POOLS OF GENETIC

countries under the Convention on Biological Diversity of 1992, as reinforced by the Nagoya Protocol to that Convention of 2010.[105] As elsewhere explained at length, the SMTAs in this international context seek to ensure public stakeholders that they will receive a fair share of the financial returns from private investments in commercial applications of genetic resources originating from provider countries under standardized terms and conditions that avoid costly and burdensome case-by-case negotiations.[106]

For present purposes, however, the principle obstacle to such an approach is that the full bundle of rights conferred by copyright laws arise automatically, without formalities of any kind, which are forbidden by the Berne Convention.[107] Even if the United States copyright law were to offer authors a menu of standard options from which they could choose, only authors who voluntarily registered their copyrights with the Copyright Office would necessarily become exposed to these options,[108] which they could accept or reject.[109] Most of the "authors" – accidental or otherwise – for whom the maximum existing bundle of rights remains unnecessarily broad would have little or no occasion to register because they were not expecting commercial benefits from their works. Because most authors who take the trouble to register will be in pursuit of some known or likely commercial opportunities, they would logically incline to opt for the maximalist bundle of rights, even if given a choice to do otherwise.

Under current copyright law, the bulk of accidental authors who would not need or want the full bundle of exclusive rights[110] would thus have little or no opportunity to accept a less encumbering package deal, unless they were already familiar with the Creative Commons licenses or other private ordering equivalents, as is typically the case with academics. If the objective remains nonetheless to make voluntary recourse to a more limited bundle of rights more widely available than at present, then perhaps one way to achieve it would be to design a set of diverse copyright notices from which authors could voluntarily choose to indicate the more limited or tailor-made bundles of rights they had voluntarily accepted from the menu of

---

RESOURCES: EQUITY AND INNOVATION IN INTERNATIONAL BIODIVERSITY LAW 315, 315–16 (E. C. Kamau & G. Winter eds., 2013).

[105] TRIPS Agreement, *supra* note 9, arts. 7–8; CBD, *supra* note 39; Nagoya Protocol, *supra* note 39.

[106] REICHMAN ET AL., *supra* note 39, chapter 3 ("Tightening the Regulatory Grip: From the Convention on Biological Diversity in 1992 to the Nagoya Protocol in 2010").

[107] *See* RBC 1971, *supra* note 8, art. 5(2) (forbidding mandatory formalities with any risk of technical forfeiture).

[108] *See* 17 U.S.C. §§ 408(a), 412 (2012) (making registration voluntary, not mandatory, and conferring some benefits, especially with regard to innocent infringement, for those who do register). *But see id.* § 411 (mandating registration of U.S. works for infringement actions).

[109] Mandatory reduction of the exclusive rights under RBC (1971), arts. 9-14ter would be seen as technical forfeiture under *id.* art. 5(1), (2).

[110] 17 U.S.C. §§ 106, 106A (2012).

options afforded by copyright authorities endowed with statutory authority to do so. Use of these notices would perforce remain voluntary,[111] as is the notice currently allowed by the 1976 Copyright Act.[112] Nevertheless, their very availability and use in practice could make an ever growing number of user communities familiar with – and more comfortable with – the practice of adopting tailor-made limitations of rights as a matter of course, and incline them to consider their real needs more carefully from the outset.

For example, scientists and other academic subcommunities could adopt or endorse one of several designated notice options for their members as a whole, subject to peer pressure or other stronger sanctions as the case may be. Funders and learned societies could require their grantees or members to similarly select specific package deals and to apply the relevant copyright notices to their published research results.[113] In time, many other creative communities or subcommunities whose members were both creators and users of common pool resources[114] could become familiar and comfortable with the standard package deals available at the federal level. If so, as awareness and use of the tailor-made options spread beyond the confines of existing private ordering initiatives, there would be a concurrent reduction of unlimited exclusive rights with their inherent risk of unforeseen obstacles to the use of the copyrighted culture over time.

The ready availability of these tailor-made options could also buttress authors against the publishers' own standard form licensing contracts, which tend to take all of the authors' exclusive rights that copyright law otherwise automatically confers on them.[115] The resulting usage patterns might also eventually influence the federal judiciary to favor greater use of liability rules, rather than injunctions, in routine actions for copyright infringement.[116] As more open access or semi-open access options became more widely used in practice, it might also alleviate some of

---

[111] *See supra* note 107.

[112] 17 U.S.C. §§ 401(a) (2012).

[113] For existing pressures by science funders in this directions, see Contreras, *Data Sharing, supra* note 23; Reichman et al., *supra* note 39, chapter 8. *See generally* Reichman & Uhlir, *supra* note 43; RECODE, *supra* note 95.

[114] *See generally* Elinor Ostrom, Governing the Commons – The Evolution of Institutions for Collective Action (Cambridge University Press 1990); Understanding Knowledge as a Commons: From Theory to Practice (Charlotte Hess & Elinor Ostrom eds., MIT Press 2006). For applications to data sharing initiatives, see generally Reichman et al., *supra* note 39, chapter 8; Contreras & Reichman, *supra* note 91.

[115] For government action to the same end in Germany, see, e.g., Gesetz über Urheberrecht und verwandte Schutzrechte [UrhG] [German Copyright Act], Sept. 9, 1965, Bundesgesetzblatt, Teil I at 1273, §§ 29–31.

[116] *Cf.* e-Bay v. MercExchange, 547 U.S. 388 (2006). *See generally* Reichman, *Green Tulips, supra* note 101.

the pressure on formal limitations and exceptions to exclusive rights, especially the bedrock doctrine of fair use.

Without laboring the point further, the proposed standard form licenses – backed by a properly reformed copyright law – could reduce transaction costs and simplify both access to and use of all those literary and artistic works whose authors do not need, or would not benefit from, the overly inclusive regime of restrictions and control that current copyright laws now implicitly make their standard deal. Those who do need such a restrictive regime should, of course, opt into it, subject to suitably designed limitations and exceptions, as occurs under existing copyright laws.[117] Conversely, if a mass of accidental "authors" empowered by digital technology were persuaded to free themselves from automatically imposed constraints on access and control they do not need or want, the process of codifying suitable limitations to, and exceptions from, the exclusive rights of commercially motivated creators might become more rational and targeted, with fewer unanticipated repercussions on either private stakeholders or the public at large. Given that all literary and artistic works will ultimately end in the public domain, the more that creative artists can access and use the copyrighted culture free of unnecessary constraints in the meantime, the more that literary and artistic pursuits are likely to flourish, at least in the light of historical practice.[118]

What neither creative artists nor the public at large need is an overly broad and intrusive regime of exclusive rights that automatically restricts everyone's ability to draw from the digitally available copyrighted culture, as if every component of that culture possessed some known or likely commercial value.[119] On the contrary, if the default rules of copyright law generated standard-form deals that encouraged most "authors" to make their works freely available in the manner outlined above, including use of a standard-form liability rule for commercial purposes, I predict that more authors and artists would actually obtain more financial returns from their outputs than under the single set of restrictive conditions that now constitutes the normative framework.[120] That prediction follows from the fact that a liability rule invites users to find new uses for literary and artistic works that authors themselves had not previously envisioned.

---

[117] *See generally* Samuelson, *supra* note 2; HUGENHOLTZ & OKEDIJI, *supra* note 17.

[118] *See* Giancarlo F. Frosio, Users' Patronage: Cumulative Creativity, Collaboration, and Fan-Authorship (2015) (unpublished SJD thesis, Duke University School of Law) (on file with Goodson Law Library, Duke Law School).

[119] For a similar mistake on the part of developing-country negotiators of the Convention on Biological Diversity, see REICHMAN ET AL, *supra* note 39, chapter 5. *See generally id.*, Part One.

[120] For the potential lottery effects flowing from liability rules that invite third parties to put an author's work to profitable uses, see Reichman, *Green Tulips*, *supra* note 101.

Whether this prediction proves accurate or not, so long as those who need a more restrictive deal can opt into it from the outset or when they need it, the general availability of less restrictive standard deals could produce a win-win situation for all concerned, with greatly reduced transaction costs and far more access to, and use of, the copyright culture than could ever be attained by means of legislated limitations and exceptions. In effect, the proposed standard deals, if widely adopted, would already have embodied the tailor-made limitations and exceptions needed by different subcommunities of authors, without the heavy-handed contractual restrictions that intermediaries tend to impose.[121]

In putting forward these proposals, I am not suggesting that copyright law has become irrelevant. On the contrary, let us not forget that copyrights actually make Creative Commons licenses workable. They may also play a key role in enabling communities of authors to contractually configure research commons to their own needs and to ensure that knowledge assets are shared under mutually agreed terms.[122]

The more that authors themselves advocate for, and implement in practice, user friendly conditions on access and use of copyrighted works, the harder it will become for publishers to claim that the existing "one size fits all" copyright regime truly promotes the interests of authors. To the extent that the *ancien regime* ceases to represent authors' real interests, it correspondingly forfeits claims to legitimacy, in which case change and adaptation to the digital universe could become mandatory, even as the role of intermediaries evolves in response to the needs of both creators and the public at large.[123]

Meanwhile, we should be asking whether the limits of limitations and exceptions to adequately address these needs tell us something more important about structural defects in the copyright paradigm itself, as handed down from the Eighteenth Century, and about the need for new directions to more fully enable digital technologies to exploit cultural artifacts.[124] Ever since Yochai Benkler, James Boyle, Jessica Litman, Pamela Samuelson, and Lawrence Lessig, among others, began sounding the alarm, it has become clear that the copyright paradigm itself needs to evolve and incorporate methodologies that, when properly triggered, would directly connect creators and users, rather than hinder collective use of knowledge assets for specified public-interest pursuits. The adjustments suggested here and elsewhere in

---

[121] *Cf.* REICHMAN ET AL., *supra* note 39, chapter 7; Reichman & Okediji, *supra* note 6.

[122] *See, e.g.*, Reichman & Uhlir, *supra* note 43, at 319–22, 396–413, 419; *see also* Niva Elkin-Koren, *Exploring Creative Commons: A Skeptical View of a Worthy Pursuit, in* THE FUTURE OF THE PUBLIC DOMAIN: IDENTIFYING THE COMMONS IN INFORMATION LAW 325, 329–31 (Lucie Guibault & P. Bernt Hugenholtz eds., 2006).

[123] *See* REICHMAN ET AL., *supra* note 39, chapter 7.

[124] *See* Ricolfi, *supra* note 96.

this volume may depart from the Romantic view of authorship, or otherwise force us to discard or revise legal tools used to rescue authors from the literally dead hands of patronage after the French Revolution. Nevertheless, it is well to remember that the sharing of knowledge assets had been the customary norm from time immemorial.[125] In adjusting an increasingly obsolete copyright regime to the needs and opportunities of digital networks, we may be rediscovering – and even recovering – foundational dimensions of human creativity that have been under-appreciated far too long.

---

[125] *See* Frosio, *supra* note 118.

11

Lessons from CopyrightX

William W. Fisher III[*]

ABSTRACT

The increasing economic and cultural importance of the copyright system throughout the world has reinforced the need to provide all persons, not just lawyers, affordable access to high-quality education about copyright law and policy. At the same time, the growing complexity of the system, attributable in part to the intricacy of its "exceptions and limitations," has made achievement of that goal more difficult. This essay describes and assesses a recent effort to combine modern educational technologies with venerable pedagogic principles to enable more of the people who are affected by the copyright system to understand it and to participate in shaping it.

Beginning in 2013, I have organized each spring an unusual course on copyright law. I will do so again in 2015 and, I hope, for at least a few more years thereafter. Because it is part of the HarvardX distance-learning initiative,[1] the course has come to be known as CopyrightX. This essay describes and assesses the venture. Among the purposes of the essay is to provide some guidance to teachers considering similar projects.

11.1. THE COURSE STRUCTURE

CopyrightX has three interlocking parts: a residential course on Copyright that I teach to roughly 100 students at Harvard Law School; an online course taught by Harvard Teaching Fellows to roughly 500 students throughout the world; and a set

---

[*] WilmerHale Professor of Intellectual Property Law, Harvard University. In October of 2014, I presented this chapter as the Peter Jaszi Distinguished Lecture on Intellectual Property at American University. The chapter has been much improved by the comments I have received from Peter Jaszi himself and from Ana Enriquez, Niva Elkin-Koren, Nathaniel Levy, Ruth L. Okediji, Diane Rosenfeld, and David Wills.

[1] Information concerning HarvardX is available at http://harvardx.harvard.edu.

of affiliated courses, most of them based in countries other than the United States. They work as follows:

During each of the twelve weeks of Harvard University's spring semester, the students in the residential course watch a ninety-minute recorded lecture that I have prepared, read some edited judicial opinions or articles,[2] and then attend two eighty-minute classes. Nine of the twelve lectures consist of surveys of the principal sets of rules in copyright law; the other three present the main theories upon which scholars (and sometimes lawmakers) rely when shaping or evaluating the copyright system. The topics of the lectures are set forth below.[3]

1. The Foundations of Copyright Law: Treaties; Originality; and the Idea/Expression Distinction
2. Fairness and Personality Theories
3. The Subject Matter of Copyright
4. Welfare Theory
5. Authorship
6. The Mechanics of Copyright
7. The Rights to Reproduce and Modify
8. The Rights to Distribute, Perform, and Display
9. Fair Use
10. Cultural Theory
11. Secondary Liability and Para-Copyright
12. Remedies

During the two live classes, I don't lecture at all, and I rarely focus on the assigned reading materials. Instead, I engage the students in Socratic discussions of case studies that raise difficult questions related to the themes of the week. All of the case studies examine real (not hypothetical) controversies. In form, most resemble the kind of case studies used in most business schools: they describe in some detail the history of a conflict and then ask students how the law would or should apply to it. (In one respect, however, my pedagogy differs from the approach typically used in business schools: I rarely provide the case studies to the students in advance. Instead, I present them in class, and students are asked to respond on the spot.) At the end of the course, the students take a reasonably traditional written examination designed to test their knowledge of copyright law and theory.[4]

The second piece of the puzzle – the online course – is free and is open to anyone over the age of 12. Enrollment, however, is limited. Persons interested in

---

[2]   The reading materials are available at http://copyx.org/hls-syllabus/.
[3]   Recordings of all of the lectures are available, in a variety of formats, at http://copyx.org/lectures/.
[4]   Examples of the exam are available at http://copyx.org/courses/harvard-law-school/.

participating must complete an application, which includes an essay question. When making admissions decisions, we look not for educational attainment, but for manifestations of intelligence, competence in the English language, and commitment to completing the course. In addition, we strive to create a group of students that is diverse along many dimensions. Partly as a result, roughly half of the people who to date have participated in the online course reside in the United States, while the others reside in ninety-three different countries. (A map showing, in dark grey, the countries that have been represented thus far appears in Figure 11.1.)

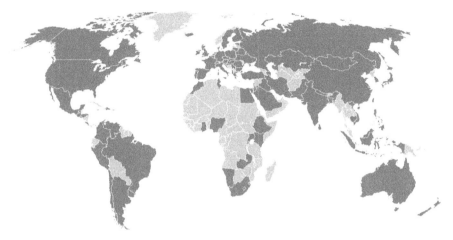

FIGURE 11.1.

Half of the online participants are men and the other half are women. Most are not lawyers but rather are engaged in fields affected by copyright law: music, film, photography, graphic art, journalism, software, library science, and so forth.

The online course is taught, not by me, but by teaching fellows. Most are currently students at Harvard Law School. A few are recent graduates of the law school or are graduate students in other Harvard departments. All have taken or audited (or are taking or auditing) the residential course described above. Each teaching fellow is given responsibility for a "section" of 25 students.[5]

The pedagogy of the online course is similar to that of the residential course. Each week, the online students watch the same recorded lecture that the Harvard students watch and read a subset of the materials read by the students in the residential course.[6] Then, on Thursday, Friday, or Saturday, the students in each online section attend a live 90-minute online seminar (using the Adobe Connect conferencing

---

[5] A list of the teaching fellows and links to their biographies are available at http://copyx.org/people/teaching-fellows/.
[6] The readings for the online course are available at http://copyx.org/copyx-syllabus/.

system[7]) in which the teaching fellow presents and then guides discussion of case studies identical or similar to those that I employ in the residential course. The meeting times of the seminars are staggered to enable students located in diverse time zones to attend. At the end of the course, the students have an opportunity to take a written examination that incorporates the principal portion of the exam given to the Harvard Law Schools students.[8] To receive a certificate of completion, an online student must both satisfy a participation requirement (by attending 10 of the 12 weekly seminars for his or her section) and pass the written exam.

Last but not least, a growing group of universities and other organizations, most of them located outside the United States, are now offering CopyrightX courses – typically to their own students or to members of their own communities. A list of the institutions that are offering such affiliated courses now (in the spring of 2015) is set forth in Table 11.1 on the following page. The asterisks indicate the courses that are offered for academic or professional development credit.

All of the affiliated courses have the following features: the teacher is a university faculty member or someone who knows a great deal about the copyright system;[9] not more than 30 students can be admitted; the students must watch the same recorded lectures as do the Harvard and online students; and the course must include at least twelve 80-minute seminars. In other respects, however, the affiliated courses vary. Most conduct their seminars in "real space," but a few meet partially or wholly online. Some use the same curriculum employed by the online sections (which focuses on U.S. copyright law), while others blend the readings I have assembled with readings designed to illuminate the copyright systems in their own countries.[10] The schedules of most of the affiliates mimic the schedule of the Harvard course and the online courses, but some adjust their starting and stopping dates to accommodate local academic calendars. Finally, the students in all of the affiliated courses are offered the opportunity to take a final examination that incorporates the principal portion of the Harvard exam but may also include questions that focus on the copyright systems of the countries or regions in which the courses are based.

In addition to the partial parallelism of their curricula, two things bind these various courses into a single community: the students in all three sectors of the course are invited to participate in an asynchronous online discussion (not open to the public); and a few times during the semester, the students in all of the courses are invited to participate – either in person or via a live, interactive webcast – in "events" where

---

[7]   For information about Adobe Connect, see www.adobe.com/products/adobeconnect.html.

[8]   Copies of the examinations given in 2013 and 2014 are available at http://copyx.org/sections/.

[9]   I review the qualifications of prospective teachers to ensure that this is true.

[10]   Some of the custom syllabi used by the affiliated courses are available at http://copyx.org/syllabus/.

TABLE 11.1.

Country	Institution	Teacher
Australia	Monash University*	George Raitt
Brazil	Institute for Technology and Society	Ronaldo Lemos
China	Renmin University*	Haijun Jin
Egypt	American University in Cairo	Nagla Risk
Germany	University of Hamburg	Wolfgang Schulz
Ghana	Advanced Information Technology Institute – Kofi Annan Centre of Excellence	Dorothy Gordon
Kenya	Content Development and Intellectual Property Trust	Alex Gakuru
Kenya	GoDown Arts Centre	Joy Mboya
India	National Law University, Delhi*	Arul Scaria
Italy	University of Turin	Giancarlo Frosio
Jamaica	Norman Manley Law School*	Sarah Hsia Hall
Netherlands	Institute for Information Law	Thomas Margoni
Nigeria	Nigeria Institute of Advanced Legal Studies	Helen Chuma-Okoro
Palestine	Palestinian Association for Protection of Intellectual Property	Mohammed Iriqat
South Africa	University of Cape Town	Tobias Schonwetter
Uganda	Makerere University	Francis Ssekitto
United Kingdom	Centre for Intellectual Property Policy and Management at Bournemouth University*	Maurizio Borghi & Argyro Karanasiou
United States	WilmerHale	Jennifer Garnett

outside speakers discuss dimensions of the copyright system. A chronological list of the topics and speakers of the events held to date appears below.

The Interests of Authors	Dale Cendali, Richard Kelly, William Landay & John Drake
IP Protection for Fashion	Jeannie Suk & Chris Sprigman
Extralegal Norms in Comedy	Dotan Oliar & Jim Mendrinos
Appropriation Art	Shepard Fairey, Marita Sturken & Geoffrey Stewart

Free Culture	Larry Lessig
Orphan Works and Digital Libraries	Robert Darnton & John Palfrey
Creativity in Music	Joshua Redman
Copyright and Development	Ruth L. Okediji
The Roles of the Berkman Center	Chris Bavitz, Felix Oberholzer-Gee,
for Internet & Society	Jeffrey Schnapp, and Stuart Shieber
Copyright in the Creative Economy	Angela Ndambuki
(hosted by CopyrightX: Kenya	
Copyright Board)	
Negotiating Copyright Treaties	Justin Hughes
Litigating Fair Use	Bruce Rich
Creativity in Photography	Abelardo Morell & Gerald Frug

As should be apparent, most of these events focus, not on the law of copyright, but on activities that copyright law affects. Partly for that reason, fewer than half of the speakers have been lawyers. Thus far, the large majority of the events have been hosted at Harvard. In the future, I hope that a growing percentage will be hosted in other countries by the teachers of the affiliated courses.

11.2. PEDAGOGIC PRINCIPLES

Many of the features of CopyrightX reflect efforts to implement principles concerning optimal forms of education. Few of these principles are novel; most have been appreciated for decades if not centuries. However, online courses commonly ignore or violate them. CopyrightX functions in part as an arena in which familiar pedagogic guidelines can be applied, tested, and refined in a rapidly developing technological environment. The main principles and the ways in which I have tried to implement them are set forth below.

1. *Active Learning*. Students do not learn well when they merely listen to or watch lectures. They are much more likely to master and retain information and ideas when they put them to use – solving problems, debating their merits and applications, and so forth.[11]

The most important of the dimensions of CopyrightX that reflect this fundamental principle is the discussion-based format. As indicated above, all of the students in all of the courses are obliged to attend and participate in interactive classes.

---

[11] The literature that confirms and elaborates on this generalization is large. See, for example, A. Renkl, *From Example Study to Problem Solving*, 70 J. Exp. Educ. 293 (2002); R. Hake, *Interactive Engagement versus Traditional Methods*, 66 Am. J. Phys. 64 (1998); Chet Meyers & Thomas Jones, Promoting Active Learning (1993).

A second, less obvious dimension is the use of teaching fellows in the online course. As indicated above, almost all of the teaching fellows are themselves students. Some have learned the material they teach in their seminars only a few days before the seminars themselves. All report that the kind of engagement with the material necessary to teach effectively, amplified by the discussions they have with me and with their colleagues concerning their lesson plans, substantially deepens their understanding of that material.

2. *The Interdependence of Theory, Doctrine, and Practice.* As most law teachers will attest, understanding law requires much more than memorizing a collection of rules. It also demands, at a minimum, securing a critical understanding of the theories that animate those rules (or could be used to change them) and acquiring an appreciation of how the rules influence behavior and the capacity to predict how they have been (or would be) applied to real controversies. Good legal education integrates work on these various levels.[12]

Several aspects of CopyrightX grow out of this principle: the weekly lectures oscillate between doctrine and theory; the classes focus on the application of doctrines and theories to case studies; and some of the events explore the impact of copyright law on fields of practice.

3. *Multiple Media.* Most people learn best when presented with information in a variety of complementary media. Partly for that reason, the recorded lectures contain little footage in which I appear as a "talking head." Most of the time, my voice is combined with (or replaced by) visual or audio material – illustrating cases, suggesting typologies of arguments, and so forth.

One unusual type of material used in the course bears emphasis. I have prepared two "mindmaps" that contain all of my lecture notes for the course. The first presents the main sets of rules that together constitute copyright law; the second presents the main copyright theories. Excerpts from these maps frequently appear as part of the background in the recorded lectures. In addition, interactive versions of the maps themselves are available to all of the CopyrightX students (and to the public at large), for use as study aids.[13] Many students have reported that this format makes the concepts easier to understand than a linear outline.

A possible reason for the apparent pedagogic value of the maps is suggested by Steven Pinker's recent analysis of the psychological underpinnings of good grammar. Pinker argues, in brief: "Syntax ... is an app that uses a *tree* of phrases to translate a *web* of thoughts into a *string* of words. Upon hearing or reading the string of words, the perceiver can work backward, fitting them into a tree and recovering the links

---

[12] For an early explication of this principle, see *Report of the Harvard Law School Committee on Educational Planning and Development* (1982) (commonly known as the "Michelman Report").

[13] Available at http://copyx.org/maps-of-intellectual-property/.

between the associated concepts."[14] Pinker derives from this insight helpful guidelines for constructing the sentences and paragraphs in a lecture or essay. But I take
from his argument a different lesson: if teaching via speech or prose entails converting a two-dimensional conceptual map into a one-dimensional string of words,
from which the student "recovers" a semblance of the original map, wouldn't it be
more efficient for the teacher to provide the student a two-dimensional, expandable
map that approximates the "web" of concepts in the teacher's head? By reducing
the errors and time associated with the steps of conversion and reconversion, this
approach should both enhance and accelerate learning.

4. *Academic Freedom.* Teachers should be given substantial autonomy in deciding
what to teach, write, and say. The conventional justification for this principle is that
it is necessary to shield teachers from political pressure and thus facilitates free intellectual inquiry.[15] But there are two additional, equally important reasons: to attract
people capable of becoming excellent teachers, one must offer them considerable
autonomy; and pedagogic progress requires experimentation, which is fostered by
according teachers freedom to try different approaches.

For these reasons, I give the teaching fellows in the online course substantial
autonomy in designing and conducting their classes. I do not provide them lesson
plans or lists of the issues they must cover. Nor do I tell them which case studies they
should use in their seminars.

To be sure, I do offer the teaching fellows guidance of several sorts. The recorded
lectures, which both they and their students watch, set forth the principal themes
of the course. All of the teaching fellows have participated in or audited classes in
which I have presented some of the case studies to Harvard Law School students.
And each Wednesday, before they teach their own classes, the teaching fellows meet
with me for eighty minutes to discuss pedagogic strategy and options. But, in the
end, they must make their own choices concerning what and how to teach.

The teachers of the affiliated courses enjoy even more autonomy. Most are experienced faculty members and thus do not need (and likely would not appreciate)
guidance in planning their classes. As indicated above, many create customized
syllabi that juxtapose U.S. law with the law in their own jurisdictions. And, like the
teaching fellows, the affiliated faculty must decide which (if any) of the case studies
to employ in their seminars.

5. *The Wealth of a Network.*[16] The top-down, one-to-many structures of most
Massive Open Online Courses (MOOCs) not only neglect opportunities for active
learning, they also forfeit the potential benefit of the substantive contributions that

---

[14] THE SENSE OF STYLE ch. 4 (2014).

[15] *See, e.g.,* Statement of the American Historical Association, July 19, 2013, available at http://blog
.historians.org/2013/07/aha-statement-on-academic-freedom-and-the-indiana-governor/.

[16] *Cf.* YOCHAI BENKLER, THE WEALTH OF NETWORKS (Yale University Press 2006).

might be made by participants other than the guru on the mountaintop. By contrast, I try to encourage such contributions.

For example, each teaching fellow is required to create or revise one case study during the semester. I provide the fellows assistance, of course; I identify cases or controversies they might select, suggest research strategies, and edit their drafts. But they do the bulk of the research and writing. A typical case study consists of a short summary suitable for distribution in class; a set of slides illustrating the controversy and germane law; and a 10-page teaching manual. The teaching fellow who creates a case study generates almost all of this material. His or her work product then goes into the basket from which the other teaching fellows, the affiliated faculty, and I draw when teaching our own courses.

This year (2015) I have extended this system to the affiliated courses. Each of the affiliated faculty has been asked to create at least one case study (either alone or with the aid of his or her students) highlighting the law of the country in which the affiliated course is located. The result will be to help all of the other teachers (including me) enrich their classes with illustrations of copyright systems in different countries.[17]

The students in the online sections and the affiliates are also important sources of material. For example, Danny Rayman of Chile and Emilio Velis of El Salvador – students in the 2014 and 2013 online course, respectively – are collaborating in the preparation of Spanish translations of the twelve recorded lectures. Ali Tahvilian, who was a student in the affiliate offered by the University of Turin in 2014, has begun a Persian translation. Other groups of students have created outlines of all or portions of the course. We strongly encourage such initiatives – and post links to their work products on our Community Contributions page.[18]

6. *Rigor.* It is often asserted or assumed that complex systems of ideas must be simplified to make them accessible to broad audiences. CopyrightX rejects that proposition. The twelve recorded lectures are pitched at levels that will meet the demanding standards of Harvard Law School students; they have not been "dumbed down" in any way. The versions of the judicial opinions read by the online students and by the students in most of the affiliated courses are the same as the versions assigned at Harvard. Finally, to obtain a certificate of completion, all students must pass an exam that incorporates the principal portion of the exam given to the Harvard students.

To be sure, we do provide students without legal training some assistance in getting up to speed. For example, the online students (most of whom are neither lawyers nor law students) are encouraged to read, prior to the course, a guide to understanding and analyzing judicial opinions.[19] And the teaching fellows frequently explain

---

[17] The first product of this new system is an excellent case study by Thomas Margoni, examining the changing standard of "originality" used in the European Union.

[18] Available at http://copyx.org/content/community-contributions/.

[19] Ana Enriquez & Tatum Lindsay, *Understanding Judicial Opinions* (June 2014), available at http://copyx.org/understanding-judicial-opinions-2/.

to their students technical features of the judicial opinions or case studies that are discussed in the seminars. But, with these aids, all students must wrestle with the most difficult questions in the field.

11.3. ASSESSMENT

How well is CopyrightX working? I will first try to answer that question from the standpoint that (for better or worse) has come to dominate evaluations of educational initiatives: how well is it meeting the expectations and needs of the students? I will then reverse field and consider the extent to which it is advancing my own goals.

Various indices suggest that, on balance, CopyrightX is satisfying reasonably well the desires of the students in all of the various components of the course. First, their course evaluations are encouraging. The mean of the Harvard Law School students' assessment of the "overall effectiveness" of the residential course was 4.66 (out of 5) in 2013 and 4.64 in 2014.[20] The students who completed the online course were similarly enthusiastic. In 2014, the mean of their evaluations of the overall effectiveness of the course was 4.57. (We neglected to ask this question in 2013.) Even more revealing are the online students' assessments of the various ways in which the course might have benefited them. The means of their responses are shown in Table 11.2.

TABLE 11.2. *How valuable[a] was your experience in CopyrightX for each of the following things?*

	2013	2014
Increasing your intellectual curiosity	4.57	4.46
Improving your ability to contribute to civil society	4.08	3.88
Improving your ability to perform well professionally	4.11	4.18
Increasing your interest in sharing your knowledge with others	4.29	4.24
Improving your self-expression and creativity	3.79	3.72

[a] This is one of the questions for which the scale was "not at all valuable" to "extremely valuable." *See* note 20.

Another indicator of the utility of the venture is the retention rate. Figures 11.2 and 11.3 show, for each year, the numbers of enrolled students who participated in each of the twelve weekly seminars, who satisfied the attendance requirement for receipt of a certificate; who took the final examination; who passed the final examination; and who received certificates of completion.

[20] The scale used in the Harvard Law School course evaluations is: 1="unsatisfactory," 2 = "poor," 3 = "fair," 4 = "good," and 5 = "excellent." All of the more detailed evaluations discussed in the remainder of the essay also use a five-point scale. For most, the meanings of the numbers are the same as in the Harvard system. A few, however, use the following scale: 1 = "not at all valuable," 2 = "somewhat valuable," 3 = "valuable," 4 = "very valuable," and 5 = "extremely valuable."

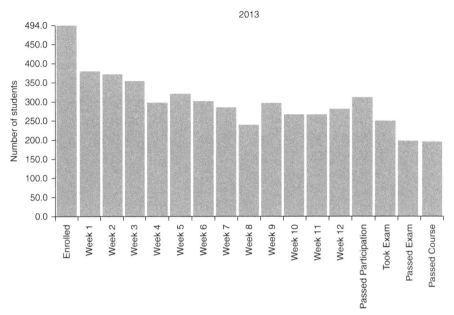

FIGURE 11.2.

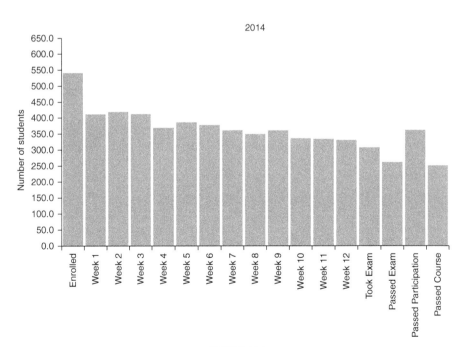

FIGURE 11.3.

Retention might be measured in a variety of ways. If one compares the number of students who attended the first weekly seminar to those who attended the last one, the retention rate in 2013 was 74 percent and in 2014 was 80 percent. If instead one compares the number of students who enrolled in the course to the number who stuck with it to the end, took the exam, and passed it – and thus received certificates of completion – the retention rate in 2013 was 40 percent and in 2014 was 47 percent. Various other comparisons might be made using the data in these charts. But by any measure, these completion rates are substantially better than those typically associated with free online courses.[21]

To be sure, various factors other than the content and pedagogy of the course contributed to high retention rate. The obligation to complete an application and the risk of being rejected undoubtedly discouraged some potential students who would not have stuck with it. And, as indicated above, one of the criteria we employed in making admission decisions was manifestation of commitment. Whatever the cause, the fact that so many students complete the course is gratifying.

Our quest for diversity in our student body does not seem to have done any harm in this regard. As can be seen from Figures 11.4 and 11.5, the retention and success rates for all groups were similar. Non-Americans did approximately as well as Americans; and retention and success rates did not vary substantially with age or educational attainment.

Of the various statistics latent in these figures, the following are perhaps the most significant: In 2013, 80 percent of the online students who satisfied the participation requirement took the final exam; in 2014, the rate was 90 percent. In 2013, 79 percent of those who took the exam passed it; in 2014, the rate was 85 percent. Those numbers were only modestly higher for lawyers than for nonlawyers.

The data we have gathered thus far from the affiliated courses are much less detailed. In particular, we do not have the benefit of standardized student course evaluations or demographic information of the sort summarized above. (Starting in 2015, we will.) For the time being, we have only two indicators of success: First, the retention rates for the affiliates were comparable to those of

---

[21] The average completion rate for Massive Open Online Courses (MOOCs) is roughly 7 percent. *See* Chris Parr, *Not Staying the Course*, TIMES HIGHER EDUCATION, May 10, 2013, available at www .insidehighered.com/news/2013/05/10/new-study-low-mooc-completion-rates. Justin Reich, however, has recently argued that this number is misleading, in part because it fails to differentiate students who, at the outset of a course, intend to complete it from those who do not. Using a sample of nine HarvardX courses, Reich found that 22 percent of the persons who said that they intended to complete the courses ultimately did so. *See Learner Retention Recasts "Low" MOOC Completion Rates* (Dec. 8, 2014), available at http://harvardx.harvard.edu/news/learner-intention.

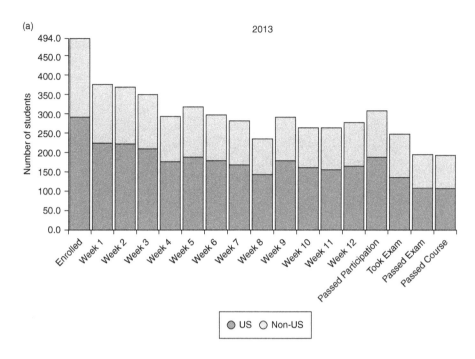

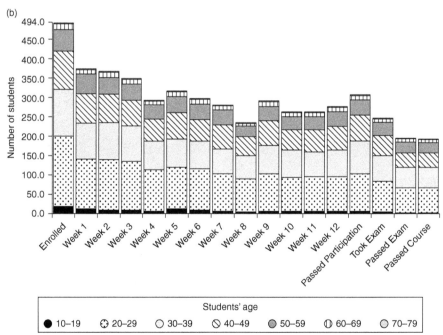

FIGURE 11.4.

(c)

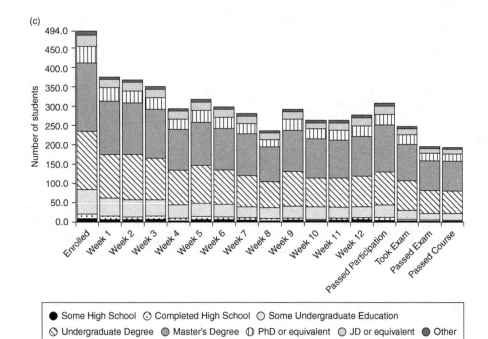

FIGURE 11.4 *(continued)*

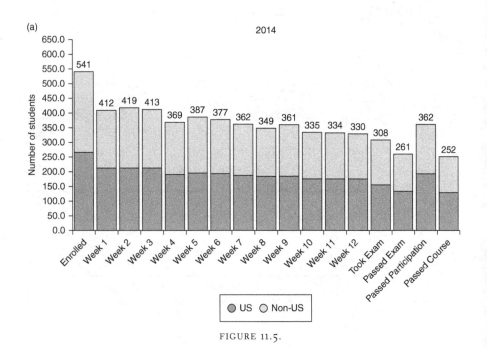

FIGURE 11.5.

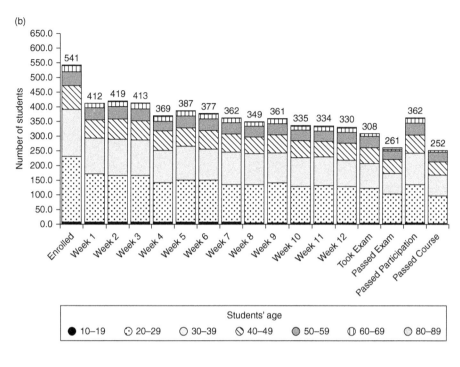

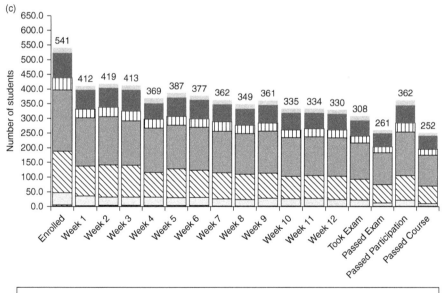

FIGURE 11.5 *(continued)*

the online courses. Second, the teachers of the affiliated courses enthusiastically endorsed them.

That CopyrightX seems to be meeting students' needs and expectations reasonably well does not mean that all of its components are optimal. Table 11.3, which shows the mean student evaluations of each of the major sectors of the course in the two years we have been in operation, makes clear that, while some parts are running smoothly, others must be adjusted.

TABLE 11.3.

	2013 Harvard course	2013 online course	2014 Harvard course	2014 online course
Instructor	4.82	4.68	4.74	4.45
Recorded Lectures	4.29	4.58	4.62	4.56
Assigned Readings	4.23	4.11	4.05	4.20
Case Studies	4.47	4.53	4.71	4.41
Live discussions				3.95
Events	4.19	4.03	4.23	3.54
Online forum		2.91		2.42
Maps	4.40		4.76	

The extensive written comments submitted by the students in the various sectors of the course are consistent with these numbers, as are the impressions of the teaching fellows.

Some of the numbers are encouraging. For example, the students' evaluations of the recorded lectures, the case studies, and the maps are affirming. These are the most innovative forms of "content" in CopyrightX, and all are rated highly.

Especially important are the high evaluations of the teaching fellows in the online course. The means of the online students' evaluations of their teachers' "overall effectiveness" were 4.68 in 2013 and 4.45 in 2014. The responses of the students to more detailed questions concerning the skills of their teaching fellows (shown in Table 11.4) buttress these aggregate assessments of their abilities.

One of the hypotheses upon which CopyrightX rests is that Harvard law and graduate students, given a modest amount of guidance and considerable freedom in crafting their lesson plans, will be effective teachers. Were this not true, the online course could not function. I am thus much relieved to find the hypothesis confirmed.

TABLE 11.4. *How would you rate your teaching fellow for each of the following*

	2013	2014
Knowledge of subject matter	4.76	4.41
Clarity and organization of presentation	4.58	4.64
Responsiveness to student questions during section meetings	4.82	4.66
Presentation/acceptance of alternative viewpoints	4.81	4.45

Less impressive are the numbers in Table 11.3 pertaining to the assigned readings and special events. Both should be improved. With respect to the assigned readings, I have edited the judicial opinions that are assigned in the 2015 version of the course much more tightly than I have done in years past.[22] (I was able to achieve this compression, without disabling students from consulting the material that I have omitted from the required readings, by using the remarkable H2O course-construction system developed by Jonathan Zittrain.[23]) With respect to the special events, I hope in the future to introduce more comparative-law material – in part by enlisting the growing group of affiliate faculty in the organization and conduct of events.

Ironically, the most discouraging set of numbers in Table 11.3 are those pertaining to the value of the asynchronous discussion forum. This is the pedagogic feature most commonly associated with online courses, so you might expect that it would be easy to do it well. Instead, to my surprise, it has proven especially difficult to organize an educationally rich online discussion. We have tried many ways of stimulating and improving conversation; thus far, none has worked well. In 2015, we are trying yet another approach. The principal adjustments we have made are: (a) concentrate all discussions in a single, plenary forum, while encouraging students in the individual online sections and affiliated courses to organize unsupervised small-group discussions using any of the many software applications suitable for that purpose; (b) structure the plenary forum in ways that will foster conversations across disciplinary and geographic boundaries; and (c) devote more of my own time to framing discussion questions and responding to students' reactions.

To summarize, CopyrightX seems to be doing a reasonably good job of meeting the needs and expectations of the students, and plans are in place for correcting its defects. I turn now to my own ambitions in the venture. They certainly include addressing the needs of the students. But three additional goals originally motivated

---

[22] The 2015 versions of the readings are available at http://copyx.org/hls_syllabus_2015/ and http://copyx.org/syllabus-for-online-sections-2015/.

[23] Available at https://h2o.law.harvard.edu.

me to undertake the project and prompt me to try to keep it going. Set forth below
are preliminary assessments of our progress on each front.

1. *Make high-quality education concerning copyright law widely accessible.* For better or worse, copyright laws increasingly affect people involved in a wide variety of
professions and activities throughout the world. Most of those people lack the time,
money, or inclination to attend law school. One of the ambitions of CopyrightX is
to provide them access to the sort of education they could receive in law school.

We seem to be doing reasonably well on this front. The diversity of the countries
from which the online students have participated, and the variety of professions
represented in our student body, are sources of pride. I am also pleased by the wide
variety of universities and institutions that will be offering affiliated courses in 2015.

However, it must be conceded that we could reach much larger audiences if we
did not limit enrollment in both the online courses and the affiliates. Roughly 1000
students participate in CopyrightX each year. That number is tiny compared with
the reach of many Massive Open Online Courses. So why don't we open our doors
wider? The principal reason is that the pedagogic model of CopyrightX depends
heavily upon close engagement of informed teachers with small groups of students.
That model does not "scale" easily.

(This disadvantage, from the standpoint of the number of people we can reach,
does have one concomitant benefit. Online courses are sometimes criticized as
threatening to the teaching profession, because they enable a few lecturers to provide instruction to enormous numbers of students.[24] This criticism may have merit
as applied to some MOOCs but is inapplicable to CopyrightX, because our pedagogic model depends upon maintaining a high ratio of faculty to students.)

In addition to diversity along the axes of geography and profession, I also hope
to reach a broad socioeconomic spectrum of students.[25] If CopyrightX did nothing
more than enhance the knowledge and skills of the economic and cultural elite in
each country, I would be disappointed. Three dimensions of CopyrightX reflect our
ambition to reach deeper:

    a. We attempt to lower the economic barriers to access by not charging tuition
       for the online course.

    b. When crafting the lectures and case studies, we try to minimize jargon and to
       provide, whenever possible, background information necessary to understand
       technical legal issues.

---

[24] *See, e.g.,* Steve Kolowich, *Why Professors at San Jose State Won't Use a Harvard Professor's MOOC,*
      Chronicle of Higher Education, May 2, 2013, available at http://chronicle.com/article/
      Why-Professors-at-San-Jose/138941/.

[25] Some of the reasons that underlie that aspiration are explored in the CopyrightX lecture on Cultural
      Theory – available at http://copyx.org/lectures/.

c. The technologies we employ in running the course have been selected or adjusted to maximize access for persons who either lack reliable broadband Internet access or who have disabilities. For example, we make all of the lectures available in both high-resolution and low-resolution formats, and we are now using closed-captioning systems for the lectures that increase their value for persons with hearing difficulties.

In combination, these initiatives have extended our reach well beyond the elite. However, on every dimension, we can and should do better. Thus, for example, we have begun evaluating the accessibility of all of the course materials to persons with disabilities. And I could do more to annotate the course materials for nonlawyers.

Finally, I have recently adjusted CopyrightX in one respect in hopes of mitigating the restrictions on access to the course. From the beginning, I have posted on the Internet all of the lectures, readings, maps, and recordings of the "events" – and have authorized other teachers and the public at large to make use of those materials in any way they wished, subject only to the restrictions in the Creative Commons attribution-noncommercial-sharealike license.[26] However, Richard Stallman has persuaded me to open the doors even wider.[27] Henceforth, users' only obligation will be to provide appropriate attribution to CopyrightX and Harvard University.[28] The purpose of this change is not to augment the revenues of for-profit educational institutions. The goal, rather, is to maximize the number and variety of educational projects and derivative works that can be built (directly or indirectly) on our foundation – and thus the set of students who might benefit from our efforts.

2. *Enhance the education of Harvard students.* This is one of the main objectives of the HarvardX program. The hope that experimentation in distance education would redound to the benefit of Harvard students is one of the main reasons why the university has been willing (thus far) to pay the very substantial costs of developing and running courses like CopyrightX.

In three respects, we seem to be advancing this goal. First, by honing the lectures and case studies to make them accessible to large, diverse audiences, I have made them more useful to Harvard Law School students. The recorded lectures are more concise, better documented, and more convenient to watch than the lectures I used to deliver "live." To be sure, I could have done this without making those materials

---

[26] The terms of this license are available at http://creativecommons.org/licenses/by-nc-sa/2.5/.

[27] The most persuasive of Stallman's criticisms of the attribution-noncommercial-sharealike license is that successive generations of noncommercial derivative works created in reliance on that license will eventually give rise to "orphan" works – in other words, works that can never be put to commercial uses because it is impossible to locate and secure permission from all of the many persons (or their assignees) who have contributed to them. *See* Richard Stallman, *On-line Education Is Using a Flawed Creative Commons License* (Sept. 2012), https://stallman.org/articles/online-education.html.

[28] The new license is available at http://copyx.org/permission/.

accessible to anyone other than my Harvard students. But, in truth, the prospect of opening my presentations to the public has nudged me to make them better.

Second, as mentioned above, the Harvard students who have served as teaching fellows have all reported that teaching their sections has improved their understanding of copyright law and policy. My own assessments bear this out. By the end of the course, the teaching fellows show greater mastery of the material than the Harvard students who have not opted to become teachers. I am also reasonably confident that the teaching fellows will retain their knowledge better and longer – although verifying this impression empirically is likely to prove infeasible.

Finally, some of the teaching fellows aspire to become full-time law teachers after graduation. Harvard Law School, like most law schools, offers potential teachers few opportunities to learn the craft. CopyrightX now provides them one arena in which they can develop and test teaching techniques – as well as to assess, in a relatively low-stakes setting, whether they truly want to become teachers.

Plainly, organizing an online course is not the only way of providing graduate students the educational and professional benefits of serving as teaching fellows. Large public universities frequently admit more than 500 undergraduates to traditional residential courses – and then hire more than twenty teaching fellows to help teach them. But this model is unavailable, at least with respect to technical subjects like Copyright, in medium-sized universities like Harvard. (I also suspect that both the challenges and the rewards of teaching are greater when one is obliged to convey difficult concepts to older students with diverse backgrounds and professions than when one teaches only undergraduates – but I have no evidence to support that intuition.)

3. *Cultivate the Wise Practice of Copyright.* Last but not least, I hope that CopyrightX will help and encourage its participants to use the copyright system wisely.

Wise practice entails, among other things, invoking or applying the law in a way that will advance its ultimate ends. That, in turn, requires knowing what those ends are. The three lectures that examine theories of intellectual property are intended, in part, to convey that knowledge.

To be sure, there is considerable disagreement among theorists concerning what goals copyright should be advancing. I do not attempt in the lectures, or in my teaching, to resolve that disagreement. Rather, I strive to inform students and viewers what the principal contentions are and thus to assist them in reaching thoughtful conclusions concerning the proper functions of the system. (Partly to afford them room to reflect, I wait until the tenth lecture to present my own perspective on the most attractive conception of those functions.)

An informed judgment concerning the ends of the system is not enough, however; at least as important is skill in determining what way of resolving or handling a dispute will advance those ends. That skill, I believe, can be acquired only through practice. One of the reasons why case studies figure so prominently in CopyrightX is to provide the students opportunities for practice of this sort. By exposing them to many real controversies, examining how the participants in those controversies did or could have employed the law, I hope not only to give students a feel for the "law in action," but also to enable them to consider and discuss what resolutions of those controversies would promote the goals of the system as a whole.

Most of the people who take CopyrightX do so because they encounter the copyright system with some frequency in their professional or personal lives and thus want to understand it better. My hope is that when after finishing the course, they confront copyright questions or disputes, they draw upon knowledge and skills of the sorts just described. Of course, it would be foolish to think that they would act as philosopher kings, with no regard for personal or institutional self-interest. Rather, my hope is that the way they act or the advice they provide others will reflect, among other things, thoughtful pursuit of the public interest – as they understand that term.

Is the course succeeding in this respect? Anecdotal evidence suggests yes. Testimonials by some CopyrightX alumni – most of them nonlawyers – suggest that their capacities to engage in wise practice have indeed been enhanced. But we have not devised a method for assessing our progress on this front systematically – and, frankly, I have little hope of doing so. Thus far, I have been proceeding primarily on faith, and will likely continue to do so.

Taking all these variables into account, I am happy with the performance of CopyrightX but see many ways in which it might be better. Generally speaking, the students seem to be satisfied, and we appear to be making good progress along all three of the axes that matter most to me. However, the course has flaws – most of which are variants of a single theme: we have not yet fully capitalized on the potential latent in CopyrightX for the creation of a vibrant global community of faculty and students engaged in the study of intellectual property. To be sure, the Harvard Law School students, the students in the online course, and the students in the affiliates do "speak" with one another in the discussion forum and the special events. But those conversations are not as common and deep as they could be. My principal overarching ambition when modifying the course will be to strengthen those ties.

11.4. RESOURCES

CopyrightX requires resources of four sorts: technology, access to copyrighted works, people, and money. The challenges we have encountered in gathering and deploying these things have implications for teachers and institutions considering launching similar ventures.

Many sorts of technology are necessary to create and run a course of this sort:

- computers, to prepare the course materials and to operate all aspects of the course;
- software, to support the application, admissions, and enrollment processes, organize and curate the course materials, administer the asynchronous discussion forum and the online seminars, track attendance, record grades, and manage the certificates of completion;
- a studio and an editing system, to produce the recorded lectures;
- cameras and related technical infrastructure, to webcast the special events;
- servers, to house and distribute the lectures and reading materials; and
- a high-capacity Internet connection to deliver all of these things to the course participants.

For this elaborate apparatus, we have relied on three related organizations: the Berkman Center for Internet and Society; EdX, a nonprofit consortium of Harvard University and the Massachusetts Institute of Technology; and HarvardX, Harvard's separate online-education initiative.[29] We have been fortunate in that many of the necessary technological tools were already owned or controlled by at least one of these organizations when we launched CopyrightX. A university that set out to create a similar course from scratch would likely find assembling such an apparatus a formidable and expensive task.

The technological burdens on the universities and other institutions that are now offering courses affiliated with CopyrightX are less severe but not trivial. They too must have computers and, if they wish to conduct their seminars online, access to conferencing software.[30] If, as I hope, the affiliates offer more webcast special events in the future, they will need even more technology.

Last but not least, to participate effectively in the course, a student must have two technological resources: a computer and a reliable Internet connection. We do our best to reduce the technological demands we place on students. For example, most of the students in the affiliates based in sub-Saharan African countries lack consistent access to the bandwidth necessary to download even the low-resolution versions of the recorded lectures – so each December, we load copies of the lectures and all of the course materials onto portable USB flash drives and mail them to the teachers of those courses. (Typically, during the first meeting of such a course,

---

[29] Descriptions of the three organizations may be found at http://cyber.law.harvard.edu/about; www.edx.org/about-us; and http://harvardx.harvard.edu/who-we-are.

[30] As indicated above, we use Adobe Connect for the online sections – and have acquired from Adobe the licenses necessary to employ their system. Some of the affiliated courses use other, less expensive conferencing systems, such as AnyMeeting (available at www.anymeeting.com).

the students take turns using the flash drive to copy the course materials onto their laptop computers.) But we cannot eliminate altogether the technological impediments to participation. The result, unfortunately, is to limit the set of people who can take the course.

The second essential resource consists of copyrighted materials. The CopyrightX syllabi contain articles and excerpts of books, the recorded lectures include many photographs and excerpts from sound recordings, and most of the case studies incorporate copies of the works over which the disputants were struggling. To reproduce, distribute, and publicly perform such things lawfully, we need either licenses from the copyright owners or privileges to use them without permission.

Overcoming this particular hurdle has been easier than one might think. The majority of the readings assigned in CopyrightX consist of edited versions of opinions issued by federal courts in the United States. Those opinions, fortunately, are not subject to copyright protection. (Obtaining copies of the opinions that are not encumbered by the contractual restrictions imposed by the dominant commercial legal-research services in the United States[31] has not always been easy, but we have managed.) The copyrights in most of the articles I assign are held by their authors, all of whom have been generous in giving us permission to use them. Finally, the fair use doctrine, although not ideal as a safe harbor for teachers,[32] is broad enough to enable us to employ – for a nonprofit, educational purpose – excerpts of contested works in our course materials.

To be sure, we have encountered occasional difficulties. Some institutional copyright owners have demanded exorbitant fees or have insisted upon conditions that made it impossible for us to use their materials in the online sectors of the course. (The most unreasonable has been Oxford University Press.) And the automated systems used by YouTube[33] and other online service providers for detecting putative instances of copyright infringement have occasionally caused those organizations to block public access to my recorded lectures, compelling me to invoke the laborious procedures that must be used to persuade the Online Service Providers (OSPs) to recant such "takedowns." But such problems have been infrequent.

Unfortunately, the creators of online courses focused on non-legal topics are likely to find it more difficult to obtain the materials they need to teach effectively. Most of the secondary sources and some of the primary sources a teacher would

---

[31] *See* LexisNexis Terms and Conditions, available at www.lexisnexis.com/terms; Subscriber Agreement for Westlaw, available at http://legalsolutions.thomsonreuters.com/law-products/_ui/common/web Resources/subscriber-agreement.pdf.

[32] *See* William McGeveran & William Fisher, *The Digital Learning Challenge: Obstacles to Educational Uses of Copyrighted Materials in the Digital Age* (2006), available at http://papers.ssrn .com/sol3/papers.cfm?abstract_id=923465.

[33] *See How ContentID Works*, available at https://support.google.com/youtube/answer/2797370.

want to assign when teaching most subjects do fall within the zone of copyright protection,[34] and securing permission to distribute such materials online will be hard or expensive.

Given the potential social value – and increasing popularity – of "distance education," one might expect the copyright system to contain a mechanism that would mitigate the difficulty and cost of using copyrighted materials for teaching. And, indeed, the copyright statute of the United States contains a provision that purports to do so, encouragingly named the "TEACH Act" (shorthand for Technology, Education and Copyright Harmonization Act). Unfortunately, the privilege created by that act to use copyrighted materials in educational settings is subject to so many restrictions and conditions (most of them the fruits of effective lobbying by publishers) that it is almost useless for online education. For example, the act authorizes only "performances" and "displays" of materials, access to those materials must be limited to enrolled students, and students must not be permitted to retain the materials for longer than the class session in which they are used.[35] Such conditions deprive the TEACH Act of any value for a course like CopyrightX. And, indeed, almost no online courses rely upon it. Until the statute is amended, teachers of online courses will be obliged either to obtain permission for most of the materials they assign or to include in their syllabi only books and articles whose authors have made them available under Creative Commons or similar licenses.

The third resource is personnel. Four people have been crucial in creating and running CopyrightX. Nathaniel Levy, a staff member at the Berkman Center for Internet and Society, has been our Project Manager from the beginning. Kendra Albert, now a Harvard law student, was the Head Teaching Fellow in 2012–2013. Ana Enriquez, a graduate of Berkeley Law School and now also a fellow at the Berkman Center, has been the Head Teaching Fellow since the summer of 2013. Ed Popko, a staff member at the Berkman Center, is our Course Technologist. Ana works full time on the venture; Nathaniel and Ed devote substantial portions of their time.

Many people outside this core team have also contributed importantly. David Karger, a Professor of Computer Science at MIT and a pioneer in the development of online pedagogies, has been a highly valuable advisor as we have built the course. The staff of the Berkman Center has helped us construct and run the course website, promote the course, and organize the special events. And the staff of HarvardX has created and edited the lectures. In short, getting CopyrightX off the ground and keeping it flying has required considerable effort from many people.

---

[34] For an exception, see *The Ancient Greek Hero*, available at www.edx.org/course/ancient-greek-hero-harvardx-cb22-1x#.VJmFFbgJtKc.

[35] For a more extensive discussion of the TEACH Act and its limitations, see Kenneth Crews, *Copyright Law and Distance Education: Overview of the TEACH Act* (Aug. 17, 2010), available at http://copyright.columbia.edu/copyright/files/2010/08/teach-act-summary-by-kenneth-crews.pdf.

We come finally to money. Running a course like CopyrightX is expensive. Our annual direct costs are now roughly $130,000. That covers the salaries and benefits of our core staff, the cost of our software licenses, and our webcasting fees. But that number understates the true cost of the course. For example, excluded from that sum is the value of my time, David Karger's time, the teaching fellows' time (they receive academic credit, not compensation), and the time of the affiliate teachers – as well as the extensive in-kind support we receive from the staff of HarvardX.

To date, roughly 40 percent of the money necessary to operate CopyrightX has come from HarvardX; the balance has come from Harvard Law School and the Berkman Center. Unfortunately, this financial model is not sustainable long term. So we are now in the process of seeking alternative sources of funds.

One potential source is law firms, some of which have strong commitments to the public interest in general and to experimentation in legal education in particular. To date, WilmerHale and Kirkland & Ellis, both law firms with strong intellectual-property divisions, have agreed to support the venture.

A second source is the set of academic institutions that offer affiliated courses. During the first two iterations of CopyrightX, we did not ask the affiliates for any financial contribution. However, in hopes of enabling the venture to survive in the long term, we have now begun to do so. Specifically, we are requiring institutions that offer CopyrightX affiliated courses for academic credit or professional-development credit to pay modest fees to help us cover our costs. To reduce the hazard that this system will prevent poorer universities from joining the community, we are engaging in differential pricing,[36] and we have exempted from the new system the ten institutions that helped us create the affiliate system. But new affiliates located in prosperous countries are being asked to help with our expenses. Monash University in Australia took the lead in developing this new arrangement. Bournemouth University in England and Renmin University in China have also recently joined the CopyrightX community under this arrangement.

The principal rationale for the new financial system is that all of the members of the growing CopyrightX community should contribute to sustaining it, to the extent they are able. Although I am persuaded by this argument, I worry that the new regime may corrode the spirit of voluntarism and sharing that has characterized CopyrightX from its inception. I very much hope not.

A more fundamental point underlies these prosaic considerations. The substantial per-student cost of running a course like CopyrightX means that distance learning

---

[36] Specifically, institutions located in countries classified as "high-income economies" by the World Bank (as of June 1, 2014) will pay a fee of $500 per enrolled student; institutions located in countries classified as "upper-middle-income economies" by the World Bank will pay a fee of $150 per enrolled student; and institutions located in countries classified as either "lower-middle-income economies" or "low-income economies" will pay no fee.

on this model will not solve the intensifying financial crisis in higher education – or at least will not solve it as quickly and decisively as the more enthusiastic advocates of MOOCs have sometimes claimed.[37] The CopyrightX model provides, we hope, a way to make higher education both better and more widely available – but not to make it dramatically cheaper. And we have not yet fully worked out mechanisms for making it financially sustainable without sacrificing its ambitions. That will be among our tasks in the next few years.

---

[37] *See, e.g.,* Fiona M. Hollands & Devayani Tirthali, MOOCS: Expectations and Reality 74–81 (2014), available at www.academicpartnerships.com/sites/default/files/MOOCs_Expectations_and_Reality.pdf.

12

Rights on the Border: The Berne Convention and Neighbouring Rights

Sam Ricketson[*]

ABSTRACT

This chapter is concerned with the relationship between authors' rights and related or neighbouring rights, and the way in which this relationship was developed in the period up to 1939. While the conditions for protection of authored works under the Berne Convention for the Protection of Literary and Artistic Works were initially quite generous, it subsequently became more difficult for later claimants, such as photographic works and works of applied art, to gain protection. But if such protection was ultimately obtained, albeit subject to significant qualifications, the doors were firmly shut against the claims of a number of other "value-adders" in the literary and artistic production chain, notably phonogram producers, performers, and broadcasters. This was on the basis that these persons or entities were not "authors" and their productions were not "works."

Accordingly, the notion of separate related or neighbouring rights protection began to be explored at the international level in a number of forums outside the Berne Union. These included: the International Institute for Intellectual Co-operation in Paris, an autonomous body associated with the League of Nations and later absorbed by the United Nations Educational, Scientific and Cultural Organization (UNESCO); the International Institute for the Unification of Private Law at Rome, more usually known as UNIDROIT; and the International Labour Office, the permanent Secretariat of the International Labour Organization or ILO in Geneva. Working through a committee of experts convoked by the International Institute for the Unification of Private Law that met in Samedan, Switzerland, in July 1939, a series of draft international instruments dealing with the protection of performers and phonogram producers, and broadcasters were produced. Two further draft instruments dealt with the protection of news items and droit de suite.

* Melbourne Law School, Victoria, Australia. Thanks to Justin Hughes and Bernt Hugenholtz for helpful comments.

The work of the Samedan Committee was cut short by the advent of World War II. Although now largely forgotten today, its influence is seen in developments after 1945 in the cases of performers, phonogram producers, and broadcasters, leading up to the adoption of the Rome Convention in 1961. More importantly, the work of the Samedan Committee, and the preparations leading up to it, cast important light on the relationship between authors' and related rights, and the emerging thinking on these issues at both the international and national levels in this early period.

≈ ≈ ≈

12.1. INTRODUCTION

For many reasons, 1939 may be a year best forgotten: at its commencement, many countries were still emerging from a worldwide depression that had endured for almost a decade, while civil wars and military invasions had already engulfed individual states in Asia, Africa and Europe; by its end, most countries were moving into the grips of an ever-widening conflagration that would not end until 1945. But in the midst of these unfolding events – and just over a month before the outbreak of war in Europe – a small group of experts convoked by the Rome International Institute for the Unification of Private Law (the "Rome Institute" or UNIDROIT) met to consider and adopt a series of draft treaties on rights neighbouring on those of authors. The location of the meeting – Samedan in Switzerland – could not have been better chosen for the purposes of reflection, reasoned deliberation, and scenic contemplation. Samedan was a small town of less than 2,000 in the Canton of Graubüunden in Eastern Switzerland (just more than 3,000 in 2015), where Romansch was still the first language of half the population, and which now, perhaps irrelevantly for present purposes, has a listing in the Guinness World Records as having the distinction of the "Smallest Permanently Licensed Bar in the World."[1]

The work of the Samedan committee receives no more than a footnote in official accounts of the history and development of neighbouring rights regimes:[2] for obvious reasons, within less than six weeks, its work looked quite irrelevant in the face of the horrors that were sweeping across Europe, and the only published account of its recommendations are to be found in the pages of the monthly journal of the International Office of the Berne Union, *Le Droit d'auteur*,[3] published in October,

---

[1] Information derived from Wikipedia at: https://en.wikipedia.org/wiki/Samedan#Heritage_sites_of_national_significance.

[2] There is one brief reference to its work in the general report of Abraham Kaminstein at the Rome Diplomatic Conference of 1961: *Records of the Diplomatic Conference on the International Protection of Performers, Producers of Phonograms and Broadcasting Organizations*, 10–25 October 1961, ILO, UNESCO, BIRPI, Paris and Geneva, 1968, at 35.

[3] Abbreviated hereafter as "DA."

November and December 1940.[4] However, awareness of the Committee's work did not disappear entirely, and significant elements of it were carried into the deliberations of the Bureaux Internationaux Réunis pour la Protection de la Propriété Intellectuelle (BIRPI),[5] the International Labour Organization (ILO),[6] and the United Nations Educational, Scientific, and Cultural Organization (UNESCO)[7] that followed in the period after 1945 and which led ultimately to the adoption of the International Protection of Performers, Producers of Phonograms and Broadcasting Organizations (the "Rome Convention") in 1961.[8] The work of the Samedan Committee therefore provides a useful prism through which to view one particular aspect of the Berne Convention: the relationship between authors' rights and rights neighbouring on these rights. Even in the digital age, this is a relationship that continues to vex policymakers and legislators, as witnessed by continuing debates about the scope of database protection and the adoption of new treaties on such matters as broadcasters' rights.

As this chapter will show, the relationship between authors' and neighbouring rights has a long history that extends back almost to the adoption of the Berne Convention in 1886. Certainly, if one were to take a snapshot of the Convention towards the end of its first half-centenary in 1933, and following its three substantive revisions of Paris 1896, Berlin 1908, and Rome 1928, it is possible to conclude that this now represented a reasonably comprehensive set of basic norms to be applied to the international protection of authors' rights. The works to be protected were defined broadly, the exclusive rights to be accorded were very similar to those under the present text of Stockholm and Paris (with the odd exception of reproduction rights),[9] a

---

4 [1940] *DA* 109–11, 121–25 and 133–38. Documents relating to the meeting are recorded in the archives of UNIDROIT under "Intellectual Property – Study V – Copyright: Reconciling the Berne and Havana Conventions," S.d.N – U.D.P. 1939, Documents 14–22, *available at* www.unidroit.org

5 "*Bureaux Internationaux Réunis pour la Protection de la Propriété Intellectuelle*" or the United Offices for the Protection of Intellectual Property was the term adopted in the 1950s to describe the two international offices that were established under the Paris Convention for the Protection of Industrial Property 1883 and the Berne Convention for the Protection of Literary and Artistic Works respectively, but which, in practice, were administered and operated together. BIRPI was the predecessor of the World Intellectual Property Organization (WIPO) which was established under its own Convention in 1967 and is now a specialised agency of the United Nations.

6 This body, founded in 1919, continued as a United Nations agency after the end of World War II.

7 This body, founded in 1945 as a specialised agency of the new United Nations, absorbed the International Institute for Intellectual Co-operation, an autonomous international organisation associated with the League of Nations: see UNESCO Archives AtoM catalogue at atom.archives.unesco.org/inernational-instiutue-of-intellectual-co-operation.

8 *See also Records of the Diplomatic Conference on the International Protection of Performers, Producers of Phonograms and Broadcasting Organizations,* 10–25 October 1961, ILO, UNESCO, BIRPI, Paris and Geneva, 1968.

9 Rome Act 1928, Berne Convention for the Protection of Literary and Artistic Works, arts. 8 (adaptation), 11 (public representation and performance), 11bis (broadcasting and other public communications), 12 (adaptations), 13 (mechanical reproductions and adaptations), 14 (cinematographic

generous term of protection based on the life of the author plus 50 years was established,[10] along with the no-formalities rule,[11] and there were some tightly drawn provisions on exceptions and limitations.[12] As an authors' charter for the non-digital age, it was an impressive multilateral achievement, with a sizeable membership of 39 countries, including many dependent territories and dominions, and an asserted coverage of "about a billion souls."[13]

12.2. GAINING PROTECTION UNDER BERNE – THE NEED
FOR AUTHORSHIP OF A LITERARY OR ARTISTIC WORK

To use a simple metaphor, the Convention was rather like a confectionary shop – once across the threshold, there were a lot of goodies on display for ready consumption – but there were limits as to who could gain access. Authorship was the entry requirement, meaning authorship of a literary or artistic work, and this is where the rub lay: like many clubs, these requirements were laid out initially in fairly generous terms, and various original applicants were admitted readily enough under what we might now call "grandparenting" arrangements. This is reflected in Article 4 of the 1886 Act, which defined the expression "literary and artistic works" as follows:

> The expression 'literary and artistic works' shall include books, pamphlets, and all other writings; dramatic or dramatico-musical works, musical compositions with or without words; works of drawing, painting, sculpture and engraving; lithographs, illustrations, geographical charts; plans, sketches, and plastic works relative to geography, topography, architecture, or science in general; in fact, every production whatsoever in the literary, scientific, or artistic domain which can be published by any mode of impression or reproduction.

This reflected what was already generally accepted both in national laws and in preceding bilateral treaties, and clearly indicates that works of an informational or utilitarian nature fell within the broad understanding of what was a "literary and artistic work" – consider, for example, the inclusion of "geographical charts; plans, sketches, and plastic works relative to geography, topography, architecture, or science in general." Indeed, the concluding words ("in fact, every production whatsoever in the literary, scientific or artistic domain which can be published by any mode of impression or reproduction") would have suggested a generous approach

reproductions and presentations), 6bis (moral rights). Reproduction rights in art. 9 were not added until the Stockholm Act of 1967.
[10]   Rome Act, art 7(1) (albeit optional at this stage: art 7(2)).
[11]   Rome Act, art 4(2).
[12]   Rome Act, arts. 9 and 10.
[13]   [1933] DA 2 (environ un milliard d'âmes).

to those works not specifically listed. Subsequent revisions of the Convention, however, were to indicate that "listing" was critical in order to ensure protection under the Convention, even if individual Union members might, at their discretion, accord protection to such productions under the general principle of national treatment. Intellectual creation and authorship, although not expressly mentioned in Article 4, were necessary conditions for protection: after all, Article 1 proclaimed, in terms that remain today, the constitution of a "Union for the protection of the rights of authors in their literary and artistic works." Post-1886, meeting the requirements of authorship and intellectual creation posed significant barriers for some new claimants for inclusion.

12.3. PHOTOGRAPHIC WORKS – AN EARLY CLAIMANT FOR PROTECTION

Foremost among these were photographic works, which failed to make the cut during the 1884–86 Conferences.[14] At this stage, there were some countries, such as France and the United Kingdom, which protected them along with other artistic works;[15] others, such as Germany, refused to accord them this status and only granted a lesser level of protection.[16] The reasons for these differences turned on the very questions of authorship and intellectual creativity identified above. With photographic works, the skill required to produce the final picture might be no more than the simple manual operation of operating a shutter or pushing a button, an option that was to place photography in the hands of everyone by the end of the century, with the development of the "Box Brownie."[17] On the other hand, there could be considerable elements of skill, both artistic and technical, involved in relation to such matters as choice and arrangement of subject, lighting, perspective, and so on. Whether these skills were those of authors was therefore something on which strong conflicting opinions could be held, and these differences came out into the open at both

---

[14] The following section draws on material in SAM RICKETSON & JANE C. GINSBURG, INTERNATIONAL COPYRIGHT AND NEIGHBOURING RIGHTS: THE BERNE CONVENTION AND BEYOND (Oxford University Press 2006), paras. 8.48 ff.

[15] Fine Arts Copyright Act 1862 (UK), s 1. Specific statutory protection was also to be found in the Spanish Law of 10 January 1879, art. 1. In France, this protection was to be found in the jurisprudence: see A. DARRAS, DU DROIT DES AUTEURS ET DES ARTISTES DANS LES RAPPORTS INTERNATIONAUX (Paris: Rousseau 1887), para. 320, and E. Pouillet [1889] DA 54. The same was true in Belgium and Italy: see P. WAUWERMANS, LE DROIT DES AUTEURS EN BELGIQUE 144 (1894) (for Belgium) and H. Rosmini [1889] DA 18, 30 (for Italy). For a general survey, see the International Office study in [1895] DA 116, 129.

[16] German Law of 10 January 1876; see further the commentary on this law in [1895] DA 116, 118. To similar effect was the Swiss Law of 23 April 1883, art. 9.

[17] See The GEH Brownie Collection, George Eastman House, Technology Archive at www.geh.org/fm/ Brownie/htmlsrc/index.html which lists the original model of the Brownie camera as being available from February 1900 at a list price of US $1.00.

the Conferences of 1884 and 1885, where the French moved for the inclusion of photographic works in Article 4.[18] This met with strong German opposition,[19] and led the commission at the 1885 Conference to propose the adoption of an interim solution, which inserted the following paragraphs in the Closing Protocol:

> 1. As regards Article 4, it is agreed that those countries of the Union where the character of artistic works is not refused to photographs engage to admit them to the benefits of the Convention concluded today, from the date of its coming into force. They shall, however, not be bound to protect the authors of such works further than is permitted by their own legislation except in the case of international engagements already existing, or which may hereafter be entered into by them.
>
> It is understood that an authorized photograph of a protected work of art shall enjoy legal protection in all countries of the Union, as contemplated by the said Convention, for the same period as the principal right of reproduction of the work itself subsists, and within the limits of private agreements between those who have legal rights.[20]

It will be seen from the second paragraph that the only photographic works which were to be protected by Union countries were those which were "authorised" photographs of a "protected work of art"; for example, a photograph of a painting, drawing, or sculpture. This was akin to protecting other kinds of derivative work, such as the translation of a literary work or the adaptation of a novel into a play, although it may be noted that the making of an unauthorised photograph, translation, or adaptation would have been an infringement of the work photographed, translated, or adapted in any event.[21] As regards other photographic works, that is, "original" photographs of such subject matter as persons, animals, landscapes, buildings, and the like, under the first paragraph protection under the Convention was limited to the extent to which such works were regarded in a given Union country as artistic works, or to the extent to which such works were protected under the terms of a bilateral agreement between the countries concerned. Thus, if country A accorded protection to these photographs as artistic works, as was the case in France and the U.K., that country was obliged to protect the photographs of authors claiming protection

---

[18] *Actes de la Conférence internationale pour la protection des Droits d'auteur réunie à Berne du 8 au 19 septembre 1884*, International Office, Berne (1884) (*Actes 1884*), at 44; *Actes de la 2me Conférence internationale pour la protection des oeuvres littéraires et artistiques réunie à Berne du 7 au 18 septembre 1885*, International Office, Berne (1885) (*Actes 1885*), at 43.

[19] *See id.*

[20] *Actes 1885*, at 43, 54–55.

[21] This provision was also anomalous in that it did not extend to photographs of protected literary works, for example, a photograph of a manuscript: STEPHEN P. LADAS, THE INTERNATIONAL PROTECTION OF LITERARY AND ARTISTIC PROPERTY (New York: Macmillan 1938), vol. I, 231–32.

under the Convention. As no condition of reciprocity was required, this protection was to be accorded, irrespective of the fact that the countries to which these authors belonged did not protect photographs or accord protection to them other than as artistic works.[22] This last point was important, because if country B protected photographs under another head, it was not obliged under the principle of national treatment to extend this protection to photographs emanating from another Union country in which artistic copyright protection was given.[23] As far as bilateral agreements were concerned, there were several of these in operation in 1886 under which photographs were enumerated among the works which each country undertook to protect.[24] These agreements, of course, had no effect so far as other Union countries were concerned (leaving aside the flow-on effect of most-favoured-nation clauses in other bilateral agreements).

It was only by stages that photographic works achieved full "list" status under Article 4 and its successors.[25] An interim position was adopted in the Berlin Act 1908, under which Article 3 specifically obliged Union countries to protect "photographic works and works produced by a process analogous to photography." The scope of this protection, however, was more limited than for literary and artistic works under Article 2 (formerly Article 4). In particular, they did not enjoy the newly accorded minimum term of the life of the author plus fifty years, with the term of protection being limited to whatever it was in the country where protection was claimed.[26] Furthermore, as photographic works were still not included among literary and artistic works under Article 2, this meant that they were not covered by those articles of the Convention which applied specifically to literary and artistic works, such as Articles 9 and 10, which were concerned with lawful borrowings.[27] In the view of some, these limitations did not matter, in view of the fact that there was now a guarantee of protection for photographic works in Union countries.[28] However, there was now an internal contradiction: if the Berne Convention was a convention for the protection of the rights of authors in their literary and artistic works, why should it extend protection to a category of subject matter which was not uniformly recognised by countries of the Union as having the characteristics

---

[22] [1895] *DA* 116, 118; LADAS, *supra* note 21, at 207–08.

[23] See *supra* note 22.

[24] See, e.g., the Spanish-Italian Convention of 26 June 1880, art 1, and the Franco-Italian Convention of 9 July 1884, art 1 (LCD, vol. II, 303).

[25] For a full discussion, see RICKETSON & GINSBURG, *supra* note 14, at 442–53.

[26] Berlin Act, Article 7, third paragraph.

[27] LADAS, *supra* note 21, at 232.

[28] In the words of the German Administration: "although opinions as to the intrinsic nature of photographic works still vary greatly, it matters little whether they are considered under national law as works of art or are submitted to any special treatment; the important thing is that their protection be guaranteed in each country of the Union": *Actes de la Conférence de Berlin 1908*, International Office, Berne (1909) ('*Actes* 1908'), at 49–50. Quoted with approval by the Commission at p. 235.

of a literary or artistic work? This, surely, was a derogation from the fundamental object of the Union, namely the protection of the rights of authors in their literary and artistic works. On the other hand, from the point of view of those countries which did treat photographs as artistic works, Article 3 of the Berlin Act was a satisfactory halfway house, a firm step in the direction of full conventional recognition which could be attained at a subsequent conference of revision. After further and ultimately abortive proposals for fuller protection at the Rome Revision Conference in 1928, this goal was finally achieved at Brussels in 1948, although the term of protection still remained a matter for the law of each country where protection was claimed.[29] A further indication that photographic works are still regarded as being of somewhat lower status, notwithstanding their elevation to Article 2(1), is to be seen in the twenty-five-year minimum term which was adopted at the Stockholm Revision Conference in 1967.[30]

12.4. OTHER EARLY CLAIMANTS FOR PROTECTION

The tale of photographic works is a salutary one. Other claimants have met with mixed success. Thus, works of architecture and choreographic works and entertainments in dumb show received a relatively easy entry into Article 2(1) in the Berlin Act 1908, without the need for any conditions or limitations on their protection. The same was true of cinematographic productions, which received protection under the Berlin Act of 1908 as literary or artistic works in cases where "by the arrangement of the acting form or the combinations of the incidents represented, the author has given the work a personal and original character."[31] There were strong proponents for the inclusion of these kinds of works, or, at the very least, there were no strong objectors. The argument of authorial status was more readily advanced and accepted in the cases of architects, choreographers, and film directors (although it may be significant that it was felt necessary, in the case of cinematographic works, to specify the particular characteristics that would confer authorial status). Likewise, there was general acceptance of the claims for protection of derivative works such as translations, adaptations, arrangements of music, and even collections of different works, as also occurred in the Berlin Act 1908.[32] On the other hand, real division of

---

[29] Brussels Act, Berne Convention for the Protection of Literary and Artistic Works, Article 7(3).

[30] Stockholm Act, Berne Convention for the Protection of Literary and Artistic Works, art 7(4) (not to be applied now, in the case of contracting parties to the WIPO Copyright Treaty 1996, under Article 9 of that treaty).

[31] Berlin Act, Berne Convention for the Protection of Literary and Artistic Works, Article 14, second paragraph. Inclusion in Art 2(1), along with "works produced by a process analogous to cinematography" occurred in the Brussels Act 1948.

[32] Berlin Act 1908, Berne Convention for the Protection of Literary and Artistic Works, Art 2, second paragraph.

opinion arose over the category of works of applied art, as many countries drew a distinction between works of art exploited within the traditional artistic sphere and works of art applied industrially in the manufacture of useful articles. Ultimately, such works were admitted to protection only after lengthy debates at successive conferences, and then on a conditional basis that essentially leaves Union countries free to determine whether they will protect them as artistic works or under *sui generis* schemes of industrial design or models protection, or both.[33]

If there are conclusions to be drawn about the nature of works and authorship from the above, they point to two things. The first is the need for the presence of some kind of personal creative contribution to a form of expression that falls generally within the literary or artistic domain (noting that the factual, informational, or "scientific" character of the final production does not prevent it from being literary or artistic in the broad generic sense of those terms). Second, this inquiry may be affected, though not necessarily fatally, by the utilisation of some mechanical means (as in the case of a camera) or the presence of some industrial purpose (as in the case of works of applied art). These broad propositions may then serve to explain why two other claimants for protection at the Berlin and Rome Revision Conferences – sound recordings (phonograms) and performers – failed to gain acceptance within the scope of the Berne Convention, even on the same tentative basis as photographic works. There is a paradox at work here, as will be seen. On the one hand, there was a "production" – the sound recording – that can readily be characterised as "artistic," as in the case of a recording of an orchestral work, but there was a perceived absence of authorial contribution to its making, in that it resulted from a process of industrial manufacture. On the other hand, performers' contributions may well be described as authorial, in that they can involve high levels of personal creativity, but there is no "production" that can be identified (other than the very transience of the performance itself). A third claimant for protection that began to be considered in the 1930s – broadcasts – entailed neither a work of any kind nor the involvement of anyone who looked remotely like an author. The history of each of these different subject matters both within and outside the Berne Union therefore requires some further consideration, as each was ultimately to become the subject, internationally, of what we now call "neighbouring rights" protection, that is, of separate rights that are related to, but are not to be classified as, those of authors.

12.5. THE CASE OF SOUND RECORDINGS

Following the invention of the phonograph by Edison in the late nineteenth century, a large industry concerned with the manufacture of sound recordings and similar

---

[33] *See also*, RICKETSON & GINSBURG, *supra* note 14, paras. 8.59 ff.

devices had come into existence by the time of the Berlin Revision Conference of
the Berne Convention in 1908. At this Conference, as the result of strategic lobbying at the national level, authors of musical works were given exclusive rights with
respect to mechanical reproductions of their works (Article 13(1)), but allowance for
the grant of compulsory licences to record manufacturers was also made (Article
13(2)), partly because of fears that music publishers (who owned most of the musical
copyrights) might exercise their newly acquired mechanical reproduction rights in a
monopolistic fashion.[34] During the Conference, though not noted specifically in the
minutes, the British delegates raised the question of whether it would be desirable
to include in the Convention a provision expressly giving international copyright
protection, in suitable cases, to the actual instruments on which the musical works
were recorded – the gramophone discs, piano rolls, and the like.[35] Against this, it was
maintained that these objects were on the borderline between "industrial property"
and copyright, and might conceivably be held to belong more properly to the former
category.[36] The matter was taken no further by the British Government at this stage,
but, prompted by the concerns of its extensive recording industry,[37] it repeated its
suggestion in more formal terms at the Rome Revision Conference in 1928. This
proposed the inclusion of the following paragraph to Article 13:

> Without prejudice to the rights of the authors of an original work, recordings, per-
> forated rolls and other instruments by means of which sounds may be mechanically
> reproduced, shall be protected as original works.[38]

This proposal was likewise criticised on the ground that it was concerned with
the protection of manufacturing, rather than authors' interests.[39] There were also
attacks on the consistency of the U.K. Government's position, as it had, at the same
Conference, opposed analogous proposals for the protection of performers.[40] The

---

[34] *See also* LADAS, vol. I, *supra* note 21, at 429–32.

[35] *Miscellaneous No 2 (1909), Correspondence respecting the Revised Convention of Berne for the
Protection of Literary and Artistic Works, signed at Berlin, November 13, 1908*, Presented to both
Houses of Parliament by Command of His Majesty, February 1909, C-4467, HMSO, London (1909)
('*Correspondence 1908*'), at 14 (report of British delegates to the Foreign Secretary, Sir Edward Grey).

[36] *Id.*

[37] *See, e.g.,* the submission by the Mechanical Music Industry of Great Britain made to the UK
Government prior to the Rome Conference: G. S. Wood, Preliminary Observations upon, and
Arguments against, the Amendments to the Berne Convention of 1886 ... proposed by the Italian
Government in conjunction with the office of the International Union for the Protection of Literary
and Artistic Works, with general suggestions for revision of that Convention along different lines,
Mechanical Music Industry of Great Britain (1927).

[38] *Actes de la Conférence réunie à Rome du 7 mai au 2 juin 1928*, International Office, Berne (1929)
('*Actes 1928*'), at 94.

[39] *Actes 1928*, at 263 (comments by the French delegation).

[40] *Id.* See further below in the principal text.

result was that no agreement was reached on the proposal, and it lapsed.[41] At that point, proposals to protect phonograms as such dropped off the Berne revision agenda, although it is odd to note that the *Association littéraire et artistique internationale* (ALAI) passed a resolution in favour of the inclusion of "phonographic works" in Article 2(1) at its 1935 Congress,[42] while the *Confédération internationale des société des auteurs and des artistes* ("CISAC") passed a resolution equally opposed at its congress of that year.[43] The Berne International Office and the Belgian Government, in their jointly prepared proposals for the forthcoming Brussels Revision Conference (to be held in 1935, though later postponed), were just as firmly opposed in the draft programme they circulated in early 1933[44] and the Berne Office repeated this critique in a note on the ALAI resolution two years later.[45] The contributions of the record manufacturer were regarded as "industrial" rather than "intellectual," notwithstanding the creative qualities of the work that was recorded, and therefore had no place within the Berne Convention (at this point, of course, the activities of great record producers such as Phil Spector or George Martin were over thirty years in the future). On the other hand, such bodies as CISAC recognised that phonogram producers, "without prejudice to the rights of authors," merited some kind of protection, perhaps in an annex to the Berne Convention that accorded them a right to prevent unauthorised reproduction and an entitlement to an "equitable remuneration" in the case of unauthorised broadcasts and uses.[46] Arguments in favour of what we would now call a "neighbouring right" now began to be expressed more forcefully, particularly by interested industry groups.[47] This development is taken up further below.

12.5.1. *Performers*

In terms of artistry and creative contribution, performers must surely come closer to the notion of authorship implicit in Article 2(1) of Berne. However, as already noted, it is harder to point to a work or "production ... in the literary, scientific, or artistic domain" that is the subject of that authorship, particularly given that the bulk

---

[41] *Id.* at 264.
[42] At Montreux-Caux from 30 January to 3 February 1935, reported in [1935] *DA* 45 and noted in *Documents de la Conférence réunie à Bruxelles du 5 au 26 juin 1948*, International Office, Berne (1951) ('Documents 1948'), at 436.
[43] At Seville from 6 to 11 May 1935: *Documents 1948*, at 437.
[44] [1933] *DA* 74.
[45] [1935] *DA* 39
[46] Congress at Stresa, 2–3 June 1934, reproduced in *Documents 1948*, at 478. Notably, this resolution referred also to communication by way of television. ALAI was less convinced, noting that this should be a matter for a separate convention rather than an annex to Berne: see the resolution of the 1937 Congress at Paris, 15–19 June 1937 reproduced in *Documents 1948*, at 509.
[47] *Documents 1948*, at 477–78 (International Congress of the Phonographic Industry, Rome, 10–14 Nov. 1933).

of performances are of pre-existing works of which the author may well be someone other than the performer. There was a conundrum here that posed clear problems for the purists of the Berne Convention, although it took time in coming to the fore. For some years, performers' claims for separate protection were unnecessary, as works could only be performed in public by the actual performers, that is, "live." However, the advent of the phonogram, and then of public broadcasting, posed an immediate threat to performers' livelihoods, as performances now could be fixed and disseminated far beyond the immediate confines of concert halls and public venues – the phenomenon sometimes referred to as "technological unemployment."[48] By way of compensation, therefore, could performers be regarded as the authors of their performances in order to stake a claim to a place in the sun under the Berne Convention? Obviously, no problem arose if the performer was also the author of the work which she performed, and the same was potentially the case where she spontaneously created an oral work in the course of her performance (at least in jurisdictions where fixation in some material form was not required). However, in the more usual situation where she performed a pre-existing work in which she had no rights, the only basis for a claim of protection under the Berne Convention was that her actual performance – the transient interpretation of a particular work[49] – constituted a literary or artistic work in its own right. This, in fact, was the approach to be found in several national laws, where the performer of a recorded work was granted protection as if this was a transformation or an adaptation of that work.[50] This elevation of performers to the status of author was exceptional,[51] but points to an important link between performers and phonogram producers once a live performance is recorded, as interpretations of the same work by different performers can result in quite contrasting recorded versions of that work that have an additional or independent commercial value arising from the contribution of the performer rather than that of the composer or record producer.[52] In some jurisdictions, this now entitles

---

[48] *See also* M. Saporta, *Les droits dits "connexes" aux droit d'auteur* 4 REVUE INTERNATIONAL DE DROIT COMPARÉ 45 (1952); G. H. C. Bodenhausen, *Protection of "Neighbouring Rights,"* 19 L. & CONTEMP. PROBS. 156, 162 ff. (1954) (pointing to studies done by the ILO immediately after World War II).

[49] Described by Stephen Ladas as a "creation of a very fugitive character": LADAS, vol. I, *supra* note 21, at 427.

[50] As in the German Law of 22 May 1910, art 1 amending article 2 of the Law of 19 June 1901 concerning the right of the author in literary and musical works: French translation in [1910] DA 86 and commented upon by LADAS, vol. I, *supra* note 21, at 427. See also art. 4, para. 2, of the Swiss Law of 7 December 1922: [1923] DA 61–2.

[51] See further the critique by LADAS, vol. I, *supra* note 21, at 427.

[52] This point is well understood by collectors of recordings of classical music who will discern vast differences in interpretations of Bach's piano works by artists such as Glenn Gould, Murray Pereia and Alfred Brendl or recordings of Wagner's Ring Cycle by Klemperer, von Karajan or Solti. In the case of more modern music, a search on YouTube for the song 'Cry me a river' will reveal an extraordinary range of recorded interpretations by singers such as Ella Fitzgerald (for whom the song was originally written in 1953), Julie London, Dinah Washington, Nina Simone, Diana Krall, Michael Bublé, Ray

performers to a share in the neighbouring right subsisting in the recording in addition to whatever rights they may have in their performances.[53]

At the international level, these matters were first discussed in some detail at the Rome Revision Conference in 1928, where the Italian Government and Berne International Office proposed that performers should be protected against unauthorised broadcasts and recordings of their performances;[54] there were also several supplementary proposals to include performances expressly in Article 2.[55] While delegates generally agreed that some kind of protection was warranted, there was no consensus on any of these proposals. It was, of course, open to any Union country to take the view that performances were, in any event, included under the general rubric of "productions in the literary, scientific and artistic domain," but there was no general acceptance of this among the delegates. In particular, the French delegation made clear its view that performers were not authors,[56] and that performances were therefore not works within the Convention. Finally, a resolution was passed that requested Union countries to consider what measures they could take to protect the interests of performers, and the matter was left there.[57] In the period following the Rome Conference, opposition to protecting performers as authors continued to be expressed by various authors' organisations, such as ALAI and CISAC.[58] Indeed, the 1933 Conference of CISAC at Copenhagen declared that the recognition of any exclusive right for performers would be "dangerous" for the exclusive rights of authors,[59] and the issue clearly concerned that other champion of authors' rights, ALAI, which called, more cautiously, for further study.[60] On the other hand, the plight of performers was picked up by the International Labour Office which, largely at the prompting of musicians' and actors' unions, now began to study the general question.[61] The strong objections from authors' groups were reflected in the 1933 programme for the Brussels Conference prepared by the Berne International Office and the Belgian Government, although there was also considerable sympathy here for the vulnerability of performers to the unauthorised fixation of their performances by third parties.[62] This resulted in a subsequent proposal in the

Charles, Joe Cocker and Justin Timberlake (whose version appears to have almost no connection to any of the others).

[53] *See, e.g.*, the *Copyright Act 1968* (Australia), ss 22(3A), 97.

[54] *Actes* 1928, at 78.

[55] *Id.* at 229, 260.

[56] *Id.* at 256, 260.

[57] *Id.* at 350.

[58] See the texts of the various hostile resolutions collected in *Documents* 1948, at 455–57 and 493–94.

[59] CISAC Congress at Copenhagen, 29 May–3 June 1933: reproduced in *Documents* 1948, at 457.

[60] ALAI Congress at Budapest, 4–10 June 1930: *Documents* 1948, at 456.

[61] Saporta, *supra* note 48, at 42–47 and accompanying footnotes. *See also Documents* 1948, at 455–6.

[62] *See also* LADAS, vol. I, *supra* note 21, at 628–30.

Brussels programme for a new Article 11*quater*, which left it to each Union country to determine the conditions under which protection for performers was to be accorded[63] – hardly an advance from the resolution of 1928. A more specific British amendment proposed that unauthorised recordings of performances of dramatic or musical works should be prevented.[64] Once again, while there was fairly general sympathy with the object of these proposals, the view was clearly emerging that the protection of performers belonged outside the Convention.[65] Final resolution of these matters within the Berne Union was to be deferred by the advent of war, but following this the Brussels Revision Conference (held in 1948) shut the door firmly on protection under Berne.[66] Thus, while acknowledging the "artistic character" of performances, the Conference satisfied itself merely with a pious resolution that studies concerning neighbouring rights, and notably those of performers, should be "actively pursued."[67] International protection of performers' rights was thenceforth to be the subject of separate treaties, first under the Rome Convention of 1961,[68] and then under the WIPO Performances and Phonograms Treaty of 1996, and the Beijing Treaty on Audiovisual Performers of 2012. This later history lies outside the scope of the present chapter, but it should be noted that, even by the mid-1930s, it was clear that performers did not belong within the framework of Berne. The notion of separate rights, analogous to those of authors but outside authors' rights regimes altogether, was now beginning to emerge. This was partly as a consequence of work that was being done outside the Berne Union, notably within the International Labour Office and by the Rome Institute (see further below). It will also be seen that the Berne International Office was receptive to this kind of approach, giving rise to the intriguing legal issue of whether such obligations could then be annexed to the Berne Convention, even if not part of the principal agreement, or whether they should be embodied in freestanding instruments. At the same time, alongside performers and phonogram producers, broadcasters were now beginning to advance their own claims for protection.

---

[63] *Documents 1948*, at 308 (new art. 11*quater*). These proposals were made by the International Office subsequent to its 1933–4 proposals, and were the subject of differing responses from Union countries that were published in [1936] *DA* 80.

[64] *Documents 1948*, at 310–11.

[65] *See also* [1936] *DA* 80.

[66] *Documents 1948*, at 313, report of discussions within the General Committee of the Conference, where proposed Article 11*quater* was eventually withdrawn, along with other proposals for protection: see further at 309–12.

[67] *Documents 1948*, at 587 (Resolution VIII, proposal of Austria).

[68] Rome Convention for the Protection of Performers, Producers of Phonograms and Broadcasting Organizations 1961. *See also* STEPHEN M. STEWART, INTERNATIONAL COPYRIGHT AND NEIGHBOURING RIGHTS 221ff. (2d ed., London: Butterworths 1989).

12.5.2. *Broadcasts*

By the time of the Rome Revision Conference in 1928, the potential of radio broadcasting in relation to the diffusion of literary, dramatic, and musical works was fully recognised.[69] One of the positive achievements of that Conference was the adoption of Article 11*bis*(1) under which the authors of literary and artistic works were given the exclusive right of authorising the communication of their works to the public by means of radio-diffusion. The exclusive right granted, however, was not absolute: in recognition of the public and social aspect of broadcasting, the possibility of it being made subject to conditions and reservations under national laws, that is, compulsory licences, was provided for in Article 11*bis*(2). There was a compromise here struck between

> two opposing tendencies – that of completely assimilating the radio broadcasting right to the author's other exclusive rights (a tendency defended especially by the British and French Delegations) and that of considering the matter subject to intervention on the part of the public authorities in order to protect the cultural and social interests linked to this specific new form of popular dissemination of intellectual works, particularly musical ones (a tendency defended especially by the Australian and New Zealand Delegations).[70]

At this stage, no specific claim for protection for their transmissions was made by the broadcasters themselves, but there was a curious French amendment advanced at the Rome Conference which appeared to address their position directly: this proposed the inclusion in Article 2(1) of "radiophonic works" (*oeuvres radiophoniques*),[71] and was subsequently modified to read as "works specially created for the purpose of radio-diffusion" (*oeuvres spécialement créées en vue de la radiodiffusion*).[72] The stated purpose of the proposal was to cover "those works *sui generis* which are neither written, nor oral, and the diffusion of which is only possible over radio (for example, the contemporaneous reporting of a football match …)."[73] On the other hand, it was open to the objection that the definition of such works by reference to their purpose hardly made them a separate category of work, and that it was always open to Union countries to accord protection under the general definition of "literary and artistic work" in Article 2(1) (subject, of course, to the requirements of national laws with regard to the matter of fixation).[74] In any

---

[69] Described as the "triumphant progress of radiophony" in the programme for the Conference: *Actes 1928*, at 76.

[70] *Actes 1928*, at 210 (general report of the drafting committee).

[71] *Actes 1928*, at 98.

[72] *Id.* at 226–27.

[73] *Id.* at 227.

[74] See the 1935 ALAI proposals for their protection and the International Office's response to this: [1935] DA 39, 45.

event, the French proposal was withdrawn after the Conference had adopted Article 11*bis*, and did not therefore proceed to a vote. The issue of whether there should be protection against unauthorised uses of the emissions of the broadcaster – usually a different person or entity from the authors of any works that were the subject of those emissions – was not addressed by the Conference, although this distinction was noted by at least one delegate.[75] In one respect, broadcasters, who might be a mixture of state-owned and private enterprises under different national laws, fared well with the Rome revision, with the adoption of Article 11*bis*(2). On the other hand, proposals for the protection of their emissions as such soon began to be considered, and were advanced by, relevant industry bodies, such as the International Juridical Congress of Radio-electricity at its conferences in Warsaw in 1934[76] and in Brussels in 1935.[77] These studies were supportive of fuller broadcasting rights for the authors of literary and artistic works and appropriate protection for performers, but also sought protection for broadcasters, within the framework of the Berne Convention, against the unauthorised "industrial" uses of their broadcasts, whether through a right of control or even a claim for equitable remuneration. While these proposals did not enter into the programme for the forth-coming Brussels Revision of the Berne Convention, outside the forum of the Berne Convention discussions of "neighbouring rights" protection in a number of areas, including broadcasts, were now getting under way, and it is to these broader developments that we must now turn.

12.6. BROADER CONCERNS ABOUT NEIGHBOURING RIGHTS

As to how such protection might look, if embodied in some kind of international agreement, national laws already provided some pointers. For example, as noted above, Germany and Switzerland had accorded limited protection to photographs under separate laws late in the nineteenth century[78] and to performers in 1910 and 1922 respectively.[79] Again, the United Kingdom in 1911 – and with no attention to

---

75 *Actes 1928*, at 227 (Norway).
76 Noted in [1934] *DA* 54–5. For the records of the Congress, see Congrès juridique international de la radioélectricité (5; 1934-04-10/1934-04-14; Varsovie). Cinquième congrès juridique international de la radioélectricité, Varsovie, 10–14 avril 1934/organisé par les soins du Comité international de la radioélectricité, 1935, at 112 ff., 129ff., and 142–43.
77 Congrès juridique international de la radioélectricité (6; 1935-07-08/1935-07-10; Bruxelles). Sixième Congrès juridique international de la radioélectricité, Bruxelles, 8–10 juillet 1935/organisé par les soins du Comité international de la radioélectricité, 1936, at 136 ff. where rights for broadcasters as well as for phonogram producers and performers were included in a draft treaty on radio-diffusion.
78 German Law of 10 January 1876; see further the commentary on this law in [1895] *DA* 116, 118. To similar effect was the Swiss Law of 23 April 1883, art. 9.
79 German Law of 22 May 1910, art 1 amending article 2 of the Law of 19 June 1901 concerning the right of the author in literary and musical works: French translation in [1910] *DA* 86 and commented upon by LADAS, vol. I, *supra* note 21, at 427. See also art. 4, para. 2, of the Swiss Law of 7 December 1922: [1923] *DA* 61–62.

doctrinal purity – had accorded a "copyright" in "records, perforated rolls and other contrivances by means of which sounds may be mechanically produced,"[80] and, in the case of performers, had extended protection through the imposition of criminal penalties in the event of unauthorised fixations of performances.[81]

However, photographers, performers, phonogram manufacturers, and broadcasters were not the only claimants for protection, either at the national or international levels, in this period. One area of concern was the protection of news (*les informations de presse*), where claims for protection under the Berne Convention had been rejected at the Berlin Conference in 1908 on the basis that these did not properly fall within the description of literary or artistic works (being simply facts or ideas) and that their protection therefore lay more appropriately within the scope of unfair competition law.[82] But attempts to include misappropriation of press reports within Article 10*bis* of the Paris Convention for the Protection of Industrial Property at revision conferences of that Convention in both 1925[83] and 1934[84] failed on the basis that their place was more properly within the literary and artistic sphere. Accordingly, there were discussions, beginning in the late 1920s and principally within the League of Nations, its associated body, the International Institute for Intellectual Cooperation (IIC) and the International Chamber of Commerce,[85] as to how such material might best be protected.[86] As will be seen, protection of press information was to become the subject of one of the draft agreements adopted by the Samedan Committee in 1939.

A further claimant for protection in this period related to the titles of literary or artistic works where these had a distinctive character. This was the subject of a proposed new Article 15*bis* of the Berne Convention in the programme that was prepared for the proposed Brussels Revision Conference by the Berne International Office and the Belgian Government in 1933.[87] As in the case of news items, this also appeared

---

[80] *Copyright Act 1911* (UK), s 19(1) (adopted, in turn, by most British self-governing dominions, such as Australia, Canada, South Africa and New Zealand). Similar laws were passed in Austria and Italy in 1936 and 1937: see further LADAS, vol. I, *supra* note 21, at 425.

[81] *Dramatic and Musical Performers Protection Act 1925* (UK).

[82] *Actes 1908*, at 251–52 (general report). *See also* RICKETSON & GINSBURG, *supra* note 14, at 497 ff.

[83] *Actes de la Conférence de la Haye de 1925*, Bureau international de la Union, Berne, 1926 ('*Actes 1925*'), at 253–54, 478–79 (report of fourth sub-committee).

[84] *Actes de la Conférence réunie à Londres du 1 mai au 2 juin 1934*, Bureau de l'Union internationale pour la protection de propriété industrielle, Berne 1934, at 289 (Czech proposal), 420–21 (report of fourth sub-committee), 469 (report of drafting committee), 477 (general report of drafting committee), 592 (text of resolution as adopted, recommending that countries should "study" the question of introduction into their laws of an "efficacious protection" against the unauthorised disclosure of news during the period of its "commercial value" and against disclosure without any indication of source).

[85] The predecessor of UNESCO.

[86] *See generally* Manley O. Hudson, *International Protection of Property in News*, 22 AM. J. INT'L L. 385–89 (1928) and see also STEPHEN P. LADAS, PATENTS, TRADEMARKS, AND RELATED RIGHTS: NATIONAL AND INTERNATIONAL PROTECTION (Harvard University Press 1975), vol. III, at 1722–23.

[87] *See* [1934] DA 27.

to have a link to unfair competition issues rather than authors' rights as it sought to prohibit commercial use by a third party where this might cause confusion. This was not
included in the Samedan drafts, and was ultimately rejected by the Brussels Conference
when it finally convened after the war.[88]

Yet another claimant for protection, although not something that we would think
of today as a neighbouring right because of its direct link to the authors of artistic
works, was the *droit de suite* or art resale royalty right. This had been first adopted
in France in 1920[89] and in several other European countries in the following years,[90]
and was a matter which had long been promoted by ALAI.[91] The matter was also
taken up by the IIIC, which advocated action on both a national and international
level.[92] At the Rome Conference, the French Government proposed the following
'*voeu*' which was based directly on the wording of a resolution passed by ALAI at its
Paris Congress in 1925:

> It is desirable that the inalienable droit de suite, established in France by the law
> of 20 May 1920 and in Belgium by that of 25 June 1921, to the profit of artists, in
> their original works which are publicly sold, should be the object of similar legisla-
> tive dispositions in other countries, on condition of reciprocity, in each of them,
> between their nationals and those of countries which have already adopted this
> measure.[93]

This proposal, modestly framed with its reference to the need for the proposed
right to be reciprocal, was nonetheless pushing the boundaries too far for the majority of Berne Union members. In particular, doubts were raised as to the connection
between this proposed right and authors' rights protection in general, in that it was a
right pertaining to the physical embodiment of the artistic work itself rather than to
the traditional incorporeal rights of making and disseminating copies.[94] A modified
text of the resolution was finally adopted as follows, but a number of delegations,

---

[88] *Documents 1948*, pp. 373–74.

[89] Law of 20 May 1920; reproduced in [1920] DA 61 and for an analysis of the law, see A. Vaunois, [1920]
       Le Droit d'Auteur 161.

[90] Belgium: Law of 25 June 1921 (reproduced in [1921] *Le Droit d'Auteur* 97); Czechoslovakia: Law of 24
       November 1926, art 35 (reproduced in [1926] *Le Droit d'Auteur* 33–34).

[91] *See* J.-L. Duchemin, *Le Droit de Suite des Artistes* (1948), 241–45 for an account of ALAI's involvement
       in the study and promotion of *droit de suite*. *See also* the resolutions of ALAI passed at Paris 1912, Paris
       1925 and Warsaw 1936: *Actes 1928*, 48.

[92] Institut International de Cooperation Intellectuelle, *La Protection internationale du droit d'auteur*
       (1928): includes the report of the IIIC sub-committee on *droit de suite*. For a commentary on the
       report, see Duchemin, *supra* note 91, at 245–49.

[93] *Actes de la Conférence réunie à Rome du 7 mai au 2 juin 1928*, International Office, Berne (1929)
       ('*Actes 1928*'), at 103.

[94] *Actes 1928*, at 283.

including those of the U.K., Hungary, the Netherlands, Norway, and Switzerland, abstained from voting on it:

> The Conference expresses the desire that those countries of the Union which have not yet adopted legislative provisions guaranteeing to the benefit of artists an inalienable right to a share in the proceeds of successive public sales of their original works should take into account the possibility of considering such provisions.[95]

Following the Rome Conference, both ALAI and the IIIC continued to study the implementation of *droit de suite* on both a national and international scale,[96] and the matter was also considered by a number of other international bodies, including the Rome Institute.[97] More particularly, the Belgian Government and Berne International Office made it the subject of a specific proposal for a mandatory new right applying to both original works of art and the original manuscripts of writers and composers, which they included in their preliminary programme in 1933 for the Brussels Revision of the Berne Convention.[98] Not surprisingly, this expanded proposal for protection received a wide range of critical responses from member states, some of which were hostile to the notion of an obligatory right generally,[99] while others objected to particular aspects of the programme proposal, such as its inclusion of manuscripts and its apparent inclusion of architectural works and works of applied art, its limitation to heirs, and the failure to link its duration to that of economic rights generally.[100] Following the postponement of the planned Brussels Revision Conference in 1936, proposals for recognition of *droit de suite* became part of an emerging agenda for protection of neighbouring rights that was considered by a committee of experts convened by the Rome Institute in April 1935.[101] This committee proposed that certain matters which were not generally regarded as part of authors' rights, but were nevertheless closely related or "neighbouring," should be dealt with in a convention or arrangement annexed to the Berne Convention. The work of this committee was to lead directly to the convening of the Samedan committee in 1939.

---

[95] *Actes 1928*, at 283.
[96] Duchemin, *supra* note 91, at 243 ff.
[97] Duchemin, *supra* note 91, at 252 ff. See further Rome Institute (now UNIDROIT), *Rapport sur le droit de suite de l'artiste*, Study VII, S.d.N. – U.D.P. 1931.
[98] Duchemin, *supra* note 91, at 301 (for text of the proposition, to be article 14*bis*) and at 250 ff. (for further background).
[99] *See* [1936] *DA* 93.
[100] [1936] *DA* 93. See also *Documents 1948*, at 362–63.
[101] Duchemin, *supra* note 91, at 252 ff. See further Rome Institute (now UNIDROIT), Comité d'experts pour les droits intellectuels. Première Session, Rome, 28–29 avril 1935, *Résumé des délibérations*, S.d.N. – U.D.P., Document 11 (see also 10). Noted also in Institut international de coopération intellectuelle. La Coopération intellectuelle/Société des Nations. Institut international de la coopération intellectuelle. 1929–39, Chronique, at 319.

Perhaps the most significant aspect of this 1930s period is the fact that quite extensive discussions were going on in various international forums, some official and
others private, about these new forms of protection, but that this was largely outside
the more "traditional" forum of the Berne Convention, which was becoming more
clearly defined than ever as a purely authors' rights convention. The "purity" of the
Berne system was also maintained in the important area of formalities, where work
on the possibility of a bridging convention between the non-registration systems of
Berne countries and the registration countries of the Pan American copyright treaties (including, most notably, the USA) was being carried out under the auspices of
the IIIC, rather than the Berne International Office.[102] This draft convention was
eventually to form the basis for the Universal Copyright Convention in the post–
World War II period. The position of the Berne International Office in relation
to all these matters is interesting, as the issues of neighbouring rights protection
and the proposed bridging convention continued to feature regularly in reports and
commentaries in its monthly publication *Le Droit d'auteur*,[103] while the issues of
further protection for performers' rights and *droit de suite* were, of course, addressed
in the programme that was being prepared for the postponed Brussels Revision
Conference. Furthermore, the Director of the International Office, Fritz Ostertag
(Director, 1926–38) is reported as being present and actively involved at most of
the relevant meetings of the IIIC, the Rome Institute, and other interested bodies
during this period. It is clear that Ostertag was keen to ensure that any proposals
for the international protection of neighbouring rights should be linked in some
way to the Berne Convention, and this also seems to have been the intention of the
other bodies that were working on these issues, including the International Labour
Office. In early April 1939, however, it was a further meeting of the Rome Institute
that took the initiative of convening a committee of experts to be held in Samedan,
Switzerland, in July of that year for the purpose of "enlarging the programme of the
Brussels Conference."[104]

12.7. THE OSTERTAG REPORT AND DRAFT PROPOSALS

By way of preparation for the Samedan meeting, Ostertag, who had recently retired as
Director of the Berne International Office and moreover had been closely involved
in the preparation of the Brussels programme, undertook the preparation of a report

---

[102] Société des Nations, Cooperation Intellectuelle, 61–62, at 61–67, *Documents, Avant-projet de
Convention universelle pour la protection du droit d'auteur* (25 Apr. 1936). See further LADAS, vol. I,
supra note 21, at 573–679.
[103] *See, e.g.,* 'Le rapprochement des Conventions de Berne et de La Havane' [1935] *DA* 100, 109.
[104] [1939] *DA* 62. See further Rome Institute (UNIDROIT), Comité d'experts pour les droits intellectuels, *Procès-verbal, Rome le 2 avril 1939*, S.d.N. – U.D.P. 1939, Document 14.

and a series of draft provisions for consideration by the committee of experts.[105] This was an elegantly formulated document that brought together most of the disparate claimants discussed above, plus several others, into one overall document and draft convention. In this regard, it is worth noting that, unlike several other Directors of the International Office, who had been employees of that office for the bulk of their working lives,[106] Ostertag had been a judge and president of the highest Swiss court (the *Tribunal fédéral*) and had only became Director at the age of 58. It is unclear whether he had had much experience with intellectual property issues up to this time, but in his twelve years as Director he had become immersed in the subject area and had been pivotal to the success of the two major revision conferences that had occurred on his watch: the revisions of the Berne Convention at Rome in 1928 and of the Paris Convention in London in 1934. He was also a prolific contributor to both *Le Droit d'auteur* and *La propriété industrielle*, and continued these scholarly (if not polemical) activities well into his retirement.[107] According to his obituary,[108] among the most significant of these contributions was his Samedan memorandum and accompanying draft texts, which were entitled, evocatively for present purposes, "Nouvelles propositions pour la Conférence de Bruxelles." This dealt with six separate subjects, several of which have not been included in our discussion so far: letters and other confidential writings (*les letter-missives et les autres écrits confidentiels*) and the rights of persons in their image (*le droit de la personne sur son image*), in addition to performers (*les artistes exécutants*), sound recordings (*les phongrammes*), radio broadcasts (*les radioémissions*), and news (*informations de presse*). Omitted from this draft was the *droit de suite*, although as will be seen this was to be added following the meeting of the Samedan committee.

Each of Ostertag's draft provisions was supported by a careful memorandum that sought to explain the basis for the proposals and their links to the Berne Convention. The provisions themselves have an economy about them that, in turn, reflects the emerging consensus that was developing about them in national laws (in this respect, Ostertag appears to have been aiming at striking a balance between what international lawyers would call codification or harmonisation with a modicum of progressive development) and the more substantive recommendations and resolutions of interested industry groups and international organisations such as the ILO, IIC, and Rome Institute. Distilling all this into 12 draft articles, he proposed the

---

[105] Published in [1939] *DA* 62–72.
[106] For example, Ernst Röthlisberger, a driven man who was the immediate predecessor of Ostertag, and Benigna Mentha (his successor): see the brief biographies of each in *1883. Paris Convention Centenary*. 1983, WIPO, Geneva 1983, at 91, 93 and 94.
[107] Although he had been retired for twelve years, M. Ostertag was the "opposite of a man of the past": obituary in [1948] *Le Droit d'auteur* 60.
[108] [1948] *Le Droit d'auteur* 60.

following provisions (these were to be elaborated upon considerably, but with some deletions and additions, in the draft texts ultimately adopted at Samedan):[109]

- Each of the listed subject matters was to be protected in other countries of the agreement (the "present arrangement") where their country of origin was one of those bound by the agreement (Article 1(1)). "Country of origin" was then defined in differing ways for each subject matter: for example, for performers it was the place where the recitation, representation, or interpretation had taken place; for phonograms, if unpublished, it was the country of which the producer was a national or the country of first publication, where publication had taken place; for broadcasts, it was the country where the emission had taken place; for letters and other confidential writings, it was the country of domicile of the author and of the recipient; for personal images or "portraits," it was the country of domicile of the person represented; and for press information, rather oddly, it was the country for which that information or news was intended (Article 1(2)).
- In the country of origin, protection was to be solely by the law of that country (as under Berne); in other countries, again following the model of Berne, protection was to be exclusively by the law of the country where protection was claimed,[110] together with the "rights specially accorded by the present agreement" (Article 2).
- The "rights specially accorded" were then spelled out as follows:
  o *For performers*, the rights to an "equitable remuneration" when their interpretation was recorded in "disks, ribbons, films, etc." or when it was broadcast by radio or by television, by loud speaker or similar devices (Article 3(1)). However, performers were to have a moral right to veto the use of interpretations that would be prejudicial to their honour or reputation (Article 2(2)). The rights accorded here to performers were limited to performances of literary or artistic works – that is, there was to be no obligation to protect unfixed or *ex tempore* performances – but it was also provided that it did not matter if the work performed had fallen into the public domain (Article 3(3)). Considerable flexibilities were further reserved to national laws with respect to group performances and the making of exceptions, as well as the mode of fixation of the level of remuneration (Article 3(4)).
  o *For producers of phonograms*, there was to be a right to prevent the unauthorised reproduction, whether made directly or indirectly, of the recording, and

---

[109] *See* [1939] DA 71–72.

[110] This did not necessarily mean national treatment, as under Berne, but this possible gap was filled in the drafts later adopted by the Samedan drafts for performers, phonogram producers and broadcasters: see principal text below.

a right to an equitable remuneration in the case of use of the phonogram in broadcasting, cinema, or other modes of public presentation (Article 4(1)). In fixing the level of this remuneration, it was provided that account should be taken of the remuneration paid to the author of the work recorded and to the performer (Article 4(4)).

o *For radio broadcasters*, the right to prevent the retransmission and recording of their broadcasts, and the right to an equitable remuneration for communications of their broadcasts to the public, by loud speaker or any other technical means, where done for a commercial purpose (Article 5).

o *For letters and other confidential writings*, these were not to be communicated to the public without the consent of the author and the recipient; in the case of one or the other being deceased, communication was not to take place without the consent of their relatives for a period of ten years following their decease (Article 6(1) and (2)). An exception was allowed for publication where this could be justified in the public or private interest and this outweighed the legitimate interests of the sender or recipient (Article 6(3)). Likewise, a further exception was allowed to national laws in the case of writings that were of interest to "national culture" (Article 6(4)).

o *For personal images*, called "portraits" in the draft text, similar rights to prevent unauthorised public disclosures were proposed, with similar exceptions, and a duration for up to the life of the person represented and ten years after death (see generally Article 7).

o *For news items or "press information" intended for agencies or newspapers*, it would not be lawful for third parties to collect this by means which were 'contrary to honest commercial practices' (Article 8).

• So far as duration of protection was concerned, terms of 30 years from the date of performance (for performers), first publication (for phonograms) and transmission (for broadcasts) were proposed (Article 9(1)), while the term of protection for unpublished letters and portraits was dealt with in Article 6 and 7 respectively (see above), and it was left to national laws to determine the length of protection for press information (Article 9(3)).

• Contracting countries were to be free to accord more extensive protection than that provided under the proposed agreement (Article 10), and it was further reserved to contracting states to determine "modalities of protection" and remedies available to protect the rights accorded under the agreement (Article 11).

• Connection with the Berne Convention was to be achieved through the application "by analogy" of the following articles of that Convention: Articles 17 (censorship and other government regulation), 21 to 26 (international office, expenses, revision, accessions and application to colonies, protectorates, etc.),

28 (ratification), and 29 (duration and denunciation) of that Convention (presumably the Rome Act). Oddly enough, none of these provisions directly touched upon the qualifications for joining the proposed agreement, for example, membership of the Berne Union, or required compliance otherwise with the provisions of that Convention. Doubtless, these would have been issues with which Ostertag was well acquainted (and this was only a working draft). Nonetheless, the question of consistency between authors' rights protections under Berne and neighbouring rights protections that might be granted under any new international arrangements were of critical importance. Much therefore turned on the meaning of the expression "connected to" the Berne Convention. In this regard, it should also be noted that Ostertag, as a former employee of the Berne International Office, emphasised that his draft was a private one that was prepared for the Rome Institute committee of experts and was in no way endorsed by the International Office (which nonetheless had no problem in publishing it in its monthly journal).[111] This may explain, however, why Ostertag omitted the *droit de suite*, from his draft on the basis that this had a place, albeit tentatively, on the programme for the postponed Brussels Conference. By contrast, this reticence did not arise with respect to his proposals concerning private letters and images, which he fully admitted were not concerned with authors' rights at all, but rather touched on rights of personal privacy and confidentiality – the maintenance of "private life" (*la vie intime*[112]). One reason for their inclusion may have been that these were matters that had already been addressed in the national laws of a number of continental countries, including his own (Switzerland), but also in neighbouring Germany and Austria[113] (which appears ironic, given the national socialist regimes in power in both countries at this time). As will be seen, these two sets of proposals were deleted in the final drafts adopted by the Samedan Committee.

12.8. THE WORK OF THE SAMEDAN COMMITTEE

Meeting in an idyllic setting, over three days, the committee of experts produced four draft instruments on performers and producers of phonograms, broadcasters, press information, and *droit de suite* (as might be expected, the proposals concerning private letters and images were not proceeded with, as being too distant from authors' rights). Ostertag's text was clearly the starting point for this, but the

---

[111] [1939] DA 71.
[112] [1939] DA 68.
[113] *See also* [1939] DA 68–9.

final work of drafting was done by a group of experts well versed in both copyright and international law, as well as national policy making and international negotiations.[114] These experts included: Mariano d'Amelio (president of the Rome Institute, and a distinguished Italian lawyer), Alfred Farner (secretary-general of the Rome Institute, and a Swiss lawyer who had been closely involved in drafting previous reports on performers' rights[115]), Piola Caselli (previously the rapporteur at the Rome Revision Conference of 1928 and a distinguished Italian jurist), Francis Déak (from the IIIC), Valerio de Sanctis (another experienced Italian lawyer and later a distinguished delegate at the Brussels and Stockholm Revision Conferences), Albert Guislain (Belgium, advocate and later a delegate at the Brussels Revision Conference), Sir William Jarrett (U.K., and former controller of industrial property), Herbert Kühnemann (Germany, and post-war president of the German Patent Office), Mario Matteuci (Italy, subsequently the secretary-general of UNIDROIT and an Italian delegate at the Rome Conference 1961), Benigna Mentha (Switzerland, a longstanding employee of the Berne International Office, and Ostertag's successor as Director), and Raymond Weiss (chief legal officer at the IIIC and subsequently a member of the French delegation in Brussels in 1948).[116]

The most thorough and accessible account of the work of the Samedan Committee is to be found in the October, November, and December 1940 issues of *Le Droit d'auteur*.[117] By this time, the immediate prospects for consideration of the draft proposals by national governments were clearly minimal (although it is noteworthy that discussions of new laws on authors' and neighbouring rights continued in both Germany and Italy after the outbreak of war, leading to the adoption in Italy in 1941 of the law that still applies today). The *Droit d'auteur* reports, written possibly by Mentha, are something like postcards to a future that must have seemed both uncertain and bleak in 1940. Nonetheless, they are valuable accounts of the work that had been done, and lay down important markers for the deliberations that were to resume fitfully in the post-war years, leading up to the adoption of the Rome Convention in 1961 and the WIPO treaties of the last twenty years. Many of the themes and approaches articulated in the Samedan drafts are to be found in these later instruments.

---

[114] [1940] DA 138.
[115] *See also* Rome Institute (now UNIDROIT), Study IX – Intellectual Property Rights: Performers' Rights, Documents 1–4 (1932, 1935, 1937, and 1938).
[116] [1940] DA 138.
[117] [1940] DA 109–11, 121–25, 133–38 (respectively). The minutes of the meeting are recorded as being in the UNIDROIT archives: Comité d'experts pour l'étude de la protection internationale de certains droits voisins du droit d'auteur, *Compte-rendu*, Samedan, 29–31 juillet 1939, S.d.N.- U.D.P. 1939 – Étude V – Droits intellectuels, Document 20, but have not been viewed by the author.

While not purporting to be a critical analysis of the Samedan drafts (a statement that is, perhaps, a little misleading as there is a considerable amount of commentary), the *Droit d'auteur* articles highlight the major difficulties facing the committee of experts.[118] In particular, what made a right "neighbouring" in the first place, and where was the line to be drawn?[119] And were the draft proposals better contained within one general instrument (as proposed by Ostertag) or should they be in a series of separate agreements to which states might sign up to on an *a la carte* basis? And what was to be the connection or link to what was already in the Berne Convention, that is, to authors' rights? With respect to the first of these questions, there were outliers at both ends of the "neighbourhood" spectrum that could be readily excluded from consideration: thus, there was little point in removing photographs from the scope of the Berne Convention, into which they had grudgingly made their way in previous revisions, although still waiting in the anteroom to Article 2(1). Likewise, it was easy to exclude private letters and images as being quite outside or "foreign" to authors' rights and therefore not "neighbouring" (although obviously worthy of protection in some other way).[120] Sufficiently neighbouring, however, were rights for performers, phonograms and broadcasts, as each of these was connected, albeit in different ways, with the exploitation of authors' rights, and these therefore became the main focus of the committee's attention. Linked to this was the *droit de suite*, although this might equally well be reconceptualised as an authors' right in the purer sense (see further below). However, it is harder to see the degree of "neighbourhood" arising in the case of press information: although retained in the Samedan drafts, this had more affinity with concepts of unfair competition than with authors' rights.

The second question, concerning the link with the Berne Convention, raised issues of a more legally technical character. Ostertag's draft had proposed that there should be a single agreement on all subjects, with an unsettled connection to the Berne Convention, other than through incorporation of the machinery provisions of that Convention – a drafting device that did not specifically address issues of consistency between the two instruments or even whether membership of the Berne Union would be a prerequisite for entry to the other agreement. An alternative to a single separate agreement was to incorporate the proposed provisions into the text of the Berne Convention itself, following the precedents already set in relation to photographs and works of applied art, thereby making it now a convention for the "protection of authors" and related rights. This did not appear attractive to

---

[118] *See*, in particular, the discussion in [1940] *DA* 109–11.
[119] "On voit que les droits voisins du droit d'auteur ne manquent pas d'une certaine variété": [1940] *DA* 110.
[120] [1940] *DA* 110.

Committee members, perhaps for no reason other than that it was preferable to keep the Berne Convention "pure" as an agreement on authors' rights alone. This was clearly the approach that had prevailed at the Rome Revision Conference and in the subsequent preparations for the proposed Brussels Revision. Another, more radical, option was to have these new provisions (whether in one treaty or in a series of treaties) as freestanding and open to all states to adhere to, regardless of whether or not they were members of the Berne Union. This approach apparently had appeal to some Samedan committee members, but the view that ultimately prevailed was that the degree of "connexion" between these subjects and authors' rights was so great that there must be consistency or compatibility between the two, that is, nothing in the proposed protections should threaten or prejudice the rights of authors.[121] Accordingly, membership of the Berne Union would be a prerequisite for joining any proposed agreement or agreements on neighbouring rights, and this was underlined by non-derogation provisos in the drafts adopted with respect to performers, phonogram producers, and broadcasters.[122]

This, then, led to a further consideration: whether the proposed agreement should be one single package or a series of separate agreements.[123] In the case of a single package (such as contained in the Ostertag draft), an important issue arising was whether countries would have to sign up to all of its provisions, or whether they would be free to pick and choose, for example, by making reservations as to particular provisions. There was some appeal in this idea, as it was clear that individual nations were at different stages in their acceptance of the need for protection of each of the proposed neighbouring rights, so that some might be prepared to protect one or more but not all, and it would clearly inhibit accessions and ratifications if this had to be on a "take it or leave it" basis. However, there had been bad experiences with reservations in the early years of the Berne Convention, where the facility to make reservations with respect to such matters as translation rights had led to the emergence of a series of "sub-Unions" between groups of Berne members, which had resulted in considerable complexity in the relations *inter se* of Berne Union members.[124] In the end, the Samedan drafts struck a balance between these competing positions: there was to be a series of subject-specific agreements to which countries might adhere separately, although Berne membership would be a prerequisite for this. Notably, however, the number of agreements was reduced to four, with performers and phonogram producers being grouped in the first, radio broadcasters being the subject of the second, press information the subject of the third, and *droit de suite* being the fourth. In each

---

[121] [1940] DA 111.
[122] *Id.*
[123] *See generally* [1940] DA 111, 121–22.
[124] *See also* RICKETSON & GINSBURG, *supra* note 14, [3.23] ff.

instance, the scope of protection was loosely based on the models provided in the Ostertag proposals, with the following variations and/or additions:

- *Performers and phonograms producers:*[125] The close interdependence between these two subjects was now reflected in their joinder here in the one agreement. The requirement of national treatment was now explicitly articulated (Article 2(1)), while the rights "specially accorded" to both were retained in similar form (an "equitable remuneration" for unauthorised broadcasting or fixations (Article 5), and a moral right of veto with respect to uses prejudicial to their honour or reputation (Article 6), in the case of performers, and exclusive rights of fixation, and rights to equitable remuneration for unauthorised broadcasts and other public communications, in the case of phonogram producers (Article 7)). Both sets of rights were expressed to be "without prejudice to the rights of the author of any literary or artistic work concerned." Independence of protection *a la Berne* was also provided for (Article 3(1)), but with the possibility of reciprocity being allowed for in the case of the provisions of the country of origin with respect to duration of protection, formalities, and any system of compulsory licensing (Articles 3(2) and 8(2)). More significantly, there was no longer any prescription as to the minimum term of protection to be accorded.
- *Radio broadcasts:*[126] Again, the requirement of national treatment was articulated (Article 2(1)), while the rights specially accorded followed those in the Ostertag draft (the rights to prevent unauthorised retransmissions and fixations of broadcasts – Article 5) but without any entitlement to an equitable remuneration with respect to other unauthorised uses, such as communications made for commercial purposes by means of loudspeaker or other modes of public communication. These rights were to be without prejudice to the rights of the author of any literary or artistic work involved. The principle of independence of protection was also introduced (Article 3), but there was no reservation with respect to the facility to require reciprocity in relation to certain matters, as in the case of performers and phonogram producers (see preceding bullet point). There was also no provision relating to duration of protection (as in the Ostertag draft), leaving this solely as a matter for the country where protection was claimed.
- *Press information:*[127] There was quite a significant elaboration here on the simple provision proposed by Ostertag. The Samedan draft followed closely the model proposed for performers and phonogram producers, with a starting point of national treatment and rights "specially accorded." Unlike the Ostertag draft, the persons entitled to claim protection were identified specifically as

---

[125] For the text of the draft provisions, see [1940] DA 125.
[126] For the text of the draft provisions, see [1940] DA 134.
[127] For the text of the draft provisions, see [1940] DA 136.

the proprietors of newspapers, journals and agencies, with the country of origin being defined as the country in which these enterprises or agencies were headquartered (Article 2, as opposed to the rather odd choice of the country for which the news was intended, as in the Ostertag draft). The rights specifically to be accorded to proprietors and agencies were also spelled out in more detail: to require that their press information should not be reproduced without an indication of its source, and that it should not be reproduced by third parties before publication if obtained by illicit means (Article 5). Certain matters were reserved to national legislation, including the right to determine what were illicit means of collecting information and to prevent, after publication, the systematic reproduction or broadcasting of such information for profit (Article 6), as well as matters of duration, formalities, remedies, and transitional provisions (Article 7). Curiously, although Berne membership was a prerequisite for joining this proposed agreement, there was no non-derogation provision inserted, as in the case of the performers, phonogram producers, and broadcasters treaties – perhaps a clear indication that the protection of press information was seen as quite unconnected with authors' rights.

- *Droit de suite:*[128] The addition of this was possibly curious, given that a proposal for protection had already been included in the draft programme for the postponed Brussels Revision Conference. However, the *Droit d'auteur* commentary notes the limited acceptance to date of this right under national laws and that it might well be better placed in a separate agreement as proposed by the Samedan Committee.[129] Under the latter's proposals, each contracting state would undertake to accord the authors of "original works of art in the field of painting, sculpture, engraving, and design, a *droit de suite* in the price of resales of their works in accordance with the provisions of the present convention" (Article 1). This was to be a personal and inalienable right of the author which would belong to his heirs after his death (Article 5). Certain matters, however, were left to national legislation to determine, including the duration of protection, the method of collection and the amount, and the means of safeguarding the new right (Articles 6 and 7). While the proposed agreement was to be open to signature only by present and future Berne Union members (Article 9), there was no non-derogation clause included, presumably on the basis that, while this was a right pertaining to authors, or more particularly visual artists, it was quite a separate right and one that was not of the same kind as the incorporeal rights of reproduction and broadcasting accorded to them under the Berne Convention.

---

[128] For the text of the draft provisions, see [1940] DA 138.
[129] [1940] DA 136–37.

12.9. THE TRAJECTORY OF NEIGHBOURING RIGHTS
PROTECTION AFTER SAMEDAN

Following the conclusion of World War II, the subject of *droit de suite* came back on to the programme for the Brussels Conference and entered into the Convention as Article 14*bis* (now Article 14*ter* of the Stockholm/Paris Act). This was extended to both original works of art and manuscripts, and became an optional requirement under the Convention, subject to reciprocity. Nonetheless, this signalled the integration of the *droit de suite* into the Convention as an author's right, albeit of an atypical kind. It slumbered in this position for a long time, with a minimum of objection but a relatively high level of disregard from most Berne Union members. In more recent years, however, there have been significant developments at the national and regional level, and *droit de suite* or arts resale royalty rights laws have come to be included in the laws of just under half of the membership of Berne, including all the states of the European Union.[130] For the most part, although clearly differentiated from moral rights and other economic rights, this is part of national laws on authors' rights. *Droit de suite*, as a species of neighbouring right, therefore had a brief life only as part of the Samedan drafts, before moving firmly into the embrace of the Berne Convention.

For performers, phonogram producers and broadcasters, the outcomes have been more mixed. Here, the Samedan drafts were of more lasting influence, as significant components of each are to be found in the provisions of the Rome Convention (1961) and WPPT (1996). In particular, post–World War II, the "ownership" or international sponsorship of these rights continued to be undertaken by the international organisations (or their successors) that had been concerned with them before 1939: the ILO in the case of performers, UNESCO (the successor of the IIIC) in the case of both performers and phonogram producers, and the Berne International Office (later called BIRPI, which was in turn taken over by WIPO) in the case of all three. So far as "perfecting" the protection of these rights, this has now been achieved with respect to performers and phonogram producers in the WPPT and Beijing Audio-visual Performers Treaty, although the completion of a full treaty in the case of broadcasters still appears elusive. But in each of them, strong traces of Samedan are evident. In particular the linking of performers and phonogram producers, the concept of a shared equitable remuneration for certain

---

[130] A recent U.S. Copyright Office study on the subject in 2013 put this figure at "more than 70," with thirteen countries in South America, sixteen in Africa, as well as Australia, the Philippines and the Russian Federation: Office of the Register of Copyright, *Resale Royalties: An Updated Analysis*, Washington, Dec. 2013, at 17. A more recent report now puts this figure at 81, which is just under half the present Berne membership of 168: see S. Ricketson, *Proposed international treaty on droit de suite/ resale royalty right for visual artists*, Academic Study prepared for CISAC, Paris, June 2015, at 10, note 17, *available at* www.cisac.org.

uses, and the notion of moral rights for performers. Technological developments, of course, have complicated matters considerably, notably so far as questions of definition are concerned – for example, what is now meant by "sound recording" and "broadcasting"? Likewise, changing views of performance practice have changed our conceptions of who is a performer, whether and to what extent this includes groups, and how far it should extend to all categories of public presenters, such as radio and television announcers, sportsmen and women, and participants in organised public events. But these are contemporary issues that fall outside the scope of the present chapter.

The other subjects considered at Samedan have now dropped out of sight, so far as discussions of neighbouring rights protections are concerned. Confidential documents and personal images raise interesting issues of privacy and rights of publicity, but have tended to find a home in national unfair competition and privacy laws rather than in any further consideration at the international level of separate intellectual property rights protections. And protection of news continues to fall between the cracks: proprietors of newspapers, journals, and the like may find an occasional solace in authors' rights laws where original works and authors can be identified, and likewise may gain protection under unfair competition laws – it may, indeed, be arguable that an obligation to protect can be deduced from the provisions of Article 10*bis* of the Paris Convention.[131] But, again, the history post-Samedan suggests that this was not a subject that could be readily slotted into a neighbouring right formulation, and accordingly it has fallen off the norm formulation agenda of WIPO.[132]

12.10. LESSONS FROM SAMEDAN?

The experience of the interwar years, culminating in the Samedan meeting of 1939, has certain lessons for us today. Up until this time, there had been a binary aspect to intellectual property rights protection at the international level, with authors' rights (Berne Convention) on the one hand, and industrial property rights (the Paris Convention) on the other. In between, however, fell other interests with a legitimate claim to protection, and it is these interests that were to become the subject of the

---

[131] *See also* LADAS, vol. III, *supra* note 85, at 1722–25.

[132] But not within certain European countries, such as Germany and Spain, as revealed by recent legislative amendments to give press publishers an ancillary right against the activities of news aggregators, such as Google: see new articles 87f-87h of the German Copyright Law 1965, proclaimed 7 May 2013 and coming into effect 1 August 2013 (see further, for an English translation of these provisions, by Dr. Ulrike, Rechtsanswalt, Frankfurt am Main, *available at* www.ulixmann .de/2013/03/27/neighbouring-right-for-newspaper-publishers-in-germany-passed/) and article 32 of the Spanish *Ley de Propriedad intelectal, as amended* (discussed on 11 Dec. 2014 in IPKat http:// ipkitten.blogspot.com/2014/12/google-announces-end-of-news-in-spain.html).

neighbouring rights conventions that came to be adopted in the post-war years. The discussions during the 1930s therefore served to articulate and highlight a number of issues of continuing contemporary relevance.

1. *The centrality of authorship:* This may, of course, be disputed by many in a post-modern age where notions of authorship and who is an author may take vastly different forms in the digital environment. But given the significant protection accorded to authors of original works under the *Berne Convention, WCT* and *TRIPS Agreement,* it is still useful to have some limits placed on the concept. Too ready admission to the status of author can have far-reaching consequences: consider, for example, the case of computer programmes which may be protected for the life of the author plus at least fifty years, free of formalities, and buttressed by a powerful body of exclusive rights. However, early possibilities for protection of computer programmes canvassed during the 1970s proposed *sui generis* regimes with more limited terms of protection and more carefully tailored rights – in other words, something that could have been readily described as a neighbouring, rather than an author's, right.[133] Would we have been any worse off for such an approach?

2. *The development of neighbouring rights regimes as alternative forms of protection:* The development of proposals for international neighbouring rights protection in the 1930s provided policy makers and legislators with a flexibility not available under the Berne system. This is well reflected in the different formulations of rights adopted in the Samedan drafts for performers, phonogram producers, and broadcasters, respectively. Importantly, it also made it easier to devise forms of protection that could be conferred directly on corporate entities, rather than individuals (as in the case of authors), with shorter terms of protection and more carefully calibrated exclusive rights and/or rights to remuneration. At the international level, of course, this freedom was qualified by the need to ensure consistency with Berne and the protection of authors' rights, and not to undermine the latter. It is noteworthy, however, that national legislators have not been so coy in adopting neighbouring rights solutions for the protection of new forms of subject matter, underlining the point that authors' rights are not the only option and, indeed, opting for something lesser can provide more appropriate and tailor-made protection regimes. Both common and civil law systems have proved to be highly creative in this regard: consider the protection given to publishers' editions (typographical arrangements) in the U.K. and Australian law,[134] computer-generated works in the U.K.,[135] scientific

---

[133] *See, e.g.,* the WIPO *Model Provisions on the Protection of Computer Software,* WIPO Publication 814(E), Geneva, 1978.

[134] *Copyright, Designs and Patents Act 1988* (UK), s 8; *Copyright Ac 1968* (Aust), Part IV, s 88.

[135] *Copyright, Designs and Patents Act 1988* (UK), s 9(3).

editions, organisers of performances, film producers, and press publishers under the German law,[136] databases and film producers in the EU,[137] and so on.

3. *The value of the respective contributions*: The discussions during the period under consideration, both within and outside the Berne Union, also raised interesting policy and philosophical challenges as to how the respective contributions of authors and others should be valued and protected. No consistent theme or explanation is readily apparent here, but the preceding discussion must suggest that there is a hierarchy of interests involved, with the starting point being the creation of some authorial production that accordingly has the largest claim to recognition. Performers, phonogram producers, and broadcasters build on these initial contributions, either through performance or interpretation in the case of performers or through fixation and dissemination in the case of the second two. There is an interconnection and dependency here that makes their respective contributions difficult to value, either in terms of formal protection or commercial worth, but the notion of a hierarchy serves to make some sense of this, in terms of a chain of production that starts at one point and moves outwards, albeit perhaps in different directions. It is by no means a complete way of looking at things, as demarcation issues still arise, for example, as to why the producers of derivative works should be treated as authors rather than under neighbouring rights regimes. However, the drafters at Samedan, and their predecessors in the various meetings that had discussed these things, were seeking to achieve a sensible and coherent taxonomy of rights that kept authorship at the centre, while assuring protection to the value-adding contributions of performers, phonogram producers, and broadcasters.

4. *The virtue of separate international agreements*: While there will always be disagreement about the matters discussed in the preceding point – why some things should be placed on one side of the line rather than the other, and why some should be more valued, in terms of protection granted, than others – the Samedan proposals do not fall too far short of present reality, in terms both of classification and methodology. They embodied a series of linked but separate international agreements for performers, phonogram producers, and broadcasters that were to apply without prejudice to the rights of authors in

---

[136] *See generally* German Copyright Act of 9 September 1965 (Federal Law Gazette Part I, p. 1273), as last amended by Article 8 of the Act of 1 October 2013 (Federal Law Gazette Part I, p. 3714), Articles 70 (scientific editions), 80 (organisers of performances), 87i-h (press publishers) and 94 (film producers).

[137] Directive 96/9/EC of the European Parliament and of the Council of 11 March 1996 on the legal protection of databases and Directive 2006/115/EC of the European Parliament and of the Council of 12 December 2006 on rental right and lending right and on certain rights related to copyright in the field of intellectual property (codified version), Article 9.1(c).

literary and artistic works. With the exception of *droit de suite*, now repatriated to Berne, and the pushing away of subject matter only loosely connected to authors' rights (confidential letters, personal images and, subsequently, news items), this remains the basic form in which authors' and neighbouring rights are organised internationally today.[138]

12.11. CONCLUSION

Quite apart from the above, there is an air of sadness, even doom, that hangs over the work of the Samedan Committee. The attendees, drawn from both sides of the approaching conflict and neutral Switzerland, must have felt keenly the irrelevance and unreality of their discussions in the light of all that was happening around them: from that perspective, the fate of authors' and neighbouring rights was very small beer indeed. Yet the work was undertaken with a clear seriousness of purpose, and the resulting drafts do not fall far short of what was to be ultimately achieved in the case of performers and phonogram producers over half a century later in the WPPT and Beijing Treaty. Although beyond the scope of the present chapter, it should also be noted that the Berne International Office continued its administration of each of the major conventions (Berne, Paris and Madrid) for which it was responsible throughout the war, and was able to resume the process of revision and review as early as 1948 with the holding of the long postponed Brussels revision of Berne. This is a timely reminder – and an important precedent in its own right – that independent multilateral agreements and institutions can continue, notwithstanding prolonged periods of belligerency, between their constituent members.

The work of the Samedan Committee is also important as a reflection of the important and often idealistic work that was being carried on at the international level in all areas of private and public law prior to 1939 by bodies such as the IIIC, the Rome Institute, and the International Labour Office, as well as in the regular international congresses of relevant interest groups. Intellectual property rights were seen as an important component of these endeavours, and much of this work was to be continued by bodies, such as UNESCO, UNIDROIT, the ILO, and finally WIPO itself, under the auspices of the United Nations after World War II. Even in the case of the tiny Berne International Office, it is salutary to see how conscientiously its officials sought to liaise with, and participate in, the meetings and deliberations of these other bodies during the 1920s and 1930s. There is a fuller story here that remains to be told, a story of those who believed in the desirability of international solutions, even in the darkest and most troubling of times.

---

[138] *See also* Rome Convention, art. 1; WPPT, art. 1(2); Beijing Treaty, art. 1(2).

13

How *Oracle* Erred

*The Use/Explanation Distinction and the Future of Computer Copyright**

*Wendy J. Gordon***

ABSTRACT

In *Oracle v. Google* (2015), the Federal Circuit addressed whether the "method header" components of a dominant computer program were uncopyrightable as "merging" with the headers' ideas or function. Google had copied the headers to ease the ability of third-party programmers to interact with Google's Android platform. The court rebuffed the copyrightability challenge; it reasoned that because the plaintiff's expression *might have been written* in alternative forms, there was no "merger" of idea and expression. But the *Oracle* court may have been asking the wrong question.

In *Lotus v. Borland* (1995), the owner of a dominant spreadsheet program sought to prevent a new competitor's program from making available a set of "command menu" headers based on the dominant program's menus. The defendant also wrote its own, original command menus, but provided the copied menus as an option to relieve customers who, migrating from the dominant spreadsheet, would otherwise have had a substantial burden to master new terms and rewrite macros.

In assessing the legality of the copying in *Lotus*, the First Circuit started its inquiry not with a question about how the plaintiff's program might have been written, but rather with how the program *actually* was written. It then identified the menu commands as "methods of operation" because they were necessary to make the actual

* Copyright © by Wendy J. Gordon 2016.
** William Fairfield Warren Distinguished Professor at Boston University, and Professor of Law at Boston University School of Law. Prof. Gordon owes thanks to Hal Abelson, David Bachman, Jim Bessen, Bob Bone, Randy Davis, Stacey Dogan, Paul Gugliuzza, Gary Lawson, Jessica Litman, Jerry Reichman, Pam Samuelson, Jessica Silbey, and David Vaver, as well as to Ruth L. Okediji and the full Okediji book group; to Abraham Drassinower and the CILP Workshop at the University of Toronto; to Frances Hanks, David Lindsay, Megan Richardson, and the other participants at the University of Melbourne presentation; to participants at the Griffith (Queensland) conference; to her colleagues at the BU faculty workshop; and to participants at her 2014 AIPLA presentation on design protection. She also owes thanks to her excellent BU student assistants for their research help, especially Kim Condoulis, Alex Lee, Melissa Rybacki, Alex Vitruk, and Yevgeniy Yalon, and to the amazing staff of the BU Law Library.

program operate a computer. The copyright statute renders "methods of operation" per se uncopyrightable, regardless of the possibility of alternatives.

Debates over the conflict between *Oracle* and *Lotus* have largely ignored a middle road that supports the *Lotus* result without the potential for overkill some observers see in *Lotus*. This middle road is a doctrine known as the "explanation/use" distinction. Laid out in the classic Supreme Court case of *Baker v. Selden* (1880), and ratified by statutory provisions of the Copyright Act including the much-ignored § 113(b), the "explanation/use distinction" specifies that a copyright owner has no power to control behaviors that belong to the domain of utility patent. Like "merger" and "method of operation," the "explanation/use" doctrine implements the deference that, pursuant to Congressional command and Supreme Court precedent, U.S. copyright law must give to patent law. However, the explanation/use doctrine operates by limiting the *scope* of the exclusive rights a copyright owner might otherwise possess, not by targeting the copyrightability of what plaintiff produced.

This chapter examines justifications for the "explanation/use distinction," and suggests a two-part test for implementing that doctrine. The chapter argues that a copyright owner should have no prima facie rights over copying behavior where (1) the goals of the copying are "use" (behavior in the realm of utility patent) and (2) the copying is done solely for goals unrelated to the expressiveness of the plaintiff's work of authorship. (The copying in *Oracle* and *Lotus* seems to have been fully indifferent to expressive values; the result might be different in a case where defendant's goals are mixed.)

This two-part test is met by the defendants in *Oracle* and *Lotus*. (1) Making a machine operate is clearly utilitarian. And as for (2) indifference to expression, both *Lotus* and *Oracle* involve someone copying a computer interface to enable users to interoperate: third-party programmers could use or design Java-enabled programs on Android, and spreadsheet users could use their prior macros on a new spreadsheet program. Interoperability is one of the few areas where indifference to expression is clear: After all, when one wants a spare key made, the elegance or beauty of the key's shape is irrelevant – all that matters is that the shape fits the lock.

≈ ≈ ≈

13.1. INTRODUCTION

The world would look far different than it does if copyright law covered functional expression without limit. Someone who imagines they can "build a better mouse trap" would need only to sketch it on paper, or draw it on a computer screen and hit "save,"[1] to secure for the purported innovation over seventy years of

---

[1] Nations differ on the extent to which "fixation in a tangible medium" is required for copyright, and as to the definition of "fixation." Under U.S. law pre-1978, saving a screen drawing to a computer disk

legal protection[2] against copying.[3] Anyone else who makes or sells a similar device would be in danger of suit.[4] By similarly simple means, any car maker or other manufacturer could eliminate competition in the making of spare parts.

Markets for physical products are not the only things that would change; so would markets for electronics and digital content. If copyright had no boundaries where functionality was concerned, a designer of a leading video game could choose one console and, by asserting its copyright, could forever[5] limit its fans to that console. Similarly a console maker could bar any "unlicensed" game from playing on its machine. Alternatively, the seller of an application program could ensure that once its customers learn the program's intricacies and prepare macros[6] based upon its

would not have qualified as a copyrightable "writing" because it could not be visually perceived from the disk except with the aid of a machine; post-1978, direct visual perception became unnecessary. 17 U.S.C. § 101 (2012) (definition of "copy"). Unless otherwise specified, all references to law are to federal law of the United States.

[2] U.S. Copyrights that come into being today have a duration of either (a) seventy years beyond the life of the author, or (b) the shorter of 120 years from creation or ninety-five years from publication (for works made for hire and some other categories). 17 U.S.C. § 302 (2012). Utility patents by contrast have a duration of no more than twenty years. 35 U.S.C. § 154(a)(2) (2012) (providing that utility patents end twenty years from filing date). Design patents are even shorter – fifteen years from the date of grant. 35 U.S.C. § 173 (2012), as amended by Patent Law Treaties Implementation Act of 2012, Pub. L. No. 91–190, § 102, 125 Stat. 1527 (2012).

The instant chapter is concerned with the intersection of copyright law with the law of utility patents. That is where the most significant conflict with copyright occurs. Design patents pose no such tension for copyrights because, like copyrights, they are supposed to be unavailable for elements that are "functional." *See* L. A. Gear, Inc. v. Thom McAn Shoe Co., 988 F.2d 1117, 1123 (Fed. Cir. 1993) ("If the particular design is essential to the use of the article, it cannot be the subject of a design patent.").

[3] There was a period when United Kingdom and Canadian law took this extreme path. *See, e.g.*, Spiro-Flex Indust. Ltd. v. Progressive Sealing Inc., 1986 CanLII 771 (BC SC), available at www.canlii .org/en/bc/bcsc/doc/1986/1986canlii771/1986canlii771.html.

Both nations now take a somewhat more patent-deferential approach to design protection.

[4] Admittedly, copyright gives rights only over "copying." By contrast, patent infringement can arise regardless of whether or not the defendant who makes and sells a version of the patented innovation has copied it or independently invented it.

But the copyright plaintiff's need to prove actual "copying" (a kind of "cause in fact") is less of a barrier to lawsuits than it once was. Given the pervasiveness of mass media, and the Internet's ability to give access largely without regard to geographic boundaries, copyright defendants find it harder to prove they never had contact with a plaintiff's work. Also, because subconscious copying can trigger copyright liability, at least in the United States, defendants cannot be sure that telling their truth on the witness stand ("I cannot remember copying and I believe I did not copy") will make a difference, even if the jury believes them.

[5] A game (if a work for hire) would have copyright for roughly a century. Each new version of the game would have a new, full-duration copyright in any distinguishable variations added since the prior version. By continually tweaking its games, a company whose copyright knew no functional boundaries could lock its fan base into a particular platform for as long as the fan base continued to exist. By the time that the original version of a game entered the public domain, there would likely be no machines left capable of playing it.

[6] A user can assign a complex set of commands to a simpler keystroke command. This is called writing a "macro." For example, in using a word processing program, someone who authors documents

keystroke commands, the customers' learning and all their macros will be worthless if they ever switch to a new provider. The makers of computers, smart phones, or game consoles could limit use of their machines only to programs, apps, and games of which the makers approve.

But copyright law does *not* cover functional expression without limit. Most of the results just described could not be achieved through copyright,[7] for both Congress and the courts have sharply limited copyright's operation in the field of functionality.[8] Copyright law defers to patent law when it comes to functional use, and patents are short-lived and hard to get.

Moreover, patent law jealously guards the public domain status of the functional works that it declines to protect. In the words of the Supreme Court, "the federal patent laws *do* create a federal right to 'copy and to use,'"[9] – a right which is applicable both to expired patents and to "potentially patentable ideas which are fully exposed to the public."[10] The patent public domain similarly assures "'the consuming public of the advantage to be derived' from free exploitation"[11] of discoveries with expired or invalid patents.[12] So, unsurprisingly, many forms of right (including copyright,[13]

---

containing many lengthy quotations might tell her program that a particular keystroke combination (say, hitting "control-alt-q" at the same time) should put highlighted text into quotation form: indenting it and making it single-spaced. Thereafter, she could properly format long quotes just by highlighting the relevant text and hitting control-alt-q.

[7] Regarding the examples just mentioned: an attractively shaped automobile bumper or muffler pipe that lacks patent can be freely copied (unless some aspect of it is a separable work of authorship, which is unlikely), 17 U.S.C. § 101 (2012) ("definition of pictorial, graphic and sculptural works"); an original drawing of a mouse trap or other functional object can have copyright as a pictorial work, but the rights of the copyright owner do not extend to control over the manufacture and sale of the objects depicted, 17 U.S.C. § 113(b) (2012); copyright's fair use doctrine, 17 U.S.C. § 107 (2012), permits the copying of copyrighted computer programs for the purpose of making a video game compatible with existing consoles. *See* Spiro-Flex Indust. Ltd. v. Progressive Sealing Inc., 977 F.2d 1510, 1523 (9th Cir. 1992) ("Accolade did not attempt to 'scoop' Sega's release of any particular game or games, but sought only to become a legitimate competitor in the field of Genesis-compatible video games. Within that market, it is the characteristics of the game program as experienced by the user that determine the program's commercial success. As we have noted, there is nothing in the record that suggests that Accolade copied any of those elements.").

[8] Many of these limits are discussed at length *infra*.

[9] Bonito Boats v. Thunder Craft Boats, 489 U.S. 141, 164–65 (1989).

[10] *Id.* (citations omitted).

[11] Kimble v. Marvel Entm't, LLC, 135 S. Ct. 2401, 2407 (2015) (quoting Scott Paper Co. v. Marcalus Mfg. Co., 326 U.S. 249, 256 (1945)).

[12] Kimble, 135 S. Ct. at 2405 (upholding the rule that royalty contracts are unenforceable to the extent they provide for the payment of royalties after the point of patent expiration). The Supreme Court in *Kimble* may have had some doubts about the wisdom of the particular rule it upheld, but did not seem to harbor doubts about the importance of the patent public domain.

[13] See, e.g., 17 U.S.C. § 102(b) (2012) (no copyright for systems or methods of operation); *id.* § 113(b) (no infringement results from building a useful article depicted in a copyrighted portrayal). These and other limits are discussed *infra*, passim.

trademark,[14] and contract[15]) are limited lest they undermine the "balance between fostering innovation and ensuring public access to discoveries" that "Congress struck" "[i]n crafting the patent laws."[16]

The boundary doctrines that enforce copyright's deference to patent are continually threatened with erosion. In particular, the recent decision in *Oracle v. Google*[17] threatens to expand copyright's reach into functionality. That decision, by the Federal Circuit, increases the ability of market leaders to use copyright law to lock out competition in a functional market – and to lock their customers, their suppliers, and producers of complementary products into patterns that might be privately profitable, but inefficient or otherwise undesirable from a social perspective.

As a social practice, lock-in is quite controversial. Business schools teach future executives how to lock in their customers and other players,[18] yet antitrust law makes some forms of lock-in unlawful.[19] Scholars debate whether various examples of potential lock-in might be socially harmful, socially useful, or irrelevant to social welfare,[20] and how the law should take lock-in into account.[21] Such arguments need not be resolved for cases like *Oracle v. Google*. That is because, in the context of computer programs, the techniques that companies use to enforce lock-in typically

---

[14] No trademark can be federally registered if it is "functional," 12 U.S.C. § 1052(e) (2012), and no unregistered trademark can give rise to suit under the Lanham Act unless the plaintiff carries the burden of proving nonfunctionality. 12 U.S.C. § 1125(a)(3) (2012); Eppendorf-Netheler-Hinz Gmbh v. Ritter Gmbh, 289 F.3d 351, 355 (5th Cir. 2002).

[15] Kimble, 135 S. Ct. at 2405 (royalty contracts held unenforceable to the extent they provide for the payment of royalties after the point of patent expiration).

[16] *Id.* at 2406.

[17] Oracle Am., Inc. v. Google Inc., 750 F.3d 1339 (Fed. Cir. 2014) [hereinafter Oracle II] (holding Java's applied programming interface (API) and its structure, sequence and organization, copyrightable as against claims of "merger" and "method of operation"). The lower court had held the copied portions of Java uncopyrightable as "methods of operation." Oracle Am., Inc. v. Google Inc., 872 F. Supp. 2d 974, 980 (N.D. Cal. 2012) [hereinafter Oracle I].

[18] *See, e.g.*, KENNETH J. SOUSA & EFFY OZ, MANAGEMENT INFORMATION SYSTEMS 41, 47–48 (7th ed., Cengage 2015).

[19] *See* HERBERT J. HOVENKAMP, MARK D. JANIS, & MARK A. LEMLEY, IP AND ANTITRUST: AN ANALYSIS OF ANTITRUST PRINCIPLES APPLIED TO INTELLECTUAL PROPERTY LAW § 21.4 (2d ed., Aspen Publishers 2010).

[20] *Compare, e.g.*, Stan J. Liebowitz & S. E. Margolis, *The Fable of the Keys*, 30 J. LAW ECON. 1 (1990), *with* Paul A. David, *Clio and the Economics of QWERTY*, 75 AM. ECON. REV. 332 (1985).

[21] One issue is the doctrinal category through which to address lock-in. The instant article makes lock-in relevant to the scope of a copyright owner's prima facie rights, but the relevance arises indirectly: What's important to this chapter's analysis is whether copying is functional, expressive, or a mixture of both, and copying done to escape lock-in is likely to be nonexpressive and purely functional.

Lock-in might also be relevant to copyrightability, to misuse, or to fair use. The Solicitor General, for example, argues that lock-in should be examined under the fair use doctrine. *See, e.g.*, Brief for the United States as Amicus Curiae, Oracle II, 750 F.3d 1339 (Fed. Cir. 2014), at 17, *available at* www .justice.gov/sites/default/files/osg/briefs/2015/06/01/14-410_google_v_oracle_us_cvsg_brief.pdf.

run afoul of a historic doctrine called the "use/explanation" distinction.[22] The doctrine distinguishes between behaviors that use a copyrighted work expressively and those that use the work without regard to its expressive virtues, simply to serve a utilitarian function.

For example, it is an expressive use when the publisher of a how-to book on home repair copies someone else's copyrighted passage explaining how to rewire a lamp instead of writing his own instructions. It is a nonexpressive use when a homeowner applies the same copyrighted passage to the task of actually rewiring lighting fixtures. Copying text to convey an explanation or to serve other expressive goals belongs to the realm of copyright; copying to build a functional invention instead belongs to the realm of patent. These basic points about the limited rights that attach to copyright in the design of physical products have important implications for computer copyright cases.

As a result of how the *Oracle v. Google* litigation has been structured, the legal community concerned with computer copyright is currently focused on issues of copyrightability. It is time to redirect our attention to include the scope of a copyright owner's exclusive right.

This chapter will show how the fundamental distinction between "use" and "explanation" can resolve disputes like *Oracle v. Google*. The chapter will also explore a much-ignored provision in Copyright law, § 113(b) that provides an explicit immunity for using copyrighted works functionally.

13.2. *Oracle v. Google*

Oracle owns the Java set of programs, and Java is ubiquitous. Third-party programmers are able to make their apps compatible with many platforms, and save time in doing so, because large numbers of platforms are crafted to respond to Java commands with predefined Java routines and subroutines. The Java routines are activated when a programmer uses a specified "method header" accompanied by a statement – in particular format – of the desired inputs for a method's operation. Platforms are typically programmed to recognize Java method headers (sometimes called "declaration code") and to implement the appropriate Java routines and subroutines (sometimes called "implementation code") in response.

---

[22] This chapter is focused on uses that are functional (because functional uses implicate patent law) and indifferent to expressivity (for the indifference removes a reason for enforcing copyright). Lock-in and the imposition of switching costs raise many other issues in addition. For example, when a copyright owner's acts of dissemination and enforcement combine in a way that negatively alters another's prospects, I argue that this does and should erode the owner's scope of right. *See generally* Wendy J. Gordon, *A Property Right in Self-Expression: Equality and Individualism in the Natural Law of Intellectual Property*, 102 YALE L.J. 1533 (1993).

Google, wanting to facilitate third-party programming for the Android phone, tried to obtain a Java license, but the parties failed to find mutually agreeable terms.[23] Much of Java is available under General Public License terms,[24] but Google apparently found the free-software license restrictions inconsistent with its business plan. Since in copyright law, unlike patent, duplication without copying is not infringing, Google therefore used independently written implementing code to substitute for Java's implementing code.[25] Wrote the lower court:

> It is the method body that does the heavy lifting, namely the actual work of taking the inputs, crunching them, and returning an answer. The method body can be short or long. Google came up with its own implementations for the method bodies and this accounts for 97 percent of the code for the 37 packages."[26]

(As for patent, Oracle brought patent claims against Google,[27] but the jury rejected them.)

It was clear that Google's clean-room code did not copy Java's implementing code (some minor items aside), and it is implementing code that does the "heavy lifting."[28] However, something significant was copied: to enable the Android platform to *recognize* what a third-party program might ask for, Google copied from Oracle's Java program many of its method headers, and by necessary implication, some of Java's selection and organization.

For example, a particular small program in Java might function to compare two integers, and tell you which one is larger. An ordinary programmer writing an app might be able to easily write this program for herself, but it's even easier to call on the Java program called MAX. A third-party programmer can call on thousands of such routines to save time – so long as the platform at which her program is aimed recognizes the "method headers" and inputs she has employed. Java's slogan is "write once, run anywhere."[29]

Google wanted its programs for the Android platform to recognize the familiar identifying language. If instead of using the Java label "MAX" and its syntax,

---

[23] Oracle II, 750 F.3d at 1350.

[24] David Turner, *The LGPL and Java*, available at www.gnu.org/licenses/lgpl-java.html (last visited June 8, 2015).

[25] Oracle II, 750 F.3d at 1350.

[26] Oracle I, 872 F. Supp. at 980, *rev'd*, Oracle II, 750 F. 3d 1339.

[27] Patents as well as copyrights can exist in computer programs under today's law. The extent of their eligibility for patent may be limited, however. *See* Alice Corp. Pty. Ltd. v. CLS Bank Int'l, 134 S. Ct. 2347, 2357 (2014).

[28] Oracle I, 872 F. Supp. 2d at 980, *rev'd*, Oracle II, quoted above in text accompanying note 26.

[29] Oracle II, 750 F.3d at 1350.

Google had given the Android subroutine that performed the same function a different name, like "LARGER," then the Android platform would be significantly harder for the Java-accustomed programming community to use. That is, without the "method headers," the third-party programmers would have found it more difficult to make their programs speak to Google's (noninfringing) implementing code. Also, lacking the "method headers" would mean that the Android platform could not be backwards compatible with existing application programs that use Java – because when one of those programs needs a subroutine to find the larger of two integers, the program calls what it needs "MAX."

In order to compete on a level playing field with platforms running Java, therefore, Google needed not only to provide functionality as good as Java's. It also needed its Android platform to recognize the known method headers and inputs (specified in Java's declaration code) that identified functions that the third-party programmers would want performed by Android's new and noninfringing implementation code.

In copying the headers, and making its own modules that mimicked Java functioning, Google also copied by necessity some organization from Java.[30] In particular, Google copied the *selection* of those functions that were important enough to be worth creating an implementation and header for them.[31]

The District Court ruled that Google only copied uncopyrightable elements of Java, and found no infringement.[32] On appeal, however, the Federal Circuit held that the headers could have copyrights (as could their organizational structure), largely because many alternative ways to express and organize the headers[33] had been open to Oracle's[34] programmers.

In so holding, Federal Circuit rejected the persuasive power of a 1995 First Circuit decision, *Lotus v. Borland.*[35] The cases posed similar issues.

In *Lotus*, a challenger to the then-dominant spreadsheet program had created a fully independent spreadsheet program, one having its own implementation code. The new program also independently wrote its own structure of commands.[36] However,

---

[30] Organizational elements are sometimes treated as potentially copyrightable compilations. *See* 17 U.S.C. § 101 (2012) ("A 'compilation' is a work formed by the collection and assembling of preexisting materials or of data that are *selected, coordinated, or arranged* in such a way that the resulting work as a whole constitutes an original work of authorship.") (emphasis added).

[31] Oracle II, 750 F.3d at 1350–51.

[32] *Id.*

[33] *See id.* at 1361 ("[M]erger cannot bar copyright protection for any lines of declaring source code unless Sun/Oracle had only one way, or a limited number of ways, to write them.").

[34] By "Oracle" here, I also include Oracle's predecessor in interest, Sun. It was Sun's programmers who largely created Java.

[35] Lotus Dev. Corp. v. Borland Int'l, Inc., 49 F.3d 807 (1st Cir. 1995), *aff'd by an equally divided Court*, 516 U.S. 233 (1996).

[36] Virtually all application programs have command hierarchies; as a common example, users might be instructed to hit the F key to open a "File" menu, on which the user might then find sub-commands such as "Save" or "Save As."

the newcomer program also allowed its users to trigger an optional interface that emulated the dominant spreadsheet's command structure. Through the emulation interface, users switching from the established spreadsheet program to the new program could utilize their existing knowledge base regarding keystrokes. In addition, many consumers had written macros to customize the earlier program to their purposes;[37] such consumers could continue using their macros on the new program only through the emulation interface. The emulator – a copied set of commands ordered in a particular way – made the users' existing macros interoperable with the new spreadsheet program.

To make the emulation interface required the new program to copy both the command headers and some organization from the market leader. The latter company sued for copyright infringement, but lost. The First Circuit held that the copied commands and their hierarchy were "methods of operation."[38] Given the statutory command that "In no case does copyright protection for an original work of authorship extend to any … method of operation …,"[39] the First Circuit held that the command hierarchy could be copied. Further, the court explained, "The fact that Lotus developers could have designed the Lotus menu command hierarchy differently is immaterial to the question of whether it is a 'method of operation.'"[40]

As mentioned above, the Federal Circuit in *Oracle v. Google* vigorously disagreed with the *Lotus* analysis of copyrightability.[41] The *Oracle* court instead ruled for plaintiff on this initial copyrightability issue,[42] arguing that because all computer programs are methods of operation, adherence to the *Lotus* holding would deny copyright for all computer programs and thus frustrate Congressional intent.[43]

---

[37] A macro is a kind of mini-program. Typically, macros are crafted as short-cuts by persons using word processors, spreadsheets, or other application programs. The user states the commands she embeds in the macro sequence by specifying keystrokes. The meaning of each keystroke depends on whatever nomenclature and command structure the application program has specified for its user interface.

[38] Lotus Dev. Corp. v. Borland Int'l, 49 F.3d at 816.

[39] *Id.* at 815–16. 17 U.S.C. § 102(b) (2012) is the cited statutory section; in full Section 102(b) states: "In no case does copyright protection for an original work of authorship extend to any idea, procedure, process, system, method of operation, concept, principle, or discovery, regardless of the form in which it is described, explained, illustrated, or embodied in such work." It is usually assumed that "ideas" and "concepts" are outside copyright because of free speech concerns (see *Eldred v. Ashcroft*, 537 U.S. 186 (2003)); that "discover[ies]" are outside copyright because they are not original (see *Feist Pubs., Inc. v. Rural Tel. Svc. Co., Inc.*, 499 U.S. 340, 348 (1991) ("facts do not owe their origin to an act of authorship")); and that Congress put "system[s]" and "method[s] of operation" outside of copyright in order to maintain patent's dominance over functionality.

[40] Lotus, 49 F.3d at 816, *aff'd by an equally divided Court*, 516 U.S. 233 (1996).

[41] Oracle II, 730 F.3d at 1361.

[42] This ruling may not be determinative of the ultimate outcome, of course. Although the Federal Circuit's decision reversed a decision that no copyright resided in the material copied from Oracle, copyrightability is only one of the relevant issues. A petition for certiorari having been turned down, 135 S. Ct. 2887 (June 29, 2015) (No. 14–410), the case is being remanded. Oracle II, 750 F.3d at 1339.

[43] Oracle II, 750 F.3d at 1361, *cert. denied*, 135 S. Ct. 2887 (June 29, 2015) (No. 14–410), *available at* www.supremecourt.gov/orders/courtorders/062915zor_4g25.pdf.

It is on the copyrightability dispute between the First and Federal Circuits that the defendant Google relied in seeking Supreme Court review. Although *cert.* was denied,[44] it is useful to see how Google's Petition for Writ of Certiorari framed the disputed question:

> Whether copyright protection extends to all elements of an original work of computer software, including a system or method of operation, that an author could have written in more than one way.[45]

These two views of copyrightability – one upholding copyright when "alternative" expressions existed, and one refusing to look for "alternatives" when faced with a method of operation – also dominated discussion of *Oracle*. Yet approaches to copyrightability need not determine the overall outcome of cases like *Oracle* and *Lotus*. Central to both *Lotus*[46] and *Oracle*[47] is the iconic Supreme Court case, *Baker v. Selden*.[48] Despite the age of the opinion (*Baker v. Selden* dates from 1880), *Baker* was a primary focus of the Supreme Court's questions during oral argument in *Lotus*,[49] and conflicting views of *Baker* stood at the core of the Federal Circuit's *Oracle* opinion and of the *Oracle* defendant's Petition for Writ of Certiorari. As will appear below, *Baker* makes important rulings on copyrightability, but it also provides a new avenue (outside issues of copyrightability) for handling some software cases.

13.2.1. An Irony

Before examining the new avenue, let us note the parallel way the Federal Circuit handled the issue of protectable subject-matter in another area. In trademark law, "functional" shapes are ineligible for trade dress protection, for the same reasons of patent-deference that limits the reach of copyright.[50] Defining "functionality"

---

[44] Oracle II, 750 F.3d at 1361, *cert. denied*, 135 S. Ct. 2887 (June 29, 2015) (No. 14–410), *available at* www .supremecourt.gov/orders/courtorders/o62915zor_4g25.pdf.

[45] Petition for Certiorari, Google, Inc. v. Oracle America, Inc., 750 F.3d 1339 (Fed. Cir. 2014), 83 U.S.L.W. 3240 at i (U.S. Oct. 6, 2014) (No. 14–410), 2014 U.S. S. Ct. Briefs LEXIS 4113.

[46] Lotus Dev. Corp. v. Borland Int'l, 49 F.3d 807, 816–7 (1st Cir. 1995).

[47] Oracle II, 750 F.3d at 1355.

[48] Baker v. Selden, 101 U.S. 99 (1880). (Much of the secondary literature gives the opinion's date as 1879. Although the case was argued in 1879, the opinion came down in 1880.)

[49] The oral argument is available at www.oyez.org/cases/1990–1999/1995/1995_94_2003

[50] The core of trademark law is "distinctiveness as to source." Protection for product shapes on the ground of "distinctiveness" is called "trade dress." No form of trade dress protection is permitted for functional configurations. 15 U.S.C. § 1227 (2012); *see also* Qualitex v. Jacobson Prods., 514 U.S. 159 (1995) ("The functionality doctrine ... forbids the use of a product's feature as a trademark where doing so will put a competitor at a significant disadvantage because the feature is "essential to the use or purpose of the article" or "affects its cost or quality." (citing Inwood Labs v. Ives Labs, 456 U.S. 844, 851 n. 10 (1982))).

has of course been the subject of much litigation. The U.S. Supreme Court in *TrafFix v. MDI*[51] ruled that the availability of alternative product shapes could *not* "save" an otherwise functional shape from being unsuitable subject matter for trademark ownership.[52] The Federal Circuit responded to *TrafFix* essentially by taking an evasive maneuver, saving questionable trademark rights in functional product shapes by re-introducing "the availability of alternatives."[53]

So when in *Oracle* the Federal Circuit took the same route as it had in trademark – validating nonpatent rights over functional subject matter by asking, "are alternatives possible?" – it perhaps should not have been surprising. The chapter will suggest that, much as the Federal Circuit attempted to evade the full import of the Supreme Court's *TrafFix* opinion for functionality in trademark law, the Federal

---

[51] TrafFix Devices v. Mktg. Displays, 532 U.S. 23 (2001).

[52] *Id.* at 25.

The Fifth Circuit case *Eppendorf-Netheler-Hinz Gmbh v. Ritter Gmbh* well illustrates the *TrafFix* approach. In Eppendorf, a syringe had a flange that was supported against deformation by a particular design for fins. The plaintiff sought trade dress protection for the fins as distinctive and nonfunctional trade dress, relying on expert testimony indicating that many different fin designs – many alternatives – could have supported the flange. The particular design was nevertheless held ineligible for trademark protection. Eppendorf-Netheler-Hinz Gmbh v. Ritter Gmbh, 289 F.3d 351, 357–58 (5th Cir. 2002) ("Eppendorf's experts concede that fins *of some* shape, size or number *are necessary* to provide support for the flange and to prevent deformation of the product.... *[T]hey are functional* as a matter of law. TrafFix, 532 U.S. at 33–34.") (emphasis added). The juridical irrelevance of alternative flange designs could not be more obvious.

Copyright uses a similar approach in the "separability" hurdle that useful three-dimensional articles must surmount in order to obtain copyright. Thus, when the Second Circuit denied copyright to sculpted mannequins used for clothing displays, the court did not ask whether the sculpted torsos could have been shaped differently. Instead, the Court looked at the shapes as they existed. Since all the elements served a function, no elements survived the separability inquiry. Thus, despite the obvious possibility of sculpting torsos differently, there was nothing to which a copyright could attach:

> [T]he features claimed to be aesthetic or artistic, e.g., the life-size configuration of the breasts and the width of the shoulders, are inextricably intertwined with the utilitarian feature, the display of clothes. [A] model of a human torso, in order to serve its utilitarian function, must have some configuration of the chest and some width of shoulders...

Carol Barnhart, Inc. v. Economy Cover Corp., 773 F.2d 411, 419 (2d Cir. 1985). Although courts vary in their definitions of "separability," no court will give copyright to a useful product shape simply because alternative shapes exist. One court seems to be flirting with including some consideration of alternatives into "separability," Pivot Point Int'l, Inc. v. Charlene Prods., Inc., 372 F.3d 913, 931 (7th Cir. 2004), but even that court's dominant inquiry is not "alternatives." Its focus is on the degree to which the design process was free of "utilitarian pressures."

The separability test – more demanding than the "merger" test that also denies copyright to works of authorship – is mandated by the definition of sculptural works in the statute. *See* 17 U.S.C. § 101 (2012) (definition of "pictorial, graphic and sculptural works").

[53] *See* Valu Eng'g, Inc. v. Rexnord Corp., 278 F.3d 1268, 1276 (Fed. Cir. 2002). *See* 1-2A GILSON ON TRADEMARKS § 2A.04 ("The Federal Circuit believes its pre-*TrafFix* test is still good law and continues

Circuit in *Oracle* now attempts to evade the full import of the Supreme Court's *Baker* opinion for functionality in copyright.

13.3. COPYRIGHT USES AND PATENT USES: *BAKER V. SELDEN*

13.3.1. *Introducing* Baker v. Selden

As mentioned, the core Supreme Court case on functional use of copyrighted works is Baker v. Selden.[54] Relied on both by the *Lotus*[55] and *Oracle* decisions,[56] the case involved the copying of accounting forms.

Selden's widow and administratrix, as plaintiff, asserted copyright in a number of books that both explained and illustrated the decedent's supposedly novel method of bookkeeping. The Selden method enabled an accountant to use fewer volumes and work more expeditiously. Baker was alleged to have copied accounting forms from Selden's books. Baker's forms differed somewhat from Selden's, but the litigants' focus was not on how similar or different the forms might have been. Rather, their focus was on whether Baker's forms enabled accountants to reach the same practical results via the same system as did Selden's.[57]

The Supreme Court was concerned lest copyright allow an end run around the requirements imposed by patent law. Patents are secured only by prior review and must be registered to give the public notice of their content; copyrights arise without either necessity. Patents last a short time; copyrights remain assertable for decades longer. Patents are supposed to issue only upon passing rigorous tests of novelty and nonobviousness; copyrights arise in virtually any doodle, letter home from camp, or amateur recording of street noise. In now-classic language, the Court wrote:

> To give to the author of the book an exclusive property in the art described therein, when no examination of its novelty has ever been officially made, would be a surprise and a fraud upon the public. That is the province of letters-patent, not of copyright.... The description of the art in a book, though entitled to the benefit of copyright, lays no foundation for an exclusive claim to the art itself. The object of the one is explanation; the object of the other is use. The former may be secured by copyright. The latter can only be secured, if it can be secured at all, by letters patent.[58]

---

to use its *Morton-Norwich* analysis that recognizes evidence of alternative designs as part of the overall mix.... The Trademark Trial and Appeal Board follows the Federal Circuit ...").

[54] Baker v. Selden, 101 U.S. 99 (1880).

[55] *Baker v. Selden* is discussed both by the majority, 49 F.3d 807 at 813–17, and by the concurrence, 49 F.3d 807 at 819. Lotus Dev. Corp. v. Borland Int'l, Inc., 49 F.3d 807 (1st Cir. 1995), *aff'd*, 516 U.S. 233 (1996).

[56] Oracle II, 750 F.3d at 1355–57.

[57] Baker, 101 U.S. at 101 ("The evidence of the complainant is principally directed to the object of showing that Baker uses the same system as that which is explained and illustrated in *Selden's* books.").

[58] *Id.* at 102, 105.

So the functional system or other useful art could not be copyrighted, even though copyright could subsist in the textual explanation or pictorial illustration of the art.

But this conclusion did not necessarily leave a work with functional goals without copyright altogether. A copyright might lose its force as against some forms of copying and yet retain its force against others. The kind of use makes a difference: a diagram that is a "necessary incident" to a system can be used freely by the public for "purposes of practical application" but not "for the purpose of publication in other works explanatory of the art."[59] This distinction has become known as the "use/ explanation" doctrine.[60]

The best-known result of the *Baker* Court's concern with keeping copyright from interfering with patent law was *Baker's* holding that systems could not be copyrightable. But copyrightability is only one of copyright's dimensions; another is the nature of the "exclusive rights" a copyright owner is granted.[61] *Baker v. Selden* operated in both dimensions: the opinion posited that even when a valid copyright existed, deference to patent would place limits on the scope of a copyright owner's rights.[62] That second aspect of *Baker*, the aspect dealing not with copyrightability but with scope of right, is this chapter's main topic.

Baker and its progeny distinguish between two types of behaviors that employ created works: uses that are suitable for copyright regulation, and uses that should be regulated solely by patent law. *Baker's* ruling that copyright owners do not have the same rights to control each type[63] of behavior provides another avenue for examining copying in suits like *Oracle v. Google*. This new avenue focuses on limiting a copyright owner's rights over functional use rather than on denying copyright to functional subject matter.[64]

---

59 *Id.* at 103. The Court writes, similarly, that, "[W]hilst no one has a right to print or publish his book, or any material part thereof, as a book intended to convey instruction in the art, any person may practise and use the art itself which he has described and illustrated therein.... And, of course, in using the art, the ruled lines and headings of accounts must necessarily be used as incident to it." *Id.* at 104.

60 As the reader may have noticed, the name of the doctrine comes from a portion of the opinion that is a bit inapposite, as the portion focuses more on copyrightability than on the scope of exclusive right:

> The description of the art in a book, though entitled to the benefit of copyright, lays no foundation for an exclusive claim to the art itself. The object of the one is explanation; the object of the other is use. The former may be secured by copyright. The latter can only be secured, if it can be secured at all, by letters-patent. Baker v. Selden, 101 U.S. 99, 105 (1880).

61 Copyright has essentially three dimensions: duration (has the copyright expired?), subject matter (is the work original, fixed in a tangible medium, and a protectable type of authorship?), and exclusive right (is the defendant accused of a behavior over which the copyright owner has an exclusive right?)

62 There is an identity between the "rights" of the owner and the "uses" that the owner controls. *See* 17 U.S.C. § 106 (2012) (granting to copyright owner exclusive rights to control use of the work via reproduction, use of the work via public performance, use of the work via public display, and so on).

63 Baker, 101 U.S. at 102.

64 At the risk of blurring definitional boundaries, it should be noted that many subject-matter questions can be stated in terms of exclusive rights, and vice versa. For example, one could say, equally, that

At first glance, this approach from *Baker* may seem as broad in its impact as the *Lotus* decision that held a computer program's command structures uncopyrightable. However, as this chapter shows below, the approach need not imperil the overall copyrightability of computer programs and would not eliminate all ability of computer-program copyright owners to bring suit against economically significant use.[65] The "rights" approach from *Baker* instead draws some helpful lines – and note that the approach has nothing to do with "alternatives," which had been key to the *Oracle* court's decision in favor of plaintiff.

13.3.2. *Significance*

Had the Supreme Court in *Baker v. Selden* enabled copyright owners to control functional uses of the utilitarian systems or devices their copyrighted works portray, a welter of unregistered private rights lasting far longer than patents and easier to obtain than patents would be awarded over utilitarian subject matters regardless of whether they met patentable standards. *Baker v. Selden* marks the place where resistance to the confluence of patent and copyright law first took mature form.[66]

Prior to that 1880 decision, designers of systems who could somehow ground those systems in graphic art had plausible claims to copyright. For example, some years before *Baker,* a case arose involving copyright in dressmaker patterns.[67] (Dressmaker patterns are two-dimensional paper drawings meant to be pinned on fabric to guide a tailor's shears.)[68] The plaintiff successfully enjoined unauthorized garment patterns that, though not identical, achieved the "same result" in terms of producing the same finished clothing.[69]

"systems are not copyrightable" or that "copyright owners have no right to control the functional copying of their systems."

   The point at issue in this chapter is whether Baker can allow the public to engage in some functional use of a program (say, uses which are "purely" nonexpressive) while allowing the computer program author to retain copyright control over other uses.

   It's easy to interpret *Baker* as requiring complete denial of copyright – after all, the opinion does say, "The conclusion to which we have come is, that blank account-books are not the subject of copyright." *Baker*, 101 U.S. at, 107. But much of the opinion leans toward a less sweeping invalidation.

[65]   This fear was expressed by the *Oracle II* court. Oracle II, 750 F.3d at 1361.

[66]   In my analysis of *Baker*, I am indebted to the work of Abraham Drassinower, particularly his book ABRAHAM DRASSINOWER, WHAT'S WRONG WITH COPYING? (Harvard University Press 2015), and the work of Pamela Samuelson, particularly Pamela Samuelson, *Frontiers of Intellectual Property: Why Copyright Law Excludes Systems and Processes from the Scope of Its Protection*, 85 TEX. L. REV. 1921 [hereinafter *Systems and Processes*]; and Pamela Samuelson, *Baker v. Selden: Sharpening the Distinction Between Authorship and Invention*, *in* INTELLECTUAL PROPERTY STORIES (Jane C. Ginsburg & Rochelle Cooper Dreyfuss eds. 2006).

[67]   Drury v. Ewing, 7 F. Cas. 1113 (C.C.S.D. 1862).

[68]   Id.

[69]   Id.

In 1880, that changed. After *Baker v. Selden,* courts continually rejected efforts to argue that similarity in system and practical result[70] could justify a judgment of copyright infringement.[71]

13.3.3. *Baker and "merger"*

The "merger" doctrine aims to preserve the public's liberty to use abstract ideas by preventing copyright from arising in a work of expression that is one of very few ways to convey the abstraction. If few or no alternative forms exist, then the particular form of expression is said to "merge" with the unprotectable idea, and the expression too becomes incapable of being owned under copyright law.

"Merger" is a troublesome doctrine, but it has some legitimacy when employed to keep copyright from locking up general and abstract ideas. The *Oracle* court took "merger" and applied it instead to functional innovation. Because the contested elements of the Java program could have been written in alternative ways, the Federal Circuit held, those elements were capable of sustaining a copyright.[72]

The Federal Circuit is not alone in using the possibility of alternatives to justify giving nonpatent protection to a functional innovation. Yet the application of "merger" in such contexts is neither mandated nor explicitly approved by any legislation, and no court has articulated a clear rationale for taking the step.

Further, much U.S. legislation and precedent would seem to weigh against seeing "merger" and its inquiry into "alternatives" as an appropriate tool for defining appropriate borders between copyright and patent law. For example, consider the requirements for protection in the law of utility patent. Patent applicants must show "utility," "novelty," and "nonobviousness," but applicants need *not* prove that

---

[70] After discussing various similarities and differences in appearance, as between plaintiff's work and defendant's, the court in *Drury* opined:

> But there is one fact that seems wholly conclusive on this question of identity, and dispenses with the necessity of a minute inquiry into the alleged discrepancies between the two plans. Some nine or ten witnesses, practical and intelligent dressmakers, well acquainted with the theory and practice of taking measurements, and cutting dresses upon the plan of these parties, testify that the two are substantially the same, and *in practice produce the same result.* Some of these witnesses swear they have cut dresses by both plans, and that when the directions of each are strictly pursued, the results are substantially the same.
>
> ... Mrs. Ewing has, with some adroitness, so arranged and transposed some parts of Mrs. Drury's diagrams as to present to the unexperienced eye the impression that they are dissimilar, but in doing this she has utterly failed to prove that there is any difference *in the principle* of the two. Drury, 7 F. Cas. at 1117 (emphasis added).

[71] *See, e.g.,* the cases reviewed *infra* at notes 113–119.

[72] Oracle II, 750 F.3d at 1361.

their invention is superior to other ways of accomplishing a goal.[73] The presence of "alternatives" does not doom eligibility for federal patent protection.

Patents exist in many different riding lawn-mowers, for example, without any of the manufacturers needing to prove that their own mower possesses elements so unique that no other product can serve as an adequate alternative. Sometimes, therefore, simply being different can suffice for a patent.[74]

This is a sensible decision for Congress to have made. Variety can produce both immediate benefits and unexpectedly valuable routes to future innovation;[75] judgments of product superiority or uniqueness are vulnerable,[76] and characteristics that make an innovation merely different today might make it uniquely important later. Monetary value, for example, is largely a matter of context, so that price and cost attributable to varying combinations of elements will alter over time as constraints and needs alter.

From the fact that Congress permits patents to be granted in innovations that have alternatives, it would seem to follow that such innovations have at least some significance. If so, it is quite arguable that the law should avoid undermining innovators' willingness to embrace the costly patent system (with its rigorous standards, disclosure requirements, and short duration) for such innovations. The patent system loses much of its appeal if an innovator can bypass it to employ a regime like copyright. (Although an owner's rights under copyright are a bit less strong than an

---

[73] *See, e.g.,* 1–4 CHISUM ON PATENTS § 4.01 (2015) ("To comply with the utility requirement, an invention need not be superior to existing products or processes.").

[74] Some qualifications are in order. For example, in determining whether or not an innovation is nonobvious, courts sometimes used to look to secondary evidence such as whether others in the field have long failed to "solve the problem." *Id.* at § 5.05. Other secondary criteria include, inter alia, length of unmet need, or (most controversially) the presence of commercial success. *Id.* As a matter of logic, an innovation with no existing alternatives will do better on measures such as "unmet need" and "unsolved problem" than can an innovation that already has alternatives on the market. Similarly, an innovation that may not have alternatives on the market now, but for which potential alternatives can be easily imagined, may well fare poorly on measures such as commercial success. The presence of actual or potential alternatives may, therefore, make some kind of difference to the likelihood that a patent will be awarded.

[75] Thus, the Tenth Circuit argues:

> [T]he framers of the patent system did not require an inventor to demonstrate an invention's superiority to existing products in order to qualify for a patent. That they did not do so tells us that the patent system seeks not only superior inventions but also a multiplicity of inventions. A variety of choices is more likely to satisfy the desires of a greater number of consumers than is a single set of products deemed "optimal" in some average sense by patent examiners and/ or judges. And the ability to intermingle and extrapolate from many inventors' solutions to the same problem is more likely to lead to further technological advances than is a single, linear approach seeking to advance one "superior" line of research and development.

Vornado Air Circulation Sys., Inc. v. Duracraft Corp., 58 F.3d 1498, 1508 (10th Cir. 1995), *cert. denied,* 516 U.S. 1067 (1996).

[76] *Id.*

owner's rights under patent law, copyright is still tempting:[77] copyrights are granted for immensely long terms of private control, are largely free of required disclosure,[78] and arise under fairly easy standards of acquisition.) In addition, many of Congress's decisions, such as the patent rule that only "novel" and "nonobvious" functional innovations should be privatized,[79] will be disregarded if courts uphold copyrights in common and obvious functional variations.

Patent Law Is a Jealous Monarch

In several cases construing the pre-emptive reach of federal patent law, the U.S. Supreme Court has stated that a functional configuration that is known to the public and is unprotected by utility patent or design patent *should not be able to find protection* under the wings of nonpatent regimes.[80] Functional products that patent law does not protect (whether because a product fails to meet standards such as nonobviousness or novelty,[81] or because its patent has expired[82]) become governed by the patent public domain, and in that domain, patent law gives rights "to copy

[77] Some readers may object that this should be parsed more closely. They might point out, for example, that the Supreme Court has indicated that, for innovations clearly ineligible for patents, allowing states to provide alternative routes to privatization would reduce neither the number of federal patent applications nor the amount of disclosure produced by the federal patent system. Kewanee Oil Co. v. Bicron Corp., 416 U.S. 470, 485 (1974) (refusing to pre-empt state trade secrecy law). *Kewanee's* logic is, however, questionable on its own terms and inapplicable here. One of the difficulties with *Kewanee's* interior logic is the real possibility that diminishing the level of disclosure produced by the patent office might be a lesser problem than the impairment of free competition resulting from non-patent protection. If so, asking how state protections would impact on the number of federal patent applicants would be beside the main point. More importantly for this chapter is that *Kewanee's* focus on the differential likelihoods of patenting various innovations is largely irrelevant to the "merger" search for alternatives. Whether or not an innovation has alternatives does not directly correlate with whether or not the innovation could obtain a federal utility patent.

[78] All patent applications must disclose their inventions. Copyright Office regulations, by contrast, allow the registrants of computer software to hide most of the code from public view. *See, e.g.,* U.S. Copyright Office, Compendium of U.S. Copyright Office Practices § 1509.1(C)(4)(b) (3d ed. 2014) (Computer Programs That Contain Trade Secret Material).

[79] The dangers of too much privatization include, inter alia, excessive deadweight loss, and this cost applies to innovations whether or not they are potentially patentable.

[80] At first the courts spoke as if patent and copyright were to be given similarly broad pre-emptive effect. *See, e.g.,* Compco Corp. v. Day-Brite Lighting, Inc., 367 U.S. 234, 238 (1964) ("when an article is unprotected by a patent or a copyright, state law may not forbid others to copy that article"). Over time, however, the patent and copyright cases were given different treatment. Although in many areas the patent statute was understood to have drawn "a balance" between protection and public domain to which states were required to defer, the 1909 Copyright Act by contrast was interpreted as leaving significant topics as to which "Congress has drawn no balance." Goldstein v. California, 412 U.S. 570–71 (1973) (declining to pre-empt California provision that prohibited the copying of sound recordings).

[81] Sears, Roebuck & Co. v. Stiffel Co., 376 U.S. 225, 226 n.1 (1964) (reiterating a District Court finding that Stiffel's lamp patent was "invalid for want of invention" – a holding that Stiffel did not challenge on appeal).

[82] TrafFix Devices v. Mktg. Displays, 532 U.S. 23, 25 (2001) (configuration for which trade dress protection was sought had been previously protected by patent).

and to use."[83] It is as if patent law were a monarch who has declared that any product she has freed must remain free of subordinate sovereigns as well.

To crown patent law the chief monarch over functionality makes considerable sense. Federal copyright[84] and federal trademark law[85] both contain provisions that *decline* to protect functional innovations and designs. Moreover, it is in the patent statutes that Congress seems to have embodied its most attentive consideration to questions of how functional innovations should be treated.

I concede that this "jealous monarch" view of patent law is not unanimously held, particularly in regard to patent/copyright relations. First, the monarchal view of patent is strongest in the pre-emption cases, where the Supremacy clause governs,[86] and the Clause is irrelevant to interactions between two federal regimes like copyright and patent. Second, the federal copyright and trademark statutes have been interpreted in various ways, with some courts being willing to inquire into a functional product's "alternatives"[87] en route to deciding whether or not to allow nonpatent protection. So the monarchal view of patent law does not reign unopposed within courts interpreting its sister statutes. Third, pre-emption cases themselves fluctuate in the strength they attribute to patent's public domain.[88]

Nevertheless, the pre-emption cases have a clear central line of argument, and the federal statutes for both copyright and trademark consistently defer to patent law for reasons best explained (in terms of both logic and history) by the same

---

[83] Bonito Boats v. Thunder Craft Boats, 489 U.S. 141, 153 (1989) (quoting Compco Corp. v. Day-Brite Lighting, Inc., 367 U.S. 234, 237 (1964)).

[84] In the copyright statute, 17 U.S.C. § 102(b) (2012) puts systems, methods of operation, and processes fully outside copyright protection; in other provisions (such as § 113(b), or the definition of PGS work in § 101), the statute actively prevents copyrights from arising, or deprives copyright owners of otherwise-applicable rights, where copyright could interfere with patent law's public domain.

[85] Under the federal Lanham Act, trademarks cannot be functional; see 15 U.S.C. §§ 1052(e), 1125(a) (3) (2012). The language is not self-defining, however; many courts distinguish between "de jure functionality," which permits protection under the Lanham Act, and "de facto" functionality that just happens to exist. The Supreme Court's most recent opinion on the topic, *TrafFix Devices v. Mktg. Displays*, 532 U.S. 23 (2001), sensibly ignores the labels of de jure and de facto functionality, and in so doing seems to unite the two categories. The *TrafFix* Court held that the possibility of alternative product shapes could not justify giving federal trade dress protection to a shape that was otherwise functional. *Id.* at 25.

[86] Bonito Boats v. Thunder Craft Boats, 489 U.S. 141, 160 (1989) (Florida statute prohibiting certain modes of copying boat designs *held* inconsistent with the patent public domain and thus pre-empted by the Supremacy Clause).

[87] The Supreme Court has criticized using an inquiry into "alternatives" to decide whether a product shape is ineligible for protection under federal trademark law, *TrafFix Devices v. Mktg. Displays*, 532 U.S. 23 (2001), and the Federal Circuit has resisted. *See* Section 13.2.1, *supra*.

[88] Compare, for example, the breadth of pre-emptive sweep in *Compco Corp. v. Day-Brite Lighting, Inc.*, 376 U.S. 234 (1964) (pre-empting state protection for certain trade dress) with the convoluted logic of *Kewanee Oil Co. v. Bicron Corp*, 416 U.S. 470, 485 (1974) (not pre-empting state protection for trade secrets).

approach: namely, that only through patent law should duties be imposed that require the public not to duplicate or sell innovative functional products. After all, nonpatent laws that privatize intellectual products have potential to undermine patent law's balance between competition and monopoly whether the laws are federal or state.

In the pre-emption area, at least one classic case makes it clear that state protection is forbidden not only for unique advances, but also for products that have alternatives. Thus, the Supreme Court wrote:

> That an article copied from an unpatented article could be made in some other way, that the design is . . . not essential to the use of either article, . . . that there may be "confusion" among purchasers as to which article is which or as to who is the maker, may be relevant evidence in applying a State's law requiring such precautions as labeling; however, and regardless of the copier's motives, neither these facts nor any others can furnish a basis for imposing liability for or prohibiting the actual acts of copying and selling.[89]

This approach to the patent public domain leaves no room for a doctrine like "merger."

Conceivably, a justification could be constructed for restricting the logic of the pre-emption cases to assessing solely the validity of state laws. The justification might also stretch to defending the practice of courts' employing "merger" to justify privatizing functional but unpatented products under federal copyright and federal trademark laws. Perhaps one could argue, for example, that patent law's public domain should defer more to cognate federal laws (such as federal copyright and federal trademark) than it does to states' attempts to create intellectual property. But such an argument would need to go much further than pointing out that the Supremacy Clause has no purchase over intrafederal relations; such a formalistic reply would ignore the fact that when *either* federal *or* state law grants exclusivity in functional products outside of patent, those grants can have very serious real-world effects.

In sum: patent law makes nothing turn on the difference between innovations that have alternatives and those that do not, and copyright and trademark states both defer to patent law. Therefore, it should at least surprise us when a court allows copyright or trademark claims to arise in an original or distinctive functional product simply because the product passes something like a "merger" test of having

---

[89] Compco Corp. v. Day-Brite Lighting, Inc., 376 U.S. 234, 238 (1964). The Supreme Court has admittedly withdrawn from some of the statements in *Compco* and its companion case Sears, Roebuck & Co. v. Stiffel Co., 376 U.S. 225 (1964). In my view, the later cases do not impair the core policy of requiring other laws to respect patent law's limits on protection. The most difficult case for my position is *Kewanee Oil Co. v. Bicron Corp*, 416 U.S. 470 (1974), but its result is explicable. I think that in *Kewanee* trade secrecy survived the pre-emption attack for reasons not rooted in logic but in practical administration of the law: it was obvious that Congress had not intended to create such a significant disruption in local commercial law.

competitive alternatives. But that is what the *Oracle* court did, and it is what other courts sometimes do as well.

The historic origins of this practice cannot be fully untangled here. Nevertheless the instant chapter does hope to accomplish two things. The first goal is to make vivid why it is problematic for courts to use the search for alternatives as if it were a sensible or natural tool – one that needs no explanation or justification – to resolve tensions between patent law and other cognate doctrines. I hope that goal has been accomplished.

The second goal is to make clear that the legal community should stop attributing to *Baker* the mess that is "merger." It is to that task that the chapter now turns.

Baker v. Selden neither gave birth to, nor legitimates, the use of "merger" in the context of functionality

Some jurists, perhaps including some on the Federal Circuit,[90] see *Baker v. Selden* as the foundation for "merger." But that reading blurs the line between "abstract ideas" (which merger addresses) and "functional systems" (which are addressed by *Baker* and a host of "useful article" and "functionality" doctrines). Regarding abstract ideas, copyright puts them in the public domain for virtually all purposes, but as for systems and methods of operation, copyright "channels" them toward patent law.[91] Under *Baker*, patent law and its "rights to copy and to use"[92] unpatented innovations seem to have a particularly strong magnetic force.

Admittedly, the *Baker v. Selden* opinion contains language about the "necessity" of using Selden's forms – language that some have interpreted as the Court assuming that few alternative accounting forms would do the job. But the relevant passage is not a finding of fact and is best explicable on purely rhetorical grounds.[93] More

---

[90] Oracle II, 750 F.3d at 1355.

[91] For a useful discussion of pitfalls and opportunities in current methods of channeling IP producers to different legal doctrines, see Mark P. McKenna, *An Alternate Approach to Channeling?*, 51 Wm. & Mary L. Rev. 873 (2009).

[92] This language, while applicable in spirit, I quote from a case decided much later than *Baker*. Bonito Boats v. Thunder Craft Boats, 489 U.S. 141, 164–65 (1989).

[93] It is true that the *Baker* opinion said that "where the art [that a book] teaches cannot be used without employing the methods and diagrams used to illustrate the book, or such as are similar to them, such methods and diagrams are to be considered as necessary incidents to the art, and given therewith to the public." Baker v. Selden, 101 U.S. 99, 103 (1880). That language is sometimes interpreted to indicate that the Court believed that few or no alternatives existed to the plaintiff's accounting form. But that language was *not a factual finding*.

Rather, it was a reply to the earlier claim by plaintiff's lawyer that his client owned the system precisely because (he alleged) the forms were necessary to the system's use. ("It is contended [by plaintiff] that he has secured such exclusive right because no one can use the system without using substantially the same ruled lines and headings which he was appended to his books in illustration of it. In other words, it is contended that the ruled lines and headings, given to illustrate the system, are a part of the book, and as such are secured by the copyright, and that no one can make or use similar ruled

importantly, the same passage indicates that even "necessary" forms *will be infringed* when they are copied in "publication in other works explanatory of the art."[94] The passage therefore is not addressing copyrightability at all.

Whether or not the "merger" doctrine is capable of safeguarding the public domain status of abstract ideas, abstract ideas were not the Court's concern in *Baker*. As intimated above, abstract ideas and patentable inventions lie outside copyright for non-identical sets of reasons. The *Baker* Court's concern was to keep an over-generous application of copyright law from undermining inventors' reasons to seek the protection of patent law. Congress had not chosen copyright (with its long term and ease of acquisition) to govern functional innovation; Congress gave that task to patent law, a realm marked by short duration, requirements of disclosure, and high standards that a government agent needed to be persuaded were satisfied.[95]

13.4. DEFINING "EXPLANATION" AND "USE"

The discussion to this point has suggested that, under *Baker*, the owners of copyright in literary and graphic works cannot employ their rights to control all forms of copying. Some copying is functional and lies within the public's freedom of action unless restrained by some law other than copyright. Thus, a copyright owner can have rights against some copying but not others: A liberty to copy can be given the public "for the purpose of practical application....,"[96] while, by contrast, copying done "for the purpose of publication in other works explanatory of the art"[97] could result in infringement. This dichotomy between infringing and noninfringing uses[98] has of course become known as the "use/explanation" distinction.

---

lines and headings, or ruled lines and headings made and arranged on substantially the same system, without violating the copyright." *Id.* at 101).

As I see it, the Court was merely turning the copyright claimant's rhetoric on its head. The claimant's lawyer had pointed to an alleged interdependence of the accounting system and the accounting forms. The lawyer had argued that the forms (a set of drawings) were necessary to the system, and that therefore the drawings' eligibility for copyright should make copyright apply to the system as well. The Court replied in kind. If such interdependence existed, the Court ruled, such that the drawings were necessary to the system, then it was the system's ineligibility for copyright that would apply to both.

For other reasons why the "merger" interpretation of *Baker* is incorrect, the best guide is Pamela Samuelson, whose scholarship is cited throughout below.

94 Baker, 101 U.S. at 103.
95 *Id.* at 102.
96 *Id.* at 103.
97 *Id.*
98 This dichotomy could be equivalently expressed. Where an owner has rights against copying, the public has duties not to copy (for "duties" are correlative to "rights"); where an owner lacks rights against copying, the public has a privilege or liberty to copy (for liberties are correlative to an absence of exclusive right in opposing parties). This vocabulary, which can be quite useful, finds its origin with Hohfeld. Wesley N. Hohfeld, FUNDAMENTAL LEGAL CONCEPTIONS AS APPLIED IN JUDICIAL REASONING AND OTHER LEGAL ESSAYS (1919).

The "use/explanation" nomenclature is fairly unhelpful. *Everything* done with a copyrighted work is in some sense a "use," so the "use" half of the term is less a description than a gesture: a hand waved toward the realm of utility patents. As for the other half of the phrase, "explanation," copying for explanation is obviously exemplary rather than exhaustive of the many kinds of copying behavior that copyright law can legitimately regulate. Scholars sometimes use the term "nonfunctional" to label the behaviors that copyright can regulate without imperilling patent law. (This chapter also sometimes employs "nonfunctional" in this way.)

But "nonfunctional," too, is mere term-of-art shorthand and, in the end, inaccurate in the context of ordinary language. Behaviors unquestionably within copyright's legitimate sphere (such as copying a work verbatim into one's blog) can serve "functions" such as educating one's readers, or advertising one's own skills, that are as important as many "functions" served by patented inventions.

So what are the behaviors beyond "explanation" that can properly be controlled by copyright? *Baker* has some suggestive answers, as does the contemporary copyright statute.

First, regarding literary or graphic works that convey the "teachings of science," *Baker* tells us that it is only use of the *expressive aspect* that copyright can enforce. When scientific and practical teachings are:

> embodied and taught in a literary composition or book, their essence consists only in *their statement. This alone is what is secured by the copyright.* The use by another of the same methods of statement, whether in words or illustrations, in a book published for teaching the art would undoubtedly be an infringement of the copyright.[99]

Legislative history tells us that Congress considered "expressiveness" the basis for copyright even for computer programs.[100] So a use on the copyright side of the line is a use that draws on the expressive aspects of a work.

---

[99] Baker v. Selden, 101 U.S. 99, 104 (1880) (emphasis added).
[100] When Congress adopted copyright for computer programs, expressiveness was key. To quote from the legislative history, using emphasis supplied by the *Oracle I* court:

> Some concern has been expressed lest copyright in computer programs should extend protection to the methodology or processes adopted by the programmer, rather than merely to the "writing" expressing his ideas. Section 102(b) is intended, among other things, to make clear that *the expression adopted by the programmer is the copyrightable element in a computer program*, and that *the actual processes or methods embodied in the program are not within the scope of the copyright law.*
>
> Section 102(b) in no way enlarges or contracts the scope of copyright protection under the present law. Its purpose is to restate, in the context of the new single Federal system of copyright, that the basic dichotomy between expression and idea remains unchanged.

> H.R. Rep. No. 94–1476, at 56–57 (1976) [hereinafter 1976 House Rep.] (emphasis added), *available at* www.copyright.gov/history/law/clrev_94–1976.pdf.
> Oracle I, 872 F. Supp. 2d at 986 (emphasis altered; footnote omitted).
> This reliance on expressiveness also appears in the rationale for the 1980 amendments. The recommendations on which Congress relied in 1980 depended on the division between "the copyrightable

The *Baker* opinion also provides some helpful examples. Not only can copyright infringement result from copying for "publication in other works explanatory of the art,"[101] the Court tells us; infringement also can arise as a result of copying the "lines of the poet or the historian's periods"[102] and from copying works of authorship whose only goal is to serve aesthetic "taste"[103] or the "production of pleasure in the contemplation" of "form."[104]

So it does not count as utilitarian "use" to produce pleasure through aesthetics and contemplation. To produce pleasure through designing a tickling machine would be another story.

It can be as difficult to define what counts as a patent-type "use" as it was to define a copyright-type "explanation." Yet it is important to identify what kinds of purposes (described with whatever specificity is possible) might suffice to activate patent's magnetic force so strongly that patent's influence makes an act of reproduction non-infringing under copyright law.

We might start by distinguishing expressive from nonexpressive uses.[105] However, *Baker* does not address all nonexpressive uses; *Baker* addresses only one subset, namely, copying behavior that lies within the domain of patent law's proper concern. Does patent law provide answers? Unfortunately not; patent law's notion of "utility" is too vague to assist and hardly self-defining. Is there some other source of criteria for

---

element of *style and expression* in a computer program and the process which underlies it." Final Report of the National Commission on New Technology Uses of Copyrighted Works 22 (1978) [hereinafter CONTU]. In 1980, Congress essentially adopted the CONTU recommendations.

[101] Baker, 101 U.S. at 104–05.

[102] *Id.* at 104.

Robert Bone has suggested that the *Baker* court was trying to distinguish between different *kinds* of works – those susceptible only to expression-oriented behaviors of the kinds with which copyright has traditionally been concerned, and those works that are susceptible to functional application of the kinds with which patent law has traditionally been concerned. It is possible that, as Professor Bone suggests, the Court may be making a teleological subject-matter distinction here, namely, that works of a particular type (poetry, history, pictures "addressed to the taste") simply have no conceivable "functions" or "uses" about which patent law should be concerned. But even so, the Court's root concern would seem to be with *types of use*.

One need not go so far as to eliminate copyrightability in order to shelter the public's freedom to use functional aspects of a copyrighted work in a functional way.

[103] Baker, 101 U.S. at 104.

[104] The Court noted, "[T]hese observations are not intended to apply to ornamental designs, or pictorial illustrations addressed to the taste. Of these it may be said, that their form is their essence, and their object, the production of pleasure in their contemplation." Baker, 101 U.S. at 103–04.

[105] By contrast, Abraham Drassinower's view of *Baker* does begin with a distinction between communicative and non-communicative use. *See, e.g.*, Abraham Drassinower, *Copyright Infringement as Compelled Speech*, Section III, Philosophy and Intellectual Property (Anabelle Lever, ed., Cambridge University Press 2012); *see also* the discussion *infra* accompanying note 126 and the sources cited therein.

identifying patent-type "use," or for identifying (something not quite its converse) the kind of "use" for which copyright is not the proper regulator?

One potential source is the contemporary statutory concept of "useful article."[106] It appears in the 1976 Copyright Act.

Coming into the mid-seventies, Congress was considering the latest of a series of copyright reform bills. When the House received the bill containing what soon became the new Copyright Act, part of the bill ("Title II") was a set of sui generis rules granting design protection for "applied art" such as the attractive design of autos, appliances, and furniture. The House jettisoned Title II. It did so in part because of concerns about monopoly.[107]

The entitlements given by Copyright are even stronger than the sui generis right that Congress had declined to create, and thus copyright posed more danger of monopoly than the rejected right. It is natural that the Copyright Act of 1976 would thus leave, as it did, a wide moat of public domain liberty around objects that meld form and function. This public-protective ring is embodied not only through narrowing the copyrightability of PGS useful articles.[108] The statute also limits the exclusive rights that attach to any

---

[106] 17 U.S.C. § 101 (2012) (definition of "useful article").

[107] In dropping the design-protection portion of the bill, Title II, the House Report gave among its reasons the following:

> [T]he Committee will have to examine further the assertion of the Department of Justice, which testified in opposition to the Title, that Title II would create a new monopoly which has not been justified by a showing that its benefits will outweigh the disadvantage of removing such designs from free public use.

1976 House Rep., *supra* note 100, at 49–50.

[108] Useful articles that seek protection as pictorial, graphic, or sculptural works ("PGS" works) must meet a demanding "separability" test:

> [t]he design of a useful article, as defined in this section, shall be considered a pictorial, graphic, or sculptural work only if, and only to the extent that, such design incorporates pictorial, graphic, or sculptural features that can be identified separately from, and are capable of existing independently of, the utilitarian aspects of the article.

17 U.S.C. § 101 (2012) (definition of "pictorial, graphic and sculptural works").

In my view, the "best" account of separability is that advanced by Paul Goldstein. The key, as he indicates, is whether forbidding competitors to copy the copyrighted portion of the useful article will make the utilitarian aspects of the item less useful. For example, will removing the "aesthetic" component make the object do its task less well, or make the object more expensive to manufacture? If so, the component is not "separable." If removing it makes no utilitarian difference, however, then it is "separable." See GOLDSTEIN, 1 COPYRIGHT § 2.5.3 (physical separability exits if the sculptural feature "can be physically separated from the article *without impairing the article's utility* and if, once separated, it can stand alone as a work of art traditionally conceived," *id.* at 2.75; conceptual separability arises when a feature "can stand alone as a work of art traditionally conceived, *and if the useful article in which it is embodied would be equally useful without it." Id.* at 2:78.1.)

In some of its cases the Second Circuit has implemented this perspective: explicitly or implicitly asking whether the useful article's functions can be equally well served were the object denuded of the portion in which copyright is claimed. *See* Carol Barnhart, Inc. v. Economy Cover Corp., 773 F.2d 411, 418 (2d Cir. 1985).

copyrights that portray useful articles – the copyright owner's rights do not control what *Baker* called "use."[109]

We might, accordingly, find some hints to fill out *Baker's* distinction between "use" and "explanation" in the current statute's definition of "useful article." The definition reads as follows:

> A "useful article" is an article having an intrinsic utilitarian function that is not merely to portray the appearance of the article or to convey information.[110]

According to this definition, it is apparently a copyright–appropriate use "to portray appearance" (or, presumably to portray any pattern of form to any sense, whether the form be, e.g., a pattern of colors, a pattern of sounds, or a pattern of dance steps). Similarly, "to convey information" is also a presumptively copyright-appropriate use. Functions beyond "appearance" and "information" lean in the patent direction. Although PGS works are especially singled out for special copyrightability hurdles[111] that do not apply to useful articles packaged in non-PGS formats, the definition is at least suggestive; it suggests that any function beyond "appearance" and "information" might be ripe for being classified as none of copyright's business.

Copyright scholars are accustomed to drawing a sharp line between "useful articles" that are pictorial, graphic or sculptural works ("PGS" works), on the one hand, and, on the other, the many other kinds of functional-but-expressive creations that appear in non-PGS parts of the copyright statute. Given legislative history, the distinction between PGS works and other works makes sense when copyrightability is on the table.[112] However, when "scope of right" rather than copyrightability is the

---

[109] *See, e.g.*, 17 U.S.C. § §113(b) and 113(c); 102(b) (2012). Subsection 113(b), discussed at further length *infra* at the section entitled "Congressional Implementation," provides in essence that "the copyright in a work portraying a useful article as such would not protect against manufacture of that article." REPORT OF THE REGISTER OF COPYRIGHTS, GENERAL REVISION OF THE COPYRIGHT LAW 14 (1961), available at http://copyright.gov/history/1961_registers_report.pdf/. *See also* 1976 HOUSE REP., *supra* note 100, at 109.

[110] 17 U.S.C. § 101 (2012). The statute gives force to the "useful article" concept most obviously in regard to Pictorial, Graphic and Sculptural ("PGS") works: useful articles that seek copyright under the PGS category must pass a separability test, section 101, and the derivative work right attaching to a copyrighted PGS work that depicts a useful article is narrow and will not cover the making of the functional articles depicted, §113(b).

More controversially, "useful article" has application in regard to functional use more generally, pursuant to a broad but plausible reading of 17 U.S.C. § 113(b) (2012). The broad reading of § 113(b) is discussed further *infra* at "Congressional Implementation."

[111] The statute gives PGS works that serve functions beyond "appearance" and "information" rough treatment when it comes to copyrightability. Useful PGS works must pass a 'separability' test, as discussed *supra* at notes 53, 108.

[112] "[A]lthough the shape of an industrial product may be aesthetically satisfying and valuable, the Committee's intention is not to offer it copyright protection under the bill. Unless the shape of an automobile, airplane, ladies' dress, food processor, television set, or any other industrial product

issue, Congress has not drawn such a sharp line. All functional-but-expressive creations owe a conflicting allegiance to both copyright and to patent; they share many
common policies; it may be time for "useful" PGS works and other "useful" works
to learn something from each other.

The *Baker*-type cases cited in copyright legislative history are in fact consistent with
what became the 1976 definition of "useful article."[113] These cases refuse to impose
liability for making a copy or derivative work that does more than portray "appearance"
or convey "information"– that is, the cases give an immunity for any version of the
copyrighted work that actually functions.

Thus, to manufacture furniture,[114] lamps,[115] or gears[116] copied from copyrighted
graphics in a competitor's catalogue does not infringe the copyrights. It also does not
infringe to build a highway/bridge interchange based on a copyrighted drawing of an
original road design.[117] These noninfringing acts of reproduction are all uses that go
beyond "conveying information" and "portraying" form; they are on the "use" side
of the *Baker* divide. Similarly, cases that did impose infringement verdicts (i.e., those
on the "explanation" side of the *Baker* divide) involved defendants whose purposes
involved only "information" or "appearance."

Thus, it did infringe to build a memorial[118] based on a copyrighted sculpture. Memorial stones only convey information (such as naming who is buried

---

contains some element that, physically or conceptually, can be identified as separable from the utilitarian aspects of that article, the design would not be copyrighted under the bill." 1976 HOUSE REP.,
supra note 100, at 55.

[113] These were cited in regard to a provision that later became § 113.

[114] Lamb v. Grand Rapids School Furniture Co., 39 F. 474 (W.D. Mich. 1889) (defendant alleged to have
manufactured church furniture depicted in another entity's copyrighted catalog and to be publishing
as advertisements graphics showing its 'own' furniture that virtually duplicated the plaintiff's original
photos; motion seeking preliminary injunction denied).

[115] Kashins v. Lightmakers, Inc., 155 F. Supp. 202 (S.D.N.Y. 1956) (no infringement results from making
lamps identical to those appearing in a copyrighted catalog). The case does not really assist in fleshing
out § 113(b), however, since the plaintiff seemed to claim no authorship in the lamp designs that were
photographed. If the plaintiff's originality subsisted only in choice of photographic angles and such, a
defendant who built the objects depicted in the photo would have used nothing of what made the photos copyrightable. In such a case, infringement would not attach whether or not the objects depicted
were 'useful'.

[116] In *PIC Design Corp. v. Sterling Precision Corp.*, 231 F. Supp. 106 (S.D.N.Y. 1964), the defendant's catalogs copied illustrations of gears from the plaintiff's catalogs. It appears that the plaintiff had designed
the gears, though no inquiry into their originality was made. The court noted that "the component parts
so pictured in all the catalogs before us are in the public domain and plaintiff has no exclusive right to
produce and illustrate them. It is the illustration that is protected, not the object itself." *Id.* at 110.

[117] Muller v. Triborough Bridge Auth., 43 F. Supp. 298, 300 (S.D.N.Y. 1942) (holding that copying a drawing of a highway/bridge interchange by building such a roadway does not infringe copyright in the
drawing).

[118] A memorial stone is not a useful article; it merely portrays appearance (e.g., angel wings) and conveys
information (about the deceased.) To copy someone else's art in a memorial can therefore infringe.
Jones Bros. Co. v. Underkoffler, 16 F. Supp. 729, 731 (M.D. Pa. 1936) (memorial copied from a photograph was held infringing).

beneath, reproducing lines of poetry, conveying descriptions and dates) and portray appearance.

Similarly, making a doll[119] based on a copyrighted comic did infringe. This too fits the "useful article" definition; stuffed dolls are not "useful" because they employ only the copied work's form and "appearance." Today's Copyright Office does not consider dolls and other toys to be "useful articles."[120]

There is of course no prescience in the old case decisions; the judges were not seeking to anticipate and apply the "useful article" definition from the 1976 Act. To the contrary, any causal relation ran in the ordinary temporal direction. The pre-1976 cases just mentioned are based on *Baker v. Selden*, and those decisions along with *Baker* are part of the source from which the 1976 definitional principle drew its legitimacy. The Justice Department's anti-monopoly position too was hardly born the moment Congress heard it; the anti-monopoly strains in IP law are rooted deeply in history.[121]

---

[119] King Features Syndicate v. Fleischer, 299 F. 533, 537 (2d Cir. 1924) (finding defendant had infringed by making a three-dimensional doll from plaintiff's two-dimensional cartoon horse "Sparky"). The court imposed liability by finding a parallel between "the production of pleasure in contemplation," mentioned in *Baker v. Selden* as a legitimate copyright purpose, and the ability of Sparky to produce "pleasure in amusement." *See also* Fleischer Studios, Inc. v. Freundlich, Inc., 73 F.2d 276 (2d Cir. 1934) (involving the Betty Boop doll).

[120] From cases like this arose the current rule treating stuffed animals and dolls as art and not as useful articles. Toys and stuffed animals are typically not considered "useful articles." Compendium II of Copyright Office Practices at 502, available at www.copyrightcompendium.com/#500.

[121] One of the crucial milestones was the Statute of Monopolies, Westminster (1624), Primary Sources on Copyright (1450-1900), eds L. Bently & M. Kretschmer, www.copyrighthistory.org. In the US, the importance of leaving nonpatented products open to all to copy was probably stated most clearly in *Sears, Roebuck & Co. v. Stiffel Co.*, 376 U.S. 225 (1964) and its companion case, *Compco Corp. v. Day-Brite Lighting, Inc.*, 376 U.S. 234 (1964).

Precursors to the 1976 Act's § 113 provide the following illustrative language:

'*** In fact, the defendant manufactures goods from designs taken from complainants' illustrations, and they say (what for the present purpose must be admitted) that their illustrations are in truth of their own goods, so that the similitude of the illustrations results from the fact that the goods are alike. The manufactures of the complainants are not patented. The defendants may lawfully manufacture just such goods. Can they not publish correct illustrations of them as adjuncts of their sale? Ought they to be restrained from doing this because the complainants, having done the same thing, have copyrighted illustrations which, while representing their own goods, represent those of the defendant also? It is clear that the books of both parties are published and used solely as means for advertisement. To say that the defendant has not the right to publish correct illustrations of its goods must practically result in creating a monopoly, in goods modeled on those designs, in the complainants, and thus give all the benefits of a patent upon unpatented and unpatentable articles. * * * It does not appear to me that such results can be accomplished in this way. It is true, there is an appearance of profiting at another's expense, and reaping what another has sown, but I can see no legal ground on which this can be prevented. The legislation, with its limitations, which public policy has approved, does not extend so broadly as to give the complainants a monopoly in the harvest in such a case.'

Kashins v. Lightmakers, Inc., 155 F. Supp. 202, 203 (S.D.N.Y. 1956), quoting from *Lamb v. Grand Rapids Sch. Furniture Co.*, 39 F. 474, 475 (C.C.W.D. Mich. 1889).

13.4.1. *Tentative Conclusion: Interoperability and* Baker

Returning to *Oracle v. Google*, it is indisputable that computer programs do more than "portray form" and "convey information." They make machines work, and when someone copies code, the copies are typically sold to people for the purpose of making other machines work. While neither of these facts about the use of computer programs is sufficient to resolve the *Oracle* case, they remind us that computer code may be a "useful article" and that like all useful articles, considerations of patent deference can and should play a strong role.

As mentioned, Baker indicates that expressive use is the kind of use which copyright law can legitimately regulate.[122] Copying an entire copyrighted computer program will of necessity make use of both expressive and nonexpressive aspects,[123] and using the copy – even using it to run a machine – could therefore infringe. Where any possibility exists that the defendant saved herself some expressive effort, and that obtaining this advantage played a nontrivial role in motivating the copying, it is not as clear that Baker will shelter her behavior.[124]

But copying that is done solely to achieve interoperability (with other programs or with previously acquired utilitarian skill) is fully indifferent to the copied program's expressive aspects. This is true both for interoperability between the copied program and the copier's program, as in *Lotus v. Borland*, or interoperability between the copier's program and third-party programs, as in *Oracle v. Google*. What matters for interoperability is not the quality of expression, but exact conformity.

If it is correct that uses indifferent to expression cannot infringe, then a proper resolution of *Oracle* and *Lotus* is clear. In neither case would the copying infringe.

This result does not turn on the value or disvalue of lock-in as a social or economic practice.[125] A logically prior matter is whether an instance of copying is related or unrelated to the copied material's expressivity. And copying to avoid lock-in certainly

---

[122] *See supra* notes 56–62 and accompanying text.

[123] Were a program to lack any expressive content, it could not have copyright in the first instance.

Whether expression in a program ever "really" exists (in the ordinary-language sense) or whether Congress conclusively deems it to exist (in the sense of a mandatory legal fiction) is a question this chapter does not address. Many scholars have addressed the inherent conceptual instability caused by Congress including computer programs among the categories of potentially copyrightable subject matter. *See, e.g.,* Lloyd L. Weinreb, *Copyright for Functional Expression*, 111 HARV. L. REV. 1149 (1998).

[124] The touchstone examples in *Baker* involve no use of expressiveness: the medicines made by reading a book, the mechanical skills learned from a book ... none copy or use the book's mode of "statement" which *Baker* teaches is the aspect to which copyright attaches.

[125] Overstating the importance of lock-in economics to the *Oracle* case is a mistake the Solicitor General made in his opposition to certiorari. *See* Brief for the United States as Amicus Curiae, Oracle Am., Inc. v. Google Inc., 750 F.3d 1339 (Fed. Cir. 2014), available at www.justice.gov/sites/default/files/osg/briefs/2015/06/01/14-410_google_v_oracle_us_cvsg_brief.pdf.

seems to be unrelated to expression. When having a key made, one doesn't care if the key is clunky or beautiful. Its elegance as a sculptural artifact is irrelevant.

All that matters is that it fits the lock.

13.4.2. *Juridical Integrity and Lack of "Fit"*

My contention, that copying for interoperability does not infringe, cuts less broadly than it may seem. To better see this, it will be helpful to examine and distinguish the perspective that Abraham Drassinower brings to *Baker v. Selden*.

In Professor Drassinower's view, *Baker* demonstrates that nonexpressive, non-communicative forms of copying should count as "nonuse"[126] – a behavior outside the copyright statutes, and thus not actionable under copyright law.[127] Only when a work is used expressively, as a communication, Drassinower argues, can the use give rise to copyright infringement. It's not that Drassinower argues that patent's public domain has "trumping" power, or that giving patent-like power to copyrights is socially costly; his argument is rather that copyright has no role beyond its proper (communicatory) sphere.

While I cannot agree with all of Professor Drassinower's contentions, I find an immensely useful starting point in Drassinower's observation that mere mechanical repetition of a particular physical or audible form does not always use the work *as a work*.[128] Sometimes, for example, it is being used as a tool (functionally) or as a fact (as evidence in a courtroom) or for some other purpose whose value does not depend on the work's expressiveness.

We all know how a person can change roles, and that different roles (spouse, employer, enemy combatant) can trigger different rights and duties both socially and under law. Similarly, a given configuration of words (or symbols, sounds, shapes, lines, or colors) can have different roles in different contexts.

A new role can change the configuration's legal significance – either because copyright is juridically concerned only with one role, namely, communication (as

---

[126] DRASSINOWER, *supra* note 66, at 13 ("[In *Baker*, t]he defendant used the forms as a tool but not as a work, and was therefore not liable in copyright... *Baker* thus turns on a crucial distinction between the work as a communicative act and its material form as its physical embodiment. Use of the physical embodiment for noncommunicative purposes does not give rise to liability.").

[127] Drassinower emphasizes that copyright would have reached the accounting form in *Baker* if it had been copied as part of an explanatory book, or copied for other reasons relating to its expressive, authorial qualities. The defendant however copied the form for reasons relating to its *inventive* qualities. The set of lines changed role from "work of authorship" to "tool" – resulting in a lack of fit with copyright, and defendant was not liable. Baker v. Selden, 101 U.S. 99, 100 (1880).

[128] *Id.* at 102 (arguing that it is an error to see "any and all uses of a work's material form" as "uses of the work").

Drassinower might have it),[129] or because the new role alters the work's economic and social impact (as policy analysts might have it).

For an example of changing roles for a copyrighted work, consider a love letter introduced into evidence in a divorce proceeding. In the litigation context, the letter's eloquence as a work of authorship is irrelevant; the literary work has become a fact, valued not for its beauty in language but for what it implies, factually, about the relationship between sender and receiver. The same copyrightable letter, now serving as a fact rather than as expression, under current law can be freely copied for evidentiary purposes in litigation.[130] It is a "fair use."[131]

There are *reasons* for granting private rights in the first instance, and rights should not be exercised for reasons that lie far afield. Functional uses, like evidentiary uses, do not reward quality of expression; they do not "fit."

If crafting exceptions to the public's duty-not-to-copy were costless and perfectly predictable, lack of fit standing alone would always suffice as ground for sheltering a defendant's activity. Instead, the process consumes some governmental and private resources, probably increases uncertainty (in both markets and everyday noncommercial behaviors), and might make unlawful copying and litigation a bit more likely.[132] Rule of Law values such as predictability might be poorly served by case-by-case insistence on "fit."

Lack of "fit" in a particular instance shows merely that enforcement will fail to further a particular law's goals. Courts often want a showing that, in addition, refusing to enforce will achieve some *affirmative* public advantage. They want something that can outweigh the extra costs involved in case-by-case recrafting of the rules.

For an example, consider negligence law. It uses the "proximate cause" doctrine to immunize defendants from liability when the harm they cause is unrelated to the dangers that made their behavior negligent in the first instance. Because there is a "lack of fit" between unforeseeable harm and imposing a duty of care, a proximate cause limitation makes sense both on juridical grounds and on economic grounds.[133]

---

[129] See generally DRASSINOWER, *supra* note 66.

[130] Copying for courtroom purposes is seen as a "fair use," recognized by cases such as Den Hollander v. Steinberg, 419 Fed. App'x 44 (2d Cir. 2011).

[131] *Id.* It would be more accurate to say that works of authorship become "facts" when copied for evidentiary purposes; unfortunately, however, clear statement about these cases is inhibited by the Supreme Court's odd ontological assertion that "facts" are "found" and never "created." Feist Pubs., Inc. v. Rural Tel. Svc. Co., Inc., 499 U.S. 340, 348 (1991) ("[F]acts do not owe their origin to an act of authorship.") On this latter point, see Wendy J. Gordon, *Reality as Artifact: From Feist to Fair Use*, 55 L. & CONTEMP. PROBS. 93 (1992).

[132] Conceivably, each case where a defendant succeeds in finding a limitation could encourage new types of copying that might hope (with less ground) to find equivalent shelter.

[133] Juridically, there is no conceptual linkage between taking reasonable care and avoiding an unforeseeable kind of harm. The proximate cause limitation makes sense economically as well, for the law is powerless to encourage people to take precautions against invisible dangers.

But because "proximate cause" is implemented on a fact-sensitive, case-by-case basis, which is costly, we expect to find more explanation for the doctrine, in addition to simple "lack of fit" – and we do. Eliminating the proximate cause doctrine, which would mean imposing liability to the extent of all unforeseeable harms caused, could bring with it demoralizing[134] and crushing burdens[135] of liability.[136] These social burdens make a difference, particularly since, given the lack of "fit" caused by unforeseeability, the burdens would not even be partially offset with gains in encouraging reasonable care. Taken together, these are weighty reasons to adopt a doctrine (called "proximate cause") to limit liability where there is "lack of fit" in personal injury cases.

I don't deny that "lack of fit" standing alone can and should warrant limiting legal enforcement in some circumstances, particularly those involving free speech and other fundamental rights. Outside the area of fundamental rights, however, few judges demand that the legislature (in crafting rights) or a particular plaintiff (in bringing suit) demonstrate a one-on-one correlation between a particular exercise of right and the policies for which the right was granted. Except perhaps for juridical purists, law must usually operate on a more wholesale level.[137]

Arguably, copyright should be one of those rare areas where "lack of fit" alone will suffice.[138] As a matter of fundamental right, overbroad copyright enforcement often threatens first-amendment values.[139] As an economic matter, copyright liability imposes obvious social costs. Monetary incentives for new authorship are generated by making it more expensive to purchase copies of, or access to, existing authorship; the increasing cost makes authorship less available both for new authors to use[140] and for consumers to purchase.

---

[134] "Demoralization cost" is a term coined by Frank Michelman to refer to *dis*incentives (effects that discourage productive activity) caused by the threat of large unpredictable losses. Frank Michelman, *Property, Utility and Fairness: Comments on the Ethical Foundations of "Just Compensation Law*, 80 HARV. L. REV. 1165, 1214 (1967).

[135] Having to pay an immense judgment can trigger costs much higher than the numbers in the judgment itself. For example, tort judgments against companies can cause prices to rise and jobs to be lost; tort judgments against individuals may mean losing a home, which in turn leaves family members vulnerable to further losses.

The same point is true on the side of potential plaintiffs: bearing a tortious injury without receiving compensation can result in disastrous follow-on costs for both businesses and individuals. *See* GUIDO CALABRESI, THE COSTS OF ACCIDENTS, 27–28 (Yale University Press 1970) ("secondary costs"). Identifying which kinds of cost are likely to be more serious in varying circumstances is the task of empirical research.

[136] I am indebted to Bob Bone here.

[137] I am indebted to discussions with Jane Ginsburg for her insistence on this point.

[138] Fundamental liberties are usually linked to avoiding important harms; when this is true, the lack of fit *means* an "extra" element of social harm is present.

[139] Admittedly, we commentators perceive these threats to free speech far more easily than do the courts.

[140] A classic statement of these issues is William Landes & Richard Posner, *An Economic Analysis of Copyright Law*, 18 J. LEG. STUD. 325 (1989).

These ever-present risks counsel that copyright's scope should generally remain within the arena where these social costs are most likely to be outweighed by copyright's positive incentive effects – which is, definitionally, the arena where the elements of the cause of action are a "good fit" with statutory purpose. Only in the area of "fit" – authorial works being used for authorial purposes – is the ability of copyright enforcement to produce more benefits than costs likely to be more than coincidental. And indeed, in copyright law, the fair use doctrine and a multitude of specific exemptions provide some shelter from simple "lack of fit." But we have no consensus on how far the shelter should extend, and at the moment it is far from complete.[141]

As an example of a "lack of fit" that might not give rise to a copyist victory, consider a hypothetical decorator who has noticed that sheet music can make visually pleasing patterns, and who begins manufacturing wallpaper that duplicates the appearance of copyrighted sheet music. In papering its customers' walls with a particular composer's clefs, eighth-notes, sharps and so on, the wallpaper maker is not using the musical work *as* a musical work. Any connection between the notes' visual appeal and the quality of the work's intended aural expression is purely coincidental. Allowing the composer to collect monies from the wallpaper maker does nothing to reward composing skill or encourage its further development.

There is no "fit."

It is possible such copying might be sheltered from liability.[142] Yet given the commercial nature of the use, and the obscurity of any claim the wallpaper might have to be serving the public interest, as a descriptive matter the defendant's likelihood of success is rather low.

By way of contrast, recall the example of copyrighted works being reproduced for evidentiary use in court. Courts understand the importance of providing factual evidence for litigation, and understand also how often the author of an incriminating document might wish to assert copyright to prevent its being copied. Establishing a rule that permits copying for evidentiary purposes serves a public interest easily understood, and therefore such copying is routinely accommodated by copyright's fair use doctrine. Judges are likely to be sensitive to the different levels of social interest at stake and, even in copyright, "lack of fit" alone will not always generate shelter for an act of unconsented copying.

---

[141] As a matter of current doctrine, a court might impose copyright liability despite "lack of fit" unless the defendant can demonstrate an additional public interest dimension that would be served by giving her the contested liberty of action. Stacey Dogan makes this point about trademark law. Stacey Dogan, *Principled Standards vs. Boundless Discretion*, 37 COLUM. J.L. ARTS 503, 506 (2014).

[142] It might, for example, be considered "transformative" under the fair use doctrine. *See, e.g.,* Bill Graham Archives v. Dorling Kindersley Ltd., 448 F.3d 605 (2d Cir. 2006) (holding it was fair use for defendant to reproduce miniaturized copies of copyrighted 'Grateful Dead' concert posters to mark a graphical timeline of the band's history).

Moreover, the Supreme Court has upheld two statutory expansions of copyright with only the roughest guess as to "fit." Both term extension and statutory restoration of public domain copyrights have doubtful ability to further copyright goals, and both statutes have implications for free speech; but when these statutes were challenged the Court declined to employ strict scrutiny.[143] These developments counsel caution, even though the judiciary's role in deploying doctrines like the "use/explanation" distinction or "fair use" is different from the role the Supreme Court plays in reviewing the constitutionality of Congressional statutes.

For such reasons, this chapter does not claim (as a descriptive matter) that a lack of "fit" between a copyright defendant's actions and copyright law's overall policy will always suffice to defeat liability. Also, given the real costs of making fine distinctions among cases, this chapter does not claim (as a normative matter) that all non-fitting cases of copying should escape liability. What the chapter does claim is that line-drawing is worth the cost when copyright threatens to control the kinds of functional uses that *Baker* saw as properly relegated to patent. Imposing liability on purely functional uses not only fails to advance the goal of incentivizing expressive activity, but such liability has the potential for undermining the patent system, with effects such as decreasing the disclosure of inventions, and shrinking free competition among unpatented utilitarian products. The result, in *Baker's* language, could be a "fraud upon the public."[144]

These are matters whose importance is difficult to understate. Therefore, when it comes to a particular kind of disjunction – between *expressive use* and *functional use*, or (putting it somewhat differently) between *authorship* and *invention* – the Supreme Court in *Baker* held that the cost of disregarding the "lack of fit" is too high.

That, I would argue, is the essential point of *Baker v. Selden.*

---

[143] *See* Golan v. Holder, 132 S. Ct. 873 (2012) (upholding the revival of certain copyrights already in the public domain); Eldred v. Ashcroft, 537 U.S. 186 (2003) (upholding the constitutionality of the Sonny Bono Copyright Term Extension Act).

In *Eldred* the Court defined its path: declining to apply a heightened degree of scrutiny. The opinion states that "copyright law contains built-in First Amendment accommodations" such as "fair use" and the idea/expression dichotomy, 537 U.S. at 219, that make lesser scrutiny appropriate. Further, to measure whether "Congress' exercise of its Copyright Clause authority" was "rational," *id.* at 206, the Court employed an extremely broad notion of what purposes federal copyright could legitimately serve. *See generally* Wendy J. Gordon, *The Core of Copyright: Authors, Not Publishers*, 52 Hous. L. Rev. 613 (2014) (criticizing *Eldred's* analysis of copyright's purpose).

[144] Baker v. Selden, 101 U.S. 99, 102 (1880).

13.4.3. *Should Mixed Uses Qualify for* Baker's *Shelter*

This chapter interprets *Baker* as resting not only on juridical coherence in Drassinower's sense, but also on consideration of social and economic cost. To obtain *Baker's* shelter, then, two elements are needed: the user's indifference to expression (that is, "nonuse" in Drassinower's sense) and interference in patent law's domain.

Must the use be purely functional, with no admixture of expressive value? From an abstract juridical perspective, as long as some expressive value inheres in the use, copyright should be able to find a mixed use (both expressive and functional) to be an infringement. Yet, concerns from outside of copyright (such as pressure from patent's public domain) might counsel against copyright owners having rights over a mixed area. In terms of *Baker's* policies, an expressive value should be capable of being outweighed or even trumped by a functional role. Under *Baker*, must copyright remain unenforced whenever the use has a functional aspect? These questions remain open, for in terms of our facts – those of *Oracle* and *Lotus* – the nature of the use is fairly "pure" in its functionality.

How do we know when a work of authorship is being used solely as a functional tool?[145] As suggested above, the answer must surely lie in determining whether the defendant is indifferent to the stylistic or expressive aspect – if the defendant would copy whatever the language or style might be, not caring in the least for the content but only for its physical effects, then the copying is of the "tool" variety and copyright law does not (or at least should not) reach it.[146]

13.4.4. *Directness*

Does the Baker rule apply only to shelter the "users" who employ the copy functionally, or does it also shelter those from whom the "users" purchased the copies? Lawyers usually think of "direct" versus "contributory" roles in terms of secondary liability. (For example, we debate whether computer programs that allow consumers to violate copyright law should be held responsible for the consumers' unlawful behavior.[147]) In discussing how far the *Baker* doctrine reaches, however,

---

[145] Within "sole" or "pure" functional use, I include functional uses that are insubstantially or trivially concerned with expression.

[146] It may be that mixed uses of copyright works should sometimes be sheltered from liability. I need not reach that question, for copying sequences of command names (*Lotus*) or method headers (*Oracle*) for purposes of defeating switching costs is not a mixed case.

[147] *See, e.g.*, Wendy J. Gordon, *Moral Philosophy, Information Technology, and Copyright: The Grokster Case, in* INFORMATION TECHNOLOGY AND MORAL PHILOSOPHY 270 (Jeroen van den Hoven & John Weckert eds., Cambridge University Press 2008).

we address the converse: whether an actor's contribution to another person's lawful act can be sheltered by the lawfulness of the assisted behavior.

The issue has significance in many areas of copyright law, particularly fair use, but within the confines of *Baker* it can be resolved straightforwardly. The defendant in *Baker v. Selden* was manufacturing account books for *sale to others*. Nothing in the opinion suggests it would have been necessary for the defendant to have used the account books himself. Similarly, when a manufacturer uses a competitor's catalogue or drawings without permission as his source for his new product line, the statute shelters not only those who *use* the product he makes, but the manufacturers, retailers and advertisers as well.[148] Therefore, precedent and statutory analogy suggest that "directness of use" is not a prerequisite to shelter under *Baker*.

13.5. RESISTANCE TO THE USE/EXPLANATION DISTINCTION

Some resistance to making distinctions among types of use is evident. One hears comments such as, "If an arrangement of lines or symbols is someone's property, the owners should be able control any use they want. That's what property is for." At one point the Nimmer copyright treatise similarly opines that "the question of liability should turn simply on whether the defendant has copied copyrightable elements contained in the plaintiff's work, without regard to the manner in which the defendant uses or intends to use the copied material."[149] This cannot be taken literally. An exemption for patent-type "use" is hardly the only copyright limitation tied to "use" issues.

13.5.1. *"Rights Over Use" as a Conceptual and Economic Fulcrum*

All of copyright operates on two dimensions – to prevail in an infringement suit, a plaintiff must prove (1) ownership of appropriate (copyrightable) *subject matter* and (2) that his or her *exclusive rights* include control over the use that the defendant has made of the copyrighted subject matter.

The overall structure of the Copyright Act thus ties the definition of a copyright owner's rights to defined uses, so that prima facie liability always varies with the

---

[148] 17 U.S.C. § 113(b) (anyone engaged in "making, distribution, or display"); *see also* § 113(c) ("In the case of a work lawfully reproduced in useful articles that have been offered for sale or other distribution to the public, copyright does not include any right to prevent the making, distribution, or display of pictures or photographs of such articles in connection with advertisements or commentaries related to the distribution or display of such articles, or in connection with news reports.").

[149] 1–2 NIMMER ON COPYRIGHT § 2.18[D][1]. The Treatise continues: "If ... copying of copyrightable expression occurs, then infringement should be found, even if the defendant employs the material for use rather than for explanation." *Id.*

nature of the defendant's use even in the statute's operative core, § 106.[150] A host of additional uses are categorized as not infringing.[151] So, for example, since only "public" performances can infringe,[152] an allegation of private performance would be dismissed as not satisfying the plaintiff's obligation to present a prima facie case. The same should be true when a plaintiff seeks copyright redress for rights that the Supreme Court or Congress has removed from the copyright owner as better relegated to patent's domain.

As already mentioned, copyright's statutory structure places emphasis on distinguishing among uses. Differences among uses are also central to how copyright functions as an economic engine.

Congress provides incentives to authors largely by helping copyright owners subject the users of their works to differential pricing ("price discrimination") according to intensity of use.[153] Copyright law embodies a set of Congressional decisions about *which uses* of a copy should be subjected to this legal power to meter (and price) types and frequency of usage.

---

[150] *See* Wendy J. Gordon, *Intellectual Property as Price Discrimination: Implications for Contract*, 73 CHI.-KENT L. REV. 1367 (1998).

It is equally hard to understand the purported irrelevance of "use" from a statutory perspective. The Copyright Act throughout varies rights and duties according to the nature of the use, starting with the basic section of copyright owner rights in Section 106, 17 U.S.C. § 106 (2012). The statute also empowers judges to make general variations by "use" in the fair use doctrine, 17 U.S.C. § 107, and variations according to use are fleshed out in the dozens of specific use-limitations embedded in the statute. *Id.* §§ 108–122.

[151] The shape of a copyright owner's exclusive rights can be determined only by examining a wide range of sections, namely 17 U.S.C. §§ 106–122, but the primary section is § 106. It is subdivided by type of use, from reproduction to performance:

§ 106. Subject to Sections 107 through 122, the owner of copyright under this title has the exclusive rights to do and to authorize any of the following:

(1) to reproduce the copyrighted work in copies or phonorecords;
(2) to prepare derivative works based upon the copyrighted work;
(3) to distribute copies or phonorecords of the copyrighted work to the public by sale or other transfer of ownership, or by rental, lease, or lending;
(4) in the case of literary, musical, dramatic, and choreographic works, pantomimes, and motion pictures and other audiovisual works, to perform the copyrighted work publicly;
(5) in the case of literary, musical, dramatic, and choreographic works, pantomimes, and pictorial, graphic, or sculptural works, including the individual images of a motion picture or other audiovisual work, to display the copyrighted work publicly; and
(6) in the case of sound recordings, to perform the copyrighted work publicly by means of a digital audio transmission.

[152] 17 U.S.C. § 106(4) (2012) (right of public performance for literary works, musical works and additional works other than sound recordings); *id.* § 106(6) (right of public performance for sound recordings).

[153] *See* Gordon, *supra* note 150.

To illustrate, consider again the right of "public performance."[154] Because the statute gives the copyright owner prima facie rights to control public performance, the copyright owner can distinguish in pricing between the person who wants to read a literary work silently to herself, and a person who wants to read the work aloud at an auditorium or on radio. The silent reader pays whatever price for the copy was charged by her bookstore or online supplier; her use is contained in the base price. By contrast, the public performer has to negotiate and pay something beyond the price of the copy in order to avoid the risk of an infringement suit. She needs to purchase a permission or set of permissions to cover her behavior, which usually means she has to disclose to the copyright owner economically meaningful data about her behavior in order to obtain a meaningful license.[155]

Conversely, because the statute gives the copyright owner no rights to control *private* performance, the copyright owner will find it harder to distinguish in pricing between, say, a person who wants to read to herself the published script of a play, and an ambitious society host who wants to have his friends perform the play during a series of dinner parties. These all are private uses under the statute,[156] and do not fall within the domain of an exclusive right. The private reader, the living-room performers, and the host may have very differing values for the text, but each pays the same (base) price for a copy, without risk of liability arising from how they are using it. Congress has decided not to help copyright owners distinguish among these home uses.

Defining the types and limits of "exclusive right" is an important part of how Congress calibrates the balance between public domain and public duty. Uses that are within the copyright domain impose duties on the general citizenry to either obtain permissions or refrain from use. Uses that are not within copyright owners' control lie in copyright's public domain.[157]

So "exclusive rights" over types of use are always crucial. It would be odd indeed if one of copyright's most important policies – to avoid interference with patent law – found expression only in the dimension of "subject matter" and none in the dimension of "exclusive right."[158]

---

[154] 17 U.S.C. § 106(4) (2012) (for literary works, musical works, and additional works other than sound recordings) and *id.* § 106(6) (for sound recordings).

[155] This brief discussion of permissions is not fully generalizable. A purchaser (rather than a seeker of specific permissions) may be better able to conceal details. But even a purchaser of copyrights needs to identify herself as such, giving the potential seller some notice of her plans.

[156] Under the statute, a place is not public if it is open only to "a normal circle of a family and its social acquaintances." *See* 17 U.S.C. §101 (2012) (definition of "publicly").

[157] That a behavior like "building a machine" is in copyright's public domain means that the behavior cannot be restrained or penalized by copyright. If a utility patent exists that covers the machine, however, the behavior is not in *patent's* public domain, and can be restrained by patent law.

[158] See the discussion of Hohfeld's terminology, *supra* note 98.
In sum, a copyright owner's claim rights over use correlate with the public's duty to refrain from such use.

13.5.2. *Further Buttressing* Baker's *Use/Explanation Distinction from Attack*

The *Oracle* court ignored *Baker's* careful distinction between different kinds of rights of control, and instead treated *Baker* as an on-off switch that determines copyrightability. The fullest articulation of the reasons for such an approach appears in the Nimmer Treatise, which argues that, "If copying of copyrightable expression occurs, then infringement should be found, even if the defendant employs the material for use rather than for explanation."[159] (Although David Nimmer, the current author of the Treatise, indicates he is rethinking its position,[160] the Treatise's provides a useful point of departure from which to crystallize discussion.)

There are several reasons why it is erroneous to reject the "use/explanation" distinction. Three reasons are matters of positive law. First, the Nimmer position relies on dicta from a 1954 case whose reasoning is itself unreliable on this score. Second, rejecting the "use/explanation" distinction ignores both the language of *Baker* itself and post-1954 instantiations of *Baker* in the courts. Third, a rejection of the "use/ explanation" distinction is puzzling because Congress explicitly adopted an immunity for practical "use" in the current Copyright Act.[161] Finally, as a policy matter, ignoring a defendant's type of use would be inconsistent with both the juridical integrity and economic logic of the copyright system.

1954 Dicta

In rejecting the "use/explanation" distinction of *Baker*, the Nimmer treatise relies heavily on the 1954 Supreme Court opinion, *Mazer v. Stein*.[162] In *Mazer*, a statuette of a Balinese dancer was employed as the base for an electric lamp, and copied for a similar use by another lamp maker.[163] The 1954 Court approved *Baker*, but gave *Baker* a reading that cautiously depended on the case's particular facts:

> Unlike a patent, a copyright gives no exclusive right to the art disclosed; protection is given only to the expression of the idea – not the idea itself. Thus, in *Baker v. Selden*, 101 U.S. 99, the Court held that a copyrighted book on a peculiar system

---

[159] The Treatise argues, NIMMER ON COPYRIGHT § 2.18; *see also id.* § 2.18 at n.44. Nimmer's claim has had some influence. *See, e.g.,* Close to My Heart, Inc. v. Enthusiast Media LLC, 508 F. Supp. 2d 963 n.3 (2007).

[160] See *infra* note 180. At one point the Treatise follows an interpretation of *Baker* far more congenial to the instant chapter's viewpoint. *See* 1–2 NIMMER ON COPYRIGHT § 2.08[1][a] (2015).

[161] 17 U.S.C. § 113(b), set forth infra at note 175, and interpreted as set forth in text accompanying note 186. This section incorporates by reference a series of cases that, largely relying on *Baker*, refuse to allow the copyright in a work that depicts a useful article – such as the copyright in a sketch depicting an automobile or the copyright in a blueprint depicting a motor – to be asserted against persons who actually make or build the useful article itself.

[162] *See, e.g.,* NIMMER ON COPYRIGHT § 2.18

[163] Mazer v. Stein, 347 U.S. 201 (1954).

of bookkeeping was not infringed by a similar book using a similar plan which achieved similar results where the alleged infringer made a different arrangement of the columns and used different headings. [164]

Nimmer points to this observation in arguing that the Supreme Court in *Mazer* stripped from *Baker*'s heritage its concerns with functional use.[165]

I think such reasoning – trying to turn *Baker*'s own language into a version of the idea/ expression dichotomy – misses the mark. As Professor Pamela Samuelson has emphasized, the Court's concern in *Baker* was not with the general principle, already recognized well prior to 1880, that copyright needed to distinguish abstract general ideas from particularized expression, but with preventing copyright from interfering with the balance between competition and incentive set by Congress in the law of utility patent.[166]

It was natural for the Court in *Mazer* to have treaded gingerly in discussing *Baker*. In *Mazer*, the Supreme Court held that the copyright in the statuette gave the plaintiff a valid copyright infringement suit against the competing lamp maker.[167] Yet lamp-making is a utilitarian kind of use, and *Baker* cautioned against extending copyright over utilitarian uses.[168] So perhaps it was fear of being accused of inconsistency with *Baker* that led the Supreme Court in *Mazer* to stick to the narrowest reading of the early case.[169]

In hindsight, however, we see that the *Mazer* Court had no reason to fear inconsistency with *Baker*. The freedom to "use" that was recognized in *Baker* only gave freedom to use *for functional purposes*, that is, freedom to copy for purposes other than explanation and the satisfaction of aesthetic "taste."[170] By contrast with *Selden's* accounting forms, the Balinese dancer's form served only "taste." The statuette's expressive form and graceful lines had no impact on function: it did not make the lamp's shine any brighter or the lamp's structure any more stable.

To further see that the statuette served no "functional" purpose, notice what happens if the statuette's expressive features are eliminated: Filing away the dancer's sculpted dress and body would leave a smooth ceramic cylinder. The cylinder could hold up the lightbulb and shade – the lamp would function as well as it did

---

[164] *Id.* at 217.

[165] NIMMER ON COPYRIGHT § 2.18

[166] *See generally* Samuelson, *Systems and Processes, supra* note 66; Pamela Samuelson, *CONTU Revisited: The Case Against Copyright Protection for Computer Programs in Machine-Readable Form*, 1984 DUKE L.J. 663; Pamela Samuelson, *Baker v. Selden: Sharpening the Distinction Between Authorship and Invention* in INTELLECTUAL PROPERTY STORIES (Jane C. Ginsburg & Rochelle Cooper Dreyfuss eds., 2006).

[167] *Mazer*, 347 U.S. at 214.

[168] *Baker v. Selden*, 101 U.S. 99, 102 (1880).

[169] *Mazer*, 347 U.S. at 217.

[170] As mentioned above, *Baker* cautioned that its "observations are not intended to apply to ornamental designs or pictorial illustrations addressed to the taste." *Baker*, 101 U.S. at 103–04.

before.[171] So enforcing copyright in the statuette posed no direct challenge to patent law: competition based on the *functions* of a lamp could proceed unimpeded whether or not the Balinese dancer shape had a copyright.[172] That being the case, the defendant in *Mazer* was not threatened by *Baker*, even if the Court in 1954 was not yet in a position to articulate why.[173]

The results of the two opinions are sufficiently consistent with each other that their statutory embodiments are near neighbors. Section 113(a) of the Copyright Act embodies *Mazer*[174] and § 113(b)[175] (which will be discussed further below) embodies *Baker*.

Baker and Caselaw Progeny

The Nimmer treatise relied on 1954 dicta from *Mazer* which depicted defendant's victory in *Baker* as resting on a lack of substantial similarity between defendant's forms and plaintiff's form. The dicta did not accurately portray *Baker v. Selden*. The Supreme Court's 1880 opinion in *Baker* showed no concern with determining how similar defendant's forms were to those of plaintiff.

---

[171] *See* Samuelson, *Systems and Processes, supra* note 66, at 1960 ("Because Stein's [plaintiff's] lamps did not function any better or worse for having Stein's statuette as a base instead of a block of wood, it is consistent with *Baker* to hold that the statuettes were, indeed, copyrightable subject matter because the artistic designs they embodied were physically as well as conceptually separable from the lamps.").

[172] That is not to claim that *Mazer*'s impact was fully costless. The *Mazer* ruling did make it more expensive for competitors to make lamps; they could not use plaintiff's lamp base as a form for "direct molding" and similar processes, or if they did, they would have to then strip off the dancer's features. However, the cost difference related only to decoration, not to function.

[173] *See* Samuelson, *Systems and Processes, supra* note 66, at 1960 ("*Mazer*'s observation about differences between the *Selden* and *Baker* forms was a simple misreading of *Baker*, not a radical reinterpretation of the case, its holding, and the holdings of *Baker*'s progeny.").

[174] Section 113(a) provides:

> Subject to the provisions of subsections (b) and (c) of this section, the exclusive right to reproduce a copyrighted pictorial, graphic, or sculptural work in copies under section 106 includes the right to reproduce the work in or on any kind of article, whether useful or otherwise.

17 U.S.C. § 113(a) (2012). Thus, under 113(a), a statuette of a dancer did not lose copyright by being fastened to a bulb.

[175] Subsection 113(b) was a response to questions such as, "[W]ould copyright in a drawing or model of an automobile give the artist the exclusive right to make automobiles of the same design?" Congress essentially answered "no." See 1976 HOUSE REP., *supra* note 100, at 109. The statute provides:

> §113 (b) This title does not afford, to the owner of copyright in a work that portrays a useful article as such, any greater or lesser rights with respect to the making, distribution, or display of the useful article so portrayed than those afforded to such works under the law, whether title 17 or the common law or statutes of a State, in effect on December 31, 1977, as held applicable and construed by a court in an action brought under this title.

17 U.S.C. § 113(b). This provision is discussed further *infra* in the section entitled "Congressional implementation" and in section 11.6.

Moreover, judicial decisions since 1954 continued to posit that the functional copying of a copyrighted design is noninfringing. As one such court said, "It is the illustration that is protected, not the object itself."[176] The post-*Mazer* precedent includes cases on which Congress relied in drafting the 1976 Copyright Act.[177]

Congressional Implementation

An absolutist approach to "copyright as property" might suggest that an owner's rights will be unvarying, and that the public has no shelter for "copying for use." Yet not only does *Baker* provide such a shelter, but Congress has also implemented *Baker* by explicitly enacting a statutory shelter as well. Subsection 113(b) provides that copyright in a drawing or model that "portrays a useful article as such" (such as a copyrighted sketch of a garment, or a copyrighted blueprint for a machine) does not grant its owner the full scope of ordinary rights to control derivative works.[178]

Subsection 113(b) directs that the copyright owner has no rights over the "making, distribution or display" of the useful article depicted.[179] This is by way of contrast to

---

[176] PIC Design Corp. v. Sterling Precision Corp., 231 F. Supp. 106 (S.D.N.Y. 1964). It is not clear that the plaintiff could have claimed originality in the design, however. A better case is Muller v. Triborough Bridge Auth., 43 F. Supp. 298, 298 (S.D.N.Y. 1942) (which predated Mazer). In *Muller v. Triborough*, the plaintiff claimed "that his copyrighted drawing [of a design to unsnarl traffic at a bridge approach] was novel and unique and originated with him." Citing *Baker*, the court characterized the design as a "system" and ruled for the defendant despite arguable similarities between the drawings and the actual roads the defendant had built. Note that no challenge was made to the copyrightability of the drawing.

[177] The primary legislative report for the current Act mentioned with approval a list of twelve cases that had appeared in the Supplemental Report of the Register of Copyright (1965) at 48. See 1976 HOUSE REP., *supra* note 100, at 109. Many of the cited cases predate *Mazer* in 1954, but some came later. See DeSilva Construction Corp. v. Herrald, 213 F. Supp. 184 (M.D. Fla. 1962); *PIC Design Corp.*, 231 F. Supp. at 110 (S.D.N.Y. 1964). Thus, the *DeSilva* court cited the major copyright treatise of its day, Ball on THE LAW OF COPYRIGHT AND LITERARY PROPERTY, which in turn explicitly relied on *Baker*. *De Silva*, 213 F. Supp. at 195–96. (Note, however, that the *Baker* rationale was only one ground of several for dismissing the plaintiff's complaint in *DeSilva*.) These cases are discussed at *supra* notes 120–23.

[178] 17 U.S.C. § 113(b) provides:

> This title does not afford, to the owner of copyright in a work that portrays a useful article as such, any greater or lesser rights with respect to the making, distribution, or display of the useful article so portrayed than those afforded to such works under the law, whether title 17 or the common law or statutes of a State, in effect on December 31, 1977, as held applicable and construed by a court in an action brought under this title.

> Section 113(b) constitutionality is open to question on the ground of vagueness. Its vagueness may not be fatal: at least one federal statute was held constitutional even though it incorporated state law not yet enacted or decided. United States v. Sharpnack, 355 U.S. 286 (1958). But § 113(b) makes reference to state and federal law in a manner so general it leaves open to question even the sources to be incorporated by reference. See, e.g., GOLDSTEIN ON COPYRIGHT § 7.4.4 (2014), especially 7:116–1120 (presenting some of the puzzles generated by the subsection's imprecision).

[179] 17 U.S.C. § 113(b).

the usual rule, under which the maker of two-dimensional portrayals (say, a draw-ing of a sculpture, or a sketch of a cartoon character) has derivative-work rights to control the portrayal being adapted into three-dimensional form. Thus, the owner of copyright in a drawing of a car can control the making of toys, murals, or movies based on the drawing, but cannot control the construction of a working automobile based on it.

Subsection 113(b) limits the rights that attach to copyrighted portrayals of useful arti-cles, but does not impact the copyrightability of the portrayals themselves. (Drawings, models, blueprints, or other portrayals of a useful article are not themselves "useful articles" because they do no more than convey information or portray appearance.[180] Since the drawings, etc., are not useful articles, in order to obtain copyright the portray-als need not pass the "separability test" to which useful articles are subject.[181]) Rather, § 113(b) leaves intact the copyrightability of any expression that depicts a useful article, and instead limits the rights that attach to owning the portrayal.

Patent law imposes many subtle limits on copyright, but the limit in § 113(b) is hit-over-the-head necessary: Should rights against copying attach to an innova-tion merely by drawing it, describing it, or modeling it in clay, few inventors would go through the expensive and uncertain route of trying to persuade federal patent examiners that their mechanical invention is "novel" and nonobvious – especially since the payoff from succeeding in the more difficult and more costly route of seeking a utility patent would be to receive a right only marginally stronger than copyright's[182] and which lasts for a term of protection far shorter than copyright pro-vides.[183] A whole area of patent law – at least, patents in mechanical configurations,[184] and perhaps other types of inventions as well – would cease to exist, and with it

---

[180] Under the statute, 17 U.S.C. § 101 (2012), "A "useful article" is an article having an intrinsic utilitar-ian function that is not merely to portray the appearance of the article or to convey information." Therefore, a work is not "useful" (in the sense of being dangerous to patent) unless it does something more than "convey information" or "portray appearance." 2 NIMMER ON COPYRIGHT § 2.18 (2015). A blueprint for a mechanical device is not a "useful article," even though the device *as built* will be a "useful article." *Id.*

[181] The copyrightability of useful articles that are PGS works depends on whether the "separability" test can be passed. 17 U.S.C. § 101 (2012) (definition of PGS works). Useful articles of other kinds might need to pass different tests, such as proof that giving copyright will not restrain competition in provid-ing the function because, e.g., ample alternatives to the plaintiff's expression exist that have equal and equivalent functional advantages.

[182] As mentioned, patent plaintiffs do not have to prove copying, but with technological change spreading works across the globe, copyright plaintiffs find it progressively easier to lead juries to find "copying" has occurred.

[183] Depending on circumstances, copyrights remain in private ownership at least for seventy years, and often for well over a century. Utility patents expire after twenty years.

[184] Subsection 113(b) is usually understood as addressing pictorial works or models that depict functional three-dimensional objects. As I argue below, the subsection is not explicitly so limited, and can also be understood as applying to non-PGS works that implicate patent issues, such as computer programs.

would also disappear the "rights to copy and to use" that patent gives to nonpatented inventions.[185] Subsection 113(b) prevents that from happening.

Here is a Copyright Office Report illustrating the subsection's impact on day-to-day objects:

> [T]he copyright in a work portraying a useful article as such would not protect against manufacture of that article…
>
> [C]opyright protection would not extend to the following cases:
>
> - A copyrighted drawing of a chair, used to manufacture chairs of that design;
> - A copyrighted scale model of an automobile, used to manufacture automobiles of that design;
> - A copyrighted technical drawing showing the construction of a machine, used to manufacture the machine;
> - A copyrighted picture of a dress, used to manufacture the dress.[186]

Thus, copyright can subsist in a drawing of a dress, in a blueprint of a car, or in a scale model of a tractor or teapot. Someone who makes an unauthorized copy of such a drawing for illustrative use in a coffee-table book would infringe the copyright, as would someone who reproduced the scale models in a toy[187] or in a new scale model. Those are not uses of functional application that threaten patent. By contrast, under *Baker* and under § 113(b), the public may lawfully employ the copyrighted drawing or model to construct working, full-size versions of the car, dress, tractor or teapot. This is certainly a special exception pertaining to "copying for use."

13.6. SUBSECTION 113(B) APPLIED DIRECTLY TO COMPUTER PROGRAMS

Subsection 113(b) does more than support the "use/explanation distinction" in *Baker*. The section can be applied on its own terms to computer copyright litigation.

---

[185] Bonito Boats v. Thunder Craft Boats, 489 U.S. 141, 164–65 (1989):

> [T]he federal standards for patentability, at a minimum, express the congressional determination that patent-like protection is unwarranted as to certain classes of intellectual property…. For almost 100 years it has been well established that in the case of an expired patent, the federal patent laws *do* create a federal right to "copy and to use." *Sears* and *Compco* extended that rule to potentially patentable ideas which are fully exposed to the public. (Emphasis in original.)

[186] REPORT OF THE REGISTER OF COPYRIGHTS, *supra* note 109. This 1961 Report was approved in the 1965 SUPPLEMENTARY REPORT at pages ix & 47–49, and that Report in turn was relied on in the drafting of Subsection 113(b) in the 1976 Copyright Act. See 1976 HOUSE REP., *supra* note 100, at 109.

[187] That making toys lies on the "copyright" side of the line was first determined in *King Features Syndicate v. Fleischer*, 299 F. 533 (2d Cir. 1924).

Programmers write human-readable code ("source code") that is then "compiled" into the binary patterns that computers can understand. The resulting binary pattern, called "object code," does more than portray information and appearance: object code runs the machine. Object code is thus a "useful article."[188] It might be argued that human-readable source code is a "portrayal" of that useful article. If so, § 113(b) might mandate that any functional copy made from source code is immune from charges of copyright infringement.

The following discussion addresses three issues: whether the subsection's language permits or requires it to be applied to computer programs; whether the section's origin in *Baker* allows the subsection to be applied to computer programs and other "literary works"; and whether § 113(b) would immunize not only purely nonexpressive uses, but also functional uses that contain a substantial admixture of expressive use.

13.6.1. *Language*

Subsection 113(b) appears in a section entitled, "Scope of exclusive rights in pictorial, graphic and sculptural works." Computer programs are not categorized not as PGS works but rather as "literary works."[189] The section title seems therefore to indicate that subsection (b) does not apply to computer programs.

However, titles do not trump plain meaning. "[A] heading ... cannot limit the plain meaning of the text."[190]

The language of § 113(b) itself does not mention PGS works. It could have done so; the language of the preceding subsection, § 113(a), quite explicitly limits itself to the PGS category.[191] The language of § 113(b) is by contrast not limited to any particular category of works.

The statute's definition of "useful article," too, is not limited to PGS works or any other particular category of works.[192] Any work that does more than "portray" form

---

[188] 17 U.S.C. § 101 ("A 'useful article' is an article having an intrinsic utilitarian function that is not merely to portray the appearance of the article or to convey information.")

[189] *See* 17 U.S.C. §§ 102(a) (subject matter), 101 (definitions) (2012).

[190] Yule Kim, *Statutory Interpretation: General Principles and Recent Trends* 31–32 CRS REPORT FOR CONGRESS (2008), available at http://fas.org/sgp/crs/misc/97–589.pdf.

[191] 17 U.S.C. §§ 113(a) provides:

> Subject to the provisions of subsections (b) and (c) of this section, the exclusive right to reproduce a copyrighted pictorial, graphic, or sculptural work in copies under Section 106 includes the right to reproduce the work in or on any kind of article, whether useful or otherwise.

In my view, subsection (b) articulates a generally applicable rule to remind courts not to let copyright erode patent via § 113(a).

[192] 17 U.S.C. § 101 (2012). ("A 'useful article' is an article having an intrinsic utilitarian function that is not merely to portray the appearance of the article or to convey information.")

or "convey information" (that is, any work that goes beyond serving the expressive functions appropriate for copyright regulation) is a "useful article"[193] – which makes sense, for any such work potentially has implications for patent.

Subsection 113(b) incorporates pre-1978 caselaw by reference, and the legislative history mentions particular cases and gives a number of examples. On the one hand, that the caselaw cited in the legislative history seems to involve only PGS works[194] might suggest the subsection should be confined to the PGS context and not extend to computer programs. On the other hand, none of the cited pre-1978 opinions expressly limits its principles only to the PGS category.

The focus on PGS fact patterns is explicable given technological context. The bulk of the cited examples date from a 1961 Report,[195] and the list of cited cases comes from a 1965 Copyright Office Report.[196] At that stage in law and technology, copyright in product shapes posed the most obvious danger to patent.[197] The same policies that in the 1960s triggered concerns with product shape, today also trigger concerns with computer programs.

An additional wrinkle is presented by Congress's actions in 1980. To see its significance, consider some background:

Recall that § 113(b) incorporates caselaw ending in 1977 – that is, cases decided *prior* to the effective date of the 1976 Copyright Act.[198] In 1977, computer programs

---

[193] I am on somewhat less secure ground here. The definition of "useful article" indicates that proper copyright functions are to convey information or "*to portray the appearance of the article.*" *Id.* The word "article" is quite general, which helps my interpretation, but the word also has connotations of physicality that work against my interpretation. Similar ambiguity afflicts the word "appearance." The term "appearance" can mean any kind of "seeming," thus standing in for all types of form. This helps my interpretation. But the word "appearance" also has visual connotations.

[194] Most of the examples and cases cited by Congress or the Copyright Office addressed whether manufacturers infringed when they based their three-dimensional functional products on two-dimensional drawings whose copyrights were owned by others. The cases are summarized in *supra* notes 113–21.

[195] REPORT OF THE REGISTER OF COPYRIGHTS, *supra* note 109. This 1961 Report was approved in the 1965 SUPPLEMENTARY REPORT at pages ix and 47–49, and that Report in turn was relied on in the drafting of Subsection 113(b) in the 1976 Copyright Act. See 1976 HOUSE REP., *supra* note 100, at 109.

[196] A list of twelve cases that appeared in the SUPPLEMENTAL REPORT OF THE REGISTER OF COPYRIGHT (1965) at 48. The primary legislative Report for the current Act mentioned this list with approval. See HOUSE REP., *supra* note 100, at 109.

[197] Ordinary literary descriptions posed little danger of giving control over systems, given *Baker's* insistence that a book copyright gave no rights over any practical sciences it might describe.

[198] Again, the statute reads as follows:

§ 113 (b) This title does not afford, to the owner of copyright in a work that portrays a useful article as such, any greater or lesser rights with respect to the making, distribution, or display of the useful article so portrayed than those afforded to such works under the law, whether title 17 or the common law or statutes of a State, in effect on December 31, 1977, as held applicable and construed by a court in an action brought under this title.

had uncertain copyright status; because machine-readable copies of literary works did not count as infringing,[199] little economically meaningful protection could attach even to programs that might in the abstract be eligible for copyright.[200] That helps explain why *Baker*-oriented caselaw (or any copyright caselaw) on computer programs would be scarce. Moreover, at the same time that Congress adopted § 113(b), it adopted a special section to govern computer programs. That special provision, Section 117, fixed the law of computer copyright also at the end of 1977.[201]

---

[199] *See* White-Smith Publishing Co. v. Apollo Co., 209 U.S. 1 (1908). This decision held that copyrights could be infringed only by persons making *visually perceptible* copies. The decision was overturned for most literary works by the Copyright Act of 1976, effective 1978. See 17 U.S.C. § 101 (definition of "copies") (1976); *see also* 1976 HOUSE REP., *supra* note 100, at 52. Computer programs, however, remained governed by 1977 law. 17 U.S.C. § 117 (1976); *see* 1976 HOUSE REP., *supra* note 100, at 116.

[200] Computer source code is visually perceptible without machine aid, and in 1977 source code probably could be federally copyrighted. But unauthorized disk copies of source code would not infringe because the contents of a CD or other machine-readable disk are not visually perceptible to the naked eye. Only with the new 1976 Copyright Act, effective in 1978, did the federal copyright statute embrace all embodiments that could be perceived "with the aid of a machine or device." 17 U.S.C. § 101 (2012):

> "Copies" are material objects, other than phonorecords, in which a work is fixed by any method now known or later developed, and from which the work can be perceived, reproduced, or otherwise communicated, either *directly or with the aid of a machine or device*.... (Emphasis added)

Therefore the federal protection available to source code would be limited (since unauthorized object code copies would not be actionable) and object code itself would be unprotectable under federal law.

   It might be asked whether state protections for computer programs pre-1978 might be relevant. In my view, they probably would not. Subsection 113(b) incorporates only caselaw "construed by a court in an action brought under this title." State copyright actions are not "brought under this title." They reach federal court under diversity jurisdiction.

   The state rights that can appear as pendent claims in an "action brought under this title" are claims sounding in state trademark law or other kinds of unfair competition. *See* 28 U.S.C. § 1338 (a):

> The district courts shall have original jurisdiction of any civil action asserting a claim of *unfair competition* when joined with a substantial and related claim under the [federal] *copyright*, patent, plant variety protection or trademark laws.... (Emphasis added)

Nevertheless, state copyright claims have been brought under a variety of labels, including "misappropriation" which is a type of unfair competition. So the potential relevance of pre-1978 state copyright law for Subsection 113(b) remains unresolved.

   Note that in 1978, the federal copyright act abolished most state copyright law. 17 U.S.C. § 301 (2012) (pre-emption).

[201] 17 U.S.C. §117 (1976) as originally enacted read as follows:

   §117. *Scope of exclusive rights: Use in conjunction with computers and similar information systems.*

   Notwithstanding the provisions of Sections 106 through 116 and 118, this title does not afford to the owner of copyright in a work any greater or lesser rights with respect to the use of the work in conjunction with automatic systems capable of storing, processing, retrieving, or transferring information, or in conjunction with any similar device, machine, or process, than those afforded to works under the

Then, in 1980, Congress amended § 117 and the copyright act's definitions[202] to bring computer programs into modern federal copyright.[203] Also, starting in 1978, machine-readable disks counted as "copies" and, if unauthorized, could infringe.[204] However, Congress did *not* amend § 113(b).

The upshot: reading the 1980 amendments in conjunction with the un-amended § 113(b), Congress could be seen as eliminating one barrier to enforcing copyright in computer programs but retaining another. It eliminated the old visual-bound definition of "copy," but retained the public's liberty to employ copyrighted portrayals of useful articles to make and sell functioning versions of those articles without authorization.

13.6.2. *Is* Baker *only for accounting forms and other PGS works?*

Baker v. Selden[205] dealt with a pictorial work. However, it was not limited to the pictorial context. To the contrary, the Court's analysis took as its touchstone the public's liberty to make machines or use systems described in books. It was from examples involving literary works that the Court built the public's liberty to reproduce *Selden's* pictorial accounting forms.

Thus, the Court writes:

> [T]there is a clear *distinction between the book as such and the art*[206] which it is intended to illustrate.... A treatise on the composition and use of medicines, be they old or new; on the construction and use of ploughs, or watches, or churns; ... would be the subject of copyright; but no one would contend that the copyright of the treatise would give the exclusive right to the art or manufacture described ... *To give to the author of the book an exclusive property in the art described* therein when no examination of its novelty has ever been officially made would be a surprise and a fraud upon the public. That is the province of letters patent, not of copyright. ...[207]

---

law, whether title 11 or the common law or statutes of a State, in effect on December 31, 1977, as held applicable and construed by a court in an action brought under this title.

    Copyright Act of 1976, Pub. L. 94–553, title I, § 117, Oct. 19, 1976, available at http://copyright.gov/history/pl94-553.pdf.

[202] In 1980, Pub. L. 96–517 inserted a definition for "computer program" into the statute, 17 U.S.C. § 101 (2012).

[203] Pub. L. 96–517.

[204] The 1980 amendments eliminated the 1977 reference point that had been embedded in § 117, and inserted a definition of "computer program" as "literary work" into § 101. Pub. L. 96–517 (1980). This made the general provisions of the 1976 Copyright Act – and its definition of "copy" – applicable to programs, so that "unaided" visual perception became irrelevant.

[205] Baker v. Selden, 101 U.S. 99 (1880).

[206] "Art" in this context refers not to aesthetics but to practical skills, as in the "arts" of husbandry, carpentry, or medicine.

[207] Baker, 101 U.S. at 102 (emphasis added).

The Court repeats and elaborates the point,[208] and returns to new literary-work examples, such as books about the art of perspective.[209]

When the Court finally turns to graphic and pictorial works (such as the accounting forms at issue in *Baker*), the opinion returns to literary works as its first and primary point of reference:

> *Had he used words* of description instead of diagrams (*which merely stand in the place of words*), *there could not be the slightest doubt* that others, applying the art to practical use, might lawfully draw the lines and diagrams which were in the author's mind, and which he thus described by words in his book.[210]

Just as a graphic design or a set of diagrams *"merely stand in the place of words"*[211] for the Court in *Baker*, so can words stand in the place of graphic designs and diagrams for § 113(b).

To see how closely § 113(b) fits *Baker's* treatment of literary works, note that *Baker's* examples could be restated using the words of the subsection: The subsection tells us that an "owner of copyright in a work that portrays a useful article as such" has no rights to control the manufacture of the useful article itself. Therefore (turning to *Baker's* examples), the "owner of copyright in a [literary] work that portrays" a medicine, system, or device, gives no rights to control those who use the book to make the medicine, employ the system, or build the device.[212]

13.6.3. *Mixed Uses*

Baker's facts seem to describe a purely functional use of the accounting forms. If § 113(b) goes further, and applies even to uses that mix functional and expressive uses, the subsection's sweep against the enforceability of programs will be broad indeed, because

---

[208] The Court writes:

> ...Take the case of medicines. Certain mixtures are found to be of great value in the healing art. If the discoverer *writes and publishes a book* on the subject (as regular physicians generally do), he gains no exclusive right to he gains no exclusive right to the manufacture and sale of the medicine; he gives that to the public. If he desires to acquire such exclusive right, he must obtain a patent for the mixture as a new art, manufacture, or composition of matter. *Id.* at 102–3 (emphasis added).

[209] *Id.* at 103.

[210] *Id.* at 103 (emphasis added). The Court wrote these works in regard to one of its many examples, namely, a "book on perspective." The opinion quickly made clear, *id.* at 104, that these observations were directed to *Selden's* accounting forms as well.

[211] Baker v. Selden, 101 U.S. 99, 103 (1880). The paragraph from which the quoted words are drawn is quoted in full just above, *supra* note 117 and accompanying text.

[212] In the Court's words, "The very object of publishing a book on science or the useful arts is to communicate to the world the useful knowledge which it contains. But this object would be frustrated if the knowledge could not be used without incurring the guilt of piracy of the book." *Id.* at 103.

most copies of computer programs will be used functionally at least in part.[213] Does §
113(b) extend to mixed uses?

The post-*Baker* cases that give meaning to § 113(b)[214] suggest it might extend so
far. The cases involved, inter alia, chairs, lighting fixtures, and other furnishings that
various defendants had "built" without permission by copying their competitors' copyrighted drawings and photos. It is highly likely that some of these copyrighted pictorial works showed furnishings that contained separable ornamental features, such as
statuettes on lamp bases or flower designs on upholstery. It is even likely that some
of the copying was motivated by a desire to capitalize on the market appeal of such
ornamental elements.

Yet the courts gave the defendants in these cases the liberty to build and sell working
duplicates of what appeared in the pictures, without regard to whether or not the portrayed objects might have contained separable ornamental features.[215] Consider a drawing of a chair that contained a separable work of authorship (such as an original design
of colors or flowers applied to the chair seat). These cases seem to suggest that the act of
constructing the article depicted cannot result in infringement even if the defendant's
chair seat bore a duplicate of the separable flower design.[216] If so, the limits that § 113(b)
puts on a copyright owner's rights apply to shelter copying that is partly motivated by

---

[213] Source code can be copied for explanatory purposes. For example, open-source licenses typically
require the sharing of source code in part to explain what a program does and how it does it. See GNU
Operating System, *GNU General Public License, Version 2*, FREE SOFTWARE FOUNDATION (Dec. 4,
2014), www.gnu.org/licenses/old-licenses/gpl-2.0.en.html.

    Copying source code for explanatory purposes without license can infringe. Section 113(b) by its
own terms has no relevance to copying done to serve proper copyright purposes such as explanation
and amusement.

[214] The cases are summarized at *supra* notes 120–24.

[215] "An article that is normally a part of a useful article is considered a useful article." 17 U.S.C. § 101
(2012) (definition of useful article). Subsection 113(b) gives rights to build whatever is depicted in the
drawing of the useful article, which according to this definition would include all parts, including
separable artistic works.

    Thus, there is no infringement when a stranger without authorization builds a chair that purposely
duplicates a copyrighted *portrayal* – even a portrayal that shows a chair designed with a separable
ornament. The rule is different if a designer does more than *portray* her design in a drawing or sketch,
but actually builds it. A stranger who builds a chair that purposely duplicates a designer's as-built chair
might infringe if the chair has an ornament that is arguably separable.

[216] Under this provision's wording, a designer who sketched a chair (for example) could not use her copyright in the two-dimensional sketch to restrain a competitor from building the chair, even if the designer
had included in her sketch elements of the chair which would be "separable" (and copyrightable) if she
built the chair. Paul Goldstein criticizes the subsection for exempting the copying of "separable" features
from a copyrighted portrayal of a useful object, but does not seem to challenge that the subsection has
that effect. 2 GOLDSTEIN ON COPYRIGHT § 7.4.4.1, 118 (2014). He suggests that a court should first assess
the copyrightable elements if any in the design being depicted, and then compare that element of copyrightable (separable) expression to the appearance of the defendant's functioning object.

    Instead, the subsection seems to provide that the designer would have to authorize the construction
of an actual chair in order to have copyright in the separable components.

expressive concerns. Giving § 113(b) such breadth for PGS works makes some sense: no one wants the utilitarian product markets to be subject to strike suits by doodlers who see some resemblance between a manufactured product and some fantasy sketches they have posted on social media.[217] If the doodlers cannot argue "separability" as a way to withstand motions to dismiss – if § 113(b) can be used even by defendants who "build" and use a portrayal's expressive content – patent law may be safer.

But for computer programs, it is dangerous to extend § 113(b) to shelter functional uses with substantial expressive content. It's hard to imagine any functional copying of source code that could survive a statute so interpreted. Also, if § 113(b) extended that far, it would make other computer-related provisions of the Copyright Act surplusage.[218]

> There are some good reasons for requiring the designer to engage in such a two-step dance. Images of useful and potentially useful articles abound, from Dufy's sailboats to Dali's melting watches. Should a designer of actual objects be afraid to take inspiration from the painters and visual fantasists who might never *make* the three-dimensional objects they have dreamed up and depicted on canvas or in print? The § 113(b) rule means that only copying from an actual useful article will make someone liable for reproducing the separable (copyrightable) parts.
>
> Nevertheless, it is undoubtedly cumbersome to withhold copyright in "separable" parts until the designer brings the useful article to life. Paul Goldstein argues as a policy matter that this aspect of § 113(b) should be altered.

[217] Note that my example here focuses on a plaintiff's sketches rather than on a plaintiff's constructed design. The law may differ for each context.

> Subsection 113(b) appears to allow members of the public to build any and all aspects of a useful article that they copy from a copyrighted drawing, whether or not any aesthetic element is "separable" from the useful components. By contrast, if the designer actually constructed the article in question, she could have a copyright in its "separable" elements.
>
> The difference in legal result may be attributable to the minor investment required to merely sketch a useful article (and thus the greater threat that, in the absence of § 113(b), sketches would pose to patent) as compared with the effort required to construct a three-dimensional article.

[218] In the 1980 amendments to § 117, Congress gave the public some liberties to use computer programs functionally. For the public to need such a specific set of liberties, Congress would seem to have been assuming that (without the specified new liberties) some functional uses of programs *could* be infringing. If § 113(b) reached mixed uses, then all but the archival portion of § 117 would be surplusage. (The liberty to make and keep an archival copy, 17 U.S.C. 117(a) (2) (2012), does not involve a functional use, and thus does not invoke either *Baker* or § 113(b).)

> By contrast, if § 113(b) reaches only uses that are very substantially or purely functional, then computer copyrights would remain enforceable against defendants whose purposes are substantially related to "style and expression." (Were copying of programs *never* done for purposes related to "style and expression," then Congress certainly *did* err – perhaps on a Constitutional level – in accepting computer programs into the list of copyrightable works!)
>
> In short, a narrow reading § 113(b) leaves untouched all copying that is done for mixed purposes of function and expressiveness. If so, § 117 provides liberties that go beyond § 113(b), and applying 113(b) to computer programs does not make § 117 surplusage.
>
> If copying for *mixed* purposes of function and expressiveness is not embraced by *Baker* or by § 113(b), a wide range of copying remains potentially open to copyright's control – that is, *Baker* leaves untouched all copying that is done for mixed purposes of function and expressiveness. If so, § 117 provides needed liberties that go beyond § 113(b), and is not surplusage.

As a policy matter, this chapter argues, § 113(b) should either be limited to purely functional and nonexpressive uses or should be limited to PGS works.

Limiting the subsection to functional uses that are fully nonexpressive is admittedly in some tension with the language of the subsection, for that language seems to treat all "portrayals of useful articles" the same. But it must be remembered that § 113(b) merely incorporates caselaw, including distinctions that the caselaw might embody. Refusing to apply § 113(b) to "mixed" uses is not inconsistent with the relevant caselaw. None of the cases I have found explicitly say that deference to patent requires giving the public a liberty to construct useful articles that have separable and copyrightable parts. Under my more narrow reading, then, the subsection would only shelter use that is both functional and fully nonexpressive.

One final note is needed, regarding the copying of "object code," that is, copying directly from the machine-readable disk to make another disk.

13.6.4. *Copying Computer Object Code*

Subsection 113(b) limits the rights of those who own copyrights in drawings and other portrayals of useful articles, and does not limit the rights of those who own copyrights in useful articles themselves.[219] And useful articles can indeed have copyrights.[220] A computer programmer typically does more than "portray" a useful article. Consider *Oracle* or its predecessor, Sun. They not only created Java source code (a "portrayal" of a useful article); they actually created an indisputably "useful article" namely, Java object code.

Even if making a functional copy of a source code (a "portrayal") is noninfringing because of § 113(b), that section is simply inapplicable to acts that copy useful articles themselves. Infringement *can* result from making a functional copy of object code.

---

[219] Note that § 113(b) is also inapplicable to cases where the defendant has copied a work that portrays an article that is *not* useful. This rule does not change even if the copy is then applied to a useful object. *See* Falk v. T. P. Howell & Co., 7 F. 202 (C.C.D.N.Y. 1888) (infringement results from copying an artistic work even though the defendant used it to decorate a chair back); 17 U.S.C. § 113(a) (2012).

[220] Useful articles can have copyright. As mentioned, "PGS works" that are useful articles can be copyrighted as to those aspects that pass a "separability" test. 17 U.S.C. § 101 (2012) (defining PGS works). "Architectural works" that are useful articles are copyrightable to the extent their features are not "functionally required." See H.R. Rep. No. 101–735, 101st Cong., 2d Sess. 20–21 (1990), *reprinted in* 1990 U.S.C.C.A.N. 6935, 6951–52. Different kinds of useful articles can thus be governed by different tests.

What tests should govern the copyrightability of computer code is of course much debated in the context of *Oracle v. Google*. This chapter does not reach that issue, but rather addresses the question of what rights should attach to code even if copyrightable.

As a factual matter, it seems unlikely that Google copied Java object code.[221] But what if a defendant also copied from object code? If so, § 113(b) drops out as a potential shelter for that aspect of the defendant's behavior.

Nevertheless, as for all copying, a copyright owner's rights over the copying of object code are governed by Supreme Court precedent, including *Baker*. If the copying was fully nonexpressive in nature, then under *Baker* no infringement of copyright would result.

13.6.5. *Does the breadth of subsection 113(b) govern?*

Baker mandates freedom to copy nonexpressively; its mandate is less clear in cases where copying is a mixed case of expressive and nonexpressive use. By contrast, § 113(b) is not limited by inquiry into the defendant's pure concern with function. It is likely that attractive features triggered some of the copying of furniture and lamps in the old cases; § 113(b) seems to mandate that the public has freedom to copy portrayals of useful articles by building the articles even if the copying was partly motivated by a desire to capture expressive elements.

Subsection 113(b) thus might sweep more broadly than *Baker* itself.

Fortunately, in cases of fully nonexpressive copying like *Oracle*, the courts need not reach the scope of § 113(b). *Baker* itself suffices. In fact, in the computer context, I think that § 113(b) functions best as an echo and reinforcement for *Baker* rather than an independent source of command. It is nevertheless time for the legal community to see that the subsection potentially has significant impact.

13.7. CONCLUSION

Copyright has no inherent interest in governing copying that is indifferent to expression, such as copying a letter to present as evidence in a lawsuit, or copying a sculptural key shape to unlock a door. To regulate such copying would be foreign to

---

[221] Source-code versions of Java commands and input specs were widely available, and evidence in the case shows that Google did indeed use the source code. For example, a "slide show" that Java prepared for litigation highlighted this colloquy (from a deposition):

Q. Did you consult the Java docs when doing your work on the API implementations for Android?
A. Yes.
Q. Okay. And where did you obtain those Java docs?
A. They're posted for free on Sun's website.

Deposition of Bob Lee, August 3, 2011, quoted in *Google Employees Consulted Sun's Copyrighted Java Materials When Implementing Android*, from Oracle Slideshow, available at www.cnet.com/pictures/oracles-slideshow-alleging-how-google-copied-java-images/2/ (last visited June 29, 2015).

copyright's interior logic.[222] From an economic perspective, also, incentives to create more or better expression can have only random correlation with copying that is motivated by expressive-indifferent concerns.

Because line-drawing among types of copying can be costly, infringement claims need not be struck down every time an act of copying does not "fit" copyright's expressive paradigm. But often a lack of "fit" is linked to significant policy concerns. In *Baker v. Selden* the Supreme Court made clear that line-drawing among forms of copying is worth the attendant costs, and *must* be done, when broad enforcement would give copyright law the power to redraw boundaries that Congress has entrusted to patent.

It is not just caselaw that demonstrates this sensitivity. The Copyright Act also includes provisions that limit copyright owners' rights out of deference to patent law.

One such Copyright Act provision, § 113(b), provides that the rights that attach to owning copyright in the portrayal of a useful article do not cover the functional use – the making or sale – of the useful article itself. Taking the section literally, it could immunize defendants who made functional copies of source code because source code is a "portrayal" of the useful article known as object code. In the recent case of *Oracle v. Google*, it appears that Google copied from source code rather than from object code; if so, Google's copying could be sheltered by § 113(b).

However, § 113(b) may sweep very broadly, and it is not certain how Congress meant its language to be interpreted. *Baker* itself can suffice to resolve *Oracle v. Google* and similar disputes. *Baker* indicates that where copying is done with indifference to expressive values, and to serve utilitarian goals of the kind that are governed by the law of utility patent, copyright infringement should not result.

Oracle v. Google, like *Lotus v. Borland* before it, involves a kind of interoperability that is needed to fight lock-in: interoperability between a newcomer program and the relevant public's habituated skills and its existing macros or other programs. In the *Oracle* case, the goal of the copying was to help third-party programmers, who were habituated to Java, more easily interoperate with Google's Android platform. Google's copying the familiar method headers from Java into Android enabled the programmers to choose whether or not to work with the Android platform on its merits, rather than being discouraged by the switching costs involved in recrafting their programming habits. In *Lotus*, the goal of the copying was to help customers of an established spreadsheet program decide whether or not to choose a new spreadsheet program on its merits, rather than being held to the old program by the switching costs involved in learning new meanings for keys and recreating macros.

---

[222] For one eloquent view of this interior logic, see DRASSINOWER, discussed *supra* at note 126 and following.

In both these cases, the plaintiff's programs were not copied because they embodied skilled expression; in both cases the defendants carried the "heavy lifting" of creating new implementation code independently. What copying occurred was not done to spare the defendants the effort, money, or other resources that would be involved in creating high-quality expression. Instead, the copying was done for the purpose of conforming with exactness to whatever the dominant program specified; the copying was done without regard to the quality, vel non, of what was copied.

Under the canonical case of *Baker v. Selden*, as reinforced by *Baker*'s progeny in both caselaw and the copyright statute, the copying in *Lotus* and *Oracle* did not infringe. And this conclusion need not follow from copyrightability, or from "fair use," but from the plaintiff's lack of prima facie right to control functional use. Going forward in *Oracle* and other cases that charge infringement of computer copyrights, *Baker*'s "use/explanation" distinction can play a clarifying role. Patent law gives the public rights to copy and to use[223] that *Baker*, its progeny, and the pattern of the copyright statute all tell us copyright should not undo.

---

[223] Bonito Boats v. Thunder Craft Boats, 489 U.S. 141, 164–65 (1989).

14

Reframing International Copyright Limitations and Exceptions as Development Policy

*Ruth L. Okediji**

ABSTRACT

There is very little that aligns the current design of international copyright law with the requirements for economic development. This chapter advances the proposition that copyright limitations and exceptions (L&Es) needed to promote economic development differ in important respects from the set of L&Es around which there is international consensus. Existing international copyright L&Es do not allow access to copyrighted works at a scale, or on terms, needed for economic development progress; they also insufficiently enable key stakeholders, such as educational institutions and libraries, to facilitate access to knowledge in support of human capital formation. The chapter highlights the need to orient the international copyright framework toward development concerns, while safeguarding local systems of cultural production. The changes suggested underscore the importance, for all countries, of new L&Es that support development and strengthening those L&Es traditionally understood to reflect the public interest.

≈ ≈ ≈

14.1 INTRODUCTION

Since the 1960s, development goals and aspirations have provided powerful rhetoric and shaped institutional and political strategies for encouraging newly independent developing countries to enact a full suite of domestic intellectual property (IP) laws, join international IP treaties, and send government officials for "capacity building"

* William L. Prosser Professor of Law & McKnight Presidential Professor, University of Minnesota Law School. For their helpful feedback and encouragement, I am grateful to Olufunmilayo Arewa, Margo Bagley, Terry Fisher, Wendy Gordon, Peter Jaszi, Keith Maskus, Tade Okediji, Jerome Reichman, and Rodney Smith.

or training programs. Development rhetoric also has conditioned developing and least-developed countries to demand formal assurances of technical assistance as a standard entitlement for their participation in the international IP framework.[1]

The international minimum standards established in the Great Conventions – the Paris Convention for the Protection of Industrial Property[2] and the Berne Convention for the Protection of Literary and Artistic Works[3] – are not, however, mid-twentieth century innovations. These foundational treaties were concluded during the colonial era and implemented in many of the colonies that now comprise the "developing" and "least-developed" countries.[4] Upon independence, the new countries could have broken away from the international IP order, but they did not. Instead, the international community successfully engaged in concerted efforts to encourage the countries to embrace the treaties' minimum standards.

There were important reasons to attract the new sovereign states, particularly in Africa, to the largely culturally homogenous membership base of the Great Conventions. Some of those reasons had to do with a felt need in the international community to overcome historical attitudes that had left these countries on the periphery of the international legal order. With respect to copyright, covert competition between international organizations for the membership of countries in Africa, Asia, and the Americas produced a new treaty, the Universal Copyright Convention (UCC).[5] Although membership was open to all countries, the treaty

---

[1] For the latest example, *see WIPO Assemblies End in Stalemate over Design Law Treaty, Budget,* Bridges Wkly. Trade News Dig., Oct. 10, 2013, at 8–9 (noting that disagreement between developed and developing countries over specific provisions regarding technical assistance and capacity building contributed to the failure to reach agreement on a Diplomatic Conference at the 2013 WIPO General Assemblies). *See also* Catherine Saez, *No Industrial Design Treaty at WIPO in 2014; Technical Assistance Still in the Way,* IP WATCH (Oct. 5, 2014), www.ip-watch.org/2014/05/10/no-wipo-industrial-design-treaty-in-2014-technical-assistance-still-in-the-way.

[2] Paris Convention for the Protection of Industrial Property, Mar. 20, 1883, *as revised* at Stockholm, July 14, 1967, 21 U.S.T. 1583, 828 U.N.T.S. 305 [hereinafter Paris Convention].

[3] Berne Convention for the Protection of Literary and Artistic Works, Sept. 9, 1886, *as revised* at Paris, July 24, 1971, 25 U.S.T. 1341, 1161 U.N.T.S. 3 [hereinafter Berne Convention].

[4] The process and consequences of extending intellectual property (IP) to the colonies have been the subject of recent scholarly attention. *See, e.g.,* PETER DRAHOS, INTELLECTUAL PROPERTY, INDIGENOUS PEOPLE AND THEIR KNOWLEDGE (2014); SARAH BANNERMAN, THE STRUGGLE FOR CANADIAN COPYRIGHT: IMPERIALISM TO INTERNATIONALISM, 1842–1971 (2013); MICHAEL D. BIRNHACK, COLONIAL COPYRIGHT: INTELLECTUAL PROPERTY IN MANDATE PALESTINE (2012); BOATEMA BOATENG, THE COPYRIGHT THING DOESN'T WORK HERE: ADINKRA AND KENTE CLOTH AND INTELLECTUAL PROPERTY IN GHANA (2011). *See also* Ruth L. Okediji, *The International Relations of Intellectual Property: Narratives of Developing Country Participation in the Global Intellectual Property System,* 7 SING. J. INT'L & COMP. L. 315, 320–25 (2003) (discussing the extension of IP to British colonies in Africa).

[5] *See* Universal Copyright Convention, Sept. 6, 1952, 6 U.S.T. 2731, 216 U.N.T.S. 132. *See also* UNESCO & WIPO, *Tunis Model Law on Copyright for Developing Countries* (1976), http://portal.unesco.org/culture/en/files/31318/11866635053tunis_model_law_en-web.pdf/tunis_model_law_en-web.pdf.

was designed for countries at lower levels of economic development than the leading members of the Berne Convention. Many developing countries, and some non-developing ones such as the United States, became members of the UCC.

The Berne Convention and the now-defunct UCC represent the dominant rationale that adoption of copyright laws will improve the material well-being of developing countries and promote their progress by incentivizing domestic creativity and authorial production. Today, in a variety of international legal and policy contexts, economic development and the public interest feature prominently as key justifications for copyright protection,[6] including in international trade agreements that now routinely include the strongest international copyright standards.[7]

Despite enduring debates about the relationship of IP and economic development, that relationship is not much better understood today than it was more than fifty years ago at the height of the independence era. What does it mean to claim that copyright law advances development? Why do development indicators in many countries reflect poorly in the areas that are supposed to be strengthened by copyright law's objectives such as promoting democratic governance, a robust marketplace of ideas, formal education and literacy?

Scholars, policymakers, and advocacy organizations need to have a clearer sense of what it is about copyright that matters for development, including why and how it matters. If appropriately designed copyright laws really have the potential to deliver dynamic development gains, legislative and policy choices about copyright

---

[6] *See, e.g.*, Agreement on Trade-Related Aspects of Intellectual Property Rights, Apr. 15, 1994, Marrakesh Agreement Establishing the World Trade Organization, Annex 1C, 1869 U.N.T.S. 299, 33 I.L.M. 1197 [hereinafter TRIPS Agreement] (recognizing the public policy objectives of national systems for the protection of IP, including developmental and technological objectives, and the special needs of the least-developed country members for maximum flexibility in the domestic implementation of laws and regulations that enable them to create a sound and viable technological base); World Intellectual Property Organization Copyright Treaty, Dec. 20, 1996, S. TREATY DOC. NO. 105–17 (1997), 2186 U.N.T.S. 121 [hereinafter WCT] (recognizing "the need ... to provide adequate solutions to the questions raised by new economic, social, cultural and technological developments" and "the need to maintain a balance between the rights of authors and the larger public interest"); *Trans-Pacific Partnership*, OFFICE OF THE U.S. TRADE REPRESENTATIVE, https://ustr.gov/trade-agreements/free-trade-agreements/trans-pacific-partnership/tpp-full-text (last visited Sept. 15, 2016) ("Having regard to the underlying public policy objectives of national systems, the Parties recognise the need to (a) promote innovation and creativity; (b) facilitate the diffusion of information, knowledge, technology, culture and the arts; and (c) foster competition and open and efficient markets, through their respective intellectual property systems, while respecting the principles of transparency and due process, and taking into account the interests of relevant stakeholders, including right holders, service providers, users and the public."); U.S. PATENT & TRADEMARK OFFICE, 2014–2018 STRATEGIC PLAN, www.uspto.gov/sites/default/files/documents/USPTO_2014-2018_Strategic_Plan.pdf ("Strong IP systems foster innovation, which in turn drives economic success.").

[7] *See* TRIPS Agreement, *supra* note 6; *see also* WCT, *supra* note 6; *Trans-Pacific Partnership*, *supra* note 6.

in developing and least-developed countries must assume a more central position in national economic planning. Those choices will likely vary country by country; the international community could help the various nations' decision-making by providing much more carefully nuanced analyses of copyright rules in view of domestic innovation prospects and development priorities.

This chapter challenges the hypothesis that the existing combination of exclusive rights and limitations and exceptions ("L&Es") permitted by international copyright law advances development. One of my central objectives is to consider the design of the international copyright system in light of what economists have learned about the conditions for economic development, and to query what changes to international copyright law those insights might require. At a minimum, this effort should facilitate more honest dialogue about the relationship between copyright and economic development. It may also help underscore where developing and least-developed countries should sensibly invest their limited economic and political capital when engaging with the international copyright framework.

Section 14.2 draws from literature in the field of development economics to frame my central argument that the current set of international copyright L&Es is ill-suited for development progress. My view of development entails economic growth and well-designed institutions that attend to distributional effects. The combination of growth, institutions and distributional concerns emphasizes that development requires progressive improvement of the material and social environments to advance human flourishing.[8] This approach to development highlights the cumulative understanding produced by several distinctive intellectual shifts in multidisciplinary efforts over the last seventy-five years to understand how societies evolve, their rate and quality of growth, and why some societies are rich and others perennially poor. The section suggests that copyright policies that potentially fuel economic growth in developing countries are not the same as the policies developed countries seek to achieve through international copyright law. In particular, L&Es that are traditionally associated with the public interest do not inevitably promote economic development. Undiscerning advocacy for those L&Es diverts resources to the cultivation of liberal values that, while important in the long run, will not readily improve the material and structural conditions that prevail in developing countries.

---

[8] *See generally* MARTHA C. NUSSBAUM, CREATING CAPABILITIES: THE HUMAN DEVELOPMENT APPROACH (2011); AMARTYA SEN, DEVELOPMENT AS FREEDOM (1999); AMARTYA SEN, INEQUALITY REEXAMINED (1992); William W. Fisher, *The Implications for Law of User Innovation*, 94 MINN. L. REV. 1417, 1466–72 (2010); Margaret Chon, *Intellectual Property and the Development Divide*, 27 CARDOZO L. REV. 2821, 2875–79, 2897–911 (2006).

Section 14.3 begins with the limits of copyright harmonization and explores the landscape of copyright L&Es at the international level. Section 14.4 recalls failed efforts to address development within the international copyright framework and the resurgence of development concerns following the conclusion of the Uruguay Round of multilateral trade negotiations. Section 14.5 considers prospects for retooling the Berne Convention's framework in support of development goals and Section 14.6 highlights considerations for doing so.

Finally, Section 14.7 offers suggestions to more successfully integrate development considerations in the international copyright framework. The initial steps proposed could give substance to the now hollow claims that international copyright potentiates economic development.

14.2 DEVELOPMENT AND THE INTERNATIONAL COPYRIGHT FRAMEWORK

14.2.1 *The Rhetoric of Development and the Institutional Context for International Copyright*

Broadly speaking, development economics is concerned with the policy choices that affect economic growth, particularly those that can explain and improve the rate and quality of economic progress in a country. There is considerable attention in the field to designing policy interventions at the national or regional level and shrinking a variety of gaps between citizens of rich and poor countries.[9] National economic development thus requires a mix of state policies and resource endowments that over time will produce political, economic, and social improvements from which all people in the country can benefit.[10]

Beginning in the 1950s, the study of development across several disciplines sought better understanding of the causes and processes of economic growth, focusing particularly on states that emerged as independent sovereigns in the post–World War II period. Among social scientists, there was heavy emphasis on the role of cultural endowments and institutions – the informal codes and norms that influence individual and group behavior – as key determinants of the development process.[11] Roughly during this same period, neoclassical growth theory

---

[9] *See* FRONTIERS OF DEVELOPMENT ECONOMICS: THE FUTURE IN PERSPECTIVE (Gerald M. Meier & Joseph E. Stiglitz eds., 2001); *see also* WORLD BANK, WORLD DEVELOPMENT REPORT 1998/99: KNOWLEDGE FOR DEVELOPMENT (1999).

[10] *See generally* THOMAS PIKETTY, CAPITAL IN THE TWENTY-FIRST CENTURY (2014).

[11] *See generally* VERNON W. RUTTAN, SOCIAL SCIENCE KNOWLEDGE AND ECONOMIC DEVELOPMENT: AN INSTITUTIONAL DESIGN PERSPECTIVE 33–67 (2003).

focused on capital accumulation as the source of economic growth. Ignoring institutions, history, and distributional consequences, neoclassical models posited that, assuming certain parameters, such as population growth or saving rates, all societies would inevitably move toward a steady state of growth.[12] If all countries operated under the same parameters, the theory claimed, there would ultimately be a convergence where poor countries reflect economic growth similar to developed countries.[13] When convergence did not occur, as evidenced repeatedly in the 1980s and 1990s, neoclassical scholars largely attributed the result to government failures.[14]

In pioneering work, Robert Solow and Trevor Swan laid the foundations of what many consider to be the beginnings of modern economic growth theory. Central to their theory was the idea that capital, labor, and technological improvements (technical change) were the drivers of short- and long-run growth. Solow's subsequent empirical work suggested technical change was the dominant of the three forces. Solow and Swan's work went on to become the conceptual foundation of much of modern growth theory, including the convergence literature that emphasized the role of technology over physical capital as the primary source of economic growth.[15] Unfortunately, insights about the development process from historical, sociological, anthropological, or political science–driven theories of societal transformation did not inform the assumptions made in growth economics.[16] This sterile set of assumptions contributed to the confidence with which international organizations encouraged – and at times imposed – a wide range of inapt economic policies and legal regimes in developing countries. Examples include copyright rules that did not respect established systems of cultural production and that, at the same time, made access to cultural goods produced elsewhere too costly to obtain.

---

[12] *See* Debraj Ray, *Development Economics, in* THE NEW PALGRAVE DICTIONARY OF ECONOMICS 469 (Steven N. Durlauf & Lawrence E. Blume eds., 2d ed. 2008) (defining conventional growth theory as an approach that "develops the hypothesis that given certain parameters ... economies inevitably move towards some steady state. If these parameters are the same across economies, then in the long run all economies converge to one another.").

[13] *See* Robert M. Solow, *A Contribution to the Theory of Economic Growth*, 70 Q.J. ECON. 65 (1956); Robert M. Solow, *Technical Change and the Aggregate Production Function*, 39 REV. OF ECON. & STAT. 312 (1957). For examples of variations to the basic model, see, e.g., Robert E. Lucas, Jr., *Why Doesn't Capital Flow from Rich to Poor Countries?*, 80 AM. ECON. REV. 92 (1990); N. Gregory Mankiw, David Romer & David N. Weil, *A Contribution to the Empirics of Economic Growth*, 107 Q.J. ECON. 407 (1992).

[14] Karla Hoff & Joseph Stiglitz, *Modern Economic Theory and Development, in* FRONTIERS OF DEVELOPMENT ECONOMICS: THE FUTURE IN PERSPECTIVE 391 (Gerald M. Meier & Joseph E. Stiglitz eds., 2001).

[15] *See* Solow, *supra* note 13. *See also* Trevor W. Swan, *Economic Growth and Capital Accumulation*, 32 ECON. REC. 334 (1956).

[16] *See* Hoff & Stiglitz, *supra* note 14, at 390–91.

As Hoff and Stiglitz note, the absence of history, culture, and distributional consequences left out "the heart of development economics."[17]

An important shift occurred with the introduction of endogenous growth theory ("new" growth theory) in the work of economists such as Paul Romer and Robert Lucas.[18] The lack of evidence of convergence toward steady-state growth across even the developed countries, and the inability of neoclassical models to account for persistent divergence in income growth rates and per capita income across countries, provided impetus for new growth economics and its attendant models.[19] As concern over income disparities between countries occupied greater attention among economists, modern growth models began including other factors in the parameters that affect long-run growth rates.[20] The early models developed by Romer, for example, emphasized the accumulation of knowledge as a source of long-run economic growth.[21] By the 1990s, the World Bank also started to emphasize factors such as knowledge, institutions, and culture to form a more comprehensive approach to development.[22]

Modern economic theory recognizes that these intangibles, alongside history and resource endowments, are important considerations in understanding and planning for development outcomes.[23] Moreover, these outcomes can differ even between two similarly situated countries.[24] The now well-established premise that "fundamentals" – resources, technology, and preferences – "are not the only deep determinants of economic outcomes"[25] and that culture, history, and institutions have a long reach into development prospects,[26] has important ramifications for international copyright law's claim as a facilitator of development.

---

[17]　*Id.* at 390.

[18]　Paul M. Romer, *Increasing Returns and Long-Run Growth*, 94 J. Pol. Econ. 1002 (1986); Robert E. Lucas, Jr., *On the Mechanics of Economic Development*, 22 J. Monetary Econ. 3 (1988).

[19]　*See generally* Paul M. Romer, *The Origins of Endogenous Growth*, 8 J. Econ. Persp. 3 (1994).

[20]　*See* T.N. Srinivasan, *Long-Run Growth Theories and Empirics: Anything New?*, *in* Growth Theories In Light Of The East Asian Experience 37, 46 (Takatoshi Ito & Anne O. Krueger eds., 1995) (listing trade policies, among others, as part of the parameters for modeling long run growth rates in new growth economics).

[21]　Romer, *Increasing Returns and Long-Run Growth, supra* note 18, at 1003.

[22]　*See* WDR 1998/1999, *supra* note 9.

[23]　*See* Hoff & Stiglitz, *supra* note 14. *See also* Ray, *supra* note 12, at 472 ("Factors as diverse as the distribution of economic or political power, legal structure, traditions, group reputations, colonial heritage and specific institutional settings may serve as initial conditions – with a long reach.").

[24]　*See* Ray, *supra* note 12, at 470–72.

[25]　Hoff & Stiglitz, *supra* note 14, at 390.

[26]　Daron Acemoglu, Simon Johnson & James A. Robinson, *The Colonial Origins of Comparative Development: An Empirical Investigation*, 91 Am. Econ. Rev. 1369 (2001) ("At some level it is obvious that institutions matter."); *see also* Douglass C. North, Institutions, Institutional Change, and Economic Performance (1990).

First, appeals to "development" in international copyright policy circles rarely provide any indication of what is meant by the term. Claims that strong copyright protection (or even *any* copyright protection) promotes development seldom attract serious scrutiny when they are made, nor are they subject to interrogation when they fail to produce promised results.[27] Intellectual property bureaucracies in developing and least-developed countries that are the targets of technical assistance programs are the least likely to raise questions. Instead, they echo similar assertions about IP and development – sometimes as forcefully as their counterparts in industrialized countries.[28]

Second, the rhetoric of economic development all but guarantees international organizations extraordinary access to senior policymakers in developing and least-developed countries. International actors of all types exert significant influence over domestic law-making processes in a model best described as "care and control."[29] Undue foreign influence is obvious in IP laws generally; in copyright the results are sometimes bizarre (such as enhanced criminal penalties for copyright infringement) and at other times mystifying (such as copyright protection for "spiritual works"). Technical assistance from international agencies has produced some creative legislative outcomes, such as a blend of fair use and an enumerated list of copyright exceptions that has appeared recently in the copyright laws of some African countries.[30] Nevertheless, many developing countries, and particularly leaders of most African countries, are remarkably unstrategic in their approach to any type of IP.

The problem is not simply that international copyright rules may be unsuited for achieving national development goals and interests. Copyright law envisions that the interests of authors and markets will align in specific ways to advance

---

[27] But see Francis Owusu, *Pragmatism and the Gradual Shift from Dependency to Neoliberalism: The World Bank, African Leaders and Development Policy in Africa*, 31 WORLD DEVELOPMENT 1655 (2003) (discussing changes in the World Bank's approach to development in Africa, including, in some instances, acknowledgment by the Bank that some of its development prescriptions had failed to produce expected results). *See also id.* at 1660.

[28] See CAROLYN DEERE, THE IMPLEMENTATION GAME: THE TRIPS AGREEMENT AND THE GLOBAL POLITICS OF INTELLECTUAL PROPERTY REFORM IN DEVELOPING COUNTRIES (2009).

[29] Michael N. Barnett, *International Paternalism and Humanitarian Governance*, 1 GLOBAL CONSTITUTIONALISM 485 (2012) (noting that paternalism is an "organizing principle" of the international order and applying the heuristic "care and control" in his analysis of paternalism in humanitarian intervention).

[30] See, e.g., The Copyright and Neighboring Rights Act, 2006 § 15 (Uganda), www.wipo.int/wipolex/en/details.jsp?id=3922. *See also* Copyright & Neighboring Rights Act, 2000 §§ 12–22 (Bots.), www.wipo.int/wipolex/en/details.jsp?id=9583; Nigerian Copyright Commission, Draft Copyright Bill 2015, http://nlipw.com/wp-content/uploads/DRAFT-REVISED-COPYRIGHT-BILL-1.pdf.

cultural progress, and that the content and direction of such progress will result from the cumulative choices of creators who are free from state intervention.[31] Like the neoclassical growth literature, leading theories of copyright protection are appreciably distant from the deeply embedded social and cultural institutions that exist in many developing and least-developed countries.[32] This would not be the case if copyright law were grounded in any serious understanding of development.

Even if copyright's vision of progress accurately portrays the role of authors in liberal societies (a proposition that has attracted important skepticism),[33] that vision is still an inadequate justification for the existing international copyright framework. The international minimum standards established in the Berne Convention, reinforced in the Agreement on Trade Related Aspects of Intellectual Property Rights (TRIPS Agreement)[34] and in subsequent bilateral and plurilateral trade agreements, *require* states to shape their domestic copyright laws consistent with the choices reflected in those standards. These international minimum copyright standards are not culturally neutral, nor are they the result of scientific investigation. True, the rules do not dictate how authors may choose to express themselves or the content of their creative works. Nonetheless, the international minimum standards define important things, such as what counts as protectable expression,[35] and the terms and conditions of access and use of protected works. Moreover, the TRIPS Agreement prescribes a universe of domestic enforcement mechanisms[36] that states

---

[31] Neil Weinstock Netanel, *Copyright and a Democratic Civil Society*, 106 YALE L.J. 283 (1996). For an important analysis of the conception of progress in IP, see Margaret Chon, *Postmodern "Progress": Reconsidering the Copyright and Patent Power*, 43 DEPAUL L. REV. 97 (1993).

[32] Daron Acemoglu and James A. Robinson, *Why Is Africa Poor?* 25 ECON. HIST. OF DEVELOPING REGIONS 21 (2010) (emphasizing Africa's institutional environment); JEAN-PHILLIPE PLATTEAU, INSTITUTIONS, SOCIAL NORMS AND ECONOMIC DEVELOPMENT (2000) (emphasizing social norms that force sharing); Ruth L. Gana, *Has Creativity Died in the Third World?* 24 DENVER J. INT'L L. & POL'Y 109 (1995) (discussing colonial history and traditional systems of creativity).

[33] Julie E. Cohen, *Copyright as Property in the Post-Industrial Economy: A Research Agenda*, 2011 WIS. L. REV. 141 (2011).

[34] TRIPS Agreement, *supra* note 6.

[35] The Berne Convention explicitly excludes miscellaneous facts having the character of mere items of press information from international protection. See Berne Convention, *supra* note 3, art. 2(8). While this exclusion is often characterized as an L&E, it is better understood as defining the outer boundaries of copyrightable subject matter. This is, in fact, precisely the way the Berne Convention treats ideas, facts, and press items; these items are not understood as "original works of authorship" and so do not qualify for protection. See also Sam Ricketson, *Rights on the Border: The Berne Convention and Neighbouring Rights*, in COPYRIGHT LAW IN AN AGE OF LIMITATIONS AND EXCEPTIONS (Ruth L. Okediji ed., 2017).

[36] TRIPS Agreement, *supra* note 6, at part III.

must provide, and requires that changes in national legislation be reported to the World Trade Organization (WTO).[37] With this level of incursion into the domestic sphere, it is hard to argue that the national or international copyright frameworks, or the types of creativity they support, are free of significant state involvement. So, to what ends is the copyright power of the state directed in developing and least-developed countries?

Even after implementation of the TRIPS Agreement, many developing and least-developed countries continue to heed development rhetoric from transnational private actors and leading copyright exporting countries. As a result, these countries have embarked on various initiatives to strengthen or redesign their copyright laws to enhance the exclusive rights granted. This rhetoric usually exaggerates the role of IP in economic development,[38] and it downplays the historical record of weak (and in some cases no) copyright or patent protection in the economic development of leading industrialized countries.[39] Yet, in a longstanding tradition, development rhetoric from international organizations helps shape the expectations of governing elites in the developing countries so that they welcome, demand, and sometimes even lead in the paternalism that has long characterized their participation in the international IP framework.[40]

---

[37] *Id.* art. 63(2) ("Members shall notify the laws and regulations referred to in paragraph 1 to the Council for TRIPS ...").

[38] *See* U.S. PATENT & TRADEMARK OFFICE, *supra* note 6 ("Strong IP systems foster innovation, which in turn drives economic success."); *see also* David Kline, *Do Patents Truly Promote Innovation?*, IP WATCHDOG (Apr. 15, 2014), www.ipwatchdog.com/2014/04/15/do-patents-truly-promote-innovation/ id=48768; W.G. Park, & D. C. Lippoldt, *Transfer and the Economic Implications of the Strengthening of Intellectual Property Rights in Developing Countries* (Organization for Economic Co-operation and Development (OECD), Trade Policy Working Paper No. 62, 2008).

[39] *See* Edmund W. Kitch, *Property Rights in Inventions, Writings, and Marks*, 13 HARVARD J.L. & PUB. POL'Y 119, 123 (1989) ("Economists, who have been the principal writers on patent policy, have concluded that if we did not have the patent system, we would be fools to create it; but because one exists, it is not clear that it is worth the trouble to get rid of it."). *See also* Keith Maskus, *Cognitive Dissonance in the Economics of Patent Protection, Trade and Development* (forthcoming, KRITIKA 2016) ("[T]he mechanisms by which intellectual property rights might build technology markets are complex and vary greatly by socioeconomic circumstances, making it extremely difficult to search for strong causal patterns in imperfect innovation data. Locating systematic impacts on growth and development is harder still."); Walter G. Park, *Do Intellectual Property Rights Stimulate R&D and Productivity Growth? Evidence from Cross-national and Manufacturing Industries Data*, in INTELLECTUAL PROPERTY AND INNOVATION IN THE KNOWLEDGE-BASED ECONOMY § 9-3 (Jonathan D. Putnam ed., 2005) (noting the controversy about whether IPRs matter for productivity growth, directly or indirectly); Chon, *supra* note 8 (citing several empirical studies that demonstrate "the actual impact of intellectual property laws on rates of innovation and economic growth, a key justification for the regulatory intervention into the public goods problem that intellectual property represents").

[40] *See, e.g.*, KAMIL IDRIS, WORLD INTELLECTUAL PROPERTY ORGANIZATION, INTELLECTUAL PROPERTY: A POWER TOOL FOR ECONOMIC GROWTH (2002).

For example, in 2007, member states of the World Intellectual Property Organization (WIPO), the organization responsible for "promoting the protection of intellectual property throughout the world,"[41] adopted a Development Agenda. Spearheaded by the developing countries, the Development Agenda is an institution-wide mandate dedicated to the integration of development considerations into its substantial normative and capacity-building activities.[42]

Almost a decade after its adoption, it remains unclear what effect the Development Agenda has had on WIPO's core mission of promoting the strongest possible levels of IP protection. There is little indication that the Development Agenda has transformed WIPO's fundamental operating procedures or ideological orientation, nor is there evidence of how the organization's programs have effectuated lasting positive change in national development planning or innovation policies. Yet, in virtually every issue or multilateral initiative seeking to address development challenges on a global scale, WIPO is there like a superhero, defending IP interests, avowing the role of IP in development,[43] and reinforcing its authority over the domestic policy choices of developing and least-developed countries.

In short, many of the developing and least-developed countries, especially in Africa, still fundamentally struggle with the relationship between copyright and economic development, and with what is possible within the constraints of the international copyright framework. As such, they have failed to translate even promising international copyright standards into effective national policies that foster innovation and enhance prospects for human flourishing.

Setting aside for the moment the significant challenge of failed political institutions,[44] policymakers in developing and least-developed countries are hard-pressed to justify investment of scarce political and economic resources into legal regimes that appear wholly removed from the institutional environment and developmental challenges they face. Furthermore, sound copyright or IP laws do not guarantee high economic returns, even quite apart from the existing fundamental misalignments. This point is not made nearly enough in the context of international

---

[41] Convention Establishing the World Intellectual Property Organization, preamble, July 14, 1967, 21 U.S.T. 1749, 828 U.N.T.S. 3.

[42] *See Development Agenda for WIPO*, WORLD INTELL. PROP. ORG., http://wipo.int/ip-development/en/agenda (last visited Sept. 15, 2016) (stating that adoption of the WIPO Development Agenda was an important "milestone" and "ensures that development considerations form an integral part of WIPO's work. The effective implementation of the Development Agenda, including the mainstreaming of its recommendations into our substantive programs, is a key priority.").

[43] *See, e.g., Millennium Development Goals (MDGs) and WIPO*, WORLD INTELL. PROP. ORG., http://wipo.int/ip-development/en/agenda/millennium_goals (last visited Sept. 15, 2016).

[44] *See generally* DARON ACEMOGLU & JAMES A. ROBINSON, WHY NATIONS FAIL: THE ORIGINS OF POWER, PROSPERITY, AND POVERTY (2012). *See id.* especially at 45–69 ("Poor countries are poor not because of their geographies or cultures, or because their leaders do not know which policies will enrich their citizens."). *See also* Acemoglu & Robinson, *supra* note 32.

norm-setting exercises where development gains are often portrayed as the inevitable outcome of adopting strong copyright and patent laws. The enduring appeal of the copyright and development narrative can be traced to the longstanding practice of using copyright to advance national goals or, more colloquially, to serve the public interest.

14.2.2 *Constructing the National Public Interest in the Design of International Copyright Law*

In 1788, one of America's founders wrote of copyright and patent laws that "[t]he public good fully coincides ... with the claims of individuals."[45] Over the centuries, notions of what constitutes the "public good" or the "public interest" have shifted. In addition, copyright law itself changed drastically. For example, the duration of ownership over a typical copyrighted work expanded from fourteen years (in 1790) to over a century (in 2016). Copyright scope and subject matters similarly exploded in breadth. Whatever one's definition of "public interest," as copyright grew, observers found it less and less easy to assume that the public good was served by granting and expanding ownership rights.

Much of today's copyright debates tries to pull the term "public interest" into a particular camp. For the camp that favors a slimmed-down copyright regime, "public interest" tends to be identified with L&Es such as compulsory licenses or freedom of ideas and facts from a copyright owner's control. In the United States and many other industrialized nations, the groups that seek to reduce copyright's girth tend to focus on those L&Es that shelter free speech concerns. More recently, this focus has included emphasis on L&Es that support creative freedom and enhance human capabilities, including favorable judicial application of fair use to user-generated works, to copying computer code to promote interoperability, and to services offered by digital repositories. These are all important L&Es but they are of a somewhat different ilk than what is required for development, moreso in environments where what is essential is building human capabilities to engage in productive social and economic endeavors.

It should be no surprise that copyright L&Es differ in their facility to advance development, especially for countries at the earliest stages of technological capacity. Yet, appropriate distinctions between copyright law's various objectives are hardly made in the persistent claims linking copyright to development. Those important distinctions are also missing in more recent well-meaning debates suggesting that fidelity to an elusive "balance" between exclusive rights and the L&Es

---

[45] THE FEDERALIST NO. 43 (James Madison), www.constitution.org/fed/federa43.htm.

a country adopts is sufficient to address any negative effects of copyright's bundle of entitlements. Even more important, the international copyright system plays a significant role in defining the extent to which any real balance can be achieved nationally.

The role of copyright limitations for human flourishing and socioeconomic development has been a key part of international copyright law since the conclusion of the Berne Convention in 1886. The process of creating an international copyright framework required identifying similarities in national laws to establish common ground for an acceptable set of minimum standards; those national standards typically included limits to the scope of protection. Even among leading proponents of strong copyright, some limits to the scope of protection were a key feature of the multilateral system contemplated by those demanding uniform minimum standards for the cross-border protection of authors.[46]

When first concluded, the Berne Convention (Berne Act) defined new international rights for authors. Those rights were juxtaposed with a strong subject matter boundary[47] and an explicit reference to the public domain.[48] The Berne Act also imposed other limits. For example, the Act limited the author's right of translation to ten years.[49] It also excluded some subject matters: an author's exclusive rights to prohibit reproduction and translation were made inapplicable to articles of political discussion, reproduction of news of the day, or miscellaneous information.[50] Other limits were linked to the prevailing national conditions in member countries in which the author sought protection. For example, the Berne Act subjected international protection to "the conditions and formalities" contained in national law,[51] and it left intact any domestic provisions regarding use of works for educational and scientific purposes.[52]

---

[46] *See* JAMES BOYLE & JENNIFER JENKINS, INTELLECTUAL PROPERTY: LAW AND THE INFORMATION SOCIETY 282–83 (2014) (translating a speech by Victor Hugo in Paris, 1878, in which Hugo recognized both the "unquestionable property of the writer" and the "equally incontestable right of the public domain"). As stated by Hugo: "Create a system of literary property, but at the same time, create the public domain!" *Id.* at 283.

[47] *See* Berne Convention for the Protection of Literary and Artistic Works, art. 4, Sept. 9, 1886, 168 Parry's T.S. 185 [hereinafter Berne Act]. *See also* Ricketson, *supra* note 35 (citing to the original version of the Convention) (noting the importance and disciplining character of the list of protected works in Article 4 despite the broad language in the Convention).

[48] Berne Act, *supra* note 47, art. 6 (citing to the original version of the Convention).

[49] *Id.* art. 5.

[50] *Id.* art. 7.

[51] *Id.* art. 2.

[52] *Id.* art. 8.

In sum, the early design of the Berne Convention included two forms of L&Es: those that carefully delineated the subject matter of authorial rights and those that preserved space for a nation to express its domestic concerns by imposing its own additional boundaries on authors' rights. At least in these two senses, the idea of a national public interest was introduced into the international copyright framework. States, not authors, defined the boundaries of the property claim, and it was states that determined the need for further conditions on the exercise of those rights in national law.

National copyright laws had, of course, long reflected a symbiosis between the grant of property rights in knowledge goods and the "public interest." In defining what was subject to the newly minted right to prohibit copying, the English Statute of Anne[53] in 1710 also declared a realm in which copyright had no claim.[54] As such, this realm belonged to the public. And notwithstanding persistent scholarly dissension about the extent to which notions of authorial "right" shared the stage with the public's interest in the Statute of Anne,[55] most commentators have a strong intuition that durational and other limits to copyright are intrinsically linked to public interest objectives. Evidence of this connection can be found in historical documents,[56] in speeches and debates from America to Europe,[57] and in the trove of scholarly literature examining justifications in support of the institution of literary and artistic property in the nineteenth century.[58] Yet the particular nature of the public interest to be served by L&Es remained unspecified, appropriately reserved for resolution through domestic political processes that typically reflected prevailing economic realities.

---

[53] An Act for the Encouragement of Learning, 8 Ann., c. 19, § 1 (1710) (Eng.).

[54] *See* Jane C. Ginsburg, *"Une Chose Publique"?: The Author's Domain and the Public Domain in Early British, French and US Copyright Law*, 65 CAMBRIDGE L.J. 636, 642 (2006) ("[T]he realm of copyright was a shoreline of uncertain contours. The Statute of Anne may have separated the waters from the lands, but it did not clearly tell us which was which.").

[55] *See* ISABELLA ALEXANDER, COPYRIGHT LAW AND THE PUBLIC INTEREST IN THE NINETEENTH CENTURY 17–18 (2010) (discussing the different scholarly views); *see also* Ronan Deazley, *The Myth of Copyright at Common Law*, 62 CAMBRIDGE L.J. 106, 108 (2003); MARK ROSE, AUTHORS AND OWNERS: THE INVENTION OF COPYRIGHT 47–48 (1993); LYMAN RAY PATTERSON, COPYRIGHT IN HISTORICAL PERSPECTIVE 143–50 (1968).

[56] *See* Letter from Thomas Jefferson to Isaac McPherson (Aug. 13, 1813), *in* 13 THE WRITINGS OF THOMAS JEFFERSON 326, 334–35 (Andrew A. Lipscomb ed., 1905).

[57] *See* sources cited *supra* and accompanying text. *See also* CARLA HESSE, PUBLISHING AND CULTURAL POLITICS IN REVOLUTIONARY PARIS, 1789–1810 (1991); CATHERINE SEVILLE, LITERARY COPYRIGHT REFORM IN EARLY VICTORIAN ENGLAND: THE FRAMING OF THE 1842 COPYRIGHT ACT (1999); EDWARD C. WALTERSCHEID, THE NATURE OF THE INTELLECTUAL PROPERTY CLAUSE: A STUDY IN HISTORICAL PERSPECTIVE (2002).

[58] *See* sources cited *supra* and accompanying text. *See also* Peter Jaszi, *Toward a Theory of Copyright: The Metamorphoses of "Authorship,"* 1991 DUKE L.J. 455 (1991).

This state of affairs might have been unobjectionable had the boundaries of copyright subject matter remained fixed. In reality, as those boundaries were enlarged, the scope for unilateral state action correspondingly diminished. One might have hoped that, over time, a distinct vision of the public interest would have emerged and would have featured more explicitly in the design of the evolving international framework for authors' rights. However, the early international compacts did not endeavor to fill the conceptual gap; the Berne Convention principally deferred to national limits enacted by the various signatory states pursuing their own conceptions of the public interest. As the Convention matured, the international framework came to adopt some of the limits recognized in most member states. But agreement on a common set of international L&Es proved elusive even for the relatively culturally homogenous members of the Berne Union.[59] This state of affairs was made more complex by efforts in the late 1960s and 1970s to accommodate developing countries, and their distinct development challenges, in the international copyright framework.[60]

Throughout its evolution, the Berne Convention focused primarily on the powers of exclusion that countries were required to grant to authors, and thus on the duties that nations were required to impose on their populations. Those duties eliminated existing liberty rights to copy or otherwise use authorial works as necessary. In the absence of a governing notion of the public interest, the negotiations during each iteration of the Berne Convention framed the meaning of "rights" as if the only rights at issue were the copyright owner's rights of exclusion, forgetting that the public has rights that also matter a great deal, such as rights to read the books, to watch the movies, and to access the underlying ideas expressed in any copyrighted work.

This model of "thick" minimum standards for author's rights and "thin" L&Es for the public has remained intact. As the Berne Convention evolved, it retained its core logic as a regime dedicated to the protection of private rights of exclusion. It also largely continued to eschew setting mandatory L&Es, leaving the mandatory authorial rights it had established without a significant counterweight, while at the same time circumscribing state power to create or strengthen L&Es nationally.

To be clear, the gradual expansion of international copyright protection to new categories of works had some limits.[61] This was not, however, accompanied by any

---

[59] *See* Sam Ricketson, The Berne Convention for the Protection of Literary and Artistic Works, 1886–1986, at 479–80 (1987).

[60] *See infra* Section 14.5 (highlighting particular problems in developing and least-developed countries and the need for development-inducing L&Es).

[61] The public interest was, for example, invoked during the negotiations leading to the Berne Convention as a basis for limits to the rights granted to authors. *See* Ricketson, *supra* note 59, at 477 ("[F]rom

overarching theory of an international public interest.[62] No effort similar to that directed to establishing common ground for authorial rights was made then, nor has one been made since, for the public interest. Instead, once the author's exclusive right to reproduce a work was formally recognized in the Stockholm/Paris revisions to the Berne Convention, international copyright law invented a device, the three-step test, to formally limit the extent to which countries could establish L&Es to this primary right.[63] Pursuant to the TRIPS Agreement, the three-step test applies to all the economic rights granted to a copyright holder. It requires WTO members to confine L&Es to "certain special cases which do not conflict with a normal exploitation of the work and do not unreasonably prejudice the legitimate interests of the right holder."[64]

The three-step test is among the most contested and contentious topics in contemporary international copyright relations, but its application has rarely been judicially verified.[65] Instead, the test is the subject of intense scholarly debate over its scope and interpretation. It is hard to imagine that the test has not, at least for copyright scholars, overtaken the U.S. fair use doctrine's claim to being the most troublesome doctrine in copyright law.

Today, building on the foundations established in the TRIPS Agreement, a slew of international economic agreements have fortified constraints on national copyright policy making, especially in the area of L&Es, by including the three-step test obligation.[66] The agreements also establish mandatory enforcement standards, making

the Berne Act on, the Convention has contained a number of provisions granting latitude to member states to limit the right of authors in certain circumstances.").

[62] Except, of course, to the extent one ascribes copyright protection per se as an expression of the public interest. *See, e.g., id.* ("Above all, it is to be remembered that the very fact that copyright protection exists, both at [the] national and international level, is an express recognition of the strong public interest that there is in the promotion of cultural, social and economic progress.").

[63] *See id.* at 479–81; *see also* Berne Convention, *supra* note 3, art. 9; Jessica Litman, *Fetishizing Copies, in* COPYRIGHT LAW IN AN AGE OF LIMITATIONS AND EXCEPTIONS, *supra* note 35 (criticizing the often repeated notion by rights holders that authors should be able to control all uses of their works and that "every appearance of any part of a work anywhere should be deemed a 'copy' of it, and that every single copy needs a license or excuse"). *See generally* MARTIN SENFTLEBEN, COPYRIGHT, LIMITATIONS AND THE THREE-STEP TEST: AN ANALYSIS OF THE THREE-STEP TEST IN INTERNATIONAL AND EC COPYRIGHT LAW (2004).

[64] *See* TRIPS Agreement, *supra* note 6, arts. 9.1, 13.

[65] For recent analyses, *see, e.g.*, Justin Hughes, *Fair Use and Its Politics – at Home and Abroad, in* COPYRIGHT LAW IN AN AGE OF LIMITATIONS AND EXCEPTIONS, *supra* note 35 (examining the relationship between the U.S. fair use doctrine and the three-step test). *See also* P. Bernt Hugenholtz, *Flexible Copyright: Can the EU Author's Rights Accommodate Fair Use?, in* COPYRIGHT LAW IN AN AGE OF LIMITATIONS AND EXCEPTIONS, *supra* note 35 (exploring prospects for new L&Es in the EU despite the three-step test).

[66] *See Trans-Pacific Partnership, supra* note 6, art. 18.65(1) ("With respect to this Section, each Party shall confine limitations or exceptions to exclusive rights to certain special cases that do not conflict with a normal exploitation of the work, performance or phonogram, and do not unreasonably prejudice the legitimate interests of the right holder."). *See also* Free Trade Agreement between the Republic of Korea and the United States of America, S. Kor.-U.S., art. 18:4, para. 1, 8 n.11, June 30, 2007,

maneuvering around internationally required copyright entitlements difficult – especially for developing and least-developed countries.[67] For example, in the realm of patents developed countries have issued threats of retaliation in response to efforts by developing countries to exercise L&Es.[68] This has created a culture of intimidation and uncertainty that effectively proscribes the use of state discretion in all of the other IP subject areas. If the L&Es recognized in the domestic laws of many of these countries were already quite anemic, the TRIPS-plus environment has placed them on life support. In short, the constraints in international copyright law considerably affect what L&Es a country may add to its domestic copyright legislation; they also curtail the possibility of altogether different L&Es for development progress.

In the developed countries, demands on the public interest justifications for copyright usually arise with respect to applications of L&Es to alleged infringing conduct. In the United States, for example, the fair use doctrine is regularly deployed to address a wide range of conduct enabled by new technologies.[69] On the other hand, in the European Union, a system of carefully designed L&Es that address specific uses of copyrighted works has traditionally been less accommodating of technological advances, although this too seems poised for change in the face of

---

modified, Dec. 5, 2010, https://ustr.gov/trade-agreements/free-trade-agreements/korus-fta/final-text; United States-Peru Trade Promotion Agreement, Peru-U.S., art. 16:7, para. 8, Apr. 12, 2006, https://ustr.gov/trade-agreements/free-trade-agreements/peru-tpa/final-text ("With respect to Articles 16.5 through 16.7, each Party shall confine limitations or exceptions to exclusive rights to certain special cases that do not conflict with a normal exploitation of the work, performance, or phonogram, and do not unreasonably prejudice the legitimate interests of the rights holder."); United States-Australia Free Trade Agreement, Austl.-U.S., art. 17:4, para. 10(a), May 18, 2004, https://ustr.gov/trade-agreements/free-trade-agreements/australian-fta/final-text ("With respect to Articles 17.4, 17.5, and 17.6: each Party shall confine limitations or exceptions to exclusive rights to certain special cases that do not conflict with a normal exploitation of the work, performance, or phonogram, and do not unreasonably prejudice the legitimate interests of the rights holder ...").

[67] *See* Henning Grosse Ruse-Khan, *The International Law Relation Between TRIPS and Subsequent TRIPS-Plus Free Trade Agreements: Toward Safeguarding TRIPS Flexibilities?* 18 J. Intell. Prop. L. 325 (2011) (highlighting the unfairness that results from lack of TRIPS flexibilities in free trade agreements). *See also* Beatrice Lindstrom, *Scaling Back TRIPS-Plus: An Analysis of Intellectual Property Provisions in Trade Agreements and Implications for Asia and the Pacific* 42 N.Y.U. J. Int'l L. & Pol. 917 (2010) (arguing that the "TRIPS-plus" trade agreements in the Asia-Pacific region "are not an appropriate vehicle for intellectual property lawmaking").

[68] *See* Ed Silverman, *Colombian Government Recommendation Puts Novartis Cancer Drug Patent at Jeopardy*, Stat (Mar. 7, 2016), www.statnews.com/pharmalot/2016/03/07/novartis-gleevec-cancer. *See also* Zack Struver, *122 Experts Defend Colombia's Right to Issue Compulsory License on Imatinib in Face of U.S. Pressure*, Knowledge Ecology International: Zack Struver's Blog (May 17, 2016), http://keionline.org/node/2563; Glynn Moody, *At the Behest of Big Pharma, US Threatens Colombia over Compulsory Licensing of Swiss Drug*, Techdirt (May 13, 2016), www.techdirt.com/articles/20160512/07462934424/behest-big-pharma-us-threatens-colombia-over-compulsory-licensing-swiss-drug.shtml.

[69] *See, e.g.*, Sony Corp. of Am. v. Universal City Studios, Inc., 464 U.S. 417 (1984); Authors Guild v. Hathitrust, 755 F.3d 87 (2d Cir. 2014); Oracle Am., Inc. v. Google, Inc., 750 F.3d 1339 (Fed. Cir. 2014).

rapid technological developments.[70] The point is that leading industrialized countries appear to rely less on L&Es than the developing countries to address problems that could be resolved by improving access to cultural goods. This apparent lack of reliance on L&Es was not the case historically and, in reality, it is not the case today. All countries need robust access to knowledge as a pathway to economic development; this was precisely the reason for the United States' long-standing abstention from Berne membership.

Pointing out that the United States did not join the Berne Convention until it reached an appropriate level of development may seem clichéd. Nevertheless, it is important to emphasize why delayed ratification was an expedient strategy. The other industrialized countries had joined the Berne Convention before the regime required expanded rules of protection for authors, limited the scope of permissible L&Es, and imposed other conditions of entry on new adherents. Eschewing Berne ratification provided the United States room to devise a range of important policy tools (e.g., copyright formalities) that, together with robust access to foreign literary works, helped establish domestic cultural industries and produce a literate and innovative society. This wasn't, as is sometimes portrayed, a matter of just "waiting for the right time" in the development arc to adopt internationally required copyright rules. The ability to shape rules and devise incentives for the development of local content industries, outside the strictures of the Berne Convention, made international L&Es less important to the national experiences of the United States and other developed countries.

Today, global rules no longer allow such domestic inventiveness; adherence to the global copyright standards is mandatory. Under these conditions, internationally recognized L&Es must be understood as far more than just another set of levers to assist copyright law's internal balancing act; they are an important component of modern economic development and growth strategy.

In the next section, I address two major challenges of copyright law for development. First, I discuss the design of the Berne Convention and implications of copyright harmonization for creativity in developing societies. To the degree harmonized copyright rules are misaligned with domestic institutions, or they override cultural or social structures, those rules squelch creative expression and hinder development of local content industries. Second, I review the landscape of international copyright L&Es to explain why the current international framework cannot sufficiently enable economic development. Insights from growth economics, supplemented by aspects of development economics, are central to my claim that L&Es that facilitate development objectives must be differently designed than those that support industrialized nations' usual notions of the public interest. The

---

[70] *See* Hugenholtz, *supra* note 65.

goal is to use the insights from these fields to highlight what type of L&Es are needed to vindicate appeals to "development goals" as a justification for international copyright law.

14.3 LIMITS OF THE INTERNATIONAL COPYRIGHT FRAMEWORK FOR DEVELOPMENT

14.3.1 *The Limits of Copyright Harmonization*

Neither economic development nor the public interest were the concern of nineteenth century international copyright law. The chief logic of the Berne-fueled international copyright system is harmonization – requiring countries to grant the same minimum rights to authors, irrespective of levels of development. The Berne Convention also ensured that harmonization of authorial rights would be progressive.[71] As early as its first iteration in 1886, the Berne Convention included a pair of levers that precluded states from undermining the agreed upon minimum international copyright standards. Articles 15 and 20 of the Berne Act addressed preexisting and future copyright agreements. These articles precluded member states from joining international copyright arrangements other than those providing greater levels of authorial rights, or otherwise not contravening Berne standards.[72]

The lock-in effects of Articles 15 and 20 "meant that no other international copyright agreement different in substance, form or orientation could successfully compete with the Berne Convention."[73] The design features resulted in a path-dependency for the evolution of the international copyright framework, effectuating the progressive harmonization and strengthening of authors' rights.[74] At the same time, these features secured the nascent regime from threats arising from shifting political or economic alignments.[75] With progressive harmonization as its fundamental organizing principle, the international copyright framework

---

[71] *See, e.g.,* Ruth L. Okediji, *Sustainable Access to Copyrighted Digital Information Works in Developing Countries, in* INTERNATIONAL PUBLIC GOODS AND TRANSFER OF TECHNOLOGY UNDER A GLOBALIZED INTELLECTUAL PROPERTY REGIME 162 (Keith E. Maskus & Jerome H. Reichman eds., 2005) [hereinafter Okediji, *Sustainable Access*].

[72] The articles were merged during the Berlin Revisions to the Berne Convention and codified as Article 20. In its current form, Article 20 provides "The Governments of the countries of the Union reserve the right to enter into special agreements among themselves, in so far as such agreements grant to authors more extensive rights than those granted by the Convention, or contain other provisions not contrary to this Convention. The provisions of existing agreements which satisfy these conditions shall remain applicable." Berne Convention, *supra* note 3.

[73] Okediji, *Sustainable Access, supra* note 71, at 154–56.

[74] *Id.*

[75] *Id.*

intentionally targeted and disciplined national discretion to adapt copyright law to specific institutional and cultural conditions.

Implicit in the earliest demands for international minimum copyright standards of protection was (and still is) the impulse to eliminate any trace of history, resource endowments, as well as culturally mediated ideas about authorship, from consideration in the national design of copyright law. Like neoclassical growth theory, copyright harmonization is driven by the fallacy that countries and societies start from the same values (or should), function within the same basic parameters (or eventually will), and will enjoy the same returns. If the result does not follow in some country, belief in the fallacy leads to blaming that nation's government as not having done enough to take care of rights holders.

Transplanting an internationally driven copyright regime to differently situated societies puts much more than authors at stake. An important body of scholarship has explored how the organization of traditional societies produced very different conceptions of "authorship" and "rights."[76] This body of work has also studied the disruption in developing and least-developed countries caused by the overlay of harmonized foreign copyright norms on deeply held local customs and beliefs about the creative process and use of creative products.[77] Much of this legal scholarship questions the conventional utilitarian account that creativity is largely a response to economic incentives.[78] Other threads in this body of scholarship highlight ways in which creativity may be structured and rewarded beyond the exclusive rights model employed in the Berne Convention.[79] Still others are concerned about how to accommodate pluralism in the design of copyright frameworks.[80] What has occupied far less scholarly attention is the displacement of the institutions that support creative activity in post-colonial societies.[81]

Much more pernicious than the disruption of local innovation methods was the disruption of institutions of creative activity – the values, techniques, and beliefs that formed distinctive cultures and that, in turn, sustained the norms that nourished

---

[76] *See, e.g.,* DRAHOS, *supra* note 4; Peter Drahos & Susy Frankel, *Indigenous Peoples' Innovation and Intellectual Property: The Issues, in* INDIGENOUS PEOPLE'S INNOVATION: INTELLECTUAL PROPERTY PATHWAYS TO DEVELOPMENT 1 (Peter Drahos & Susy Frankel eds., 2012); BOATENG, *supra* note 4; MICHAEL BROWN, WHO OWNS NATIVE CULTURE (2004); Gana, *supra* note 32.

[77] *See* Gana, *supra* note 32, at 141–42. *See also* DRAHOS, *supra* note 4.

[78] *See, e.g.,* JESSICA SILBEY, THE EUREKA MYTH: CREATORS, INNOVATORS, AND EVERYDAY INTELLECTUAL PROPERTY (2014); Mark A. Lemley, *IP in a World Without Scarcity,* 90 N.Y.U. L. REV. 460, 492 n.160 (2015) (citing sources).

[79] *See, e.g.,* Megan M. Carpenter, *Intellectual Property Law and Indigenous Peoples: Adapting Copyright Law to the Needs of a Global Community,* 7 YALE HUM. RTS. & DEV. L.J. 51 (2004).

[80] *See id.*

[81] *But see* Gana, *supra* note 32, at 128.

innovation in these societies.[82] Scholars, including myself, have talked about this disruption in the past tense – as a historical event that occurred at colonialism and then stopped. To the contrary, the "hyper-harmonization"[83] of copyright law, at the rate observed in the TRIPS Agreement and since, facilitates an ongoing and persistent erosion of systems of organization and social governance that stand at odds with copyright's utilitarian emphasis. This emphasis makes copyright particularly useful in the mobilization of capital in developed countries that, in turn, fuels political appetite for ever stronger copyright entitlements.[84] Copyright harmonization might thus be better understood as a reflection of, and reaction to, processes of globalization. Those processes compel the reorganization of factors of production in a way that privileges certain forms of creativity, especially those that can be commercialized on a large scale uninhibited by the demands of cultural or sociological values.[85]

That our dominant justifications for copyright law include its role in advancing the political and social conditions that make mobilization of capital possible, while also advancing values such as freedom of speech or privacy, curiously makes copyright law more palatable even to its harshest critics. These cherished liberal values gild the proverbial lily by presenting copyright law as both desirable and ideal for all countries. The erosion of native innovation cultures and innovation institutions thus continues unabated and appears, even to copyright minimalists, to be a small price to pay in exchange for promoting the causes of free speech, the public domain, or freedom of association. In the meantime, efforts to reap the supposed benefits of implanting copyright and other forms of IP more systematically in developing and least-developed countries also remain mostly unsuccessful, at least if measured by substantial improvements in levels of innovation in those regions.[86]

---

[82] See DRAHOS, *supra* note 4. *See also* Gana, *supra* note 32, at 140.

[83] DANI RODRIK, THE GLOBALIZATION PARADOX: DEMOCRACY AND THE FUTURE OF THE WORLD ECONOMY (2011) (using the term "hyper-globalization").

[84] *See* Cohen, *Copyright as Property in the Post-Industrial Economy, supra* note 33.

[85] *See id.* at 148 ("[T]he incentives for capital that copyright supplies support the mass culture industries and mass culture markets which in turn have distinct and well-studied substantive preferences and inclinations" (citations omitted)).

[86] Measures of innovation are notoriously difficult. One much criticized measurement is IP (patent and trademark) filings, which has serious shortcomings. Other measurements could be total factor productivity (TFP) which includes technology but much more. Here, I am referring to levels of patent filings, and also the capacity to absorb and use technical or scientific information to improve goods or services. A close review of IP statistics published by WIPO, and the yearly Global Innovation Index, shows the persistence of an innovation divide between high-income and low-income countries. *See* THE GLOBAL INNOVATION INDEX 2016: WINNING WITH GLOBAL INNOVATION (Soumitra Dutta, Bruno Lanvin & Sacha Wunsch-Vincent eds., 2016) [hereinafter GII]. *See also id.* at 149–68. Particularly interesting is the increase in the rate of foreign (nonresident) filings in middle-income developing countries. High rates of foreign filings usually demonstrate strategies to secure overseas markets, and to leverage exclusive rights against local or regional competitors. Many low-income countries do not have patent examination offices, but they offer the full term of exclusionary rights

This ongoing destabilization of institutions of creativity – the cultural fabric in which creative processes are unleashed and productively applied – may be one of the reasons for the ineffective exploitation of copyright regimes for wealth creation even in some of the leading developing countries.[87]

Conversely, global reinforcement of specific forms and standards of creativity through copyright harmonization, such as notions of "originality," requirements for "fixation" of works,[88] and the fetishizing of copying,[89] may be a significant reason for copyright law's tremendous capacity to attract capital in the developed countries, especially in the United States.[90] Copyright harmonization privileges and prioritizes the specific cultural context, institutional environment and value choices reflected in leading neoliberal societies. As a result, model features of copyright law derived from international minimum standards are ill-fitted for many of the institutional environments in which copyright is expected to take root and flourish.[91] Copyright law, when transplanted through processes of harmonization, must adapt to new cultural and institutional environments or face cultural and economic irrelevance.[92] In such relatively inhospitable conditions, harmonized copyright law cannot easily mobilize domestic mass culture in receiving countries, but it can serve as an instrument of

---

to patentees who obtain local protection simply by registering the patent in a regional office. *See, e.g.,* ORGANISATION AFRICAINE DE LA PROPRIÉTÉ INTELLECTUELLE (OAPI), www.oapi .int. Formed in 1977, the sixteen member states do not have patent granting systems. OAPI grants a single patent valid in all member countries. *See also* MARGO A. BAGLEY, RUTH L. OKEDIJI & JAY A. ERSTLING, INTERNATIONAL PATENT LAW AND POLICY 132–33 (2013). Other examples of "pure" registration systems include Nigeria, Uganda, and South Africa. *Id.* at 614–15. Such systems, while they can be more efficient administratively, "may fail to enhance the overall amount or quality of technical skill or information in circulation in the local market." *Id.* at 615. Moreover, weak IP administrative systems significantly undermine the ability of developing and least-developed countries to shape global IP rules and how those rules might undermine knowledge spillovers and other public interest or development gains from the patent system. *See generally* PETER DRAHOS, THE GLOBAL GOVERNANCE OF KNOWLEDGE: PATENT OFFICES AND THEIR CLIENTS (2010) (arguing that patent offices largely serve the interests of multinational companies).

[87] This point is analogous to Dani Rodrik's observation that open markets are successful only when they are embedded within social, legal, and political institutions that attract legitimacy because they represent a broad spectrum of the society. The need for such representation requires governments to intervene with more and effective regulation, broader social safety nets and, in the case of copyright, additional L&Es as needed. *See* RODRIK, *supra* note 83.

[88] The Berne Convention does not require fixation for the works enumerated in Article 2(1). However, Article 2(2) leaves it to the discretion of member states to require fixation as a condition of protection. As a practical matter, most countries have a fixation requirement for certain, but not all, categories of works. *See* Ricketson, *supra* note 35, at 239–43 (discussing protection for oral works and the compromise in Article 2(2) which arose in the context of fixation for choreographic works).

[89] *See* Litman, *supra* note 63.

[90] *See* Cohen, *Copyright as Property in the Post-Industrial Economy, supra* note 33 (arguing that copyright is better understood as an incentive for capital).

[91] *See* BOATENG, *supra* note 4. *See also* Gana, *supra* note 32.

[92] *See* BIRNHACK, *supra* note 4; BOATENG, *supra* note 4.

access to goods from those cultures in which copyright has been successful. In short, without appropriate limits, and absent mitigating national policies, copyright harmonization has disproportionately adverse effects in countries that are poor or institutionally weak, creating divergent development prospects even where countries arguably started with similar endowments.[93] The kind of deep harmonization and strong enforcement obligations contained in international IP frameworks, such as the TRIPS Agreement and other more recent plurilateral treaties,[94] are millstones around the proverbial necks of many developing and least-developed countries.

There are important benefits to the harmonization of basic copyright norms, particularly to encourage cross-border flows in knowledge goods.[95] Enforceable obligations by the state to recognize and enforce property entitlements influence decisions by firms about what kind of cultural goods to invest in, how much to invest, and where to invest. Further, in the digital economy, clearly defined rights – for users and creators – are important inputs in key decisions about the scalability of business models, how to navigate the competitive landscape, and the type of enforcement possible to preserve the highest returns on investment. However, to have positive effects for all countries, the international copyright framework needs to anticipate long-run outcomes from rules of copyright law when applied in different socioeconomic conditions. Or, alternatively, it should provide tools that can allow for flexible adjustment when it becomes clear that a particular set of rules will not produce desired outcomes.

There is no question that modern copyright harmonization is in tension with what contemporary growth theory suggests will best align with national development efforts. Copyright harmonization takes as fixed the conditions for creativity in all societies, regardless of institutions, knowledge, history, resource, or other endowments. It concludes that the only inputs needed for creativity to flourish are more exclusive rights, and wholly ignores not only other factors that may affect the productive use of knowledge, but also the broader context in which knowledge goods may or may not produce expected economic and social returns.

14.3.2 *Existing Limitations and Exceptions in the Berne/TRIPS Framework*

The project of harmonizing authors' rights necessarily affected the kind of L&Es recognized by the Berne Convention. The ad hoc approach to the public interest, and the absence of developing countries in the period of the Convention's expansion, produced a scheme of L&Es that insufficiently addressed development

---

[93] *See generally* Ray, *supra* note 12, at 470–72.
[94] *See Trans-Pacific Partnership, supra* note 6.
[95] P. BERNT HUGENHOLTZ & RUTH L. OKEDIJI, CONCEIVING AN INTERNATIONAL INSTRUMENT ON LIMITATIONS AND EXCEPTIONS TO COPYRIGHT 11 (2008).

needs. Further, existing international L&Es have not been retooled for the digital environment, creating both opportunities and challenges for developing and least-developed countries.

The Berne/TRIPS framework determines what L&Es can be adopted at the national level. In an earlier work, I analyzed the structure, content, and conditions of the L&Es in the Berne Convention.[96] To summarize briefly, there are two broad categories of Berne L&Es – compensated and uncompensated. This simple categorization has been upset by the extension of the three-step test that, as noted earlier, establishes the outer limits of sovereign discretion to adopt new L&Es. The three-step test under the TRIPS regime also subjects preexisting L&Es to challenge under prevailing WTO jurisprudence.[97]

A strong argument can be made, supported by historical evidence and state practice,[98] that L&Es existing in national laws prior to the 1967 revision to the Berne Convention are beyond the reach of the TRIPS Article 13 three-step test, which prohibits any L&Es unless they represent "special cases" that "do not conflict with a normal exploitation of the work" and "do not unreasonably prejudice the legitimate interests of the right holder." Arguably, one right that isn't within the scope of the historical carve-out is the reproduction right. I will return to this claim regarding carve-outs and its implications for development later. What is important to note here is the cloud of uncertainty generated by the three-step test regarding L&Es that states can legally adopt under current international rules.

Beyond the three-step test, the basic structure of L&Es in the Berne Convention remains important for how policymakers might craft and utilize new L&Es to promote economic growth and development. I focus first on uncompensated L&Es because adopting new L&Es in this category is likely to incur the strongest disapproval of the developed countries. Yet, uncompensated L&Es must be part of a newly configured international copyright framework, even for the developed countries.

(i) Uncompensated Limitations and Exceptions in the Berne/TRIPS Framework

Uncompensated L&Es are largely clustered around activities consistent with promoting or securing liberty interests. By ensuring that certain uses of copyrighted works are beyond authorial control, and can be undertaken at no economic cost,

---

[96] Ruth L. Okediji, *The International Copyright System: Limitations, Exceptions and Public Interest Considerations for Developing Countries* (UNCTAD-ICTSD Project on IPRs and Sustainable Development, Issue Paper No. 15, 2006), *available at* http://unctad.org/en/docs/iteipc200610_en.pdf.

[97] *See, e.g.,* Panel Report, *United States – Section 110(5) of the US Copyright Act,* WTO Doc. WT/DS160/R (June 15, 2000).

[98] *See* Vienna Convention on the Law of Treaties, art. 31(3)(b), May 23, 1969, 1155 U.N.T.S. 331. *See also* Appellate Body Report, *Japan – Taxes on Alcoholic Beverages,* ¶ 13, WTO Doc. WT/DS8,10,11/AB/R (adopted Nov. 1, 1996).

these L&Es encourage the liberal exercise of personal freedoms, encourage markets for book reviews, commentary, or criticism, which facilitate a robust marketplace of ideas, and they leave the basic building blocks of creativity – ideas and facts – in the public domain.

Some uncompensated L&Es reinforce copyright's subject-matter boundaries. For example, Article 2 of the Berne Convention, which defines literary and artistic works, excludes "news of the day" and "miscellaneous facts having the character of mere items of press information" from the Convention's ambit.[99] Such works can be the subject of *national* copyright laws; however, Berne Union countries are not under any obligation to protect authors of such works unless, consistent with the national treatment principle, domestic authors of such works are protected.[100]

The Berne Convention further leaves it up to member states to decide whether to grant copyright protection for "official texts of a legislative, administrative and legal nature, to official translations of such texts,"[101] and to decide whether "works of applied art and industrial designs and models" are entitled to copyright protection.[102] Finally, the Berne Convention allows countries to impose fixation as a threshold requirement for the protection of literary and artistic works[103] and to impose additional requirements for works of applied art, designs, and models.[104]

Beyond these subject-matter exclusions in the Berne Convention are what might be described as "liberty-enhancing" L&Es. These L&Es are crucial for the protection of individual autonomy and necessary for the realization of personal freedoms. In addition to empowering individual access and use of copyrighted works, liberty-enhancing L&Es recognize and protect institutions, such as the press, that are necessary to ensure wide dissemination of ideas.

For example, the Berne Convention leaves it to the discretion of member states to adopt legislation excluding, wholly or in part, "political speeches and speeches delivered in the course of legal proceedings" from the protection required by the Convention.[105] Also, member states can determine the conditions on which "lectures, addresses and other works of the same nature which are delivered in public may be reproduced by the press, broadcast, communicated to the public by wire and made the subject of public communication ... when such use is justified by the informatory

---

[99] Berne Convention, *supra* note 3, art. 2(8).
[100] *Id.* art. 5(3).
[101] *Id.* art. 2(4).
[102] *Id.* art. 2(7). *See also* J. H. Reichman, *Design Protection in Domestic and Foreign Copyright Law: From the Berne Revision of 1948 to the Copyright Act of 1976*, 1983 DUKE L.J. 1143, 1146 (1983).
[103] Berne Convention, *supra* note 3, art. 2(2).
[104] *Id.* art. 2(7). *See also id.* art. 7(4) (dealing with protection for photographs); Ricketson, *supra* note 35 (noting the strict application of the list of works in Article 2 of the Berne Convention).
[105] Berne Convention, *supra* note 3, art. 2bis(1).

purpose."[106] Moreover, the Berne Convention allows the free use of quotations, "provided that their making is compatible with fair practice, and their extent does not exceed that justified by the purpose, including quotations from newspaper articles and periodicals in the form of press summaries,"[107] the use of copyrighted works by way of illustration for teaching purposes,[108] and reproduction by the press ("the broadcasting or the communication to the public by wire of articles published in newspapers or periodicals on current economic, political or religious topics, and of broadcast works of the same character").[109]

These provisions of the Berne Convention allow member states to enact legislation permitting uses of copyrighted works on the conditions outlined.[110] In the context of news reporting under Article 10bis(2), a member state that enacts these L&Es is free to do so with no conditions at all.[111] Liberty-enhancing L&Es thus enable and facilitate competition, freedom of information, and political and cultural engagement.

Finally, countries may adopt uncompensated L&Es to the reproduction right, subject of course to the three-step test. The significant contestation over the scope and meaning of the test, and the uncertainty of whether a particular L&E satisfies the test, make reliance on this standard practically unworkable for many countries, including the developed countries. However, in practical terms, the flexibility granted by other provisions in the Berne Convention provides ample room to address a variety and diversity of liberty interests.[112] In my view, the inhibiting effect of the three-step test is directed at enacting new and/or non-liberty enhancing L&Es, including development-inducing L&Es.[113]

(ii) Compensated Limitations and Exceptions in the Berne/TRIPS Framework

Compensated L&Es in the Berne/TRIPS framework respond to a different set of concerns than the uncompensated L&Es summarized above. Article 11bis(1) and Article 13 address broadcasting rights and reproductions of musical works,

---

[106] *Id.* art. 2bis(2).

[107] *Id.* art. 10(1).

[108] *Id.* art. 10(2).

[109] *Id.* art. 10bis(1).

[110] Quotations under Article 10(1) may be made for any purpose and are subject only to the condition that the use should be consistent with expectations of fairness in light of the reason for which the quotation is being made.

[111] Article 10bis(2) provides "It shall also be a matter for legislation in the countries of the Union to determine the conditions under which, for the purpose of reporting current events by means of photography, cinematography, broadcasting or communication to the public by wire, literary or artistic works seen or heard in the course of the event may, to the extent justified by the informatory purpose, be reproduced and made available to the public."

[112] *See* Pamela Samuelson, *Justifications for Copyright Limitations and Exceptions, in* Copyright Law in an Age of Limitations and Exceptions, *supra* note 35.

[113] To be clear, compensated L&Es do not enjoy any special status vis a vis the three-step test. For historical reasons having to do with the evolution of the music industry, the international copyright

respectively. Article 11bis grants authors the exclusive right to authorize the broadcast of their works, or other communication to the public by "wire," "rebroadcasting," "loudspeaker," or "any other analogous instrument transmitting, by signs, sounds or images, the broadcast of the work."[114] Where an author withholds permission to exercise these rights, or for other reasons permission is unavailing, use of the work may occur on conditions determined by domestic law. In such cases, a competent authority must set equitable remuneration for the author.[115]

Similarly, under Article 13, a Berne member state can derogate from the general right of reproduction with regard to musical works.[116] So long as reproduction of the work and words was authorized by the author, subsequent reproduction by others is allowed if national law so prescribes. The Convention allows countries to establish conditions on the right to reproduce a musical work and the lyrics, subject to a right of remuneration which can be set by an independent authority. For example, in the United States, a compulsory license is available for a recording artist to make a "cover" (i.e., a mechanical reproduction) of a musical work written by someone else and released by a different recording artist.[117] These L&Es reflect consideration by Berne member states of the rival interests among various market actors in the music industry. To mediate those competing interests, the Convention allows countries to establish liability rules in place of exclusive rights, allowing authors and other actors in the recording industries to co-exist in a dense network of relationships that prevails in many countries today.

(iii) Implied Limitations and Exceptions in the Berne/TRIPS Framework

Finally, the Berne/TRIPS framework recognizes implied exceptions. The most notable relate to Article 11, which grants a public performance right to musical and literary works.[118] The L&Es applicable in this context are generally referred to as "minor reservations" or "de minimis" exceptions.[119] So-called minor reservations bear upon the scope of the public performance right, allowing states to permit activities such as public concerts at festivals, musical performances during church services, or concerts by military bands.[120]

---

framework allows countries to adopt somewhat different L&Es for musical works. With regard to other categories of works, the fact that compensation is paid to a rights holder will factor into the three-step test analysis, but will not, by itself, be sufficient to justify the L&E. See SENFTLEBEN, *supra* note 63.

[114] Berne Convention, *supra* note 3, art. 11bis(1).

[115] *Id.*

[116] *Id.* art. 13

[117] 17 U.S.C. § 115 (2012 & Supp. 2014).

[118] *See* Berne Convention, *supra* note 3, art. 11(1). Implied exceptions also apply to Articles 11bis, 11ter, 13, and 14.

[119] For the importance of the minor reservations doctrine, *see* Panel Report, *supra* note 97.

[120] *See* RICKETSON, *supra* note 59, at 533–37. Most of these L&Es cover practices that predated recognition of the public performance right in the Berne Convention.

Finally, there are implied exceptions to the right of translation, although there is far less clarity about the scope of this exception and state practice on this matter differs considerably.[121] The great divergence of practices suggests that developing and least-developed countries can exercise appreciable unilateralism in providing knowledge goods to citizens in local languages as needed. Yet, they do not.

(iv) Limitations and Exceptions in the Digital Copyright Regime

The case for more robust copyright L&Es in all countries has become more pressing than ever before. The constellation of rapid technological changes, cultural and social expectations, and the rise of new intermediaries have created opportunities for courts and administrative agencies to formulate and recognize new L&Es not explicitly authorized by the Berne Convention.

Shortly after the TRIPS Agreement, two new copyright treaties were concluded under WIPO's auspices. The WIPO Copyright Treaty (WCT)[122] and the WIPO Performers and Phonograms Treaty (WPPT)[123] are directed at the protection of authorial interests in the digital environment. As courts in the developed countries struggled to adapt copyright law to digital technologies, L&Es occupied center stage in a global battle over the terms on which the digital copyright landscape should be configured.[124] A large part of this battle was about how to share the economic returns associated with unprecedented opportunities to exploit knowledge and information goods.

The Agreed Statements to the WCT provide some clarification, and pay homage to the idea of a dynamic interpretation of the Berne Convention's universe of international L&Es.[125] Specifically, the Agreed Statements allow ratifying states "to carry forward and appropriately extend into the digital environment limitations and exceptions in their national laws which have been considered acceptable under the Berne Convention."[126] Moreover, states may "devise new exceptions and limitations that are appropriate in the digital network environment."[127]

---

[121] *See* Berne Convention, *supra* note 3, art. 11(2). *See also* SAM RICKETSON & JANE C. GINSBURG, INTERNATIONAL COPYRIGHT AND NEIGHBORING RIGHTS: THE BERNE CONVENTION AND BEYOND § 13.83 (2d ed. 2005) (noting the varying national interpretations and the illogical result of providing express limitations for reproduction rights but not for translation rights).

[122] WCT, *supra* note 6.

[123] World Intellectual Property Organization Performances and Phonograms Treaty, Dec. 20, 1996, S. TREATY DOC. NO. 105–17, 2186 U.N.T.S. 203 (1997).

[124] *See* Pamela Samuelson, *The US Digital Agenda at WIPO*, 37 VA. J. INT'L L. 369 (1997).

[125] Diplomatic Conference on Certain Copyright and Neighboring Rights Questions, *Agreed Statements Concerning the WIPO Copyright Treaty*, WIPO Doc. CRNR/DC/96 (adopted Dec. 20, 1996) [hereinafter Agreed Statements], www.wipo.int/edocs/mdocs/diplconf/en/crnr_dc/crnr_dc_96 .html.

[126] *Id.* concerning art. 10.

[127] *Id.*

New information and communication technologies and networked digital platforms hold great promise for human flourishing[128] even in the most desperate communities around the world.[129] These technologies facilitate a wide range of interactions, offering unprecedented opportunities for the expression of civil and political freedoms, wider cultural engagement, and new forms of social and economic retooling. Information technology platforms and the wealth of information and knowledge they enable constitute central drivers in the formation of new kinds of human and social capital.[130]

To the extent legal entitlements for authors impede use of or access to the wealth of technological and information goods available in a global digital economy, copyright law has earned a dubious reputation as an enabler of development and as a tool for public welfare.[131] This opprobrium is expressed keenly among a set of stakeholders dependent on L&Es to employ new business models, or to provide goods and services to consumers engaged in a wide range of productive activities. For these nontraditional stakeholders in the copyright system, assertions about restoring copyright's role to promote the public interest have far less to do with authorial interests and much more to do with their need for robust L&Es, especially L&Es adapted to the digital environment.

The Berne/TRIPS framework and the WCT are directed at legislative action by states. But courts, not legislatures, have been at the forefront of determining how to apply doctrines created for the print era to the digital arena. Not only has this involved considerations of how these doctrines "fit" new technologies, but new actors, new uses, and new interests have emerged to challenge many aspects of the traditional fabric of copyright law, including established definitions.

---

[128] *See generally* JULIE E. COHEN, CONFIGURING THE NETWORKED SELF: LAW, CODE, AND THE PLAY OF EVERYDAY PRACTICE (2012); OECD, SUPPORTING INVESTMENT IN KNOWLEDGE CAPITAL, GROWTH AND INNOVATION 35 (2013).

[129] *See, e.g.*, WORLD BANK, WORLD DEVELOPMENT REPORT 1998/1999: KNOWLEDGE FOR DEVELOPMENT (1999) [hereinafter WDR 1998/1999]; WORLD BANK, BUILDING KNOWLEDGE ECONOMIES: ADVANCED STRATEGIES FOR DEVELOPMENT (2007) [hereinafter BUILDING KNOWLEDGE ECONOMIES]; Richard Heeks, *ICT4D 2.0: The Next Phase of Applying ICT for International Development*, 41 COMPUTER 26 (2008); Richard Heeks, *Emerging Markets: IT and the World's "Bottom Billion,"* 52 COMMUNICATIONS OF THE ACM 22 (2009); OECD, SUPPORTING INVESTMENT IN KNOWLEDGE CAPITAL, GROWTH AND INNOVATION (2013).

[130] *See* Julie E. Cohen, *Configuring the Networked Citizen, in* IMAGINING NEW LEGALITIES: PRIVACY AND ITS POSSIBILITIES IN THE 21ST CENTURY 129 (Lawrence Douglas, Austin Sarat & Martha Merrill Umphrey eds., 2012). *See generally* COHEN, CONFIGURING THE NETWORKED SELF, *supra* note 128.

[131] *See e.g.*, Peter S. Menell, *This American Copyright Life: Reflections on Re-Equilibrating Copyright for the Internet Age*, 61 J. COPYRIGHT SOC'Y U.S.A. 235 (2014) (addressing the "dismal state of copyright's public approval rating").

In some developed countries, for example, the rise of citizen journalism has expanded the concept of "journalism" to website blogs and Twitter, and raised prospects for application of the Berne Convention's L&E for reporting current events to anyone who captures newsworthy items and shares them on social media.[132] The notion that only established media conglomerates or officially constituted communicative organizations can carry out journalistic functions simply has no staying power in a culture suffused with information that fuels all kinds of interaction – political, social, and economic.[133]

Adjudicated cases and administrative rulings provide limited guidance to users, but even courts and agencies lag behind the wealth of ingenuity catalyzed by information communication technologies. Seemingly inexhaustible new sources and forms of creative expression make it not only feasible, but inevitable, that the application of L&Es to new technologies will disturb previously settled notions of permissible conduct. Expectations of copyright law's boundaries for user behavior in digital space are being rapidly transformed as copyrightable content relentlessly mediates consumer interaction in every sphere of life. So, notwithstanding restrictions arguably imposed by the international copyright framework, developed countries are in an "age of experimentation"[134]; and they are flexing national discretion accordingly. Courts and, in a

---

[132] *See* England and Wales Cricket Board v. Tixdaq [2016] EWHC 575 (Ch) [114] (Eng.) (holding that section 30(2) of the U.K. Copyright, Designs and Patents Act of 1988 and article 5(3)(c) of the EU Information Society Directive "are not restricted to traditional media and that 'citizen journalism' can qualify as reporting current events"). *See also* Slater v. Blomfeld [2014] NZHC 2221, [2014] 3 NZLR 835 [54] (N.Z.) (concluding that a website blog can be a news medium if it disseminates news to the public about recent events of interest to the public and has a regular commitment to the publication of news); Leveyfilm v. Fox Sports, No. 13 C 4664, 2014 WL 3368893, at *10 (N.D. Ill. July 8, 2014) (finding that a citizen's use of an album cover image on her website was fair use on the basis of "news reporting" because it accompanied an article about an ongoing lawsuit associated with that album cover); Caner v. Autry, 16 F. Supp. 3d 689, 703 (W.D. Va. 2014) (finding that a citizen's act of uploading a video to YouTube was fair use for the purpose of criticizing a public figure and that "First Amendment protections, advanced by the fair use defense, have never applied to some bizarre oligarchy of 'qualified' speakers"); Patricia Aufderheide, *Journalists, Social Media and Copyright: Demystifying Fair Use in the Emergent Digital Environment*, 9 J. Bus. & Tech. L. 59, 69 (2014) (arguing that the current legal environment concerning fair use and news reporting sends "confusing signals about the expectations even of ordinary users and citizen journalists at a time when journalists are turning increasingly to [social media]").

[133] *See* Heythrop Zoological Gardens Ltd. v. Captive Animals Protection Society, [2016] EWHC 1370 (ch) [60] (Eng.) ("Today, campaigning organisations carry out an important journalistic function."). *See also Cool Story, Bro: Is Every Citizen a Reporter?*, Yale L. & Tech. (Nov. 13, 2011), www.yalelawtech .org/uncategorized/cool-story-bro-is-every-citizen-a-reporter ("With the rise of online journalism, barriers to entry in reporting have completely collapsed."); William F. Woo, *Defining a Journalist's Function*, 59 Nieman Rep. 31, 33 (2005), http://1e9svy22oh333mryr83l4s02.wpengine.netdna-cdn.com/ wp-content/uploads/2014/03/winter2005.pdf (arguing for a functional definition of journalism: "At its core, the functional definition of journalism is much like the functional definition of a duck. If it looks like journalism, acts like journalism, and produces the work of journalism, then it's journalism, and the people doing it are journalists. Whoever they are.").

[134] Ruth L. Okediji, *International Copyright Law Reform: Prospects and Pathways* (University of Minnesota Working Paper, 2016).

few cases, legislatures recognize that significant economic potential lies in empowering both authors and users of copyrightable content. There appears so far to be little appetite to curb the cultural and political engagement possible through access to information, thus making copyright L&Es central to the realization of any number of socio-economic policies and to the functioning and growth of consumer markets.[135]

Enumerated L&Es and open-ended standards, such as the fair use doctrine, are being stretched to accommodate the myriad possibilities for improving access to knowledge in a content-driven and data-saturated economy.[136] From debatable applications of the scope of transformative fair use[137] to recent decisions affirming the legitimacy of music sampling[138] and to protection for new ways libraries and cultural institutions may serve patrons,[139] national copyright L&Es are in flux. Moreover, legal construction of a zone of "user rights" has gained momentum in a number of countries,[140] and has increasingly captured the attention of copyright scholars.[141] Whether the law formally acknowledges it, users *are* forcing a change in copyright law. And this is good. Among other things, concerted efforts to position users more centrally in copyright law's discourse, something not quite envisioned by the Berne Convention, illustrate the imprudence of restricting the right to make national policy interventions. Ultimately, neither technological change nor user behavior can be fully cabined by international rules that bear no resemblance to the reality of daily life.

---

[135] *See* COHEN, CONFIGURING THE NETWORKED SELF, *supra* note 128, at 2–5.

[136] *See* Authors Guild v. Google, Inc., 804 F.3d 202 (2d. Cir. 2015), *cert. denied*, 136 S. Ct. 1658 (2016).

[137] *See* Cariou v. Prince, 714 F.3d 694 (2d Cir. 2013).

[138] *See* VMG Salsoul, LLC v. Ciccone, 2016 WL 3090780 (9th Cir. June 2, 2016); Bundesverfassungsgericht [BVerfG] [Federal Constitutional Court], 1 BvR 1585/13, May 31, 2016, www.bundesverfassungsgericht .de/SharedDocs/Pressemitteilungen/EN/2016/bvg16-029.html.

[139] *See* Authors Guild v. Hathitrust, 755 F.3d 87, 99 (2d Cir. 2014) (applying fair use and concluding "[w]e have no reason to think that these copies are excessive or unreasonable in relation to the purposes identified by the Libraries and permitted by the law of copyright. In sum, even viewing the evidence in the light most favorable to the Authors, the record demonstrates that these copies are reasonably necessary to facilitate the services HDL provides to the public and to mitigate the risk of disaster or data loss."). *See also Authors Guild*, 804 F.3d at 221 ("Complete unchanged copying has repeatedly been found justified as fair use when the copying was reasonably appropriate to achieve the copier's transformative purpose and was done in such a manner that it did not offer a competing substitute for the original ... If Google copied less than the totality of the originals, its search function could not advise searchers reliably whether their searched term appears in a book (or how many times)."); Uma Suthersanen, *Introduction to Part II 'Digital Libraries and Online Licensing,'* in GLOBAL COPYRIGHT: THREE HUNDRED YEARS SINCE THE STATUTE OF ANNE, FROM 1709 TO CYBERSPACE 169–75 (Lionel Bentley, Uma Suthersanen & Paul Torremans eds., 2010); Dame Lynne J. Brindley, *Phoenixes in the Internet Era – The Changing Role of Libraries*, in GLOBAL COPYRIGHT, *supra*.

[140] *See* Michael Geist, *The Canadian Copyright Story: How Canada Improbably Became the World Leader on Users' Rights in Copyright Law*, in COPYRIGHT LAW IN AN AGE OF LIMITATIONS AND EXCEPTIONS, *supra* note 35.

[141] *See e.g.*, Niva Elkin-Koren, *Copyright in a Digital Ecosystem: A User Rights Approach*, in COPYRIGHT LAW IN AN AGE OF LIMITATIONS AND EXCEPTIONS, *supra* note 35. Geist, *supra* note 140.

Some patterns of accepted user practices in relation to copyrighted works have emerged; these include use of works that facilitate access to knowledge, that reflect new forms of creativity, or that are important to the proper functioning of the Internet. In the developed countries, these wide ranging and diverse activities – from mass digitization projects to habitual posting of content on social media sites – are presumed to be justifiable within the Berne/TRIPS framework. It is not clear that the Berne/TRIPS L&Es can be extended this far, but it hardly matters since developed countries are less likely to be questioned about their motives for such L&Es. Nevertheless, not even under the most generous interpretation of the three-step test can many of the activities currently framed as user rights and freedoms, particularly activities on social media, be easily justified under the Berne/TRIPS framework.

In other regions, citizens engage in new activities in the digital arena without the pretense of legal cover. New services, new business models, and new ideas all flourish in a somewhat hedonistic digital culture. Consider, for example, the now routine practices of forwarding emails, embedding hyperlinks in text, uploading or downloading pictures and other media, or altering images to communicate new ideas and expression. Where the gap between user behavior and formal law increases to such an extent that conduct constituting formal violations of copyright law simply becomes an integral part of engagement with mass culture, efforts to assert authorial interests against these practices run the serious risk of further eroding public trust in the assertion that the rules exist for the public's welfare.[142] This erosion of public trust has already tempered copyright enforcement strategies in the digital era. But realizing the gains of copyright hedonism, and potentially building productive businesses around it – as we have seen happen with fair use – will eventually require clarity of norms and a more sustainable means to organize creative activities.

International copyright law is ill-suited to continue to provide the touchstone, as it now does, for determinations of the conditions that require adjustments to domestic copyright law, whether such changes are needed to eliminate barriers to economic growth, address social inequalities, or respond to rapid technological change.[143] Like its national counterpart in the developed countries, international copyright law must accommodate the needs and expectations of states in a globalized networked economy to effectuate legitimate social, cultural, and, especially, development objectives.

---

[142] *See id.; see also* Menell, *supra* note 131.
[143] *See* Hugenholtz, *supra* note 65 (noting "the increasing gap between the rules of copyright law in Europe and the social norms that are shaped by states of technology").

14.4 FINDING DEVELOPMENT IN THE INTERNATIONAL COPYRIGHT FRAMEWORK

14.4.1 *The Case for Development-Inducing Limitations and Exceptions*

Economists have placed important emphasis on human capital as a necessary input for innovation and economic development. In the Romer-Lucas model described in Section 14.2, investment in human capital is essential for the development of new knowledge and technologies.[144] Knowledge spillovers are critical for enhancing overall societal knowledge which, in turn, promotes technical change. In further elaborations of the fundamental insights of these scholars, several reports suggest that economic growth occurs (and is sustainable) in economies that make strong investments in human capital.[145] Such investment encompasses formal and informal education, ideally producing applicable and appropriable advancements in an economy with a research sector and a base stock of knowledge that enables the production of new information leading to final goods.[146] Romer's work eventually identified ideas (nonrival goods) as the primary source of economic growth.[147] He adverts: "[i]n a world with physical limits, it is discoveries of big ideas ... that make persistent economic growth possible. Ideas are the instructions that let us combine limited physical resources in arrangements that are ever more valuable."[148]

The size and quality of a country's human capital stock is affected by accessibility to the ideas contained in creative and scientific works. Although ideas are not copyrightable, the cultural goods that contain them are; people must be able to engage with these ideas in order to learn from and build on them. Formal education is one context in which this engagement best occurs. Government supply of education is especially important in a world where ideas are a dominant source of wealth

---

[144] *See* Lucas, *supra* note 18; RUTTAN, *supra* note 11, at 146–48; *see also* Joseph E. Stiglitz, *Knowledge as a Global Public Good*, *in* GLOBAL PUBLIC GOODS: INTERNATIONAL COOPERATION IN THE 21ST CENTURY 308, 312 (Inge Kaul, Isabelle Grunberg & Marc Stern eds., 2003) ("Initial knowledge is a key input into the production of further knowledge ...").

[145] *See* BUILDING KNOWLEDGE ECONOMIES, *supra* note 129. *See also* ANDREAS SAVVIDES & THANASIS STENGOS, HUMAN CAPITAL AND ECONOMIC GROWTH (2008); GII, *supra* note 86; Eric A. Hanushek and Dennis D. Kimko, *Schooling, Labor-Force Quality, and the Growth of Nations*, 90 AM. ECON. REV. 1184 (2000).

[146] *See* Romer, *Endogenous Technological Change*, *infra* note 185

[147] *See* Paul M. Romer, *Idea Gaps and Object Gaps in Economic Development*, 32 J. MONETARY ECON. 543 (1993). *See also* Paul M. Romer, *Why, Indeed, in America? Theory, History, and the Origins of Modern Economic Growth* (Bureau of Econ. Research Working Paper No. 5442, Jan. 1996).

[148] Paul Romer, *Two Strategies for Economic Development: Using Ideas and Producing Ideas*, 6 WORLD BANK ECON. REV. 63, 64 (1992), https://paulromer.net/wp-content/uploads/2013/10/Two-Strategies-for-Economic-Development-Using-Ideas-and-Producing-Ideas.pdf.

and productivity.[149] Copyright plays a role in government efforts to encourage and facilitate the spread of ideas because this is an integral part of copyright's structural function.[150] Reading a book and being able to apply the concepts, information, and ideas in the book to improve one's life are intrinsic aspects of any meaningful notion of access. Both are needed for education to have taken place.

In theory, educated consumers are better able to use L&Es to continue to improve their material well-being and to become productive members of society.[151] Education begins with literacy. According to one World Bank study, at least 30 percent of a population must be literate for development to occur.[152] Literacy may be achievable today without adjusting copyright laws since there are many works in the public domain that can help teach people how to read. But concepts of literacy should extend beyond the mere ability to read. Technological, social, and cultural literacy are key components of a country's productive capacity in the digital economy, including its capacity to absorb data effectively. For example, in a study of education reform in Senegal, the authors found evidence that tertiary education increased the income of graduates and decreased the mismatch between the quality of skills demanded and supplied.[153] Other studies reinforce the idea that access to knowledge and education is especially critical for a country's capacity to absorb technical information,[154] to leverage its comparative advantage in certain sectors,[155] and to cultivate a cadre of citizens sufficiently skilled to participate in global supply chains.

Access to knowledge does not require free access to knowledge goods, although cost certainly is a key determinant. In addition to cost, the terms of access (including literacy and availability in local languages) must ensure that educational attainment is available to as many citizens as possible. Without a sufficiently literate and educated society, countries simply cannot be well-positioned for growth and development in a global knowledge economy.[156] International copyright reforms are not the

---

[149] *See* Robert Barro & Jong-Wha Lee, *Sources of Economic Growth*, 40 CARNEGIE-ROCHESTER CONFERENCE SERIES ON PUBLIC POLICY 1 (1994).

[150] *See* Netanel, *supra* note 31.

[151] *See* Acemoglu, Johnson & Robinson, *supra* note 26.

[152] *See* BUILDING KNOWLEDGE ECONOMIES, *supra* note 129 (citing WORLD BANK, INFORMATION AND COMMUNICATION TECHNOLOGIES, POVERTY AND DEVELOPMENT: LEARNING FROM EXPERIENCE (2003)).

[153] *See* Dorothée Boccanfuso, Alexandre Larouche, & Mircea Trandafir, *Quality of Higher Education and the Labor Market in Developing Countries: Evidence from an Education Reform in Senegal*, 74 WORLD DEV. 412–24 (2015).

[154] *See id.*; *see also* Francesco Caselli & Wilbur John Coleman II, *The World Technology Frontier*, 96 AM. ECON. REV. 499 (2006).

[155] *See* Glenda Kruss, Simon McGrath, Il-haam Petersen & Michael Gastrow, *Higher Education and Economic Development: The importance of Building Technological Capabilities*, 43 INT'L J. EDUC. DEV. 22 (2015).

[156] *See* STANLEY L. ENGERMAN & KENNETH L. SOKOLOFF, ECONOMIC DEVELOPMENT IN THE AMERICAS SINCE 1500: ENDOWMENTS AND INSTITUTIONS (2011) (finding that education, suffrage,

only necessary policy initiatives to address the economic growth and development challenges of developing and least-developed countries, but the global copyright rules are an important piece of the puzzle. At a minimum, the global rules influence the extent to which countries can coordinate and encourage international knowledge diffusion.[157]

In sum, to meaningfully address development goals, copyright law must (1) facilitate the production of knowledge consistent with a robust public domain; (2) facilitate access to information; (3) assist in the formation of human capital and absorptive capacity by; (4) supporting access to knowledge and education. These conditions for development are not novel to Africa, Asia or the Americas: all countries have, at different points in history, had these same requirements. The importance of these conditions – particularly access to education – for development were recognized long ago by the developing countries. However, historical efforts to adapt the international copyright framework to tackle this issue have repeatedly failed.

14.4.2 *Past Efforts to Address Development Interests in the Berne Convention*

The most serious efforts to address the needs of developing and least-developed countries within the international copyright framework date back to the 1967 Stockholm Revision. There, members of the Berne Union reluctantly agreed to a Protocol establishing a compulsory licensing scheme to facilitate access to copyrighted works for developing countries.[158] For these countries, facing the need to educate large populations and build literate societies, bulk access to copyrighted works and in local languages was a high priority. None of the preexisting L&Es in the Berne Convention could accommodate such uses, and nothing in the history of the Berne Convention afforded guidance for bulk access and use of copyrighted works.

---

and land policies are the most important explanations for the divergence in the development and growth paths of the Caribbean and Latin America).

[157] *See* CLAUDIA GOLDIN & LAWRENCE KATZ, THE RACE BETWEEN EDUCATION AND TECHNOLOGY (2008) (arguing that economic advancement in the United States over the last two centuries has been a race between technology and education).

[158] See Berne Convention, *supra* note 3, app. *See also* Barbara A. Ringer, *The Stockholm Intellectual Property Conference of 1967*, 14 BULL. COPYRIGHT SOC'Y U.S.A. 417 (1966–1967) (describing the process leading up to the Stockholm Revision as "five full weeks of crises and continuous negotiation … Signing ceremonies at the end of major diplomatic conferences are supposed to be formal occasions aimed at relieving tensions, healing wounds, and restoring harmony, but this one was different … [P]hotographers caught some worried looks. It was becoming apparent that after weathering a hurricane and making it into the harbor the Stockholm Conference was in some danger of sinking at the dock.")

This was not a surprise. As discussed earlier, most developed countries were sufficiently mature by the time the Berne Convention evolved to the point of constraining their ability to freely use foreign copyrighted works for local educational needs.
Others, notably the United States, simply stayed outside of the Union long enough
to have adopted most of its domestic L&Es. Indeed, when the United States ratified
the Berne Convention,[159] long after most developing and least-developed countries,
it was presumptively insulated from any expectation that its domestic L&Es would
change.[160] Thus, in significant ways, it is the shared cultural and political sensibili-
ties of the developed countries that has most deeply shaped the ideology and normative substance of the international copyright framework; it has been those countries'
need for, experience with, and historical bargains over L&Es that shaped the Berne
Convention's modern orientation. These countries made sure that the international
copyright framework did not prevent them from using copyright as part of a national
policy toolkit to advance their economic growth and development.

The situation was very different for developing countries. The Stockholm Protocol
addressed the need for bulk access to copyrighted works by allowing those countries
to issue compulsory licenses "for the purpose of teaching, scholarship, or research"
with a right to compensation set at rates appropriate for the using country.[161] It also
permitted compulsory licenses for producing translations of protected works.

Once described as an instrument "patched together at the last minute with spit
and chewing gum," the Stockholm Protocol was destined to fail.[162] Only three
countries (all of them developing) ratified the entire Stockholm Protocol; nine
countries (all developed) rejected the Revision; and twenty-six countries accepted
only the administrative provisions.[163] The principal reason was economic; at stake
was the future of textbook markets in countries with large populations. Publishers
were firmly resistant to the compromise that made it possible for developing countries to join the international copyright system.[164] That resistance was expressed
strongly to the governments of the exporting countries, resulting in domestic pressure to reject the Protocol.[165]

---

[159] *See* The Berne Convention Implementation Act of 1988, Pub. L. No. 100–568, 102 Stat. 2853 (1988).

[160] *See* Ruth L. Okediji, *Toward an International Fair Use Doctrine*, 39 COLUM. J. TRANSNAT'L L. 75
(2000) (noting that the international community, including WIPO, did not dispute the compatibility
of the fair use doctrine because it wanted the United States to join the Berne Convention).

[161] *See* Berne Convention, *supra* note 3, app. art. II(5).

[162] *See* Ringer, *supra* note 158, at 428–33 (describing the main provisions of the Protocol).

[163] *See* Okediji, *Sustainable Access*, *supra* note 71, at 157.

[164] *See* Ringer, *supra* note 158, at 429 (citing to and partially quoting Ronald E. Barker, Secretary of the
British Publisher's Association). *See generally* Ndéné Ndiaye, *The Berne Convention and Developing
Countries*, 1 COLUM.-VLA J.L. & ARTS 47 (1986–1987); Irwin A. Olian, Jr., *International Copyright
and the Needs of Developing Countries: The Awakening at Stockholm and Paris*, 7 CORNELL INT'L L.J.
81 (1973–1974).

[165] *See* Ringer, *supra* note 158, at 418 (noting that there was "an explosion of angry comments in the
English press" in reaction to the Appendix).

The emphatic disfavor of the influential private sector foreclosed any possibility that developed countries would support the exercise of the rights granted in the Protocol.[166] In the 1971 Paris Revision to the Berne Convention, the Protocol was replaced by the Berne Appendix.[167] The Berne Appendix established a complex system for compulsory licensing of copyrighted works also to address bulk access needs in the developing and least-developed countries.[168] It did not fare much better than the Protocol. As a source of international copyright law to advance economic growth and development, the Appendix, like the Protocol before it, has also been a failure.[169] On the rare occasion that an importing country sought to use the Appendix, the risk of reprisals or trade sanctions forestalled such efforts.[170]

Nonetheless, the Appendix is still part of the international copyright framework.[171] Continuing reference to the Appendix in major international copyright instruments strongly supports claims that the rights recognized remain an important part of the governing international rules.[172] How to extricate these rights from the complex system in which they are entangled, so they can be sensibly used to address the development challenges for which they were formulated, remains a central challenge of international copyright law.

14.4.3 Why Does Copyright's Development Role Require an International Solution?

Reaction to the unprecedented mandatory rules for IP protection in the TRIPS Agreement elicited immense backlash among human rights advocates and nongovernmental organizations. A global network of civil society, human rights advocates, and nongovernmental organizations emerged after the TRIPS Agreement to claim the international copyright system as a vehicle for human development.[173] This

---

[166] *See id.* at 429–30.

[167] *See* Berne Convention, *supra* note 3.

[168] *Id.* app. *See, e.g.*, Okediji, *Sustainable Access, supra* note 71, at 162.

[169] *See* Okediji, *Sustainable Access, supra* note 71.

[170] *See* Alberto Cerda Silva, *Beyond the Unrealistic Solution for Development Provided by the Appendix of the Berne Convention on Copyright* 23–24 (Pub. Int. J. Intell. Prop. Research Paper No. 2012-08, 2012)

[171] *See e.g.*, TRIPS Agreement, *supra* note 6; Agreed Statements, *supra* note 125.

[172] *See* Ringer, *supra* note 158, at 433 ("The fundamental alternative facing the delegates at Stockholm was whether to enlarge the base of the Berne Union to accommodate all of the countries of the world, importers as well as exporters, or whether, to preserve the requirements for the traditionally high-level protection as the price of admission to the Berne. The choice, in a way, was between compromising or even sacrificing authors' rights under certain circumstances as against barring a substantial part of the world from the copyright club ..."). *See also* Abraham L. Kamenstein, *Statement of the U.S. Delegation on the Berne Convention*, 14 Bull. Copyright Soc'y U.S.A. 435, 436 (1966–1967) ("A country at a certain stage of development is faced with alternatives, and the immediate needs and demands of its citizens obviously have to take first place.").

[173] *See* Amy Kapczynski, *The Access to Knowledge Mobilization and the New Politics of Intellectual Property*, 117 Yale L.J. 804 (2008).

loosely organized and effective international coalition was partly a project of resistance to the capture of global rulemaking processes by private economic interests.[174] But it was also an advocacy movement, galvanized by the threat to the human aspirations of developing and least-developed country citizens posed by property-like entitlements in knowledge goods. "Access to knowledge" and "access to medicines" became organizing heuristics for challenges to IP policy choices that left millions dying or unable to participate in social, economic, or cultural life because they were unable to afford the costs of books and medicines.

This network of actors and its allies also sought to challenge the influence of rights holders over the norm-setting processes that shaped the production of knowledge goods in the developed countries. The concept of a "global public interest" came to represent concerns about national and international copyright norm-setting processes. The domestic public interest that justified national copyright laws in most of the industrialized countries, and concern for development objectives in the least-developed countries, were blended in the global efforts to resist further expansion of copyright protection. "Development" and the "public interest" became synonymous in the advocacy strategies directed against copyright maximalism, at least partly in recognition that effective resistance would require coordination of national and international strategies. Since the TRIPS Agreement, this resistance has largely focused on the scope of copyright L&Es.

As noted earlier, the L&Es established in the Berne/TRIPS framework, and that are allowed in the national laws of WTO members, speak principally to the values important to liberal democratic societies. While many of these L&Es are also important for human flourishing, the capacity to exploit them for productive purposes requires (or assumes) a set of conditions that are yet to emerge in many developing and least-developed countries. More importantly, those conditions may not emerge for a long time – not only because domestic legal or constitutional traditions may lean heavily against them, but also because the institutions needed to support the exercise of L&Es need to be cultivated. At least two reasons having to do with the conditions in many developing and least-developed countries urge action for international L&Es that are specific to development. These are coordination problems and the lack of institutions that can channel returns to the appropriate sectors.

(i) Coordination Problems
Coordination problems exist when there is a structural misalignment between government policies and the regulatory frameworks in place to achieve intended policy objectives. For example, institutions that secure private property or that provide

---

[174] *See generally* SUSAN K. SELL, PRIVATE POWER, PUBLIC LAW: THE GLOBALIZATION OF INTELLECTUAL PROPERTY RIGHTS (2003).

education for women are critical for creating efficient and inclusive labor mar-kets.[175] However, if there are no effective methods to secure and enforce property rights, or if gender discrimination precludes women from joining the labor force, the institutions that support property or women's education will not produce ideal returns in that society.[176]

All countries have some coordination problems, but these are particularly acute in environments characterized by weak institutions, under-enforcement of laws, and under-investment in research and development (R&D). These features are pres-ent in many developing countries, and especially in the least-developed countries. In developing countries that exhibit strong coordination problems between institu-tions and markets, almost any government intervention can produce externalities that further cripple growth prospects.[177] Implementing international copyright rules domestically, without appropriate L&Es, is just one example.

Coordination problems require regulatory frameworks that reconcile policy objectives with institutional design, most usually through some form of government intervention. Copyright classically serves such a function, and is well understood as a type of government intervention to address a public goods problem.[178] The classic utilitarian justification for copyright law goes something like this: entitlement-like protection provides incentives for individuals to engage in creative processes, but levels of protection higher than necessary to induce investment in the produc-tion of knowledge goods depresses social, cultural, and technical advancement.[179] Moreover, a complete absence of legal protection insufficiently encourages invest-ment in the creative enterprise.[180]

That is all fine and good. But there are other coordination problems related to the design of copyright law. For example, without L&Es copyright enforcement may inhibit even those uses that are socially desirable, including criticism, social commentary, and free speech. Moreover, copyright owners could limit competi-tion by preventing copying that is necessary for developing interoperable consumer

---

[175] *See id.*
[176] *See* Hernando de Soto, The Mystery of Capital: Why Capitalism Triumphs in the West and Fails Everywhere Else (2000).
[177] *See* Hoff & Stiglitz, *supra* note 14.
[178] *See* Stiglitz, *supra* note 144, at 312.
[179] *See, e.g.,* Stan J. Liebowitz & Richard Watt, *How to Best Ensure Remuneration for Creators in the Market for Music? Copyright and Its Alternatives,* 20 J. Econ. Surv. 513, 525–37 (2006) (discuss-ing economic and technological alternatives (or additions) to copyright to obtain remuneration and protection for creative works). *See also* Jane C. Ginsburg, *The Role of the Author in Copyright,* in Copyright Law in an Age of Limitations and Exceptions, *supra* note 35 (discussing self-publishing by authors and alternative pricing models to obtain remuneration for creative works, including "pay-what-you-want" schemes and "freemium" subscription models).
[180] *See id.*

products.[181] Either copyright L&Es permit such conduct or countries have to adopt other regimes, such as antitrust, to address abuses of the monopoly position that property entitlements may afford.

The insight that enforcement of property rights is not always optimal is a familiar one.[182] Negative externalities associated with copyright protection and enforcement can produce coordination problems, the correction of which requires a mix of institutions and resources. L&Es can serve as levers that prevent or mitigate these externalities, better enabling copyright law to produce socially optimal returns. But if the international copyright framework constrains adoption of domestic L&Es, as it currently does, those externalities can be significant and, in turn, lead to other coordination challenges.

A good example is L&Es in national copyright laws to support access to educational materials.[183] The scenario is not complicated; in most countries, the cost of educational materials for primary education is borne by the government.[184] In low-income countries, the cost of such materials can be prohibitive, contributing to low quality education. The situation usually worsens as children advance from primary school to tertiary education where the cost of textbooks makes them inaccessible to most families. An insufficiently educated workforce has implications for the labor market and for domestic productivity.[185] Firms are unable to employ workers with suitable technical skills,[186] and so are less likely to adopt technologies that require skilled labor.[187]

In the absence of copyright L&Es, and absent fiscal resources that enable governments to fully subsidize the cost of education, enforcement of copyright in educational materials produces negative effects on the size of the labor market

---

[181] See Pamela Samuelson, *The Past, Present and Future of Software Copyright Interoperability Rules in the European Union and United States*, 34(3) Eur. Intell. Property Rev. 229 (2010).

[182] See David de Meza & J.R. Gould, *The Social Efficiency of Private Decisions to Enforce Property Rights*, 100 J. Pol. Econ. 561 (1992).

[183] See WIPO, Standing Comm. on Copyright & Related Rights, *Study on Copyright Limitations and Exceptions for Libraries and Archives*, WIPO Doc. SCCR/30/3 (June 10, 2015) (prepared by Kenneth D. Crews), www.wipo.int/edocs/mdocs/copyright/en/sccr_30/sccr_30_3.pdf.

[184] See *Economics of Education*, World Bank (Aug. 25, 2014), www.worldbank.org/en/topic/education/brief/economics-of-education ("The provision of schooling is largely provided and financed by governments.")

[185] See Paul Romer, *Endogenous Technological Change*, 98 J. Pol. Econ. S71 (1990). *See also* Peter Klenow, *Ideas versus Rival Human Capital: Industry Evidence on Growth Models*, 42 J. Monetary Econ. 3 (1998); Expert Group on Future Skills Needs, Tomorrow's Skills: Towards a National Skills Strategy (National Skills Strategy Research Rpt. No. 5, 2007) (discussing the situation in Ireland), www.dhet.gov.za/Archive%20Manuals/Ireland/Towards%20a%20national%20skills%20strategy.pdf#search=McGrath.

[186] See See Boccanfuso, Larouche & Trandafir, *supra* note 153.

[187] See Caselli & Coleman, *supra* note 154 (finding a relative skill bias in cross-country technology differences).

because fewer citizens can be educated. Other negative effects on the labor market include depressed wages, in turn exacerbating gaps between rich and poor (potentially with racial, gender, or ethnic implications), and reinforcing dysfunctional institutions.[188]

This unadorned account of the potential effects of lack of access to educational materials is to make clear a simple point: educational L&Es can help to address distributional considerations by making it likely that more families can afford to educate their children.[189] At a minimum, mandatory educational L&Es (which I argue for below) provide a strategic baseline for governments that wish to bargain with publishers over the price of educational materials. Such L&Es could also, for example, safeguard policy space to adopt special rules (such as local production of textbooks) to enhance access to the latest scientific and technical educational resources. Moreover, within this same L&Es space, governments likely could explore a range of policy options to address areas where poverty levels mean citizens can only afford a price of zero for educational materials.

It is possible to consider the inability of a household to pay for available educational materials as an externality – one arising from the inability, for example, to borrow against future income, get the desired level of education, and pay society back in the future through income taxes. This view, however, ignores the role of education in empowering members of society as a good in itself. Enabling citizens to develop a range of capabilities and to exercise a variety of rights is also essential for development. A robust body of economic research has shown that sustained production and use of knowledge is a material determinant of productivity and economic growth.[190]

In a world in which countries are obligated to maintain and enforce strong copyright laws, getting copyright policy "right" – that is, identifying and implementing the appropriate mix of legal, regulatory, and technological tools – is a critical aspect of ensuring that coordination problems related to copyright are minimized, and that copyright potentiates ideal rates of consumption of a wide range of cultural goods.

---

[188] *See generally* Tazeen Fasih, Linking Education Policy to Labor Market Outcomes 8–9 (2008); Paula S. Rothenberg, Beyond Borders: Thinking Critically About Global Issues 324–25 (2005); Michael W. Elsby, Bart Hobijn & Aysegul Sahin, *The Labor Market in the Great Recession* (Nat'l Bureau of Econ. Working Paper No. 15979, 2010).

[189] *See* Susan Isiko Strba, A Model for Access to Educational Resources and Innovation in the Developing World, *in* Intellectual Property, Trade and Development: Strategies to Optimize Economic Development in a TRIPS-Plus Era 287, 288 (Daniel J. Gervais ed., 2d ed. 2014).

[190] *See* Derek H. C. Chen & Carl J. Dahlman, *Knowledge and Development: A Cross-Section Approach* (World Bank Policy Research Working Paper No. 3366, Aug. 2004), http://info.worldbank.org/etools/docs/library/117333/37702_wps3366.pdf.

(ii) Institutions

Since Douglass North's path-breaking work, the study of institutions has played a significant role in analyses of prospects for growth-inducing economic organization.[191] Institutions are generally defined as formal laws, rules, and legal frameworks. The lack of institutions, or the presence of weak institutions, can make externalities a major challenge for development.[192] Economists have shown that coordination failures caused by the lack of institutions and exacerbated by other factors (history, culture, ethnic rivalries, etc.) are particularly challenging for development progress and need to be carefully addressed.

Legal scholars and economists have made the case for institutions, including strong property rights, as important drivers of economic growth.[193] This rationale has been extended with equal force to intellectual property rights. But as already noted, where property enforcement is maximized, with no L&Es or other mitigating policies, countries may actually *lose* expected development benefits because there are no institutions to channel those benefits.

Consider the example of coordination problems in R&D spillovers.[194] Spillovers can have strong positive effects on the production of technology in other firms and ultimately improve the overall production of consumptive goods.[195] How does this happen? Mechanisms such as L&Es facilitate leaks of privately conducted research into the commons or "public pool." This may occur as a result of many other factors such as employee mobility,[196] publications,[197] or in the course of educational training (both formal and informal). One of the most important ways that leaks occur, however, is via a robust public domain. In principle, the more aggregate private research is conducted, the greater the stock of ideas from which every producer can

---

[191] *See* Douglass C. North, Institutions, Institutional Change, and Economic Performance (1990). *See also* Institutions, Property Rights, and Economic Growth: The Legacy of Douglass North (Sebastian Galiani & Itai Sened eds., 2014).

[192] *See* Acemoglu, Johnson & Robinson, *supra* note 26.

[193] *See generally* Acemoglu & Robinson, *supra* note 44; Douglass C. North, Structure and Change in Economic History (1981); Adam Smith, The Wealth of Nations (Edwin Cannan ed., 1994).

[194] *See* Hoff & Stiglitz, *supra* note 14, at 401.

[195] *See id.; see also* Lucas, *supra* note 18; Mark Lemley & Brett Frischmann, *Spillovers*, 107 Colum. L. Rev. 257 (2006).

[196] Edward M. Bergman & Uwe Schubert, *Spillovers and Innovation, Environment and Space: Policy Uncertainties and Research Opportunities, in* Spillovers and Innovations: Space, Environment and the Economy 157 (Gunther Maier & Sabine Sedlacek eds., 2005).

[197] *See, e.g.*, National Institutes of Health, *NIH Public Access Policy*, U.S. Dept. of Health & Human Serv. (last updated Mar. 18, 2014), https://publicaccess.nih.gov.

draw.[198] More producers of knowledge goods can lead to greater competition and net welfare gains to society. And the more that aggregate research is driven by a robust public domain, the greater the range and diversity of ideas and products likely to arise as a result.

The number of cell phone applications available today is an example of net welfare improvements associated with a commons, in which neither copyright nor patent laws are barriers to software developers who must deploy their goods on existing proprietary technological platforms. In the *Oracle v. Google* litigation,[199] Oracle sought damages against Google for the latter's use of its copyrighted software. Although Google initially sought to license the software, negotiations were unsuccessful.[200] Google nevertheless copied 7,000 lines of code to ensure interoperability.[201]

As Professor Wendy Gordon argues, the use of L&Es to limit the scope of Oracle's copyright claims was essential for preserving the patent/copyright divide, ensuring that certain kinds of knowledge remain free of copyright's easy grant of long-lived exclusivity. She goes further to argue for a limit that would make such determinations much earlier in litigation, facilitating entry of competitive (or complementary) goods in the market, and reducing the economic costs imposed on a defendant. For small or foreign companies, defending a lawsuit against Oracle, or against other technology giants would have been improbable, even though the public gain could be significant.

The Federal Circuit's decision "increase[d] the ability of market leaders to use copyright law to lock out competition in a functional market – and to lock their customers, their suppliers, and producers of complementary products into patterns that might be privately profitable, but inefficient or otherwise undesirable from a social perspective."[202] Professor Gordon's argument that copyright owners should have no prima facie rights over copying of functional works, nor over copying "done solely for goals unrelated to the expressiveness of the plaintiff's work of authorship,"[203] reinforces the importance of copyright law's design. The

---

[198] *See* Hoff & Stiglitz, *supra* note 14, at 401. *See also* Romer, *Increasing Returns and Long-Run Growth, supra* note 18, at 1007.

[199] *See* Wendy J. Gordon, *How Oracle Erred: The Use/Explanation Distinction and the Future of Computer Copyright, in* Copyright Law in an Age of Limitations and Exceptions, *supra* note 35 ("The world would look far different than it does if copyright law covered functional expression without limit.").

[200] Oracle Am., Inc. v. Google, Inc., 750 F.3d 1339, 1350 (Fed. Cir. 2014).

[201] *Id.*

[202] *See* Gordon, *supra* note 202.

[203] *See id.* at 376.

Ninth Circuit, applying the fair use doctrine, affirmed Google's right to copy the lines of code, in effect acknowledging the welfare benefits of permitting Google's behavior.

Reasonable minds will differ over whether this outcome is consistent with the universe of L&Es in Berne/TRIPS. The point is that even in the most innovative and productive industrialized countries, courts and legislators have rationalized, or, perhaps ignored, what may be inconsistencies between domestic L&Es and Berne/TRIPS obligations.[204] In fact, most developed countries do not look to the Berne/TRIPS L&Es as the final arbiter of what constitutes appropriate domestic copyright policy, whether in respect to domestic L&Es or other copyright doctrines. This is especially true of the United States, but increasingly, also, of the European Union.

This subtle irreverence for the ostensibly disciplining authority of the Berne Convention is not just an arrogant exercise of sovereign power; it could be a proper exercise of sovereign responsibility for promoting the welfare of its citizens. Developing countries should be allowed to do the same. In some cases, developing countries should be mandated to do the same. The right to devise, test, retool, and constantly improve domestic copyright laws and policies should be unequivocally recognized in international copyright law.

14.5 THE CASE FOR DEVELOPMENT-INDUCING LIMITATIONS AND EXCEPTIONS

14.5.1 *Distinguishing the Public Interest, Creativity and Development*

The questions that occupy development and growth economics strongly implicate the objectives and rules of copyright law. Yet, rarely are the copyright policy options or legislative choices recommended for developing and least-developed countries examined in view of relevant insights from these subfields.[205] Whether current models of copyright law play the same role in economic growth in all societies is an unresolved and under-studied question.[206] And the abysmal results of over six decades of copyright and "development" advice from a wide range of sanguine international actors appear not to have made an impression on those same actors

---

[204] *See, e.g.,* Panel Report, *supra* note 115.

[205] For an important exception, *see* Chon, *supra* note 8. *See also* Ruth Gana Okediji, *Copyright and Public Welfare in Global Perspective*, 7 IND. J. GLOBAL LEGAL STUD. 117 (1999).

[206] *See* B. ZORINA KHAN, THE DEMOCRATIZATION OF INVENTION: PATENTS AND COPYRIGHTS IN AMERICAN ECONOMIC DEVELOPMENT 1790–1920 (2009). *See also* Frank Thadeusz, "No Copyright: The Real Reason for Germany's Industrial Expansion?," SPIEGEL ONLINE INTERNATIONAL (Aug. 18, 2010,

who mostly continue to advocate IP policies that have been domestically unworkable.[207] Perhaps it is because the other challenges to development – corruption, weak or nonexistent institutions, infrastructure deficits, and the failure to invest in public goods – seem to be far more substantial problems than copyright law. And indeed they are.

But countries are still making investments in copyright law and administration; indeed, TRIPS obligations require it. Any developing country accused of a TRIPS violation cannot point to the well-known, overwhelming development challenges in defense, nor will those challenges forestall authorized trade reprisals that will undoubtedly follow noncompliance with TRIPS. If countries cannot point to the more obvious (and arguably more urgent) development challenges to justify their failure to comply with TRIPS rules, then those rules must continue to attract enduring scrutiny for their role – however small – in constraining environments that best advance human flourishing.

The economic development question is especially significant in light of unrelenting pressure for developing and least-developed countries to adopt the strongest levels of copyright protection, despite persistent knowledge and innovation gaps between them and the developed countries.[208] A different, new set of L&Es in international copyright law could help address these gaps. To do so, however, development-inducing L&Es must address different kinds of users, a larger scale of use, including by government agencies, and the cost of bulk access to copyrighted works. The existing landscape of international copyright L&Es does not deal with these types of considerations, and consequently is insufficient to aid the development process.

Earlier in Section 14.2, I discussed the fact that although conceptions of the public interest existed in some domestic copyright laws, there was no systemic effort to identify or coordinate the different national policy objectives to formulate an ideal of the international public good in the Berne Convention. The choice to limit the international copyright system to identifying a minimum basis for the protection of copyrighted works was an intentional means of empowering states to

---

04:52 PM), www.spiegel.de/international/zeitgeist/no-copyright-law-the-real-reason-for-germany-s-industrial-expansion-a-710976.html; Linsu Kim, Learning and Innovation in Economic Development (1999); Nagesh Kumar, *Intellectual Property Rights, Technology and Economic Development: Experiences of Asian Countries* (Commission on Intellectual Property Rights, Study Paper 1b, 2002).

[207] With respect to Africa, the same observation could be said of most post-independence policy recommendations. *See, e.g.,* Owusu, *supra* note 27. *See also* Jonathan D. Ostry, Prakash Loungani & Davide Furceri, *Neoliberalism: Oversold?,* 53 Fin. & Dev. 38 (2016) (focusing on failures of capital account liberalization and austerity policies).

[208] *See* GII, *supra* note 86, at 111–12.

adopt locally relevant policies that could most secure the stable progress of their own societies. In other words, states were (and still are) responsible for working out their own notions of the public good.

A regime requiring the protection of authorial works in all countries had the benefit of discouraging cross-border copying; it also served to encourage states to invest in cultivating an authorial class of their own. In addition to significant investments in public goods, investment in a domestic institutional culture also materialized through the adoption and exercise of L&Es. Today's developed countries shaped their domestic copyright law to match specific national interests; to the extent those interests reflected values and policy goals that stood in tension with the rights of creators, the tensions were typically addressed through L&Es. Any L&E so adopted was, by default, treated as part of the "public interest" zone permitted by the international framework for states to operate unilaterally. Thus in most developed countries, the public interest came to mean whatever different interest groups could successfully wrest from the scope of copyright protection, usually through a process of legislative compromise. That the international framework both permitted and facilitated a country-specific definition of the public interest was a crucial aspect of the Berne Convention's foundational success, particularly since copyright law could not run afoul of values that reinforced the political and cultural underpinnings of liberal states.[209]

In short, the traditional account that holds that the copyright legislation and policy tools of commonwealth countries were designed to advance some thoughtfully conceived idea of the public interest in a way different from the civil law countries may be exaggerated.[210] But there is some evidence that in its early years in common law countries, copyright was tolerated because the alternatives seemed worse,[211] and because many important goals besides the production of creative works were encompassed within copyright law's framework.[212]

---

[209] See, e.g., Netanel, *supra* note 31, at 341–64.

[210] *See generally* PAUL GOLDSTEIN & P. BERNT HUGENHOLTZ, INTERNATIONAL COPYRIGHT: PRINCIPLES, LAW, AND PRACTICE 19–22 (3d ed. 2013) (observing significant overlap between continental droit d'auteur systems and copyright systems in some respects). *See also* Paul Edward Geller, *International Copyright: The Introduction*, in INTERNATIONAL COPYRIGHT LAW AND PRACTICE 13, 15–16, 27 (Lionel Bently ed., 2015) ("Conventional wisdom distinguishes between the laws of copyright and of authors' rights. However . . . key issues are best analyzed as arising in closely interrelated families of such laws, in which copyright and authors' rights often overlap.").

[211] *See* Thomas Babington Macaulay, *Speech in the House of Commons* (Feb. 5, 1841), *in* SPEECHES AND LEGAL STUDIES: THE COMPLETE WORKS OF THOMAS BABINGTON MACAULAY 235, 240–41 (1900) ("It is good that authors should be remunerated; and the least exceptional way of remunerating them is by a monopoly. Yet monopoly is evil. For the sake of the good we must submit to the evil; but the evil ought not to last a day longer than is necessary for the purpose of securing the good.").

[212] *See id.* at 251–52.

Authorial protection has, therefore, always served private interests while also advancing state interests in a variety of other areas, including education, freedom of the press, privacy, and cultural policy.

There is considerable variation among developing and least-developed countries' capacity to leverage the international framework to promote public and private interests equally. Even when L&Es are styled as rules – thus requiring little or no institutional sophistication to apply them – rarely are they invoked by the developing and least-developed countries. In particular, least-developed countries are ineffective in asserting their rights of residual sovereignty to shape domestic implementation of international copyright L&Es. Reasons for this include the misalignment between the design of copyright law and the domestic institutional environment.[213] Other reasons relate to the failure of policymakers to adopt policies that strategically integrate IP in national development planning, including the failure to encourage consumers to access and use knowledge goods.

One might logically inquire why developing countries do not adopt the posture of the developed countries and simply graft L&Es that facilitate development into their national laws. In my view, the need for government agencies to be actively involved in leveraging L&Es for development, and the scale at which access and use of works must occur for human capital formation, makes it highly unlikely that development-inducing L&Es can be informally adopted or casually deployed. Something more formal is needed to both encourage and defend efforts by willing countries to use copyright law as part of a strategic industrial policy in the digital and non-digital arenas. Now that it is clear that trade, not authors, provides the dominant rationalization for international copyright rules, developing and least-developed countries are entitled to no less of an opportunity than the developed countries had to strengthen their competitive abilities for the knowledge economy by reframing international copyright L&Es as development policy.

Two preliminary points provide helpful support for my arguments that current international L&Es and related conceptions of the public interest are insufficient for development purposes.[214] First, while the Berne/TRIPS framework allows for uncompensated L&Es, countries may choose to provide compensation to rights holders. Countries may not, however, convert compensated L&Es into uncompensated access regimes. Compensation is conventionally viewed as a legitimate interest of a rights holder; stripping copyright owners of the right to demand compensation for use of

---

[213] *See supra* Section 14.3.
[214] A major area where the Berne L&E framework and TRIPS is especially insufficient is in response to the needs of science. *See* Jerome H. Reichman & Ruth L. Okediji, *When Copyright Law and Science Collide: Empowering Digitally Integrated Research Methods on a Global Scale*, 96 Minn. L. Rev. 1362 (2012).

their works would, at the least, be considered a violation of the minimum standards model. Such an act certainly would be deemed a violation of the three-step test.[215]

Second, the existing body of uncompensated L&Es (liberty-enhancing) recognized in the international framework provides an important set of limitations to copyright law that benefits all countries. Even for developing countries that are currently unable to usefully engage those L&Es, the breadth of activities they support in the developed countries makes knowledge and information more richly available in global markets. Uncompensated L&Es serve as important signposts for the importance of limits to copyright's bundle of entitlements. Free uses, in particular, signal that the societal interests at stake are too significant to subvert solely to authorial interests. These are all important antecedents for development-inducing L&Es. By using a combination of standards and rules for uncompensated L&Es, the international framework appears to provide ample flexibility to shape the contours of domestic copyright laws and to infuse those laws with locally relevant norms and values.

Copyright L&Es carry immense potential for effecting an innovation culture within the distinctive and relatively weak or nonexistent institutional environment prevalent in developing and least-developed countries. Limitations and exceptions consistent with local institutional conditions, and which map onto domestic values, are more likely to strengthen domestic capacity for the production of knowledge goods, while also providing essential support for development planning. Moreover, for development purposes, L&Es must address issues of scale, cost, and language. In regards to resolving issues of scale, this could mean, for example, that liability rules may be preferable to property rights in certain sectors such as education or scientific publishing; or it may mean that where the supply of public goods is implicated, regulatory interventions in conjunction with industry "best practices" could be a significant improvement over the status quo.

Examples already exist in developed countries such as the adoption of best practices in documentary film making, various fair use guidelines, and other forms of private-ordering.[216] These flexible pathways to norm-setting in developing and least-developed countries are important, not only to provide much needed clarity in fledgling markets, but also to foster the embrace of legal or technological disruptions

---

[215] *See* TRIPS Agreement, *supra* note 6, art. 1 ("Members may, but shall not be obliged to, implement in their law more extensive protection than is required by this Agreement, provided that such protection does not contravene the provisions of this Agreement.").

[216] *See, e.g.,?* Documentary Filmmakers Statement of Best Practices in Fair Use, *available at* http://cmsimpact.org/wp-content/uploads/2016/01/Documentary-Filmmakers.pdf; CONFERENCE ON FAIR USE, FINAL REPORT (1998), Appendix J, *The Fair Use Guidelines for Educational Multimedia*, *available at* www.uspto.gov/sites/default/files/documents/confurep_o.pdf.

that catalyze innovation. As soft instruments, guidelines encourage experimentation in the specific contexts in which L&Es need to be deployed, and they facilitate more seamless integration of local values into transplanted copyright rules. Additionally, such tools can help formalize customs and practices that, although widely practiced, lack legal certainty and thus are less helpful as evidence of alternative policy approaches to regulating creative industries.

The Nigerian film industry provides a useful example of how culturally coherent L&Es and private ordering can facilitate domestic innovation structures. Ranked by some sources as among the top three movie industries in the world based on volume of movies and revenues,[217] this industry, dubbed "Nollywood," so far has thrived "outside of copyright."[218] The industry's success is in large part due to the socially complex space compelled by Nigeria's tenuous mix of formal and informal rules of governance in economic transactions. This profoundly cultural project is governed by informal networks of power, where relationships operate to secure sufficient returns to investment against a backdrop of weakly enforced laws.[219] In this environment, neither creators nor financial investors look to copyright law to inform business models or to shape economic relationships that are defined much more by ethnicity and class than by legal norms.

Many of the doctrines of copyright law, particularly its emphasis on the centrality of the author and exclusive rights, would reconfigure and disrupt strongly held traditional expectations (such as the right to lay claim on, or otherwise share a relation's property). Conventional copyright discourse cannot be easily reconciled with deeply embedded institutions, including extended familial relations or kinship ties, that permeate business relations and secure longstanding distribution networks for cultural goods. These ties are far more powerful than legal code. And while kinship networks may find little room in the Berne Convention's vision for copyright law, they function within a set of informal copyright L&Es that served to facilitate, and then later consolidate, the basis for this remarkable film industry. These "L&Es" include an exception to the exclusive right

---

[217] Funke Osae Brown, *Nollywood Improves Quality, Leaps to N1.72trn Revenue in 2013*, BUSINESS DAY ONLINE (Dec. 24, 2013), www.businessdayonline.com/nollywood-improves-quality-leaps-to-n1-72trn-revenue-in-2013; Jake Bright, *Meet 'Nollywood': The Second Largest Movie Industry in the World*, FORTUNE (June 24, 2015), http://fortune.com/2015/06/24/nollywood-movie-industry.

[218] Nonetheless, industry stakeholders have persistently sought stronger copyright protection. *See* Bright, *supra* note 217.

[219] Interview with Nollywood Producer Charles Igwe, Workshop on Nigeria's Digital Economy and the Copyright System: Challenges and Opportunities for Strategic Growth in the Information Age, Ikeja, Lagos, Nigeria (June 15, 2015).

to distribute, exceptions to the right to reproduce and to publicly perform and display works, as well as various forms of what might loosely be called 'fair use.'

Nollywood's remarkable success often is used to illustrate limits of the incentive rationale for copyright law. This explanation misses at least two very significant things. First, as I have already noted, kinship and relationship networks may explain the limited role of copyright in Nollywood's success. The high likelihood of repeated interaction between agents disciplines behavior far more effectively than weakly enforced copyright laws.

Second, it is precisely because copyright law, through L&Es, leaves ideas and other public domain materials "free as the common air" to be used by others, that Nollywood creators can exercise the creative discretion they do. These creators did not formally rely on the L&Es allowed by the Berne/TRIPS framework – most Nollywood business and creative leaders likely are unaware that those L&Es even exist in Nigerian copyright law. Rather, local institutions and values had *already* schooled consumers and creators to ignore any attempt to enclose mass culture, and instead to understand sharing, borrowing, and remixing practices as legitimate (or at least uncontrollable) exercises of creativity. As one of Nollywood's leading producers described it, "we were learning the rules set by the rest of the world – not because we wanted to follow those rules, but because we wanted to break them. The [Nigerian] economy would simply not support what those rules required, so we learnt very well what the Americans, Chinese, the Indians and so on, were doing. And then we returned to Nigeria and we [shattered] all of that to become what we are today."[220] In short, intense competition, not copyright, shapes and directs lawful creative activity in this dynamic industry.

A similar account can be told of the rise of tecnobrega in Brazil.[221] There, as in Nollywood, creative business models facilitated by networks of distributors leveraging specific cultural conditions, expectations, and practices made this music genre a distinctive global phenomenon.[222] These national examples suggest that strong proprietary grants that conflict with innovation structures informed by cultural values may actually suppress, not incentivize, innovation. The business models of creative industries in the global South that defy copyright's key assumptions can do more than offer powerful illustrations of the fact that authorial incentives

---

[220] *See* Kate Douglas, *Meet the Boss: Charles Igwe, CEO, Nollywood Global*, HOW WE MADE IT IN AFRICA (Nov. 19, 2014), www.howwemadeitinafrica.com/meet-the-boss-charles-igwe-ceo-nollywood-global.

[221] RONALDO LEMOS & OONA CASTRO, THE PARAENSE TECNOBREGA OPEN BUSINESS MODEL (2008).

[222] Chris McGowan, *The Muse of Tecnobrega Boosts Brazil's Latest Musical Export*, HUFFINGTON POST: THE BLOG (Jan. 9, 2012), *available at* www.huffingtonpost.com/chris-mcgowan/tecnobrega-brazil_b_1079308.html.

need not comprise the strongest property rights possible. These business models, and the competition that follows their adoption,[223] also offer assurances that policymakers should consider narrower copyright protection in order to incentivize investments in other kinds of innovation, such as in new kinds of funding models or in new distribution strategies. Both Nollywood and tecnobrega have contributed positively to economic growth and development; these sectors employ more people, create more cultural goods, and invest in technologies more than copyright theory suggests is possible without a system of strong entitlements.

In short, international copyright law's irreverence for local creative systems can influence choices by firms about where to direct investments, what form those investments are likely to take and what technology is selected and deployed in the production and distribution of cultural goods. It may mean, as it has in Brazil, Nigeria, and elsewhere, that firms who otherwise might rely on copyright to provide high returns on their economic investments are less likely to replace tested and proven traditional systems with transplanted copyright rules that are devoid of cultural legitimacy. Such a swap likely would not be good business sense, at least not in the short run.

International copyright law's irreverence for the local also undermines the possibility of reconciling copyright – including L&Es – to domestic institutional capacity. As a result, locals and policymakers are far less vested in copyright than they otherwise might be. Ignoring copyright has worked so far for Nollywood and, perhaps, a few other industries, but it may not work for all. Reconciliation of copyright rules and domestic institutions may encourage domestic private interests to harness copyright tools to create conditions that enable human development and enable flourishing of a wide range of sectors and industries.[224]

14.5.2 *Mismatched Berne/TRIPS Limitations and Exceptions*

Developing and least-developed countries need different L&Es than those that are likely to attract the indulgence of their developed country trade partners, or the deference of multilateral dispute settlement processes. One difference lies in the beneficiaries of L&Es for development. In most developing countries, and certainly in

---

[223] *See* Bright, *supra* note 217 (describing how numerous countries in sub-Saharan Africa now offer different platforms for distribution of film content).

[224] *See* G.A. Res. 70/1, Transforming our World: the 2030 Agenda for Sustainable Development (adopted Sept. 25, 2015) (creating the Sustainable Development Goals to "end poverty, protect the planet, and ensure prosperity for all," www.un.org/sustainabledevelopment/sustainable-development-goals).

the least-developed countries, schools, libraries, and museums, where they exist, are the most likely (and sometimes the only) gateways to knowledge acquisition. These institutions should be direct targets of international copyright L&Es, but currently are not. In addition to the institutions that should be targeted, development-inducing L&Es must differ in kind, in scale, and in form (rules versus standards). Because much of what we know about the development process centers on the foundational role of education and access to knowledge, particularly for long-term growth,[225] international copyright L&Es for educational institutions should be mandatory.

There are at least five important reasons why the legacy of L&Es from the international copyright framework has proven ineffective from a development perspective. First, the flexibility of the various types of L&Es in the Berne/TRIPS framework requires domestic legislation for citizens to meaningfully experience or exploit them. They are written too broadly to give direction to individual users, and so member states must translate them domestically. This is a challenge for countries that lack institutional capacity to engage meaningfully with these rules. Moreover, domestic implementation of the rules requires some exercise, however minimal, of national discretion.

The uncertainty involved with regard to the specific limits of that discretion, and the real risk of drawing unfavorable attention from industries in the developed countries, makes the effort to apply Berne/TRIPS L&Es seem ill-advised to policymakers in developing countries. Judicially developed L&Es under flexible standards, such as the fair use doctrine, or L&Es promulgated by administrative tribunals or agencies in the developed countries may avoid the scrutiny of WTO trading partners. However, such political grace is far less likely to be extended to the practices and customs (arguably L&Es in their own right) that abound in developing and least-developed countries.

Burdened by the TRIPS progeny, enacting domestic L&Es is now, at best, a risky and uncertain enterprise given the three-step test.[226] There have been important initiatives, such as the Max Planck Declaration on the Three-Step Test,[227] and other extraordinary scholarly efforts demonstrating the test's malleability.[228] These arguments rarely penetrate the circles of policymakers in the developed countries. It is their opinions that matter most since they are the ones who communicate threats to their counterparts in developing or least-developed countries.

---

[225] *See supra* Sections 14.3, 14.4, and 14.5. *See also* Building Knowledge Economies, *supra* note 129; WDR 1998/1999, *supra* note 9.

[226] *See* TRIPS Agreement, *supra* note 6, art. 13.

[227] *See* Christophe Geiger et al., *Declaration: A Balanced Interpretation of the "Three-Step Test" in Copyright Law*, 39 Int'l Rev. Intell. Prop. & Competition L. 707, 708 (2008).

[228] *See* Christophe Geiger, Daniel J. Gervais, Martin Senftleben et al., *The Three-Step-Test Revisited: How to Use the Test's Flexibility in National Copyright Law*, 29 Am. U. Int'l L. Rev. 581 (2014).

Nor do scholarly arguments sway the political elite in developing countries, whose interaction with international "experts," with international institutions offering funds for "capacity building," or whose exposure to political pressure (including threats of retaliation) almost routinely result in retreat from ambitious copyright law reform initiatives. The stalled Brazilian copyright reform[229] and the controversial efforts of the South African government to overhaul its copyright law are recent examples.[230] In the current global environment, the presumption of flexibility and compromise possible at national levels seems to have disappeared and has been replaced, instead, with the chilling effect of the three-step test and other trade pressures.[231]

Second, even if political realities empowered states to define the application of Berne/TRIPS L&Es in their territories, the nature of these L&Es cannot fully support economic growth and development. Only two of the L&Es contemplated in the Berne/TRIPS framework have direct implications for the formation of human capital: the teaching and the translation exceptions.[232] These L&Es impact the technical and cultural capacity of poor countries to engage with, absorb, and productively utilize new knowledge assets developed in richer countries.[233] Nonetheless, the L&Es have rarely been exercised by the developing and least-developed countries.

Third, there seems to be little appetite internationally for addressing the application of Berne/TRIPS L&Es to the digital environment. Professor Justin Hughes's caution about the potential difficulty for countries to translate flexible standards into domestic gains[234] is equally applicable to the digital arena. Adapting international L&E standards to the digital context presupposes a level of legal and technical proficiency that simply is lacking, certainly in the least-developed countries. Given these practical conditions, the WCT's preservation of domestic policy space to develop

---

[229] *See* INTERNATIONAL INTELLECTUAL PROPERTY ALLIANCE, *Brazil, in* 2016 SPECIAL 301 REPORT ON COPYRIGHT PROTECTION AND ENFORCEMENT 66–75 (2016), www.iipawebsite.com/rbc/2016/2016SPEC301BRAZIL.PDF (identifying 2015 as a year of legislative stasis on copyright issues and recommending attention to enforcement reform legislation in 2016). *See also* Mariana Giorgetti Valente & Pedro Nicoletti Mizukami, *Copyright Week: What Happened to the Brazilian Copyright Reform?*, CREATIVE COMMONS (Jan. 18, 2014), https://br.creativecommons.org/copyright-week-en (explaining that Brazil's copyright reform process lost momentum due to Brazil's political turmoil and civil society's shift of focus to other priorities, such as privacy and surveillance).

[230] *See Inside Views: South Africa: New Prominent Pro-IP Academic Comes Out Against Government*, Intellectual Property Watch (Mar. 23, 2016), www.ip-watch.org/2016/03/23/south-africa-new-prominent-pro-ip-academic-comes-out-against-government-2. *See also* Charlie Fripp, *Final Text of Copyright Amendment Bill to be Put Before Parliament This Month*, HTXT.AFRICA (July 7, 2016), www.htxt.co.za/2016/07/07/copyright-bill-parliament-july (providing a.pdf of the bill and explaining that it has been both praised and criticized).

[231] *But see* Geiger, Gervais & Senftleben et al., *supra* note 209, at 581–626.

[232] *See supra* Section 14.4.

[233] *See* GII, *supra* note 86.

[234] *See* Hughes, *supra* note 49.

new L&Es in the digital context rings hollow. The extent to which developing and
least-developed countries access digital knowledge goods will depend in large part
on the exercise of L&Es and user behavior in the developed countries that makes
cultural goods available in global markets.

Fourth, international L&E standards typically envision *individual* uses related to
private exercises of liberty. Even with institutional capacity, liberty-promoting L&Es
require political commitment to a certain vision of a progressive society. Economic
growth can aid in the social transformation that usually precedes embrace of liberal
values in traditional societies. L&Es that can fuel such growth arguably should be
prioritized in the short term, moreso since liberty-enhancing L&Es are not designed
to provoke commitments to liberalism, but instead more likely suggest that those
commitments already exist.

Finally, with the diminished powers of countries to shape copyright law for locally
distinct environments, the old model of deference to nationally determined L&Es,
while international rules prescribe ever stronger rights for copyright holders, is simply unworkable for development. This model preys on the weaknesses of importers
of knowledge goods who lack institutional capacity to adopt, utilize, and enforce
the international L&Es. As already noted, these countries also face distinctive challenges in their domestic institutional environment.

I propose a different model for development progress. I suggest rule-like L&Es
at the international level that can be implemented flexibly in the local context.
Moreover, some of these international rules should be mandatory for all countries,
ensuring that spillovers from the developed countries can further improve the volume and quality of knowledge goods circulating in global markets.

14.6 REFRAMING INTERNATIONAL COPYRIGHT LIMITATIONS AND EXCEPTIONS FOR DEVELOPMENT

14.6.1 *Steps toward a Redesign of International Copyright Law*

Justifications for copyright law have managed to remain intact despite significant
shifts in the understanding of economic growth and development. Moreover,
resistance by the developed countries to policy interventions that can support
development goals through copyright law has become stronger at precisely the
time when dynamic technological change urges flexibility in the international
copyright framework. The prospects for developing and least-developed countries to benefit from global R&D spillovers, to participate in international scientific collaborations, and to reduce the innovation divide are brighter than at
any other time in history. Turning these prospects into realizable gains, in part,

requires addressing barriers to knowledge acquisition and facilitating the diffusion of knowledge across borders. International copyright law is not the only hurdle to these goals, but it is an important one. Efforts by various stakeholders to address the global knowledge and innovation gap would benefit from renewed attention to the international copyright framework and, especially, a redesign of international copyright L&Es.

Scholars usually describe L&Es as purposive tools to aid copyright law in achieving its public interest ends.[235] This view has been important in efforts to counter the dominance of copyright maximalism in developed countries. But it may have done disservice to the needs of developing and least-developed countries. L&Es can help correct copyright's tilt toward stronger property rights; but designing L&Es primarily as balancing tools is a second-best approach to resolving a fundamental mismatch between what society formally desires from copyright – production and dissemination of cultural goods – and the multifaceted and complex institutional demands that are vital to the development process. Conceiving of L&Es as a tool to achieve copyright goals reduces the pressure to design copyright to serve socially beneficial goals. It allows copyright law to grow unhindered because, after all, it is assumed that whenever there is an imbalance, some L&E will fix it.

If copyright law is to have an important role in promoting economic growth and development, it has to look different in developing countries. International copyright law should both enable and support this difference. After all, international copyright law is a social institution. And like all social institutions, there is an expectation that it will be fair and will facilitate attainment of collective and individual goals under conditions most conducive to the fullest expression of human flourishing.

Below I offer a set of possible first steps toward aligning international copyright law for development.

(i) Strict Enforcement of Copyright's Boundaries in a Local Context

The literature on endogenous growth has important implications for the design of copyright law. First, copyright's idea/expression distinction[236] is much more fundamental to development than one might expect. Although the principle has only recently been codified in international copyright law,[237] most developed countries have long recognized copyright protection only in expressive works of authorship

---

[235] *See e.g.*, Shyamkrishna Balganesh, *Foreseeability and Copyright Incentives*, 122 HARV. L. REV. 1569, 1578 (2009); DAVID L. LANGE and H. JEFFERSON POWELL, NO LAW: INTELLECTUAL PROPERTY IN THE IMAGE OF AN ABSOLUTE FIRST AMENDMENT (2009). *See also* Eldred v. Ashcroft, 537 U.S. 186 (2003).

[236] *See* TRIPS Agreement, *supra* note 6, art. 9(2) ("Copyright protection shall extend to expressions and not to ideas, procedures, methods of operation or mathematical concepts as such.").

[237] *See id.*

and not in the underlying ideas.[238] And since copyright legislation in developing and least-developed countries is rarely drafted by local experts, but involves direction and commentary from WIPO, the idea/expression distinction is typically featured in the laws of these countries as well. This is the good news.

One might rationally think of the idea/expression distinction as sufficient to address the emphasis on ideas as the most important driver of economic growth.[239] Certainly, excluding ideas from copyright protection is a key part of maintaining a robust public domain from which all creators can freely draw. But the idea/expression distinction needs to be implemented locally to favor scientific use and discovery in these countries. Leading arguments for the public domain emphasize this productive function.[240] If the public domain furthers creative production because it makes the building blocks of creativity accessible, then a disciplined copyright system tailored to the formal and informal structures of the local community is essential to improve the size, quality, and diversity of the public domain.

(ii) Harmonizing the Education Exception

The central role of education in economic growth and development has already been mentioned, but it can hardly be overstated. In the digital context where panic over copyright's deficiencies for the digital age led to new international rights being grafted onto the copyright system, countries nevertheless still acknowledged the need for balancing the rights of authors against "the larger public interest, *particularly education*, research, and access to information."[241] Even in the developed countries, educational L&Es fall far short of what they should be to prepare citizens for a knowledge economy.[242]

---

[238] *See* GOLDSTEIN & HUGENHOLTZ, *supra* note 111, at 220 ("Every mature system withholds protection from ideas ...").

[239] *See* Romer, *The Origins of Endogenous Growth, supra* note 19, at 1004.

[240] *See* Jessica Litman, *The Public Domain*, 39 EMORY L.J. 965 (1990). *See also* James Boyle, *The Second Enclosure Movement and the Construction of the Public Domain*, 66 LAW & CONTEMP. PROBS. 33 (2003).

[241] *See* WCT, *supra* note 6, preamble.

[242] *See, e.g.*, William McGeveran & William W. Fisher, III, *The Digital Learning Challenge: Obstacles to Educational Uses of Copyrighted Material in the Digital Age* (Berkman Center Research Publication No. 2006–09, Aug. 2006), http://ssrn.com/abstract=923465. *See also* Andrew J. Rotherham & Daniel Willingham, *21st Century Skills: The Challenges Ahead*, 67 EDUC. LEADERSHIP 16 (2009) (addressing challenges arising from the fact that the U.S. copyright regime locks up content and creates immobilizing certainty for educators, which is in direct contrast to what educators feel twenty-first-century students need); U.S. GOV'T ACCOUNTABILITY OFFICE, GAO-05-325SP, 21ST CENTURY CHALLENGES: REEXAMINING THE BASE OF THE FEDERAL GOVERNMENT 23 (2005) ("If we are to compete effectively in a growing, knowledge-based economy, our educational system must equip children with appropriate skills to meet high standards and provide means for adults to continue to learn new skills and enhance their existing abilities.")

The education exception, such as it is, remains one of the least harmonized areas in the international copyright system.[243] Ordinarily this should be advantageous for developing countries given the arguments I've made in this chapter about the challenges of harmonization. But in this instance harmonization would actually be incredibly useful for all countries.[244] In this regard, much work needs to be done.

There is no single L&E for education in the Berne/TRIPS framework. Instead, there are L&Es that support activities relevant to education.[245] These include, for example, L&Es for personal use and the quotation right. Limitations and exceptions for personal use in relation to educational activities are the most well-established provisions in the national laws of Berne member states.[246] There are also L&Es that address reproduction for educational purposes, school performances, and recordings of educational communications such as for online classes.[247] The collage of liberty-enhancing L&Es in the international copyright framework covers most uses of copyrighted works by individual students or instructors, particularly when those activities take place in the context of formal classroom instruction and training.

But L&Es for education fall far short of what should exist, and of what could reasonably improve government efforts to supply education. For example, there are no specific L&Es for schools or educational institutions as such, nor for making copies for students or for distributing protected works. There are no L&Es addressing circumvention of technological protection measures or rights management information for educational purposes.[248] Other than the Berne Appendix,[249] there are no specific provisions for translation of educational materials, which is an important issue for many developing and least-developed countries.

---

[243] *See* WIPO, *Study on Copyright Limitations and Exceptions* for *Libraries* and *Archives, supra* note 183.

[244] *See* Ruth L. Okediji, Presentation at the University of California Berkeley Symposium: Copyrightable Subject Matter in the Next Great Copyright Act (Apr. 4, 2014) (partial transcript available, http:// tushnet.blogspot.com/2014/04/next-great-copyright-act-conference.html) (calling for an unequivocal copyright exception for education in U.S. copyright law). *See also* Kevin L. Smith, *Of Bundles, Bindings, and the Next Great Copyright Law: Peer to Peer Review,* LIBRARY J. (Apr. 17, 2014), http://lj .libraryjournal.com/2014/04/opinion/peer-to-peer-review/of-bundles-bindings-and-the-next-great-copyright-law-peer-to-peer-review.

[245] *See* Okediji, Presentation at the University of California Berkeley Symposium: Copyrightable Subject Matter in the Next Great Copyright Act, *supra* note 244; McGeveran & Fisher, *supra* note 242; U.S. GOV'T ACCOUNTABILITY OFFICE, *supra* note 242.

[246] *See* DANIEL SENG, DRAFT STUDY ON COPY RIGHT LIMITATIONS AND EXCEPTIONS FOR EDUCATIONAL ACTIVITIES (World Intellectual Property Organization, May 2016).

[247] *Id.; see also* Smith, *supra* note 244; M. Mitchell Waldrop, *Massive Open Online Courses, aka MOOCs, Transform Higher Education and Science,* SCIENTIFIC AMERICAN (Mar. 13, 2013), www .scientificamerican.com/article/massive-open-online-courses-transform-highereducation-and-science.

[248] SENG, *supra* note 246.

[249] *Id.*

The state of affairs regarding L&Es for education requires serious attention from governments and from the international copyright framework. The cost of knowledge as well as other requirements that shape how knowledge can be used are shaped by copyright obligations that, too often, constitute barriers to educational institutions, teachers, and students.

In the digital environment, copyright is an impediment to routine educational activities such as uploading and downloading documents, forwarding email, posting links to websites,[250] watching online videos, participating in Massive Open Online Courses (MOOCs), and much more. Many initiatives to harness the power of information communication tools in the educational context currently operate in the shadows of national and international copyright obligations. Using MOOCs as an example, students enrolled in these classes are downloading, sharing, distributing, and posting content online, both in the digital "classroom" and with other students around the world.[251] It is a good example of how the exercise of L&Es in one country could benefit populations in other countries; indeed, in the digital environment, least-developed and developing countries rely on L&Es exercised in the developed countries, as much as they might on L&Es enacted in their own domestic copyright laws, to gain access to knowledge and information.[252]

An important implication of the Romer-Lucas contributions to endogenous growth theory is that to sustain economic growth, there must be significant spillovers or other sources of increasing returns to capital arising from technical changes.[253] An educated workforce reflects returns to capital in the form of better employees, new ideas circulating in society, greater purchasing power due to greater numbers of wealthier citizens, and a better informed and productive society. On the other hand, barriers to education limit the positive externalities that could otherwise benefit

---

[250] *See* Case C-466/12, Svensson v. Retriever Sverige AB, 2014 CURIA 76 (Feb. 13, 2014) (holding that a search engine that searched the contents of news websites and offered hyperlinked results did not infringe the copyright holders' exclusive rights). *But see* Case C-160/15, GS Media BV v. Sanoma Media Netherlands BV (Sept. 8, 2016), http://curia.europa.eu/juris/document/document.jsf?text=&docid=183124&pageIndex=0&doclang=EN&mode=lst&dir=&occ=first&part=1&cid=398970 (holding that determinations of the legality of hyperlinks require ascertaining whether the links were "[P]rovided without the pursuit of financial gain by a person who did not know or could not reasonably have known the illegal nature of the publication of those works on that other website or whether, on the contrary, those links are provided for such a purpose, a situation in which that knowledge must be presumed.").

[251] Some sources show that foreign student enrollment in many MOOCS is higher than U.S. enrollment. *See* Waldrop, *supra* note 247.

[252] The same observation is true in relations between developed countries, and across countries at different socioeconomic levels. Differences in copyright rules may, for example, allow citizens in Country A to access cheaper products from Country B because Country A adopts an international exhaustion rule. Such arbitrage is contemplated by the rules in the TRIPS Agreement which adopts no rule on exhaustion. *See* TRIPS Agreement, *supra* note 6, art. 6.

[253] *See* Cohen, *Configuring the Networked Citizen*, *supra* note 130. *See also* RUTTAN, *supra* note 11, at 147.

growth and development such as skilled labor markets[254] and, possibly, higher rates of citizen participation in political and economic markets.[255]

In all countries, even leading developed ones such as the United States, educational L&Es require attention .[256] Efforts to formulate a coherent L&E standard for education, particularly for online educational activities, could be an important step in providing the legal framework necessary to facilitate access to knowledge. Also important is the development of private ordering techniques that release knowledge goods from the source and make them available to users without consent.[257]

Today, a constellation of factors – government subsidies, tax policies, L&Es, constitutional or human rights claims, other legal regimes – ensure that most citizens in the developed countries have access to knowledge and cultural goods. Increasingly, however, evidence suggests that even for these countries, newly designed (or broadly applied) copyright L&Es constitute part of an important set of policy levers needed to advance economic growth in a knowledge economy.[258]

Addressing access to education and knowledge in developing countries will require a combination of policy instruments ranging from compensation schemes for producers of educational materials, educational L&Es, and public investments in cultural institutions such as libraries, archives, and museums. Every government needs to do more, and part of "more" includes copyright reform to enhance educational quality, opportunity, and access.

(iii) Maximizing Use of Authorial Works for Human Capital Formation
The diffusion of knowledge is critical to ensure a dynamic interplay between the public domain and the production and introduction of new goods in society. As Professor Jessica Litman put it, "[t]he most important reason we want authors to create and communicate new works is that we hope people will read the books, listen

---

[254] *See* Joseph E. Stiglitz, *The Theory of "Screening," Education, and the Distribution of Income*, 65 Am. Econ. Rev. 283 (1975) (arguing that the key role of education is to produce human capital and to screen individuals by ability since educational credentials separate people in the labor market).

[255] *See* Kenneth Arrow, *Economic Welfare and the Allocation of Resources for Invention*, *in* The Rate And Direction of Inventive Activity: Economic and Social Factors 609, 616 (1962) (arguing that because invention is a risky endeavor, it will not be undertaken if the cost of the information prerequisite to the process is too high).

[256] *See, e.g.*, McGeveran & Fisher, *supra* note 242; Rotherham & Willingham, *supra* note 242; U.S. Gov't Accountability Office, *supra* note 242.

[257] Jerome H. Reichman, *The Limits of "Limitations and Exceptions" in Copyright Law*, *in* Copyright Law in an Age of Limitations and Exceptions, *supra* note 35.

[258] *See, e.g.*, Computer & Communications Industry Association, Fair Use in the U.S. Economy: Economic Contribution of Industries Relying on Fair Use (2007), www.ccianet.org/wp-content/uploads/library/FairUseStudy-Sep12.pdf; OECD, *supra* note 128.

to the music, see the art, watch the films, run the software, and build and inhabit the buildings. That is the way that copyright promotes the Progress of Science."[259] The presence of knowledge goods in a society is necessary, but not sufficient for producing new goods and technologies; enhancing productive output requires that knowledge goods actually be used. The development of human capital requires steady access to knowledge goods – as Ruttan observes, "the production of human capital is intensive in its use of human capital."[260]

Economic growth is potentiated not just because new goods are added to society, but also because knowledge helps to shape the structural conditions in society, making it better equipped to absorb new ideas and to leverage them productively. In one measure of global innovation, least-developed countries ranked lowest in human capital and research, and in knowledge and technology outputs.[261] Earlier research on sources of growth in developing countries regularly found the ratio of productivity growth to economic growth to be much smaller in those countries, and led to the belief that this was due to inappropriate forms of technology being transferred.[262] While scholarly and policy emphasis among economists has shifted to the role of multinational enterprises and transnational production chains in technology transfer, the capacity to absorb technical knowledge remains foundational to economic growth. Such capacity is crucially linked to education and improved skills in the labor force.[263]

Copyright's bundle of exclusive entitlements and L&Es requires reliable domestic institutions to capture and secure the gains produced through the creation and diffusion of knowledge and knowledge goods. Put differently, institutions are necessary to ensure appropriate returns to a country of its national copyright law. To facilitate maximum returns, international copyright law should support national choices both through flexible standards and rule-like L&Es. Where countries fail to adopt L&Es, the international copyright framework could supply them. This gap-filling role is especially crucial for development progress in countries that are still in the embryonic stages of institution building and that continue to struggle with extreme human capital and resource constraints.

Eventually, the goal is for countries to retain sufficient domestic power – with explicit international support – to craft the best balance between institutions and cultural endowments under their domestic copyright laws. What seems clear, however,

---

[259] *See* Litman, *supra* note 63.
[260] *See* RUTTAN, *supra* note 11, at 134.
[261] *See* GII, *supra* note 86, at 35.
[262] *See* RUTTAN, *supra* note 11, at 143.
[263] Chon, *supra* note 8. *See also* SEN, *supra* note 8; Robert I. Lerman, Signe-Mary McKernan, & Stephanie Riegg, *The Scope of Employer-Provided Training in the United States: Who, What, Where,*

is that a generalized, "cut and paste" approach, whether to copyright entitlements or to L&Es, cannot adequately support the use of copyright as part of development policy. Mechanically plugging L&Es into national copyright laws will not be sufficient to make real gains in development progress. Allowing for other factors, especially differences in modes of economic organization and whether a specific developing country has restructured its institutions differently from what existed under colonial conditions will determine how well a country can meaningfully develop L&Es to pursue specific development strategies.

In some countries, changes in resource endowments may suggest that existing L&Es are sufficient; other countries may need more rights to be recognized and enforced. We won't know what might produce the best results for each country or region without careful analysis of, among other things, existing institutions (including traditional innovation systems), and human capital and resource endowments. This level of analysis may yield national policy recommendations foreclosed or constrained by the international copyright framework – and that prospect is an important part of what this chapter seeks to challenge.

Policymakers and international organizations recognize the importance of helping developing and least-developed countries benefit from emerging patterns of global R&D collaborations, to strengthen their capacity to absorb international R&D spillovers, and to participate in the internationalization of science.[264] Attention to the L&Es in the international copyright system might offer a small, but important, step in achieving these goals.[265]

14.6.2 *Mandatory International Limitations and Exceptions*

Positive externalities from increased access to and use of copyrighted works could be enhanced if a new set of international L&Es along the lines I have proposed are mandatory. For developing and least-developed countries, mandatory L&Es for cultural institutions are especially important. Such institutions – libraries, museums, and archives – represent a significant source of knowledge goods for populations in many regions.[266]

In 2010, WIPO's standing committee for copyright and related rights (SCCR) adopted a work plan on "text-based" work for libraries and archives, education, and

---

and How Much?, in JOB TRAINING POLICY IN THE UNITED STATES 211–44 (Christopher J. O'Leary & Robert A. Straits eds., 2004).

[264] *See* Reichman & Okediji, *supra* note 214.

[265] *See id.*

[266] *See* James Afebuameh Aiyebelehin, *General Structures, Literatures, and Problems of Libraries: Revisiting the State of Librarianship in Africa*, Paper 832, LIBR. PHIL. & PRAC. 1 (2012), http://digitalcommons.unl .edu/cgi/viewcontent.cgi?article=2108&context=libphilprac. *See also* Stella E. Igun, *Digital Libraries in Africa: Evolution, Status, and Challenges*, INT'L J. DIGITAL LIBR. SYS., Apr. 2012, at 13, 17.

persons with disabilities.[267] This work plan so far has produced the first mandatory international instrument for copyright L&Es. In June 2013, WIPO member states concluded the Marrakesh Treaty to Facilitate Access to Published Works by Visually Impaired Persons and Persons with Print Disabilities (Marrakesh Treaty).[268] The Marrakesh Treaty requires contracting parties to establish exceptions to the right of reproduction, the right of distribution, and the right of making available under the WCT, to facilitate the availability of accessible format copies for persons who are print-disabled.[269] It is an unprecedented treaty in a number of regards: structurally, it upsets the dominant "rights only" model of international copyright law that has proliferated in recent years by mandating a specific L&E for the benefit of users of the copyright system; instrumentally, it uses copyright law to effectuate a human rights end; and normatively, it prescribes a method of implementation that presumptively complies with the three-step test.[270] Something similar is necessary for educational institutions and for libraries, museums, and archives.

Like the traditional press, the role of libraries has been significantly transformed by digital information technologies.[271] The breadth and range of services libraries can offer, and the global populations they can serve, afford meaningful prospects for cultural and economic growth everywhere.[272] In many countries, libraries and archives are the institutional frontlines of culture and information; they represent the most accessible and dependable source of information, scientific materials, and knowledge.

In Europe, international, cross-border collaborations are increasingly a key source of leading research outputs. The Association of European Research Libraries – La Ligue des Bibliotheques Europeene de Recherche (LIBER) – states that "over 40% of research outputs from France and Germany are from international research collaborations."[273] The U.S. Library of Congress has

---

[267] *See* WIPO, Standing Comm. on Copyright & Related Rights, *Conclusions*, WIPO Doc. SCCR/21/ CONCLUSIONS (Nov. 12, 2010), http://wipo.int/meetings/en/doc_details.jsp?doc_id=147798.

[268] Marrakesh Treaty to Facilitate Access to Public Works For Persons Who are Blind, Visually Impaired, or Otherwise Print Disabled, *adopted* June 27, 2013, WIPO Doc. VIP/DC/8 Rev., www.wipo.int/ treaties/en/ip/marrakesh [hereinafter Marrakesh Treaty].

[269] Agreed Statements, *supra* note 125, art. 4.

[270] *See* Laurence H. Helfer, Molly K. Land, Ruth L. Okediji, & Jerome Reichman, The World Blind Union Guide to the Marrakesh Treaty to Facilitate Access to Published Works by Blind and Otherwise Print Disabled Persons (2017).

[271] *See e.g.*, Wendy Pradt Lougee, Diffuse Libraries: Emergent Roles for the Research Library in the Digital Age (2002).

[272] *See generally*, *Library and Information Services in Africa in the 21st Century*, 64 Library Trends 1–177 (2015), https://muse.jhu.edu/issue/32727 (analyzing libraries in Africa).

[273] *See* WIPO, Standing Comm. on Copyright & Related Rights, *Statement of LIBER* (May 1, 2014) WIPO Doc. No. SCCR/27 (partial transcript available at http://blogs.ifla.org/sccr/2014/05/01/ liber-statement-on-cross-border-uses-at-sccr-27).

exchange arrangements with over 5,000 institutions worldwide[274] in order to, among other things, foster exchange of materials. Since 1962, it has maintained overseas offices "to acquire, catalog, preserve, and distribute library and research materials from countries where such materials are essentially unavailable through conventional acquisitions methods."[275] Libraries are key agents in providing opportunities for knowledge accumulation and, ultimately, in facilitating the development of skilled labor that is important for national economic growth prospects.

The absence of harmonized L&Es for libraries is increasingly a key impediment to access to knowledge goods. According to one study, "exceptions for libraries and archives are fundamental to the structure of copyright law throughout the world, and [] the exceptions play an important role in facilitating library services and serving the social objectives of copyright law."[276] Over two-thirds of WIPO's membership have a statutory exception for libraries that typically addresses the making of copies (usually single copies) of works for readers, researchers, and other library users, and the making of copies for preservation of materials in the collections.[277] Other exceptions address the ability to make copies for replacement of works that have suffered damage or loss. The European Union's 2001 Directive adds to these traditional exceptions an express authorization for libraries to make digitized copies of works available on-site to users for research and study.[278]

Still, libraries have been hampered in what they can do with the digital communication tools available. As with education, no single library exception reflects the full spectrum of activities or uses that could enhance the degree of knowledge goods in circulation globally.[279] Moreover, there remains significant variation across countries concerning the type of libraries that can make legitimate copies directly available (publicly funded, publicly accessible, or all libraries), what can be copied (full text articles, extracts, published versus unpublished works), the conditions under which copies can be made, and the kind of copies that can be made (electronic, reprographic).[280] Some countries have no statutory exceptions for libraries.[281]

---

[274] *Exchange of Library Materials*, THE LIBRARY OF CONGRESS, www.loc.gov/acq/exchange.html (last visited Sept. 16, 2016).

[275] *Overseas Offices*, THE LIBRARY OF CONGRESS, www.loc.gov/acq/ovop (last visited Sept. 16, 2016).

[276] WIPO, *Study on Copyright Limitations and Exceptions for Libraries and Archives, supra* note 186.

[277] *Id.*

[278] Directive 2001/29/EC, of the European Parliament and of the Council of 22 May 2001 on the Harmonization of Certain Aspects of Copyright and Related Rights in the Information Society, 2001 O.J. (L 167) 10–19.

[279] *See* Teresa Hackett, *Time for a Single Global Copyright Framework for Libraries and Archives*, WIPO MAGAZINE, Dec. 2015, www.wipo.int/wipo_magazine/en/2015/06/article_0002.html.

[280] *See id.*

[281] *See id.*

The situation is even dimmer for archives. Most archives lack permission to make copies for research or study, or to make copies for preservation. A series of proposals at WIPO for mandatory L&Es[282] are meant to harmonize the landscape and to position these cultural institutions to serve new and dynamically evolving needs of users.[283] Thus far, very little progress has been made.

Mandatory L&Es for libraries, archives, and other educational and cultural institutions are essential to facilitate both liberty-enhancing and development-inducing goals. A digitally globalized environment makes content distribution and cross-border sharing remarkably feasible. It is important that harmonized L&Es benefit the institutions from which people most often access knowledge goods. The increasingly collaborative nature of international research and scholarship, catalyzed by the growth of the Internet and digital communication, will certainly continue driving cross-border demand for content in libraries and archives.[284]

Moreover, when multiple countries have shared (or comparable) institutions, histories, languages, or cultural heritage, the library or archive in one country may have historical information or cultural goods that are highly valuable to people in other countries. Due to the absence of internationally harmonized, mandatory L&Es for educational and cultural institutions people may be prevented from accessing such valuable content given the territorial nature of copyright law. For example, libraries faced with requests from overseas institutions refuse to provide materials for copyright reasons, even though those requests are made in accordance with the law of the source country, and even if the requested materials are not available from any other source. So long as the receiving country does not have a similar L&E, source libraries often cannot meet the request for materials.[285] Explicit cross-border provisions are needed that deviate from territoriality when territoriality constitutes a barrier to access to knowledge.

---

[282] *See* WIPO, Standing Committee for Copyright and Related Rights, *Working Document Containing Comments on and Textual Suggestions Towards an Appropriate International Legal Instrument (in whatever form) on Exceptions and Limitations for Libraries and Archives*, WIPO Doc. SCCR/26/3 (Dec. 16–20, 2013), www.wipo.int/edocs/mdocs/copyright/en/sccr_26/sccr_26_3.pdf.

[283] *See* Int'l Fed'n of Libr. Assoc., *Treaty Proposal on Limitations and Exceptions for Libraries and Archives* (Dec. 6, 2013), www.ifla.org/files/assets/hq/topics/exceptions-limitations/tlib_v4_4.pdf. For facts and figures on the international landscape of L&Es for libraries and archives, including a survey of 188 countries, see WIPO, *Study on Copyright Limitations and Exceptions for Libraries and Archives, supra* note 186. *See also* WIPO, Standing Comm. on Copyright & Related Rights, *Draft WIPO Treaty on Exceptions and Limitations for Persons with Disabilities, Educational and Research Institutions, Libraries and Archives*, WIPO Doc. No. SCCR/22/12, www.wipo.int/meetings/en/doc_details .jsp?doc_id=189479.

[284] *See* Suthersanen, *supra* note 139. *See also* Hacket, *supra* note 279.

[285] *See, e.g.*, WIPO, Standing Comm. on Copyright & Related Rights, *Statement of German Library Association Association (Deutscher Bibliotheksverband)*, WIPO Doc. No. SCCR/27 (May 1,

The education example also emphasizes this point. Despite the magnitude of new educational models in the online environment, copyright law hinders maximum exploitation of these possibilities because educational activities rely on a patchwork of exceptions. In the absence of an international L&E for education, national L&Es for education in developed countries could have a positive effect on development in least-developed countries.[286] However, the patchwork of exceptions in most national laws constitutes a barrier to access in the domestic context, wasting the magnitude of opportunities available to supply this essential public good nationally and globally.[287]

One might argue that a system of licensing would be a better alternative to mandatory L&Es to promote bulk access to cultural goods[288] – and particularly to pursue the kind of objectives I identify as important for economic growth and development. Many journals and electronic publications are already offered freely online.[289] Additionally, open source development of educational materials is on the increase, and some may view this as a superior option to mandatory L&Es. These are all important solutions and worth exploring, but none can replace the role of a mandatory L&E that establishes a normative baseline for further policy prescriptions. A mandatory L&E targeted at educational institutions, which deals specifically with access to educational materials and educational uses for digital and non-digital works, should be part of a larger set of tools to address the pressing need for education in developing and least-developed countries.

These ideas about education, libraries, and archives appeal to the possibility of an international instrument specifically dedicated to L&Es. In previous work exploring prospects for an international L&Es instrument, Professor Bernt Hugenholtz and I identified some reasons for bringing coherence to the unregulated space of copyright L&Es.[290] We concluded that a global approach to L&Es is necessary:

> i) to facilitate trans-border exchange, both online and in traditional media, by eliminating inconsistency and uncertainty, and for encouraging uniformity of standards

2014) (giving examples). *See also* WIPO, Standing Comm. on Copyright & Related Rights, *Statement of the Australian Library and Information Association (ALIA)*, WIPO Doc. No. SCCR/27 (May 1, 2014) (same).

[286] *See, e.g.,* William Fisher, *Lessons from CopyrightX, in* COPYRIGHT LAW IN AN AGE OF LIMITATIONS AND EXCEPTIONS, *supra* note 35.

[287] *See* McGeveran & Fisher, *supra* note 242.

[288] *See* Raquel Xalabarder, *Digital Libraries in the Current Legal and Educational Environment: Towards a Remunerated Compulsory License or Limitation?, in* GLOBAL COPYRIGHT, *supra* note 139. *See also* J.A.L. Sterling, *Online Exploitation and Licensing: General Reporter's Summary and Proposals for Discussion, in* GLOBAL COPYRIGHT, *supra* note 139.

[289] *See, e.g.,* DIRECTORY OF OPEN ACCESS JOURNALS, https://doaj.org.

[290] *See* HUGENHOLTZ & OKEDIJI, *supra* note 95.

of protection and transparency; ii) to alleviate institutional weakness of States who need diffusion most (DC's and LDC's); iii) to counteract the recent shift to bilateralism and regionalism in international copyright policymaking and; iv) to constrain unilateral ratcheting up of global standards. A new international instrument with a broad membership offers an opportunity to eliminate anticompetitive effects associated with differing levels of protection across national jurisdictions while also consolidating recent gains in integrating public interest goals into the international copyright system.[291]

We also offered some minimum goals of an international approach to L&Es such as (i) elimination of barriers to exchange, particularly in regard to activities of public information service providers; (ii) facilitation of access to tangible information products; (iii) promotion of innovation and competition; (iv) support of mechanisms to promote/reinforce fundamental freedoms; and (v) provision of consistency and stability in the international copyright framework by promoting the normative balance necessary to support knowledge diffusion. Ideally, an international instrument on L&Es should be: (a) flexible; (b) leave some room for cultural autonomy of nation-states, allowing diverse local solutions; and (c) be judicially manageable.[292]

The L&Es agenda at WIPO should be viewed as a crucial part of the longstanding attempts to align copyright law with broader welfare concerns. This agenda should not stop at WIPO, but should be advanced at national and regional levels. Moreover, developing and least-developed countries must themselves become more attuned to the tradeoffs involved when new international L&Es are proposed in international fora. Given the weak political appetite for L&Es at WIPO, simply adding L&Es to international copyright law, the way we might adorn a Christmas tree with ornaments, imperils prospects to undertake the kind of serious reform necessary for copyright in developing countries to accomplish its central purpose: the encouragement of learning for development.

14.7 CONCLUSION

The existing roster of international L&Es is poorly adapted to the central challenge of developing and least-developed countries namely, the formation of human capital required for economic development. Limitations and exceptions that promote the public interest by securing privacy, facilitating civic and social engagement, and ensuring freedom of expression, are important elements of the liberty interests copyright is intended to foster in pluralist societies. These liberty-enhancing L&Es

---

[291] *Id.* at 4.
[292] *Id.*

have enjoyed considerable acceptance in the international copyright system and they should continue to be strengthened.

But in a world of limited political capital, developing and least-developed countries must choose among a set of priorities. Personal freedoms play an important role in developing human capital, but without economic growth and development, the full benefits of liberty cannot be appropriated in the broader economy. What is needed in addition to liberty-inducing L&Es are new international L&Es that strengthen the capacity of developing and least-developed countries to absorb and utilize knowledge inputs.

To the extent copyright law is an integral aspect of shaping the conditions necessary for human flourishing, and thus foundational for national economic development, the design of international and national copyright law matters a great deal. The pressure to harmonize copyright law (and the long practice of doing so) only in the direction of strengthening exclusive private rights has made it unnecessarily difficult to adjust the system to accomplish goals that are important for the welfare of developing and least-developed countries.

Read in the most ambitious light, my arguments here suggest that current international copyright law imposes an externality on society at large. Wherever there are bright minds in sub-Saharan Africa, or in other regions in the global South, an overly restrictive international copyright framework will be one factor (not the only factor by any means, but certainly a factor) making it more difficult for those minds to be trained, developed, and to become productive assets for society at large.

Scholars and the international community must return to an honest dialogue: one that has the potential to infuse countries with a genuine capacity to demand and implement international copyright norms consistent with their own development aspirations.

Index

CPSIA information can be obtained
at www.ICGtesting.com
Printed in the USA
LVHW111957070119
603028LV00002B/277/P